EARLY CHILDHOOD EDUCATION

An International Perspective

EARLY CHILDHOOD EDUCATION
An International Perspective

Edited by

Nechama Nir-Janiv
Ministry of Education and Culture
Tel Aviv, Israel

Bernard Spodek
University of Illinois
Champaign, Illinois

Doreen Steg
Drexel University
Philadelphia, Pennsylvania

Associate Editors

Mima Spencer and Paula Wagemaker
ERIC/EECE
Urbana, Illinois

PLENUM PRESS • NEW YORK AND LONDON

Library of Congress Cataloging in Publication Data

International Congress on Early Childhood Education (1980: Tel Aviv, Israel)
  Early childhood education.

  "Proceedings of the International Congress on Early Childhood Education, held January
6 — 10, 1980, in Tel Aviv, Israel"—T.p. verso.
  Includes bibliographies and index.
  1. Education, Preschool—Congress. 2. Education of children—Congresses. I. Nir-Janiv,
Nechama. II. Title.
LB1140.A13I57 1980   372'.21   82-5256
ISBN 0-306-41007-9   AACR2

Proceedings of the International Congress on Early Childhood Education, held
January 6 — 10, 1980, in Tel Aviv, Israel

© 1982 Plenum Press, New York
A Division of Plenum Publishing Corporation
233 Spring Street, New York, N.Y. 10013

Printed in the United States of America

PREFACE

   Possibly more than any other field of education, early childhood education has been an international phenomenon. The great
pioneers of the field--Friedrich Froebel of Germany, Maria Montessori
of Italy, Margaret McMillan and Susan Isaacs of England--all saw
their influence expand well beyond the borders of their native lands.
Froebelian kindergartens, Montessori schools, and nursery schools
designed along the English model have flourished in many lands during
this century and the last.

   The international perspective is no less important in early
childhood education today. The research work done in the United
States in the 1960s and 1970s, along with the development of different conceptual models of early childhood education, had an impact on
early childhood education research, policies, and practices throughout the world. Ideas from many lands continue to influence the field
as information becomes available through national journals, the ERIC
system, and such international journals as OMEP's *International
Journal of Early Childhood*.

   Thus, the International Congress in Early Childhood Education
convened in Tel Aviv, Israel, in January 1980 represented and extension of existing international perspectives in the field rather
than a new thrust. The Congress provided opportunities for scholars,
researchers and practitioners to present their ideas and report their
work. It afforded an opportunity for each one to interact with others
in the same field who might ordinarily have been separated by thou-
sands of miles or who might be familiar by name only.

   The papers that are included in this volume were selected from
among those presented at that Congress and are the work of early
childhood educators from Europe, the Middle East, Africa, Asia, North
and South America, and Australia. They provide testimony to the true
international nature of the Congress. Unfortunately, it was not
possible to include every presentation because of space limitations.
In addition, many presentations that were made orally or that included
the use of audiovisual materials did not translate well into the
medium of the printed word.

Even more unfortunate is the fact that there is no way to communicate the richness of the interactions among participants and the observations and visits that were provided to schools and other institutions.
These will continue to exist only in the memories of the participants.

There are many individuals and groups whose support of this volume
should be acknowledged. The many people who participated in the
Congress and who worked to make the Congress a reality cannot all be
acknowledged. Special notice, however, must be given to the members
of the Israel Organizing Committee and Advisory Board and the International Advisory Board. The support of the Ministry of Education and
Culture of the State of Israel must also be acknowledged. In addition,
all of the presenters and participants of the Congress contributed,
whether directly or indirectly, to this volume. Special thanks must
be given to the Van Leer Foundation for their support which enabled this
volume to be produced in English and translated into Hebrew, and to
the Editorial Board for its assistance. Plenum Press provided the
support and encouragement needed to produce this book. Finally and
most important, a special thanks needs to be given to Mima Spencer,
Paula Wagemaker, Sheila Ryan and Tillie Krieger who were responsible
for the technical editing and index preparation of the volume. Their
care and concern contributed much to the final product.

                              Bernard Spodek
                              University of Illinois
                              Urbana-Champaign

INTRODUCTION

Zevulum Hammer

Ministry of Education and Culture
Jerusalem, Israel

In Israel we recognize the value of early childhood education.
We see it as a foundation and basis for the education which will
follow. We value the research and the wonderful work done both in
this country and abroad which paves the way for work in early childhood education.

I would like to say a few words concerning education and Jewish
tradition. The will to learn does not grow in a vacuum. It is often
futile to attempt to cultivate an appreciation of knowledge through
techniques which relate to a person's cognitive development alone.
The will to learn and to explore new avenues of thought, the patience
to read a text carefully and analytically, the perseverance to master
rigorous intellectual disciplines--all these are related to a person's
self-image and vision of life. In order to perceive oneself as a
student in the fullest sense, one must feel self-dignity and worth
and believe that what one thinks and does, makes a significant difference both to oneself and to others.

I share Martin Buber's view that a person's "I" consciousness is
fundamentally relational. Although the influence exerted on a child
by his home environment is not unchangeable, there is often a relationship between a person's self image and the human environment in
which he was reared. A person's self-image will be different if the
world he discovered as a child was responsive and loving or if it was
cold, mute, and rejecting.

The psychological conditions which allow for the development
of discipline and openness in a formal school environment develop
in the person during his or her childhood. Discipline has meaning

to a person who feels personal dignity and inner security.

The Hebrew word for dignity, Kavod, is related to the word Kaved, which means weight. If my existence has weight, if I cannot be dismissed easily, then I experience myself as worthy and dignified. Dignity and self-respect grow when others are responsive to one's needs and feelings. A silent, uncaring childhood environment contributes to the development of the lonely, isolated self who doubts his own worth and integrity; and when such doubt grips a person, the motivation to learn and discover is weakened and often destroyed. One has no access to culture, unless one believes in the integrity and trustworthiness of human beings. Learning also requires the courage to enter into an uncharted future, to enter a world which one cannot totally control and to be open to novelty and surprise. The belief that the future may reveal new possibilities is essential for the learning experience.

One of the roles of informal frameworks of experience in general and of early childhood education in particular is to create a human environment where one does not feel easily ignored. It is a fatal error to believe that we can cultivate a will to learn in our students if we ignore the truth that the will and the intellect are part of a total human being. Bringing the whole human being to bear on the learning experience is a great challenge facing human societies in terms of how they deal with children. The world of education revolves around "grace" in terms of trust in others. One cannot begin the learning process without trust, and trust is difficult to create in school unless it was cultivated during a child's preschool years of development. Mother, father, siblings, friends, and preschool teachers are all significant figures who mediate the significance of interdependency to the growing child.

The ultimate purpose of these people is to create a trusting character base upon which the quest for knowledge and personality may be grafted. I am very pleased that this International Congress on Early Childhood Education is taking place in Israel, where we are striving to merge spirit with body and to integrate the spirit, will and intellect of our people into a unified whole. As a society, we seek to forge a community which reflects a balanced, organic wholeness. We long for Shalom--peace--which is derived from the word Shalem, wholeness and completeness. We trust that your deliberations will enrich our common quest for personal and collective integrity and wholeness.

We must understand the inescapability of trust; communication between people entails trust. Even the rudiments of the Aleph-Beit-- the key to language, literature and higher forms of cultural expression--are embedded in a social context. If one cannot trust his teacher in principle, then one cannot trust the printed word. The suspicious child whose primary experience of life was that of being manipulated and abused because of weakness and helplessness may have great difficulty adjusting to a reality which demands that he accept his dependence on others and that he trust and grow on the basis of what others transmit to him. Deeply rooted suspicions, fear and lack of trust are inimical to the development of the freedom and spontaneity so needed for any healthy learning experience.

CONTENTS

Early Childhood Education Foundations

Children's Development

Teacher Education

Parents, Family, and Home Intervention

Children's Learning

Social Environment of Children

Early Childhood Education Programs

Tests and Testing

Evaluation

EARLY CHILDHOOD EDUCATION: A SYNOPTIC VIEW

Bernard Spodek

University of Illinois
Urbana-Champaign

As I was about to prepare this paper I chanced to be reading Theodore H. White's *In Search of History: A Personal Adventure* (1978). White, who is probably best known for the books he has written about American presidential election campaigns ("The Making of a President" series), had written an autobiography laced with personal recollections of famous men. The most interesting parts of the book are about White's personal beginnings. White grew up in the slums of Boston and he shares his perceptions of that time, of the culture around him, and of his own roots in transitional American-Jewish culture.

White comments that the many different sects of Jews, although they may quarrel with one another, are tied together by the thread of the *Shma*--the incantation "Hear, O Israel, the Lord our God, the Lord is One." The *Shma* sustained Jews through the persecutions of the Crusades and during the medieval period when Jews were burned at the stake for their beliefs. The *Shma* was the call of courage passed down from one century to another.

White reminds us that the *Shma* is the unity of all happenings, the idea begun in prehistoric times that there was only one God and that God gave order to the universe. This idea formed the mind set of all great Jewish thinkers who sought to create one theory to explain the varied phenomena they observed. Those thinkers who went out into the larger world were often bearers of an all-embracing theory as unifying as the *Shma*. White cites as examples the compelling ideas of Einstein, Christ, Marx, and Freud. He concludes that the passion of Jewish thinkers for a single, universal theory in every field of knowledge has frequently proved subversive to settled establishments and order.

1

White's view of the importance of the *Shma* in Jewish tradition, is well documented. His view of the importance of similar synoptic, integrative theories is also well documented. Comprehensive theories have impacted on many fields and have moved thought and research along with them. Proposing new integrative theories often results in what Kuhn (1970) has called "scientific revolutions," since new theories help scientists view the world in ways that were not possible before. Such theories also provide a unity to a field of inquiry or of human endeavor. But whether the development of such integrative theories is the sole cultural baggage or inherited cultural characteristic of a single ethnic group is open to question.

The idea of searching for the integrative statements that hold a field such as early childhood education together is intriguing. Is it possible to tease out of the traditions and practices of early childhood education those elements that have served an integrative function? In what way is the early childhood education field unified? Perhaps the one thing that brings its members all together is that they are all concerned with young children. Thus, there might be something unique in the way that they serve. Yet within the age range of three through eight, and even more so as we have extended early childhood education downward to birth, there is a vast difference. The way one serves two-year-olds is vastly different from the way one serves seven-year-olds, for example.

In 1933 Grace Langdon published a doctoral dissertation: *A Study of Similarities and Differences in Teaching in Nursery School, Kindergarten and First Grade*. Of the thirty-one conclusions arrived at by observation and analysis, thirty identified differences in teaching the three grades. Only one set of conclusions dealt with similarities of teaching:

> 17. On each of the three age levels there is an emphasis on learning the rules, regulations, and customs of the group and conformity to them, and these acts are considered important for each of the three levels. (P. 274)

I believe that the similarities and differences found by Langdon over forty-five years ago would be observed by a researcher making a similar study today. Within early childhood education there are vast differences between what we do to children and what we expect of them, simply as a function of age.

If we cannot find unity in the nature of the children we serve, or the ways in which we behave towards these children, perhaps then we can find an integrative theme in the kind of service provided. The institutions we define within the field of early childhood education include nursery schools, kindergartens, primary grades of elementary school and day care centers.

The primary grades are conceived of as providing academic instruction. Although, as originally defined, these classes were limited to teaching the "three r's," by the turn of this century their focus had widened to include art and music as well as science or nature study in their curriculums. While the broadening of the curriculum can be attributed to many causes, a number of educators have felt that at least one important cause was the inclusion of kindergartens in the public schools and their resulting influence on these schools. (Vandewalker, 1907). Nevertheless, the kindergarten and primary grades have always been distinct from one another and continue to be.

The kindergarten itself was designed as an educational institution, although Froebel's concept of early education was different from the concept we hold today. Froebel viewed education as a supporter of development, a result of self-activity. Froebel's education was designed to help the child grasp universal concepts related to man, God and nature through the use of materials and activities that symbolized those universals (Lilley, 1967).

Many of the early American kindergartens were sponsored by private schools, in some cases German-language schools developed to serve the German-American population. The kindergarten movement spread throughout the American community; many private English-speaking kindergartens were established and public schools slowly adopted kindergartens as well.

But kindergartens were soon used to serve other than a basic educational purpose. The church considered the kindergarten as a valuable means for carrying on its work. A number of churches incorporated kindergartens into their parish work. In addition, church missionaries used kindergartens to reach socially isolated minority groups in America, as well as foreign groups abroad. Kindergartens were established by American missionaries in cities in Brazil, Rhodesia, China, Japan and Turkey, to name but a few countries. Miss Annie L. Howe, who was sent to establish a mission kindergarten in Kobe, Japan, is credited with providing the first translation of Froebel's works in Japanese (Vandewalker, 1908).

Kindergartens were sponsored by the Women's Christian Temperance Union to provide aid to families in locations "where the drink habit had worked its greatest havoc." Kindergartens were also incorporated into many of the early settlement houses, institutions established to provide aid, comfort and social services to poor and immigrant families in the slums of many American cities. Labor unions and businesses also sponsored some of the early American kindergartens.

While the variety of sponsors probably aided the development of kindergartens in America, there were also disadvantages resulting

from this variety. One was the confusion created in the minds of
many between the idea of a kindergarten which was an educational
institution and the crèche or day nursery which served a child caring
function. Another was the lowering of standards of quality, since
many kindergarten sponsors stretched their resources to serve as
many children as possible and to provide that service as a labor of
love. Training was often inadequate for those serving in kindergartens as were the physical and monetary resources available (Vandewalker, 1908).

In addition, the nature of kindergarten practice became diversi-
fied, with practice reflecting the purposes of the sponsors. Thus,
church-related kindergartens were more concerned with teaching children religious precepts, while settlement house kindergartens were
more concerned with meeting broad social needs. The confusion between education and philanthropy was evident.

Almost a quarter of a century after Vandewalker described the
proliferation of sponsors and services related to kindergartens, the
contributors to the 28th Yearbook of the National Society for the
Study of Education, *Preschool and Parental Education* (Whipple, 1929),
identified an even broader array of purposes for the nursery school,
then a relatively new educational institution in America. These
included:

Philanthropy--The Ruggles Street Nursery School was established
in Boston in 1922 along the lines of the nursery school envisioned
by Margaret McMillan in England to serve the needs of poor children.

Research in Educational Curriculum and Methods--Nursery schools
at Teachers College, Columbia University, and the Bureau of Educational Experiments (later to become Bank Street College) were designed "to study the growth needs of children in order to determine
educational programs, procedures and materials" (p. 28).

Home Economics--Laboratory nursery schools were opened at the
Merrill-Palmer School of Homemaking in Detroit, Iowa State College,
Cornell University, and at other institutions to educate young (i.e.,
college age) women in the care and training of children. Nursery
schools were also established in private women's liberal arts
colleges, such as Vassar and Smith, as a result of pressure to offer
a curriculum for the woman who would become a homemaker and parent.

Cooperation of Parents--One of the first nursery schools in
the United States was established by a group of faculty wives at the
University of Chicago "to offer an opportunity for wholesome play for
their children, to give mothers certain hours of leisure from child
care, and to try the social venture of cooperation of mothers in
child care" (p. 29). Althea Bass reports that mothers felt the
need for children to experience group play and sometimes the super-

vision of adults who were not their own mothers. The mothers also
needed to know other children and to see the effectiveness of their
home training when their own children joined a group (Forest, 1927,
pp. 299-300). Cooperative nursery schools were also reported at Smith
College, and in Cambridge, Massachusetts.

Research in Child Development--The Iowa Child Welfare Research
Station established a nursery school for the "maintenance of a constant
group [of children] which could be observed daily under favorable
conditions for a period of several years" (p. 32). Other institutions established nursery schools to support a wide range of investigations of childhood needs and characteristics.

Teacher Training--Nursery schools were established to provide
practice facilities for those wishing to become nursery teachers,
as well as to give those studying to become primary and kindergarten
teachers an opportunity to observe and work with younger children.

Supplements to Child Guidance Clinics--The North Bennett Industrial school in Boston established a Play School for Habit Training
in 1922. In 1926 the Guidance Nursery School was opened in connection
with the Yale Psycho-Educational Clinic. Children with specific behavioral problems were admitted to these nursery schools, including
those with "records of temper tantrums, enuresis, habitual grouchi-
ness or just bad judgment" (p. 33).

The 1929 Yearbook dealt separately with day nurseries, as they
called day care centers. The day nursery had one primary purpose:
"the day care of children who remain part of a family unit but who,
for social or economic reasons, cannot receive ordinary parental
care" (p. 87). Centers were categorized by their sponsorship:
philanthropic, commercial, industrial, and public school. The
philanthropic day nursery was the most prevalent kind at the time.
The authors of the yearbook took care to distinguish between the nursery school and the day nursery, with the day nursery viewed as serving a relief function, providing aid to families rather than being
primarily concerned with the needs of children. It was felt, however,
that the day nursery program could be strengthened by incorporating
within it a nursery school program.

This distinction is also found in Ethel Beer's book, *The Day
Nursery* (1938), first published about a decade later. Beer suggests
that a differentiation should be made between the staffs of these
institutions. The nursery school teacher was viewed as inadequate
in background and training to properly envisage the total needs of
the day nursery program.

During the forty years that have passed since the publication
of the 28th Yearbook of the National Society for the Study of Education, nursery schools and day care centers have served a range of

purposes. As a result of the depression of the 1930s, many local
taxing agencies in the United States found themselves lacking in
funds. Included in these were local school systems which reduced
the number of teachers in their employ to lower expenses. The
federal government provided support for the establishment of nursery
schools as one way of providing work relief for these unemployed
teachers.

World War II followed the depression. In order to increase the
number of women in war work, and thus extend the labor force, the
federal government provided support for the establishment of day care
centers in communities that had felt the impact of war-related in-
dustries. This was not a new use of day care for children, for the
1929 N.S.S.E. Yearbook states:

> It is significant that they [day nurseries] were at first,
> like so many other forms of child welfare, a by-product of
> war. It was in Philadelphia in 1863 that the first permanent
> day nursery was established to care for the children of women
> needed to manufacture soldiers' clothing and to clean in
> hospitals. Men were at war; industries needed workers; women
> were urged or forced to become breadwinners; children were
> neglected. The last two factors have continued to be the im-
> portant elements in all-day nursery expansion (p. 91).

While day nurseries were reported as early as 1854, it is interesting
that over the past century the need for national defense has carried
more weight than the concern for family integrity in arguments about
the provision of day care for young children.

The next major impact of federal legislation on early childhood
education saw education for young children serve yet another purpose.
In 1965 the Head Start program was established in the United States
under the Economic Opportunity Act. This program, conceived of as a
comprehensive child development program, was established as part of
the community action program, a tool in the War on Poverty fought
to create the "New Society."

Most recently there have been major changes in the sponsorship
and purpose of day care centers in the United States. More day care
centers are being operated as commercial ventures, a major change
from the situation in 1929 when the majority were philanthropic.
In addition, day care is seldom considered to be "relief" today.
With the increase in the number of women in the work force in our
country, and with the changing status of women, day care is viewed
as a legitimate alternative to home care. Thus, day care has come
to serve the purpose of providing a child rearing service comparable
to that provided in the home nurseries of wealthy families in an
earlier era.

Do the varied purposes served by different early childhood programs affect these programs in ways that separate them into different
fields or different segments of a single, though diverse, field?
After all, one can argue, all these programs deal with young children
who have the same basic needs. One can also argue that, although different purposes are served by different programs, each program has
within it a kernel of educational service. The programs differ in
what is provided over and above that service.

Yet all of us who have worked in schools or agencies that serve
children directly know that the resources of these agencies are far
from limitless. Decisions need to be made about how to use the
resources that are available. Decisions also need to be made as to
the number of persons to be employed and the level and kind of competency these persons should have. It is in this decision-making process that purpose determines priorities. It is in these decisions
that basic values become manifest. When education is less important
than child care or community service, the agency will be less concerned with the educational background or teaching competence of
those who work with children and more concerned with other attributes.
It is not that one set of criteria or one set of purposes is better
than others, but that a particular set of purposes will ultimately
lead to a different kind of service being offered to young children.

If the unity and integrity of the early childhood field is
found neither in the nature of the children who are served by the
field nor in the kinds of services provided nor in the kinds of agencies
and sponsorship of service, then where might it be found? Perhaps
the nature of the ideas underlying the field, the theory and philosophy of early childhood education, is the appropriate source of unity.

Unity was one of the key ideas underlying early childhood education from its inception. Central to the idea of early education as
conceived by the early kindergarteners was the conception of man as
Gliedganzes, a word coined by Friedrich Froebel himself. "The word
Gliedganzes means a member of a whole who is potentially commensurate
with the whole to which as member he belongs, but who can make this
potentiality actual only in and through active membership" (Blow,
1913, p. 9).

The concept of *Gliedganzes* contains three distinct implications.
The first is "that which is generic or the reproducers of the species
in lower forms of life, becomes Ego in man. The second implication
is that this generic Ego or universal self is not only the ideal
Human, but the devine . . . The third and final implication is that
this immanent-transcendent God is one with the absolute first principal through which is given its being" (Blow, 1913, p. 10).

Froebel developed a kindergarten theory that unified man, God
and nature. This theory was presented to young children through a

series of symbolic materials and activities. The method of learning
was through self-activity. Each child constructed his conception of
unity as a result of his own active involvement in the kindergarten.

    During the era of the Froebelian kindergarten, it could truly
be said that one set of ideas and ideals undergirded all of the
programs for young children. However, by the end of the nineteenth
century, new philosophies of education, new ideas and understandings
regarding children, their ways of learning and their ways of developing were to provide alternative ways of thinking about the education
of young children that led to modification and revision of kindergarten theory.

    In the United States, influenced by the progressive education
movement and the child study movement, a reform was proposed by forward thinking kindergarteners. While they suggested that they only
wished to provide alternative practices to bring kindergarten activity more in line with Froebelian philosophy, in effect they were
proposing an alternative philosophy. While the method of self-activity remained an integral part of the new kindergarten program,
the key element around which programs were to be built was not the
unity of man, God and nature, but rather the social life of the community and the social experience of the child (Hill, 1913).

    New ideas about the education of young children were being de-
veloped in Europe at this time that were to be major influences in
early childhood education. Maria Montessori abstracted knowledge of
children from the developing field of anthropology, and knowledge of
programming from a fledgling field of special education, to create
the Montessori method. While this method has remained isolated from
the mainstream of early childhood educational thought, it has had
profound influences on the nature of programming and on the development of physical supports for early childhood education, especially
in the design of materials and equipment.

    In England, the nursery school was evolving, designed as a
social service for needy children. Its developers made use of the
ideas of Froebel and Montessori in the creation of this new institution. They also made use of the new insights about children being
generated from the field of child study. Even psychoanalytic theory
was called upon as a source of knowledge about children in this early
era of thinking about programs for young children.

    From the earliest period of its development, the nursery school
was closely linked with the child development movement in the United
States. Many of the leaders in the field of early childhood education
consider themselves developmental specialists. Many of the presidents
of the National Association for Nursery Education, and later of the
National Association for the Education of Young Children, for example, can be identified as developmentalists rather than educationists.

During this time, however, nursery school practice and early childhood educational practice were not derived from developmental theory. No single comprehensive theory of child development existed with which all early childhood practitioners identified. Rather, a number of theoretical positions including maturationism, psychoanalytic theory, Gestaltism, and others had influenced the field. From no one of these theories, by the way, could educational practice in nursery schools and kindergartens be extracted, although each could be used to justify some practice.

The range of theoretical positions in child development that were used to justify early childhood practice proliferated in the 1960s. Following the call for more powerful programs of preschool education to serve as compensation for children being reared in poverty and to improve the chances of these children's success in formal school, a wide range of early childhood program models was developed. Many of these models justified their practices by recourse to developmental or learning theories, as earlier program models had. But the newer models used theoretical positions such as constructivism, behaviorism and a range of eclecticisms that were different from those advocated by earlier early childhood practitioners.

The language of early childhood education during this time was only indirectly related to the language of child development. Early childhood education is based upon such concepts as "individuality," "freedom," "child interest," "need," "play," "activity," "creativity," "child-centered programs," and "growth." The idea of "development as the aim of education" (Kohlberg & Mayer, 1972), a basic progressive education concept, is what connects education with development and it is with the growth metaphor that the educationist and developmentalist have found common ground.

But each of the concepts just identified is ill-defined. The term "play," for example, is defined and used in several dozen ways in the literature. The practitioner, however, does not look for a single precise definition before working with children, and helping them play. As a matter of fact, it may very well be that it is just this looseness of definition that allows a wide range of early childhood educators to accept the centrality of these concepts to the field. These words do not in fact represent clearly defined concepts that are tied together in a neat, testable theory, but rather they serve as slogans, as rallying points for practitioners who use them to identify with particular ideological positions in relation to what is important in the experiences we provide for young children.

Just as I was not able to find a unifying theme in the kinds of services and clients we have in the field of early childhood education; just as I was not able to find a unifying theme in the purposes for which we establish early childhood programs; so I could

not find a unifying theme in the ideas that underlie the field of
early childhood education unless I was willing to limit my search
to the ideas being proposed a century back. I am forced, it seems,
to accept the fact that early childhood education is not one thing.
It consists of many kinds of services, presented to many types of
clients, by a diverse group of practitioners, through agencies under
varied sponsorships, aimed at achieving a broad range of purposes.

If this statement is accepted, then can there be a unifying
force, whether a set of ideas or ideals, that underlies the field
and its practices? What kinds of conclusions can we arrive at?
What kinds of guidance can we provide those who study our field?
Given the diversity of the field, as I found it, I could not come
up with one single conclusion. Therefore, I would like to present
three endings to this presentation.

The first is based on a fable, "The Blind Men and The Elephant."
The story, as it has been told and retold, concerns a group of blind
men who came upon an elephant. No one of them could see the entire
animal, so by touching its separate part, each concluded what it was:
"A snake," thought the one who touched its tail. "A wall," thought
the one who touched its side. "A tree trunk," thought the one who
touched its leg. And so on. Each individual experienced only a
part of the whole yet each thought his part was the whole.

As early childhood educators, we each operate in only one part of
a vast, diverse field. Our inquiries tend to be limited. There is
a danger that we will overgeneralize from what we know, that we will
think of what we experience and come to understand as the totality
of the field, and that we will see simple interactions of the variable
that we may study as basic explanations of major effects. Each
generalization of this type would be a distortion of reality. Yet
each inquiry, each study, each insight can contribute to our understanding of the whole, if placed in its proper perspective, and combined with insights and understandings derived by others.

The second ending is also based on a fable. It was used in Laws'
Introduction to the *Report of the Committee of Nineteen on the Theory
and Practice of the Kindergarten:*

A father had three sons whom he loved equally well. This
father owned a precious ring--said to be endowed with power
to bring highest blessings to its owner. Each one of the sons
asked the father to bestow the Ring on him after the father's
death. The father, in his great love for his sons, promised
the Ring to each one. In his old age, the father sent for a
jeweler and asked him to make two rings exactly like the
precious Ring owned by him. The jeweler assented, and after a
while he brought the three rings to the father who could not
distinguish the precious Ring from the other two, so well were

they made. When the time came that the father died, he called
each of his sons separately to him, blessed him, and gave him
a ring. After the father's burial, the three brothers met, and
each one claimed the birthright and the ownership of the genuine
ring. Finally, when they could not decide which was the original
one, they went to a Judge, who gave the decision in the form of
advice, viz., 'As the true Ring is said to have the magic power
of making the owner beloved and esteemed by God and man, and as
each of you three brothers believes his ring to be the genuine
or original one, so let each one, untouched by his prejudice,
strive to reveal the power of the Ring in his life by loving
peaceableness, and by charity and sincere devotion to God; and
when in later generations the power of the true Ring reveals
itself, I will call upon you again, before the "seat of Judgment."
A wiser man than I may be there and speak.' (p. xv)

In the field of early childhood education, we have many theories
expounded. We have heard many purposes suggested. We have been
told that many roles are the proper ones for our services. The
diversity can be confusing, but it is not necessarily bad. While
each of us may believe that his position is the right one, and act
accordingly, at some later generation we may all be called on to the
"seat of Judgment" to finally learn which of us indeed has the true
Ring.

My third and final ending derives from research, rather than
fable. I had recently come across a study of English infant school
classrooms, *All Things Bright and Beautiful?* by Ronald King (1978).
King, a sociologist, did an ethnographic study of early childhood
classrooms, theoretically based on the work of the sociologist,
Max Weber. King's study was designed to understand the ways in
which teachers typify their situations, that is, give meanings to
them. King suggests that the reality of the classroom teachers'
world is constructed through teachers' ideology. It is the belief
system of the teachers which led them to a set of common definitions
of their situations, and led them to share a common language and set
of concepts. This system was highlighted by the one teacher who was
employed in the school who did not share their definitions; he was
not "infant trained."

Although I am not convinced that the source of common beliefs
lies within professional preparation I do believe that, as a group,
early childhood educators hold a common belief system. The shared
values and definitions, the concepts and slogans we use, help us to
define the world of early childhood education in a common way. While
there are disagreements among members of the field, there is still
something shared that holds us together. My colleagues in other
departments at my university, for example, tell me that they can tell
whether a student is specializing in elementary education or early

childhood education even though the two specializations are in the
same department and no official distinction is made between them.

Perhaps it is this common set of definitions, this common set
of beliefs, that unify the field. Despite the fact that we may do
different things, work in different settings, serve different purposes, and feel responsible to different agencies, the fact that we
define ourselves as unified, that we decide to hold beliefs in common,
ties us to one another and makes us a field of early childhood education. Perhaps in this sense we still accept the idea of Froebel, the
importance of unity within diversity.

REFERENCES

Beer, E.S. *The day nursery*. New York: Dutton, 1938.
Blow, S. First report. In *The kindergarten: report of the committee
    of nineteen on the theory and practice of the kindergarten*.
    Boston: Houghton-Mifflin, 1913.
Forest, I. *Preschool education: a historical and critical study*. New
    York: Macmillan, 1927.
Froebel, F. *The education of man*. New York: Appleton, 1896.
Hill, P.S. Second report. In *The kindergarten: report of the commit-
    tee of nineteen on the theory and practice of the kindergarten*.
    Boston: Houghton-Mifflin, 1913.
Holmes, M.J. (Ed.). *The kindergarten and its relation to elementary
    education*. 6th Yearbook of the National Society for the Scientific
    Study of Education, Part II. Bloomington, IL: Public School
    Publishing, 1907.
King, R. *All things bright and beautiful?* New York: Wiley, 1978.
Kuhn, T.S. *The structure of scientific revolutions* (2nd ed.). Chicago:
    University of Chicago Press, 1970.
Langden, G. *A study of similarities and differences in teaching in
    nursery school, kindergarten, and first grade*. New York: John
    Day, 1933.
Laws, A. Introduction. In *The kindergarten: report of the committee
    of nineteen on the theory and practice of the kindergarten*.
    Boston: Houghton-Mifflin, 1913.
Lilley, I. *Freidrich Froebel: a selection from his writings*. Cambridge
    University Press, 1967.
Owen, G. *Nursery school education*. New York: Dutton, 1920.
Selleck, R.J.W. *English primary education and the progressives:
    1914-1939*. Boston: Routledge & Kegan Paul, 1972.
Vandewalker, N.C. History of kindergarten influences in elementary
    education. In Holmes, M.J. (Ed.). *The kindergarten and its rela-
    tion to elementary education*. 6th Yearbook of the N.E.E.S.E.,
    Part II. Bloomington, IL: Public School Publishing Co., 1907.
Vandewalker, M.C. *The kindergarten in American education*. New York:
    Macmillan, 1908.

Whipple, G.M. (Ed.). *Preschool and parental education.* 28th Yearbook of the National Society for the Study of Education. Bloomington, Illinois: Public School Publications Co., 1929.

White, T.H. *In search of history: a personal adventure.* New York: Warner, 1978.

TOWARD SOLUTIONS FOR PROBLEMS OF

EARLY CHILDHOOD EDUCATION

J. McVicker Hunt

University of Illinois at Urbana-Champaign

The same basic goal has animated the recently instituted efforts of both Israel and the United States of America in early childhood education. For different historical reasons, both nations have faced the incontrovertible fact that a substantial portion of children enter school without the knowledge and skills required to cope effectively with school. In consequence, many children drop out without having acquired the knowledge and skills and values required for productive employment in industrialized economies or for responsible citizenship. A major share of such children come from families where the parents are both uneducated and poor. The goal of early childhood education has been to provide these children with the knowledge and skills required to cope effectively with the tasks of school learning and ultimately to prepare them for a role both productive and responsible in the mainstream of our societies.

This goal is like a mountain. From the vantage point of distance, an ascent looks like a single climbing task. Yet, once embarked upon, the ascent becomes a succession of climbing tasks, each one revealed by success with its predecessor.

The first obstacle to such a goal consists of the beliefs that intelligence is fixed and that the early development of human beings is determined once and for all by heredity at conception. So long as these beliefs are held, such a goal is unthinkable. Once we realize the plasticity in early psychological development, our ignorance of what experiences are important for early psychological development looms as the obstacle. When knowledge of these important experiences has been gained, lack of a tested technology of early education becomes the obstacle. Even when the importance of parental influence in such a technology has been recognized, how to involve and teach

15

parents to be effective educators of their infants and young children appears as an obstacle. At every level, moreover, obtaining and maintaining the interest and financial support for ongoing research on how young human beings grow psychologically and for the development of an educational technology for infancy and the preschool years is a continuing obstacle.

BELIEFS IN FIXED INTELLIGENCE AND PREDETERMINED DEVELOPMENT

     The effort of early childhood education with the ambitious goal of equal opportunity was launched only recently. Infants and preschool children have always been dependent, but almost exclusively upon their parents. The state has felt obliged to assume responsibility only for those who are unable to learn and grow because of serious defects at birth. Although failure in school had long been observed to be especially common among the children of uneducated parents of poverty, their failure was considered an inevitable consequence of their defective heredity. Francis Galton's (1869) *Hereditary Genius* was a watershed in this domain. It implicitly attributed imbecility to heredity as well. Malthus (1798) had taken this position earlier in his famous *Essay on the Principles of Population*. Moreover, because Malthus expected the population to advance geometrically while the sources of food increased arithmetically, he opposed all charity. Charity, he contended, would foster an increase in the rate of population growth. Thus in the end charity would merely increase and prolong the agonies of the incompetent poor in their competition with those more competent.

     This view was presupposed from the beginning in the studies of individual differences launched by Francis Galton (1883) with his *Inquiries into Human Faculties*. Alfred Binet and Theodore Simon (1905, 1911), on the other hand, were educators. They considered the intellect to be plastic. From their measure of the development of intelligence they hoped to obtain information that would enable them to improve the educational process. Once Wilhelm Stern (1912) hit upon the idea of dividing the measure of mental age by the chronological age to obtain the IQ, however, the Binet-Simon measure of intelligence readily lent itself to a Galtonian interpretation. The IQ was conceived to be an essentially fixed dimension of each child. In effect it was interpreted to be a measure of the child's potential as well as of her or his past achievements. Thus, the debate over the constancy of the IQ was launched. Moreover, so long as most people in authority accepted the constancy of the IQ and the implicit underlying beliefs that intelligence is fixed and psychological development predetermined by heredity, the idea of using early education to help the children of uneducated parents of poverty to cope effectively with the learning tasks posed by the schools was unthinkable. Variations in home conditions had little or no relevance to that value of equal opportunity established by the fathers of the U.S. Constitution as a basic tenet of governmental responsibility.

In his book entitled *The Children's Cause*, Gilbert Y. Steiner (1976) has attributed the change in this interpretation to two books that have had political as well as scientific influence. But the political influence is due only to an accident of history. One of these books assembled the accumulated evidence against the beliefs in fixed intelligence and predetermined development (Hunt, 1961). The other book reviewed the evidence concerned with stability and change in human characteristics (Bloom, 1964). While both of these books and others went somewhat beyond assembling the evidence "to suggest that existing policy did not adequately meet society's responsibility to children" (Steiner, 1976, p. 26), the evidence and the suggestion could have had little or no political effect had not John Kennedy, newly elected to the Presidency of the United States, been sensitized by having a mentally deficient sister.

President Kennedy decided early to launch his War on Poverty. However, not until several months after the passage of the Economic Opportunity Act and the appointment of his brother-in-law Sargent Shriver as director of this agency was early education considered as part of that War on Poverty. The catalyst for this consideration was Dr. Robert E. Cooke, Professor of Pediatrics at the Johns Hopkins University School of Medicine, who served as pediatrician for the Shrivers and also had a mentally deficient child. Given the mandate to recommend a program for children, Cooke assembled a panel of experts to consider what programs might be effective in increasing the opportunities for children of the poor. The panel recommended preschool programs and thus "largely by chance, the knowledge provided in the specialized writings of Bloom, Hunt, Cooke, and Jean Piaget found its way into policy" (Steiner, 1976, p. 28). The consequence: the Office of Economic Opportunity (OEO) launched Project Head Start in the summer of 1965. OEO planners authorized about $17 million for an estimated 100,000 children. Such was the popularity of the Head Start Program, however, that 561,359 children were actually enrolled in 11,068 centers that summer.

In 1961, I wrote that "in the light of the evidence now available, it is not unreasonable to entertain the hypothesis that, with a sound scientific educational psychology of early experience, it might become feasible to raise the average level of intelligence as now measured by a substantial degree...[and] 'this substantial degree' might be of the order of 30 points of IQ" (Hunt, 1961, p. 27). Nevertheless, I was highly ambivalent about the launching of Project Head Start. It is one thing to discern that something may be possible, and quite another to know precisely how to do it. While I and others like me were delighted to have the U.S. federal government interested in early childhood education, we also feared that overselling the effects of early experience without having the "sound scientific educational psychology" for infancy and early childhood might lead to a failure that would foreclose opportunities for better prepared efforts later.

The earliest reports about Project Head Start from the field were favorable. Four-year-olds from the uneducated families of poverty

showed academic gains not to be found in children of comparable background without Head Start experience. On the other hand, the unrealistic hope that a summer or a year of preschooling in Head Start could
enable children of uneducated families of poverty to compete on equal
terms with those from educated families of the middle class was demonstrated to be false. Moreover, the findings of such large-scale surveys
as that by the U.S. Commission on Civil Rights (1967) and by the Westinghouse Corporation (Cicarelli, 1969) showed that Head Start programs
not only failed to fulfill the unrealistic hopes for catch-up, but had
produced only temporary gains.

A variety of factors other than a lack of a tested educational
technology limited the accomplishment of Project Head Start (see Hunt,
1975, p. 281ff).[1] On the other hand, Project Head Start led to a variety
of significant, related enterprises that should be included within its
accomplishments. These include the investigations of class differences
in child-rearing and innovations in compensatory education and in the
prevention of incompetence (see Hunt, 1975, pp. 285-303). Such was the
popularity of Project Head Start that early in the fall of 1966 the
White House appointed a multidisciplinary task force to examine the
federal government's role in early child development and to recommend
what it should be. The task force produced a report entitled *A Bill
of Rights for Children* (Hunt et al., 1967), which recommended the
Parent and Child Center Program for younger children and the Follow-
Through Program for older ones (Hunt, 1975).

The transitoriness of any gains from compensatory education would
be expected from a theory in which the rate of development is a function
of the development-fostering quality of a child's interaction with her
or his physical and social environment. In Project Head Start and in
the various programs of compensatory education, the student-teacher
ratio has typically been reduced to about 5 to 1. Moreover, the
teachers were usually given heavy responsibility for direct guidance
and active stimulation of the learning process. When this guidance
and stimulation were removed, the children became dependent for the
development-fostering quality of their experience on their uneducated
parents and the public schools where the student-teacher ratio typically
ranged between 25 and 35 to 1.

Although public and professional reactions to the disappointing
evaluations of Project Head Start were mixed, one important reaction
consisted of revisiting the beliefs in fixed intelligence and predetermined development. Arthur Jensen (1969) opened his well known paper
by saying, "Compensatory education has been tried and it apparently has
failed." A major share of his paper thereafter was devoted to an
explication of the heritability of IQ and scholastic achievement, which
he claimed explains why compensatory education "apparently has failed."
He went on to revisit the explanation of class and race differences in
terms of the assumption of biological inevitability, traditional from
the days of Parson Malthus through World War II.

Jensen's paper had wide circulation and was influential in government quarters. It not only revived and reheated the old controversy over the relative importance of heredity and environment, but increased the difficulty of obtaining funds for the support of programs concerned with early childhood education. Such reactions mean that the traditional beliefs in fixed intelligence and predetermined development have not been adequately disposed of. Let us turn, therefore, to some of the newer evidence of plasticity in early psychological development and to the fact that the nature of an infant's early experience can markedly alter her or his characteristics at age three.

New Evidence of Plasticity in Early Psychological Development

First, some investigators have employed a strategy of intervention that consists of providing experiences intended to foster psychological development by increasing its rate. These interventions of an educational nature have yielded not only evidence of plasticity, but some information about the nature of early development and the kinds of experience that foster it.

The first of these is my own program carried out with a number of collaborators for the most part in the orphanage of the Queen Farah Pahlavi Charity Society in Tehran. A letter from my old colleague and friend Wayne Dennis led me to this orphanage in 1958. With the letter was a dittoed copy of a prepublication (Dennis, 1960) describing orphanages in Tehran, where about 60% of the infants in their second year were not yet sitting alone; about 80% of those in their fourth year were not yet walking. At that time I was working on what ultimately became papers entitled "Motivation Inherent in Information Processing and Action" (Hunt, 1963) and "Intrinsic Motivation and Its Role in Psychological Development" (Hunt, 1965). I was formulating educated guesses about the role of such motivation in the psychological development of infants during their first and second years. The nature of my guesses suggested that orphanages caring for infants from birth on would provide about the only facility I could think of for testing their validity. The orphanage that Dennis described seemed ideal. To make a long story short, it took eight years to find a suitable Iranian collaborator and the funds to support the research program, which lasted from the summer of 1966 through the end of 1975 (Hunt, Mohandessi, Ghodssi & Akiyama, 1976).

Orphanage Program in Tehran

This program employed what I have termed "wave design," which I used for both investigative and ethical reasons. It gave those caring for the controls no opportunity to imitate the educational intervention employed with the treatment group and avoided the dubious practice of withholding a promising educational service from one group of infants

while providing it for another. The experiment consisted of five
waves, or samples, in which each successive wave was started more than
a year after the preceding one. The original control wave used the
customary rearing practices of the orphanage.

The subjects were foundlings, infants without known relatives.
Probably the progeny of illegitimate matings, these infants were taken
from the Municipal Orphanage of Tehran, whence they had come from having
been deposited on either the floor of a Mosque or a police station.
Each successive sample or wave was taken from the Municipal Orphanage
when the infants were still less than 30 days old. Only those without
detectable pathology of any kind were chosen.

The independent variables were the educational interventions. For
the 15 foundlings in the first or control wave, there was no intervention other than the repeated examining with the ordinal scales (Uzgiris
& Hunt, 1975) with which we measured development (Hunt et al., 1976).
The second wave of 10 foundlings received what we intended to be audiovisual enrichment, which was to have consisted of music and mother-
talk delivered through speakers attached to the sides of the cribs.
When the apparatus was working, the infant could turn these speakers
on by pulling on a string attached to her or his wrist with a plastic
bracelet. The visual portion consisted of a mobile, which the infant
could activate by shaking him or herself. This effort was abortive
because the apparatus was not maintained. The third wave of 10 foundlings received "untutored" human enrichment. This consisted of reducing the typical infant-caregiver ratio of between 30 and 40 to 3 to
10 to 3. The enrichment was "untutored" because the caregivers were
given no instructions and were allowed to do whatever came naturally.
It was planned in part as a form of enrichment to be compared with the
audiovisual kind, and in part to provide a base-line rate of development for comparison with that obtained with caregivers taught a way
to foster early development. The fourth wave of 20 foundlings received
the audiovisual enrichment originally planned for the foundlings in
wave II, with the apparatus being maintained.

Before the fifth wave was assembled, it had become clear that the
foundlings in waves I and II had reached age three without either expressive or receptive language. The absence of expressive language
was easy to discern, for during their entire third year only two of
the 25 ever used her or his voice for anything but crying or yelling.
Through illness, these two had become pets of one or more of the caregivers. Moreover, only these two ever spontaneously named objects before three years of age. The evidence for lack of receptive language
was more difficult to come by. It came from having either the caregivers or examiners, both highly familiar to these children, give very
simple verbal directions such as "Go to the man," or "Put the paper
[which was lying on the floor] on the table." Such directions led only
to blank looks and no action. Yet when I would look at a child, smile,
and make a gesture of approach, two kinds of reaction were obtained:

either withdrawing and crying or a tentative approach. Both showed appreciation of the meaning of the gesture absent from the verbal instruction. None of these infants ever put the paper on the table in response to the request. Yet some of those who would approach me could be induced to put the paper on the table through repeated gestures.

The "tutored" human enrichment was employed with the 11 foundlings in wave V. This approach was suggested by a theory, gleaned from the literature, that language acquisition is epigenetic in nature, that phonology is acquired through imitation, that semantics is acquired by association of phonological patterns heard with parts of the body touched, or actions, events and objects experienced concretely, and that elementary syntax is probably a creative use of phonological and semantic achievements in the interest of communication for various purposes (Hunt, 1981). The caregivers were taught to use the Badger learning programs for infants (Badger, 1971a) and toddlers (Badger, 1971b). These programs call for responsiveness to the needs of infants as soon as expressed and also for providing them with materials that match their individual levels of achievement and interest. The original version of these programs had been employed for educational day care with offspring of the poorly educated parents of poverty served by the Parent and Child Center at Mt. Carmel, Illinois. Because the original version had advanced object construction without advancing vocal imitation and language acquisition, experiences designed to foster these latter skills were inserted into these programs.

In the hierarchy comprising the epigenesis of language acquisition, according to my hypothetical scenario, the associative coordination required for the development of semantics requires previous attainment of a minimal level of permanence in objects and an interest in hearing and imitating vocalized sounds. Imitation also goes through epigenetic transformations, which in turn reflect those of intrinsic motivation (Hunt, 1965). Infants become interested in what they have come to recognize through earlier encounters before they become interested in what is new or novel for them (Hunt, 1965; Greenberg, Uzgiris & Hunt, 1970). Infants thus show interest and respond in kind when they hear recognitively familiar sounds vocalized by adults well before they become interested in what to them are unfamiliar phonemic patterns. This response is termed "pseudo-imitation."

In implementing this scenario, we supplemented the Badger learning programs by teaching the caregivers to imitate the cooing and babbling sounds of the foundlings in their care. This started vocal games, which were expected to foster the facility of infants' vocal systems. When the infants were observed to play the game with a number of such patterns, the caregivers were instructed to begin playing "follow-the-leader." When the infants could follow from one familiar vocal pattern to another with facility, the caregivers were to model sounds they had never heard the infant make. At the same time, the caregivers were instructed to talk about the caregiving processes as they conducted

them. As the infants began to imitate novel phonemic patterns, the
caregivers were to touch parts of their bodies and simultaneously name
the parts touched. The paradigm was, "Now I am going to wash your
ear." As the caregiver's vocal emphasis came to the word "ear," her
washcloth was to make contact with the infant's anatomical ear, and so
with hands, nose, knees, and so forth. This is as far as explicit instructions in the fostering of the vocal imitation and language went. I
was also as far as the caregivers went. Without special instruction,
it did not occur to them to ask the foundlings in their care to point
to parts named, or to name parts touched, or to discuss plans and wishes

Two features of importance in this program of investigations are
that the interventions are longitudinal and that a variety of different
aspects of psychological development have been assessed. As a corollary
to the longitudinal nature of the intervention, the program took into
account the epigenetic nature of infant development, particularly that
of imitation and language. The various aspects of development assessed,
sometimes only through partially systematized observations suggested by
clinical impressions, have included: (1) motor development, (2) cognitive
development, as assessed by the seven Piaget-inspired ordinal scales of
Uzgiris and Hunt (1975), (3) language achievement, and (4) social attractiveness. The ordinal scales include: (a) Object permanence, (b) Development of Means for Obtaining Desired Events, (c) Vocal Imitation,
(d) Gestural Imitation, (e) Operational Causality, (f) Object Relations
in Space, and (g) Schemes for Relating to Objects. These methodological
features are the basis for some important serendipitous findings.

RESULTS

The results from the Uzgiris-Hunt scales have come in terms of the
means and standard deviations of the ages in weeks at which the foundlings of these five waves attained an intermediate and the top step on
each of the seven scales (Hunt et al., 1976, pp. 200-201). In summary,
each successive wave except the second, which received the abortive attempt at audiovisual enrichment, attained the top steps on these scales
at mean ages younger than did the infants in the preceding waves.
Properly administered, the audiovisual enrichment enabled the foundlings in wave IV to attain the intermediate steps on the Uzgiris-Hunt
Scales considerably younger than did those of waves I and II and also
well ahead of those in wave III, who got the untutored human enrichment. In fact, the wave IV foundlings were not far behind those of
wave V in attaining the intermediate steps, a finding which suggests
that mechanically administered, audiovisual enrichment can be fairly
effective in fostering development during the first 6 to 9 months of
life. Not so thereafter. The foundlings of wave V showed by far the
greatest advances in mean ages of attaining the top steps on all seven
of the Uzgiris-Hunt scales.

When one compares the mean ages of attaining the top steps in the
seven scales by these foundlings of wave V with those of waves I and

II, the differences range from 34 weeks for the scale of Object Permanence, to 87 weeks for that of Gestural Imitation. The mean of
these differences between the mean ages of attaining the top steps on
the seven scales is 63 weeks, or nearly a year and a quarter. Each of
these mean ages for attaining top steps can be transformed to an IQ-
ratio by using for mental age the mean ages at which home-reared children attain these top steps and dividing such estimates of mental age
by the mean chronological ages at which the foundlings in each of the
waves attained the steps (see Hunt, Paraskevopoulos, Schickedanz, &
Uzgiris, 1975). When this operation is performed, the mean difference
of 63 weeks becomes a difference of approximately 47 points in the
mean IQ ratios. Since performances on composites of Piagetian tasks
show a high correlation with performances on standard tests of intelligence (Humphreys & Parsons, 1979), this gain of 47 points of IQ ratio
probably approximates the gain in IQ that would have been found with
standard psychometric tests. It is also interesting to note that on
five of these seven scales the foundlings of wave V attained the top
steps at somewhat younger ages than did a sample of home-reared infants
from predominantly professional families of Worcester, Massachusetts.
This finding suggests that their rate of past development, as assessed
by IQ strategy, was probably of the order of 130.

   Serendipitous Findings: Measuring these several branches of psychological development simultaneously and repeatedly in longitudinal strategy produced two serendipitous findings with substantial significance
for both theory of development and early pedagogy. First, the more
standardized is the development-fostering quality of experience, the
lower is the standard deviation of the ages at which infants attain
steps on these scales (Hunt et al., 1976). This finding corroborates
findings from cross-sectional studies where the standard deviations of
the ages of children at the various levels of development decreased
with the degree of standardization of the development-fostering quality
of their experience independently assessed. In such studies, it was
especially interesting to note that the standard deviations in the ages
of children at the upper levels of these ordinal scales were larger than
those of orphanage-reared children even though the mean ages of those
home-reared were substantially below those of orphanage-reared infants
(Hunt, 1980, p. 56ff).

   The second finding provided evidence of specificity in the relationship between kinds of experience and kinds of developmental advance
or retardation. For instance, the untutored human enrichment received
by wave III markedly hastened the development of posture and locomotion
without advancing development along any of the Piaget-inspired scales.
Nearly all of the foundlings in waves I and II failed to sit up during
their first year and failed to stand and cruise around their cribs until they were about 80 weeks old, whereas those in wave III not only
sat up earlier, but were standing and cruising on the average by 41
weeks of age (Hunt et al., 1976). The particular sensorimotor organizations that are used and extended to cope with the circumstances en-

countered develop most rapidly. Thus the original Badger learning
programs used in the day care provided by the Parent and Child Center
of Mt. Carmel, Illinois, served to advance the mean age (73 weeks) at
which the offspring of poorly educated parents of poverty served by
the Center achieved the top step on the scale of Object Permanence
nearly half a year ahead of the mean age (98 weeks) at which the top
step was achieved by the home-reared infants of predominantly professional families in Worcester, Massachusetts. But the Badger programs
left the Mt. Carmel infants five months behind the Worcester infants
in achieving the top step on the scale of Vocal Imitation. Much better
knowledge of such specific relationships between kinds of experience
and kinds of developmental advance are needed for the design of more
effective programs of early education.

   Language Achievement: In language achievement, the advancement of
the foundlings in wave V over those of waves I and II was even more
dramatic. On the scale of Schemes for Relating to Objects, only one
of the 15 foundlings in wave I and only one of the 10 in wave II ever
spontaneously named an object before 169 weeks of age. On the other
hand, all 11 of those in wave V spontaneously named objects in the
examining situation at an average age of 90 weeks. This is only four
weeks later on the average than this landmark was attained (86 weeks)
by the home-reared infants from predominantly professional families
in Worcester (Hunt, 1980; Hunt et al., 1976).

   The difference is marked, but perhaps the contrast of wave V with
waves I and II in language achievements can best be communicated with
some vignettes of individual behavior. I had become accustomed to the
foundlings' lack of language even at age three from observing those
in waves I and II. On the day that I first entered the playroom of
wave V when they were between 17 and 22 months of age, they greeted me
by saying, "Hello," in unison at a signal from one of their caretakers.
The contrast was striking. Before being shown to the playroom on this
occasion, I had been held for an exasperatingly long time at the customary tea ceremony in the office of the directress. It turned out
that this delay was occasioned by an effort to get these foundlings to
say in unison, "Hello, Dr. Hunt." That was too many syllables. The
caretakers and examiners had to settle for "hello."

   Following this "hello," Cambiz, the oldest of wave V, astounded me
by approaching with his arms thrust upward and uttering a word which
I learned was Farsi for "up." The gesture was clearly a request to be
picked up. No infant in any of the other waves had ever shown such
trustful behavior. When the chief examiner invited me to see the examining room, Cambiz resisted being put down, so I carried him along.
Through a window opposite the door of entry, one could see a sprayer.
Cambiz excitedly shouted, "Ab, ab, ab," the Farsi word for water.
This was a beautiful example of spontaneous naming.

   When I sought to get Cambiz to imitate the English word "water,"

he remained so excited with seeing the sprayer and shouting "ab" that
it was impossible to get him to pay attention to my modelings of
"water." I therefore backed into the hall out of sight of the sprayer.
He then readily focused his attention on my saying "water." Moreover,
he responded with "awter," a fair approximation. When, after about four
modelings, with continued failure to include the initial "w," I changed
my model to "wah, wah," Cambiz immediately replied in kind. When I
followed this by another modeling of "water," he immediately followed
with a rendition of "water" as clear as my model.

The next vignette concerns Shabnam, the youngest in wave V and
then somewhat less than 18 months of age. As the chief examiner was
demonstrating that Shabnam could readily imitate the names of each of
the infants in the group, she came to Yass. I had had no opportunity to
see Yass because she had been adopted and removed from the orphanage in
1974. Shabnam had been uttering clear imitations of the names modeled
by the examiner. However, when the examiner said, "Yass," Shabnam's
manner changed abruptly. She twisted in my arms, reached and looked
toward the door, and said, "Yass rafteh." This is a sentence; it means
"Yass gone." I am satisfied that no one had schooled her in the construction of such a sentence. Yet she reflected in it a state of af-
fairs for which she had full cognitive appreciation; Yass had been her
special friend.

Shabnam's performance prompted me to ask how many words she knew.
No one knew the answer. So I asked how one would say in Farsi, "What
is it?" After getting the examiner's answer, I would gently pull
Shabnam's hair or touch the features of her face, parts of her body,
the garments she wore, and utter my best imitation of the Farsi for the
question, "Een chi eh?" Shabnam surprised the examiner and me by responding quickly with the names for all these except her elbow. When I
touched her elbow and asked the question, she looked distressed. Her
distress seemed to imply a sense that she *should* know, and the examiner
quickly responded by supplying the Farsi word for elbow. On another
occasion, I determined in the same fashion that she also knew the Farsi
names for table, chair, the various dishes, and the utensils used in
caretaking. When I listed the objects I had asked her to name and
counted them, there were more than fifty that she had named.

Moreover, when such a procedure was employed with the nine other
foundlings of wave V still available, they too could name correctly at
least fifty items involved in the caretaking process. No attempt was
made to test vocabulary limits, but several of the older infants also
showed considerable semantic mastery of the elementary abstraction of
colors, and one showed perfect mastery by naming repeatedly the reds,
yellows, greens, and blues as I pointed to them in pictures along the
wall. When one considers that only about a quarter of the 4-year-olds
in Head Start programs show semantic mastery of this elementary abstraction (Kirk, Hunt & Lieberman, 1975), this must be seen as no mean
achievement for orphanage-reared foundlings.

There is yet another aspect of language achievement worth noting. At approximately age two, these foundlings of wave V who had not yet been adopted were judged to be substantially better at imitating the pronunciations of strange three-syllable words, modeled for them by the chief examiner, than were the children remaining from wave III, who had received the untutored human enrichment and were then four years of age (Hunt, 1981).

The absence of language, both receptive and expressive, in the infants of waves I and II at age three demonstrates dramatically the importance of the role of experience in language acquisition. This lack calls into serious question the impugning of the importance of experienc in language acquisition by such psycholinguistic theorists as Chomsky (1959) and Lenneberg (1966). The fact that all 11 of the infants in wave V spontaneously named objects before they were two years old, and nearly as soon as did the home-reared children from predominantly pro-fessional families in Worcester, attests that the procedures taught the caregivers to foster vocal imitation and semantic mastery were indeed effective.

Social Attractiveness: The caregivers' tutoring affected language acquisition beyond expectations. But the effect of this intervention on the social attractiveness of the foundlings in wave V was quite un-expected. No ready metrics exist for measuring such phenomena. Never-theless, the contrast of wave V with waves I and II in social attrac-tiveness was most obvious in the domain of interaction with adults, es-pecially with strange adults. Sound cinemas could have rendered highly palpable this contrast. Unfortunately, sound cinemas were not planned for and probably would have been unfeasible. Nevertheless, I can report what I observed, and these observations get at least a degree of confir-mation from snapshots of the children taken without any expectation of their providing evidence of this contrast in social attractiveness.

The foundlings of waves I and II wore glum expressions, failed to play with toys, and indeed showed no evidence of preoccupation with either things or people. The children initiated no interactions with adults and seldom with other children, and were wary of or withdrawn fro any adults but their accustomed caregivers or examiners. Four of these children from waves I and II are pictured in the upper half of Figure I.

The children of wave V, on the other hand, wore alert and interes-ted expressions. They were almost always interacting with toys or peopl of their own choice and tended to approach with interest almost any adult who came within view or earshot. Four of them are pictured in the lower row of Figure I. The one on your left is Cambiz, who approached me immediately after the "Hello" incident with the request to be picked up. Note his obvious enthusiasm for striking the ball hung from the ring in the ceiling. The second from the left is Parvis. Note his interested preoccupation with the stacking toy. The third is Monee. Note the evidence of initiative in his gesture of request or demand of

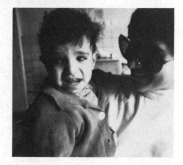

Figure I.   Foundlings from the Municipal Orphanage of Tehran

the adult standing by. On your right is Shabnam, the youngest one,
who said "Yass rafteh." Note her unsolicited wave to me as I took her
picture. The social attractiveness of these children was confirmed by
several childless couples in Tehran who chose 7 of the 11 foundlings of
wave V for adoption. On the other hand, of the 57 foundlings who served
in the preceding waves, only two were ever adopted. These two were chosen before they were six months old because they were pretty babies.
The 7 from wave V were adopted because they were attractively responsive
2-year-olds.

This contrast between the developmental achievements of the foundlings in wave V with waves I and II constitutes evidence of the tremendous plasticity in psychological development during the first two or
three years of life. In terms of the IQ, this difference as transformed
appears to approximate 47 IQ points of roughly three standard deviations
one more standard deviation than I had expected from the evidence
available in the late 1950s. One cannot possibly predict the future
development of these two groups of children without knowing the
development-fostering quality of the experiences they will encounter in
their future lives. But unless the interested, out-going 2-year-olds
of wave V meet with conditions that squelch their well developed initiative and trust, or unless those of waves I and II are fortunate
enough to receive very powerful therapeutic encouragement, the observed
contrast between these two groups can be expected to endure indefinitely

The Milwaukee Program

Evidence confirming both the degree of plasticity obtained in this
Tehran program and this predicted persistence of the contrast has come
from the longitudinal intervention in Milwaukee, Wisconsin, conducted
by Heber, Garber, and their collaborators. This program began with an
epidemiological study of the census tract where about a third of the
mentally retarded known to the Milwaukee schools are found (Heber, Dever
& Conry, 1968). The intervention program was based on a selection of
88 consecutive births where the mother also had at least one child age
six years. The total number of children was 586.

It turned out that 45.4% of the mothers with IQs below 80 contributed 78.2% of the children with IQs below 80. When Heber and collaborators plotted the IQs of the children as a function of age, they found
the IQs from consecutive testings of the children of mothers with IQs
above 80 to be roughly constant, but those of children of mothers with
IQs less than 80 dropped progressively from 95 on the infant tests to
about 80 by age 4 and to about 65 by age 14. From these findings, it
appeared that "the source of the excess prevalence of mental retardation appeared to be the retarded parents residing in the slum environment, rather than the slum itself" (Heber, 1978, pp. 42-45).

Jensen (1969) has cited these data of Heber et al (1968) as evi-

dence that intelligence is largely fixed by heredity. Heber, on the
other hand, considered the possibility "that the mentally retarded
mother residing in the slum creates a social environment for her offspring which is distinctly different from that created by her next-door
neighbor of normal intelligence" (Heber, 1978, p. 45). Thus he and his
collaborators proceeded to identify 40 mothers with IQs of 70 or less
who had newborns. These mother-infant dyads were assigned to either a
treatment group for intense rehabilitation or to a control group. The
program for the treatment group had two aspects: (1) education, vocational rehabilitation, and home-and child-care training for the mother,
and (2) an intense, personalized educational intervention with the
infants beginning when they were about three months of age and continuing until they entered public school at about 66 months of age. This
intervention is described as having a cognitive-language orientation,
which was implemented through the encouragement of reciprocal interaction and informal prescriptive teaching techniques.

    During the first year, a consistent one-to-one teacher-child re-
lationship was maintained. Gradually during the preschool years this
relationship was changed to groups of from 10 to 12 children, each with
three teachers in a more traditional classroom setting. Contact was
also maintained continuously with the mothers in the control group.
The control mothers also received some counsel with problems of housekeeping and employment, but not with child care. The children in both
groups participated in the same schedule of repeated testings keyed to
each child's birthdate and carried out every two months from age 6
months to 24 months and then monthly to age six.

    Results: As measured by the Gesell scales, the development of
the two groups of infants was roughly comparable during the first year,
but by 22 months of age, those receiving the educational intervention
averaged 4.5 to 6 months in advance of the controls on all four of the
Gesell schedules. By that time, the controls had fallen well below
Gesell's norm on the Adaptive Language Schedule. By age 3 years those
receiving the educational treatment scored substantially better than
the controls in every measure of language proficiency employed. By age
4.5 years the treated group was approximately a standard deviation above
the norm of the Illinois Test of Psycholinguistic Abilities, while the
controls were approximately a standard deviation below this norm. On
the Cattell and Stanford-Binet Tests of Intelligence, the mean IQs of
the two groups differed little at age 12 months. However, during the
second year the IQ increased for the treated group, but decreased continuously to age 30 months for the controls. At age 6 years, the mean
IQ of the treated group was 120.7 (SD = 11.2; lowest IQ = 109), while
that of the control group was 87.2 (SD = 12.8), a difference of somewhat more than 30 IQ points.

    Once the children entered public school at an average age of
about 66 months, the early educational interventions ceased. Thus,
those in the treated group became completely dependent upon their

poorly educated parents and the public schools for the development-
fostering quality of their experience. The two groups of children
have been examined annually with the Wechsler Intelligence Scale for
Children for the years following their school entry. During the first
year in school, when the development-fostering quality of the experience of the treated group changed radically, their mean IQ dropped
about 8 points, whereas the mean IQ of the controls dropped only from
87 to 82. At age 108 months, after the three ensuing years into the
follow-up, the mean IQ of the treated group (108) remains approximately
30 points above that (79) of the controls. The lowest IQ of treated
children at age 96 months was 88; of the 20 controls at this age, 13
had IQs below 75 (Heber, 1978, p. 60). The fact that the differences
induced by the early education persisted in the Milwaukee study suggests that the contrast found in the foundlings of wave V and of waves
I and II in their third year is very likely to persist indefinitely.

One may ask whether the contrast between the treated and the control groups in the Tehran and Milwaukee programs could have resulted
from the samplings of infants. While wave design fails to control
conditions that may change with time, three facts support the validity
of the Tehran contrast. The foundlings in each wave came from that
population of foundlings in the Tehran orphanage. The changes in
the mean ages of achieving the steps on the scale through five successive waves match precisely those that would be expected from the theoretical qualities of the development-fostering quality of the experiences provided. Moreover, the more standardized the rearing conditions,
the smaller were the standard deviations in ages of attaining the
upper steps on the ordinal scales.

It is true that the treated and control groups in the Milwaukee
program may not have been strictly random samples from the finite
population of 40 mother-child dyads, as Page (1972) has contended, but
the only trait measured on which the difference at birth was significant was body weight. No evidence of correlation between birthweight
and subsequent intelligence exists to my knowledge, when birthweights
are within normal limits. Moreover, Garber and Haber (1973) have
reported a variety of data indicating that the family-based conditions
of these two groups of infants were highly comparable, including the
IQs of the mothers. Further studies in educational interventions are
needed, employing those experiences that have been found to be most
effective in fostering development when properly matched to the existing developmental achievements of infants and young children. We
also need appreciation of the rules for that matching such as those
used in the Tehran program (see p. 8, 2nd paragraph).

The North Carolina Study

A third very recent study by Ramey and Haskins (1980) has taken
special care to observe the methodological strictures of random sam-

pling of simultaneous treatment and control groups from a specified
small population of children at high risk. One major finding is an
absence of decline in test scores for the group receiving the early
educational treatment versus the decline present in those who did not
receive it. The second major finding is the absence of the commonly
found correlation between the IQs of mothers and their children when
the children received the early educational treatment. Thus, effects
of early education on various aspects of what is measured as intelligence are present even when the treatment and control groups are formed
simultaneously by randomized sampling from a small, finite population.
On the other hand, children receiving the early educational treatment
in this North Carolina study did not attain scores well above the test
norms. Thus, the contrast between the final scores of the treated and
the control subjects was considerably less than the contrast in either
the Tehran or the Milwaukee program. Although Ramey and Haskins also
emphasized the importance of language, the effect of language achievement that they obtained from their early educational intervention was
considerably less than that in either the Tehran or the Milwaukee study.
These Carolina investigators started their intervention later than did
the investigators in Tehran and Milwaukee, took no account of the epigenetic nature of language development, and did not provide experiences
appropriate to each level of such development. I am confident that
their failure to find contrasts as large as those found in Tehran and
Milwaukee rests not on the rigor of their statistical sampling, but on
weaknesses in the age, timing, and nature of their educational treatment.

     Despite still remaining uncertainties, this new evidence of plas-
ticity in early psychological development, plasticity considerably
greater than the old evidence suggested, should be highly encouraging
to everyone interested in our hopes for early education. From such
findings, I am inclined to believe that every human infant born without detectable pathology has the hereditary potential to acquire all
the knowledge, skills, and values required for productive participation
in the mainstream of any culture on earth. Note, however, that this
statement is no paraphrase of the extreme environmentalism of John B.
Watson. It does not mean that any infant can be reared to become anything or to be an intellectual giant such as Aristotle, Isaac Newton,
or Albert Einstein, nor a 7-foot basketball star. Moreover, still
largely wanting is that condition of "a sound scientific educational
psychology for infancy and early childhood" required before raising the
level of intelligence by a substantial degree becomes feasible.

THE OBSTACLE OF IGNORANCE ABOUT EARLY CHILD DEVELOPMENT

     Although investigation during the past twenty years has im-
proved our understanding of early psychological development, belief
in old fictions continues to confuse us. It is worth stating some
of these fictions and at least indicating the nature of the evi-

dence contradicting them.

According to one fiction, each infant develops from conception as a whole or, in Arnold Gesell's language (1954, p. 339), "as an integer." In his sound cinema, *Life Begins,* Gesell made this fiction even more explicit with his statement that "maturation proceeds apace along all systems simultaneously." Not so. Providing infants with an opportunity to use any system markedly hastens the rate at which that system develops. Providing infants at 5 weeks of age with mobiles to look at brought on the blink response by a mean age of 7 weeks; in the controls it did not appear till a mean age of 10.4 weeks (Greenberg, Uzgiris & Hunt, 1968). In similar fashion, providing infants with visual targets that they can reach and touch hastens markedly the development of eye-hand coordination (White, 1967). At the Tehran orphanage, when the infant-caregiver ratio was reduced, caregivers carried the infants about, thereby giving them an opportunity to use their balancing mechanisms. When placed in strollers, the infants were able to put weight on their legs and to practice the stepping scheme. As a result, posture and locomotion were markedly advanced without, however, advancing achievement along any of the Piaget-inspired scales (Hunt et al, 1976).

While such evidence belies the assertion that infants "develop along all systems apace," such advances from use need not have appreciable influence on the rate of overall development unless those systems advanced participate in coordinations that mark the epigenetic transformations of behavioral structure. For instance, educational intervention advanced the achievement of top-level object permanence of the offspring of poorly educated parents of poverty in Mr. Carmel nearly six months ahead of this achievement in home-reared children from predominantly professional families of Worcester, but left the Mt. Carmel infants five months behind those of Worcester in attaining the top step on the scale of Vocal Imitation. Without advancement in both object construction and vocal imitation, language acquisition was substantially delayed in the Mt. Carmel infants. When given tests of intelligence in their fourth year, they were retarded (mean IQ in low 80s). Thus early psychological development is not a single stream but a complex of relatively independent streams or branches. This fact provides for the epigenetic nature of early psychological development.

According to two contentions competing for more than a century, both the form and the rate of early psychological development are chiefly a function of heredity or chiefly a function of environment. Both are fictions. Although heredity guarantees which species a fertilized ovum will become and continuously influences every aspect of development, it guarantees little or nothing about the form or rate of intellectual and motivational development in infancy. Nor, I believe, does heredity guarantee the ultimate level of competence to be attained. Moreover, the influence of the environment comes about only indirectly as the intimate proximal material and social circumstances influence which neuromuscular systems get used, when coordinations are called for

and adaptive modifications are demanded. The mighty muscles and hands
of Longfellow's village blacksmith did not develop automatically from
the time he spent in the environs of his anvil and bellows-augmented
fire; they grew in their use as he swung his hammer to shape the heat-
softened iron on the anvil and as he lifted the hooves of the horses
for shoeing. Unfortunately, as the unexpectedness of findings of specific relationships between kinds of experience and kinds of developmental advance illustrate, knowledge of what intimate, proximal experiences yield what developmental advances is still very limited.

Another set of fictions about development have their origin in
what has been termed "drive theory." I want to summarize here an alternative theory in some detail. According to the fictitious drive
theory, organisms are inactive unless stimulated by a homeostatic need,
pain or sex, or by some innocuous stimulus associated with one of these
"primary drives." Such motivational systems do indeed exist. It was
the merit of Abraham Maslow (1954) to point out that such motives form
a hierarchy. In his theorizing, Maslow used findings from animal
studies to show how eating and drinking to satisfy hunger and thirst
can be inhibited by painful stimulation, that sexual behavior can be
inhibited by hunger and thirst, and that interest in knowing can be
dominated by stimuli producing sexual arousal. Thus, drive-based motives do exist. What is fictitious about drive theory is that animals
and people cease to be active in the absence of such stimuli. Even
though Freud (1905) was probably the most notable source of emphasis
on the importance of early experience in psychological development, his
theory of psychosexual development was based upon "instincts [or drives]
and their vicissitudes" (Freud, 1915).

Suffice it here to say that Freud's theory, which described an
epigenetic sequence of libidinal investments in oral, anal, and phallic
zones and functions, has failed to survive the dissonance of objective
evidence (see Hunt, 1979, pp. 112-115). Moreover, these past twenty
years have seen the emergence and evolution of a theory of "motivation
inherent in information processing and action" (for review, see Hunt,
1963). Above I referred in passing to the fact that this motivational
system itself appears to have an epigenetic course of development
(Hunt, 1965). At birth, attention is attracted primarily by changes in
the characteristics of on-going receptor inputs. As the objects, places,
and persons within the life space of an infant are repeatedly encountered, representative central processes, or memories, are gradually
formed. Those objects, places, and persons for which recognitive familiarity is developing become attractive (Greenberg, et al., 1970;
Weizmann, Cohen & Pratt, 1971; Wetherford & Cohen, 1973). With further
exposure, these familiar objects, persons, and places become passé and
the infant turns her or his attention to what is new and novel in the
familiar context.

Elsewhere (Hunt, 1965, 1970) I have pointed out that recognitive
familiarity provides a highly plausible motivational basis for such

autogenic and repetitive activities as hand and foot watching, babbling, and pseudo-imitation in which the infant responds in kind when a familiar vocal pattern is modeled for him. Similarly, interest in what is novel within a familiar context supplies a plausible motivational basis for the inclination of infants to explore new territory and to be interested in unfamiliar objects, and for genuine imitation of unfamiliar gestures and vocal patterns.

The onset of interest in what is new and novel in a familiar context leads to what I have termed the "problem of the match" (Hunt 1961, pp. 267-288). Whether perceptions of novel circumstances will foster the development of an infant's understanding is a function of the degree of discrepancy between the information that he or she has already mastered and that coming in the new encounter. Similarly, in the domain of action, what is attractive is a matter of an optimal degree of discrepancy between skills achieved and the action-demands of the circumstances encountered. When these discrepancies are too small, the result is boredom, and no development occurs. When the discrepancy is too large, the infant or child cannot cope with the demands for adaptive modifications in her or his existing achievements. Distress results, and the child attempts to escape from the situation. When the degree of discrepancy is optimal, the child becomes interested. The demands on his knowledge and skills are within his capacity for adaptive modification, so in meeting them the child develops. Providing new situations that match the developmental achievements of children by creating copable demands for adaptive modification becomes a major problem for caretakers, parents, and teachers who would maximize the development-fostering quality of a child's experience. In the present state of our ignorance about early development, behavioral signs of interest are perhaps the best cue available for knowing whether a proper match is being achieved (see Hunt, 1980, p. 8 ff).

The unexpected effects of social attractiveness from having the caretakers imitate the vocal cooings of the infants in their charge has suggested that my formulation of the epigenesis in the motivation inherent in information processing and action needs modification (Hunt, 1981). In this earlier formulation (Hunt, 1965), no attempt was made to differentiate separate processes from motivation inherent in information processing and the motivation inherent in spontaneous action. In the former, recognition appears to develop gradually through repeated perceptual encounters with situations. In the case of action, what appears to be important are the perceptual encounters contingent with the spontaneous actions of the infant. When a spontaneous act serves merely to produce a perceptible change in the ongoing receptor inputs, that change appears to attract the attention of the child and to help associate the act with the effect.

R. W. White (1959) has contended that producing such an effect, termed "effectance," has pleasing emotional value. But the unexpected

and spectacular effects of having the caretakers imitate the vocal
cooings of the infants in their charge suggests that even more attractive and reinforcing, especially for very young infants, is having a
spontaneous action produce an effect that is recognitively familiar.
The exquisite delight that very young infants take in reciprocal gestural and vocal games suggests that any joy there may be from producing
an effect is more than doubled when that effect is recognitively familiar. One can properly speak of such an effect as being highly reinforcing. It reinforces, however, not only the readiness of the motor
act to recur, as Skinner (1953) has claimed. It also creates expectations that serve as the experiential basis for intentional action.
Thus, begins the establishment in an infant of that generalized sense
of an "internal locus of control of reinforcement," which Rotter (1966)
has emphasized leads toward an emotional attachment in infants to those
human beings who imitate them, and fosters in their imitators a fondness
for themselves.

    Such experiences may be seen to serve as a source of intentional
action when, in the course of repeated sequences of spontaneous vocalizations that are imitated, a memory for the sequence of events is produced. Since the central processes underlying memory run off more
rapidly than do the events, they provide a basis for the expectations.
Once an infant begins to act in order to obtain an anticipated event,
she or he is acting intentionally. That the reciprocal interaction of
the vocal games resulting from caretaker imitations of the spontaneous
vocalizations of infants fosters initiative and trust in the infants is
illustrated by the outgoing behavior of the foundlings of wave V and
its lack in those of waves I and II. That this reciprocal interaction
also fosters affectional attachment in caretakers for the infants cared
for is attested by the fact that the caregivers of wave V at the Tehran
orphanage claimed they could not have loved a child of their own body
more than they had come to love the foundlings in their charge. One
could readily be skeptical of such reports were they not substantiated
by the tears of grief that occurred in each caretaker in the days following the adoption of one of the infants in her charge.

    Freud (1905, 1933) attributed the affection of an infant for its
mother to the gratification of hunger at her breast. Harlow (1958),
however, found monkey infants more concerned with contact comfort than
with food. Recent pediatric studies have found reciprocal interaction
of infants with their mothers, to which such terms as "communication,"
"conversation," dialogue," and the "dance of life" have been applied,
beginning very early (Brazelton, Tronick, Adamson, Als & Wise, 1975;
Travarthen, 1974, 1977) to be a major factor in emotional attachment.
When newborns are left with their mothers in the lying-in hospital,
such mutual interaction has appeared as early as three weeks of age.
Papousek and Papousek (1977) have considered it to provide not only
the origins of emotional bonding between mother and child, but also
to be the basis for a "cognitive head start." However, the unexpected
findings concerning both emotional bonding between the foundlings and

their caregivers and the development of social attractiveness in the
foundlings of wave V in the Tehran study indicates that this early
period immediately after birth, while sensitive indeed, need not be
truly critical. Despite the fact that the caregivers never saw the
foundlings in their charge before they were about a month old, the emotional bond developed. Moreover, even though the foundlings were 30
weeks behind the home-reared infants of Worcester in achieving pseudo-
imitation, they achieved genuine vocal imitation slightly ahead of the
Worcester infants and developed an unusual degree of trust and initiative
that seems to account for their unusual degree of social attractiveness
(Hunt, 1981a).

A related fiction is the belief that if children are caught up to
the norm in academic skills, they should thereafter remain caught up.
Such a belief fails to take into account that development is ever a
process of adapting and coping with changing circumstances of increasing complexity. When the development-fostering quality of experience
is reduced for some, as is the case with those children who have had
compensatory education and then must depend on their poorly educated
parents of poverty and the public schools, their rate of development
will inevitably be slowed, while the rate of development of children
of educated parents will be maintained by that higher development-
fostering quality of experience which gave them their original advantage. Plasticity can cut both ways.

Perhaps evidence recently uncovered from a series of long-term
follow-ups of the academic performances of comparable children who
did and did not have experiences of compensatory preschool education
(Bronfenbrenner, 1974; Lazar, Hubel, Murray, Rosche & Royce, 1977);
Lazar & Darlington, 1978; Weikart, Epstein, Schweinhart & Bond, 1978)
may be making a fiction of the earlier finding that effects of compensatory education do not persist. If I understand this evidence correctly, it is a new source of hope for compensatory education in the
fourth and fifth years. In general, these studies agree that certain
effects of compensatory education do persist indefinitely. A consortium of twelve research groups that pioneered in compensatory education
have collaborated now in follow-up studies of the outcomes of their
earlier programs. The findings of this Consortium of Developmental
Continuity (1977) are based upon information from approximately 3,000
children of poorly educated parents of poverty. Within this number
are both those who participated in early compensatory education and
those who served as controls. Those children who participated have
surpassed their controls on the Stanford-Binet Test of Intelligence
for only about three years after the programs ended, and they surpassed
the controls on achievement tests only in the domain of mathematics
no later than the fourth grade. Yet the proportion of children who
participated that had later to be assigned to classes for special education has been substantially smaller than that of children who do not
participate. Moreover, the proportion of participants who had to repeat grades has also been substantially smaller than that of non-

participants. This evidence of persistence of effects held for all
categories of children from poorly educated parents of low income.

A later consortium report (Lazar & Darlington, 1978) carried the
follow-up through from 10 to 20 years, depending on the dates during
which each compensatory program took place. Again, evidence of persisting effects as measured by tests of intelligence and academic achievement had disappeared within three or four years. Yet only about half
as many of those who participated in preschool as of the control children had to be assigned to special education. And fewer of the former
than of the latter had to repeat grades. Such benefits held equally
for both sexes, for black and white, and were not limited to those with
higher initial IQs. Moreover, the statistical analyses uncovered little
evidence that the differing characteristics of the programs made some
more helpful than others. A report by Weikart et al. (1978) of the
High/Scope programs supports each of these points.

Inasmuch as the gains in academic achievement and IQ while early
educational programs are in force are substantially greater for those
that drill on language and other academic skills, this absence of differential in the persisting effects is very interesting. It suggests
that the effects which persist may reside more within the motivational
domain than in the cognitive. One such hypothesis holds that it is the
opportunity to develop attachments to adults outside the family that
persists and contributes to the motivation to accept the demands and
meet the standards of the teachers in the schools. Another hypothesis
holds that the greater opportunity for young children to choose and
start their own activities in the freer curricula may help to foster
that self-winding initiative which enables them to achieve on their
own better than do those children who were heavily drilled in the academic skills.

Favoring the latter hypothesis are tentative findings from a still
unpublished follow-up by Badger on the effects of training teenage
mothers of illegitimate children for effective parenting during the
first year of their firstborn's lives. During that year, these teenage mothers were taught much of what was taught the caretakers of the
foundlings at the Tehran orphanage. The infants gained substantially
over their controls in their first year, but the gains washed out during
the second year when their mothers returned to school and left their
infants with untrained caregivers. Yet when the Kent Oral Emergency
Test was administered to these children and their controls when they
entered kindergarten some four years later, two-thirds of those whose
mothers had been trained for effective parenting were above the norm,
while two-thirds of those whose mothers were merely visited at home
were below the norm. This still tentative finding suggests that the
effects of the experiences that foster initiative and an internal sense
of control may be highly persistent unless the children experience
circumstances in which their initiative or will is punished.

Other evidence relevant to this point has come from correlating assessments of the rearing conditions within infants' homes with the measures of the developmental advancement of infants being reared there. The hypothesis that experiencing pleasurable feedback from spontaneous actions and vocalizations fosters initiative and an inner sense of control has received support from the finding of correlations that approximate +0.6 between the prevalence of inanimate materials and people that are responsive to the spontaneous actions of infants within homes, on the one hand, with measures of persistence in goal-striving by the infants at six months of age, on the other hand (Yarrow, Rubenstein & Pedersen, 1975). It would appear that intentionality, initiative, and trust can be acquired very early. The persistence of such achievements may well result from the independence they give the infant. Once they are acquired, an infant is enabled to control to a considerable degree his experience, and this permits developmental advancements to persist. Here I suspect that the findings from the studies of partial reinforcement (Jenkins & Stanley, 1950) may well be pertinent. If they are, experiences of frustration of goal-striving, so long as they do not become permanent enough to extinguish striving, will encourage the persistence of initiative and striving for self-chosen goals. A personal trait of courage in the face of obstacles may be the result (Hunt, 1981).

Other Correlations between Rearing Conditions and Development

Several kinds of rearing conditions are positively correlated with developmental advancement in desirable traits. For instance, "Child given training in one or more skills," "Home contained an adequate supply of small manipulable items the child is allowed to play with," and "Mother spontaneously vocalizes the names of objects examined by child in observer's presence," all correlated positively with the levels of development at ages 11, 15, 18 and 22 months assessed with a modified version of the Uzgiris-Hunt scales (Wachs, Uzgiris & Hunt, 1971). Similarly, "Father helps take care of the infant" is also positively correlated with advancement on several of the scales. These correlations are substantial: they range from +0.35 to +0.76, with most of them between +0.4 and +0.6. Similar evidence has also been reported by Bradley and Caldwell (1977), Wachs (1978), White (1978), and White and Watts (1973).

Conversely, this strategy has uncovered rearing conditions inimical to developmental advancement. For instance, in the study of Wachs et al. (1971), when "There is a high level of adult activity in the home" or when "Mother and infant go visiting almost daily," the correlations with measures of development are negative and they range from −0.29 to −0.82. Such negative correlations are already present at 7 months of age, and they continue to exist through testings at 11, 15, 18, and 22 months. Since these rearing conditions probably mean that the mothers are relatively inattentive and unresponsive to their infants, these correlations represent evidence on the negative side for the importance of responsiveness from both human and inanimate conditions to the spontaneous actions of infants.

Another instructive negative correlate of infant development consists of a continuous or highly prevalent auditory input of high intensity, and particularly one of loud human vocalizing that is irrelevant to the infant's spontaneous actions and functioning. In the study of Wachs et al. (1971), such negative correlates included "High sound level in the home" and "Television on most of the time." For these conditions showing negative correlations with assessments of development the hampering effects are already evident by age 7 months. By ages 18 and 22 months, the correlations range from -0.37 (with vocal imitation) to -0.81 (with foresight) and they are substantial for all branches of development involving initiative and appreciations of meaning.

A home condition described as "Child never restricted," which probably indicates lack of adult attention to whatever the infant does and what Reuven Feuerstein (1979) might term a "lack of adult mediation of the infant's experience," shows a high negative correlation (-0.64) with advancement on the scale of Vocal Imitation and also negative correlations with the development of foresight (-0.4) and with performance on the scale of the Development of Means for Obtaining Desired Events at age 22 months. Conversely, conditions suggesting that the parents have interacted vocally and instructively with their infant show substantial positive correlations with advancement on both the scale of Vocal Imitation (+0.4) and with such an indication of development in understanding as foresight (+0.7).

With vocal noise prevalent and irrelevant to an infant's developing expectations and interests, her or his inclination to orient and attend to adult speech might well be expected to become habituated or extinguished. Receptor inputs to which the orienting response, or attention, has been extinguished serve poorly or not at all as conditional stimuli or as cues in learning (Maltzman & Raskin, 1965). Inasmuch as such irrelevant vocal noise tends to become considerably more common in homes of the uneducated poor than in those of the educated middle class, it is hardly surprising that children of the uneducated poor at ages of 4 and 5 years have turned out to be less attentive and understanding of adult talk and less discriminating of vocal patterns than children of the educated middle class (Hunt, 1969, pp. 202-214). Moreover, there is evidence that this inimical influence on early development persists through the high-school years. In a cross-lagged panel analysis of cognitive measures for four grade levels, listening scores in grade four showed a correlation of +0.73 with an intellectual composite at grade 11 (Atkin, Bray, Davison, Herzberger, Humphreys, & Selzer, 1977). Such evidence helps to highlight how important it is for intellectual development to reinforce very early the interest of infants in human vocalizing and spoken communication.

Yet another kind of experience inimical to development consists of making approbation or love contingent upon a child's making adaptive modifications of his knowledge and skills that are painfully difficult or beyond her or his capacity. Based on the discrepancy concepts underlying the "problem of the match" already synopsized above, Hunt and Paraskevopoulos (1980) have correlated measures of the accuracy of mothers' knowledge of what their children know and can do with assessments of their children's development. For a set of test items graded in difficulty from the third to the ninth years, one interviewer asked the mothers to predict what their 4-year-olds would actually do on each one, and another administered the tests to their children. The number of maternal errors in prediction correlated -0.80 with the measures of child development in terms of the numbers of tests passed. Most of the relationship, however, was a matter of reporting test behavior more advanced than their children manifested. The correlation of number of these overestimations of their children's performances with the number of test items passed by the children was -0.77. For underestimations, the correlation was only -0.07. Perhaps the moral can be stated as follows: "Being unrealistically ambitious for our children hampers their development." They need mothers who observe accurately what they can do and who provide experiences that match their children's existing abilities and coping capacity. Or when their problems are too difficult, children need help and understanding.

Applications toward a Pedagogy for Infancy and Early Childhood

These remarks toward a pedagogical technology can be only suggestions based on recent findings concerning what hampers and what facilitates early intellectual and motivational development. Despite continuing limitations in our knowledge of the details of the relationships between kinds of experience and kinds of development in the first three years (see Hunt, 1977, 1980; 1978), these past two decades have made progress in uncovering knowledge that deserves to be applied by parents and by caregivers in early daycare. Here are a few principles.

First of all, real differences in achieved competence exist between the children of the poorly educated parents of poverty on the one hand, and those of the relatively well educated and affluent parents of the middle class on the other hand. The evidence from our Tehran study indicates that such differences need not be biologically inevitable. The odds are heavy that their existence represents a lack of equal opportunity for the children of poverty to learn and grow.

Second, the opportunities most likely to be in short supply for the children of poorly educated parents with low incomes are opportunities for pleasurable experiences from their spontaneous actions and opportunities for repeated encounters with a wide variety of actions, objects, persons, and places. Also likely to be absent or less frequent are experiences that foster development of the vocal system, the capa-

city to imitate, and a wide phonological repertoire, experiences that
foster semantic mastery or the symbolizing in words of everything for
which the toddler has developed cognitive appreciation, and experiences
providing a child with opportunities to use his phonological and semantic skills in communication with adults. When these skills are developed early, they increase what is measured by tests of intelligence,
enhance a child's inner sense of control and self-worth, help her or
him to solve everyday quandaries, and establish trust in others.

    Third, these experiences should come in a sequence that takes
into account the readiness of the infant for them. Readiness, however,
is not merely a matter of age, but of the amount and quality of past
experience and the developmental achievements they have enabled the
child to master. For caregivers, parents, and teachers this is the
"problem of the match." The best evidence I know that a solution of
this problem has been approximated resides in behavioral evidence of
positive interest on the part of infants in situations encountered.
Here the behavioral signs of interest must be distinguished from the
boredom with information and things that have become too familiar and
with challenges already completely mastered, and from the distress
which comes from being called upon for adaptive modifications in
already-made achievements beyond the child's capacity.

    Fourth, it appears that the earlier an educational intervention
is begun, the greater the impression it can make. But this is true
only if those providing the intervention appreciate the epigenetic
nature of early development and have provided a reasonably good solution for the problem of the match. This means permitting an infant or
young child to accept or reject interaction with any situation provided
to foster development and/or to help her or him to cope with the demands
of the situation provided. The dramatic effects obtained at the orphanage in Tehran illustrate what is made possible by starting an intervention early and taking into account in its sequencing the epigenesis in
early development with reasonably good solutions to the problem of the
match.

    Fifth, involving parents, especially mothers, as well as infants
in educational interventions helps not only to increase the magnitude
but also the persistence of the gains. It has been argued that "in the
early years of life, the key element [is] the involvement of parent and
child in verbal interaction around a cognitively challenging task"
(Bronfenbrenner, 1974, p. 54; see also 1968, 1972). Certainly a child's
parents are the most relevant persons in his early development. Moreover, both biologically and legally, parents have the basic responsibility for the early education and welfare of their children. Yet it
is the nature of the intimate proximal experiences provided for the
child that is important.

    Sixth, if one attempts to synthesize starting educational inter-
ventions early with parent involvement, one is inevitably led to con-

sider the problem of recruiting and teaching parents, and especially
mothers, to be effective in fostering the psychological development of
their children during infancy and early childhood.

THE OBSTACLE OF INVOLVING PARENTS

     In the course of biological evolution, *Homo sapiens* have been
equipped instinctively for reproduction. The pleasures of sex, which
evolved eons ahead of that sense of responsibility for progeny, helps
to guarantee the survival of the species. On the other hand, human
values as reflected in all of the great religions and cultures of history have been shifting the emphasis from survival of the species as
such to the quality of life for individuals. In the course of this
process, sex has been restricted, and in some religions, the ideal has
been to limit sex to intended procreation. Such is the motivational
strength of the sex impulse and such are the pleasures of sexual activity, however, that these limitations have never been widely successful, not even when sex outside the prescribed limits has been made
taboo or a sin to be punished by eternal damnation. In consequence
of this conflict between biological human nature and the demands and
strictures of human culture, a substantial proportion of infants arrive
when their progenitors are poorly prepared to care for them and to
foster their early psychological development.

     The organization of child care and the fostering of development
is far more dependent upon learning and therefore far more subject to
cultural influence than is the sexual behavior that leads to reproduction. This cultural influence shows in variations in child-rearing
practices and in beliefs about the nature of infants and what practices
are appropriate or required. It is likely that the Christian doctrine
of original sin, early formulated by St. Augustine and strongly emphasized by John Calvin, was postulated to explain that behavior of infants and young children which irritated their parents. When Calvin
observed the rebellious behavior of 7-year-olds being taught to read
with the Bible as the textbook--a horrible solution to the problem of
the match--he regarded it as an example of original sin and saw it as
a justification for corporal punishment--beating the devil out of the
students.

     Discipline has always been a topic of great interest, if not top
interest, to parents. Concern commonly focuses on what kind of punishment will be most effective. Unfortunately, punishment is a rotten
way to foster development. It interferes with a pleasurable, rewarding relationship between parent and child; it fails to indicate what
actions are appropriate and effective; and it fails to encourage any
understanding of the relationships involved. In a sense, the need for
punishment represents a failure to develop that delightful reciprocal
interaction already described. Once reciprocal games are established,
if such homely care-taking operations as bathing, dressing, feeding,

and toileting are accompanied by vocal games, not only is the infant's development fostered, but the infant's responsiveness rewards the mother and also the father, as Smilansky so strongly emphasizes (this volume).

Nevertheless, once the infant begins to creep and toddle, she or he can, when bored with the sameness of a place and the objects at hand, get into trouble seeking what is more novel and therefore attractive. Moreover, developing manipulative skills enables the infant to break or damage objects of value. Three devices are useful at this difficult stage. One consists of barriers that prevent the infant from getting to places of danger. A second is to remove breakable objects of value from the child's life-space. But a third, and an important one it is, consists of providing a variety of materials of interest to the child for play.

Even so, the task of the mother or caretaker calls for continuing vigilance and responsiveness. When a toddling child encounters situations with which he cannot cope, the mother must discern what a child is striving to do, and through quick interchanges indicate how the child can achieve his goal. She must momentarily drop what she is doing, diagnose a problem to produce a solution, or just share enthusiasm (White & Watts, 1973). Such attentive vigilance and responsiveness is exhausting. It calls for a high energy level.

The obstacles to involving some mothers from the poverty sector in training for more effective parenting come from their already established beliefs about what is needed and proper in adult behavior with children, from the conflicting social demands on their time and energies, and in a few from their self-centered, narcissistic needs.

Many beliefs encapsulated in the aphorisms of our culture advocate parental behavior inimical to infant and child development. Some of these are: "Let the babies cry it out, it develops their lungs," "Never talk baby-talk to a child," "Children should be seen and not heard," "Spare the rod and spoil the child." One gets the impression that such aphorisms on child-rearing tend to be more prevalently believed among those relatively less well educated. This might be expected because those without at least high school are unlikely to have their beliefs influenced by the information available in books and magazines or even in daily newspapers.

For many women of the poverty sector, the demand on their time and energy from a combination of housekeeping along with a job outside the home and/or conflict with a husband or other persons in the home may be so absorbing as to make child care exceedingly difficult.

A few young women are so engrossed with their self-centered narcissistic needs that they find it exceedingly difficult or even impossible to be responsive to the needs of their infants or to the task of learning how to fulfill them.

During the 1940s and 1950s, it became almost a fad for members of such professions as home economics, psychoanalysis, psychiatry, clinical psychology, and social work to use lecturers in an attempt to influence the child-rearing practices of parents to prevent the development of neuroses and psychoses. It quickly became evident that the parents of those children most likely to be at risk, and especially those with little education and low incomes, seldom appeared in the audience. The National Institute of Mental Health in the U.S. Department of Health, Education, and Welfare supported a substantial number of pilot programs in which an attempt was made to influence the child-rearing of uneducated parents of poverty through something resembling group therapy. The results of those projects recommended by the Study Committee, which I chaired, were exceedingly poor as is evidenced by the difficulty in obtaining the final reports legally required for these grants. This difficulty appeared to result from embarrassment of principal investigators by their failures.

The first evidence of success in influencing the quality of parenting that I know of came with the pioneering approach of Gray and Klaus (1965), who invited mothers into compensatory education classes. The mothers had an opportunity to observe and discuss what the teachers were doing. These mothers were also visited at home to encourage them to use what they had learned during the class observations and discussions. Measurement of the effects showed that the mothers' participation influenced not only the development of the target children, but also the development of older and younger children within these families through a process termed "vertical diffusion." There was also evidence of "horizontal diffusion;" children of neighbors with whom these mothers had face-to-face interaction showed developmental advances significantly greater than the children of comparable families in another community where the mothers could have no such interaction with those participating in the classes.

This pioneering effort encouraged the 1966 White House task force to recommend that Project Head Start be extended down the age scale in a program of Parent and Child Centers (Hunt et al., 1967). A later, seventh-year report contained evidence of somewhat more than the typical persistence of gain from the compensatory education in this study. This persistence may be attributable to the involvement of the mothers.

Since the pioneering of Gray and Klaus, at least nine studies have appeared on the effects of parent-child intervention from the first or early in the second year of life through elementary school in families of limited education and low income. These studies have focused simultaneously on mother and child. Random assignment to treatment and control groups was observed in seven of these. Such intervention eliminated the gradual drop in developmental quotient

or intelligence quotient with age observed in the control groups
(Gordon, 1971; Levenstein, 1976). The results in differences between
the treated and control groups in the IQs of the children at the end
of treatment were of the order of 20 points. Most of these programs
also included mother-child dyads who entered the program when the
children were somewhat older. The magnitude of the differences at the
end of treatment was inversely related to the age at which the dyad
entered the program. In other words, the greatest gains were made by
the children who were enrolled when they were less or only slightly
more than a year old.

Intervention with parents appears to have little effect on intellectual development after children enter school, but those children
who were involved in intensive programs of parent-child intervention
gained substantially more in Follow-Through Programs that extended
Project Head Start up the age scale (Gilmer, Miller & Gray, 1970;
Radin, 1972; Stanford Research Institute, 1971). Moreover, Becker's
summary (1974) of findings from an evaluative study of ten sponsors
in 137 Follow-Through schools and 117 comparison schools by Abt and
Associates notes, among other things, that participation during the
fourth and fifth years in Head Start programs enhances the gains of
children in the Follow-Through Program.

Programs of parent-child intervention help the mother as well as
their children. They tend to increase the affection between them,
and perhaps through giving the mother a sense of success in her role
as a parent they enhance her sense of self-worth and of being a competent person capable of improving her own situation. Such mothers
commonly set about learning new skills to improve their economic
status. They develop the courage to be leaders in confronting government authorities with demands for their legal rights. Such findings
have been reported by Badger (1977), Gilmer, Miller and Gray (1970),
Gordon (1971), Karnes, Teska, Hodgins and Badger (1970) and
Levenstein (1976).

Unfortunately, the families willing to become involved in such
parent-child intervention programs typically come only or largely from
the upper levels of the relatively uneducated poor (Klaus & Gray, 1968;
Radin & Weikard, 1967). Although Levenstein reports a high level of
success with her recruitment, she has not attempted to recruit such
mothers whom Heber and Dever found to be the source of 80% of the children with IQs below 80 at 6 years of age. In Israel, Lombard (this
volume) admits that her project has not tried to recruit those of
least competence from the poverty sector of the Israeli population.
Yet the educational intervention of Heber and his collaborators, which
began within 3 months after the birth of the sample of 20 such children, enabled them to achieve IQs of 124 by age 66 months. Such a
finding indicates that even infants with a genetic potential to be
among the brightest fifth of the population may acquire the functional
equivalent of mental deficiency in such homes. Can the mothers in

such homes be recruited and taught to be effective caretakers and educators of their offspring?

THE OBSTACLE OF RECRUITING MOTHERS OF GREATEST RISK

So far no direct answer can be given to this question. Yet Badger's (1977) early effort to recruit and train unmarried adolescent mothers from the poverty sector of Cincinnati, Ohio, has produced a promising approach. The pediatricians of the Medical School at the University of Cincinnati found the offspring of such mothers to be at especially high risk for ill health and developmental retardation. On the basis of her work with the mothers in the program (Karnes et al., 1970) and in the Parent and Child Centers, Badger was invited to recruit a sample of these adolescents for classes in effective parenting. The plan called for recruiting girls with the prescribed age, education, and economic status in 48 consecutive births. From examining her own experience as a mother, Badger decided that she had been most intensely concerned with her children on the first or second day after she had given birth. This experience prompted her to approach each adolescent mother assigned on the first or second day after she had given birth. All of the first 48 approached and invited to participate in either classes or home visits accepted the invitation. More than 700 girls have since been approached, mostly by other workers whom Badger has taught. Less than 1% of them have declined the invitation to participate. About 10% ultimately fail to join the program, and about half of these have sensible reasons. Another 10% attend the classes too seldom to receive much benefit. Yet another 10% may attend more than half the classes but are too self-centered or confused to profit. The remaining 70% have taken a new lease on life. Probably as a consequence of the rewards of feeling successful as a mother, they return to school to acquire new skills to increase their employability. This leaves the care of their infants to the grandmothers or others untaught. In consequence, the rate at which the infants develop during their second year decreases. Nevertheless, two-thirds of those infants whose mothers attended more than half of the classes for their first year earned scores above the norm on the Kent Oral Emergency Test of Intelligence when they entered school at approximately 5 years of age. Two-thirds of the controls, on the other hand, earned scores below the norm, as already noted above.

Badger's work illustrates the principle that scientific investigation can help solve the social problem of involving parents as well as the developmental and educational problems of early childhood education. It was unfeasible to give tests of intelligence to these young women. Hence it is impossible to know with precision how many of them had IQs under 80 and thus belonged to that class which Heber, et al. (1968) found to be the source of 80% of those children with IQs below 80 who must be assigned to the costly and all too often unsuccessful business of special education. It is therefore impossible to estimate with precision the proportion of that 80% for whom training in effective parenting would be expected to prevent functional mental deficiency.

It may well be that even approximating the goal of equal opportunity for those experiences that foster early psychological development will call for the provision of educational day care for the infants of women who lack the motivation to participate in classes for effective parenting and to attend to what is being taught. How many there are, we do not know. Were our societies to provide a program in which all mothers of firstborn infants are invited to participate in such classes, the process would have the advantage of indicating early the infants at greatest risk. The program would provide an earlier and perhaps almost as accurate a means of identifying those infants for whom educational day care should be provided as the screening tests that measure developmental achievements (Hunt, 1981c). Earlier identification should help to prevent a substantial share of the retardation that shows on the screening tests. Once the retardation is evident on such tests, therapy that is both difficult and expensive is required to repair it.

If evidence of the importance of such early experiences continues to accumulate, perhaps the law may be changed to make educational day care mandatory for the progeny of those parents who lack the educational background, the concern, and the ability to attend to the teaching of effective parenting. But yet another obstacle consists of convincing the taxpayers of the need for the programs required to equalize opportunities for all children to learn during their infancy and preschool years.

THE OBSTACLE OF LIMITED FINANCIAL AND SOCIAL SUPPORT

An ambitious project like Head Start can be launched largely on hopes if there is at least evidence that the hopes are realistic. Even though the evidence for the realism of our hopes has increased substantially during the past two decades, there is as yet little evidence that, during the 15 years since the decision was made to launch the project, the proportion of children reaching school age with functional equivalents of mental deficiency has been reduced significantly. How long then will such hopes be maintained? How is the financial support to be obtained for the ever extending process of research and development required to mount these obstacles?

A likely answer to this question is coming from recent evidence that the early efforts at compensatory education have been cost effective. In their cost-benefit analysis of the Ypsilanti-Perry Preschool

Project, a program of compensatory education conducted during the early 1960s, Weber, Foster and Weikart (1978) found three sources of benefit to offset the costs of the preschool effort. First, the children who participated required less costly forms of education as they progressed through school than did comparable students who did not participate. Fewer of them required special education and none required institutional care. Second, when life-term earnings were projected on the basis of differences in school progress and IQ scores, those who had participated in preschool education had substantially higher projected life-time earnings than did nonparticipants. Third, the released time of the parents of participants was considered to be another economic benefit. Together these benefits resulted in a 9.5% internal rate of return to the investment for one year of preschool compensatory education, higher for girls (12.0%) than for boys (8.6%).

According to this analysis, the benefits from reduced future educational costs alone are sufficient to pay for one year of preschool education. This pioneering study of the economic profitability of one of the earliest preschool intervention programs brings highly encouraging results. Such findings help appreciably toward halting the waning of enthusiasm based on hopes. Indeed, these findings have resulted in a Report to the Congress of the U.S. by the Comptroller General (1979), "Early Childhood and Family Development Programs Improve the Quality of Life for Low-Income Families."

Other considerations are also encouraging. For instance, I have been interested in the issue of whether participation in parent education has any effect on the likelihood of child abuse, which appears to have been on the increase during the last two decades. In part, the new evidences of increase may derive from better detection and an increase in the number of child protection agencies. Beginning in 1975, I began asking pediatricians, social workers in family-service and child-protection agencies, and officers of our courts whether they personally knew of instances of child abuse in which either the mother or the father had participated in classes for parenting or in parent-child programs for infant education. I have also asked many of my acquaintances this question.

Although such an approach has limited validity, it is nevertheless of some interest that I have at this writing uncovered not a single instance in which parents guilty of child abuse are known to have participated in any such program. Even though the strategy of such informal investigation has the common disadvantage of proceeding from effect to hypothetical cause, the complete absence of a critical incident carries some little force. This absence suggests that a substantial portion of the money now going for the treatment of child abusers by child protection agencies, the courts, and correctional facilities might better go toward the education for parenting when the first child is born.

United Services for Effective Parenting

Just such considerations prompted Badger to organize the social agencies of Cincinnati to provide continued access to support for the young children and their parents. The child protection agency, the schools, and some of the social-work agencies agreed to assign some of their existing staff to provide this continuation of support for parents and early education. The result has been a nonprofit corporation entitled United Services for Effective Parenting (USEP). The genius of this plan is that each agency has assigned part of its existing staff, originally hired for therapeutic services, to carry out the preventive services.

Throughout the past few decades, starting with the Kennedy-Johnson War on Poverty, the source of innovation in the domains of education and welfare has usually been the U.S. federal government. New services are organized and paid for with federal funds. All too often when the federal funds cease, the services cease. USEP reverses this process. The various agencies begin by volunteering without extra federal support to commit part of their existing therapeutic personnel to preventive services. Insofar as these preventive services are successful, the need for more expensive therapeutic service should decrease. Service-givers are typically professionals with a vested interest in what they do. What is remarkable about USEP is the fact that it is a consortium of professionals who have accepted the possibility, even the hope, of change.

Finally, it is of great interest that the USEP concept has spread to 19 other urban communities and is spreading to communities in other states. Moreover, the federal agencies of education and welfare have complimented the concept with strong evidences of interest and with inquiries about how to hasten its spread.

CONCLUSION

I hope my discourse has brought encouragement to all who are working in the vineyard of early education. I believe we are about to reach the top of the first ridge on the way to achieving the pinnacle of our hopes of equalizing learning opportunities for our children during their preschool years. Although the debates will continue for some time, the force of the evidence against beliefs in fixed intelligence and predetermined development are becoming irresistible. I must admit, reluctantly, that achieving the summit is not for my generation, but we have recognized the inequities that exist and have seen their relevance to our values.

I believe we have improved our understanding of the nature of psychological development during infancy and early childhood. Although considerable ignorance remains, several findings of the last two

decades appear highly relevant to and applicable in early education. I
believe we have learned a good deal about the importance of involving
parents in the educational process of their preschool children. I
believe we have learned that such involvement is not only important
for fostering the developing competence of the children, but that it
can be a source of joy and reward for the parents. Furthermore,
progress has been made in learning how to recruit parents into education for effective parenting.

Finally, we have the beginnings of evidence that even compensatory education for children during the year before they enter kindergarten may be cost-effective. This realization should help to halt
the waning of enthusiasm for early educational programs. We may even
be seeing the very beginnings of turning away from therapeutic programs toward preventive programs.

FOOTNOTE

1. See for more extensive review and the references to the original
    literature relevant. The word "see" before author and date of
    publication is used consistently here for this purpose. Without
    "see," original literature is being cited.

REFERENCES

Atkin, R., Bray, R., Davison, M., Merzberger, S., Humphreys, L., &
    Selzer, U. Cross-lagged panel analysis of sixteen cognitive
    measures at four grade levels. *Child Development*, 1977, *48*,
    pp. 944-952.
Badger, E.D. *Teaching guide: Infant Learning Program*. Paoli, PA:
    The Instructo Corporation, 1971a.
Badger, E.D. *Teaching guide: Toddler Learning Program*. Paoli, PA:
    The Instructo Corporation, 1971b.
Badger, E.D. The infant stimulation/mother training project. In
    B.M. Caldwell and D.J. Steadman, (Eds.), *Infant education: A
    guide for helping handicapped children in the first three years*.
    New York: Walker & Co., 1977.
Becker, W.C. Early indications of positive outcomes. Washington,
    D.C.: National Follow-Through Sponsor's Presentation, Educational
    Staff Seminar, 14 February, 1974.
Binet, A., & Simon, T. Méthodes nouvelles pour le diagnostic du niveau
    intellectuel des anormaux. *Année Psychol.*, 1905, *11*, pp. 191-
    244.
Binet, A., & Simon, T. Le measure du developpement de l'intelligence
    chez les jeunes enfants. *Bulletin de la societé libre pour
    l'étude psychologique de l'enfant*. Paris: 1911.
Bloom, B.S. *Stability and change in human characteristics*. New York:
    Wiley & Sons, Inc., 1964.

Bradley, R.H., & Caldwell, B.M. Home observation for measurement of
    the environment: A validation study of screening efficiency.
    American Journal of Mental Deficiency, 1977, *81*, pp. 417-420.
Brazelton, T.B., Tronick, E., Adamson, L., Als, H., & Wise, S. Early
    mother-infant interaction. In *Parent-Infant Interaction*, Ciba
    Symposium No. 33. Amsterdam: Associated Scientific Publishers,
    1975.
Bronfenbrenner, U. When is infant stimulation effective? In D.C.
    Glass (Ed.), *Environmental influences*. New York: Rockefeller
    University Press, 1968.
Bronfenbrenner, W. Developmental research in public policy. In J.M.
    Romanshyn (Ed.), *Social service and social welfare*. New York:
    Council on Social Work Education, 1972.
Bronfenbrenner, U. A report on longitudinal evaluations of pre-
    school programs. Vol. II: *Is early intervention effective?*
    DHEW Publication No. (OHD) 76-30025, 1974.
Chomsky, N. Review of *Verbal Behavior* by B.F. Skinner. *Language*,
    1959, *35*, (1), pp. 26-58.
Cicarelli, V.G., et al. *The impact of Head Start: An evaluation of
    the effects of Head Start on children's cognitive and affective
    development* (2 vols.). Bladensburg, MD: Westinghouse Learning
    Corp. (Distributed by Clearinghouse for Federal Scientific and
    Technical Information, Springfield, VA 22151), 1969.
Comptroller General of the United States. *Early childhood and family
    development programs improve the quality of life for low-income
    families: A report to the Congress of the United States*. Washing-
    ton, D.C.: General Accounting Office, HRD-79-40, 1979.
Consortium on Developmental Continuity. *The persistence of preschool
    effects*. Final Report, Grant No. 18-76-07843 to the Administra-
    tion for Children, Youth and Families, Office of Human Develop-
    ment Services, U.S. Department of HEW, 1977.
Dennis, W. Causes of retardation among institutional children: Iran.
    Journal of Genetic Psychology, 1960, *96*, pp. 47-59.
Erikson, E.H. *Childhood and society*. New York: Norton, 1950.
Feuerstein, R. *The Learning Potential Assessment Device (LPAD)*.
    Baltimore, MD: University Park Press, 1979.
Freud, S. 1905. Three contributions to the theory of sex. In A. A.
    Brill (Transl. & Ed.), *The basic writings of Sigmund Freud*.
    New York: Modern Library, 1938.
Freud, S. 1915. Instincts and their vicissitudes. In *Collected
    papers, Vol. 4*. London: Hogarth, 1950, pp. 60-83.
Freud, S. *New introductory lectures on psychoanalysis*. (Transl.
    by W. J. H. Sprott). New York: Norton, 1933.
Galton, F. *Hereditary genius: An inquiry into its laws and conse-
    quences*. London: Macmillan, 1869.
Galton, F. *Inquiries into human faculty and its development*. London:
    Macmillan, 1883.
Garber, H., & Haber, R. *The Milwaukee project: Early intervention as
    a technique to prevent mental retardation*. Storrs: The University
    of Connecticut, National Leadership Institute, Teacher Education/

Early Education, 1973.

Gesell, A.   The ontogenesis of infant behavior.   In L. Carmichael (Ed.),
    Manual of Child Psychology. New York: Wiley, 1954, Ch. 6.

Gilmer, B., Miller, H.O., & Gray, S. W. *Intervention with mothers
    and young children: Study on intra-family effects*. Nashville,
    Tenn.: CARCEE Demonstration and Research Center for Early Edu-
    cation, 1970.

Gordon, I. J.   Early child stimulation through parent education.   In
    I. J. Gordon (Ed.), *Readings in research in developmental psycho-
    logy*. Glenview, IL: Scott, Foresman, 1971, pp. 146-154.

Gray, S. W., & Klaus, R. A. An experimental preschool program for
    culturally deprived children. *Child Development*, 1965, *36*,
    pp. 887-898.

Greenberg, D. J., Uzgiris, I. C., & Hunt, J. McV. Hastening the
    development of the blink-response with looking. *Journal of
    Genetic Psychology*, 1968, *113*, pp. 167-176.

Greenberg, D. J., Uzgiris, I. C., & Hunt, J. McV. Attentional pref-
    erence and experience: III. Visual Familiarity and looking time.
    Journal of Genetic Psychology, 1970, *117*, pp. 123-135.

Harlow, H. F.   The nature of love. *American Psychologist*, 1958, *13*,
    pp. 673-685.

Heber, F. R.   Sociocultural mental retardation: A longitudinal study.
    In D. Forgays (Ed.), *Primary prevention of psychopathology, Vol.
    II. Environmental influences*. Hanover, NH: University of New
    England, 1978, Chap. 4, pp. 39-62.

Heber, F. R., Dever, R. B., & Conry, J.   The influence of environmen-
    tal and genetic variables on intellectual development.   In H. J.
    Prehm, L. A. Hamerlynch, & J. E. Crosson (Eds.), *Behavioral
    research in mental retardation*.   Eugene, OR: University of
    Oregon, 1968.

Humphreys, L. G., & Parsons, C. K.   Piagetian tasks measure intelli-
    gence and intelligence tests assess cognitive development.
    Intelligence, 1979, *3*, pp. 369-382.

Hunt, J. McV. *Intelligence and experience*. New York: Ronald Press,
    1961.

Hunt, J. McV.   Motivation inherent in information processing and action.
    In O. J. Harvey (Ed.), *Motivation and social interaction: The
    cognitive determinants*. New York: Ronald Press, 1963, pp. 35-94.

Hunt, J. McV.   Intrinsic motivation and its role in psychological
    development.   In D. Levine (Ed.), *Nebraska Symposium on Motivation*,
    13, pp. 189-282. Lincoln: University of Nebraska Press, 1965.

Hunt, J. McV.   Toward a theory of guided learning in development.   In
    R. H. Ojemann & K. Pritchett (Eds.), *Giving emphasis to guided
    learning*. Cleveland, OH: Educational Research Council, 1966,
    pp. 98-160.

Hunt, J. McV. et al. A bill of rights for children. White House Task
    Force, J. McV. Hunt, Chairman, 1967. Unpublished report in the
    L. B. Johnson Library, Austin, Texas, and available through the
    Educational Resources Information Center, University of Illinois,
    Urbana, IL 61801.

Hunt, J. McV. *The challenge of incompetence and poverty: Papers on the role of early education.* Urbana, IL: University of Illinois Press, 1969.

Hunt, J. McV. Reflections on a decade of early education. *Journal of Abnormal Child Psychology,* 1975, *3,* (4), pp. 275-330.

Hunt, J. McV. Specificity in early development and experience. Annual Lecture in Developmental Pediatrics. Omaha, NE: Meyer Children's Rehabilitation Institute, University of Nebraska Medical Center, 1977.

Hunt, J. McV. Developmental psychology: Early experience. In *Annual Review of Psychology,* 1979, *30,* pp. 103-143.

Hunt, J. McV. *Early psychological development and experience.* Worcester, MA: Clark University Press. (Volume X, 1976--Heinz Werner Lecture Series), 1980a.

Hunt, J. McV. Implications of plasticity and hierarchical achievements for the assessment of development and risk of mental retardation. In D. Sawin, E. C. Haskins, II, L. O. Walker & J. H. Penticuff (Eds.), *The exceptional infant (Vol. IV): Psychosocial risks in infant-environment transactions.* New York: Brunner/Mazel, Inc., 1980b.

Hunt, J. McV. The experiential roots of intention, initiative, and trust. In H. I. Day (Ed.), *Advances in Intrinsic Motivation and Aesthetics.* New York: Plenum Publ. Corp., 1981a.

Hunt, J. McV. Language acquisition and experience (Tehran). Urbana, IL: University of Illinois, Department of Psychology: 1981c (Unpublished manuscript).

Hunt, J. McV., Mohandessi, K., Ghodssi, M., & Akiyama, M. The psychological development of orphanage-reared infants: Interventions with outcomes (Tehran). *Genetic Psychology Monographs,* 1976, *94,* pp. 177-226.

Hunt, J. McV., & Paraskevopoulos, J. 1980. Children's psychological development as a function of the inaccuracy of their mothers' knowledge of their abilities. *Genetic Psychology Monographs,* (in press).

Hunt, J. McV., Paraskevopoulos, J., Schickedanz, D., & Uzgiris, I. C. Variations in the mean ages of achieving object permanence under diverse conditions of rearing. In B. L. Friedlander, G. M. Sterritt, & G. E. Kirk (Eds.), *The exceptional infant (Vol. 3): Assessment and intervention.* New York: Brunner/Mazel, 1975, pp. 247-262.

Isaacs, N. The why questions. In S. B. Isaacs, *Intellectual growth in young children.* New York: Harcourt Brace, 1930.

Jenkins, W. O., & Stanley, J. C., Jr. Partial reinforcement: A review and critique. *Psychological Bulletin,* 1950, *47,* pp. 193-234.

Jensen, A. R. How much can we boost IQ and scholastic achievement? *Harvard Educational Review,* 1969, *39,* pp. 1-123.

Karnes, M. B., Teska, J. A., Hodgins, A. A., & Badger, E. D. Educational intervention at home by mothers of disadvantaged infants. *Child Development,* 1970, *41,* (4), pp. 925-935.

Kirk, G. E., Hunt, J. McV., & Lieberman, C. Social class and preschool language skill: II. Semantic mastery of color information. *Genetic Psychology Monographs*, 1975, *91*, pp. 299–316.

Klaus, R. A., & Gray, S. W. The early training project for disadvantaged children: A report after five years. *Monographs of the Society for Research in Child Development*, 1968, *33* (4), Ser. No. 120, 1–66.

Lazar, I., & Darlington, R. B. (Eds.), *Lasting effects after preschool.* Final Report, HEW Grant 90c-1311, to the Education Commission of the States, 1978.

Lazar, I., Hubble, V. R., Murray, H., Rosche, M., & Royce, J. *The persistence of preschool effects.* Final Report, Grant No. 18-16-07843. Washington, D.C.: U.S. Government Printing Office, Stock No. 017-000-00202-3, 1977.

Lenneberg, E. H. The natural history of language. In F. Smith & G. H. Miller (Eds.), *The genesis of language: A psycholinguistic approach.* Cambridge, MA: MIT Press, 1966, pp. 219–252.

Levenstein, P. The mother-child home program. In M. C. Day & R. K. Parker (Eds.), *The preschool in action* (2nd ed.). Boston: Allyn & Bacon, 1976.

Malthus, T. R. 1798. An essay on the principle of population (7th ed.). London: Reeves & Turner, 1872.

Maltzmann, I., & Raskin, D. C. Effects of individual differences in the orienting reflex on conditioning and complex processes. *Journal of Experimental Research in Personality*, 1965, *1*, pp. 1–16.

Maslow, A. *Motivation and personality.* New York: Harper, 1954.

McCarthy, D. Language development in children. In L. Carmichael (Ed.), *Manual of child psychology* (2nd ed.). New York: Wiley, 1954, Ch. 9.

Page, E. B. Miracle in Milwaukee: Raising the IQ. *Educational Researcher*, 1972, *1*, (10), pp. 8–16.

Papousek, H., & Papousek, M. Mothering and the cognitive head-start. In H. R. Schaffer (Ed.), *Studies in Mother-Infant Interaction.* New York: Academic Press, pp. 63–85.

Radin, N. 1972. Three degrees of maternal involvement in a preschool program: Impact on mothers and children. *Child Development*, (in press).

Radin, N., & Weikart, D. A home teaching program for disadvantaged preschool children. *Journal of Special Education*, 1967, *1*, pp. 183–190.

Ramey, C. T., & Haskins, R. The modification of intelligence through early experience. *Intelligence*, (in press).

Rotter, J. B. Generalized expectancies for internal versus external control of reinforcement. *Psychological Monographs*, 1966, *80* (1), Whole No. 609.

Skinner, B. F. *Science and human behavior.* New York: Macmillan, 1953.

Stanford Research Institute. *Longitudinal evaluation of selected features of the National Follow-Through Program.* Washington, D. C.: Office of Education, Department of HEW, 1971.

Steiner, G. *The children's cause*. Washington, D.C.: The Brookings
     Institute, 1976.
Stern, W. 1912. The psychological methods of testing intelligence.
     (G. M. Whipple, Transl.) Baltimore: Warwick & York, 1914.
Trevarthen, C. Conversations with a two-month-old. *New Scientist*,
     1974, *62*, pp. 230-235.
Trevarthen, C. Descriptive analyses of infant communicative behavior.
     In H. R. Shaffer (Ed.), *Studies in Mother-Infant Interaction*.
     New York: Academic Press, 1977, pp. 227-270.
United States Commission on Civil Rights. *Racial Isolation in the
     public schools, Vol. I*. Washington, D.C.: U.S. Government
     Printing Office, 1967.
Uzgiris, I. C., & Hunt, J. McV. *Assessment in infancy: Ordinal scales
     of psychological development*. Urbana, IL: University of Illinois
     Press, 1975.
Wachs, T. D. Relationship of infants' physical environment to their
     Binet performance at 2.5 years. *International Journal of
     Behavioral Development*, 1978, *1*, pp. 51-65.
Wachs, T. D., Uzgiris, I. C., & Hunt, J. McV. Cognitive development
     in infants of different age levels and from different environ-
     mental backgrounds: An exploratory investigation. *Merrill-
     Palmer Quarterly*, 1971, *17*, (4), pp. 283-317.
Weber, C. U., Foster, P. W., & Weikart, D. P. *An economic analysis of
     the Ypsilanti Perry preschool project*. Ypsilanti, MI: High/Scope
     Educational Research Foundation, 1978.
Weikart, D. P., Epstein, A. S., Schweinhart, L., & Bond, J. T. *The
     Ypsilanti preschool curriculum demonstration project*. Ypsilanti,
     MI: High/Scope Educational Research Foundation, 1978.
Weizmann, F., Cohen, L. B., & Pratt, R. J. Novelty, familiarity, and
     the development of infant attention. *Developmental Psychology*,
     1971, *4* (2), pp. 149-154.
Wetherford, M., & Cohen, L. B. Developmental changes in infant visual
     preferences for novelty and familiarity. *Child Development*,
     1973, *44*, pp. 416-424.
White, B. L. An experimental approach to the effects of experience
     on early human development. In J. P. Hill (Ed.), *Minnesota
     Symposia on Child Development*. Minneapolis: University of
     Minnesota Press, 1967, pp. 201-226.
White, B. L. *Experience and environment: Major influences on the
     development of the young child, Vol. II*. Englewood Cliffs,
     NJ: Prentice-Hall, 1978.
White, B. L. *Newsletter II*, 1980 (2).
White, B. L., & Watts, J. C. *Experience and environment: Major in-
     fluences on the development of the young child*. Englewood
     Cliffs, NJ: Prentice-Hall, 1973.
White, R. W. 1959. Motivation reconsidered: The concept of compe-
     tence. *Psychological Review*, 1959, *66*, pp. 297-333.
Yarrow, L. J., Rubenstein, J. L., & Pedersen, F. A. *Infant and
     environment: Early cognitive and motivational development*.
     Washington, D.C.: Hemisphere Publ. Co., 1975.

TOWARDS EDUCATION OF A NEW GENERATION:

SOME THOUGHTS

Yaacov Rand

Bar-Ilan University
Israel

This paper is more related to policy making than specific experimental findings and is based on personal educational experience
accumulated over many years. Although the ideas are not necessarily
novel, they merit a renewed consideration and a reformulation in
terms of present needs and problems.

The three divisions of the paper are: (1) a short and concise
description of some characteristic features of modern society pertinent to education in general, and to early childhood education in
particular; (2) a discussion of the importance of the cognitive
processes to the general adaptation of the individual living in
such a society; and (3) some suggestions of ways in which society
should--and could--cope with the educational problems which are of
paramount value to the individual and society.

We should start by a statement which expresses a well-known
phenomenon: The more a society is technologically developed, the
greater the number of individuals in the society who have severe
difficulty in keeping pace with societal demands. More and more
individuals are considered to be low achievers or underachievers,
and the educational system in countries with high technology has
to deal with masses of students considered problematic from different points of view. More traditional societies which are less
achievement-oriented are less confronted with problems of inadequate functioning, especially in the cognitive area. The etiolog-
ical factors for this phenomenon are probably inherent in modern
life, and some of them are noteworthy.

For example, a society with a high level of technological devel-

opment is a society of specialization. In other words, appropriate
social and professional placement requires higher levels of basic
functioning that necessitate long-term and continuous investment
both from the individual and from the society. Professions are
undergoing a continuous--and rapid--process of differentiation
that places considerable strain upon the individual, both while
striving towards placement and in order to progress or even to
maintain his acquired position. Specialization is based upon the
capacity of the individual to perform tasks of a high level of complexity, to handle complicated technical instruments, to adapt them
continuously to new situations and difficulties, and to make rapid
decisions based upon highly differentiated configurations of relevant variables.

Another aspect of this problem is the explosion of knowledge.
Education today--even though less than 30 years ago--is still burdened with a heavy load of routines accumulated over many centuries
of teaching, namely, teaching towards knowledge of "facts." Certainly, knowledge of facts is important to the individual, but
today there is growing awareness that knowledge of facts alone
is not sufficient for proper functioning and adequate adaptation
of the individual to life. Rapid changes in society require continuous reevaluation of what is "true" or "important to know." It
becomes evident that more important than a body of facts may be
the individual's capacity to adapt knowledge of how to learn and
how to benefit from being exposed to a world of stimuli with which
he must cope, while maintaining his role of a subject that acts
upon his environment. Feuerstein, Rand, Hoffmann and Miller (1980)
list a variety of cognitive functions which are deemed necessary
prerequisites for appropriate cognitive functioning of the individual while he is being confronted with highly complex configurations of stimuli. The acquisition of these and other appropriate
cognitive functions becomes more and more essential and education
has made only the very first steps in this direction.

I should introduce at this point an additional variable which
is of a sociopsychological nature: anonymity. Modern society is
mainly an anonymous society. Dense population conglomerations and
highly extended possibilities--as well as motivations--for geographical and social mobility contribute considerably to the development
and enhancement of anonymity as a characteristic feature of the
individual in society. The individual has to rely heavily upon
himself and his own capacities in order to be able to cope with and
overcome difficulties in areas of importance to his future or to
his current well-being. Anonymity is also considered to have a
strong impact upon the value system of the individual because ex-
trinsic social barriers are often weakened, and behavior has to be
guided from within, from the interiorized elements of the normative
social rules. Anonymity also considerably increases the importance

of personal capacities and achievement in the individual's struggle
for survival. In the extreme, it might be said that in modern
society it is no longer the "individual in society," but rather
the "individual against society" that is prevalent. Social support
is far from adequate in too many cases, even from the proximal--and
therefore, the most meaningful--frameworks.

The last point to be mentioned refers only to a certain part
of modern society, but is becoming more widespread and is nowadays
characteristic of many societies. I refer to democracy. Life in
a democratic society, although it has its obvious advantages, also
puts a heavy psychological burden upon its members. It is true
that psychological difficulties may turn out to be advantageous to
the individual, provided one makes necessary investments in order
to prepare him to cope properly with such difficulties. In a
democratic society, the individual is frequently under stress, due
to the continuous need to make decisions and to choose between different alternatives as an autonomous human being. The act of
choice is much more frequent in a democratic society than in an
autocratic one, because life in a free world is less predetermined
and preoriented by extra-individual factors, whether social or
political, so that the individual must rely heavily upon his own
will and capacities to make decisions.

A democratic society is also highly heterogeneous in many
respects. I would like to mention here only a few that are
pertinent to daily life. Divergent philosophical systems and
ideologies are publicly expressed and brought to extensive--and
often vehement--confrontations. Political ideals and leadership
try to impose themselves continuously, due to the permanent need
for people to struggle to acquire power and to maintain positions
already acquired. Commercial advertising impinges continuously
upon the individual, requiring him to use extended discriminatory
power in order to make appropriate daily decisions. Opportunities
for mobility in many important areas are numerous and have to be
under constant scrutiny and consideration. All these require a
high level of psychological differentiation--in Witkin's terms--
(Witkin, Dyk, Faterson, Goodenough & Karp, 1962) in order to be able
to function appropriately and to adequately choose efficient alternatives from a wide spectrum of possibilities.

The characteristics of modern society just mentioned, as well
as others, have special bearing upon education in general, and upon
early childhood education in particular. It is clear today that in
the last three decades, educational and psychological thought have
undergone meaningful revisions, emphasizing again--as in classical
psychology--the importance of the cognitive processes to the adaptation of the individual to his environment and to life. At the
beginning of this century, Freud and his school called our attention

to the connotative variables of the human personality and underlined their strong impact upon the adequate psychological functioning of the individual. This was perhaps the most important discovery in psychology at that time. However, the result was an over-
emphasis of those variables which were then considered the only
important ones for adaptation. Today, although the importance of
these variables is not denied, the cognitive aspects of human functioning are becoming more salient in the framework of adaptation.
Piaget's theory and the growing flow of both critical and supportive research on cognitive theories are an expression of this trend
and a catalyzer towards further accumulation of knowledge of a
descriptive nature and elaboration of systematic interventions
geared to improving the cognitive capacities of the individual.

Cognitive functioning is perhaps the most important factor
for academic achievement and subsequent social and professional
placement of the individual. Without adequate cognitive functioning, the individual is doomed to continuous and self-perpetuating
failure across a relatively long period--the school years--and,
furthermore, such failure has a very strong impact on life per se.
School certificates that are supposed to reflect one's cognitive
capacities are main keys to open or to close options in professional
and personal areas of life. Self-image is formed, structured, and
maintained on the basis of cognitive achievement. A self-concept
of a "failing person" that an individual may carry with him from
school and throughout life will probably be reinforced by social
feedback and other life experiences which he will have to face.

It is necessary to mention here one very important aspect of
human development which may be considered a bridge between the
cognitive and the affective aspects of personality--namely, the
identification process. In an open and free society such as the
one in which we live, identification models are of a highly heterogeneous nature, impinging upon the individual from a great variety
of sources. This heterogeneity, in terms of normative behaviors,
attitudes, values, and general life orientation, requires the
individual to have highly elaborated and refined cognitive processes
in order to establish and structure his "self-identity." It is
through a cognitive process that the individual may select differentially some of a model's attributes and reject some others, to
make the integration process consonant with what he has already incorporated and internalized. Struggle for "self-identity" may be
much more difficult, therefore, in a free society than in a more
authoritative one where models with which one can identify are both
more homogeneous and mutually supportive.

The identification process is of tremendous social, and therefore educational, importance. This is especially true for societies
that absorb or try to integrate individuals having divergent and

deeply anchored cultural roots. Although an adequate level of
cognitive functioning does not insure a smooth development of the
identification process, it is nevertheless an important and necessary
ingredient. An individual with a low capacity to properly elaborate
on this process may impair his psychological and social development,
thus impeding his general adjustment to life and to society, and in
many cases resulting in socially deviant behavior.

So far, we have discussed the importance of cognitive functioning for the individual's adaptation to himself and to his environment. In fact, early childhood education has always emphasized the
importance of cognitive functioning; many programs (formal and informal) have been geared towards its improvement. Some of them
have been empirically tested and found to be successful as measured
during--and immediately after--the implementation of educational
intervention. Nevertheless, we must be aware of the fact that
despite these successes, very few of the obtained results endured
over time. This is especially true for cognitive variables as
many follow-up studies of successful intervention experiments
found that acquired gains faded away over relatively short periods.
The Head Start program, with all the controversies it has aroused,
is one example of this phenomenon, although strong arguments still
persist as to the reasons for it, and different views have been expressed in relation to differential criterion measures (Clark &
Clark, 1973, 1975). These findings are of special importance because the assumption is that early interventions, due to the plasticity of the very young individual, result in gains of a more permanent nature as compared with later interventions.

Therefore, the search for new avenues has to continue so as to
enable individuals to cope with the complexity of cognitive education. Some basic assumptions might be useful in the crystallization
of our ideas.

1. Cognitive functioning is one of the most important factors
in the individual's adaptation to himself and to his environment.

2. The human system is an open system and is subject to modification by environmental intervention.

3. Subsystems of the human personality are of a configurational
nature and are mutually interdependent. Therefore, intervention in
one area may result in meaningful modification in other psychologically adjacent areas.

4. Educational intervention in the cognitive area should be
geared mainly towards development of the individual's capacity to
learn and to become a source for information via his own autonomous
activity. This goal can be obtained by enriching his repertoire

of cognitive strategies and organizational systems to cope with complex worlds of stimuli. I refer here to what is called by Reuven Feuerstein and his school "Mediated Learning Experience" (see Feuerstein & Rand, 1974; Feuerstein, Rand, Hoffman & Miller, 1980).

5. Intervention has to be of a holistic nature, impinging upon the individual from a great variety of sources, including informal, but meaningful social settings.

6. Education, even in informal settings, such as family, can no longer be left to sheer chance. It is the role and the duty of society to find ways and to activate processes to make informal education in all its aspects, especially in the cognitive area, as efficient and systematic as possible.

7. Education cannot limit its efforts to the present generation only. Extended intervention should be geared towards creating optimal conditions that will allow more sound and efficient education from the very start of life. These efforts should be extended to the present generation of parents and to prospective parents.

With these assumptions in mind, an old but relevant Jewish dictum should be remembered: "If one wants to properly educate a child, he will have to start with his grandfather. ...." Even though practically it is difficult to implement this dictum, we should not neglect its wisdom and we must find ways to put its general idea into practice.

It seems to me that the key problem of cognitive development is anchored in what happens to the child in his interactions with his family, especially with his parents, from the beginning of his life. The contention that every adult becomes capable of assuming the educational role--especially in the field of cognition--the very moment such a role is imposed upon him, is more than questionable. Rather, we may assume that the opposite is true for very wide segments of the population. Therefore, society can no longer continue to ignore this problem and to act--as it does--on the basis of such an erroneous assumption. We should perhaps recall that the first kindergarten established by Froebel in Germany in the 19th century was mainly geared towards education of the mothers. It was only later that children were brought into the kindergarten and social investment was directed towards professional preparation of the kindergarten teacher.

Therefore, I would like to suggest a radical reorientation of the educational process in different settings to serve the needs of early childhood education, according to the following guidelines:

1. Preparation of individuals for parenthood must become an integral part of the educational process through all its formal

stages. It is inconceivable that high school programs, for example, invest so much in subject matter that is of limited use in daily life and at the same time ignore almost completely the preparation of the individual for the vital role of being a parent, a role that will be fulfilled by practically all individuals attending secondary school.

2.   In the educational framework, special attention has to be paid to the cognitive area. Parents are the most powerful mediators in the world of the young and rapidly growing child. Ways to provide a child with efficient "Mediated Learning Experience"--in Feuerstein's terms--must be acquired systematically. Investment in this direction can be highly fruitful and beneficial to both parents and their offspring.

3.   When children are in the 6th to 8th grades, special programs should be introduced relating to preparation for family life and to child-rearing practices within the family. Today, what is called sex education, especially when centered just on basic information in the field, is quite superfluous and in many cases even undesirable. Education towards parenthood in the broader meaning of the term may arouse positive motivation towards fulfilling the role of parenthood and be highly beneficial in many respects.

4.   Special courses on parenthood preparation should be initiated in all communities for young parents and nonmarried youngsters. Such courses must also offer opportunities for young parents to discuss problems concerning their family life and children's education with others who face similar difficulties, as well as with professionals who are capable of advising and supporting them. As a result, these courses may be able to fulfill a prophylactic role and help parents overcome problems in their initial stages.

I am aware that such a program is neither exhaustive nor easy to implement in the situation of our own country nor in that of many other countries. But the very moment we accept its basic assumptions, we may find many ways to implement such a program on a large-scale basis even with limited financial resources. We should perhaps approach this issue, as we do so many times in this country, by implementing it gradually, piece by piece, and in a relatively short period we may discover that something very essential has changed in our society. It is my deepest belief that this is extremely necessary and also practically feasible. It is probably inherent in the human being's nature to be modifiable, and our strong belief is that this is true at all ages. We, the educators, the parents, and certainly the children and youngsters, are amenable to modification via environmental intervention. We must also believe that it is in our capacity to act efficiently in order to reach those meaningful modifications that are felt to be so necessary for the present generation, as well as for the generations to come.

BIBLIOGRAPHY

Clarke, A.M. & Clarke, A.D.B. What are the problems? An evaluation
    of recent research relating to theory. In A.D.B. Clarke and
    A.M. Clarke (Eds.), *Mental retardation and behavioral theory.*
    Edinburgh: Church and Livingstone, 1973, pp. 3-22.
Clarke, A.M. & Clarke, A.D.B. *Mental deficiency: The changing outlook.*
    3rd ed., New York: Free Press, 1975.
Feuerstein, R. & Rand, Y. Mediated learning experiences: An outline of
    the proximal etiology for differential development of cognitive
    functions. In L. Goldfine (Ed.), *International understanding:
    Cultural differences in the development of cognitive processes.*
    1974, pp. 7-37.
Feuerstein, R., Rand, Y., Hoffman, M.B. & Miller, R. *Instrumental
    enrichment.* Baltimore: University Park Press, 1980.
Witkin, H.A. , Dyk, R.B., Faterson, H.F., Goodenough, R.D., & Karp, S.A.
    Psychological differentiation. New York: John Wiley and Sons,
    Inc., 1962.

EXPERIMENTAL AND OBSERVATIONAL STUDIES

OF PRESCHOOL CHILDREN'S MEMORY*

Marion Perlmutter

University of Minnesota

This paper contains a summary of our recent research on the
development of memory in preschool children. We have been interested in assessing the mnemonic abilities of preschool children,
ascertaining the nature of memory improvement that occurs during
this time span, and understanding the factors that contribute to
this development.

Our research strategy has been to compare younger with older
preschool children in their performance of tasks designed to tap
memory skills. Generally the younger children have been between
2 1/2 and 3 1/2 years of age and the older children between 4 1/2
and 5 1/2 years of age. Our tasks are usually designed as "games."
The games have included considerable warm-up and practice to ensure
that the children are comfortable in the situation and that they
understand the task.

Our first studies (Perlmutter & Myers, 1974, 1975, 1976) were
designed to assess the recognition capacities of young children.
We presented 18-item lists of toy objects to the children and then
gave them yes-no recognition tests on 36-item lists containing the
original 18 objects plus 18 new ones. Figure 1 shows the percentage
correct recognition for each age group in each of three recognition
studies. As can be seen, performance tended to be very good, al-

---

*Much of this research was supported by a grant to Marion Perl-
mutter from NICHHD (HD-11776) and the University of Minnesota's
Center for Research in Human Learning grants from NICHHD (HD-01136)
and NSF (BNS-75-03816).

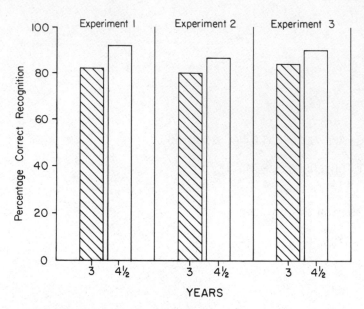

Figure 1. Mean percentage correct recognition

though there were significant improvements with age. Apparently
young children have rather good recognition memory capacities.
They can encode and retain substantial amounts of information, and
when the information is again presented, they are cognizant of their
previous experience with it.

Next, we carried out a series of recall studies (Perlmutter &
Myers, 1979) designed to assess the recall capacities of young
children. We presented 9-item lists of toy objects to the children
and then tested their free recall. Figure 2 shows the percentage
correct recall for each age group in each of three experiments.
Performance tended to be very poor. In addition, there were again
age-related improvements in performance. These data show real mnemonic deficits in young children. While the recognition data indicated that these children could encode and retain information and
recognize it when it was again presented, the recall data indicated
that they are less skillful at retrieving information that is no
longer present.

Our next goal was to analyze some of the factors limiting children's recall. One obvious difference between recognition and recall that could contribute to the discrepant performance is the
stimulus support available at time of testing. In recognition tasks
the stimulus is before the children and they have only to indicate
that it was previously seen. On the other hand, in recall tasks the
stimulus is no longer before the children and they have to cognitively

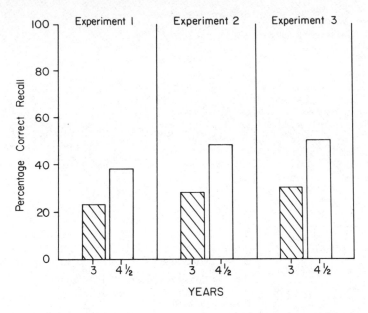

Figure 2. Mean percentage correct recall

generate it. Thus, one of our lines of research has been to manipulate stimulus support at testing. We believed this would improve recall and might be especially beneficial to younger children who might have particular difficulty mentally generating the information that our recognition studies showed they retain.

One of our first indications of how effective stimulus support could be for young children came from a recall study (Perlmutter & Ricks, 1979) in which we varied the colors of items. After testing the children with our standard free recall procedures and obtaining our now expected poor levels of performance, we decided to test the children's color recall by telling them the name of each item and asking them to tell us its color. This task provided a test of recall where information about color had to be cognitively generated, but since the name was provided, the child had considerable stimulus support. As can be seen in Figure 3, color recall was substantially higher than item recall. Moreover, when this stimulus support was provided, the age difference was substantially reduced.

In our next series of experiments (Perlmutter, 1980) we were interested in assessing the effects of category cuing on young children's recall. Category cuing would provide some stimulus support, but of a less concrete nature. Children were presented 9-item lists of pictures. After free recall testing the children were tested for cued recall by providing category labels. Category labels always improved recall (Fig. 4). Also, there were age X recall measure

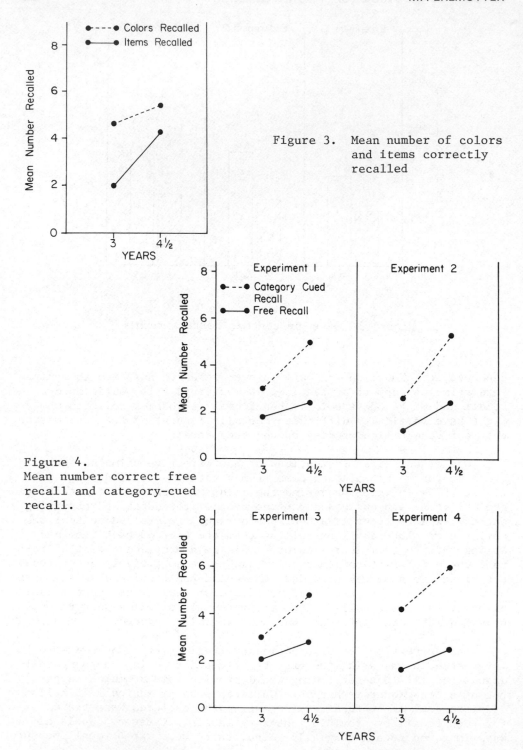

Figure 3.   Mean number of colors
and items correctly
recalled

Figure 4.
Mean number correct free
recall and category-cued
recall.

interactions, but in the direction opposite to our previous study on stimulus support. Older children profited from category cues more than did younger children. This finding is actually consistent with some of our other research showing that the memory of older preschool children is somewhat more semantically atuned than that of younger children (Perlmutter & Myers, 1979).

The category cuing effects suggest that the young children had encoded the category membership of items. A further manipulation of one of our category cuing studies enabled us to examine possible differences in category cuing when category labels had or had not been provided during presentation. Somewhat surprisingly, providing category labels at presentation did not lead to stronger category cuing effects at testing (Table 1). Perhaps children were already proficient at encoding category membership.

Table 1. Mean number recalled when category cues were present at presentation and test or only at test

	Category cues	
	Presentation & test	Test only
Younger subjects	4.52	4.69
Older subjects	7.35	7.52
Combined over age	5.94	6.11

In a further series of studies (Perlmutter, Shork, & Lewis, 1980), we examined both category and color cuing. Children were presented 12-item lists of pictures and then either cued with item colors or categories. Both of these types of cues were effective, although category cues tended to be more effective than color cues (Fig. 5).

Since the designs of these studies included color- and category-orienting tasks, we could again compare conditions in which the specific cue was known to be present in the encoding environment with conditions in which the cue was not necessarily encoded. The encoding specificity hypothesis (Tulving & Tompson, 1973) leads to the prediction of an advantage for conditions in which the cue type matches the orienting task. There was a slight advantage for conditions in which orienting task and cue matched; however, this difference was never significant (Table 2). Encoding specificity does not appear to be a very adequate characterization for very young children.

In our next series of experiments (Perlmutter, Sophian, Mitchell, & Cavanaugh, in press) we developed a cuing condition that we believed

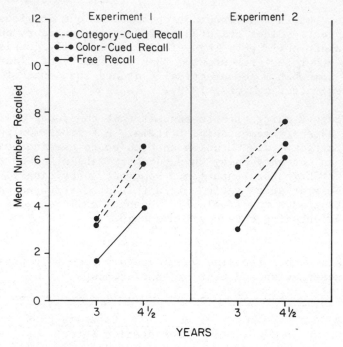

Figure 5.   Mean number correct free recall, category-cued recall,
            and color-cued recall

would be more likely to benefit the younger children. These cues
were pictures of related objects that were usually also present at
presentation. Since the pictures seemed to provide more concrete
stimulus support than category or color cues, we expected more
dramatic improvement in young children's performance. The results
look quite similar to our category or color cues; we expected more
dramatic improvement in young children's performance. The results
look quite similar to our category cuing studies (Fig. 6). Related

Table 2.   Mean number recalled when orienting task and cue were same
           or different

| | Orienting task and cue | | | |
| | Experiment 1 | | Experiment 2 | |
	Same	Different	Same	Different
Younger subjects	1.72	1.58	2.80	2.38
Older subjects	3.44	2.76	3.78	3.40
Combined over age	2.58	2.16	3.30	2.90

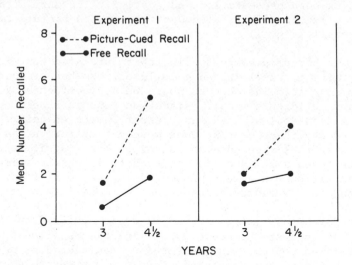

Figure 6. Mean number correct free recall and related context-cued recall

pictures cues were effective, and more so for older children.

The results shown in Table 3 provide a hint about what was occurring. Related picture cues were no more helpful if they had been present during presentation and testing than if they were present only during testing. Apparently the children had simply translated the related picture cues into category label cues, and thus the semantically related age X memory measure interaction was again obtained.

In order to determine whether the related picture cues that were present during presentation were merely used as category cues or were also functioning as context cues reinstating the encoding environment, a subsequent experiment in the series included a compari-

Table 3. Mean number recalled when related context cues were present at presentation and test or only at test

| | Related context cues | |
	Presentation & test	Test only
Younger subjects	2.00	2.92
Older subjects	3.92	3.67
Combined over age	2.96	3.00

son of the effects of unrelated and related picture cues that were
present during both presentation and testing. The unrelated context cues had little effect, although the related picture cues facilitated recall (Fig. 7).

It was rather perplexing to find that unrelated context cues
did not facilitate recall in young children. We had of course predicted that such stimulus support would be very effective in facilitating young children's recall, since the support should have
reinstated a good deal of what was present during encoding. One
hypothesis of why these context cues were not effective was that
they were never really encoded as context. That is, it is quite
plausible that young children do not tend to integrate stimulus
information, at least not when presented in the form of pairs that
we used; thus the unrelated context cues were of little help.

In the next study in the series we again compared the effects
of related and unrelated context cues. In this experiment, however,
while our related context was presented as had been done previously,
as cue-target pairs, our unrelated context was present in a manner
that was integrated with the target (e.g., a ball in a wagon). The
integrated unrelated context was especially effective, and indeed
reduced age differences somewhat (Fig. 8). When context was integrated with the target, we again found the kind of stimulus support
effect found in our earlier color recall study.

In general, then, our experimental research with preschool
children has demonstrated quite adequate encoding and retention
skills at a very young age. However, these young children are not
particularly facile at accessing their considerable information
stores; their retrieval skills apparently are not well developed.

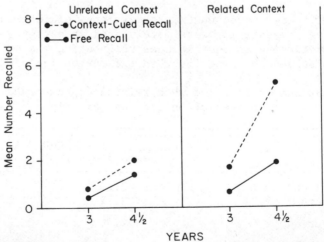

Figure 7.   Mean number correct free and context-cued recall (uninte-
            grated, unrelated context and related context)

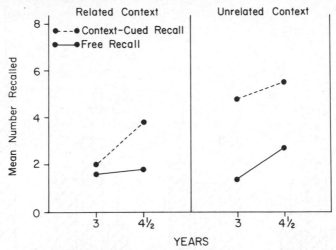

Figure 8. Mean number correct free and context-cued recall (related
           context and integrated, unrelated context)

Moreover, while providing young children with stimulus support is
often facilitating, generalizations about the effects of contextual
support are not simple, since young children often do not integrate
context in the way that older children and adults do.

     Yet, informal observations suggest that information about the
past is often evident in the everyday behaviors and conversations of
young children. Since we believe that understanding such naturalistic memory is essential, we decided to attempt to document and analyze young children's real-world memory use.

     In a diary study of infants of 7, 9, and 11 months (Ashmead &
Perlmutter, 1980), we relied upon trained parents to record their
infants' everyday use of memory. We were especially interested in
determining who or what cued memory episodes and the infant's role
in them. Figure 9 shows the mean percentage of each age group's
memory episodes that appeared to be cued spontaneously, by physical
cues, social cues, or both physical and social cues.

     All infants showed some spontaneous, apparently uncued memory.
However, the spontaneous episodes seemed to be least common among
7-month olds. The percentage of socially cued episodes were also
least common among 7-month olds, although the percentage of physically cued episodes was most common in this age group, as was the
percentage of physically and socially cued ones. In general, then,
7-month olds seem less sensitive to purely social cues.

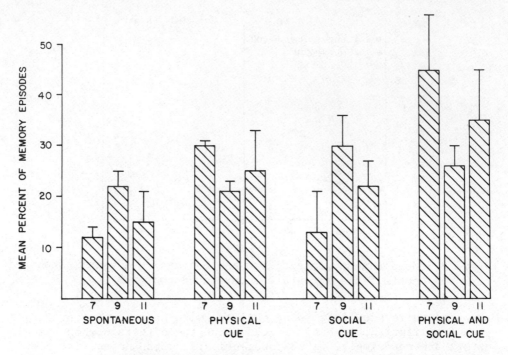

Figure 9.   Mean percentage of memory episodes cued spontaneously,
            physically, socially, or both physically and socially

        Another question concerned how active the infants were in the
memory episodes. If the infant did something that appeared to be
remembered, the episode was considered active; if the infant simply
reacted to something remembered or expected, the episode was considered passive. Figure 10 shows the mean percentage of each age
group's memory episodes in which the infant appeared to play an
active role. In many of the episodes that parents recorded, infants
did play an active role. Moreover, there was a clear age trend,
with older infants actively involved in higher percentages of memory
episodes than were younger infants. We think this evidence of infants remembering to do something, rather than simply reacting to
familiar or strange situations, is indicative of something like recall memory. That is, the infants appeared to generate remembered
information. This sort of memory is more advanced than the infant
recognition memory studied in laboratory experiments (Werner & Perlmutter, 1979). Since infants generally are not credited with having
such generative memory skills, we believe this naturalistic approach
has been particularly useful in exposing a fuller range of their
abilities than is typically acknowledged.

        Our naturalistic studies of older preschool children's memory

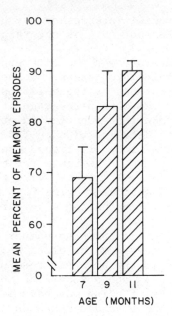

Figure 10.   Mean percentage of memory episodes in which infant played
             an active role

also point to more extensive memory than is observed in the laboratory.
In a study of 3- and 4-year-olds' conversations with adults (Todd &
Perlmutter, 1980), we have tried to determine the amount and kind
of information about the past that preschool children communicate to
adults, the time periods over which the children retain information,
and the elicitors of memory.

     The results of this study suggested that young children recall
considerable amounts of information during conversations occurring
under relatively natural conditions. Moreover, the information
appeared to be highly accurate. The highest level of error that
parents detected in the events conveyed by their children was 5%.
While the parents occasionally indicated that the structure of the
information was distorted in some way, that is, the order of events
may have been incorrect, they believed that the basic statements
were for the most part highly accurate.

     The memory information provided by the children covered a wide
variety of events ranging from routine occurrences, such as playing
with toys, to novel experiences, such as airplane rides. It was
interesting to find that social situations appeared to be important
sources of information, with the children mentioning other people
in more than 70% of the episodes. These data thus point to the
importance of social encounters for the young child and suggest that

methodologies based on social interaction may be effective in investigating memory development in this age range.

Another issue of interest was the time span over which young
children are able to retain information. To help address this issue
we relied upon parents' datings of the episodes that their children
reported. Table 4 shows the mean percentage of episodes and number
of memory units per episode that occurred in each of three time
intervals. A majority of datable episodes (60%) occurred within a
month prior to the conversation, 11% 1 to 3 months earlier, and 29%
more than four months earlier. The range for the oldest event recalled by each child was 8 to 17 months, with the age of the child
at the time of the oldest episode ranging from 2 years, 3 months for
a 3-year-old to 2 years, 11 months for a 4-year-old.

A suprprising finding was that the number of memory units per
question was actually greater for the older episodes, with events
occurring more than four months prior to testing containing about
twice as much information as those occurring more recently. Parent
reports suggested that this finding may have been due in part to the
fact that some episodes had been discussed during the intervening
time. However, this could not account entirely for the results, because the parents reported that many episodes had not been mentioned
since the time of occurrence. For example, the parents of a 4-year-
old, who related an incident that had occurred 17 months earlier,
were very confident that the incident had not been discussed during
the interim because it concerned a frightening experience for the
child and they did not wish to remind the child of it. The event,
as related by the child, was quite detailed despite the long time
interval. In addition, the child still displayed a strong level of
emotion in relating the event. It is possible that the emotional
state of the child at the time of encoding had contributed to the
relatively high level of recall over an extended time period. In
general, the children often related events that were charged with
emotion or were highly exciting. This suggests that the connection
between emotional state and the probability of subsequent recall may
be an interesting area for future research.

Table 4. Mean percentage of episodes and number of memory units per
          episode that occurred in each of three time intervals

	% Episodes	Mean number Memory unit/episode
Less than 1 month	60	6.2
1 to 3 months	11	4.0
More than 4 months	29	11.9

Finally, we were interested in determining what seemed to elicit information from the children's memory. Perhaps it is not surprising that approximately one half of the memory episodes elicited in the conversational study were in response to direct adult questioning. In pursuing this question of what elicits young children's use of memory we also carried out a questionnaire study (Warren & Perlmutter, 1980) in which parents of 3- to 5-year-olds were surveyed about the things they deliberately teach their children to remember. We were impressed with the amount of explicit memory training reported to take place, even before formal schooling. The percentage of parents who indicated direct teaching of various types of information are as follows:

Age	100	Other names	94
Colors	100	Songs	92
Animals	99	Stories	92
Letters	98	Seasons	77
Body parts	97	Address	75
Full name	97	Birthdate	56
Numbers	96	Phone number	40

In summary, we believe that while our research with preschool children has pointed to some limitations in their memory skills, it has also indicated that even at a very early age, children retain extensive information about diverse events. Moreover, young children apparently retain this information over very long time intervals. Finally, we believe that social encounters may be particularly salient for the young children. Analysis of social interactions may be fruitful for elucidating the factors that lead to cognitive development.

BIBLIOGRAPHY

Ashmead, D., & Perlmutter, M. Infant memory in everyday life. In M. Perlmutter (Ed.), *New directions in child development: Naturalistic approaches to children's memory*. San Francisco: Jossey Bass, 1980.

Perlmutter, M. Development of memory in the preschool years. In R. Greene and T.D. Yawkey (Eds.), *Early and middle childhood: Growth, abuse, and delinquency and its effects on individual, family, and community*. Westport, CN: Technomic Publishing, 1980.

Perlmutter, M., & Myers, N. Recognition memory development in two- to four-year-olds. *Developmental Psychology*, 1974, *10*, 447-450.

_____. Young children's coding and storage of visual and verbal material. *Child Development*, 1975, *46*, 215-219.

_____. Recognition memory in preschool children. *Developmental Psychology*, 1976, *12*, 271-272.

_____. Recall development in two- to four-year-olds. *Developmental Psychology*, 1979, *15*, 73-83.

Perlmutter, M., & Ricks, M. Recall in preschool children. *Journal of Experimental Child Psychology*, 1979, *27*, 423-437.

Perlmutter, M., Schork, E., & Lewis, D. Effects of orienting task on preschool children's acquisition and retrieval. Unpublished manuscript, 1980.

Perlmutter, M., Sophian, C., Mitchell, D.B., & Cavanaugh, J. Cuing preschool children's recall. *Developmental Psychology*, in press.

Todd, C., & Perlmutter, M. Reality recalled by preschool children. In M. Perlmutter (Ed.), *New directions in child development: Naturalistic approaches to children's memory*. San Francisco: Jossey Bass, 1980.

Tulving, E. & Thomson, D.M. Encoding specificity and retrieval processes in episodic memory. *Psychological Review*, 1973, *80*, 352-373.

Warren, L., & Perlmutter, M. A questionnaire study of preschool children's memory. Unpublished manuscript, 1980.

Werner, J.S., & Perlmutter, M. Development of visual memory in infants. In H.W. Reese and L.P. Lipsitt (Eds.), *Advances in child development and behavior* (Vol. 14). New York: Academic Press, 1979.

DEVELOPMENT OF CHILDREN'S MORAL DELIBERATIONS:

IMPLICATIONS FOR EARLY CHILDHOOD EDUCATION*

Michael Siegal

University of Queensland
Australia

INTRODUCTION

It has been noted since ancient times that parents should have an important positive impact on children's moral development. Aristotle even once claimed that parents exert more influence than any friendship between unrelated persons. But notwithstanding the wisdom of the ancients, the extent to which parent-child relations contributes to children's sense of right and wrong remains an issue of longstanding controversy. In fact, many modern developmental psychologists have sought to minimize the positive role of direct adult instruction and teaching. Among these are such pacesetting and provocative figures as Jean Piaget and Lawrence Kohlberg.

For Piaget (1932, 1967, 1971), adult instruction can naturally reinforce development, but ordinarily instruction acts as a constraining obstacle to be overcome with the experience gained in peer group interaction. For Kohlberg, the relationship between the moral development of parents and their children is exceedingly modest (Haan, Langer, & Kohlberg, 1976). Indeed, he has emphasized that "a specific relation to a specific good parent is neither necessary nor sufficient for normal or advanced moral development, since father's absence, father's moral level, and use of "good" child-

---

*This research was supported by a grant from the University Research Grants Committee of the University of Queensland (No. 048248 TR). The assistance of Mary Murdoch and Dulcie Singh is gratefully acknowledged, and many thanks are due to the staff and students of St. Ignatius School, Brisbane, for their fine cooperation and enthusiasm.

rearing techniques, however defined, do not predict to such maturity"
(Kohlberg, 1969, p. 471).

Here Kohlberg unmistakably rules out massive effects of a
specific parent-child relationship for moral development. From this
theoretical stand, he has proposed that moral development is primarily a function of cognitive development, which in turn is stimulated by a variety of role-taking opportunities and by contact with
high levels of moral reasoning. Kohlberg singles out a way in which
adults can promote these experiences: by guiding classroom debates
among primary and secondary school children on hypothetical moral
dilemmas. Thus the adult's role is often a rather indirect one.
It consists of encouraging moral development by broadening children's
role-taking experiences with the cognitively more sophisticated
moral reasoning often encountered in the peer group, rather than
by directly transmitting a set of substantive moral principles or
by acting as a stalwart model of moral behaviour.

Yet despite the wide appeal of Kohlberg's writings, somewhat
surprisingly, his theory incorporates no strong, direct, positive
role for the adult. If this role is in fact nonexistent, perhaps
it is because of the measurement error problems that have plagued
the Kohlberg theory since its inception (Colby, 1978), and because
of an uncertain empirical basis that has been a target for critical
notices and reviews (Crockenberg & Nicolayev, 1979; Kurtines &
Greif, 1974; Philips & Nicolayev, 1979; Rubin & Trotter, 1977; Siegal,
1980). These problems may also have given rise to so modest an observed relationship between moral reasoning and actual moral behaviour. Sad to say, the problems are probably not endemic to the
particular area of moral development, but apply similarly to the
evaluation of the general social development fostered by early
childhood intervention programs (Zigler & Trickett, 1978).

There is indeed little doubt that intelligence contributes to the
child's moral reasoning. This point is underscored by both Piaget and
Kohlberg and has been supported in the research (Keasey, 1975; Lee,
1971; Whiteman & Kosier, 1964). But in order to obtain a more comprehensive picture of the intricate workings of moral development, it
is necessary to consider other factors. Besides cognitive development, these factors include the strength of parental identification
and the possible range of conflicts that the child confronts, since
reasoning is often inconsistent across different conflict types.

The purpose of the present study was to examine this three-
factor model. Designations for characterizing both the cognitive
capacities of children and the complexity of moral conflicts
originated from Piaget (1970) and were borrowed from amongst those
discussed elsewhere (Chandler, Siegal & Boyes, 1980). Children's
cognitive development was characterized by using Piaget's well known
terminology: preoperational, concrete operational, and formal

operational intelligence. As the child passes through each level
of intelligence, he is able to solve progressively more abstract
problems.

The range of increasingly complex moral conflicts was also subdivided into three categories: individual rituals, collective rules,
and principles. These distinctions are less well known and merit
definition. The term "ritual" is used by Piaget and here to describe
a kind of idiosyncratic prerule experienced by young, preoperational
children as endowing certain behaviors with a sense of self-
obligation. Obligations of this sort control behaviors and are
less abstract or formal than are collective rules or laws. Feeling
that one ought to brush one's hair fifty times before walking to
school is an example of a childish ritual that is individual and
particularistic. Feeling that one ought, on some particular occasion, to be an early riser without obliging the same of others
is one approximate adult equivalent. By contrast, "collective
rules" are generally applicable and inter-subjective. These rules
operate as component features of more coordinated systems of obligations, such as a bill of rights or a criminal code. As features of
larger systems, some such collective rules may coexist, while others
should contradict and make logical impossibilities of their opposites.
By this account, the attainment of concrete operations should con-
cur with the ability to comprehend collective rules. Finally,
"principles" (or "meta-rules") are statements about relationships
between rules. They pertain to still more general abstract value
schemes for arbitrating conflicts involving other principles, rules,
or rituals. According to Piaget, the attainment of formal operations
is characterized by the comprehension of principles, which by definition are abstract and propositional in structure. The advent of
formal operations usually occurs early in adolescence. At this time,
the adolescent becomes capable of hypothetical, future-oriented
thinking. He is able to evaluate the rules as they are in comparison to utopian possibilities.

Given this tripartite framework for characterizing the range
of possible moral obligations, conflicts between these different
sorts of obligations can include those between rituals and rules,
rituals and principles, and rules and principles. By this account,
there should be a structural "match" between a child's level of
cognitive development and the complexity of the conflict. Preoperational children should tend to prefer ritual-oriented solutions
over those oriented towards rules and principles. Concrete operational children should prefer rule-oriented solutions to ritual- or
principle-oriented ones. And formal operational children should
prefer principle-oriented solutions over rule-oriented ones and
rule-oriented solutions to ritualistic ones. But this is all too
simplistic, since cases of regression are by no means infrequent
in such stage-structural models, and these may be accounted for by
the acute or chronic debilitating effects of external socialization

factors (Bearison, 1974). For this reason, the strength of parent-
child identification was incorporated as a factor in the present
model.

In his studies on the effects of parent-child relations, Hoffman (1971, 1975) has found that identification with a specific
parent is associated with children's rule-following and altruistic
behavior. These findings dovetail with those reported in several
other studies (Bixenstine, De Corte & Bixenstine, 1977; Mussen,
Rutherford, Harris & Keasey, 1970). Thus it would seem that a
specific relationship with a parent should accelerate a child's
moral development, whereas development should be retarded by the
lack of such a relationship. In the study reported here, children
were given stories to represent (1) a conflict between a ritual
and a rule, (2) a conflict between a ritual and a principle, and
(3) a conflict between a rule and a principle. It was expected
that children's level of cognitive development and strength of
parental identification would contribute to the structure of the
deliberations underlying their choice of action.

METHOD

Subjects

The original subjects of this study were 90 children attending
a Roman Catholic primary school located in an upper-middle-class
suburb of Brisbane, Australia. The children were all given Form
C of the Concept Assessment Kit (Goldschmidt & Bentler, 1968) as a
measure of concrete operations. Those who passed both the conservation of area and conservation of length tasks in the kit were
given Inhelder and Piaget's (1958) pendulum task, a measure of
formal operational reasoning. Performance was scored according to
the criteria detailed by Somerville (1974). The children were also
given Hoffman's (1971) identification index items, which aim to
measure the child's orientation toward parents; the children were
asked to say whom they admire, whom they would want to be like as
a grownup, and whom they take after mostly.

From their responses on these measures, 48 children were
chosen as comparatively clear cases of both cognitive and identification types. The preoperational children (age range = 5 years 10
months to 9 years 8 months; x = 7 years 0 months) were those who
failed both concrete operational tasks. The concrete operational
children (age range = 7 years 8 months to 12 years 6 months; $\bar{x}$ =
9 years 11 months) passed both tasks, but were unable to identify
the length of the string as the operative factor in the pendulum
problem. The formal operational group (age range = 6 years 5 months
to 12 years 3 months; $\bar{x}$ = 10 years 0 months) was not only able to
identify the string length correctly, but also could exclude other

variables.

At each cognitive level there were eight high-identification and eight low-identification children. The high-identification children were those who named the same parent on two or three of the identification items. As might be expected, both boys and girls named same-sex parents more often than opposite-sex parents. The low identification subjects were those who named a parent only once or not at all. Almost invariably these children named other adults who ranged from singer Elvis Presley to actress Cheryl Ladd.

Because of the amount of testing necessary to locate clear cases, it was impossible to assign an equal number of boys and girls to each subgroup. Boys were underrepresented: there were four among the low-identification preoperational children, three in the high-identification preoperational group, two in each concrete operational group, and three and one in the low-identification and high-identification concrete operational groups, respectively.

Procedure

The children were seen individually in a room of a wing ad-jacent to the main school building. The stories representing various conflict types were tape-recorded and played in a random sequence. The boys heard stories with male characters and read in a male voice, while the girls heard female character versions read in a female voice.

The story in which a ritual was contrasted with a rule in-volved a child attending a summer camp who had made a bargain with himself never to eat squash because he didn't like it. The child had to decide whether to comply with the rule of the camp that he should finish everything on his plate (including squash) and thus break the bargain he had made with himself; or to keep to his bargain, break the camp's rule, and refuse to eat the squash.

In the ritual-principle story, a child had made a bargain with himself never to lend his brand-new bicycle to anyone. A friend then asked to let him borrow the bike in order to deliver a spare set of car keys to his parents on the other side of town to replace those they had lost. The child had to decide whether to break his bargain and help the friend and his parents by lending the bike or to keep to his bargain and refuse to lend it.

The rule-principle story involved a child who saw a friend in his class cheat. The child had to decide whether to comply with a school rule that all instances of cheating must truthfully be reported to the teacher, which would mean that his friend would be thrown out of the class, or to break the school rule to protect his friend.

Following each story, the children were asked to repeat the
character's choices. All could do so without difficulty. Then
they were asked to say what the character should do, to justify
the decision, and to state and evaluate any other course of action
that the story character might have taken. The child's responses
were noted by the experimenter and tape-recorded.

RESULTS

The children's choices and justifications on the stories were
scored in three categories: ritual, rule, and principle oriented.
A ritual-oriented justification consisted of using a particular
personal preference to arbitrate a conflict (e.g., "He doesn't
like squash so he should not eat it." "He should tell on his friend
because he doesn't like him." "He didn't lend his friend the bike
because he was selfish.") A rule-oriented justification consisted
of simply using the consequences of a rule violation as a basis for
deliberation, while a principle-oriented justification required the
spontaneous generation of a hierarchy of generalizable moral values
implying simultaneous consideration of the two aspects to the problem (e.g., "It's worse to lose a friend than tell." "Helping the
friend and her parents is important and probably nothing would
happen to the bike.") Two judges independently scored the responses
with a 99% agreement.

Cognitive Development

The results incidated that cognitive development was associated
with the level of children's justifications in all three conflicts.
Five of the 16 preoperational children gave a ritual-oriented justification in maintaining that the story character should not eat
the squash, as opposed to only one in the concrete operational group
and none in the formal operational group. The remainder of the more
cognitively advanced children claimed that the character should
eat the squash, because following the camp's rules and staying at
the camp and out of trouble are more important than not eating squash.

A similar pattern was evident on the ritual-principle story.
Only five out of 16 preoperational children gave a rule or principle-
oriented justification for lending the bike; the others focused on
a specific personal preference and claimed that, because the friend
was dislikable or untrustworthy or that the bike was brand-new, it
should not be borrowed. By contrast, all of the concrete operational
and 12 of the formal operational children reasoned that helping
others is a correct generalizable course of action.

With regard to the rule-principle conflict, 10 of the preoperational children responded that the story character should protect

his friend and not tell. The comparable numbers in the concrete
and formal operational groups were eight and nine respectively, and
so choices did not vary significantly with cognitive development.
But for this story conflict, a number of children somewhat unexpect-
edly generated a principled justification for invoking the rule.
Thus level of justification often differed from direction of choice.
Only one child out of the 16 in the preoperational group gave a
principled justification for his choice, as opposed to three concrete and 10 formal operational children.

Strength of Identification

The incidence of principled justifications in the formal operational group was to a striking extent related to the strength of
identification. In the ritual-principle conflict only four of the
eight low-identification children claimed that the story character
should help his friend, as opposed to all eight of the high-identification children (Fisher Test, $p < .04$). The others said that the
story character shouldn't lend the bike because he didn't like his
friend or his friend's parents, or that the bike would get broken.
Not one of the low-identification children mentioned that the situation was an emergency, as compared with three of the high-identification subjects.

It is even more instructive to turn to the results of the rule-
principle conflict. Here only two out of the eight low-identification, formal operational children gave principled justifications
(such as "You shouldn't tell because it destroys friendship," and
"Friends are more important"), in contrast to all eight of the high-
identification children (Fisher Test, $p < .01$).

Six of the eight children in the low identification group gave
nonprincipled responses. The following excerpts from the subjects'
protocols speak for themselves:

1.   She told on her friend. She might not have liked her.
2.   She told the teacher because it's breaking a rule.
3.   You should protect your friend. If not you could get
beaten up.
4.   You should protect your friend so no one should find out.
5.   Obeying the rule is sensible.
6.   It's a rule to tell the teacher.

Responses of the high-identification, formal operational children are clearly richer and more thoughtful:

1.   If it's a friend you should not tell . . . but it's fair

to tell on a person who cheats.
2. You rather should not lose a friend than tell.
3. You should tell for your friend's own good.
4. It's good for your friend to tell.
5. She didn't report it. The friend should report it on her own.
6. You shouldn't tell because the teacher should be in the room herself and find out. You might not want to get your friend into trouble and she might not have seen you cheating.
7. She didn't tell because she wanted to be friends . . . hoped someone else might have seen her cheat.
8. If she told she could lose her friend and all others too.

These children spontaneously generated a hierarchy of moral values. Unlike the low-identification children, they made little mention of the immediate consequences of a rule violation as a basis for deliberation.

The effects of identification strength may be limited to the formal operational group, especially in view of the evidence, which suggests that adult influence on moral judgment development may possibly increase as children grow older and mature intellectually. In both the preoperational and concrete operational groups, there were no differences between the high-identification and low-identification children. Perhaps then, the relationship between cognitive and moral development approaches a necessary but not sufficient one (c.f. Kohlberg & Gilligan, 1971). An advanced intellectual development is not surprisingly an important part of moral development. But it may remain an insufficient part unless it is accompanied by parental identification, and thus by a strong direct adult influence.

DISCUSSION

As predicted, both the level of cognitive development and the strength of parental identification are associated with the structure of children's moral deliberations. A sizable proportion of preoperational children prefer ritual-oriented to rule- or principle-oriented solutions. By contrast, both concrete and formal operational children generally prefer rules to rituals; and while the concrete group generally prefers rules to principles, the reverse is the case for the formal group. Most strikingly, the extent to which formal operational children use principled justifications is highly related to the strength of their identification with a specific parent. This finding is consistent with Hoffman's (1975) claim that altruistic children have at least one parent, usually of the same sex, who communicates altruistic values and serves as a model for moral behavior. Contrary to Kohlberg, identification through direct adult instruction may in many cases serve to impart a strongly empathic, perspective-taking quality to children's moral judgments.

Some limitations to the present study should be mentioned.
The range of conflicts was represented by only one story to represent each of the three possible conflict types. Further research
should employ a larger number of clearly representative items.
This is no easy matter but, as Warnock (1971, p. 2) points out, the
vagueness inherent within many moral conflicts should not in itself
paralyze their study. What is important is that some cases should
be clear, not that all should be.

In addition, all the data were scored on the basis of children's
own responses. It would be worthwhile in subsequent studies, for
example, to examine the relationship of teachers' and peers' ratings
of children's behavior to the structure of children's moral deliberations.

But even with such limitations in mind, it seems clear, as
Damon (1979) has pointed out, that the study of moral development
cannot be reduced to the study of physical cognition. While the
stimulation of cognitive development is an important component of
moral development, an individual--no matter how intelligent--must
at some point observe and emulate the actions of others. It may
be that the child who has the cognitive capacity for principled
moral deliberations still requires a strong parental identification
to bring the promise of intellectual development to fruition in
reasoning and behavior.

Both Piaget and Kohlberg have claimed that traditional educational practice is dangerous, because direct attempts to inculcate
adult moral values discourage cooperation and encourage a thought-
less conformity to rules (Kohlberg & Mayer, 1972; Piaget, 1971,
pp. 178-180). Yet if parental respect and identification is a
decisive factor in children's moral development, the alternative
peer group debate method may be a needlessly ineffective method of
moral education. To consolidate the gains of the formal operational
child, it would seem highly desirable to foster a parent-child
identification. This is an edifice that almost certainly would
profit by a foundation during early moral education, and one that
requires the direct, active involvement of parents as well as teachers. The effectiveness of early moral education programs might
be enhanced by the adult's knowledge of the child's level of cognitive development and the types of conflicts that he or she confronts.

BIBLIOGRAPHY

Bearison, D. J. The construct of regression: A Piagetian approach.
    Merrill-Palmer Quarterly, 1974, *20*, 21-30.

Bixenstine, V. E., De Corte, M. S., & Bixenstine, B. A. Conformity
    to peer-sponsored misconduct at four grade levels. *Developmental
    Psychology*, 1976, *12*, 226-236.

Chandler, M., Siegal, M., & Boyes, M. Moral behaviour: Continuities
    and discontinuities. *International Journal of Behavioural De-
    velopment*, 1980, *3*, 323-332.

Colby, A. Evolution of a moral-development theory. *Moral development:
    New directions for child development, Number 2*, San Francisco:
    Jossey-Bass, 1978.

Crockenberg, S.B., & Nicolayev, J. Stage transition in moral reason-
    ing as related to conflict experienced in naturalistic settings.
    Merrill-Palmer Quarterly, 1979, *25*, 185-192.

Damon, W.   Why study social-cognitive development? *Human Development*,
    1979, *22*, 206-211.

Goldschmidt, M. L. T., & Bentler, P. M. *Concept assessment kit*. San
    Diego: Educational Testing Service, 1968.

Haan, N., Langer, J., & Kohlberg, L. Family patterns of moral reason-
    ing. *Child Development*, 1976, *47*, 1204-1206.

Hoffman, M. L. Identification and conscience development *Child De-
    velopment*, 1971, *42*, 1071-1082.

_____. Altruistic behaviour and the parent-child relationship.
    Journal of Personality and Social Psychology, 1975, *31*, 937-
    943.

Inhelder, B., & Piaget, J. *The growth of logical thinking from
    childhood to adolescence*. New York: Basic Books, 1958.

Keasey, C. B. Implications of cognitive development for moral reason-
    ing. In D. J. DePalma and J. M. Foley (Eds.), *Moral development:
    Current theory and research*. Hillsdale, N.J.: Lawrence Erlbaum,
    1975.

Kohlberg, L.   Stage and sequence: The cognitive-developmental ap-
    proach to socialization. In D. A. Goslin (Ed.), *Handbook of
    socialization theory and research*. Chicago: Rand McNally,
    1969.

Kohlberg, L., & Gilligan, C. The adolescent as philosopher: The
    discovery of self in a postconventional world. *Daedalus*,
    1971, *100*, 1051-1086.

Kohlberg, L., & Mayer, R. Development as the aim of education.
    Harvard Educational Review, 1972, *42*, 449-496.

Kurtines, W., & Greif, E. B. The development of moral thought:
    Review and evaluation of Kohlberg's approach. *Psychological
    Bulletin*, 1974 *81* 453-470.

Lee, L. C.   The concomitant development of cognitive and moral modes
    of thought: A test of selected deductions from Piaget's
    theory. *Genetic Psychology Monographs*, 1971, *83*, 93-146.

Mussen, P., Harris, S., Rutherford, E., & Keasey, C. B. Honesty and
    altruism among preadolescents. *Developmental Psychology*, 1970,
    3, 169-194.

Philips, D. C. & Nicolayev, J. On assessing Kohlberg's stage theory
    of moral development. In D. B. Cochrane, C. M. Hamm, & A. C.
    Kazepides (Eds.), *The domain of moral education*. New York: The

Paulist Press, 1979.

Piaget, J. *The moral judgment of the child*. London: Routledge & Kegan Paul, 1932.

_____. *Six psychological studies*. New York: Random House, 1967.

_____. Piaget's theory. In P. Mussen (Ed.), *Carmichael's manual of child psychology, 3rd edition*. New York: Wiley, 1970.

_____. *Science of education and the psychology of the child*. New York: Penguin, 1971.

Rubin, K. H., & Trotter, K. T. Kohlberg's moral judgment scale: Some methodological considerations. *Developmental Psychology*, 1977, *13*, 535-536.

Siegal, M. Development of children's reliance on adult advice. Paper presented at the Society for Research in Child Development, San Francisco, 1979a.

_____. Socialization and the development of adult respect. *British Journal of Psychology*, 1979b, *79*, 83-86.

_____. Kohlberg vs. Piaget: To what extent has one theory eclipsed the other? *Merrill-Palmer Quarterly*, 1980, *26*, 285-297.

Siegal, M., & Boyes, M. C. The comparative effects of adult and peer group influence on children's moral judgments. *British Journal of Educational Psychology*, 1980, *50*, 103-111.

Somerville, S. C. The pendulum problem: Patterns of performance defining developmental stages. *British Journal of Educational Psychology*, 1974, *44*, 266-281.

Warnock, G. J. *The object of morality*. London: Methuen, 1971.

Whiteman, P. H., & Kosier, K. P. Development of children's moralistic judgments: Age, sex, I.Q. and certain personal-experiential variables. *Child Development*, 1964, *35*, 843-850.

Zigler, E., & Trickett, P. K. IQ, social competence and the evaluation of early childhood intervention programs, *American Psychologist*, 1978, *33*, 789-798.

YOUNG CHILDREN'S DIFFERENTIAL PERCEPTIONS

OF THEIR PARENTS

Anne Silcock and D. Royce Sadler

University of Queensland
Australia

INTRODUCTION

This paper addresses the question, "How do young children perceive their parents?" It reports the findings from one section of an investigation of children's perceptions of parents and self. The study included 600 children 6- to 8-years-old in Brisbane, Australia.

Our work with University students studying developmental psychology and early childhood education, as well as discussions with parents and children, have highlighted apparent discrepancies between ways of investigating children's perceptions of their parents. Research findings based on structured questionnaires, rating scales, and interviews are at variance with results from naturalistic studies of children and their spontaneous comments during observation. Accordingly, this study attempted to tap young children's perceptions of their parents, using free responses as well as a structured approach. Accurate information on how children perceive their parents is essential for understanding the process of socialization and children's social and personal development.

Twenty-five years ago a study by Ausubel, Balthazar, Rosenthal, Blackman, Schpoort, and Welkowitz (1954) revealed that the ego structure of children is affected by their perceptions of parents' behaviors, rather than by the behavior as an objective environmental event. Serot and Teevan (1961) stated that both theory and research into parent-child relationships have failed to recognize that "the child reacts to his perception of the situation and not directly to the situation itself." (p. 337) In another study, Dubin and Dubin (1965) pointed out that "there has been widespread

91

failure even to realize that it is not only parent behavior to which
the child responds but also his perception of parent behavior."
(p. 809) They noted a tendency to assume that children respond
uniformly to parental child-rearing practices. This assumption ig-
nores the possibility that parental behavior may be interpreted differently by parents and by children and that what the child coes and
what he becomes is in response to his perception of parent behavior.

The next development of relevance to this research was Bell's
(1968) study on a reinterpretation of the direction of effects in
studies of socialization. He said that while "it seems eminently
plausible to visualize the human parent as the vehicle for the
transmission of culture and the infant as simply the object of an
acculturation process" (p. 81), the implied unidirectional effect
from parent to child disregards research suggesting that the characteristics of infants and children evoke different behavior in
the same adult. The unidirectional effect fails to consider that
specific acts of maternal caregiving could be accounted for more
satisfactorily by the behavior of the infant rather than by the
mother's general attitude towards child rearing.

Bell postulated that, instead of fixed techniques for social-
izing children, parents have a repertoire of actions, any one of
which may accomplish an objective. The activation of particular
elements in the mother's repertoire requires both cultural pressures
and stimulation from the child. He theorized that there are hierarchies of actions and that different children induce responses from
different levels of these hierarchies. The child then reinforces,
or fails to reinforce, the parent behaviors that he or she evokes.

Brazelton (1978) also emphasized the power of newborn infants
in shaping their mother's behaviors. He said: "The particular
kind of infant with which she is faced in the neonatal period must
determine which mothering reactions she will draw from her repertoire." (p. 106)

In his 1971 paper, Bell further developed the notion of the
child as a participant in a social system, stimulating as well as
being stimulated. In the same year Harper (1971) reviewed the
effects of mammalian offspring on their caretakers and suggested
the application of the same behavior analysis to parent-offspring
relations in man. Osofsky (1971), using a structured laboratory
situation, showed that parental behavior differed in response to
different child behaviors, and Berberich (1971) demonstrated that
children's responses shape the teaching behavior of adults.

More recently Bates (1975) and Cantor and Gelfand (1977) have
shown the significant effects of imitation and responsiveness in
children upon adult behavior. Cantor and Gelfand state: "The
present results portray the child as one who helps to create his

social world. A child who fails to attend to and converse with
adults is seen by the adults as less socially attractive and even
as less intelligent than the pleasant, sociable child." (p. 237)

It was against such a background of stimulating ideas that the
present research was undertaken.

THEORETICAL FRAMEWORK

The study of children's perception of their parents has elements in common with clinical psychology and the concept of identi-
ication, and shares an area of overlap with both cognitive development and personality theory. However, the twin psychological areas
of attribution theory as expounded by Jones, Karouse, Kelley, Nisbett,
Valins, and Weiner (1971) and De Charms (1968), and person perception as developed by Livesley and Bromley (1973), Newcomb, Turner,
and Converse (1966), and Bruner and Tagiuri (1954) appear to provide
the most useful umbrella. Both areas have their roots in Heider's
(1958) theoretical writings in the psychology of interpersonal relations and Festinger's (1957) theory of social comparison processes.
Kellsy (in Jones, et al., 1971) attempted to formulate a theoretical
framework for attribution theory, while person perception defines
an area of empiricalinvestigation. These areas share a perspective
with a strong practical orientation and emphasize the type of methodology that elicits free and unrestricted descriptions of real people
in real situations. Each attempts to understand relationships between and attribute causes to human behaviors.

For Jones, et al. (1971), "Attribution theory deals with the
rules the average individual uses in attempting to infer the causes
of observed behavior." Their empirical studies into the basic processes involved in perceiving the self, other persons, and the settings in which people function deal with areas of behavior such as
success and failure and the direction and intensity of emotion.
Livesley and Bromley (1973) define person perception as "how we
'perceive' or 'cognize' other persons--their intentions, attitudes,
traits, emotions, ideas, abilities and purposes, as well as their
overt behavioral and physical characteristics." (p. 1) The authors
assert that people "assimilate a wide range of perceptual data
about people into reasonably valid and stable schemata which have
the function of initiating and guiding (their) responses in relation
to them." (p. 3) Their research studies focussed on the developmental psychology of person perception through the investigation
of the simpler concepts and organization of children's and adolescents' ideas about people. It is in this latter area that the
present research makes a contribution.

Yarrow and Campbell (1963) suggest that "children appraise
others in interactional terms, along lines of personal significance."

(p. 69) The impressions that children form of "significant others,"
especially of parents and peers, are likely to establish patterns
for characteristic styles of interacting with people in the wider
social environment. Considering the importance of these perceptions,
it is surprising, as Livesley and Bromley point out, "that there
has been no systematic analysis of children's concepts of human
behavior and personality comparable to the study of their concepts
of the physical world or of space, number and causality." (p. 53)
They suggest that the developmental psychology of Piaget and Werner
and the cognitive psychology of Bruner could provide a general conceptual orientation for research into the growth of children's
understanding of people.

INSTRUMENTATION CONSIDERATIONS

      Beach and Wertheimer (1961) propose a "free response" approach
to the study of person cognition. In experiments in person perception, subjects are typically asked to make judgments about a
particular person in a given situation, using fixed scales that
require them to make judgments on dimensions they would not ordinarily use. Beach and Wertheimer question interpretations based on
dimensions whose meaning and salience may be unclear, atypical, or
nonexistent to the subject. They dispute whether the results from
studies that use artificial or synthetic stimuli, presented by means
of film, recordings, photographs, drawings, stories, lists of adjectives, and so on, can be generalized to the perception of real live
people.

      Instead, Beach and Wertheimer advocate the practice of desig-
nating a specific class of people, asking subjects to choose someone
they know who fits this class and to describe the chosen person
using any terms or dimensions they wish. The relative frequency of
use of different dimensions by a given subject reflects their relative salience. The free-response data are content analyzed in an
attempt to discover relationships.

      The authors also suggest that a subject's responses on inap-
propriate dimensions are based on stereotypes, while judgments made
on dimensions considered appropriate are more specific to the person
being judged. Beach and Wertheimer's recommendation is that fixed-
scale research should be preceded by free-response, content-analysis
studies to aid in decisions as to which scales or dimensions are
appropriate for the subjects, the people, and the situation involved.

      Willems and Willems (1965) discussed the comparative validity
of data yielded by three different methods: standardized individual
interviews, card sorts, and check lists. Their conclusion was that
coded interview data represented a free, unaided recall of the desired material, the card-sort data a stimulated forced-choice recall

with a sorting of the given items, and the check-list data a stimulated forced-choice recall with a simple yes/no marking of items.

A consistent tendency was found for the coded interview data to provide the most valid empirical indication of their objective, i.e., forces towards participation in behavior settings. As this method was time consuming and required by far the most work, a strong negative relationship was found between the ease of gathering and the validity of the data. Willems and Willems state: "If one postulates a real or valid set of responses, unique to the individual subject, then the coded interview method provides the most freedom for subjects to respond in terms of their own sets of experiences. In the card-sort and check list methods, the response sample was prearranged, abstracted and restricted." (p. 70)

In reviewing research into children's perceptions of their parents, Livesley and Bromley (1973) drew attention to the somewhat artificial nature of the methods used. Rating scales, structured questions, and structured response alternatives to pictorial stimuli, they said, place severe constraints upon the child's responses. They believe that research into the area of person perception has been retarded by highly structured and tightly controlled laboratory experiments that require subjects to form judgments using dimensions they do not normally use. "The use of fairly natural and unstructured situations minimizes the risk of our being misled by false assumptions or experimental artifacts and it allows us to identify the key variables which can be studied subsequently under more closely controlled conditions." (p. 67)

Livesley and Bromley were confronted by three research problems in the collection of free descriptive data from representative samples of subjects: (1) how to systematically observe and record the way children perceive and conceptualize people; (2) how to develop procedures for classifying and systematizing both the contents and the organization of these impressions; and (3) how to explain any developmental changes that are revealed. They selected content analysis as "the technique most free from methodological preconceptions, and the one most likely to reveal the full range of possibilities for future investigation." (p. 11) Substantial use was made of content analysis in the present study.

METHODOLOGY

Subjects, Instrumentation, and Procedures

Six hundred children (100 each of 6-, 7-, and 8-year-old boys and girls) attending three Brisbane primary schools that draw children from lower, middle, and upper-middle class backgrounds served as subjects.

A free-response task and a structured questionnaire on parent
perception were administered to subjects in their classrooms.
Teachers were present and assisted, if required, with spelling.
The free-response task on the first page consisted of six, well-
spaced, two-word phrases. Three of these read "Mothers are ..." and
three read "Fathers are ...." Children were asked to complete each of
the six sentences. They were asked to write given name, age, and
school in the space provided.

The structured questionnaire consisted of 37 questions. Subjects were asked to write either M (mother) or F (father) against
each item according to which parent the question made them think
of. Meanings of words were given when requested.

Content Analysis: In their content analysis, Livesley and
Bromley (1973) differentiated between central and peripheral statements. Central statements are more abstract and generalized,
include personality characteristics and behavioral consistencies.
Peripheral statements refer to external qualities such as appearance, skills, social roles, and social relationships. Statements
were rated as either central or peripheral, using these criteria.
They were then classified into the categories defined by Livesley
and Bromley, using the 12 of their 33 categories that appeared to
be appropriate to the data.

Three categories were subdivided. Items categorized as C10
specific behavioral consistencies or C20 evaluations were coded as
positive or negative. Items in category P27 mutual interaction were
allocated to the category P27(b) if they related specifically to
parental care-giving. Accordingly, 15 categories were used to encode children's perceptions of their parents. Items appropriate to
six of the above categories were classified as central and the
remaining nine as peripheral statements.

Reliability: The usefulness of a set of categories depends
upon their comprehensiveness and upon the extent to which different
coders, and a single coder at different points in time, can consistently assign statements to categories. Inter-coder reliability
was assessed by comparing three coders' categorizations of 360
responses selected by taking 10 response sheets chosen at random
from each of the six age/sex strata, and coding each of the six responses (three for father, three for mother) from each child. The
three judges were two principal investigators and one graduate research
assistant. The agreement between the first author and the research
assistant was 80%, and between the two investigators 72%. This represents a high level of agreement between judges.

Two separate codings of the 360 statements by the first author
separated by some eight weeks resulted in 79% agreement. These results indicate that the coding of open responses can be carried out

with adequate reliability. An improvement can be expected in future
research when the Livesley and Bromley categories are made more
operational in terms of the responses from young children and when
the judges have had more coding experience.

Relative Validity of Instruments Used: In section 3, it is
argued that open responses are likely to be epistemologically more
in harmony with children's perceptions of their parents than are
responses to structured questionnaires. An exception occurs when
the structured instrument evolves from earlier open responses (so
that it taps the characteristics the children feel are salient)
and is couched in words familiar to and understood by the children.
Obviously, a structured instrument must make certain assumptions
about child vocabulary. It appears that, for young children whose
vocabulary is naturally limited, the terms used must have simplicity and contemporaneity. The structured instrument used in this
study now appears to us to have limited validity for a number of
technical reasons. These will be examined one by one.

Unfamiliar characteristics of words: The descriptive terms
used in the structured questionnaire were taken directly from the
literature. As it turned out, some terms were relatively unfamiliar
to the children in the Brisbane sample. In particular, words such
as "rouses," "spoils," and "frowns" had to be explained. While
in common use a generation or two ago, the term "rouse" is rather
uncommon in Australian society today, even among adults. The unfamiliarity can, in principle at least, be overcome by proper explanation.

Quite another issue is whether a child ordinarily thinks of
its mother or father in terms of the concept explained. Clearly,
there are two problems: unfamiliarity of the term used as descriptor, and the use of that descriptor as a parent attribute. Imagine
the puzzled response from an adult who is asked the question:
"Who thinks irregularly, your mother or your father?" One does
not normally use a term such as "thinking irregularly" about any-
body. In any case, the term is ambiguous and to ask someone to
nominate father or mother in response is probably absurd.

Granted that some of the structured items were unfamiliar or
irrelevant to children in one way or another, the children were
nevertheless required to respond. It is speculated that children
who have never perceived their own parents in the ways suggested
in the structured instrument may respond not with perceptions about
mother or father, but with their perceptions of culture-stereotypic
mother-father roles.

Ipsative measures: Clearly, when the response is restricted
to either-or, serious limitations are placed on the patterning of
outcomes. For example, if father receives a high score on one set

of items, mother must receive a low score on the same set. An alternative way of stating the problem is this: for every choice of
father, the choice of mother must be rejected.

   Unit of measurement: A final distortion is that produced by
dichotomization in the unit of measurement. The differential between perception of father and mother must inevitably be recorded
as one unit, even if the child's perception of his parents is ambivalent.

   Mismatch: The incongruence between structured-item data and
free-response data is shown grphically in Figure 1. Four discrepancies are glaring. Category C20+ was not represented at all in
the structured item, yet more than one-third of the children's free
responses were classified here. Almost as dramatic were categories
C10- and P24, while the discrepancy for C9, though smaller, was
still notable. Details of these discrepancies are given in Section
5.

   In the early stages of data analysis, such discrepancies were
not anticipated. By historical accident, the structured data were
analyzed first, but the researchers are now convinced that these
data are much less useful than was first thought, and only a brief
summary of the results is given here. It is our belief that the
structured data grossly overemphasize the importance of characteris-

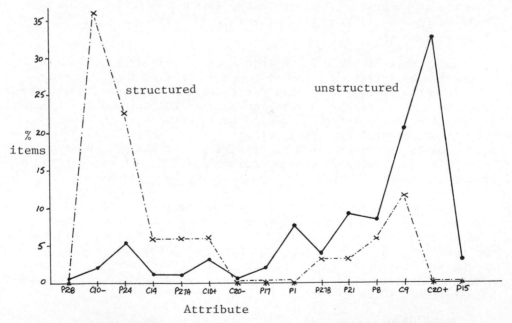

Figure 1.   Proportions of responses in each of the 15 categories
             used in analyzing the structured and unstructured data.

tics, particularly negative ones, not seen as relevant or salient by the children. The unstructured data are, we believe, closer to the children's real perceptions, even though young children do tend to make frequent use of somewhat vague descriptors such as "good" and "nice."

All research with young children where verbalization is heavily involved in data acquisition is bedevilled by the restrictions of limited vocabulary. Whether apparent shifts in perception and conceptualization with increasing age are a function of more sophisticated powers of verbalization remains to be researched. In the present study we are forced into making a sizable assumption: that children's perceptions are roughly coextensive with what the children can articulate or can at least recognize in articulated form. All in all, we put our money on the unstructured data; most of the findings dealt with in this paper are based on the free responses of the children.

DISCUSSION OF RESULTS

Use of Content Categories and Central/Peripheral Statements

Two of the 15 categories, positive evaluation (C20+), e.g., "good" and "nice," and general personality attributes (C9), e.g., "helpful" and "kind," accounted for more than half (52.4%) of the 3,600 responses of the 600 subjects. These descriptions therefore occurred most frequently in the perceptions and conceptualizations that 6-, 7-, and 8-year-old Australian children had of their parents. The descriptions are classified as psychological or central statements by Livesley and Bromley, as opposed to nonpsychological or peripheral statements such as physical descriptions and social interactions. The authors state: "The central versus peripheral contrast is analogous to that of "abstract versus concrete" in cognitive psychology and seems to be associated with levels of conceptual competence in interpersonal relationships." (p. 106) They believe that the ability to use central terms to describe people is advantageous, because effective and sensitive social interaction depends upon the ability to discern regularities that underlie specific diverse behavioral acts, and to take situational effects into account when arriving at expectations about an individual's actions.

Four peripheral categories together accounted for 30% of the total responses: social roles (P21), which was broadened to include functional parental roles such as "housekeeping" duties; appearance (P1); physical condition (P8); and effect upon and relations with others (P24). In the parent perceptions of these 6- to 8-year-olds, these categories were clearly of lesser significance than the main central categories C20+ and C9 described above. With occasional variations, these four peripheral categories occupied the same rela-

tive position in perceptions of fathers and of mothers by boys and
by girls at each age. The exceptions were the 8-year-old boys, who
recorded somewhat greater diversity of response for mothers, and
the 7-year-old girls who referred to the social roles of mothers
more frequently than any other group. Nine of the 15 content categories were used only infrequently. Except for the two negative
ones, these will not be dealt with in this paper.

Comparison of Free Response and Structured Questionnaire Data

Negative behavioral consistencies (C10-) and negative evaluation
(C20-) accounted for 2.1% and for 0.7%, respectively, of the total
free response data. Thus the subjects rarely expressed negative
perceptions of parents. In strong contrast, C10- was the most
frequently used category in responses to the structured questionnaire, accounting for 36% of the total responses. Structured questionnaires and similar instruments that are customarily used to measure young children's perceptions of parents frequently present an
abundance of items with negative connotations, such as "Who punishes
you?" "Who are you scared of more?" "Who gets mad?" and "Who spanks
you?" Accordingly, children are forced to make negative evaluations
of one or the other parent in responding to these items. Responses
with negative affect seldom occurred in the free-response situation
where the children were allowed to express their own perceptions
in their own words without coercion from the form of the testing
instrument.

Perceptions of Fathers

Sex Differences: About 45% of the boys' and girls' perceptions
of their fathers was associated with the two major categories. Boys
used positive evaluation and girls used personality attributes
somewhat more often than did the opposite sex. Negative evaluations
of fathers were very infrequent, accounting for about 5% of the boys'
and 2% of the girls' responses.

Thus both boys and girls perceive fathers predominantly in terms
of positive evaluation, using words such as "good," "nice," "terrific,"
"special," and "important" and with personality attributes such as
"kind," "loving," "helpful," "understanding," and "generous." A
small number of boys and less than half as many girls perceived
fathers as "angry," "rough," or "cranky."

Age Differences--Boys: Percentages of responses of 6-, 7-, and
8-year-old boys in the two major categories are presented in Table 1.

Table 1.   Percentages of boys of different ages responding with posi-
           tive evaluations (C20+) and personality attributes (C9)
           about their fathers.

Categories	6 yr	7 yr	8 yr
C20+	38.0	28.7	24.0
C9	6.0	17.3	22.3
	44.0	46.0	46.3

N = 100 boys at each age.

Descriptions of fathers predominantly in terms of evaluations such
as "good" and "fantastic" decreased with age, while the application
of personality attributes such as "trustworthy" and "generous" increased dramatically between 6 and 7 years and still further by 8
years.   This change probably reflects the increased cognitive sophistication of concrete operational children relative to 6-year-
olds.   Livesley and Bromley found that the most significant increase
in the use of central statements occurred between 7.10 and 8.10
years.   This sample of 300 Australian boys of ages 6 to 8 years recorded highly similar usage of central statements, except for the
dramatic increase in the use frequency of concepts describing personality attributes as noted.   The rarely occurring negative comments
were found least often with 7-year-olds and most often with 8-year-
old boys.

   Age Differences--Girls: The two major categories accounted
for nearly half of the responses at all age levels.   An inverse
relationship in the use of the two major categories at 6, 7, and 8
years, similar to the effect for boys, is shown in Table 2.   Again,
7-year-old subjects show a dramatic increase in the use of personality
attribute terms compared with 6-year-olds.   However, girls show a
further dramatic increase in their ability to conceptualize between
7 and 8 years.   In fact, the 8-year-old girls recorded a somewhat
higher percentage of central statements and considerably higher
usage of personality attribute terms than the other five groups
of subjects, reflecting perhaps the reported verbal superiority of
girls.

   Negative responses were almost nonexistent among 6- and 7-year-
old girls while 8-year-old girls recorded the same percentage (5%)
of negative appraisal of fathers as did 8-year-old boys, an interesting finding which suggests that age of subjects and not sex may be
the relevant variable here.

Table 2.   Percentages of girls of different ages responding with
           positive evaluations (C20+) and personality attributes (C9)
           about their fathers.

Categories	6 yr	7 yr	8 yr
C20+	35.0	27.7	21.0
C9	7.0	19.0	28.3
	42.0	46.7	49.3

           N = 100 girls at each age.

Perceptions of Mothers

    Sex Differences: Nearly 60% of the responses of boys and girls
fitted into the two major content categories, a considerably higher
figure than occurred in their perceptions of fathers. Again, boys
used positive evaluation and girls used personality attributes more
frequently than did the opposite sex. No sex differences were found
in the use of negative responses. It is notable that fewer than 1%
of boys' and girls' perceptions of mothers expressed negative affect.

    Thus boys and girls perceive mothers more often than not as
"nice," "good," "terrific," and "special" and with personality attributes such as "helpful," "kind," "gentle," and "soft-hearted." Boys'
and girls' negative evaluations of mothers were almost nonexistent,
suggesting generally harmonious relations between these young children
and their mothers.

    Age Differences--Boys: At each age central statements (Table 3)
accounted for more than half the responses, rising to 63.7% at 8 years.
Again, there is an inverse relationship between the frequency of use
of positive evaluation and personality attribute terms, with a striking increase in the latter at age 7 and a further gain at 8 years.
Like girls, boys appear to function at a more sophisticated cognitive
level at 7 years, compared with 6 years. In boys' perceptions of
mothers, words like "good" seem to be characteristic of 6-year-olds,
while greater diversity, e.g., "wonderful" and "special," are characteristics of the older boys. One 8-year-old described mothers as
"sweethearts" and another said they were "hearers and listeners."
Negative evaluations of mothers were almost nonexistent at each age.

    Age Differences--Girls: The now familiar pattern of parent per-
ception was found in girls' perceptions of mothers (Table 4). The
two major content categories accounted for more than half of the
responses. With increasing age there was an inverse relationship
between the frequency and use of the categories, highlighted by
dramatic increases in the use of personality attribute terms at 7

Table 3.   Percentages of boys of different ages responding with posi-
           tive evaluations (C20+) and personality attributes (C9)
           about their mothers.

Categories	6 yr	7 yr	8 yr
C20+	48.3	37.4	31.7
C9	6.3	23.3	32.0
	54.6	60.7	63.7

        N = 100 boys at each age.

years and again at 8 years.   The most significant finding was the high
proportion of central statements used by 8-year-old girls, exceeding
that of any other group.   A remarkable 43% of their 300 descriptions
of mothers dealt with personality attributes, which were usually expressed in phrases rather than in single words.

        Evidence from the present study offers strong support for Brier-
ley's (1966) findings on the use of personality constructs in children's descriptions of other people.   Her classification of the
responses of 270 children, aged 7, 10, and 13 years, into six main
categories, revealed marked age differences in the number of personality constructs employed.   She said: "It is only in the oldest
age group that these occur at all frequently, and then in girls more
than in boys." (p. 73)   As our oldest girls are only one year older
than Brierley's youngest ones, their performance is remarkable.

        A further noteworthy result was the high use of personality
attributes by 6-year-old girls in their perceptions of mothers.
For them, this category ranked second in frequency of use, whereas it was fifth in 6-year-old boys' descriptions of mothers and
sixth in both 6-year-old boys' and 6-year-old girls' perceptions

Table 4.   Percentages of girls of different ages responding with
           positive evaluations (C20+) and personality attributes
           (C9) about their mothers.

Categories	6 yr	7 yr	8 yr
C20+	43.3	29.0	24.7
C9	12.7	25.0	43.0
	56.0	54.0	67.7

        N = 100 girls at each age.

of fathers.   Perhaps 6-year-old girls are more dependent upon their
mothers than are the other groups.   As with boys, negative evaluations of mothers were exceedingly infrequent.

Differential Perceptions of Parents on Two
Major Categories Positive Evaluation (C20+)

One-third of the 3,600 perceptions of parents fell within the
positive evaluation content category.   Figure 2 shows the differential
responses to fathers and to mothers on this variable.   For both sexes
at each age level more items such as "good," "fantastic," and "wonderful" were directed to mothers than to fathers.   This phenomenon
was most marked for 6-year-old subjects and least apparent at age 7,
especially for girls.   Dubin and Dubin's (1965) review of research
into children's social perceptions revealed that, over a wide range of
ages, mother is preferred to father.   Evidence from the greater percentage of positive evaluation and the small percentage of negative
evaluation directed towards mothers as compared with fathers in this
study tends to support these earlier investigations.

Using the sentence beginning "My father" and "My mother" to evoke
attitudes towards parents, Harris and Tseng (1957) found more favorable attitudes to mothers than to fathers among a large sample of 9-
year-old children.   A sharp drop in favorableness occurred between
ages 9 and 10 and remained relatively unchanged until late high-
school years.   The authors attributed this drop to a shift away from
"the young child's uncritical fondness for parents to a more objective judgment." (p. 408)   It would be interesting to investigate
this phenomenon 20 years later.

Hawkes, Burchinal, and Gardner (1957) examined the views of
750 preadolescents (11-year-olds) to ascertain their relationships
with their parents.   They found that both parents were rated favorably by all the children and that mothers were uniformly rated more
favorably than fathers, especially by the girls.   Droppleman and
Schaefer (1963) used a group of scales to measure components of love,
nurturance, and affection.   They found that mothers were rated significantly higher than fathers by the 165 boys and girls 12 to 14
years of age.   In the present study the discrepancy between positive
evaluations of fathers and mothers was greatest for boys.

Boys of every age group used a higher percentage of positive
evaluation terms for mothers than for fathers.   Perhaps not surprisingly, 6-year-old boys registered the greatest disparity in this
regard.   However, both 7- and 8-year-old boys made relatively higher
use of this content category for mothers than for fathers.   This
finding is interesting, if father is assumed for 7- and 8-year-old
boys to be the major person with whom they identify, the source of
derived status, and the parent with whom they share ever increasing
interests and concerns appropriate to their common sex role.

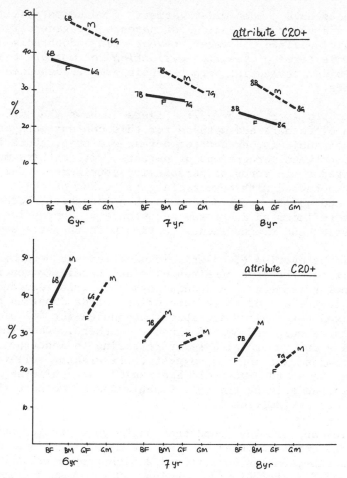

Figure 2.   Perceptions of 6-, 7-, and 8-year-old boys and girls
           (B,G) of their fathers and mothers (F,M) on category
           C20+, positive evaluations.

     Seven-year-old girls discriminated least of all between mothers
and fathers on this dimension. Interestingly, these girls also
recorded particularly low levels of negative evaluation for both
parents. The descriptions of 8-year-old girls also revealed a
smaller disparity between mothers and fathers on the positive evaluation category.

     The exceedingly high occurrence of words denoting positive eval-
uation in the responses of 6-year-olds (averaging 42% of the total
responses) can be accounted for in part by the frequency with which
they responded with "nice" and "good" when compared with the older
subjects. While these terms clearly imply positive evaluations of
parents, they are perhaps "low-level" concepts that feature promin-
ently in the younger child's vocabulary. According to the data, the

older subjects have a much wider variety of concepts available for
selection, and their descriptions of parents are generally more subtle and individualized. However, 6-year-olds undoubtedly use considerably more terms of positive evaluation for mothers than do 7-
and 8-year-olds, reflecting perhaps their greater dependence upon
their mothers.

Personality Attributes (C9): Figure 3 shows the differential
perceptions of fathers and mothers for this content category. For
all groups of subjects, except for 6-year-old boys, there is a marked
discrepancy between perceptions of parents, with mothers more often
being referred to in terms of personality attributes. The greatest
discrepancy occurred with 8-year-old girls: 28% of their responses
to fathers and 43% to mothers were in this category. Perhaps this
discrepancy reflects an increased acceptance of appropriate sex role
characteristics and closer identification with the same-sex parent.

The two categories of positive evaluation and personality attributes reflect the core of Livesley's and Bromley's central or
psychological statements. Although boys and girls recorded the same
percentage in the use of these categories, words denoting positive
evaluation and personality attributes accounted for 46% of the
responses to fathers and 59% of those to mothers. Does the use of
more abstract and generalized terms referring to inner psychological
qualities to describe mothers suggest their greater salience for
children in the 6- to 8-year-old age range? Are children more aware
of the person underlying the role functioning of mothers than they
are of fathers as individuals?

Livesley and Bromley found that although a greater number of
central statements were used to describe males than females, those
used to describe females constituted a higher proportion of the
total number of statements (41% against 39%). A much greater discrepancy occurred in this study, where the males and females described were fathers and mothers.

Differential Perceptions of Parents on Four
Minor Content Categories Social Roles (P21)

Social roles ranked third in frequency of use of the 15 categories by all subjects. This category relates to group and organizational membership and to occupational roles. It was extended in
the present study to include family and parental roles such as
"husband," and functional aspects such as "cooking the meals."

As shown in Figure 4, fathers rather than mothers tended to be
designated by social roles, e.g., "men who work for money." The
discrepancy was smallest at age 6 and became more pronounced with
increasing age. Seven-year-old girls used this category more frequently than did any other group. The divergence between the sexes

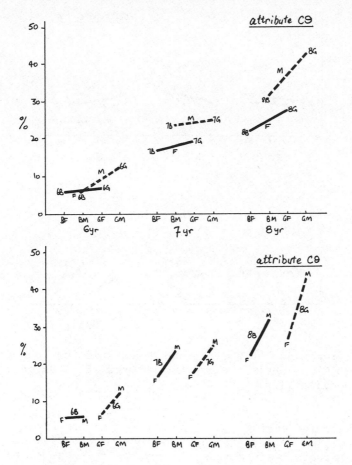

Figure 3. Perceptions of 6-, 7-, and 8-year-old boys and girls
(B,G) of their fathers and mothers (F,M) on category
C9, general personality attributes.

was greatest for 8-year-old boys. Because the social roles category
accounted for less than 9% of the data, vocational and family roles
were not investigated separately.

Physical Condition (P8): Peripheral statements describing
health, physical fitness, and strength characterize this category.
Responses describing fathers as "grown up boys" and mothers as
"sweet ladies" or "human beings" were also coded under physical
condition. This category accounted for 7% of the data, marginally
less than physical appearance (P1).

However, the category did differentiate between perceptions
of fathers and mothers for all groups except the youngest girls

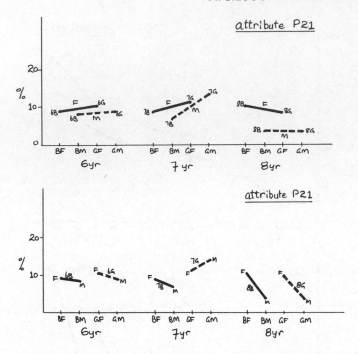

Figure 4.   Perceptions of 6-, 7-, and 8-year-old boys and girls
             (B,G) of their fathers and mothers (F,M) on category P21,
             social roles.

(Fig. 5). With increasing age of subjects, particular aspects of
physical condition, e.g., "strong," were used with greater frequency
to describe fathers, with 8-year-old boys using these statements for
fathers twice as often as for mothers.

    Appearance (P1): This category was used somewhat more often to
describe mothers than fathers by subjects of each age, with the
greatest difference shown by 8-year-old boys. Thus while fathers
were described as "handsome" and occasionally as "pretty" (and by
a 7-year-old boy as "hairy" and by an 8-year-old boy as "white, brown,
and black") mother's appearance was more often alluded to, generally
by terms such as "pretty" or "beautiful" (or "butterful"!). As seen
in P1 above, fathers rather than mothers were more often described
in terms of strength and health.

    Effect Upon and Relations with Others (P24): Responses in this
category did not discriminate between fathers and mothers, except
for 6-year-old boys, who scored mothers somewhat higher than they
scored fathers.

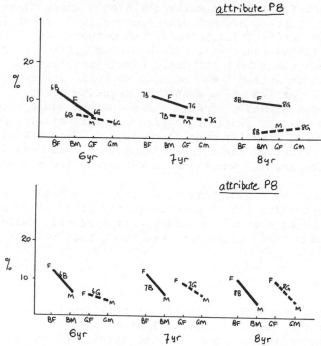

Figure 5.   Perceptions of 6-, 7-, and 8-year-old boys and girls
            (B,G) of their fathers and mothers (F,M) on category
            P8, physical condition.

Negative Categories--Negative Behavioral Consistencies (C10-) and Negative Evaluation (C20-)

Summing the two negative categories revealed that about 5% of
boys' responses to fathers were negative, as were about 2.5% to
mothers. About 2.5% of girls' descriptions of fathers and 1.5% of
their responses to mothers were negative. Although the proportions
of negative responses were very small, the highest amount was directed
by boys to fathers, and the lowest amount by girls to mothers.

Nearly half of the total expression of negative feelings by
boys came from 8-year-olds, and one-third was expressed by 8-year-
olds towards fathers. Girls recorded about half the amount of negative affect that boys registered. Two-thirds of this originated with
8-year-old girls, and nearly half of the negative feelings of girls
was directed by 8-year-olds towards fathers. Thus, much of the negative feelings recorded by 6- to 8-year-olds took the form of criticisms of fathers by the oldest boys and girls. Maybe fathers rather
than mothers tend to frustrate their 8-year-old children as they
become increasingly peer-oriented.

Research findings regarding children's expressions of negative attitudes to parents are somewhat equivocal. Gardner (1947) found that fathers were criticized more than mothers, and Du Valle (1937) and Goldin (1969) found that more positive attitudes are expressed about mothers than about fathers. Harris and Tseng (1957) in a study of 3,000 students from lower primary through high school found that the small proportion of boys showing negative attitudes towards parents decreased steadily through childhood and adolescence, while the correspondingly small proportion of girls showing negative attitudes increased steadily over these years. Emmerick (1961) found that girls perceived the mother as somewhat more positive than they perceived the father, whereas boys perceived the converse.

The study by Kagan, Hosken, and Watson (1961) of children's symbolic conceptualization of parents (using pairs of picture stimuli that differed on eleven dimensions) revealed that children were reluctant to assign "bad" characteristics to either parent.

CONCLUSION

The most significant finding of this study was the great disparity between children's perceptions of parents, as revealed by the free-response technique, and the structured questionnaire. Use of the free-response method resulted in sizable differential perceptions of parents on only two of the 15 categories employed. Negative perceptions of parents were infrequent.

In contrast, researchers who rely upon the structured questionnaire and similar instruments--a "more popular procedure of forcing the child to pick between father and mother" (Kegan et al., 1961) --customarily find that children view fathers as more punitive and as a more frequent source of power, threat, and fear arousal. Mothers on the other hand, are seen as friendly and nurturant (Kagan, 1956; Kagan & Lemkin, 1960). The authors believe that the free-response technique has more validity as a measure of parent perception.

The overwhelmingly positive response to parents by these 6- to 8-year-old children suggests that the family is still their primary source of security and satisfaction and the center of their world.

BIBLIOGRAPHY

Ausubel, D.P., Balthazar, E.E., Rosenthal, I., Blackman, L.S., Schpoon S.H., & Welkowitz, J. Perceived attitudes as determiners of children's ego structure. *Child Development*, 1954, *25*, 173-184.
Bates, J.E. Effects of a child's imitation versus nonimitation on adults' verbal and non-verbal positivity. *Journal of Personality and Social Psychology*, 1975, *31*, 840-851.

Beach, L., & Wertheimer, H. A free response approach to the study of person cognition. *Journal of Abnormal and Social Psychology*, 1961, *62*, 367-374.

Bell, R.Q. A reinterpretation of the direction of effects in studies of socialization. *Psychological Review*, 1968, *75*, 81-95.

Bell, R.Q. Stimulus control of parent or caretaker behavior of off-spring. *Developmental Psychology*, 1971, *14*, 63-74.

Berberich, J.P. Do the child's responses shape the teaching behavior of adults? *Journal of Experimental Research in Personality*, 1971, *3*, 92-97.

Brazelton, T.B. Effect of maternal expectations on early infant behavior. In: J. T. Gibson and P. Blumberg (Eds.), *Growing Up: Readings on the Study of Children*. Reading, MA: Addison-Wesley, 1978.

Brierley, D.W. Children's use of personality constructs. *Bulletin of the British Psychological Society*, 1966, *19*, 65-72.

Bruner, J.S., & Tagiuri, R. The perception of people. In: G. Lindzey (Ed.), *Handbook of Social Psychology*. Cambridge, MA: Addison-Wesley, 1954.

Cantor, N.L. & Gelfand, D.M. Effects of responsiveness and sex of children on adults' behavior. *Child Development*, 1977, *48*, 232-238.

De Charms, R. *Personal causation*. New York: Academic Press, 1968.

Droppleman, L.F., & Schaefer, E.S. Boys' and girls' reports of maternal and paternal behavior. *Journal of Abnormal and Social Psychology*, 1963, *67*, 648-654.

Dubin, R., & Dubin, E.R. Children's social perceptions: a review of research. *Child Development*, 1965, *36*,809-838.

DuValle, E.W. Child-parent social distance. *Sociology Society Research*, 1937, *21*, 458-463.

Emmerick. W. Family role concepts of children ages six to ten. *Child Development*, 1961, *32*, 609-624.

Festinger, L. *A Theory of Cognitive Dissonance*. Evanston, IL: Row Peterson, 1957.

Gardner, L.P. An analysis of children's attitudes towards fathers. *Journal of Genetic Psychology*, 1947, *70*, 3-28.

Goldin, P.C. A review of children's reports of parent behaviors. *Psychological Bulletin*, 1969, *71*, 222-236.

Harper, L.V. The young as a source of stimuli controlling caretaker behavior. *Developmental Psychology*, 1971, *4*, 74-88.

Harris, D.B., & Tseng, S.C. Children's attitudes towards peers and parents as revealed by sentence completions. *Child Development*, 1957, *28*, 401-414.

Hawkes, G.R., Burchinal, L.G., & Gardner, B. Pre-adolescents' views of some of their relations with their parents. *Child Development*, 1957, *28*, 393-399.

Heider, F. *The psychology of interpersonal relations*. New York: John Wiley. 1958.

Jones, E.E., Kanouse, D.E., Kelley, H.H., Nisbett, R.E., Valins, S., & Weiner, B. (Eds.), *Attribution: Perceiving the Causes of Behavior*. Morristown: General Learning Press, 1971.

Kagan, J. The child's perception of the parent. *Journal of Abnormal and Social Psychology*, 1956, *53*, 257–258.

Kagan, J., Hosken, B., & Watson, S. Child's symbolic conceptualization of parents. *Child Development*, 1961, *32*, 625–636.

Kagan, J., & Lemkin, J. The child's differential perception of parental attributes. *Journal of Abnormal and Social Psychology*, 1960, 440–447.

Livesley, W.J., & Bromley, D.B. *Person perception in childhood and adolescence*. London: John Wiley, 1973.

Newcomb, T.M., Turner, N.H., & Converse, P.E. *Social Psychology*. London: Tavistock, 1966.

Osofsky, J.D. Children's influences upon parental behavior: An attempt to define the relationship with the use of laboratory tasks. *Genetic Psychology Monographs*, 1971, *83*, 147–169.

Serot, N., & Teevan, R. Perceptions of the parent-child relationship and its relation to child adjustment. *Child Development*, 1961, *32*, 373–378.

Willems, E.P., & Willems, G.J. Comparative validity of data yielded by three methods. *Merrill-Palmer Quarterly*, 1965, *11*, 65–71.

Yarrow, M.R., & Campbell, J.D. Person perception in children. *Merrill-Palmer Quarterly*, 1963, *9*, 57–72.

SOME DIMENSIONS OF CREATIVITY IN
YOUNG CHILDREN

Mildred C. Robeck

University of Oregon

STATEMENT OF THE PROBLEM

The difficulty of defining and measuring creativity in young
children is widely known. Adults often describe the expressive acts
of childhood as spontaneous, imaginative, and creative; then bemoan
the disappearance of such creativity during the school years. Wilson
and Robeck (1968) suggested that the freshness and originality in
young children's speech and painting might result partially from
naivete regarding the conventions of the society and partially from
the perceptual egocentrism of the age. These authors were concerned
that young children, when entering kindergarten for the first time,
should be encouraged to enjoy problem solving activities that could
also be extended into creative self-direction in various areas of
the curriculum. They defined creative self-direction as the fusion
of cognitive conceptualizations (in the Piagetian sense) and affective conceptualizations (the recognized need to produce something
that is not only one's own but is also identifiable with oneself).
This definition of creativity in childhood as a higher level of
functioning than conceptualization made possible the expansion of
activities for the expression of creativity based on cognition.
Eleven items were structured into three levels of learning for the
kindergarten: Associative Learning, Conceptualization, and Creative
Self-Direction. These levels were subsequently used to research
creative functioning.

PURPOSE OF THE PAPER

This report synthesizes and discusses the relationship of
creativity to cognitive development, free activities in the pre-

113

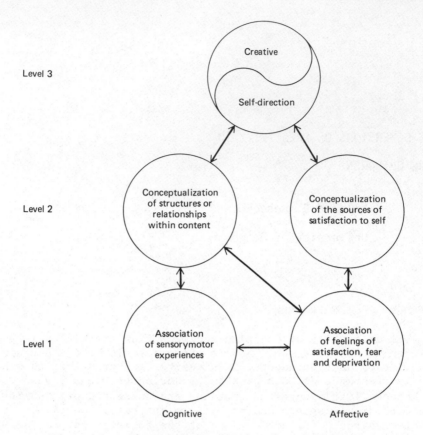

Figure 1.   The Learning-Motivation Construct

school, conforming-nonconforming choices, intelligence, conceptual
tempo, and humor.   The subjects were children from 3 to 7 years old.
Two of the studies were conducted by the author and two by doctoral
students who graduated with specialization in Early Childhood Education.   The research focussed on the following questions:

1.   What is the relationship between creative self-direction
     and cognitive development?
2.   Can the "creative behaviors" of young children be reliably
     observed and measured?
3.   What is the relationship of creativity, humor and concept-
     ual tempo?
4.   Are there cultural differences (in Native and Caucasian
     Americans) which are reflected in creative abilities?
5.   What are the implications of differences between verbal and
     figural abilities for the education of young children?

SUMMARIES OF THE RESEARCH

1. Having developed kindergarten items which define the levels
of children's functioning as (1) Associative Learning, (2) Conceptualization, or (3) Creative Self-Direction, Robeck and Wilson (1964)
validated the children's end-of-year scores at each level of functioning against chronological age (CA), mental age (MA), and IQ as
measured by the Stanford Binet Intelligence Scales. The kindergarten
scores were obtained from recorded observations made by the regular
teachers and referred to as KELP (Kindergarten Evaluation of Learning Potential) scores. Correlations (r's) between the Binet MA and
creative self-direction were .73 ± .07; and between the Binet IQ
and creative self-direction were .67 ± .08. Correlations between
total KELP scores were only slightly higher. Analysis of variance
demonstrated that the creativity score was found to contribute 29.6%
of the total variance, only slightly below that of the associative
and conceptual learning scores. The correlations of KELP and CA
were in the range of .12 to .24, suggesting a high relationship of
MA and creative self-direction, but a negligible relation to CA.

2. Keily (1974) developed an observation scale for quantify-
ing the creative behavior of children during their spontaneous activities in the preschool. Her student teachers showed initial
reliability coefficients (Spearman rho) ranging from .79 to .91 in
separate observations of children's creative behavior at four sites,
one of which enrolled Native American children. Another correlational analysis produced r's of .66 and .56 (both significant beyond
the .01 level) between creativity (Level 3 scores from KELP) and
Starkweather's (1964) test of conformity and nonconformity. Keily's
correlations of these instruments with her teacher observation
scale were more modest, but significant. These findings indicate
that children's creative behavior can be described, observed, and
is reasonably consistent over the time span of a school year.

3. Gilbert (1977) using the Torrance Tests of Creative Think-
ing--in particular, the Figural Test (1972) and the Verbal Test
(1974)--analyzed the relationship of creative thinking to humor
and to conceptual tempo in a sample of 120 first grade students.
Using the Brodzinsky (1974) tests of humor comprehension and humor
appreciation she found humor appreciation did not correlate significantly with creativity scores. Humor comprehension was correlated to creativity, but this relationship disappeared when IQ
(WISC-R) was partialled out. Four categories of conceptual tempo,
as identified by Kagan (1965), were also correlated with creativity
tests. When separated by category, reflective children were highest on creativity, followed by fast-accurate, impulsive, and slow-
inaccurate subjects. Again, when IQ was held constant, the relationship of conceptual tempo and creativity disappeared. When step-
wise regression analysis was used to predict creativity the most
powerful predictors were (1) the negative weighting of errors on

the conceptual tempo test; (2) performance IQ on the WISC; (3) age; and (4) Comprehension subtest. When the WISC subtests themselves were analyzed similarly for power in prediction of creativity the most powerful were Coding, Block Design, Arithmetic, Vocabulary and Comprehension, in that order. The analyses further confirmed a significant relationship between creativity and intelligence.

4. Comparisons of creative abilities in Native American children and their Caucasian classmates have been undertaken at the kindergarten level (Robeck, 1971). Comparison of total KELP scores and creativity scores show no differences between these two groups. However, an analysis of functioning in English shows the native Indian children to be superior (.01 level) in listening abilities, while lagging (not significant) in expressive English. KELP unfortunately does not provide an easy analysis of figural abilities. Inspection of the summary test booklets provides some clinical evidence that Indian children show creative self-direction in non-verbal areas which even out their total creativity scores when compared with Caucasian kindergarteners.

CONCLUSIONS AND IMPLICATIONS

When these four studies are considered together, the conclusion seems justified that intellectual development is significantly related to creativity in young children (3 to 7 years old). These studies did not explore the potential leveling off of IQ effects at the superior levels. The age factor as a predictor of creativity (within the age range of first graders) should be explored further, since this finding was not consistent with the kindergarten studies. Piaget's periods of cognitive development might offer some explanation for age differences on certain types of items. Our kindergarten studies produced slightly higher correlations when MA rather than IQ was used. These studies further suggest that a potentially fruitful area of research concerns the figural versus verbal abilities in young children of different ethnic origins. Such cognitive styles have already shown up in tests for early identification of gifted children (Robinson, 1979). The implications for early education are tremendous if cultural differences along these lines are replicated.

BIBLIOGRAPHY

Brodzinsky, David Michael. The role of conceptual tempo in the child's comprehension and appreciation of various types of cartoon humor. Unpublished doctoral dissertation, State University of New York at Buffalo, 1974.
Gilbert, Christiane P. Creativity, conceptual tempo, humor and IQ in first grade children. Doctoral dissertation, University of Oregon, Eugene, 1977.

Guilford, J.P. Creative abilities in the arts. *Psychological Review*, 1957, *64*, 110-118.

Kagan, Jerome. Reflection-impulsivity: The generality and dynamics of conceptual tempo. *Journal of Abnormal Psychology*, 1966, *71*, 17-24.

Keily, S. Margaret Mary. Identifying creative abilities in preschool children. Unpublished doctoral dissertation, University of Oregon, Eugene, 1974.

MacKinnon, Donald W. Personality and the realization of creative potential, *American Psychologist*, 1965, *20*, 273-281.

Robeck, Mildred C. Comparison of red Indian and white American children on language functioning. Report to the California Educational Research Association, San Diego, CA, November, 1971.

Robeck, Mildred C., & Wilson, John A.R. *Kindergarten evaluation of learning potential: Summary test booklet*. New York: McGraw-Hill, 1969.

Robinson, Halbert B., Roedell, Wendy C., & Jackson, Nancy E. Early identification and intervention. In *The gifted and the talented*. Seventy-eighth yearbook of the NSSE, Part I, Chicago: University of Chicago Press, 1979.

Starkweather, Elizabeth K. Creativity research instrument designed for use with preschool children. *Journal of Creative Behavior*, 1971, *5*, 245-255.

Torrance, E. Paul. *Torrance Tests of Creative Thinking: Figural Test*. Lexington, MA: Personnel Press, Ginn, 1972.

Torrance, E. Paul. *Torrance Tests of Creative Thinking: Verbal Test*. Lexington, MA: Personnel Press, Ginn, 1974.

Wallas, G. *The art of thought*. (Rev. and abr. ed.) London: Watts, 1945.

Wilson, John A.R., & Robeck, Mildred C. Creativity in the very young. In William B. Michael (Ed.), *Teaching for creative endeavor*. Bloomington, IN: University of Indiana Press, 1968.

AUDITORY ATTENDING SKILLS*

Sarah S. Van Camp

University of Delaware

The phonics approach to reading has been extant in the United
States since the early 1800s, when it was introduced in an attempt
to regularize an American language. In the past 100 years the pendulum has swung back and forth between the "look-say" approach to
reading and the phonics approach, with elaborate rationale developed
for both. Chall's *Learning to Read: The Great Debate* (1967), a
three-year study of these two approaches, suggests that teaching
children to decode (phonics) rather than using a total visual program appeared to result in better readers by third grade. DeHirsch,
Jansky and Langford (1966) familiarized educators with the role that
auditory discrimination, among other factors, plays in the reading
process and in the prediction of reading failure. These findings
were repeated in deHirsch, Jansky and Langford's *Preventing Reading Failure* (1972).

Robinson (1972) reported on the results of a study comparing
the reading progress of pupils identified as having high visual-
high auditory, high visual-low auditory, low visual-high auditory,
and low visual-low auditory abilities when they entered first grade.
A total of 232 of the children attended schools using a "look-say"
approach to reading, and 216 attended schools employing a phonics
approach. At the end of third grade neither method for teaching
reading surpassed the other. Auditory discrimination made a signif-

---

*Grateful appreciation is expressed to the following undergraduate
and graduate students who assisted in the testing: Matilda Bixby,
Mary Donovan, Constance Forrest, and Sharmon Jordan. Support for
the 1972 and 1976 study was provided by the General Faculty Research Funds of the College of Graduate Studies and Research, University of Delaware.

119

icant contribution to reading, while visual perception did not, regardless of teaching method.

Deutsch (1964) correlated various measures of visual discrimination and the Wepman Auditory Discrimination Test with good and poor readers from grade levels I, III, and V. She found that poor readers had more difficulty with auditory discrimination, greater difficulty in shifting from one modality to another, and were more inefficient at a serial learning task with auditory stimuli than with visual. Deutsch also underlined the influence of social class in language acquisition.

Birch and Belmont (1964, 1965) developed a research design requiring children to match a pattern of events in one modality with a pattern of events in another modality, for example listening to a tapping pattern and then picking out a visual representation of the same pattern. Variations of this have been done by Beery (1967) and Blank (1968). Golden and Steiner (1969), using the revised edition of the Illinois Test of Psycholinguistic Abilities (1968), investigated the relationship between specific auditory and visual functions and reading performance. They concluded that poor readers appear to be lacking in auditory rather than in visual functions. Mira (1968) reported that, when 24 children, half of them disabled learners, were presented electrical switches that required increasing strength of response to produce either visual or auditory stimuli, definite modality preferences were noted.

Hall (1967) constructed a paired-associates test of visual and aural material to be given to kindergarteners and second graders. The results suggested that children do not learn faster aurally than visually. Otto (1962-63) studied the differential effects of verbal and pictorial representations of stimuli upon responses evoked in 80 fourth graders. The results suggested that (1) pictorial presentation of stimuli tends to evoke more responses than verbal presentations of the same stimuli, but that the magnitude of the difference is influenced by the particular stimuli used, and (2) responses evoked by the pictorially presented stimuli tend to differ in nature from responses evoked by verbally presented material.

Kling (1968) devised a test to examine the possibility that there is a direct relationship between audition and vision in terms of frequency, duration, and amplitude. The conclusions from this study suggested that individual differences in the sensory modes are not necessarily highly correlated. Dykstra (1966) studied the auditory discrimination abilities of 632 first-grade children. His overall conclusion was that presently available auditory discrimination tests were significantly related to reading achievement, but that their main value was in predicting which child might encounter

difficulty in learning to read. Bruininks and Clark (1972) tested
first-grade retarded and nonretarded disadvantaged children in
auditory and visual paired-associate learning. They found that the
visual and the auditory-visual scores were higher than the auditory
alone.

Two studies of giving verbal feedback and positive reinforcement on the Wepman Auditory Discrimination Test have been reported.
The results of these studies were diametrically opposite. Dahle
and Daly (1972) gave two forms of the Wepman Test to 26 Educable
Mentally Retarded children, using reinforcement on the second form
but not on the first. They found that reinforcement did not appear
to make any significant difference to the score. Berlin and Dill
(1967) found that verbal feedback made a significant difference in
the scores of lower-class black children, but not with the lower-
class white children. Elenbogen (1972) theorized that upper-class
children, whom she considered verbally sophisticated, did better on
the Wepman Auditory Discrimination Test than did lower-class
children. She composed a new version of the Wepman test, using the
same phonemes to make nonsense words. The social class differences
disappeared when the second nonsense form was administered. She
concluded that a new auditory discrimination test was needed, one
without language clues.

Vellutino, DeSetto and Steger (1972) developed a new version
of the Wepman Test to balance the ratio of "Same-Different" responses to the test. (The Wepman Test has 30 "Different" scores and 10
"Same," with the former being scored.) In the test developed by
Vellutino and DeSetto, 15 items were "Different" and 15 were "Same."
They judged from their study that they achieved better results with
this balanced test.

Using 162 subjects, Ritchie and Merklein (1972) compared the
efficiency of the Verbal Auditory Screening Test for Children (VASC),
developed by Griffing, Simonton, and Hedgecock in 1962, with a
pure-tone threshold test as a technique to identify hearing impair-
ment among preschool children. Ritchie and Merklein concluded that
the pure-tone test was more effective than the taped recording of
spondaic words delivered at progressively attenuated levels as
utilized in the VASC. Marquardt and Saxman (1972) examined the
relationship between language comprehension and auditory discrimination with 30 kindergarten children having numerous misarticulations
and 30 others having proficient articulation. They found that
language comprehension and auditory discrimination were significantly correlated within the articulation error group, but not with the
articulation proficient group.

Groff (1975) questions the present emphasis assigned to auditory
discrimination tests or exercises. Newcomer and Hammill (1975) summarized research findings of fifty different studies relating to the

predictive and diagnostic validity of the Illinois Test of Psycholinguistic Abilities (ITPA). They consider that its value is limited
to gathering broad, descriptive information about certain learning
characteristics of school-age children, but caution against its use
as a determiner of academic failure or as a prescriptive tool for
remediation. Newcomer and Goodman (1975), in a study of 57 children
who were assigned auditory and visual scores on the basis of a battery
of tests for each modality (including sections of the ITPA), found
that most children, regardless of modality preferences, appear to
benefit from instruction with visual materials. They also suggest
that low auditory learners can be expected to have the most serious
academic difficulties and will benefit from as many meaningful associations to new materials as the teacher can demonstrate.

Gickling and Joiner (1974), using the Auditory Factor I from
the Kinesio-Perceptual Test II and the Spache Diagnostic Reading
Scales with 49 institutionalized mentally retarded subjects developed an Aspiration Coding Task (modified from the Wechsler Intelligence
Scale for Children [WISC]) in an effort to analyze auditory ability
and aspiration in predicting specific reading deficits. They concluded that reading instruction for slow and primary learners should
stress auditory skills backed up by visual input. Rude, Niquette,
and Foxgrover (1975) investigated the retention of basic visual and
auditory discrimination skill in 119 kindergarten children over the
summer months. Their findings suggest that the visual discrimination ability appears to increase. The change in auditory discrimination was negligible.

PILOT STUDY--1970

The present study was begun in 1970. Various aspects of auditory and visual processing were examined, and a test based upon
elements of the International Code (Morse) was developed. Using
taped telegraphic circuit stimuli and identical photographic slide
stimuli, the primary investigator tested 83 kindergarten and first-
grade children in an attempt to assess favored modalities in prereading
and beginning reading subjects. Two forms of the test were developed;
Pearsonian correlations showed a statistically significant test-re-
test reliability (p < .001). Subjects were also given the Wepman
Auditory Discrimination Test and the Perceptual Speed Test of the Primary Mental Abilities Test, Science Research Associates. Correlations
between these tests and the auditory and visual test already described were generally positive and statistically significant at
the 1% level of confidence. Scatter diagrams indicated that in
each of the four classrooms tested (two kindergarten and two first
grade) approximately 25% of the children had a preferred modality,
generally visual, although a few children had the reverse. This
finding suggested that for some children a beginning reading pro-

gram that stresses auditory decoding might be inappropriate.

Further investigation as well as refinement of the test was indicated from these preliminary findings. The auditory task was
deemed more important than the visual in view of the paucity of instruments in this field and the difficulties inherent in such sub-
jectively oriented assessments. Item analysis was used to identify
the best indicators, and a new version of the Auditory Attending
Task (AAT) was developed in the spring of 1972. The term "auditory
attending task" seemed to be the best description of the procedure and
its expected outcomes because of the subjective and largely non-
visible aspect of auditory processing, and because of the controversies surrounding such appellations as "auditory memory," "auditory processing," and "auditory sequencing."

A cassette tape was made of a male voice giving instructions,
samples, trial runs, and finally the test itself, a series of elec-
tronic impulses. The Auditory Attending Task consists of sets of
signals based upon the International Code (Morse). The generated
tones have a frequency of 1000 Hertz and are electronically designed
for exact time durations. The "dit" lasts 1/10 of a second, the "da"
3/10 of a second, and the interval between each signal 3/10 of a
second. The interval between sets of signals is 5/10 of a second.
Two sets of signals are played, and the subject is asked to nod only
if both sets are exactly the same. The level of difficulty in the
15 items ranges from 2 impulses in each set to 4 and lasts approximately 6 minutes. After the preliminary instructions are understood, the tape may be stopped only to allow the subject to answer,
but no further instruction is given. Subjects are scored on the
number correct.

1972 STUDY

The AAT was administered in the spring of 1972 to 251 elementary school children in three different schools chosen for variation in ethnic and socioeconomic population. Soundproof rooms
were used, and tests were individually administered by one of two
experimenters. The children were screened for hearing loss by the
school nurse using standard audiometric tests. In each school, one
kindergarten class, one first grade, and one group of learning
disabled children were tested, plus a control group to match the
learning disabled for age, race, and sex.

A teacher rating scale consisting of ten items on a zero to
five scale was developed. It covered general classroom behavior,
attending behavior, attitude towards school, large and small muscle
coordination, and academic achievement (above or below grade level
in five curriculum areas). Approximately 50 teachers participated
in the assessment.

Results--1972 Study

     There is a small rise, from 9 to 11, in median scores from
kindergarten to first grade, with a mean of 2.30 for the total population. Correlations between total correct and the variables of
race, age, and sex were not statistically significant. Teacher rating correlated with total correct at the 5%-level of confidence for
all grades. Teacher rating had a statistically significant correlation with sex ($p < .05$) and with race ($p < .01$). Between teacher
rating and age there was a negative correlation significant at $p <$
.001 for all schools. An item analysis was computed for school 3,
showing a Kuder-Richardson reliability of 0.77. Fourteen percent
of the total population "tuned out," that is, they attended to the
task and understood the directions, but were unable to discriminate
between the signals.

FOLLOW-UP STUDY--1975

     In the spring of 1975 a follow-up study was made of the kinder-
garten and first-grade children from the 1972 study. This population
consisted of 44 males and 38 females, with 17 black males and 20 black
females. The mean age was 9 years, 10 months. New means were computed for the 1972 study on the basis of the scores of the 82 subjects
carried into the follow-up study.

Results--1972-1975

     The mean score for the Auditory Attending Task for the 1975
study was 12.70 with an SD of 1.51. This contrasted with a mean of
10.71 and an SD of 2.42 for the same children enrolled in the 1972
study. Total Correct 1972 and Total Correct 1975 showed an F value
of 5.349 (80 df p < .05; t = 2.31 80 df p < .05). However, stepwise
regression analysis gave an R-Square of 0.06; only 6% of the variation
in Total Correct 1975 was accounted for by Total Correct 1972. The
relationship was therefore considered not significant.

     Although the primary purpose of the study was to investigate
auditory attending skills, Teacher Ratings were deemed important as
an informal measure of teacher assessment of the child's ability to
attend (listen, follow directions, etc.) as well as to achieve within each classroom setting according to teacher expectation and
measures of academic achievement. A Pearsonian correlation of Teacher Rating 1975 with Teacher Rating 1972 gave a value of 0.585, significant at the 0.001 level and suggesting reliability in this rating scale. However, stepwise regression analysis gave an R-Square
of 0.34; only 34% of the variation in Teacher Rating 1975 was accounted for by Teacher Rating 1972. With an arbitrary R-Square of

0.50 or more, the relationship was considered not significant.

DISCUSSION

    Some of the mental operations believed to be involved in the
decoding process of reading have commonly been identified under
broad designations of auditory and visual skills. Although there
is general agreement that both are intimately connected with the
art of reading, defining the components of either skill is perhaps
a futile task at this time. Research studies on the mechanisms of
the brain and understanding of the role that the cerebral hemi-
spheres play in modality preference and operation is still in its
infancy. Genetic influence has been suggested by Annett and Turner
(1974), Satz, Fennell and Jones (1969), and Levy and Naglaki as reported by Sperry (1975). The work of Sperry raises the question
of whether there is an optimal time for training and retraining
in the maturation process.

    The work of the present investigator over the past six years
is provocative. A possible value of the AAT lies in its use as a
classroom instrument to be administered by the teacher as a guide
to auditory attending skills as well as to the skills associated
with following directions. The investigator has concluded that
administration of the AAT should not be attempted for subjects with
a mental age of less than 6 years. The problems of interpreting
directions and of being sure that the child understood the concept
of same-different were noted. By the beginning of first grade,
most normally achieving children seem to understand this concept.
It appears that this would be the most productive time to administer
the AAT before formal reading instruction begins. Perhaps the
most significant finding of this study was that auditory attending
ability does not appear to be related to sex, race, or socioeconomic
class.

    One would anticipate that a visual approach to the beginning
reading process, with supplementary auditory, tactile, and aesthetic
experiences also provided, would breed success. However, the work
of Chall (1967), deHirsch et al. (1966, 1972), Deutsch (1964),
Gickling and Joiner (1974), and Newcomer and Goodman (1975) reported earlier, as well as the studies of countless other researchers,
suggest that to neglect the auditory component in reading is to produce seriously crippled readers.

    In the final analysis, no one really knows what cerebral mech-
anisms are activated in the complicated process that eventuates in
total communication skills. Until we learn more about this process,
teachers of beginning reading will probably experience the best success in following the dictum of Orton (1937) to involve all of the

sensory and perceptual skills that one can, the auditory surely being one of the foremost.

BIBLIOGRAPHY

Annett, M., & Turner, A. Laterality and the growth of intellectual abilities. *British Journal of Educational Psychology*, 1974, *44*, 37-46.

Berry, Judith. Matching of auditory and visual stimuli by average and retarded readers. *Child Development*, 1967, *38*, 827-33.

Belmont, L., & Birch, H. Lateral dominance, lateral awareness and reading disability. *Child Development*, 1965, *36*, 57-71.

Berlin, C., & Dill, A. The effects of feedback and positive reinforcement on the Wepman Auditory Discrimination Test scores of lower class negro and white children. *Journal of Speech and Hearing Research*, 1967, *10*, 384-389.

Birch, H., & Belmont, L. Auditory-visual integration in normal and retarded readers. *American Journal of Orthopsychiatry*, 1964, *34*, 852-61.

Blank, M. Cognitive processes in auditory discrimination in normal and retarded readers. *Child Development*, 1968, *39*, 1091-1102.

Bruininks, R.H., & Clark, C.R. Auditory and visual-paired associate learning in first grade: Retarded and non-retarded children. *American Journal of Mental Deficiency*, 1966, *76*, 561-67.

Chall, Jeanne. *Learning to read: The great debate*. New York: McGraw-Hill, 1967.

Dahle, A.J., & Daly, D.A. Influence of verbal feedback on auditory discrimination test performance of mentally retarded children. *American Journal of Mental Deficiency*, 1972, *76*, 586-590.

deHirsch, K., Jansky, J.U., & Langford, W.S. *Predicting reading failure*. New York: Harper and Row, 1972.

Deutsch, C.P. Auditory discrimination and learning: social factors. *Merrill Palmer Quarterly of Behavior and Development*, July 1964, *10*, 277-296.

Dykstra, R. Auditory discrimination abilities and beginning reading achievement. *Reading Research Quarterly*, Spring 1966, 5-34.

Elenbogen, E.M. A comparison of social class effects in two tests of auditory discrimination. *Journal of Learning Disabilities*, April 1972, *5*, 209-212.

Gickling, E.F. & Joiner, L.M. Complex interactions of an auditory ability and aspiration in predicting specific reading deficits. *American Journal of Mental Deficiency*, 1974, *79*, No. 2, 162-168.

Golden, N.E., & Steiner, S.R. Auditory and visual functions in good and poor readers. *Journal of Learning Disabilities*, Sept. 1969, *2*, 476-481.

Groff, P. Reading ability and auditory discrimination: Are they related? *The Reading Teacher*, May 1975, *28*, 742-746.

Hall, V.C. *Acquisition and transfer differences between kindergart-
    eners on orally and visually presented paired-associates us-
    ing an A-B, A-C design, Project #2 of Head Start Project,
    November 1967.* Syracuse University, New York (ERIC Document
    ED 026-139).

Kling, M. Some relationships between auditory and visual discrimi-
    nation. *California Journal of Educational Research,* Sept.
    1968, 170-181.

Larsen, S.C., Rogers, D., & Sowell, V. The use of selected percep-
    tual tests in differentiating between normal and learning dis-
    abled children. *Journal of Learning Disabilities,* 1976, *9,*
    85-90.

Marquardt, T.P., & Saxman, J.H. Language comprehension and auditory
    discrimination in articulation deficient kindergarten children.
    Journal of Speech and Hearing Research, 1972, *15,* No. 2, 382-
    389.

Mira, M.P. Individual patterns of looking and listening preferences
    among learning disabled and normal readers. *Exceptional Chil-
    dren,* May 1968, 649-658.

Newcomer, P.L., & Goodman, L. Effect of modality of instruction on
    the learning of meaningful and non-meaningful material by audi-
    tory and visual learners. *Journal of Special Education,* 1975,
    9, No. 3, 261-268.

Newcomer, P.L., & Hammill, D.D. ITPA and academic achievement: A
    survey. *The Reading Teacher,* 1975, *28,* 731-740.

Orton, S.R. *Reading, writing and speech problems of children.* New
    York: Norton, 1937.

Osborn, J.D., Osborn, D.K., & Brown, M.H. Testing procedures and
    auditory discrimination. *Childhood Education,* 1976, *52,* 284-
    286.

Otto, W. The differential effects of verbal and pictorial represen-
    tation of stimuli upon responses evoked. *Journal of Verbal
    Learning and Verbal Behavior,* 1962-63, *1,* 192-197.

Piaget, J. *Six Psychological Studies.* New York: Random House, 1967.

Ritchie, B.C., & Merklein, R.A. An evaluation of the efficiency of
    the verbal auditory screening for children (VASC). *Journal of
    Speech and Hearing Research,* 1972, *15,* No. 2, 280-286.

Robinson, H. Visual and auditory modalities related to methods for
    beginning reading. *Reading Research Quarterly,* Fall 1972,
    8, No. 1, 7-39.

Rude, R.T., Niquette, S., & Foxgrover, P. The retention of visual
    and auditory discrimination reading skills. *Journal of Educa-
    tion Research,* 1975, *68,* 192-195.

Satz, P., Fennell, E., & Jones, M. Comments on a model of the in-
    heritance of handedness and cerebral dominance. *Neuropsycho-
    logia,* 1969, *7,* 101-103.

Sperry, R.W. Left-brain, right brain. *Saturday Review,* Aug. 9, 1975,
    2, 30-33.

Thurston, T.G. Primary Mental Abilities Test. *Science Research As-
    sociates,* 1963, Chicago, Ill.

Vellutino, F.R., DeSetto, L., & Steger, J.A. Categorical judgement
     and the Wepman Test of Auditory Discrimination. *Journal of
     Speech and Hearing Disabilities*, May 1972, *37*, 252-257.
Wepman, J.M. Wepman Auditory Discrimination Test. *Language Research
     Associates*, 1958. *Chicago, Ill.*

HELPING OTHERS LEARN TO TEACH: SOME PRINCIPLES AND TECHNIQUES FOR INSERVICE EDUCATORS

Lilian G. Katz

University of Illinois
Urbana-Champaign

HELPING OTHERS LEARN TO TEACH

Most programs for young children make provisions for the in-service education of staff members. Those of us engaged in helping others learn to teach may be directors of Head Start, day care or teachers' centers, CDA[1] field trainers, consultants, college instructors or curriculum coordinators. All of us confront similar situations, issues and problems and have to make similar choices as to which content will be most helpful for teachers.

The purpose of this paper is to present some principles, assumptions and techniques that might be useful for teacher educators whether working with inservice teachers or caregivers, CDAs or even prospective teachers. Often the person participating in inservice education is not in a traditional student role--working with an abstract or theoretical set of topics organized into formal lectures. Instead, the learner is an adult with strong involvement in the object of the interaction--namely, her[2] own teaching behavior.

Throughout this paper the term "principle" is used as defined by R. S. Peters (Peters, 1970) to mean that which makes a consideration relevant. Principles are not ironclad, fail-safe rules to be applied mindlessly, but are intended to guide practitioners, to be qualified by such phrases as "under some circumstances" or "as the situation warrants." Although these phrases are not repeatedly mentioned below, each principle outlined in the discussion that follows should be considered with appropriate qualifiers in mind.

PRINCIPLES FOR THE SELECTION OF FOCUS

All of us who teach, at whatever level, have to face the fact
that we cannot offer our learners all the possible advice, suggestions, commentary, information or praise that might be helpful or
instructive to them. When we work with people in any situation, we
are constantly making choices concerning the nature of the interactions occurring. The potential content of human relationships is
so broad that some choices have to be made concerning which content
is most relevant, appropriate and useful at any given time in any
given situation. Similarly, there are probably more than a dozen
right or effective ways to respond in any given situation and probably just as many ineffective ways. Since we cannot respond in all
the ways that are possible, choices have to be made. Obviously
many different factors affect those choices. Some choices are made
out of a sense of history (e.g., this is how we have always done it).
Other decisions are based on what it is thought that teachers either
want or expect or will attend to carefully. Some choices reflect
philosophical commitments. The principles outlined below are recommended for use when considering what content to focus on when interacting with teachers you want to help.

1. Focus on the teacher's understandings of her own situation:
The term understandings is used here to refer to the teacher's ideas,
thoughts, constructions, concepts, assumptions or schemata about
such things as how children learn, what "works," how she affects
her pupils, what she expects of herself, what others expect, her
role, duties and so forth.

We suggest that the most useful course of action available to
inservice educators may be to focus on helping teachers develop
understandings that are more appropriate, more accurate, deeper and
more fully differentiated than they had previously been (see Katz,
1977). The rationale underlying this principle is that the focus
on understandings helps the teacher acquire knowledge, ideas, insights or information she can keep and use after the inservice educator has left the scene. Directives, prescriptions, instructions or
even orders might also address the problem the teacher is trying to
cope with, but their value is likely to be of short duration. It
seems reasonable to assume that modified understandings are more
likely to help the teacher to generate new behaviors than prescriptions and directives. For example, a teacher complained that she
had been unable to stop one of her kindergarteners from persistent
hitting of several others in her class. When asked what approaches
she had tried so far, she explained that she had already hit the boy
as hard as she dared in order to "show him how much hitting hurts."
In such a situation, the inservice educator might want to simply
prohibit the teacher's hitting by citing a rule or regulation or a
philosophical position. However, the teacher in this example seems

to have an inadequate understanding of a kindergartener's ability
to abstract from his own pain on being hit the important of not hitting others. In this case, the teacher's understanding of the
situation she is trying to cope with could be improved by suggesting to her that when adults hurt children (by hitting them) and provide a model of hurting others, they are unlikely to convince
children that it is not all right for them to do so.

Other aspects of the teacher's understanding of children's
responses to censure and her knowledge of alternative ways of handling the disruptive behavior of children might also be addressed by
the educator. While a directive might "change" the teacher's behavior in a particular incident, only modification of teachers'
understandings is likely to have enduring value and can thus serve
as a basis for action in subsequent situations that are similar.

An underlying presupposition here is that an inservice educator is someone who has more useful, appropriate, accurate or differentiated understandings than the teacher being helped. The tacit
acknowledgment that such differences exist legitimates the educator's
authority to provide inservice training.

2. *Focus on strengthening worthwhile dispositions:* Widespread
enthusiasm for performance-based teacher education, and for compe-
tency-based education in general, seems to be associated with the risk
of underemphasizing the development of desirable dispositions in
learners. We suggest that when deciding what responses to make to
teachers it is reasonable to choose those which are likely to strength-
en enduring dispositions thought to be related to effective teaching.
Similarly, responses to teachers should focus on weakening those
dispositions which might undermine effective teaching. By dispositions we mean relatively stable "habits of mind" or tendencies to
respond to one's experiences or to given situations in certain ways.
Some examples of dispositions likely to be related to effective teaching include inventiveness or resourcefulness, patience (i.e., longer
reaction times), friendliness, enthusiasm, etc. Some dispositions
likely to undermine effective teaching include tendencies to be im-
petuous, unfriendly, hypercritical and so forth.

Two suppositions provide the rationale for this principle.
First, as already suggested, it seems obvious that we cannot teach
all the knowledge, skills, methods, techniques, etc. which are of
potential use to teachers. This being the case, it seems advisable
to teach teachers and caregivers in such a way as to strengthen
their dispositions to go on learning, to be resourceful and to be
inventive long after the inservice educator's work with them is
over. Second, while we indeed want to help teachers with specific
skills and methods, it is important to do so without undermining
their "self-helpful" dispositions. In short, we should guard

against helping a teacher acquire competencies in a way that might strengthen or engender a disposition to be dependent, uninventive and/or helpless.

   3.   *Focus on competencies already acquired:*   In our eagerness to be "change agents," we may overlook the possibility that the teachers we work with may already have the competencies appropriate for, or required of, a given situation.   In such cases the focus should be on helping the teachers to use already available competencies more reliably, consistently, appropriately or confidently. For example, a kindergarten teacher might be sufficiently skilled at guiding a discussion with her pupils, but may vary too greatly in her performance from one occasion to the next.   If so, she probably does not require a module on discussion skills, but perhaps a fuller or better understanding of the causes of her own performance fluctuations, or assistance in becoming more alert to cues which cause her to perform so variably.   She might be helped, at least temporarily, by the suggestion that she refrain from leading discussions except when classroom conditions are optimum for her.   In that way the teacher may be able to consolidate and increase mastery of a skill she already has before trying it out under less than optimum conditions.   Similarly, teachers of young children are often exhorted to "listen" to the children.   It is reasonable to assume that all teachers have such "listening" competencies in their repertoires, although they may employ them inappropriately and/or inconsistently.

   In yet another case a teacher may have the skills required in a situation but fail to use them with sufficient confidence to be effective.   For example, if the teacher's actions betray a lack of confidence when she is setting limits, or redirecting or stopping disruptive behavior, children may perceive mixed signals, challenge her and thus exacerbate the situation.   In such cases the inservice educator's role becomes one of "shaping" and/or supporting the teacher's efforts to practice and strengthen already available behavior, rather than focusing on the acquisition of new competencies.

   4.   *Focus on building long term relationships:*   This principle refers to those situations in which an observation of a teacher prompts us to offer "corrections" of the teacher's behavior.   Sometimes, in our eagerness to be helpful and to establish our own credibility, corrections are offered too hastily.   Although in certain situations it may be appropriate to make corrections, there is often the risk of losing the opportunity to go on helping that teacher over a longer period of time by alienating her through premature corrections.

   5.   *Focus on providing moderate amounts of inspiration:*   Many of the teachers we are trying to help can cope admirably with the complex tasks and responsibilities they face.   They may not require

new techniques, packages, or gimmicks but simply need occasional
encouragement or reinforcement to enable them to sustain their
efforts and to maintain enough enthusiasm to keep working at an un-
glamorous and perhaps under-appreciated job. Excessive sapping of
courage or enthusiasm, at times approaching depression (i.e., believing one's efforts have no effects), is a potential cause of ineffectiveness, no matter how many competencies the teacher has.
Such ineffectiveness may depress enthusiasm and reduce courage even
further, which, in turn, may again decrease effectiveness, starting
a downward spiral. The inservice educator may be able to intervene in the downward spiral by providing moderate inspiration,
encouragement and support.

It seems important that the inspirational message be specifically related to the work setting and its specific characteristics
rather than being a generalized message of good will. It is also
suggested that supportive and encouraging messages contain real and
useful information about the significance of the teacher's efforts.
For example, it is likely to be more useful to say something like
"those new activities really seemed to intrigue the older girls in
your class . . ." than to say "you were great." Furthermore, it may
be wise to provide inspiration in optimum rather than maximum amounts
so that a teacher does not become "hooked" or dependent on it, thus
undermining her disposition to be self-helpful in the long run.

GENERAL TECHNIQUES FOR WORKING WITH TEACHERS

The principles outlined above are intended as overall guides or
decision making rules to help those of us who are inservice educators
select responses to inservice teaching situations. The general techniques described briefly below are intended to help the inservice
educator further the goals implied by those principles.

1. *Maintain an optimum distance from the teachers you are
working with:* Many educators consider closeness, warmth and suppor-
tiveness essential and valuable attributes of their relationships
with learners. Research seems to support the contention that warmth,
for example, is related to teacher effectiveness. However, we suggest that inservice educators may be tempted to make the error of
being too close to their teachers. An optimum (rather than maximum)
distance is recommended for several reasons. First, excessive
closeness may inhibit or limit the teacher educator's ability to
evaluate the teacher's progress realistically. Indeed, in such
cases the teacher educator may be unable to help the teacher confront
serious weaknesses, or may fail to perceive the weaknesses at all.
Secondly, if the teacher educator becomes too close to the teacher
he or she may unintentionally impinge on the teacher's right to
privacy, a right which deserves protection. Thirdly, there is some
danger that if we become too close to one of the teachers in the

134 L. G. KATZ

group we are working with, we might inadvertently make disparaging remarks about another in the set and thereby undermine our own credibility and effectiveness. Finally, if we allow ourselves to become too close or involved with the teachers we are working with, we may find ourselves emotionally "burned out" in a few months (Maslach & Pines, 1977) and suffer not only personal stress, but also lose the ability to be effective on the job.

2. *Cultivate the habit of suspending judgment on your observations:* There is a strong tendency among those of us who are teachers to pass judgment on what we see in the classroom. We tend to judge not only the rightness or goodness of what we see, but also whether the teacher is doing things "our way" or not. Such assessments seem to come naturally. We recommend, however, that if the intention is to stimulate and support someone's development, then, instead of passing judgment, we ask ourselves such questions as: How can I account for what I am observing? Why is the teacher responding to the situation in this way? Why is this happening? In seeking answers to such questions, rather than judging the events observed, we are more likely to learn those things which will increase our capacity to help the teacher. It might be helpful to practice making up answers to the questions and guessing possible causes. Then the "guesses" could be inspected for plausibility. When a reasonably persuasive guess or answer had been formulated, an appropriate method for helping the observed teacher could be selected and tried.

This technique is recommended for several reasons. First, it includes two features: it can help you to resist the temptation to pass judgment and also encourage you to inspect your observations more closely, which in turn will help slow down your response to the situation, thereby reducing any tendency you might have to overreact. Secondly, asking how the observed behavior might be accounted for is likely to lead to learning more about the people you are trying to help, and to increase your insight into how the teacher defines her situation. Obviously there are many reasons why teachers do what they do. Sometimes the teacher's reason for her action is that what she is doing appears to "work" (for her); perhaps what she is doing is all she *knows* how to do in a given situation. Often a teacher does what she does because she thinks that the director or the principal wants her to do it, even though that may not necessarily be the case. Some teachers do what they do because they think that the parents want them to do it, or the evaluators, or colleagues, or visitors. . . or their own teachers did these particular things, and so forth. Attempts to account for the observed behavior should help the inservice educator to make more informed decisions about what to do next to help the teacher observed.

This technique is related to the more general principle of timing (Katz, 1977) which asserts that the longer the latency before a teacher responds to the learner, the more information the teacher has, and the more likely she is to make better decisions about the next steps. The latency issue seems especially relevant to inservice educators because they often enter classrooms "off the streets"— so to speak—without prior information concerning the antecedents of the situation observed. The temptation to pass judgment rapidly may lead to important errors in assessing teacher needs and competencies.

3. *Phrase suggestions in experimental form:* Most teaching involves occasions when the most appropriate response to the learner is to make a suggestion. When giving suggestions to teachers it is helpful to phrase them in the form "Next time Y comes up, try X . . . and see if it helps". Depending on the situation, you might want to add something such as "X helps some teachers in this kind of situation . . . if you find it doesn't help, we can think about something else to try . . .".

This technique is recommended for several reasons. First, it can be expected to strengthen the teacher's disposition to be experimental, inventive and resourceful. Furthermore, when a suggestion is offered with the implication that it is *the* solution or *the* answer to the problem, and the teacher's later attempt to use the suggestion fails, her sense of frustration and defeat may be intensified rather than diminished. Similarly, it is advisable to make suggestions which the individual teacher can be expected to try successfully, or, if she fails, she should be able to understand why this was so. If suggestions require much greater sophistication than the teacher has, then she can only fail and intensify her sense of helplessness.

Another reason for recommending this technique is that when you make suggestions in terms of what to try "next time" you minimize the likelihood of humiliating or embarrassing the teacher over the incident just observed. Some inservice educators are so eager to get teachers to analyze their own "mistakes" following an unsuccessful teaching episode that they might inadvertently embarrass them, which in turn could undermine the teacher's disposition to go on learning, trying, inventing and seeking the best methods for themselves.

4. *Avoid the temptation to stop a pattern behavior:* From time to time we observe teacher behavior which we think should be stopped "cold". Without quarreling with the rightness of the teacher educator's position, we recommend a two-step approach for such situations. First, we can ask whether in such situations the behavior observed really endangers any child. If the answer is a clear "yes," then we must use all the resources at our disposal to bring the behavior to a halt. If the answer is ambiguous ("maybe" or "no") then the next step is to help the teacher to try out and to

practice alternative strategies with which to replace or supplant
the old patterns.

If we succeed in stopping a teacher's behavior in advance of her
sufficient mastery of a new pattern, she may be left without alternative methods of coping with the situation, which may cause her children
behavior to become worse, and increase her own feelings of frustration
and failure. Occasionally, this sequence of events is followed by
a type of "backlash" (i.e., a strengthened conviction that the old
pattern was really *the* right one after all).

5. *Help the teacher to redefine her job so that it is achiev-*
able: From time to time, inservice educators work with teachers who
have defined their jobs so that they have to "do everything" in sight
and only a super-heroine could achieve the objectives. For example,
many teachers of young children think their job requires them to
"love all the children in their classroom." It is reasonable to
assume that they do not have to love or even to like all the children
they teach — they *do* have to respect them all. The latter is not
always easy, but is far more achievable than universal love.

The point is that when a teacher defines her job so that the
potential for achievement (and therefore satisfaction) is very low,
she is likely to experience a decrease in responsiveness and sensitivity, which decreases her effectiveness, which in turn depresses
satisfaction which further diminishes achievement and satisfaction.
Thus, a downward spiral seems inevitable. (Seligman, 1975).

The inservice educator can assist the teacher by helping her to
clarify her own purposes and settle on some boundaries for her
responsibilities and her authority. Successful assistance along
these lines should increase the teacher's sense of effectiveness and
satisfaction which, in turn, should increase her responsiveness and
sensitivity which, in turn, should lead to heightened effectiveness
and satisfaction.

6. *Act as a neutralizer of conflicts:* Once in a while we
find ourselves in a situation marked by intra-staff conflicts. In
such situations we are often tempted to align ourselves with one side
or the other but if we give in to that temptation we may lose our
effectiveness in the long run. A technique which seems useful on such
occasions is to remind the complaining parties as gracefully as possible of their superordinate (and shared) objectives, to encourage
them to keep their minds and energies focused on their long range
common responsibilties. Similarly, it seems useful to resist the
temptation to follow up rumors or in any other way to transfer
potentially inflammatory information. It is also helpful to avoid
reinforcing complaining behavior. One has to sort out and select
those complaints which are legitimate and deserve to be followed up
and which ones simply reflect the possibility that complaining is

one of the ways some people know of getting others' attention.

7. *Use demonstrations of skills cautiously:* Modeling is a useful tool for inservice educators, and opportunities to demonstrate one's skills are often also opportunities to strengthen one's credibility as an educator. But modeling is not without some risks. For example, as inservice educators, many of us have had the experience of entering a day care center or preschool class in which (for whatever reason) the situation is out of control. Because we have worked with children for many years we may know how to bring order to the scene in a flash. In addition, being a relative stranger may increase our power to obtain obedience. But such a demonstration of skill may cause some teachers to look at the scene and say to themselves "I'll never be that good" or "Why is it so easy for her/him?" and to become more discouraged and insecure. Or, in the case of demonstrating our skill with older children, occasionally there is a risk that the demonstration will make the teacher look incompetent in the eyes of her own pupils.

8. *Share your understanding of a teacher's perceptions:* Keep in mind that we do not always know how the teachers we work with perceive us. We may know that we are kind and warm, sincere and helpful, and generous and giving, but we are unlikely to always be perceived that way! Some teachers may be afraid of us, even though we don't see ourselves as threatening in any way. If we sense that this kind of reaction is occurring, it is helpful to let the teacher know that we understand this feeling, that we have had experience with similar feelings, and that we realize teachers might look at us with apprehension, suspicion or even fear. Acknowledging the possibility of such perceptions may be a technique by which to diffuse the excessive stress teachers sometimes experience when they are observed. Furthermore, the shared insight may clear the way to selecting more useful and constructive contents for the relationship between the teacher and the inservice educator.

9. *Resist the temptation to "use" teachers to get to the children:* Of course all inservice educators ultimately hope to get something accomplished for the children. But our role should not be defined as "getting to the kids through the teachers". If you want to help children (and no doubt you do), then do so directly. Try not to "use" teachers. Instead, focus on helping the teachers as persons worthy of your concern and caring in their own right. Try to define your role as someone who helps and works with teachers for the teachers' benefit. When this is done whole-heartedly and well, the children the teachers work with will also stand to benefit.

CONCLUDING COMMENTS

In the course of employing the principles and techniques enu-

merated here, several assumptions might be useful. First, it seems
useful to assume that not all teachers can be helped by any one teacher
educator. Occasionally an assignment includes a teacher who constitutes a "chronic case" for a given teacher educator. Such a teacher
drains large portions of energy yet somehow nothing really seems to
help. While this teacher takes much time and thought, although making
no progress, there are other teachers for whom we are responsible
who are waiting to respond to our help and who seem likely to make
developmental advances with relatively modest effort on our part.

We suggest that on such occasions it is a good idea to take the
time to think through very deliberately whether or not we see any
potential for the growth of the chronic case teacher under *our*
guidance. If the assessment is ultimately a positive one, make a "go"
decision, and mobilize all the professional resources you have for
the task at hand. If the assessment is ultimately negative, make a
"no-go" decision, and try to refer this teacher to other agents or
sources of assistance.

The usefulness of the assumption that none of us can teach
everyone equally effectively resides mainly in the apparent effects of
scrutinizing one's own thoughts and feelings about the case, and
making a clear choice or decision. Once the go/no-go decision has been
made, then the energy apparently drained in agonizing over the case
seems to become available for work with those teachers who are ready
to respond to help. Indeed, the content of a relationship which is
"chronic" and unsatisfying becomes focused on the pain and frustration
it engenders instead of upon the problems of improving the teacher's
effectiveness. Furthermore, it appears that when a "go" decision
has been made, we begin to notice some positive attributes of the
teacher in question, which, in turn, tends to improve our responses
to her, which seems to lead to more positive responses on our part.
Thus, a positive "snowball" can be set into motion by engaging in
deliberate scrutiny of our own thinking about the difficult or chronic
cases we encounter.

Furthermore, it seems useful to always hold to the assumption
that every teacher we work with has her own inner life of concerns
and dreams, wishes and fantasies, hopes and associations, and so forth
just like all of us. We do not have to know the content of that life.
It is not our business. But if we respect the fact that it is there,
we are more likely to treat the teacher with dignity and with respect,
which is not only essential in teaching, but also ethically correct.

Another assumption that seems useful is that every decision made
when teaching contains its own potential errors. If we decide not to
"correct" a teacher for the sake of building a long term relationship
(as suggested above) we may make the error of letting the teacher
continue to perform incorrectly. If we "correct" her immediately,
we risk the error of undermining a relationship which could stimulate

significant long-term development which has an impact on a teacher's
entire career. Similarly, if we demonstrate to a teacher our own
skills in working with children, we may strengthen our credibility,
but we may make the error of causing the teacher to feel ashamed or
less confident of her own competence. On the other hand, if we pass
by opportunities to demonstrate our skills, what we teach may be dis-
counted as coming from an inadequate, high-minded and impractical or
naive source, and therefore our ideas and suggestions may be dismissed
out of hand.

      Until such time as we can devise approaches and techniques that
are error-free, we might accept the assumption that every choice or
decision contains some errors; then we can think through what those
errors might be and select the ones we prefer to make. This assumption
should free us to make deliberate choices about the appropriate content
of our work with teachers, and to proceed with sufficient confidence
to help them strengthen their own teaching abilities and self-confidence.

FOOTNOTES

      [1] CDA is the acronym for Child Development Associate, the staff
training program sponsored by the Administration for Children, Youth
and families, HEW.

      [2] The feminine gender is used to simplify sentence construction;
the welcome presence of male staff members in early childhood education is hereby acknowledged.

BIBLIOGRAPHY

Katz, L. G. Challenges to early childhood educators. In L. G. Katz,
      Talks with Teachers. Washington, D.C.: National Association for
      the Education of Young Children, 1977.
Maslach, C. & Pines, A. The burn-out syndrome in the day care setting.
      Child Care Quarterly, 6, 1977.
Peters, R.S. Concrete principles and the national passion. In N. F.
      Sizer and T. R. Sizer, (Eds.), *Moral Education*. Cambridge:
      Harvard University Press, 1970.
Seligman, M. E. *Helplessness: On depression, development and death.*
      San Francisco: H. W. Freeman and Company, 1975.

AN ATTEMPT TO BRIDGE THE GAP BETWEEN THEORY AND PRACTICE
IN EARLY CHILDHOOD TEACHER EDUCATION

George Harrison

Natal Training College
South Africa

In this paper I hope to convey to you some of my disquiet at what sometimes passes for teacher education and to describe an attempt to make courses more relevant and valuable to student teachers. As the title implies, this is essentially a practical presentation.

My uneasiness about teacher education began some sixteen years ago when a somewhat cynical colleague, hearing of my appointment as an educational psychology lecturer at a college of education, remarked: "Ah, he's going to his eternal rest!" My own training had been largely theoretical and so, along with my colleagues, I too proceeded to indulge myself by pouring forth much educational theory broken only by brief forays into schools to supervise students on teaching practice. Colleagues in other faculties worked like beavers, talking at great length about the best use of creative areas, garden activities, fantasy, and cognitive areas. Of course great hunks of apparatus were made, films were shown, visiting lecturers talked and, in case the students were not being stretched enough, academic courses were to be studied in depth. And children? Well, courses in developmental psychology, in-depth observation of children while on teaching practice, and much discussion about them took care of that.

The result of all these typically earnest activities that occur in many teacher education courses in Africa, Britain, and North America, as I have seen for myself, is frequently a jigsaw puzzle in the minds of students. Often only the exceptional student can fit it all together and see the relevance of the pieces of theory. Many students find it all a buzzing confusion and frequently question the relevance of the whole operation, while weak students yearn for

the limited teaching practice and the end of the long four-year
trail. I believe that there is a lack of coherence in most courses
or as Weber et al. (1973) put it, "Program components are determined more by tradition than function." There is a yawning gap
between theory and practice; this is the great bogey of teacher
education.

Faced with this familiar problem in my own 70-year-old college,
we have tried to bridge the gap by the use of case studies, simulations, action mazes, decision-making analyses, and role-plays. The
contents of all these activities are based firmly on classroom reality
and link the behavior and development of young children in a school,
the school itself, the social background, the educational authority,
and the teacher as a professional with educational, psychological,
and sociological theory. The theory is demonstrated to be a helpful
and often indispensable aid in the solution of both mundane and
knotty problems in the nursery school. Under the heading of "School
Dynamics" in three years of a four-year course, two hours per week
are spent on these activities, which supplement normal education
lectures and, of course, normal teaching practice.

We found that if students are to become fully involved in this
program of discussion, of wrestling with the manifold problems of
the very young child, of sharpening their minds on the minds of
fellow students, of becoming motivated, sentient people able to
deal with the linking of theory and practice of education, it is
necessary to provide preliminary human relations training. For the
programme to be meaningful so that students can internalise their
learning, it is imperative that students should be actively stimulated to probe, to question, to relate well to others, and, what is
fundamental, to be able to understand themselves. Using group dynamics
principles, tutors in the School Dynamics program generate groups with
lives of their own before tackling practical teaching or simulated
school incidents. The tutors do this by first sharing experiences far
removed from the decision-making areas of the classroom. Once students
feel at home analyzing their own actions and those of their groups,
they are in a better position to consider in depth the kinds of situations and problems in the typical nursery school.

Johanson (1979) sums up the nature of the program in these
words:

> To be a successful teacher involves sharing a great deal of
> oneself with others and trying to understand why other people,
> and especially children, behave as they do. Teachers are in
> daily contact with their pupils and colleagues, and very
> often with the parents. The more open, free and friendly they
> are able to be, the more they will enjoy the work and the more
> successful they will be. Human relations are every bit as
> important as the imparting of knowledge and skills.

In order to facilitate the discussion of child behavior, child development, and the child's social and educational setting, we decided to use the highly motivating simulation technique. Using the ideas of Cruickshank (1967, 1969, 1971), Walford (1975), and techniques used in business management education, we created a fictitious nursery school complete with children and modelled firmly on a typical nursery school of our province and district. Here we have a setting where tutors and education lecturers can join in dialogue with students to discuss practical matters affecting the children, the school as a social organism, home and society, the educational system, and our professional roles. Extensive information is provided in written form and by means of slide-tape programs, taped interviews with parents and staff, taped role plays, and spontaneous role plays. Tutors, lecturers, and students with the same background knowledge can thus work on common issues, and lecturers can introduce students to relevant theory, readings, and research that can be directly helpful to the practical situation under discussion.

As I cannot bring you into Natal Training College to see the programme in action, let me try to describe an actual situation we discussed with second-year students in 1979. In this way you will gain a clearer idea of organization and see the learning potential of the technique. Of course not all situations are considered in exactly the same way because as teachers we know the necessity of ringing the changes.

The situation under discussion was this:

Martin Hendrichs arrived at school in the morning proudly carrying 10 cents, which the mouse had brought him when he put his tooth into his slipper the previous night. Pierre Stanley Smith promptly told him that the mouse had nothing to do with the money and it was a "rubbish story." Martin dejectedly put his money away in his locker. Later that day Carome Royden runs up to tell you that Daniel De Beer has taken the money out of Martin's locker and that Martin is in tears. You suspect that Carome may be telling you a tale and you are aware that Daniel is at times treated as the scapegoat. You look up to see Daniel with flushed cheeks looking rather embarrassed. What should you do?

The students met in plenary session in a large hall; they were arranged in their tutorial groups, six students in a group. They were familiar with the files of Martin, Pierre, Carome, and Daniel. So that what follows can be intelligible and show you the practical and theoretical being welded together, here is a very brief thumbnail sketch of the four children.

Daniel is an illegitimate child in a children's home. The

mother neglected the child, subsequently married, and the child was
badly treated by the unstable husband. Child welfare intervened.
Mother is emotionally immature; child sees her occasionally. At
school Daniel is confused, unsure of himself, and unhappy. He is
frequently a scapegoat who accepts unkindness apathetically. He is
the oldest in the group. Reports refer to withdrawal or overreaction
and being aggressive at times. He is classified as "dull normal."

Martin is well adjusted, friendly, and well liked; good, stable
home background.

Pierre is extremely bright. He relates well to his teacher
and peers. Both parents are well-to-do professional people.

Carome is reserved and correct. She dislikes noise or mess,
is unable to relax and play as a child. At home she is treated as
a mini-adult, and spends much time with her grandmother. She does
not fit in with her peer group.

The senior tutor orientated the students to the situation in
these terms:

> After the events of the morning you realise just what respon-
> sibility is involved in teaching a lively group of 5-year-
> olds. You recall little Martin with his bright-eyed excite-
> ment as he told you of the tooth-mouse, and then the total
> disillusionment on his face when he was told it was rubbish.
> Will he still believe the story or will he feel deceived?
> Carome Royden — rather a self-righteous little miss — is she
> a sneaky tell-tale or was she correct in telling you about
> Daniel? Poor Daniel, he always seems to be on the losing
> end. As these thoughts tumble in your mind, you make your way
> to the staff room where Mrs. Cartwright is relaxing at lunch-
> time after seeing off the last child in her group. Mrs. Cart-
> wright, as you know, is in charge of the 3-year-old reception
> class and has a 2-year Nursery Nurse Diploma from the United
> Kingdom, but the Diploma is not recognised by the Central Edu-
> cation Authority. She has had 25 years of experience with
> young children. She has two children, both recently married.
> You....

At this point, there was a role play of conversation between
Mrs. Cartwright and the young teacher in which the matter of the
tooth-mouse myth was discussed quite forcibly. Father Christmas
and the stork myths were inevitably included; the whole question
of being honest with children was raised. Even the question of
belief in the existence of God entered the picture.

The role play was interrupted so that students and tutors
could have a "buzz" session on their attitude to the tooth-mouse

myth and the two conflicting parental attitudes that were revealed.
Their thinking was recorded for a report back at the end of the
session.

The role play continued with a discussion about Daniel's guilt
and his being an institutionalized child. These factors were then
discussed by the groups who reported back to the plenary session.
During the discussion, time was devoted to examining the files and
to readings while the tutors made appropriate contributions. Finally,
the senior tutor drew together the threads of the discussion. Here is
an extract dealing with Daniel, but of course many of these points
were amplified later in educational psychology lectures.

A critical aspect of the field into which the child is born and
in which it grows to maturity is the invisible field consisting
of attitudes, feelings, expectations, wishes, and ideas that
the important people in his environment have regarding him.
Is he welcome or unwanted? Are his parents loving, or cold
and disinterested? With Daniel the answer is obvious. The
view generally accepted is that a child sees and evaluates himself as he thinks others see and evaluate him. The accepted
child feels positive towards others, whereas rejected children
tend to see themselves as inferior and inadequate.

In implicit personality theory (and here references were provided) every perceiver has a relatively constant set of typical
expectations about the organisation of personality, which are
reflected in his perception and judgement of others. But what
if these theories are wrong and based on stereotypes and super-
stitions? Look at Amy Cartwright in her perceptions of Daniel
as an institutionalized child. The influence of our general
opinion about a person on our evaluation of his specific actions
is called the halo effect. A generally positive evaluation of
somebody tends to lead to an overestimation of desirable traits
and an underestimation of undesirable traits. Conversely, a
negative evaluation of Daniel causes an overestimation of a
cluster of further negative traits that possibly do not exist.
(Further references were provided at this point.)

Two aspects of stereotyping are apparent: (1) the tendency
to generalise about certain groups, for example, students
are irresponsible, women are bad drivers, you can't trust
institution children; (2) the tendency to ascribe the characteristics associated with a group to individual members of
that group. Thus the perceiver will tend to attribute all the
characteristics she associates with an institutionalised child
to Daniel, even if there is no objective justification.
Daniel is constantly labelled with a variety of negative
labels: he is regarded as being slow and dull, a passive
follower; he is unoriginal, unenthusiastic, and negativistic.

Through being part of a minority group and different, he becomes the prime target for scapegoating. Whether Daniel is guilty or not, he tends to take the blame, in this instance for taking money. (Information is provided at this point on "self-fulfilling prophecy" research.)

Daniel's reaction to this situation is formed by his perceptions of the attitudes and feelings underlying the actions and words of others. How do you think Daniel will react to discovering what others think of him? Through interaction with others, he defines himself and discovers his nature and potential. Negative expectations of a child will lead to a poor self-concept. His feelings of self-rejection, inferiority, and helplessness need to be replaced with feelings of esteem and respect for his human dignity. This is your challenge. So how should you help Daniel? (Reference here to educational research.)

At this stage of moral development, a child is developing a conscience or superego. He is forming a standard for acceptable behavior, largely through identification with the parent. Studies show that high levels of conscience are related to a warm, rewarding, and nurturant parent-child relationship. (References given.) Knowing Daniel's situation, how can we deal with this problem? If we ignore it, presuming that he has taken the money, he will probably repeat the behavior.

If we directly confront him with "Did you take the money?" he will probably deny it, and then what is the next move? Instead, approach the child and present him with an opportunity to save face; for example, "Did you play a trick on Martin and hide his money? Poor Martin is so sad and upset that I am also very upset. Let us give him back the money."

Daniel might have three possible reactions to this approach. (1) If he has the money and gives it back he will have saved face and been made aware of the fact that he has made someone sad and that taking money is unacceptable behavior. (2) If he has the money, yet denies this, he is still made aware of the fact that it is unacceptable to hurt people by taking their belongings. (3) If he is innocent, no harm has been done. There still remains the problem of Daniel having to live with unjust accusations.

I have dwelt at some length on this situation to illustrate the kinds of insights a student can obtain by facing a practical problem in this way, having to make a decision, and being obliged to refer to educational theory to help her make a wise decision. I hardly need point out the way in which this technique focuses on children as individuals.

The incidents cover a wide range of difficulties commonly faced by the nursery school teacher. Some of them are organizational, others are as diverse as difficulties with identical twins, imaginary friends, tricky behavior, relationships with colleagues, parents, the education department, exceptional children, care of pets, awkward questions, health problems, and so forth.

Another technique currently being investigated at my college is the "action maze" as outlined by Zoll (1969). The maze begins with a statement of a problem a teacher might be encountering; for example, it could concern a stuttering child. Some action must be taken — again decision making — and the student involves herself in the exercise as the person facing the child's problem. Her first action is to decide what to do by selecting one of a number of alter- natives, next to which are page references directing her to the next step, which usually means a further decision.

The student keeps a record of the path taken, including the dead ends, to resolve the problem, and with her tutor analyzes the factors considered at each of the decision points. In addition, the student refers to literature that possibly influenced her decisions, and so theory enters the scene. The path down which one individual student proceeds in taking action to resolve a difficulty may well differ from that of other individuals, as there is no one path in real life for the solution of problems. Much depends not only on the individual's own actions and attitudes at each decision point, but also on her own background and professional knowledge. A link with the group communication program described earlier can clearly be discerned here.

Action mazes are a far cry from reading and hearing about education because the student becomes personally involved and the objective of the task is abundantly clear. Students learn how to make wise professional decisions instead of simply contemplating them. The work of Bishop and Whitfield (1972) is valuable in this area as well.

Other techniques for linking theory and practice are to be explored by my lecturers, for example, video-simulated problems, in-basket exercises. It should be emphasized that all the techniques mentioned in this paper are underpinned by lectures and readings. Professor Paul Hirst (1974), discussing this kind of work, maintained that, "This is not to say that there would be no lectures or classes devoted to philosophy or psychology in isolation, only that the con- tent of such work would spring from and run alongside collaborative work on practical issues."

And what has been the students' reaction? Here is a brief summary. Comprehensive questionnaires were completed by students at the end of 1979. The following questions brought forth very positive responses from more than 95% of the students: 1. Do you think that the experience of "School Dynamics" made a contribution towards your awareness of problems in the last teaching practice? 2. Do you think this experience is likely to be of use to you as a practising teacher? 3. Do you feel that worthwhile conclusions resulted from your discussion of situations? 4. Would you welcome more time in which to study the readings in greater depth with tutors?

On the subject of the readings, there was a positive response to the suggestion that students might be able to purchase the book! The one overwhelmingly negative response was to a suggestion that the size of tutorial groups be increased for a greater sharing of ideas. It was clear from the surveys of staff and student opinion that this program should be refined and expanded. The six most effective techniques as far as students were concerned were in order: role-play, guest speakers, close study of personal files, tape-slide programmes, panel discussions, and readings.

In ongoing research Ter-Morshuizen (1979) has, among other things, been examining two interesting topics related to the teaching of very young children and to the incidents and simulator. She has conducted a statistical analysis to determine (1) whether student teachers' evaluations of their pupils are based on superficial variables such as appearance, names, home background, and what is important for an examination of the simulation technique, and (2) whether they treat the simulated children as real children. It appears from preliminary statistical results that the students do in fact use the same superficial variables for the simulated as for the real children: they look on the simulated children as if they were real. This result confirms staff observation of the way in which students speak of the "children" and the situations as if they exist.

This kind of attempt to bring theory and practice together in early childhood teacher education involves much time, effort, and expertise. Materials have to be generated within the college to suit the needs of the area. Students and staff also have to be clear on the objectives of the course and of the case studies and devised situations. The rewards are increased student motivation, greater staff collaboration, and far more relevance and coherence in the course as a whole.

You may like to try out these ideas in your courses. I have found they work.

BIBLIOGRAPHY

Bishop, A. J., and Whitfield, R. C. *Situations in teaching*. London: McGraw Hill, 1972.

Cruickshank, D. R. *Teaching problems laboratory*. SRA Chicago, 1967.
_____. *Inner-city simulation laboratory*. SRA Chicago, 1969.
_____. Teacher education looks at simulation. In P. J. Tansey, (Ed.) *Educational aspects of simulation*. London: McGraw-Hill, 1971, 185-203.
Hirst, P. *Times higher education supplement*. 1974, 26, 4.
Johanson, S. K. A group communication programme in teacher education at Natal Training College, *Consulto*, Nov. 1979, *3*, 69.
Ter-Morshuizen, K. Unpublished ongoing M.Ed. Research, University of Natal, 1979.
Walford, R., *Coalstream*. University Department of Education, Cambridge, 1975.
Weber, W. A. et al., *C.B.T.E. A guide to competency based teacher education*. Westfield, Texas: 1973.
Zoll, A. A. *Dynamic management education*, Addison-Wesley, Reading, MA: 1969.

THE EARLY CHILDHOOD TRAINING COURSE

FOR BEDOUIN EDUCATORS

Rivka Dagan

Ministry of Education and Culture
Israel

The first Bedouin kindergarten was begun only six years ago
in Tel-Sheva, a modern Bedouin village near Beer-Sheva, with equipment provided by the Education office. The education laws had to
be explained to the Bedouin parents who had to be persuaded that
kindergarten education was important.

Since then, more and more school directors have requested the
Education office to institute kindergartens in their districts.
Today there are 21 kindergarten classrooms throughout the Northern
Negev from El-Huzzeil near Kibbutz Shuval to Tel Kassif near Arad,
a few miles from the Dead Sea.

Because the children live long distances from the schools their
main transportation to school is provided by little donkeys. At the
schools the donkeys can be seen patiently waiting in their special
parking areas until the children are ready to go home. Some children
arrive in family cars but no camels are to be seen around the school.
The desert ship is slowly disappearing from this area's landscape.

The extent to which the kindergarten has won a place in the
parents' minds as a preparation for future success in school is
evidenced by the growing number of Bedouin kindergartens. Because
of parental expectations special emphasis is placed on intellectual
development so that parents will be convinced that sending their
children to kindergarten is useful and profitable.

It has not been easy because Bedouin children have never gone
to kindergarten before nor have they had the opportunities to manipulate, to play, and to achieve the various levels of development
that children usually achieve in their earlier years. The Bedouin

151

children had to jump immediately into their chronological age group.

In monthly meetings, and individually, the teachers and I have tried to find ways to fulfill the children's needs. Didactive games and task accomplishment were emphasized. I asked the teachers to send home the children's finished work and teachers reported that the children were very proud when their parents complimented them on their progress.

I also asked the teachers to build the educational program around the Bedouin environment, the Bedouin nature, their habitations, their customs, their animals. To that end, I encouraged them to make home visits as it is not the custom of Bedouin mothers to come to school. I advised the teachers to arrange the doll corner like a Bedouin living room with carpets and pillows, and to dress the dolls in the beautiful embroidered dresses of the Bedouin so that the children would identify themselves with the doll corner. The children were very excited about the doll corner which reminded them of their homes; before they entered the doll corner they took off their shoes as they did in their own homes. The satisfaction the teachers saw on the children's faces gave them the feedback they needed and the strength to continue to work in the Negev, far away from their own homes.

The teachers were (and some still are) modern Arabian young ladies from the Galilee and so-called "triangle villages." (These villages are situated in an area between Haifa and Tel-Aviv. This geographical area is shaped like a triangle--hence the name.) They were sent by the Education office to work in the Bedouin section of the Negev after they graduated as a condition of their receiving work later on as educators in their home villages. In addition to the problems all new young teachers face these Arabian young ladies were homesick. Also, they did not know the Bedouin dialect so at the beginning the children did not understand them and they did not understand the children. Young Bedouin girls worked in the kindergarten as helpers and acted as interpreters.

The Arabian teachers were also not familiar with the Bedouin habits and customs which are different from their own. After two years in the Negev, when they finally had become adapted and knew the customs and dialect, they asked to be transferred to places near their home villages. These problems, as well as many absences from work, made it difficult to maintain a high level of kindergarten education.

The school directors who were responsible for the kindergartens were aware of these problems and decided to do something about them. When, on a typical stormy desert day, Dr. Nechama Nir, the Chief Inspector in Israel for the Early Childhood Education Department of the Ministry of Education and Culture and Bar-Ilan University,

came to visit the Bedouin kindergarten, two of the directors suggested that the Bedouin girls who acted as helpers, and who often sub-
stituted for the teachers when they were absent, should be trained
in a special course so that they could teach the children themselves.
The Bedouin girls knew the children, they understood the children's
language, were highly motivated, and would not leave the area.

Dr. Nir was enthusiastic about the idea for it provided a temporary answer to an urgent problem. With her active help and per-
suasion many bureaucratic technicalities were dissolved and the
special course was begun with myself as the tutor.

It was not easy to persuade the Bedouin fathers to send their
daughters to Beer-Sheva for the course. I spoke with a Sheik whose
two daughters wanted to take the course and told him that if he would
give his permission he would set a most important example for the
other fathers. The Sheik agreed that I could use his name to
convince other Bedouin fathers but only on the condition that I
would be responsible for the girls and that no males would teach
them. We found a quiet place for class and the fathers and brothers
who came at the beginning to see if everything was under control
were satisfied.

The teachers (all women, of course) and I did not know on what
level the course would be conducted. Fortunately, five Bedouin
young ladies who had graduated from high school joined the course
and the level of study naturally rose. The students came twice a
week for four hours each day. We began last year with teaching
Arabic language, Arabic literature, and Moslem culture taught by an
Arabian teacher. There were also lessons in Hebrew language, geography, psychology (T-group), and kindergarten theory and methodology.

At the beginning the girls were very shy but gradually they began to feel at ease and to know one another. They came from different Bedouin tribes which had very little contact with one
another but after a few months the girls began to feel like a real
group. We encouraged them to ask and say whatever they wanted to.
Eventually these girls, who at first were very suspicious of us,
began to have confidence in our good intentions.

In addition to the formal lessons we went several times to observe kindergartens in Beer-Sheva where we were very well accepted
by all the children and staff. Afterwards, I saw that the Bedouin
young ladies applied what they had seen during these observations
in their own kindergarten classrooms. In the summer there were ten
days of continuing courses which included handicraft lessons and
gymnastics and outdoor games.

At the end of the first year we asked the students what they
thought about the course: did they like it? Was the material

difficult for them to understand? Were they satisfied with their
teachers? One student wrote: "I am very happy that I am in this
course because if I did not have the opportunity to be here, who
knows, maybe not in ten years, maybe never, would I have the
chance to go out and learn." Another student wrote: "I cannot
accept the idea about the differences between Jews and Arabs. I
heard that Jews didn't like Arabs but after the Jewish teachers
have taught us I don't see any differences."

The second year we received a few more girls who had heard
about the course and wanted to join us. Today we have 25 students.
Since the Education office needed kindergarten teachers from the
North, five of these girls are already working as kindergarten
teachers. The others are continuing as helpers or are coming at
least twice a week to the kindergartens to observe. Consequently,
all the students have the opportunity to gain practical experience
in the kindergarten classroom. The second year lessons are on a
higher level than last year's and we require more homework in
hygiene, citizenship, science, psychology, and educational theory
and methodology. At the end of this second--and last--year the
students will take examinations and only those who pass successfully
will be able to work as kindergarten teachers though they will be
asked to continue their studies until graduation. Since the studies
were not at the required level the kindergarten teachers will continue to study while they are working.

This course is, of course, a temporary solution. In the
future we hope that Bedouin girls who graduate from high school
will enroll as a group in a regular seminar for educators as a
group of their own. The goal is for Bedouin kindergarten children
to some day have their own educators who will know their language,
dialect, customs, and habits and who will remain in the Negev.

SOME FACTORS AFFECTING TEACHER BEHAVIOR
AND PUPIL PERFORMANCE*

Dina Stachel

Tel Aviv University
Israel

The changes in education which occurred in the sixties were brought about by scientific and technological modernization, social and economic development and the democratization of the elementary level of education. These changes presented educators with new needs and demands for educational reforms (Adar, 1956, Feitelson; 1953; Nafthali, 1972) in curricula, teaching methods, and the organization of the educational system. In the area of curricula the change was manifested in the development of new programs in science and mathematics for the elementary school level (Gagné, 1965; Goodlad, 1966; Karplus, 1965; Schools Council, 1970), and in the development of a variety of specific programs for the kindergarten level.[1] In the field of teaching strategies were adapted to the individual differences among students (Brickell, 1964; Pinder, 1966; Standing, 1966). At the organization level, the new emphasis was on the development of alternative learning set-ups within one organizational structure and the adaptation of learning methods to the various organizational types.

However, in spite of financial resources invested in curricula development and in the implementation of innovative techniques and technologies, many of the programs failed to meet the expectations of their developers (Goodlad, 1964).

Major efforts during the sixties were directed toward changing the isolated elements in education, such as the teacher, the program

---

*This article is based on a Ph.D. dissertation carried out under the supervision of Prof. D. Chen and Dr. W. Harlen, Tel Aviv University, School of Education, 1977.

and the physical set-up of the classroom. Each of these elements
was studied separately within a limited framework (Goodlad, Von
Stoephasius & Klein). Most of the innovative ideas did not pene-
trate an entire educational system, however, and since they were
not an integral part of the system, they had only partial and limited influence.

In the present study, an empirical attempt was made to introduce a new science program into the educational system, to observe
the effects of this change, to try to understand the causes, and
to formulate a model which would clarify the relationships among the
variables of change and their outcomes. The new science program,
MATAL,[2] differs in its goals, content, and teaching methods from
the program presently existing in the kindergarten.

This new program is characterized as follows:

a) The content is related to various disciplines, in contrast
    to programs based on a distinct disciplinary approach.
b) Internal structure of the material is reflected in a defined
    system of graded concepts for learning purposes, and the
    activities are structured in a sequence with increasing
    levels of difficulty in ccntrast to the existing programs
    which are based on an eclectic, unstructured approach with
    the concepts submerged under much diffused information.
c) The character of the program requires a change from tradi-
    tional teaching strategy. Since the program is based on
    activity and on learning through discovery, the teaching
    material must be adapted to the individual differences in
    the children's ways of learning. The program is graded and
    structured to permit the child's learning pace to be taken
    into consideration. The teacher is required to make a
    transition from collective (frontal) activity to group and
    individual activities and a transition from teaching aimed
    mostly at imparting information to the development of ways
    of thinking and understanding how to learn.

The program is closely coordinated with mathematical skills and
there is an emphasis on language development throughout the program
as children need language to react to and represent what they discover in their environment. An attempt is also made to integrate
concrete experiences with the creative arts to encourage the child to
spontaneously express his individual experiences with the materials
of his choice.

The kindergarten classes for 5-year-olds were chosen as a target for change, since the kindergarten is a system administratively
and educationally independent within the educational system and thus
can be more easily controlled for experimental purposes. The kindergarten is supervised by a hierarchical structure which includes the

central administrative office, the central supervision of kindergarten office and the direct supervisor. Authority is exerted
through a vertical one-way flow of institutionalized input; from
the central system through the direct supervisor into the kindergarten. Therefore, introducing any change into the kindergarten
is entirely dependent upon acceptance of the change by the control
system.

    This structure is illustrated in Figure 1.

    Our strategy for change was based on a system approach with
system components identified as the central supervisory office,
the direct supervisor, the kindergarten teacher and the students.
Input was related to the content of teaching, the teaching and the
organization. In terms of content, the input was a new program

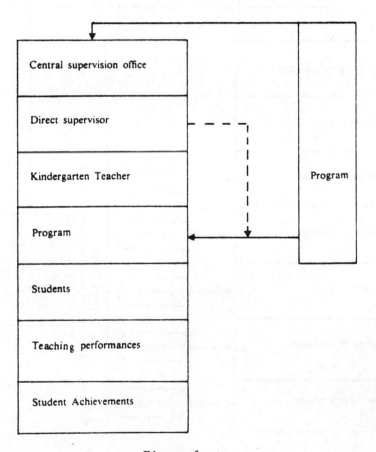

Figure 1.

and new teaching materials. In the field of teaching, a different
teaching strategy, a new program for training courses and a new
program for guidance were developed. As opposed to the vertical
flow of input which characterized the existing model, input in the
research model was horizontal and simultaneously directed towards
all the identified components of the system. Through this approach
we attempted to have the output expressed as a change in classroom
processes, teaching performances and student achievements.

The new model is illustrated in Figure 2.

In order to help the teacher implement the program the research
staff arranged for:

. Preliminary exposure of the teachers to the program content
and teaching strategies through a course held the year before

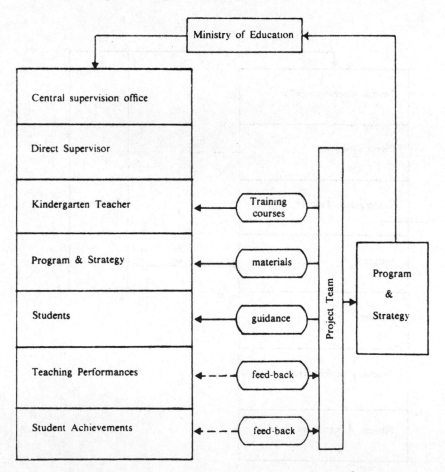

Figure 2.

the program was implemented.

. Fostered the supervisors' awareness of the objectives and
content of the program through explanatory lectures, courses
and guided visits to trial classes.

. Supplied the teacher and students with all the equipment
necessary for the implementation of the program and initiated
a supportive system of teacher-trainers composed of teachers who
demonstrated mastery of the theoretical background of the program and who were successful in program implementation. The
teacher-trainers assisted the new implementers in their classes
and helped in facilitating the transition period at the initial
stage of implementation.

. Developed a circular feed-back system in order to evaluate
the program and the implementation model. The feed-back system
included the kindergarten teachers, the teacher-trainers who
guided the kindergarten teachers, the supervisors who visited
the classes and observed the teachers, the teacher-trainers,
and the observers of the project who visited the classes and
observed the processes of implementation and the outcome.
In this model major emphasis is given to the interaction among
the components of the system as a means of bringing forth change
in the kindergarten.

Before the experiment[3] took place, two primary hypotheses were
formulated:

1)   The kindergarten is a system: educational change will be
     achieved through the operation of a change factor and the
     involvement of all the components of the system in making
     the change.
2)   The level of change will be lowered if a supporting change
     agent is not present among the components of the system.

We further assumed that within each one of the two treatments
which follow from these hypotheses variation in the levels of change
will result from the attitudes of the supervisors to the program and
the supporting change agent and their relations with the change
agent. Therefore, two secondary hypotheses followed the major ones:

3)   Negative attitudes of the supervisors towards the elements
     of change will lower the level of change, even with the
     existence of the supporting change agent.
4)   Positive attitudes of the supervisors towards the elements
     of change will raise the level of change, even with the
     absence of the supporting change agent.

SUBJECTS AND METHODOLOGY

In order to examine the above-mentioned hypotheses, two groups
of kindergarten classes were chosen. The two groups consisted of 20
classes each--a total of 872 students. The classes were located in
the Tel Aviv region and the central region of the country. The 40
teachers were chosen according to their professional status (all
were qualified teachers), tenure, and their supervisor's evaluation.
The ten supervisors participating in the experiment each supervised
four classes: two classes of Group A and two classes of Group B.
Four teacher-trainers worked with the 20 classes of Group A.

Group A: This group included the teachers, the students, and
the supervisors. In this group, the change was introduced through
the entire supporting system; that is, the project team and the
change agents (the teacher-trainers). The teachers attended extensive training courses prior to the implementation of the program.
Further extensive training was given throughout the implementation
period concerning the subject matter related to the program and
special treatment of problems which followed the implementation
process. Intensive guidance was given by the teacher-trainers who
supported the teachers by their pragmatic implementation of the
program in the classroom. Their work was on an individual and concrete level. An extensive course was available for the supervisors,
conducted by the project team and dealing with the principles of the
program and ideas for change and innovation.

The work in Group A was characterized by having the daily activities of the program carried out with either small groups of six
children or with individual children. Teaching was based mostly
on self activity of children who could use objects and materials
suggested in the program and available in their immediate environment. The teacher received individual guidance in her class on the
theoretical and pragmatic aspects of the program such as explanation and extension of the written material; explanation of concepts
unknown to the teacher; help in adjusting the activities suggested
in the program to the level of the class or group; organization of
learning space; organization of learning time; and use and maintenance of equipment. The teachers visited various schools and observed the work of different teachers. They were also engaged in
discussion groups to exchange ideas and clarify problems.

Group B: This group included the teacher, the students, and
the same supervisors as in Group A. The written program and the
mateirals were sent to the kindergartens, but the teachers did not
attend any course prior to the implementation, nor did they receive
any assistance throughout the implementation period.

In this group the program was carried out in a fashion similar
to the existing kindergarten practices in which content is chosen

by the teacher, activities are predominantly verbal and characterized by frontal class work, and experimentation is usually accompanied by frontal demonstrations presented by the teacher. Except for activities related to dramatic or constructive play,
"group" activities exist mainly in the field of creative arts where
children are found sitting in groups but are most often working individually.

To evaluate the changes in the educational system, ten measuring instruments were designed with which we attempted to measure
attitudes of the participants, knowledge of the teaching team, teaching performances in the classroom, utilization of time, students'
achievements, and interpersonal relationships. The relationships
among the various components of the system were analyzed using
cluster analysis, which was programmed for classifying qualitative
data.

The relationships between the components of the system and the
objects of the research are illustrated in Figure 3.

FINDINGS

The major hypotheses were empirically established: the kindergarten operated as an educational system and change occurred when
the change factors operated in all of the components of the system.
The role of the change agent was significant. The analysis of the
findings for the entire population revealed the existence of relationships among the factors of change (input), processes, and output.
Within this framework, the following profiles can be described:

   (1) Maximum output, as measured through change in student
        achievement and teaching performance, was achieved by
        the presence of the supporting change agent (teacher-
        trainers), a high level of teacher knowledge of the pro-
        gram, and positive interpersonal relationships between the
        change agent and the operating elements in the system.
   (2) A decrease in the relative levels of output, as measured
        above, was related to the absence of the supporting change
        agent (teacher-trainers), the absence of interpersonal
        relationships between the operating elements in the system,
        and an inferior level of knowledge on the part of the
        teacher.

Analysis of the findings for the population of Group A revealed the
following profiles:

   (3) Maximum output, as measured through change in student
        achievement and teaching performance, was achieved by the
        presence of the supporting change agent (teacher-trainer),

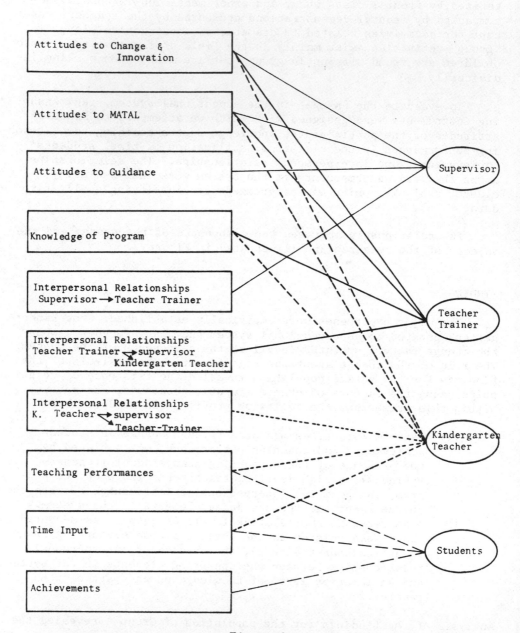

Figure 3.

a high level of teacher knowledge of the program, and
positive interpersonal relationships between the change
agent and the operating elements in the system.

(4)   No change in the relative level of output, as measured
above, was achieved through the presence of the supporting change agent, an average level of knowledge on the part
of the teacher, and a negative attitude of the supervisor
towards the program and the change agent.

Analysis of the findings for the population of Group B revealed
the following profiles:

(5)   No change in the relative output was related to the absence
of the supporting change agent, an average level of knowledge on the part of the teacher, and a positive attitude
of the supervisor towards the new program and positive interpersonal relationships with the teacher.

(6)   A decrease in the relative level of output, as measured
above, was related to the absence of the supporting change
agent (teacher-trainers), the absence of interpersonal
relationships between the operating elements in the system,
and an inferior level of knowledge on the part of the teacher.

On the basis of these findings, a model was developed which
suggests a qualitative relationship between the change which operates
in the system and the variables of the system. The model was described as follows:

$$C = F \cdot \frac{t N_s P}{R(r_1 r_2 \cdot \cdot \cdot r_n)}$$

Key

C   = Level of change in the system
t   = Time devoted to the implementation of the change
Ns = Number of sub-systems
P   = Permeability of the system
R   = General resistance of the system to change
r_1, r_2 = Resistance of sub-systems

It can be generalized that the level of change is in direct
ratio to the time devoted to the implementation of the change, the
number of sub-systems into which the change is introduced, and the
amount of permeability of the total system. The level of change is
in inverse ratio to the general resistance of the system (or its sub-
systems).

The details of the changes which took place in the system can be summarized as follows:

(1) The attitudes of the two groups of teachers towards the new program demonstrated a tendency to concentrate on an average, accepted system; no major qualitative change occurred during the experiment.

(2) The teachers of Group A, who received assistance from a supporting change agent, exhibited more openness towards change and innovation in early childhood education.

(3) The attitudes of the supervisors towards teacher-trainers demonstrated reserve and lack of involvement.

(4) The test of knowledge of the program had a total of 26 possible points. Teacher-trainers achieved an average mark of 20.5; Group A teachers averaged 16.4 and Group B teachers achieved an average mark of 12.5.

(5) A qualitative improvement in teaching performance and in student achievements was observed in Group A, in contrast to a qualitative decrease in the same measures in Group B.

(6) Utilization of time on class work and group work devoted to activities of the MATAL Program was higher in Group A.

(7) A low correlation existed between the teacher's level of knowledge of the program and change in the students' achievements. A low correlation existed between the amount of time spent on class work and group work activities related to the program and the change in students' achievements.

IMPLICATIONS OF FINDINGS

From this research it seems that in order to introduce a change initiated outside the direct educational system, the following acts should be taken into consideration:

A. Supplying the teachers with all the resources necessary for the implementation.

B. Exposing the entire staff of participants to the contents of change through courses held prior to the implementation.

C. Centering the content of the courses in three areas; basic knowledge of the subject matter; pragmatic skills; and attitudes.

D. Developing a support system, the major objective of which is to help during the primary stages of the implementation.

E. Introducing the change simultaneously in all the components of the educational system.

F. Fostering interpersonal relationships, especially among the upper levels of the educational hierarchy.

G. Developing a circular feedback system in order to receive
information about the level of implementation and to locate
problems occurring during the process.

FOOTNOTES

1. See Bereiter & Engelmann, 1966; Camp, 1973; Evans, 1971; Nimnicht,
1973; Spodek, 1973; Weikart, Dennis, Lawser & Weigerink, 1970;
in Israel--Bilski-Cohen, 1974; Fajans-Glick, 1975; Lombard,
1973; Smilansky, 1973; Stachel, 1975.
2. The MATAL kindergarten science teaching program is part of the
elementary science project developed at Tel-Aviv University in
conjunction with the Israel Center for Science Teaching and
the Ministry of Education and Culture.
3. The experiment continued throughout an entire school year from
October 1974 until the end of June 1975.

BIBLIOGRAPHY

Adar, L. A study on the scholastic difficulties of immigrant children.
Megamot, Behavioral Science Quarterly, 1956, *7,* 139-180 (Hebrew).
Bereiter, C., & Engelmann, S. *Teaching disadvantaged children in the
preschool.* Englewood Cliffs, NJ: Prentice Hall, 1966.
Bilski-Cohen, R., & Melnik, N. *The use of creative movement for the
development of concept formation and intellectual ability in
young culturally disadvantaged children.* Jerusalem: The Hebrew
University of Jerusalem, School of Education, 1974.
Brickell, H.N. State of organization for educational change: A case
study and a proposal. In M.B. Miles (Ed.), *Innovation in education.* New York: Bureau of Publications, Teachers College, Columbia University, 1964.
Camp, J.C. A skill development curriculum for 3- 4- and 5-year-old
disadvantaged children. In B. Spodek (Ed.), *Early childhood
education.* Englewood Cliffs, NJ: Prentice Hall, Viewpoints
and Alternatives Series, 1973.
Schools Council. Early experiences. *Dialogue No. 6,* August 1970.
Evans, E.D., *Behavior analysis procedures in contemporary influences
in early childhood education.* New York: Holt, Rinehart and
Winston, 1971.
Fajans-Glick, S. The intensive method for deprived children. *Hed
Hagan, Periodical for Early Childhood Education,* 1975, *40,* 62-
69.
Feitelson, D. *Causes of scholastic failure among first grades.* Jeru-
salem: Henrietta Szold Institute, 1953 (Hebrew).
Gagné, R.M. Psychological issues in science--A process approach.
In *The psychological bases of science--A process approach.*
Washington, DC: American Association for the Advancement of
Science, 1965.

Goodlad, J.I. *School curriculum reform in the United States*. New York: The Fund for the Advancement of Education, 1964.

Goodlad, J.I., von Stoephasius, R., & Klein, F. *The changing school curriculum: A report from the Fund for the Advancement of Education*. New York: 1966.

Karplus, R. *Theoretical background of the science curriculum improvement study, SCIS*. Berkeley: University of California, 1965.

Lombard, A.D. *Home instruction program for preschool youngsters (HIPPY). Final Report*. Jerusalem: The Hebrew University of Jerusalem, 1973.

Nafthali, N. *The socially and culturally disadvantaged child in early childhood in Israel: Characteristics and compensatory curricula*. Jerusalem: Van Leer Foundation, Seminar on Curriculum in Compensatory Early Childhood Education, 1972.

Nimnicht, G. Overview of responsive model program. In B. Spodek (Ed.), *Early childhood education*. Englewood Cliffs, NJ: Prentice-Hall, 1973.

Pinder, R. Non-streaming in comprehensive schools. Conference Report. *Forum*, 1966, *9*(1), 4-9.

Smilansky, S., & Shepathiah, L. *Preventing scholastic failure of culturally disadvantaged children through reading instruction in kindergarten*. Jerusalem: The Henrietta Szold Institute. Research Report No. 171, Publication No. 524, 1973 (Hebrew).

Spodek, B. *Contemporary models in early childhood education*. Englewood Cliffs, NJ: Prentice-Hall, Viewpoints and Alternative Series, 1973.

Stachel, D. The structure of "Matal" Program for kindergarten children age five. *Hed Hagan*, 1975, *40*(1), 47-61 (Hebrew).

Standing, E.M., *The Montessori revolution in education*. New York: Schocken Books, 1966.

Weikart, D.P., Dennis, J.D., Lawser, S.A., & Weigerink, R. Longitudinal results of the Ypsilanti Perry Preschool Project. Ypsilanti, MI: *Monographs of the High Scope Educational Research Foundation*, 1970, Project No. 2494.

HOW ONE CITY GOT PARENTS INVOLVED

Evelyn A. Benas

Merritt College
Oakland, California

INTRODUCTION

The city of Oakland in the State of California, USA, extending along the mainland side of San Francisco Bay, opposite the Golden Gate and the cosmopolitan metropolis of San Francisco, is an urban community of some 360,000 persons. Oakland is a city of many diverse ethnic, language and socioeconomic groups, a significant number of working mothers and a growing population of single parent households.

This paper is based upon experiences gained and information acquired while working with children and parents from Oakland. Conclusions drawn in the paper derive from personal and clinical studies, spanning more than a decade of experience, rather than from research, per se.

The primary purpose of this paper is to describe how both preschool children and their parents can be involved in a program which strengthens parenting skills and provides healthy growth and development opportunities for children.

OBJECTIVES

The objectives of this dual program include the following:

1) To increase knowledge not only of the development and behavior patterns of one's own preschool child, but also of general human development; and to apply this new information when necessary.

2)   To enable parents to see the value of using newly acquired
skills and knowledge at home as a way of enhancing the healthy
growth and development of their child. For example, by observing and discussing how play influences all areas of a child's
development (physical, social, emotional, intellectual), parents
become aware of the importance of play to their child. As parents no longer perceive play as just a way of occupying a child's
time, the value of play takes on a different and more important
meaning than before. Many parents begin to critically evaluate
their child's play at home and by doing so consciously begin
providing in the home environment a schedule, space, materials,
and equipment conducive to play experiences far richer than
previously offered.

3)   To work with parents and their preschool children in order
to improve the child's health, nutrition and successful development during the early years and beyond. Physical, social,
emotional and intellectual development are usually intertwined
and often a child's success in physically climbing something,
such as a tree, may affect later academic success. For instance,
most parents understand how a child's confident mastery of a
jungle gym helps physical, social and emotional development.
However, many parents cannot relate successfully climbing a
jungle gym with intellectual development, let alone, future
mastery of academic subjects. However, by discussing how a
preschooler learns to control bodily movements in space by
climbing and then relating this activity to the spatial skills
needed when learning to read or write or compute, parents gain
an understanding of growth and development as an intertwining
continuum.

4)   To give preschool children enrichment experiences.

5)   To help strengthen or teach parents skills designed
to   help the child, and to open new areas of thought regarding children's behavior and learning. The intention is not
to   make parents into teachers, or group leaders, although
many develop such ease with the children that they are encouraged to take some formal training and education and to continue working with children professionally.

LIMITATIONS OF THIS PAPER

1)   This paper describes only one type of parent education
class--the parent-child observation class.

2)   A history of adult education in California, USA, under
the aegis of which parent-child observation classes evolved,

is not covered.

3) No attempt is made to discuss parent education classes
elsewhere in the United States.

4) Further, no attempt is made to compare adult education
with early childhood education philosophies nor to analyze the
literature of these two disciplines.

5) No effort is made to discuss the variety of early childhood,
child development, or parent education programs now common in
the United States.

6) The paper is limited to gaining an understanding of how the
parents of preschoolers are successfully involved in a program
with their children and the benefits derived from this involvement.

7) Concepts and conclusions presented in the paper are empirical,
and are drawn from more than ten years of personal classroom and
administrative experiences. While this approach is legitimate
for purposes of this paper, it in no way eliminates the desire
and need for further research on the subject.

THE PROGRAM: A PARENT-TEACHER PARTNERSHIP

A) General Information

The program differs in many ways from other parent education
programs in the state of California. The children comprise our
laboratory class, in which parents are able to observe their own
child at play, to participate in the children's program as "parent-
teachers," and to interact in parent group discussions.

B) Definitions

There are three major participants in this program: parents,
children and teachers. For the purpose of this paper these participants will be defined as follows:

Parent: Either the mother or father or guardian or relative of
a child or a paid caregiver who has continuous daily responsibility
for the care of the child. At one time, parent-child observation
classes were designed to serve only mothers and their preschool
children. Inclusion of fathers or other relatives was rare, usually
reserved for a special occasion. Gradually, fathers and other relatives became class members; however, it was several years after their

acceptance that paid caregivers were also welcomed.

Children: Preschool age boys or girls (age 2 1/2 to 5 1/2 years) who are attending the programs with their parent.

Teacher: Credentialed adult educators, male and female, who have obtained a B.A. degree or higher and have acknowledged expertise in early childhood education and child growth and development. This expertise may have been gained through formal education or relevant field experience or a combination of both. Two teachers, responsible for one parent-child observation class and working as a team, rotate responsibility equally between the children's nursery school program and the parents' observation and discussion program.

C. Program Structure

The parent-child observation project includes at least seven classes for parents (about 240 parents). Each class meets one morning a week for three hours in a community facility which provides opportunity for both indoor and outdoor activities. These classes include a program of planned activities with the child as the participant and the parent as the observer. This constitutes half of the three-hour class. The other half of the class-time is spent by the parents in discussion with the teacher on various aspects of preschool development while the children's program continues.

A parent is more likely to attend class and be receptive to ideas if all her young children are with her and are receiving good care. Consequently, we accept not only all preschool children from any one family but also infants. Infants, however, are not allowed in the program, but are cared for (usually by a grandmother), in a special infant room, thereby enabling parents to participate in the program.

We do not separate the children by ages. Although the mixing of ages makes it more difficult for the teachers to develop a workable program, it does create a more realistic situation for parents and hence is of more value in terms of parent education. (It is likely that this practice is also more valuable in terms of what children learn from each other.) What better way to teach parents the developmental stages of their children than to have parents see these stages unfold before their eyes in the behavior and activities of the children? Age groupings do occur during snack or special activities and, more often than not, most children choose activities appropriate for their age or skills without undue adult direction. At the beginning of the morning the parents observe their own child's actions and relationships to other children and

adults. In most instances, they record their observations on simple
record sheets which are used later in discussion periods.

D. Program Philosophy

     Our general philosophy in the parent-child observation program
is to involve parents in a different way from the more familiar
nursery school, day care center, parent-cooperative nursery school,
or the government-funded Head Start Programs. We offer a different
dimension in parent education. Parents observe their own child at
play and keep a weekly record. At the end of the year, parents
write a summary of observations, providing, in essence, a record of
their children's growth and development.

     Each week, parents talk about what happens with their children
either at home or at school. This use of observation of and discussion on child growth and development and family life helps adults
of varied backgrounds feel comfortable within the program.

     The program encourages adults to actively participate and self-
learn rather than to passively listen to "experts" talk about what
should be done with children. Having parents watch everything that
is going on makes teachers and parents active partners in the process of parent education.

     The program supports parents' willingness to do the best pos-
sible things for their children as it is this desire that truly
opens the door for adult learning. Adults do not easily change
closely held personal convictions, especially in so highly an emotional area as family lifestyles and child rearing practices.

     The program is designed to aid parents utilize at home the de-
velopmental understandings and teaching techniques they have gained
in the parent-child observation class.

     As parents observe their children, they are encouraged to ques-
tion teacher techniques and philosophy. For example, parents might
ask why teachers did a certain thing in a certain way with children.
In answering these questions teachers are able to offer child growth
and development theories which directly relate to a specific parent
and her/his child. In addition to this type of individual interaction between parent and teacher, each week's observations are read
and the teachers make comments or give answers to questions noted.

     Over and over again it is emphasized in class that everybody
is learning--child, parent and teacher (sometimes teacher most of
all). Teachers do not claim that their rules and techniques are
perfect nor that they should necessarily be accepted by the parent.

Teachers do encourage questions and comments about what is done in the program and, while acceptance of the program's philosophy is hoped for, teachers fully realize that adults change their attitudes very slowly in areas of deep personal meaning. For instance, child-rearing practices such as attitudes towards discipline, especially spanking, have deep personal meaning to many parents. Since one class rule is never to spank a child, parents who believe in spanking as a way to properly rear a child must be allowed to voice unhappiness over the rule and be expected to question it with intensity.

Despite this realization, it is asked that parents abide by the rules and techniques used within the nursery school. The rules are as follows:

1) A child is never spanked, threatened or punished.

2) Children are never left unsupervised.

3) No child is allowed to hurt another child, himself or an adult.

4) No child is allowed to do anything that would endanger himself or another child.

5) No child is allowed to be destructive to nursery school property.

In all fairness, a child may be truly creative when he paints a wall or takes a chair apart. However, from an adult view point such activities are expensive and therefore are limited in our program.

Apart from rules the general assumption within the program is that "what is not forbidden is allowed." In such an atmosphere, creativity, intellectual curiosity, problem-solving, individuality, and self-discipline flourish. Parents are not unaware of the interactions they observe as children play in this environment. Parents, even if they do not carry all our theories into the home situation, gain new understandings of how different approaches to child rearing influence a child's behavior, growth, development, and learning style.

E. The Children's Program

In order to observe children, our program is set up to allow for the maximum amount of freedom for the children. Adults are asked to step back, to permit only a minimum amount of direction of children, and to let children interact among themselves naturally.

Essentially, the program attempts to create a "child's world" which is safe and interesting.

To do this, an inter-disciplinary approach, incorporating many theories dealing with many elements of human development, is used to build a creative program. For instance, reference to and use of are made of the theories of people such as the following: Gesell and Ames (importance of physical developmental stages); Erikson (personality development as related to childhood and society); Piaget (intellectual developmental stages); Montessori (use of special toys and techniques to aid intellectual development); Mead (an anthropological viewpoint); Ginott, Baruch, Bettleheim, Redl (sociological and psychological approaches to behavior, discipline, and family relations); Brazelton and Spock (health standards and an overall philosophy to childrearing, beginning with infancy).

Based on a summation of this information, the program stresses play activities which teach children something. However, a concern is held for what children are learning not only from the educational point of view, but also from the human point of view. Therefore, each activity in the program has some value for the children's total development.

All program activities are set up in such a way that parents are able to duplicate them at home. (Modeling behavior for parents to observe and duplicate is a continuing teaching priority.)

F. The Adult Program

As with the children's program, personality development, physical development, emotional development, intellectual development, and social development are all considered equally important parts of the adult education program. It is felt that the quality of the children's program determines the quality of the adult education program. Consequently, the structure of our dual program is designed to ensure that every effort is made to "practice what we preach."

Parent-child observation classes involve the parent in a weekly three-fold child development and parent education program.

1) As an observer and recorder, the parent writes a 30 minute observation of his/her child while playing.

2) Under supervision of the teacher, parents themselves become teachers in the nursery school program.

3) When not participating as a parent-teacher, the parents become students, lead by the teacher in a 90 minute discussion group. About 20% of the students become "parent-teachers" every fourth to sixth week. Eighty percent of the students are participants in the observation and discussion periods.

THE ROLE OF THE PARENT

I. The Parent as an Observer and Recorder
    of His/Her Own Child

     Observations are usually written, but may be oral. Observing
one's own child is a key method used to develop new parenting skills
which will help the parent understand the meaning of his/her child's
behavior. Observations also provide a means of introducing theories
of growth and development to parents in a non-threatening way.

     To facilitate observing and recording a few simple things, such
as pencils, observation sheets, and a heavy folder used as a writing
board and file, are provided for parents. In addition, children wear
name tags, color-coded to differentiate age groupings. (Both folders
and tags are stored in the classroom.)

     Parents are encouraged to write down whatever they see their
children doing. Teachers read each weekly observation and jot down
encouraging comments on how to see more or what a certain behavior
might mean developmentally.

     Many parents are initially hesitant or resistant toward writing
a weekly record. Some feel it is a waste of time; others are concerned about grammatical and spelling mistakes, or whether the teacher will be able to decipher their handwriting. Some comments have
been, "What is there to write about?", or, "I can't spell." However, parents are reassured that the teacher's interest in the observation is in getting to know the child better and in having the
parent utilize the observations in her class work and at home. The
writing of observations begins slowly and cautiously, but resistance
and hesitancy gradually diminish as the mother becomes involved, and
at times enthralled, watching her own child.

     Sometimes, however, writing or recording is impossible, be-
cause the parent is unable to read or write, or cannot express observations fluently in the English language. A variety of methods
have been used to combat this problem. One blind mother, for instance, came with a friend. The friend observed the child and later
read these daily observations to the mother. The mother transcribed
the notes into braille for a permanent record of her daughter's
activities. In another instance, parents in one class were asked
to simply observe certain things their children were doing and to
later review their observations orally during the discussion time.
The observation and discussion sessions have continually revealed
that parents, whether illiterate or literate, are keen observers
of their own children.

     Observing during class time allows parents to become aware

of actually how much they can learn about their child by simply
watching them, while recording gives them a permanent and ongoing
record of their children's activities and behavior. This dual
act of observing and recording offers a rare opportunity for parents to compare their children's behavior from week to week and to
raise to a conscious level the full value of observation as a tool
for positive parenting.

Recording also gives parents a chance to analyze their own
thoughts about their children as well as to develop answers to
questions such as, "Why is this happening?", "How come he acts this
way?", "How well does my child play with other children?". Since
one of the objectives of the class is to allow children to interact with the minimum of adult intervention, only teachers and "parent-teachers" are accountable for the children's activities. This
allows the "observing parent" to be free of responsibility while she
records her child at play.

Despite this stress on non-active interaction during the observation period, most mothers are physically very close to their
child and the proximity appears reassuring to both. Although a
child is free to go to his/her mother at any time, contrary to
creating dependency, as one might predict, the opposite appears true.
Children play with freedom and confidence, seemingly oblivious to
mother.

Since one of our "rules" is not to use textbooks, parents discover, by using their own observation skills, how 2-, 3- and 4-year-
olds differ. Over a three week period, utilizing a special observation form, all parents observe children by age groupings. (This is
also a relatively non-threatening way of having mothers observe one
another's children.) Each successive week, all 2-year-olds, 3-year-
olds and 4-year-olds are observed. Observations are discussed in small
groups and a certain behavior is identified: for example, how many
times did a child contact his/her parent, another adult, another
child? The groups then come together to compare their findings.
A large chart is made as each age group is studied. In the fourth
week, all age groups are compared and an attempt is made to generalize patterns of behavior. For instance, it is observed yearly how
frequently 2-year-olds contact the parent, such contacts becoming
less frequent by age 3 and almost non-existent by age four. ("Oh,
my two year old isn't spoiled or babyish, he's acting his age!"
is not an uncommon self-discovery comment.)

Parents become aware of general principles of growth and development in their children by using their own powers of observation
and analysis. Without exception, regardless of literacy or education, each group doing this unit inevitably identifies (with almost
textbook precision) most of the characteristics of growth and develop-

ment found during the preschool years. At a recent reunion of my
classes, many parents brought along their observation folders. Even
after ten years, these observations were valued.

Observations are used in many ways throughout the year, and at
term's end the parents choose and compile a description of some
particular area of their children's development.

The following seem to be valid conclusions arising from the
observation sessions:

1) Most mothers find it threatening to have some person other
than herself observe or judge her child; and

2) while most observations are seldom "objective," most
parents are keen observers, and their recording skills progressively improve in clarity and definitiveness. The parent's
recordings are generally accepted without criticism.

II. The Parent As A Teacher

Each week at least five parents become teachers within the
children's program. The credentialed parent education teacher is
responsible for the overall nursery school schedule and the supervision of parents working with the children. Parents select their
teaching days and activities, and usually participate eight to ten
times during the school year. Upon arrival, each teaching-parent
selects the card describing a specific activity responsibility,
while each observing parent takes an observation folder. The teaching-parent dons a red apron and begins working with the children.

The red apron enables children to identify those adults who
are ready and able to help them. There are often as many as 35
adults on the premises. Long before children learn the identities
of individual adults, they understand the meaning of the "red apron."

Parents are not expected to perform as if they were credentialed teachers, but rather to use their own talents and parenting skills
in a nursery school setting. They are, however, under the direction
of a credentialed teacher and constrained by some simple rules.
These rules help provide an atmosphere in which children and adults
may grow in skills and self-satisfaction. With the diversity in
parenting styles, religion, ethnicity, economic status, amount of
education, age, and marital status, developing a harmonious environment was a challenge. Nevertheless, by working alongside the parents
to find a solution to this challenge we arrived at a workable answer.

The answer was that parents are not expected to change their
child-rearing values, but only to abide by these rules for the sake

of class harmony during the three hour work period. Most parents, though some very reluctantly, agree to try new means of discipline.

At the end of the day, parent-teachers and the teacher meet for a review of successful or disastrous activities, puzzling or pleasing behavior of children and general concerns. Many of the themes covered during discussion are reintroduced at these short meetings, thus encouraging parents to utilize principles of growth and development in their practical work with children.

Being a "parent-teacher" may be frightening to those inexperienced in handling groups of children. However, these parents are maintaining homes, providing their families with a myriad of services and bringing in added income from outside employment. Consequently, transferring these valuable life experiences to preschool routines is not as insurmountable as many would expect. Parents are encouraged to choose those activities with which they feel comfortable or enjoy. By using the strengths and interests of the parent students, the children's program is enriched, and parents gain a new appreciation of their homemaking or career skills. Gradually, feelings of competency increase as parents become more responsive to trying new techniques with children or considering another's point of view as worthy of respect.

The program does not employ tests or grades to assess progress of either parent and/or child. Instead, learning is measured by changes in the behavior or attitudes of the mother and/or the child. Inasmuch as the child is involved in only three hours of school a week, changes must be attributed to parental influences rather than the teacher's. As parents participate, they become familiar with materials, and how and when to use them. Hopefully, such familiarity will make it easier for parents to transfer nursery school activities to the home environment.

When parents don red aprons, they take on a role unfamiliar to their children. Helping children handle feelings of jealousy, envy, or anxiety as they share their parents with other children is made easier in the warm and supportive environment of the class. Parents are also disquieted when their usually gentle child hits, or their carefree child clings, or their cheerful child mopes. These behaviors are unsettling, especially when parents know many a pair of eyes are upon them and their child. The teachers try to reduce stress by encouraging parents to meet their child's needs with an extra hug or other such extra attention. In addition, these experiences become discussion period themes and parents share with one another how they feel when their child interferes with participation duties or how they have successfully handled such situations.

As parents become more at ease and experienced with the group of children, they begin to realize that participation is not the

drudgery it first appeared to be, but rather that it is intimately
tied to their observation and discussion activities and is a very
practical way of learning more about children and themselves. Many
parents, because of the participation experience, are now pursuing
careers in child care, recreation or teaching.

III. <u>The Parent as a Group Discussion
      Participant</u>

Program staff are concerned at the beginning of each semester
as they wonder how they will be able to lead interesting discussions
with parents who exhibit such diverse needs and goals. As parents
and staff meet week after week, however, it is not long before an
atmosphere of warmth, support and acceptance develops and it is
realized that discussion times serve not only to share information
about parenting theories, but also to learn more about one another
as parents and people.

As the semester progresses, discussions tend to reflect what
is of relevant interest to parents. To ascertain these interests
a course outline, evaluated yearly by the parents and re-written at
timely intervals by the teacher, is used as a general guide and
evaluation tool. As parents make their needs, concerns and questions known, teachers incorporate specific problems into broader
general topics.

Discussion time is informal, a time for simple refreshments
and relaxation. Sometimes guest speakers are invited, or movies,
role-playing or "buzz" group techniques are used. At one time a
class decided that parents should bring something homemade to the
discussions--something that would reflect a person's ethnic or
religious heritage or geographical roots. With the teacher's encouragement, parents talked about their "time honored" values in
a rapidly changing world. In a less serious vein, recipes were
exchanged, as were traditional ways of celebrating holidays. Many
discussions are delightfully entertaining and even funny, others
quite deep, serious and at times personal. The teacher must be constantly alert to maintain his or her position as a discussion facilitator, not a group therapist.

Discussion time is not always used for talking. Activities
observed by parents are often introduced. For example, following
observation and discussion of how children use art materials
(paints, finger-painting, clay) parents are encouraged to use these
same materials. Experiencing what their child may be feeling, and
gaining an insight into the delight and satisfaction which comes
with using art materials gives parents a chance to do more than
discuss the value of art in the life of a child. Other bonuses of

this practice often accrue. Some parents who have never played with art materials, even as children, soon change their attitudes about using such "messy" materials, and not only provide these materials at home for their children, but also seek out adult classes for themselves.

Parents consider discussion time the "highlight" of their week. They look forward to talking with other adults, relaxing and having a break from the routines of mothering and homemaking. Involving parents and keeping them involved are best done when topics meet needs pertinent to their lives, and the lives and well-being of their children and families. For instance, during one discussion, the question was raised as to how important good eyesight is to overall development. After sessions, which included movies and speakers from local agencies and a general discussion, the mothers voted to have an eye-screening program presented in class. An optometrist tested the eyes of all of the children in each family. A very shy, clinging child was diagnosed as being extremely near-sighted. On the first day to class with his new glasses, he walked out in the yard he had once feared, hopped upon a tricycle and pedaled away. That marked the first day his mother attended the discussion period without having her son come looking for her in a panic. No lecture by the most renowned health expert could have been more convincing as to the importance of early detection of eye defects than the change in behavior parents saw in this little boy. Eye screening and eventually hearing and speech testing became annual events in most classes.

IV. The Role of the Father

Fathers must be involved if the program is to have optimum success. It is much easier for new ideas to be introduced within the family if the father is supportive of these ideas. We have not been able to develop a viable program for fathers because of our budget. However, we have tried several very successful activities with fathers. For the past five years, classes have met with fathers for a once-a-year group discussion. The men wanted more such discussions. After the fathers came to this "Discussion for Dads" our entire program improved.

The men began to support their wives when new ideas were suggested at home. Husbands told their wives that they felt attending parent-child observation class was important and they were proud of the extra effort on the part of their wives. Men became more involved in what their children were doing and did more things with their children. Husbands would regularly ask their wives what happened at nursery school and what topics were discussed by the mothers. More recently, if working arrangements permit, fathers

attend class regularly in lieu of another adult. In one instance
traditional roles were switched with the father becoming a house-
husband and the wife continuing her highly successful and well paying career in the fashion industry.

V.   Parent Recruitment

A variety of methods (generally those the supervisor and teachers
believe will appeal to the adults of each particular neighborhood)
are used to recruit parents into the program. One method used is
the written announcement. Worded in simple language, announcements
are usually presented either in Spanish and/or Chinese with English.
Television, radio and newspaper coverage are solicited, speaking before community groups is used, and referrals from pediatricians,
clinics and social work agencies are welcome.

The most effective recruiters, however, are parents themselves.
They make class activities known throughout their neighborhoods by
creating posters and bringing friends and neighbors to visit classes.

Since many adults either cannot or do not read notices, effective recruiting has to be the product of a multi-dimensional continuous campaign. In the economically deprived neighborhoods unusual
approaches such as sponsoring early childhood fairs or contacting
mothers personally are used.

VI.   Reasons Why Parents Attend Class

In surveying program participants, it was found that most
parents appeared to attend class for the purpose of offering their
children a good nursery school experience. Other reasons for coming
ranged from a need to "get out of the house," loneliness, a desire
to help their children learn English or as referrals from medical
or social workers.

CONCLUSIONS

A) The program is cost-effective since hundreds of families
are served without duplication of staff or equipment.

B) Continued parental involvement, often spanning each successive sibling's preschool years, attest to the program's value to
parents.

C) Positive parenting is encouraged, while at the same time
healthy development of children is enhanced. One of the special

values of the class is that it affords mothers an uninterrupted period of time in which they may quietly observe their children without being responsible for their supervision. Mothers see their children in new ways as they play in an environment in which there is a minimum of restraint on creative imagination and impulse. As mothers observe their children, they are also observing how the environment is designed, how materials and equipment are used and how the teacher interacts with their child.

This role of the teacher is of especial importance. By designing the total environment to be adaptable to the home and by being a role-model the teacher is setting the stage for parents to question and challenge what they see. This enables parents to analyze incidents, react to teacher techniques and discuss possible alternatives. To operate in such a situation it is essential that the teacher be well anchored in early childhood theories, knowledge and research and to be able to translate these into the skills needed to give young children a happy and positive learning experience.

Should a teacher base her program or actions upon personal convictions rather than theory, it becomes difficult for parents to question or debate an incident since they risk attacking the teacher's values. However, in an atmosphere in which parents question theories, observe them in action, and practice them as class members, insights into how one parenting technique may enhance growth and development better than another begins to develop. If what is modeled at nursery school takes root in the daily life of the family, positive parenting skills will continuously enhance the healthy development of the child.

D) Varying socioeconomic, ethnic and language groups attend the program. How to get mothers involved in preschool programs seems to be an almost universal question and concern. Because parent-child observation classes are part of adult education, compulsory attendance is not required. Consequently, if parents do not attend, classes are cancelled. Teachers spend much time and thought to ensure that coming to class is attractive to mothers. This becomes more complex when the group is heterogenous. Major factors which attract parents are a high quality children's program, a convenient location and a discussion group centered upon the needs of parents. Classes housed in neighborhoods served by public transportation attract the widest range of diversity in backgrounds. Some classes are opened with the specific intent of serving one particular group. For instance, the program has classes in economically deprived areas or for Spanish-speaking and Chinese-speaking mothers as well as for Native American and Black parents. Sites for these classes are usually housed in a familiar community center or church. When feasible, parent education students are a part of other adult classes in which they learn English, sewing or job skills.

There is value to each type of class grouping. To attract
and motivate parents, it is important to offer a choice. When parents are in control of choosing the group most comfortable to them,
attendance is usually high and interest is sustained.

E) In lieu of mother, the father, grandparents or other relatives attend. Until recently, only mothers came to the observation
class, but changing lifestyles, changing sex roles and more working
mothers caused us to open enrollment to any adult who has continuing
responsibility for the care of a child.

Essentially no child is excluded from a nursery school experience just because the mother is unable to attend. Children of working mothers came with paid caregivers or relatives, but it was not
unusual to have working mothers attend class on their day off. One
nightshift nurse came to class directly from her job. Grandparents
attending class provided younger mothers with valuable perspectives
concerning child rearing. The youngest grandmother was 40 and she
came with her daughter of four and her three-year-old granddaughter.

F) Broader community interests and self-improvement is evident.
As the semester progresses, immediate and pressing concerns about
child rearing and family problems are usually addressed. Gradually,
parents become ready to explore areas beyond the stated class goals
of growth and development, child rearing, parenting, and family life.
What evolves is an "informal agenda" which may range from the sharing
of interests and hobbies to more sensitive concerns of a personal
nature. This sharing of hobbies or special talents is usually fun
and a time of keen involvement leading many parents to discover new
skills and satisfactions.

In presenting topics of community concern, parents expand their
narrower role of "parent-learner" to the broader one of "concerned
citizen." It is not unusual to witness a shy, retiring woman develop into a more self-assured person as she shares in the presentation of arguments, discussion of issues and advocation of positions.
Parent observation classes, in a sense, become training grounds for
future community and school leaders.

Personal problems are part of the informal agenda as it is
almost impossible to keep them from being introduced. A parent may
be burdened with a concern and turn to the class for help: "My
husband wants to have his ill mother come and live with us. She
requires constant care . . . what am I to do?" "We are getting a
divorce . . . how can I begin again in a job and still care for my
children?" "My husband is on duty 6,000 miles away, the children
need him and I'm so lonely." "I don't think I love my children, I
feel so ashamed of feeling this way."

These deeply personal issues demand of each listener an ability

to grow in empathy and understanding. No small degree of personal
courage is sometimes needed to expose these problems. From these
discussions a community resource file began as parents shared information explaining social services available in our community.

Long before there was a law mandating the inclusion of handicapped children into tax-supported preschool programs, our class
accepted children with severe hearing and speech problems, epilepsy,
neurological handicaps, cerebral palsy, physical disfigurements and
personality disorders. Each child was a new challenge and learning
experience. Adults found themselves learning how to work with the
handicapped and consequently enriching their own mothering skills.
Some benefits were long term as in the case of one mother who became very interested in helping a deaf child. She discovered she
was talented in learning and using sign language. This led her
into an unexpected career as a translator for the deaf and mute,
as well as an innovator of a sign language program for her child's
elementary school.

In another situation, a mother of a handicapped child, sensing
her child was being rejected by many of the children and parents,
chose to tell the group about her little girl's problem. After
hearing of the Herculean efforts and sacrifices made by the mother,
many of us found new dimensions to the word love. Because the pediatrician recommended our program, the mother enrolled, even though
she expected rejection and hostility. Certainly, not every mother
was accepting; however, much warmth and understanding slowly replaced
the isolation surrounding this mother and child. As group support
increased, this handicapped child became the source of new and positive learning experiences for us all.

These are but two of many examples which serve to illustrate
how continued participation in observation classes has broader
benefits for the parents and the community than the basic curricula
would indicate.

G) Parent education, including preparation of the preschool
child for his school experience, is feasible with parents in economically deprived communities. When these parents are shown how they
can help the young child prepare to cope successfully with the preschool experience, and are shown in a manner which makes sense to
them, they are similar to any other group of parents in their efforts
to help the child achieve.

H) Parents show more awareness of growth and development in
their children and of their own responsibility in aiding this process after they participate in the program.

I) There is an increase in parental understanding of the role
of the parent as the child's first and primary teacher. Observa-

tions show that parents possess the ability to recognize the importance of all areas of growth--cognitive, social, emotional and
physical.

J) Teaching the non-English speaking child to understand and
speak in English is simplified when mothers are also exposed to
English. Children show less hesitancy in attempting to speak English
than the adults and language differences never seem to impede interaction between the children.

K) Many parents with limited concepts of routine and order,
of spatial relationships and the use of play materials as a method
of developing such concepts come to understand play as a primary
learning method for children. As parents analyze the educational
and developmental purposes behind the use of creative materials,
puzzles, dramatic play, block building, and the importance of reading aloud to children and encouraging conversation and listening
skills, they become increasingly able to accept their own responsibility for providing these positive play experiences at home.

In the final analysis, the program described in this paper
demonstrates how parents can be successfully involved in the preschool program of their youngsters by blending two educational
disciplines--early childhood and adult education into one program.
In essence, this program may well offer a solution to the often asked
question, "How do you involve parents?"

BIBLIOGRAPHY

Almy, M. and Genishi, C. *Ways of studying children.* New York:
    Teacher's College Press, Columbia University, 1979.
Auerbach, A.B. *Parents learn through discussion: Principles and
    practices of parent group education.* New York: John Wiley &
    Sons, Inc., 1968.
Brazelton, T.B. *Infants and mothers: Differences in development.*
    New York: Dell Publishing Co., 1969.
_____. *Development of adult education in California.* Sacramento,
    CA: California State Department of Education Bureau of Publica-
    tions, 1951.
_____. *Parent participation nursery school standards: A guide for
    the operation of cooperative parent participation nursery
    schools.* Sacramento, CA: Bureau of Publications, 1968.
_____. *Partners in education: Adult education/early childhood
    education through parent education.* Sacramento, CA: Bureau of
    Publications, 1976.
_____. *Parents can be partners.* Sacramento, CA: Bureau of Publi-
    cations, 1978.
_____. *Adult education handbook for inservice teacher training.*
    Sacramento, CA: Bureau of Publications, 1979.

_____. *Establishing parent education programs*. Sacramento,
    CA: Bureau of Publications, 1979.
_____. *Handbook on adult education*. Sacramento, CA: Bureau of
    Publications, 1979.
_____. *State preschool guidelines*. Sacramento, CA: Bureau of
    Publications, 1979.
Cohen, D.H. and Stern, V. *Observing and recording the behavior of
    young children*. New York: Teacher's College Press, Columbia
    University, 1978.
Coletta, A.J. *Working together: A guide to parent involvement*.
    Atlanta, GA: Humanics Limited, 1977.
Croft, D.J. *Be honest with yourself: Self-evaluation handbook for
    early childhood education teachers*. Belmont, CA: Wadsworth
    Publishing Co., 1976.
_____. *Parents and teachers: A resource book for home, school
    and community relations*. Belmont, CA: Wadsworth Publishing
    Co., 1979.
Fargo, J. and Pickarts, E. *Parent education: Toward parental compe-
    tence*. New York: Appleton-Century-Crofts, 1971.
Hendrick, J. *The whole child: New trends in early childhood educa-
    tion*. St. Louis, MO: C.V. Mosby Co., 1979.
Hymes, J.L. *Notes for parents*. Sierra Madre, CA: Southern California
    Association for the Education of Young Children, 1977.
_____. *Effective home-school relations*. Sierra Madre, CA:
    Southern California Association for the Education of Young
    Children, 1979.
Markun, P.M. *Parenting*. Washington D.C.: Association for Childhood
    International, 1973.
McAfee, O. and Nedler, S. *Working with parents: Guidelines for early
    childhood and elementary teachers*. Belmont, CA: Wadsworth Pub-
    lishing Co., 1979.
Morrison, G.S. *Parent involvement in the home, school, community*.
    Columbus, OH: Chas. E. Merrill Publishing Co., 1978.
Sierra Madre Community Nursery School Association. *Nurturing human
    growth: An approach for parents and teachers of young children*.
    Sierra Madre, CA: Sierra Madre Community Nursery School Associ-
    ation, 1978.

LEARNING IN THE FAMILY CONTEXT: RESEARCH ON PARENTS'
PERCEPTIONS OF THEIR ROLE AS EDUCATORS OF YOUNG CHILDREN

Roberta Jean Goldberg

University of California
Los Angeles

INTRODUCTION

Parents are children's first teachers. Starting from birth
and continuing throughout early childhood, parents are the primary
agents for children's daily learning in every sphere of development.
Many of these teaching/learning interactions shared between parents
and young children may appear mundane or inconsequential. Yet, they
have been shown to stimulate development, foster interest and expectation for future learning, and relate to children's measured learning, cognitive and social skills.

Furthermore, many parents report that these early educational
exchanges--when parents teach their children--are totally unmotivat-
ed and unplanned. Parents simply do these things in the course of
routine child rearing. They often do not identify these instances
as constituting teaching, nor do they see how these fleeting exchanges amount to anything related to teaching or learning.

On the other hand, some parents make deliberate efforts to
teach their children things which they feel will help their children's
development. This is particularly the case as children approach
school age and parents, consciously or unconsciously, begin to prepare their children for school. In so doing, they take on the role
of educator of their young children.

An investigation of parents' roles in the early education of
children has been going on for several years. This research has
included gathering information about things parents do to prepare
their children for school, what they think children should know before entering school to facilitate success at school, and which

agents they feel are responsible for this preparation.

As is evident from the following brief literature review, the above focus is a departure from past research on parents' roles in children's early learning.

HOME ENVIRONMENT VARIABLES RELATED TO LEARNING

General aspects of the home environments in which preschool children grow up have been found to relate to their later academic achievement. Several studies have demonstrated that the provision of early learning materials in the home (Bing, 1963; Moore, 1968), early reading to children (Miller, 1970), encouragement of language development (Jones, 1972), encouragement of academic achievement (Marjoribanks, 1972), and parents' interest in children's school experiences (Douglas, 1964) are all related to academic achievement in school-aged children.

With preschool populations, recent studies have focused on more subtle aspects of parent-child interaction during learning situations in the home which promote intellectual competence. For instance, based on behavioral observations, White and Watts (1973) have shown that children who were high in competency at the age of 3 were distinguished from children low in competency mainly in the nature of the intellectual interactions they shared with their mothers until the age of 2. Mothers of competent toddlers (a) interacted with them more, (b) engaged in more intellectually stimulating activities with them, and (c) taught them more often than mothers of less competent toddlers.

The daily routines of more and less intellectually competent toddlers have also been shown to differ. With a large sample of English children, Lawson and Ingleby (1974) found that children of higher I.Q. at 3 years of age (a) engaged in less general play, (b) spent less time alone or separated from family members, (c) spent less high intensity (one-to-one) and low intensity time with their mothers, and (d) received more moderate attention from everyone in the family.

In summary, these studies identify general aspects of the home which contribute to the child's learning in school, as well as characteristics of adult-child interaction which facilitate intellectual growth during the preschool years. We have much less information, however, about which preacademic and related cognitive skills children have when they enter school, how and where they learn these skills, and, particularly, the role that parents play in the acquisition of these skills.

Stevenson, Parker, Wilkinson, Heigon and Fish (1976) found that

the number and letter skills that children had before they entered
kindergarten proved to be good predictors of what they would learn
in the course of their first three years of instruction. No information was obtained, however, to indicate where (nursery school or
home) or how (television or taught by parents) children had acquired
these skills.

Delores Durkin has reported some clues based on findings from
a longitudinal study of children who learn to read before first
grade (Durkin, 1963). According to parent questionnaires, early
readers received some beginning reading instruction by one of their
parents or a sibling. Mothers of early readers reported identifying
words when asked, talking about words, pointing words out when reading, and asking questions about the content of stories, whereas
mothers of non-early readers did not. Also, parents of early readers attributed early reading to the availability of paper and pencils and reading materials in the home. The most influential agent
in teaching early readers to read was mother (93%), whereas the influence of siblings or fathers was negligible.

Most importantly, mothers of early readers expressed a feeling
that it was their responsibility to teach their children. They
indicated that interacting with children in academic and non-academic activities was part of daily life and important for children's
general development. They made a conscious effort to provide these
experiences for children.

Parents' attitudes about their contribution to children's early
development have been shown to vary across social class groups. Lower
class parents, in contrast to middle class parents, report that they
have little influence over their children's development, that children's abilities are set at birth and are not responsive to experiential input, and that children are not able or not inclined to communicate before they can talk (Hess & Shipman, 1965; Tulkin & Kagan,
1972). These attitudes will influence the kind of educational environment which parents provide for their children as well as the
degree to which they use themselves as teaching agents for young
children.

There is also strong evidence from the evaluation of Head
Start and Planned Variation early education programs in the United
States and from the Home Instruction Program for Preschool Youngsters (HIPPY) in Israel (see Lombard, 1973) that mothers can be
taught to be effective teachers of their children and that their
teaching efforts can benefit children's developing skills. The most
effective compensatory education programs appear to be those which
engage mothers in teaching or learning how to teach their children
in the home (Bronfenbrenner, 1976). Mothers in these programs have
reported changes in their ability to contribute to their children's
development as well as changes in their attitudes about the educa-

tional value of both educational materials and their own interactions
with children (Madden, Levenstein & Levenstein, 1976; Scheinfeld,
Bowles, Tuck & Gold, 1970).

Except for Durkin's work in the early 1960s, no recent investigator has actually asked parents what their children consider to be
important for school, how the children learn these things, and who
should be responsible for teaching children such important skills
and attitudes about learning. Similarly, in the last ten years it
has been rare for an investigator to ask parents of preschoolers
what kinds of activities they engage in to prepare children for
school and how much time in a routine week they might spend in such
preparatory activities. Thus, there is almost no current information
about the role that parents play in the early learning of their
children based on specific teaching practices or general perceptions
of their teaching role. Finally, little is known about the relationship between what parents do with children to prepare them for
school and children's actual performance on achievement measures, or
how children's performance may vary based on the different practices
or roles parents may assume in the early education of their children.

To answer some of these questions, several exploratory studies
have been conducted. What is special about these studies is that
parents were asked directly what they were doing to prepare their
children for school. Through this method, information about the
preparatory activities parents engage in with their children is obtained as well as information about parents' perceptions of what appropriate preparation is and their role in carrying out such preparation.

STUDY I: PRESCHOOL PREPARATION

The first study was undertaken to collect descriptive information about what parents do with preschool age children to prepare
them for kindergarten. Within the framework of a larger study,
parents were asked 1) if they were preparing their children for
kindergarten, 2) how they were preparing their children for kindergarten, and 3) what specific things (for example, numbers, letters)
which children knew would prepare them for school, and how they had
learned these things (for example, from parents, siblings, television, nursery school, learning materials in the home). Information about the amount of time parents spent in a week in preparatory activities was also available from mothers' weekly estimates
as well as from 24-hour time diaries kept by the mothers. Children
were tested in their schools with a multiple battery of tasks tapping cognitive and school related skills. In addition, teachers
rated a variety of children's abilities. This information was
compared to the preschool preparation data to explore possible
relations between parental preparation and children's skills and

abilities.

The sample consisted of ninety-three 4- and 5-year-old children
and their mothers who had an average of two years post-high school
education.

A majority (80%) of mothers indicated they were preparing their
children for school. Mothers' preparation fell into two distinct
groups: 1) mothers who prepared their children by teaching academic
skills such as numbers and letters and other similar concepts; and
2) mothers who prepared their children by teaching them non-academic
things, such as familiarizing them with school, teaching informa-
tional, self-help skills and social, adjustment skills, and physical
preparation such as going shopping for school clothes or purchasing
a lunch pail and school supplies. These two groups of mothers were
very consistent in reporting which set of preparatory skills, exclusive of the other, they were exposing their children to, and the
reasons they gave for their preparatory activities.

Most (93%) mothers reported that their children knew their
numbers and letters. When asked how their children learned numbers,
the agents mentioned were ordered 1) parents, 2) television, and
3) nursery school; for learning letters, the agents were ordered
1) parents, 2) nursery school, and 3) television. In contrast to
the variety and distribution of agents responsible for children
learning number and letter skills, parents reported they mainly
(75% of the time) taught their children other things preparatory
for school.

More educated mothers reported less academic preparation of
their children, while less educated mothers reported more academic
preparation. However, the two groups of mothers did not differ
in their non-academic preparation.

Working mothers were no different from non-working mothers in
the amount of academic preparation they reported. They did, however, report less preparation of children in non-academic areas.
The more hours a week mothers worked, the more frequently television
and nursery school were mentioned as agents for preparing children
for school.

Mothers' preparation of their children for school, both academically and non-academically, was closely related to their estimates for preparatory activities from the 24-hour time diaries.
Mothers reported spending a little over one hour a week reading to
their children and less than two hours a week teaching their children activities in preparation for kindergarten. Mothers watched
TV with their children for approximately three hours during the
week, an activity which consumed more time than the time spent in
teaching and reading combined.

Preliminary results showed that preschool preparation was related to children's preschool skills. The greater number of agents
mothers reported as contributing to youngsters' acquisition of skills
other than knowledge of numbers and letters per se (including verbal
and numerical concepts, other cognitive and perceptual skills, and
classroom skills such as following instructions), the better they performed on verbal tasks, ability to solve problems, and reading and
arithmetic achievement. More educated mothers, in general, reported
more of the above agents than did less educated mothers. However, as
the latter group of mothers gained an awareness of the number of agents
responsible for children learning these other things, their children's
scores increased significantly.

In summary, the findings suggest that the time mothers spend
in preparatory activities, the kinds of preparation children have,
and the agents of preparation utilized vary across parents, and
that mothers' education level and employment status influence parents' attitudes and practices about preparation. As a result, the
second study focussed on the degree to which parental beliefs about
their role in the early education of children determine the amount of
time parents spend in preparatory activities.

STUDY II: PARENTS' PERCEPTIONS OF THEIR ROLE AS EDUCATOR

In this second study (see Dunn, 1980) parents of 4-year-olds
were interviewed regarding their beliefs about preschool preparation
and daily diary information was collected from mothers. Beliefs,
time use and demographic characteristics were studied in relation
to children's scores on a battery of tasks and ratings similar to
those used in Study I.

Parents were found to spend very little time didactically teaching their children (an average of 2.5 minutes per weekday), which
confirms the findings of the Preschool Preparation Study above.
It should be noted that wide variation existed among families, with
some parents spending no time at all didactically teaching their
children and other parents spending up to approximately a half hour
per day on such activity. "Number of informal educational exchanges"
rather than time, however, was strongly correlated with children's
verbal scores. (This measure was obtained by having mothers describe
anecdotally, in their diary forms, educational interactions that
they shared with their children during the day.)

Parents' beliefs about preschool preparation proved to be excellent predictors of children's scores. Mothers who stated that
it was their job to teach their children letter and number skills
had children who scored higher on these skills. Teachers also
rated these children higher on comprehending class discussions and
verbal ability. Furthermore, when fathers said that they felt that

it was their job to teach these same skills or related ones, their children scored higher on ratings of following instructions, pursuing new activities, persistence, and self-reliance. Finally, when parents indicated that they were teaching their children at home, the children rated higher on interest in their learning environment. These findings suggest that parents' perceptions of their own teaching roles may greatly influence the development of preschool academic skills and social skills that will be essential for effective learning in the school environment. Note, too, that mothers' and fathers' efforts seem to contribute in distinct ways to children's preschool achievement.

It should also be mentioned that there was some evidence that parents' preschool preparation beliefs dictated their time use. For example, mothers who felt that preschool preparation was more their responsibility than the nursery school's responsibility spent more time reading with their children.

SUMMARY, APPLICATIONS AND IMPLICATIONS

The results of our studies indicate that parents differ in their preparation of children for school and differ in their attitudes about who is responsible for this preparation. It seems imperative that those of us who work with young children recognize these facts. In particular, staffs of early childhood centers need to investigate the assumptions of parents and staff about what their roles are.

These ideas need to be explored between teachers and parents and a division of labor established, or at least goals established. Of the numerous things which children need to learn, parents need to be encouraged to do those things which they are capable of, and to be guided in how to do things in areas in which they can improve. It cannot be assumed that children will eventually end up with all of the experiences which are valuable for development unless consideration is given to what pieces are missing in a child's experience, how these gaps can be filled, and who should take the responsibility for assuming the job. Parents, as crucial agents in children's early learning, must be consulted and considered in this effort, even though in many instances, professional educators will be required to stimulate and guide parents.

Our studies have also demonstrated that didactic learning of numbers and letters is not the only thing which is important for success in school. The data presented here confirm that skills (other than just number and letter skills) that children had acquired were more highly related to cognitive development and academic achievement than number and letter skills. Children need many other experiences to increase both their motivation to learn

and their curiosity about the world. Parents and teachers need to
encourage these kinds of experiences for children. Educators need
to help parents recognize that mundane, daily, routine activities
with children are tremendously important for their children's development. Parents also need to be assisted in maximizing the effect of these daily exchanges between parents and children.

A mother's own education has been found to greatly influence
her perception of her role as educator, as well as influence what
she actually does with her child vis à vis learning. Unfortunately,
to date we do not have comparable data on fathers. Essentially, opportunities for mothers to receive formal and informal education as
well as to learn how to engage their children in specific educational
activities must be a major focus of early childhood education. Early
childhood centers could become places for educating both parents
and children. Admittedly, this is not a new idea--many fine research
and demonstration projects such as HIPPY have implemented parent programs, but, as indicated by the studies described in this article,
there are too few of these kinds of programs. A general education
program might include basic literacy programs, assistance in acquir-
ing a high school diploma or some college education and training
for parents to become better teachers of their children. Such a
program should be an intrinsic part of contemporary child care programs.

Early childhood educators have a big job ahead of them: they
must determine what role they have in the early experience of
children, and help parents identify and select their roles in this
sphere more confidently.

BIBLIOGRAPHY

Bing, E. Effect of childrearing practices on development of differ-
      ential cognitive abilities. *Child Development,* 1963, *34,* 631-
      648.
Bronfenbrenner, U. Research on the effects of day care on child
      development. *Toward a national policy for children and families.*
      Report of the Advisory Committee on Child Development. Washing-
      ton, D.C.: National Academy of Sciences/National Research
      Council, 1976.
Durkin, D. Children who read before grade one: A second study.
      Elementary School Journal, 1963, *64,* 143-148.
Douglas, J.W. *The home and the school: A study of ability and
      attainment in the primary school.* London: MacGiblon and Kee,
      1964.
Dunn, N.E. Parental beliefs on preschool preparation, parents' time
      use, and preschool achievement. Unpublished doctoral disser-
      tation, University of Pennsylvania, 1979.

Hess, R.D., & Shipman, V.C. Early experience and the socialization
    of cognitive modes in children. *Child Development*, 1965, *36*,
    869-886.
Jones, P. Home environment and the development of verbal ability.
    Child Development, 1972, *43*, 1081-1086.
Lawson, A., & Ingleby, J.D. Daily routines of pre-school children:
    Effects of age, birth order, sex and social class, and develop-
    mental correlates. *Psychological Medicine*, *4*, 1974, 399-415.
Lombard, A.D. *Home instruction program for preschool children:
    Final report*. Jerusalem, Israel: The National Council of Jewish
    Women Center for Research in Education of the Disadvantaged,
    1973.
Madden, J., Levenstein, P., & Levenstein, S. Longitudinal I.Q. out-
    comes of the mother-child home program. *Child Development*, 1976,
    47, 1015-1025.
Marjoribanks, K. Environment, social class, and mental abilities.
    Journal of Educational Psychology, 1972, *63*, 103-109.
Miller, W.M. An examination of children's daily schedules in three
    social classes and their relation to first-grade reading achieve-
    ment. *California Journal of Educational Research*, 1970, *21*,
    100-110.
Moore, T. Language and intelligence: A longitudinal study of the
    first 8 years. *Human Development*, 1968, *11*, 88-106.
Scheinfeld, D.R., Bowles, D., Tuck, S., Jr., & Gold, R. Parents'
    values, family networks, and family development: Working with
    disadvantaged families. *American Journal of Orthopsychiatry*,
    1970, *40*, 413-425.
Stevenson, H.W., Parker, T., Wilkinson, A., Hegion, A., & Fish, E.
    Longitudinal study of individual differences in cognitive de-
    velopment and scholastic achievement. *Journal of Educational
    Psychology*, 1976, *68*, 377-400.
White, B., & Watts, J.C. *Experience and environment: Vol. 1*. Engle-
    wood Cliffs: Prentice-Hall, 1973.

EFFECTS OF A HOME INTERVENTION PROGRAM

ON MATERNAL LANGUAGE

Rachel Inselberg
Western Michigan University

Jolene Oswald
Kalamazoo Public Schools
Kalamazoo, Michigan

The consistency of positive effects on children resulting from
various types of parent education programs has been impressive
(Clarke-Stewart & Apfel, 1979). There is ample documentation that
parenting programs can produce immediate effects on children's
cognitive performance and development (Bronfenbrenner, 1974; Chilman,
1973; Clarke-Stewart & Apfel, 1979). IQ gains have been shown to
remain stable for several years after program termination (Gilmer,
Miller & Grey, 1970; Gordon, Guinagh & Jester, 1977; Levenstein,
1977), although gradual reversals have also been noted (Gutelius,
1977; Lally & Honig, 1977; Schaefer & Aaronson (1977).

An assumption basic to intervention programs involving parents
is that only when a parent or parents are helped to become intervention agents can cognitive progress in the child be sustained.
Yet, while changing maternal behavior is considered important, it
has often been ignored in program evaluations. Among the changes
that have been noted are IQ gains in mothers (Miller, 1967),
greater provision of educational materials in the home by program
mothers (Radin, 1972), more positive attitudes on the part of mothers
toward their children and increased verbal interaction with them
(Falender & Heber, 1975; Gordon, 1971; Heber, Garber, Harrington,
Hoffman & Falender, 1972; Wright, Honig, Lally & Tse, 1975), as
well as increasing social contacts and community involvement (Gilmer
et al., 1970; Karnes, Teska, Hodgins, & Badger, 1970).

Less attention, however, has been focused on specific changes
in maternal language, which is assumed to provide a basis for
children's precise conceptualization. If we accept as valid past
findings indicating that the language in educationally disadvantaged
homes is restricted and lacking in specificity (Bernstein, 1961;

197

Blank & Solomon, 1968; Brown, Cazden & Bellugi-Klima, 1969; Hess &
Shipman, 1965; Nelson, Carskaddon, & Bonvillian, 1973) rather than
merely representing phonological deviations (Houston, 1970), then
the promotion of differentiated and elaborated language in parents
involved in intervention programs becomes significant.

The objectives of the present study were to determine whether
(1) the language used by mothers who participated in a home intervention program with their children was more specific and reflected
a greater number of higher-order mental processes than the language
used by control mothers not exposed to the program, (2) program
mothers had become more verbal in general than the control mothers,
as reflected in greater word production, and (3) more time was spent
by the program mothers than the controls in reading to their children.

METHOD

Subjects

The experimental and control groups consisted of 15 mothers
each. They were randomly assigned to either group before the
initiation of the program from a list of low-income families with
preschool children in a midwestern city in the United States. The
list was compiled from school files, referrals from Head Start, the
Department of Social Services, and the Health Department, as well
as from a survey of families in low-cost housing areas. Both sets
of mothers were, on the average, 26 years of age and had 10 years
of schooling and 4 children. Sixty percent of the experimental
group were black and the rest were white or members of other minority groups. The respective percentages for the control group
were 53 and 47. Welfare payments were the sole source of income
for 40 percent of the experimental mothers and an identical percentage of the controls. Seventy-three percent of the experimental
mothers and 67 percent of the controls were full-time homemakers,
while the rest were employed either part time or full time.

Forty percent of the experimental mothers' children who participated and 53 percent of the control children were female. The
mean ages of the children at pretest were 30.6 months for the experimental group and 29.9 for the control group. The initial mean
Peabody Picture Vocabulary Test verbal IQ was 77.0 for the experimental children and 91.8 for the controls, the difference being
significant at the 0.008 level (t=2.84).[1] The post mean verbal
IQs were 92.3 for the experimental group and 92.4 for the controls,
the difference in the mean gain scores, namely, 15.3 for the experimental group and 0.6 for the controls, between the two groups being
significant at the 0.005 level (t=3.05). Applying the analysis of
covariance, which takes into consideration initial differences, the

adjusted postperiod mean verbal IQ was 95.4 for the experimental children and 89.2 for the control children, the difference being no longer
significant.[2]

PROCEDURE

The experimental mothers and their children participated in a
home program in which procedures developed by Levenstein (1969) were
followed. A homeworker, who visited them twice a week, demonstrated
the use of a toy or book in order to promote specific language between
a mother and child. The homeworker used not only simple but also more
sophisticated sentence constructions, and reflected higher-order mental processes such as classifying and reasoning. The homeworker did
not teach a mother directly but acted as a model and encouraged verbal
interaction between the mother and child. A total of five homeworkers
were involved, their weekly activities being monitored by two coordinators. Each mother-and-child pair participated in a total of 46 sessions during the program year, which approximated the local public
school calendar. None of the controls was exposed to any aspect of
the program.

Both groups of mothers were interviewed prior to and at the end of
the program year. The interviews were conducted by the coordinators,
with the experimental and control mothers being randomly assigned and
approximately equally divided between the two of them. During the preperiod and postperiod interviews, the mothers were asked to respond to
open-ended questions on hypothetical situations that involved seeking
help with a child-rearing problem, preparing their children for school
attendance, and solving problems faced by their children. The questions were the same as those used in a study by Hess and Shipman (1965).
The mothers also indicated the frequency with which they read to their
children, from "none at all" to "almost daily." In addition, they
were asked to tell a story to their children, using pictures provided
by the interviewer.

During the initial interview, the mothers were asked to tell a
story, using the black and white lion card included in the Children's
Apperception Test. At posttime they told stories using the same lion
card, as well as a new picture (child card) which was a drawing in
color on an 8½ by 11 inch white poster board, showing a brightly
attired child engaged in block construction. The blocks were of various sizes, colors, and shapes. Thus, the experimental design utilized
was randomized subjects, pretest and posttest. An exception was the
posttest-only design used in storytelling with the child card in
order to avoid some pretest reactivity in storytelling (Ary, Jacobs,
& Razavieh, 1972).

The interviews were taped, and transcribed at a later date. To
determine the extent of the mothers' word production, their answers

to the open-ended questions and stories were analyzed by counting the
number of words used, excluding repetitions and verbal tics such as
"you know" and "uh." The stories were further analyzed for specificity and descriptiveness by counting the nouns and adjectives used
as well as references to the concepts of color, shape, size, texture,
number, and relationship. A reference could consist of a word or
group of words. Sometimes a reference, such as the word "bigger,"
could be classified in more than one category. While "bigger" refers to size, it also refers to the size relationship between two
items. Space words such as on, in, and behind were categorized
under "relationship." Ordinal numbers were coded both as "number"
and "relationship."

The extent to which the mothers reasoned, associated, showed
divergent thinking, classified, or asked questions was determined
by analyzing their stories for manifestations of these mental processes
and indicating the frequency of their occurrence. Specifying a cause
and effect relationship was considered an indication of reasoning,
as in the statements, "The big blocks are placed at the bottom so that
the building will be steady," and "The lion needs the cane for walking because he is old and weak." The mothers were considered to be
associating when an event or condition they identified in a picture
was related to another event or condition external to the picture, as
in the comment, "The lion is thinking about where her grandchildren
are; sometimes, I also wonder where you are when you are gone for a
long time," or "The child is building with blocks; you also like to
play with blocks."

Divergent thinking was considered to be manifested when the
mother offered more than one way of describing a situation, such as
suggesting more than one kind of block construction, namely a boat
or an apartment building. Classification was evident when the
mother took into account a property or properties of a given class,
as in the comment, "This is a purple block and here is another purple block," or "This animal is a cat, not a dog." A given statement could be classified in more than one category of mental processes if it met the criteria for inclusion in more than one category. The analysis of responses was done by two individuals, one
of whom did it "blind." The interscorer agreement was 92 percent.

As the direction of differences was specified in favor of the
experimental mothers, one-tailed t-tests were used to arrive at
significant differences in the extent of the two groups of mothers'
word production, noun and adjectival usage, references to various
concepts, and manifestations of higher-order mental processes.
The chi-square test was used to determine differences in the varying frequencies with which the experimental and control mothers
reported reading to their children.

RESULTS

The extent of the mothers' verbal responses in answering questions
on hypothetical situations and in storytelling during the preperiod
and postperiod interview is presented in Table 1. No significant
differences were noted at pretest and posttest in the mean word production by both groups of mothers in their responses to questions
about identifying sources of help when faced with a general child-
rearing problem, preparing their children for the first day of school,
and handling a school problem facing the child. The mean word pro-
ductions of the two groups in storytelling with the lion card were
also not significantly different. On the other hand, the experimental mothers used more than one and a half times as many words when
storytelling with the child card, the difference being significant.

Findings on the specificity of maternal language in storytelling
are given in Table 2. No significant differences were found between
the two groups in the various categories at pretest, when storytelling with the lion card. However, at posttest the experimental mothers referred to size to a significantly greater degree.

Using the child card at posttest, the experimental mothers
used significantly more nouns or labels and adjectives. The mean
noun usage of 12.1 words by the experimental mothers was almost twice
that of the controls. In addition, the mean usage of 7.5 adjectives
by the experimental mothers was more than three times the mean of
2.3 adjectives used by the controls. The experimental mothers also
emphasized color and size to a significantly greater extent, their
reference to color being sixteen times greater and their reference
to size being more than double the references made by the controls.
Although the difference in the usage of words denoting shapes did
not approach significance ($p < 0.07$, $t = 1.48$), some of the experimental mothers did call their children's attention to various shapes,
while none of the controls did so. The experimental mothers also
used words signifying number more than twice as often as did the
controls, although the difference was not significant. Neither
group of mothers made any reference to texture, while the frequency
of terms denoting relationships used by both groups was similar.

The frequency of higher-order mental processes reflected in storytelling is presented in Table 3. When using the lion card, the experimental and the control mothers did not show any significant differences in the frequencies of higher-order mental processes reflected in their stories at pretest. However, at posttest the experimental mothers reasoned and associated to a significantly greater extent.
With the child card, the experimental and the control mothers did
not show any significant differences in the extent to which they
reasoned, associated, showed divergent thinking, classified, or asked questions.

TABLE 1. Extent of mothers' verbal responses to questions and storytelling

Mean Word Production

Situation	Pretest		Posttest	
	Experimental	Control	Experimental	Control
	N = 15	N = 15	N = 15	N = 15
Seeking Help With				
Child-rearing Problem	33.2	34.9	32.5	37.6
Preparing For School	48.3	57.9	43.6	56.9
School Problem	47.9	60.5	47.1	59.4
Storytelling				
Lion Card	69.3	69.4	64.6	61.3
Child Card (Posttest Only)			82.3*	49.3
			(1.81)	

NOTE - The number in parentheses is the t-value.

*p < 0.05 (one-tailed)

TABLE 2. Specificity of maternal language in storytelling

Mean Usage

Category	Lion Card				Child Card	
	Pretest		Posttest		Posttest Only	
	Exper[a]	Cont[b]	Exper	Cont	Exper	Cont
	N = 15	N = 15	N = 15	N = 15	N = 15	N = 15
Total Nouns	10.7	10.8	9.8	10.1	12.1* (1.88)	7.2
Total Adjectives	2.5	2.7	5.4	3.9	7.5** (2.93)	2.3
Color	0	0	0.1	0.1	3.3** (2.97)	0.2
Shape	0	0	0	0	0.3	0
Size	0.4	0.3	1.9* (1.71)	0.5	2.5** (2.59)	1.1
Texture	0	0	0.1	0	0	0
Relationship	1.5	1.9	2.8	2.5	2.1	1.6
Number	0.3	0.1	0.6	0.7	1.0	0.4

NOTE - t-values given in parentheses.

[a] Experimental

[b] Control

*p < 0.05 (one-tailed)
**p < 0.005 (one-tailed)

TABLE 3. Mental processes reflected in storytelling by mothers

	Mean Occurrence					
	Lion Card				Child Card	
	Pretest		Posttest		Posttest Only	
Mental Process	Exper[a] N = 15	Cont[b] N = 15	Exper N = 15	Cont N = 15	Exper N = 15	Cont N = 15
Reasoning	0.3	0.5	1.0** (2.28)	0.4	0.3	0.2
Associating	0.3	0.2	0.6* (1.70)	0.2	0.7	0.6
Divergent Thinking	0.1	0.3	0.2	0.3	0.9	0.8
Classifying	0.1	0.3	0.1	0.2	3.2	2.2
Questioning	0.8	1.2	2.0	2.4	2.7	1.7

NOTE - t-values are in parentheses.

[a]Experimental

[b]Control

*$p < 0.05$ (one-tailed)

**$p < 0.02$ (one-tailed)

No significant differences were noted initially in the reported
extent to which the two sets of mothers read to their children: 40
percent of the experimental group and 47 percent of the controls
indicated reading to their children almost daily or two to three times
a week.   However, at posttest almost all of the experimental mothers
(14 mothers or 93 percent) reported that they read to their child
"two or three times a week" or "almost daily"; only one read to her
child once a week or less. In contrast, only about half of the control mothers (7 mothers or 47 percent) indicated reading to their
children at least two to three times a week, and about the same number of mothers (8 mothers or 53 percent) read to their children only
infrequently, once a week, once a month, or less. The differences
in frequencies between the two groups were significant at the 0.02
level (chi square = 7.78; 1 $d.f.$).

DISCUSSION

The present findings are in accord with previous conclusions
that changes can be brought about in parents who participate in
intervention programs. But while past studies have focused mainly
on changes in parents' general attitudes and behavior toward their
children (Falender & Heber, 1975; Gordon, 1971; Heber et al., 1972;
Wright et al., 1975), the present study indicates that greater specificity in mothers' language can be achieved even after only a
school year of program involvement (46 sessions, 2 per week). The
program mothers used more labels and descriptive terms, referring to
color and size to a greater degree when telling a story to their
children than did the controls. Such findings gain added significance when viewed against recent findings that complex, descriptive,
and interrogative maternal language is associated with children's
competence in cognition, language, and social relations, but not
with the mother's socioeconomic status (Clarke-Stewart, VanderStoep,
& Killian, 1979). The progress in the present experimental children's
verbal IQ could perhaps be attributed in part to the achievement of
greater specificity in maternal language.

On the other hand, what seems to be more subject to change in
maternal language are those aspects signifying what is visible and
concrete. No differences were noted between the two groups in their
reference to the more abstract concepts of number and relationships.
Except for one experimental mother who referred to texture twice,
none of the mothers called their children's attention to texture.
As the stimulus was simply a drawing or a print, one would have had
to imagine and transcend the immediate stimulus in order to refer
to texture.

Only two significant differences out of ten comparisons at posttest were found in the extent to which the two groups of mothers
reasoned, associated, showed divergent thinking, classified and asked

questions. It would therefore appear that the conscious demonstration of such mental processes when verbally interacting with a child is more difficult to promote. It should be recalled that the program did not call for direct, didactic teaching (Levenstein, 1969). Rather, the homeworker simply interacted with the child, thus demonstrating and indirectly acting as a model for a mother to follow. Whether the use of abstract referents and conscious demonstration of such mental processes are more likely to result from direct, didactic teaching rather than from indirect methods would be a significant question to explore. A study of mothers of developmentally delayed youngsters (Bricker & Bricker, 1973) showed that those aspects of maternal teaching styles receiving attention and comments were more subject to modification in a laboratory setting. The duration of program participation would also be an important consideration. Perhaps a single program year is not sufficient for the promotion of some aspects of elaborated language usage.

It is perhaps also significant that the experimental mothers' language was more specific when telling a story using the child card than when using the lion card. The child card, which was more sensorial, shared many characteristics with the program materials, perhaps resulting in greater transfer. It might therefore be important for future studies to take into consideration the characteristics of the test stimulus.

In total, while the program mothers did not seem more talkative than the controls when answering questions, they were more verbal to some extent when interacting with their child. Furthermore, their language was more specific and descriptive, although seemingly confined to a concrete level. They also reported reading to their children more frequently in spite of the similarity to the controls in their employment status and number of children. Whether such desirable changes can be sustained and further changes brought about with longer program participation would be a fruitful subject for further investigation.

FOOTNOTES

1. It will be recalled that the mother-child dyads were randomly assigned to groups. However, random selection does not guarantee similarities, only the elimination of bias (Ary et al., 1972).
2. This means that the experimental children had caught up with the controls and the treatment was effective (McNemar, 1969).

BIBLIOGRAPHY

Ary, D., Jacobs, L., & Razavieh, A. *Introduction to research in education*. New York: Holt, Rinehart, & Winston, 1972.

Bernstein, B. Social structure, language, and learning. *Educational Research*, 1961, *3*, 163-176.

Blank, M., & Solomon, F. A tutorial language program to develop abstract thinking in socially disadvantaged preschool children. *Child Development*, 1968, *39*, 379-389.

Bricker, D., & Bricker, W. *Infant, toddler, and preschool research and intervention project report--*Year III. Nashville, TN: George Peabody College for Teachers, 1973. (ERIC Document ED 089 529.)

Bronfenbrenner, U. *Is early intervention effective? A report on longitudinal evaluations of preschool programs* (Vol. II). Washington, D.C.: DHEW Publication No. (OHD) 74-24, 1974.

Brown, R., Cazden, C., & Bellugi-Klima, U. The child's grammar from I to III. In J.P. Hill (Ed.), *Minnesota symposium on child psychology*. Minneapolis: University of Minnesota Press, 1969.

Chilman, C. Program for disadvantaged parents. In B.M. Caldwell and H.N. Ricciuti (Eds.), *Review of child development research* (Vol. III). Chicago: The University of Chicago, 1973.

Clarke-Stewart, K.A., & Apfel, N. Evaluating parental effects on child development. In L. Shulman (Ed.), *Review of research in education*. Itasca, IL: F.E. Peacock, 1979.

Clarke-Stewart, K.A., VanderStoep, L.P., & Killian, G.A. Analysis and replication of mother-child relations at two years of age. *Child Development*, 1979, *50*, 777-793.

Falender, C.A., & Heber, R. Mother-child interaction and participation in a longitudinal intervention program. *Developmental Psychology*, 1975, *11*, 830-836.

Gilmer, B., Miller, J.O., & Gray, S.W. *Intervention with mothers and young children: Study of intra-family effects*. Nashville, TN: DARCEE, 1970.

Gordon, I. *A home learning center approach to early stimulation*. Gainesville, FL: Institute for Development of Human Resources, 1971 (Grant No. MH 16037-02).

Gordon, I.J., Guinagh, B., & Jester, R.E. The Florida Parent Education Infant and Toddler Programs. In M.C. Day & R.K. Parker (Eds.), *The preschool in action* (2nd ed.). Boston: Allyn & Bacon, 1977.

Gutelius, M.F. *Mobile unit for child care supervision*. Interim Rep. R01-MH-9215. Ely, VT: 1977.

Heber, R., Garber, H., Harrington, S., Hoffman, C., & Falender, C. *Rehabilitation of families at risk for mental retardation*. Madison, WI: Wisconsin University, 1972.

Hess, R., & Shipman, V. Early experience and the socialization of cognitive modes in children. *Child Development*, 1965, *36*, 869-886.

Houston, S.H. A reexamination of some assumptions about the language of the disadvantaged child. *Child Development*, 1970, *41*, 947-963.

Karnes, M.B., Teska, J.A., Hodgins, S.A., & Badger, E.D. Educational intervention at home by mothers of disadvantaged infants. *Child Development*, 1970, *41*, 925-935.

Lally, J.R., & Honig, A.S. The Family Development Research Program.
    In M.C. Day & R.K. Parker (Eds.), *The preschool in action* (2nd
    ed.). Boston: Allyn & Bacon, 1977.
Levenstein, P. The mother-child home program. In M.C. Day & R.K.
    Parker (Eds.), *The preschool in action* (2nd ed.). Boston:
    Allyn & Bacon, 1977.
Levenstein, P. *Toy demonstrator's "VISIT" handbook*. Mineola, N.Y.:
    Family Service Association of Nassau County, Inc., 1969.
McNemar, Q. *Psychological statistics* (4th ed.). New York: John Wiley
    & Sons, 1969.
Miller, J. Research, change, and social responsibility: Intervention
    research with young disadvantaged children and their parents.
    Demonstration and center for early education papers and reports,
    Vol. 2. Nashville, TN: George Peabody College for Teachers,
    1967.
Nelson, K., Carskaddon, G., & Bonvillian, J. Syntax acquisition:
    Impact of experimental variation in adult verbal interaction
    with the child. *Child Development*, 1973, *44*, 497-504.
Radin, N. Three degrees of maternal involvement in a preschool pro-
    gram: Impact on mothers and children. *Child Development*, 1972,
    43, 1355-1364.
Schaefer, E.S., & Aaronson, M. Infant education project: Implementa-
    tion and implications of the home-tutoring program. In M.C.
    Day & R.K. Parker (Eds.), *The preschool in action* (2nd ed.).
    Boston: Allyn & Bacon, 1977.
Wright, C., Honig, A.S., Lally, J.R., & Tse, M.S. *A videotape in-
    home study of the social and educational teaching styles of
    mothers and their five-year-olds*. 1975. (ERIC Document ED 110163.

PARENTS' GOALS AND PRESCHOOL EDUCATION

Mary S. Lewis

Administration for Children, Youth & Families
Department of Health and Human Services
United States

Preschool program options for families in Israel are far greater than those available to families in the United States today. The largest preschool program in America is Project Head Start, a comprehensive child development program begun in the summer of 1965. It is the last remnant of President Lyndon S. Johnson's "War on Poverty" and has served more than six million children since it began. The term "comprehensive" means that Head Start is more than an educational program; it is designed to bring health care, social services, nutrition, and psychological services to preschool disadvantaged children and to involve their parents and/or community people as volunteers and paid employees in the program. Head Start was originally a small eight-week summer enrichment program aimed at helping poor children catch up with their more advantaged peers by the time they entered school together. The initial response to this program was overwhelming and now almost every county in the United States has a Head Start program. Head Start is a social action program designed to equalize educational opportunity for the very young through early medical screening and psychological assessment, by feeding hungry children and by providing social services to their families. In the area of parent involvement, however, there is still a long way to go.

To this day the parent involvement component of Head Start is a challenge as conscientious staff continually seek new ways to bring parents into the program. Several demonstration programs are being operated to see if timing of activities or more comprehensive services might be effective ways of involving parents. The first programmatic spin-off provides services to parents of children even younger than Head Start's 3- to 5-year-olds. These Parent-Child Centers provide comprehensive services to families

with children from birth to three years. Some 33 of these centers
operate today in order to help families understand the needs of
infants and toddlers.

Home Start was another special demonstration program designed
to bring Head Start comprehensive services to parents in the home.
This method of delivery of service was contrasted with the usual
one in which families received services through their children who
attended Head Start classrooms. The intent of this demonstration
and the current home-based programs which emerged from it was to
help parents understand and become better at their role of being
the first teacher of their children.

The Home Start program involved weekly visits from a Home
Visitor in order to bring information about available community
services and better nutrition, to arrange to get the family to the
doctor and the dentist or perhaps into job training and to show the
parent how to help the child learn. Generally, the home visitor
made use of ordinary household items as teaching aids rather than
bringing toys into the home. An exception was the introduction of
reading material, since books are well-established incentives for
reading. Great emphasis was placed on showing parents how to capi-
talize on teachable moments by calling attention to events, asking
questions of and talking with the child about colors, shapes, positions, changes, memories, contrasts and predictions of ordinary
household activities. For instance, parents learned how to discuss
right and left, large and small, under and over with their children.
The children also learned how to set the table or sort beans or
participate in other necessary chores.

A third example of a Head Start demonstration program is the
Child Family Resource Program (CFRP) which serves families with
children from birth to eight years. This is an umbrella program
in which all manner of programs are brought together under one
roof, as it were, to provide infant stimulation, preschool education, day care, after school care, referrals for job training,
better nutrition, and family health care. There are fifteen CFRPs
operating today (1979) around the United States. This program has
been highly successful in its mission and may be the prototype of
future programming. It is understandable that a family system designed to serve only 3- to 5-year-olds is neglecting other elements
which infringe dramatically on the well-being of the target child.

BACKGROUND OF THIS STUDY

One of the premises of Project Head Start in the United States
for the past fifteen years has been that the young child needs the
active participation of his parents and other adults from the community in his early group learning experiences. When familiar

adults join him in the classroom, he feels more comfortable and his
psychic energy is freed to help him learn. While parents are volunteering in the classroom and helping the teachers manage the activities, it is assumed that they will also be able to ask questions
about child behavior, observe the group of children, compare their
own child's behavior with that of other children the same age, and
absorb the principles of early childhood education. As an aside,
the opportunity of being in a helping situation on a regular basis
describes the cooperative Nursery School experience of many middle-
class parents in the United States during the past 50 years.

In demonstration programs and in Head Start proper, parent
involvement has been a constant challenge. How to bring it about?
How to increase it? Who is involved? (The parents who need it the
most never come!) If parent involvement is low, what are some of
the reasons for it? Some are obvious: parents work or have too many
other children to bring to the center or to leave at home; single
parents who must be both father and mother are too busy; there is
a cultural bias against participation of lack of emphasis on this
component by management; and finally, teachers who don't really
know how to work with adults may deter parents. Might it be also
that the program focuses on activities considered trivial or un-
important by the parents? While the Kirschner study in 1970 documented the positive impact on community institutions of Head Start
programs which involved parents from the inception of planning and
goal setting, such programs were few in number. Nowhere have
Head Start parents equalled the program changes brought about by
middle class parents who are a significant voice in the conduct of
early schooling.

However, there is a major difference between middle class
parents and parents in Project Head Start. The largely middle
class cooperative Nursery School parent body finds itself in a
compatible situation with the staff. What they see being taught
is what they expected to see; it is appropriate to the values they
hold for themselves and their children. They see activities designed to produce open, expressive, creative, inquiring children;
they see independent, responsible behavior being reinforced. This
behavior is held to be the precursor of success in school. These
parents want their children to ask questions, try new things, move
into the larger group with self-confidence and grow in self-reliance with good humor and ease. On the other hand, most Head
Start parents have another view of the world and thus expect preschool activities to be structured differently. A different set of
goals may be the key to lack of participation. Both groups value
education as a means of achieving the good life but see quite different methods as being necessary to attain such a goal.

Why talk about the goals parents want? Goals indicate a course
of action. When goals are known, a curriculum can be developed and

a program implemented.   In 1972 the fourth Annual Gallup Poll of
Public Attitudes Toward Education surveyed 1500 people; 26% were
educators and the rest were lay public.   Two of every five respondents mentioned "preparation for jobs" as a key goal of education.
Yet a group of professional educators listed high in importance the
following: pride in work; a feeling of self-worth; intellectual
curiosity; and respect for others.   Low goals for this group were
proper management of money, resources and property with "preparation for a job" last on their list (Spears, 1973).

A second study was done by Gallup in 1974 for the Child Development Associate Consortium, a group which judges competency in a
selected group of those who work with groups of young children.
This study, "Gallup Survey of Parents' and Pre-School Professionals'
Attitudes Toward Pre-School Educational Program Goals and Objectives,"
showed a marked difference in choices between the 1184 parents who
were interviewed and the 776 professionals who completed questionnaires.   The professionals rated highest the goal "sense of individuality and self-worth" while the parents rated "a good attitude
toward school, respect for rules and legitimate authority, and being
prepared for school" as their three top choices.   Note the differences
in choice between those who have achieved economic success and those
who want their children to share in the benefits of education and
improve their life opportunities.

WHAT HEAD START PARENTS WANT

A third study differed from the two previously cited in that
it began with parents' goals (Lewis, 1978).   One hundred and forty-
nine goals were elicited from a total of 360 Head Start parents in
California, Arizona and Nevada.   A master list of the thirty most
frequently listed goals was copied, translated into Spanish and then
distributed to parents who were asked to respond.   Responses from
1619 Head Start parents in California were then contrasted with
choices made by early childhood professionals from the same list of
goals.

Here again the experts were united in their conviction on what
was good for young children.   They wanted children to play, to develop social skills, trust and independence and to have good self-
concepts.   Head Start parents wanted their children to be responsible and helpful in the home, to respect all people, to follow instructions, to learn English and to prepare for school.   The two
groups agreed on only one goal.   Each thought "develop physical
skills" was least important.

It seems that economically disadvantaged people in Project
Head Start were interested in qualities that would make their children succeed in school.   They know that school success means the

children will be able to find jobs in later life. The goals they
chose are all directly related to skills needed to earn a living.
The experts' choices related to qualities which describe a mature,
caring person. Thus the two sets of goal choices relate to two
aspects of a successful human being. The choices in each set of
goals come from what is thought to be important by each group of
people. On the one hand, Head Start parents represent people who
constantly struggle to make a living and want their children to
zero in on traits they believe to be tied to school (and later
economic) success. On the other hand, the experts, people already
very successful in school, chose goals which describe a person who
can function independently yet be concerned for others in the group.

SUMMARY AND RECOMMENDATIONS

     Both parents and experts want children to be successful in
life. Each group is bound by its own experience in ranking early
childhood program goals in order of importance. Head Start parents
are guided by their own life experiences and experts base their
choices on a wide experience with children in preschools and the
opportunity to view change in these children over time. Both viewpoints are valid. The task for all of us who work with families
of young children is to reconcile these two viewpoints through our
educational efforts.

     It is necessary to recognize what parents want for their chil-
dren. What they think is important is the way it is. What goes on
in the other twenty or more hours of the day when the child is with
his family is of much greater importance in the long run than what
happens when the child is with us. Thus we need to concentrate on
helping parents understand the reasons for what we are doing in the
classroom. We need a greater focus on the teacher as a facilitator
of growth — growth for the adult as well as growth for the child.

     Teachers need to listen more to parents and to accept what is
said as valid as a means of increasing communication and enlarging
the opportunity for growth, understanding and change. A special
time each day might be set aside for the teacher and the parent
volunteers to talk about what happened in the classroom. Just being in the classroom is not enough for parents. Parents need to
have their questions answered after observing their own child and
other children. Questions and discussions which direct or focus
attention on an aspect of growth which directly influences a goal
held by the parent will serve the cause of greater mutual understanding between teacher and parent.

     Teachers need more training in understanding cultural differ-
ences and the specific cultural mores of the parent group with
which they work. At the same time, teachers must appreciate the

wide range of individual differences within the parent group. Thus, teacher training should provide opportunities for students to teach in situations very different from their own backgrounds.

Parents need opportunity for guided observation of their children in a setting where their own goals are accepted. They may need assertiveness training to learn to explain what is important to them. This process takes time; thus, programs should be designed to keep families for two or more years. Parents change over time just as teachers do. The task is to keep both groups open to each others' point of view for the benefit of the children for whom both parents and teachers are responsible.

BIBLIOGRAPHY

Gallup, George. Fourth annual Gallup poll of public attitudes toward education. *Phi Delta Kappan*, September 1972.
Gallup, George. *Gallup survey of parents' and pre-school educational program goals and objectives*. The Gallup Organization, Inc., Princeton, NJ: 1974.
Kirschner Associates, Inc. *A national survey of the impacts of Head Start centers on community institutions*. Albuquerque: May 1970 (ERIC Document 045 195).
Lewis, Mary S. *Congruence of goals for early childhood between Head Start parents and experts,* 1978 (ERIC Document 171 368).
Spears, Harold. Kappans ponder the goals of education. *Phi Delta Kappan,* September 1973.

HIPPY: A HOME INSTRUCTION PROGRAM FOR

PRESCHOOL YOUNGSTERS

Avima Lombard

Hebrew University
Jerusalem, Israel

INTRODUCTION

This paper describes an enrichment program developed in Israel for preschool children. The program is HIPPY (the Home Instruction Program for Preschool Youngsters). It was developed in 1968-71 at the Hebrew University School of Education's Research Institute for Innovation, sponsored by the National Council of Jewish Women.

HIPPY is a home-based enrichment program in which a mother works with her young child from the time he is 4 to 6 years old, on a particular set of educational activities. She receives these educational materials in weekly packets from a paraprofessional aide, herself a mother of a preschool child and a member of the same community. The aide is selected by a professional coordinator, chosen locally, whose qualifications include higher education and experience in working with mothers and their children. This local coordinator is guided in her work by a regional coordinator who is selected from among the local coordinators by the national administrator of HIPPY. The regional coordinator supervises the local coordinators in the 20 to 25 locations that make up her region and works in conjunction with the national administrator, who is based at the Research Institute of the Hebrew University of Jerusalem.

The program is aimed at educationally disadvantaged children. Families selected for the program are of Afro-Asian origin, have a low level of education (less than 10 years) and fall into the lower ranges of the economic scale. They are generally large, intact families, where five or more children per family is common. Their homes are small, often three rooms or less.

WORKING WITH MOTHERS

A mother who joins HIPPY meets weekly with the paraprofessional aide, who instructs her in how to administer the materials to her child. These weekly meetings alternate between private home visits and group meetings. The aide visits the mother at an appointed time every other week, bringing with her the workbook and packet of materials for that week. She uses role-playing, in which the aide and the mother take turns playing the roles of mother and child, to instruct the mother in the use of these materials. This ensures that the mother is fully familiar with the materials. When the mother is illiterate or for some other reason is unable to cope with written materials alone, an older sibling chosen by the mother assumes the teaching role, and the training session with the aide takes place with this sibling, but in the mother's presence. The mother is encouraged to participate to the limit of her abilities, since it is she who is the major focus of the program.

In the course of each contact there is time to discuss problems which bear on both the mother's and the child's participation in the program, such as difficulties with specific activities or the child's lack of concentration. The problems often surface when the aide checks through the previous week's workbook; they may also be raised by the mother herself.

The Ministry of Education provides the list of eligible families from among those whose children are registered in local preschool classes. The local HIPPY coordinator makes the initial contact with each family in a home visit, at which time she explains the program to the mother and the mother, in turn, decides whether she wishes to join.

When making her first visit to a family, the local coordinator also tries to assess the mother's ability to act as a paraprofessional aide. If she feels that the mother would function well in this role she discusses this possibility with her. The mothers who are selected to serve as aides are trained by the coordinator in weekly in-service training meetings.

Each mother who contracts to join HIPPY must commit herself to regular attendance at the bi-weekly meetings with her aide and the ten to fifteen other mothers in the aide's care, and to a minimal token participation fee. At the start of each meeting the aide reviews, with each mother, her child's work for the previous week, and shares problems with her from time to time as they arise. In the discussion that follows, mothers may share information on problems and suggest "solutions that work" from their own experiences. The group as a whole then reviews the next week's materials, using the same role-playing technique employed by aide and mother in the home.

In the second part of the group meeting, which is directed
by the local coordinator, several aides and their mothers join together in a general educational activity. This may be a lecture,
a demonstration, or an activity relevant in some way to the parental
role. Topics are suggested by the aides, the local coordinator,
or the mothers. These topics include health and hygiene, children's
books and games, the school system, home handicrafts, home economics
and preparation for holidays. The sustained absence of a mother
from her group meetings, particularly in combination with her not
working steadily with her child at home, may result in her being
asked to leave the program—although considerable effort would
first be expended by the aide to help the mother remedy the situation.

EFFECTS OF HIPPY ON CHILDREN

The effects of HIPPY on children have been systematically
studied over the years. The original study was conducted in the
Hatikva quarter of Tel Aviv during the years 1969-1973. There were
140 preschool children in the study, of whom 60 children were in
HIPPY in addition to preschool. Examination of the school performance of all of the children over the years indicated that
children who had home instruction performed better than those who
did not. In second grade, a year after their completion of the
program, the home instructed children performed significantly better
on tests of math and reading achievement. These differences are
found again in the fifth and ninth grades. However, the later
comparisons do not produce differences which are statistically significant. Replication studies have confirmed the original findings that HIPPY improves disadvantaged children's school performance.

The children are now in ninth grade and we find that the
HIPPY participants, like their American counterparts who were in
Head Start, are significantly less apt to be found in special education classes or to be held back in grade. In the light of the
fact that all the Israeli children studied had at least one year
of prekindergarten, the above findings are of particular interest.
The data reported by the Consortium on Developmental Continuity
(Lazar, Hubbell & Murray, 1977) give clear evidence of the impact
of preschool on disadvantaged children. The data from HIPPY show
that the impact can be increased through additional home-based
activities with the mother.

EFFECTS OF HIPPY ON MOTHERS

As could be expected, HIPPY also has an impact on the participating mothers. From reports by HIPPY mothers and aides, as well as

from coordinators and other community representatives, it appears
that mothers who participate for two or more years do undergo
changes in behavior and attitudes, the most evident of which are:

1.   They view their children differently in that they perceive
them more as individuals, express more warmth to the target child,
and evidence more interest in their children's education. They say
such things as:

> Now she wants to draw, to work, to be active. She has
> learned colors and geometric forms, and it was only after
> starting the program that she began collecting and glue-
> ing things. Before she used to do that only in nursery
> school; I didn't know that she needed to work and draw
> at home, too. Her vocabulary has grown.

> I see my child enjoying his work and I enjoy that.

> I spend more time with my child, and this gives me a good
> feeling and encourages her.

2.   The regularity and intensity of their participation increases over time, that is they are more likely to complete the
weekly assignment with their children, to attend the group meetings
more regularly, and, once at the meetings to participate more actively.

3.   Their view of themselves changes, and this change is accompanied by a change in how they are viewed by their families. Mothers
report that they feel more appreciated at home. For example, one
husband spoke of how pleased he was with the results of the program,
and said that he had a new appreciation of his wife, while another
made sure his wife was not disturbed during her work with the HIPPY
child. He brought in the washing, prepared tea and provided small
necessary things such as glue and pencils, so his wife would be able
to work steadily with the child.

In a small study undertaken to examine the impact of HIPPY on
mothers' self-concept, an Israeli adaptation of the Tennessee Self-
Concept Scale (Fitts, 1965; Frankel, 1976) was administered to
fifty mothers when they began HIPPY, and in the following two years.
Mothers who participated in HIPPY for two or more years improved
their self-concepts while those who did not stay in the program
showed a drop in their self-concepts. The differences between the
two groups of mothers was statistically significant.

4.   There is an increased participation in away-from-home activities. More mothers seek and participate in educational programs
for their own advancement and are also more active in community activities.

Three out of four mothers in one first-grade parents' community, for example, were found to be HIPPY participants. HIPPY mothers of children in another first-grade class organized a committee to work with the principal and some of the teachers in their school on a program to continue HIPPY when they "graduated" at the end of the year.

Aides told about mothers who, when faced with the challenge of working on the HIPPY materials with their children, opted to enroll in evening classes so as to acquire the reading skills necessary to work without the assistance of an older child. The data on the impact on mothers are extensive and varied. The examples cited above merely highlight the areas of major impact. The mothers freely speak of their sense of accomplishment and their pleasure in participation in the program.

HIPPY AIDES

HIPPY aides are themselves mothers of preschool children, and participate in the program both as mothers and as teachers of other mothers. In the course of their work they undergo the same kinds of changes as do all the mothers. For them, however, the program provides a much more intensive impact, producing additional changes:

1. The aides acquire new status and respect in their community. An aide reported her feelings about this as follows:

Today, when a child meets me in the street and calls out to me "Teacher, I've finished the workbook, could you bring me another?" I am very pleased to hear him call me this way. I am a simple housewife who began to work and to go out of the house because of HIPPY. I feel wonderful. Until yesterday I was this boy's neighbor; today I am his teacher.

2. The aides develop skills in dealing with problems arising out of the teaching situation. An aide who worked with a young Indian mother of four who could neither read nor write explained and read out the story for the week, moving about and dramatizing all the actions in order to help clarify the words, thereby making it possible for the mother to tell the story to her children.

3. The aides acquire increased self-confidence, both in themselves as women and in their work as aides. They especially note the relationship between this newly found self-confidence and their sense of making a contribution to their community.

The program has made me more independent, more sure of myself, more aware of exactly what I can contribute to someone else.

I have a feeling of making a contribution to the group, my self-confidence has grown, and I have learned patience and understanding.

4.   There is a change in the relationship between the aides and their husbands. While the initial reactions of husbands is frequently one of impatience and jealousy when their wives are involved with things out of the home, most of the aides report improvement in the relationship over time.

Evening work is a problem for my family, but the big plus is that my husband now assumes more of his share of family obligations. He feeds and puts the children to bed. For me that's the greatest thing. And I know that, although they keep it a secret, he and the children are proud of me.

5.   The aides' work in HIPPY arouses desire for further education. Aides seek out and attend community courses in a variety of subjects and have been instrumental in providing the impetus for the provision of special enrichment courses for HIPPY aides around the country.

CONCLUSION

This brief report on HIPPY has been presented as an example of a successful home-based educational program which provides parents with learning activities to do with their children in addition to what the children learn in their preschool classes. The participation of both mother and child in these graded HIPPY activities produces a positive interactive effect. As the mother observes her child's mastery of each task her sense of satisfaction grows, and this, in turn, enables her to be a better teacher for her child.

A word of caution is appropriate at this point. Parents of disadvantaged children participate in parent-education programs under the assumption that in so doing they are contributing to their child's future success. If their participation does not bring about changes in the child's school performance, there is likely to be an increased feeling of inadequacy and failure, and this, in turn, may result in a pulling back from further contact with the educational establishment. To the extent that parent-school communication is important for stability and continuity in the child's school career, the parent-education program will have proven to be countereffective for the child.

We, in HIPPY feel that the contract we offer participating mothers is honest and carefully thought through. There is little chance that the parents will fail to see positive changes in their children and we know that the children have a better chance for school success.

BIBLIOGRAPHY

Fitts, W.H. *Manual for the Tennessee self concept scale.* Nashville, TN: Counselor Recordings and Tests, 1965.

Frankel, Yaacov. *Adaptation of Tennessee self concept scale.* Ramat Gan, Israel: Bar-Ilan University, 1976.

Lazar, I., Hubbell, V.R., & Murray, H. *Summary report: The persistence of preschool effects. A long-term follow-up of fourteen infant and preschool experiments.* (DHEW Publication No. OHDS 78-30129). Washington, D.C.: U.S. Government Printing Office, 1977.

THE PARENT AS PARTNER IN THE EDUCATIONAL ADVANCEMENT

OF PRESCHOOL-AGE CHILDREN

Sara Smilansky and Leah Shepathiah

Tel Aviv University & Szold Research Institute
Israel

INTRODUCTION

The School System is Interested in Cooperating with Parents

The school views children's parents as important partners in its educational activity. Teacher and parents share the same goal, which is for the children to make progress. Both devote energy, time, and talent to help children develop and succeed in their studies.

In this situation, where a shared basic interest exists, the teacher (whether in school or in kindergarten) asks the parents to share in the school system's efforts. Parents are asked to supervise their child's homework; if the child has difficulties in his or her studies, the parents will be asked to help or to make sure someone else helps the child. Sometimes parents are invited to school or to the kindergarten to learn new teaching methods in various subjects so that they will be able to help their children at home. Teachers assume that parents are capable of learning and understanding the teaching methods, and capable also of helping their children.

In asking parents to help in enriching and teaching their children, teachers recognize that the home has several important advantages over the formal school system:

1. Parents can give their children individualized help in their studies; they can identify difficulties and deal with weak

points.   In school the teacher has limited time for individualized
work.

2.   The child is at home for many hours during the afternoon
and evening, and the parent can use these hours for short study
periods whenever most comfortable for both parent and child.

3.   The attention and interest parents show while helping
children in their studies act as important positive reinforcers of
learning activity in the classroom.   It is possible that this point
is more important than the learning that actually takes place at
home with the parents' help.

While there are many positive aspects to involving parents in
their children's studies, there are also many severe problems.   It
is important to be aware of these when planning to gain the parents'
cooperation in the process of fostering and teaching their children.

In this article we will present the problems; describe a research
program undertaken in order to study the subject; and propose an
approach that focuses on parents--their needs, preferences, attitudes--
even when our contact with them is meant to advance their children,
and not to advance the parents themselves.

Parents Ready to Cooperate

Most parents in Israel attach great importance to their children's
success in their studies.   This is true and evident for both educated
and uneducated parents.   The child's status at home is principally
determined by his or her success or failure in school.   A child who
is a good student and gets along well in school is forgiven difficulties and failures in other aspects of life.   On the other hand,
when a child behaves in ways that characterize a "good child,"
such as helping parents, being considerate of brothers, and being
friendly, but does not succeed in school and does not receive good
grades, the parents do not attach much importance to good deeds and
good behavior.

Both educated parents, who come from homes where the value of
education was stressed, and uneducated parents are aware of the decisive importance of education in Israeli society.   In addition, many
parents who have little education themselves want their children to
achieve what they failed to achieve themselves.   They see the school
as one of the main instruments for the advancement and social status
of their children.

The child's success in school directly and immediately influences
the parents' social status.   They can take pride in their child's success in front of neighbors and relatives.   In this way parents express

their feeling that they are successful parents, seeing that they
brought into the world and raised a child capable of dealing with
the aims presented by the school. When a child achieves an education
and succeeds in the educational field, the parents are assured that
their child will grow to have a successful life. On the other hand,
when the child has difficulties at school, the parents' self-confidence
is shaken, and their self-image as good parents is weakened. Parents
tend to feel guilty because of their children's difficulties. And they
are full of fears concerning their children's future and integration
into society.

It can be said that teachers have a partner who fully shares
the school's aims. The parent population greatly values the school's
role in the scholastic, emotional, and social development of their
children and in preparing them to be educated and cultured adults.
Given the children's great importance to parents, the parents are
especially sensitive to matters concerning the school. They expect
much from school and from the teachers in all that concerns the
child's achievements in the scholastic, social and emotional areas. In
this situation, where teacher and parent share a common interest, the
necessary basis exists for actively involving parents in the educational advancement of their children.

Conflict between Parental and Teaching Roles

For these reasons, parents usually respond positively when the
system asks them to cooperate actively, and they express readiness
to accept various tasks suggested by the system. But in practice
many of the parents cannot fulfill the demands made of them for two
reasons:

1. *The home-family system has aims and problems of its own.*
In dealing with the home system, parents experience stresses and
sometimes even great difficulties. Parents carry much responsibility
connected with providing for the family's day-to-day existence. They
have problems of their own as human beings and as a married couple.
They have ties and commitments to the extended family and to friends.
Parents feel they have a right to find satisfaction in their lives.
They have needs, wishes, and priorities concerning their free time
and the financial means at their disposal. They expect to find satisfaction in raising and fostering their children and in their children's company. Without discussing this point further, the family
can be seen as a system having its own aims, organization, and
pattern in which the parents must invest a great deal of energy.

When parents are asked to teach their children at home, an additional burden is put on them; they are given a new role that had
not been part of the function of the family system. In practice,
new difficulties are created in addition to those existing already

in the framework of the home system's usual function.

3. *There is an essential conflict between fulfilling the role of parent and the role of teacher.* Anna Freud explains the essential differences between the role of mother and the role of teacher. She claims that the attempt to turn the mother into a teacher inevitably leads to conflict. She describes the child's psychological passage from the home atmosphere, characterized by the mother's limitless love, to the school atmosphere, characterized by the teacher's limited love and attention. Freud talks of the importance of this difference in a child's development. In her opinion, the teacher's role is not that of a "mother substitute." If teachers play the mother's role, they will receive reactions from the child that are suitable to the mother-child relationship, but not to the relations between the child and another adult, such as the teacher. If, as teachers, we take the mother's role, the child will expect from us attention and endless affect; he or she will wish to get rid of all other children in the class, to stay only with "mother," and to be only hers in the class.

Anna Freud suggests, therefore, that teachers develop a certain distance in their relations with children to prevent them from feeling jealous. When there is confusion and lack of clarity between the roles of parent and teacher, learning for children becomes impossible. Learning does not require the characteristics of motherhood. These characteristics only confuse the child. In Freud's opinion, teachers should be neutral, objective people who do not build strong emotional and libidinal relations with the children. The teacher should be less "woman," less "loving," less "caretaker" than the mother; she should be accepting and attentive, express expectations, and give praise. In other words, teaching and learning require a certain emotional distance both on the teacher's side and on the child's side. A dimension of objectivity is needed that is impossible and nonexistent in parent-child relations.

Besides the differences already mentioned between the mother-child and teacher-child relationships, other differences exist that arise from the structure of the home and the school and from their behavioral precepts: the school as a framework for many children of the same age versus the home, where there are no other children of the same age; a relation of limited duration with the teacher (till the end of the class or school), versus the relation with the mother that lasts till the day of her death; differences in the dimensions of space and environment at home and in school, and so forth.

These differences create totally different experiences in children's relationships with their teacher as compared with the mother-child relationship. These differences express the range, wealth, and multiplicity of relations in human society. In this

sense a "teacher" is not a "mother," and a "mother" is not a
"teacher." And also a "pupil" is not a "son," and a "son" is not
a "pupil." These differences in roles, in areas of relations, in
the essence of relations, and in rules of behavior present children
with alternative systems of relationships, developing their cognitive and emotional skills, their discriminative ability, and their
capacity for discriminant adaptive reactions.

Clearly, the attempt to pass on to parents teaching roles involves many problems. Not all parents can solve the basic conflict
between parental and teaching roles, even if only for a limited
number of hours per week. Even giving parents good supervision does
not ensure their ability to fulfill the role assigned them. Only
some parents can bridge the contradiction between the differing
functions and harmonize them.

And indeed, many people who work with parents report that parents experience feelings of frustration and guilt at not being able
to fulfill the teaching and fostering roles assigned them by the
school or the kindergarten. The parents' attempt to fulfill the
role may at times introduce much tension into the home and sometimes
may create severe conflict between parents and children during the
afternoon hours. The parents' awareness of the importance of helping their children is not a guarantee of success, while failure
in fulfilling the role is in such cases accompanied by feelings of
guilt.

In order to study this subject and to understand the problems
and the positive aspects of having the parents share in the educational advancements of their children, an experimental research
program was undertaken.[1] Its focus was on having parents teach
their kindergarten children the elements of reading, parallel with
the kindergarten teacher's work. The experiment also continued in
first grade, but here mainly the results of work in the kindergarten
will be reported.

DESCRIPTION OF THE RESEARCH

Background and Aims

The research dealing with involving the parents in teaching
their children to read was based on experience gained in two previous experiments in which parents shared in the general intellectual fostering of their children in kindergarten classes for 5-year-
olds and 4-year-olds.[2]

Previous experimental research had brought to light some important results:

1. Regarding parents' readiness to cooperate, experience generally had been positive. Most parents responded positively to a request to cooperate in fostering their children. The few parents who expressed reservations were not opposed to the activity in itself, but raised personal reasons that prevented them from cooperating. It became apparent that one cannot expect cooperation and devotion in "problem" families, for example, families where relations between husband and wife are bad or where there is severe chronic illness. The experiments showed that one need not be afraid of asking families with many children to cooperate. There, too, one often finds great parental devotion. The conclusions regarding cooperation were that uneducated parents have the basic motivation necessary for involving them in fostering their children; they are very interested in their child's progress; and some of them are willing to make the effort to attain this purpose.

2. Regarding the children's achievements, the results were not very encouraging. At the end of the experiment, no differences in general intelligence were found between the experimental groups and the control groups. When differences in achievements were listed for the specific study units on which children and parents had worked, it was found that children who studied with their parents at home had higher achievements in certain skill areas than the control children who studied only in the kindergarten. The experiments explained the nonsignificance of the achievements of children in the experimental groups as due to the short duration of the experiment. This did not make it possible for parents to adapt to the role of teacher, to find suitable methods of work, and to organize their day at home so as to enable them to devote sufficient time and attention to the one child.

At this point it was decided to undertake longitudinal research involving parents in fostering their children. The research began with kindergarten children and concentrated on teaching them reading. Since this is a skill that by its very nature requires continuity, it seemed suitable for testing when the children reached first and second grade. This report focuses mainly on the first stage: parents teaching their children to read in kindergarten.

The longitudinal study was to provide detailed answers concerning four areas that should be examined by every project involving parents in fostering and teaching their children:

• Degree of cooperation. Will parents cooperate over a long period of time—a year, two years, or longer? Will they grow tired after a time? When? Which parents will continue to cooperate? In other words, what are the background variables connected with continued cooperation in the long run?

• Quality of the learning situation. Will the study activities at home take place in a good atmosphere and will both parent and child enjoy the activities, although they will be centered around the reading and writing skills that are essentially verbal? Will the child have to be compelled to do the activities? Who among the family members will be the one who teaches reading, and who will influence the degree of cooperation and achievement? To what degree will this activity lay a burden on the home? What are the main difficulties standing in the way of the parent's and child's study activities?

• Attitude to the study units. Will uneducated parents be able to teach the child to read? Up to what stage? Will parents prefer teaching reading because of its practical use over other fostering activities that will be suggested to them?

• The child's achievements. Will the parents' teaching influence the children's reading level? In which stages?

Population

The experiment took place in all four kindergartens in a residential area in central Israel. Kindergartens in a similar neighborhood in the same part of the country served as the control groups. Experimental and control groups were organized in this way for two reasons: (1) To ensure that most children in the experimental group would continue to study in the same schools in the neighborhood so that it would be possible to continue the experiment in grades 1 and 2; and (2) to ensure the isolation of experimental group families from control group families to prevent control group families from "catching on" to the teaching and learning activities tested in the experimental group.

After house visits to each of the 125 children in the kindergartens targeted for the experiment, 80 families agreed to participate. A total of 68 children from these families actually took part in the experiment; the rest dropped out for various reasons at the very start. The 68 experimental children were matched in pairs with 68 children in the equivalent neighborhood whose parents had also agreed to take part in the experiment. The matching was done by a number of variables: sex, education of parents, number of children in the family, child's position in the sibling group (in descending order). The experimental population resembled the control population in most variables. This was a population with a low socioeconomic background. About a third of the mothers in the experimental group worked as simple manual workers (except for one mother who was a skilled worker and one who was semi-skilled), and about two-thirds were housewives.

Process of the Experimental Work

As mentioned above, house visits were made to all of the kindergarten children in the experimental and control neighborhoods in
order to ask the parents to take part in the experiment. Parents
were told that they were being asked to help the kindergarten
teacher to prepare the child for school. The advantages the parents
have over the kindergarten teacher in the ability to help the child
were emphasized. The matter was presented so as not to make the
parents feel they were being tested or that the educational institution was coming to teach them how to be better parents. On the
contrary, the educational institution was asking the parents' help
in fulfilling its function. Parents were told they would have to
give half an hour per day, every day except Friday and Saturday for
working with the child, and would have to come to meetings in the
kindergarten once every two weeks in the evening to receive materials
and instructions. Parents in the control group were notified later
on by letter that the said activity would not take place because of
lack of funds.

The experiment lasted six months. The parents were invited
to come once every two weeks, so that the maximum number of group
meetings was twelve. Meetings were held during the evening hours
so as to enable working mothers and fathers to participate.

The kindergarten teacher invited all the parents of children in
her class to the first meeting. She opened the meeting, presented
the experimenter to the parents, praised the experimenter's ability
and knowledge of working with children and parents, and spoke of
how important she thought it would be for parents to come to all of
the meetings. The teacher described what the parents would have to
do in the course of the activity and the importance of this activity
for the children. After this opening, the teacher left and the
parents stayed on with the experimenter.

The materials the parents were given focused mainly on teaching
reading. The focus was thus on the systematic learning of a given
skill as distinct from fostering general ability. Reading is
suitable for continuous action; it is a significant study unit that
contributes to scholastic success at school. Also, the child's
progress is here immediately visible, serving as intrinsic reinforcement to the effort put into the learning by both parent and
child. An additional advantage is that reading achievements can be
reliably tested, and therefore the influence of the parents' activity will be considerable, even if relatively small.

The study units for reading included varied materials:

• Cards with words printed in them, so that the child could
play with the words, matching them, arranging them in sentences,
reading them, and gluing them onto paper to form reading booklets

• Cards with pictures printed on them so that the child could cut out the pictures, glue them onto cardboard, and match them with printed words

• A game called "Let's play and learn to read"

• Pictures for games of matching, generalization, and contrasts

• Printed words for games of matching, generalization, and contrasts

• Booklets graded by difficulty and reading level adapted to the kindergarten curriculum and to the children's achievements

In addition to the teaching of reading, other fostering units were included, similar to those used in the two previous experiments (cards and games for developing perceptual skills, discrimination, and generalization; concepts of quantity, etc.).

When the parents came to the biweekly meetings, they told the experimenter individually how they had dealt with the material, what was too difficult and burdensome, and what was easy and enjoyable. During the conversation with an individual parent, the experimenter found out how the parent had acted, and, if necessary, gave instructions. When the entire parents' group met, a group discussion took place on how the teaching at home was progressing. Then the experimenter described the new material she had brought that day and different efficient ways to use it with the children at home. She also described additional ways to use the materials the parents had been given on previous occasions.

When parents missed one meeting, the experimenter would immediately send a post card, saying she was sorry they had not come to the last meeting, that she was keeping the materials for them, and that she expected to see them at the next meeting. If a parent did not come to an additional meeting, the experimenter visited him or her at home and tried to encourage the parent to come to the next meeting.

At the end of the 6-month activity period, all parents were interviewed and information was gathered concerning cooperation, the learning situation, and the attitudes towards the different study units. In addition, all experimental and control group children were given an individual reading test to check their achievement. The interviews and tests, in addition to the record of parents' attendance at meetings, served to evaluate the experiment.

RESEARCH RESULTS

We will report here what we learned from the experimental

activity with parents in kindergarten, in all four areas that
constituted the aim of our research: (1) The parents' cooperation,
(2) the learning situation at home, (3) the parents' attitude to
the different study units, and (4) oral and comprehension reading
achievements of the experimental children (whose parents participated in the activity) as compared with the control children (whose
parents had agreed to participate, but were notified that the activity would not take place).

Results Concerning Parents' Cooperation

Data presented here concerns parents' actual degree of devotion
to the learning activity at home as expressed in three measures:
number of biweekly visits to the kindergarten, number of days per
week on which parents taught their children, and average amount of
time per day devoted to learning. We will also present data on
the relation between degree of devotion and parents' background
data.

Degree of devotion to the activity. The number of visits by
the parents to the biweekly meetings served as a central measure
for evaluating the parents' degree of cooperation. The distribution
of number of visits is presented in Table 1.

Table 1. Distribution of experimental population by number of visits
          to biweekly meetings

No. of Visits	No. of Families	% of Families
1-3	18	26.5
4-6	28	41.2
7-9	10	14.7
10-12	12	17.6
Total	68	100.0

It appears that a fourth of the families did not actually perform the fostering activity. Since they missed an absolute majority
of meetings, they did not receive the instruction materials.
Another 41% of the families participated little and came to meetings, at most, once a month. Thus, although parents expressed
readiness to participate and were in part even enthusiastic about
the program, we see that in practice there are many obstacles in
the way of performing the activity. In effect, the difficulties
are greater than the wish and readiness to cooperate. Only about

the 32% who attended 7-12 meetings can it be said that they cooperated and were devoted. Many of those who missed meetings expressed their sorrow over this and said they had difficulty coming in the evening because of fatigue at the end of a workday or because of difficulties at home.

In the interview held at the end of the activity, parents' reports about the amount of time devoted in practice to studying served as an additional measure of the degree of devotion. Almost half of the parents devoted 4 days per week or more to the activity (Table 2). Most parents taught for 30 minutes or more each time (Table 3).

Table 2. Population distribution by number of days per week devoted to studying (in percentages)

No. of days	1	2	3	4	5	Not fixed	Total
% of families	1.8	14.0	22.8	1.8	45.6	14.0	100

Table 3. Population distribution by average amount of time devoted to studying per day

Amount of time in minutes	15	30	45	60	Not fixed	Total
% of families	20.3	42.2	18.7	4.7	14.0	100

Even if we take into consideration the possibility that parents' reports exaggerated in a positive direction, it can be stated that at least some of the families showed satisfactory devotion to the activity, notwithstanding the difficulties with which these families had to deal (low education level, many children, difficulties in Hebrew and reading, problems with organizing time, etc.). The devotion of part of the population proves that the parents are strongly motivated to act for their children's progress. But the results also suggest the existence of problems and difficulties that prevent some of the parents from devoting themselves to the teaching task. As we shall see later, a low degree of devotion is explained both by a heavy load and by difficulties in satisfactorily fulfilling a teacher's role.

   Background data connected with devotion to the activity.   A
question arises: What characterizes families that cooperate? To
answer this question, we tried to examine the relation between background data about the child and his or her family and degree of
readiness to cooperate in performing the activity. It appears that
the child's sex and also the parents' country of origin are con-
spicuously related to cooperation. This relationship is expressed
both in the initial agreement to participate in the experiment and
in the actual devotion (number of biweekly visits). Parents of
sons are apparently more ready to take upon themselves the role of
teacher than are parents of daughters (Table 4). Among those who
agreed to cooperate, parents of sons also showed greater devotion,
but the difference was not statistically significant (Table 5).

Table 4. Agreement to participate in the experiment by sex by child[a]

	Parents of sons	Parents of daughters	Total
Agreed	45	35	80
Did not agree	16	29	45
Total	61	64	125

[a]$\overline{X}^2 = 4.14$, $p < .05$

Table 5. Degree of devotion to activity by sex of child

Sex of child	Degree of devotion			Distribution (%) Total
	Small	Medium	Great	
Male	34.2	36.6	29.2	100
Female	51.7	33.4	14.9	100
Total	41.8	34.3	23.9	100

These results confirm the accepted opinion that parents from Near Eastern and North African countries do not attach the same importance to the education of daughters as to the education of sons. Only thus can one explain the higher proportion of agreement to cooperate on the part of parents of sons and the devotion in practice to performing the activity of those who agreed.

Another interesting result is the relation between country of origin and cooperation. The proportion of those agreeing to participate in the activity was higher for parents from Yemen, in comparison to the rest of the population (Table 6).

Table 6. Agreement to participate in the experiment, by father's country of origin

| | Origin of father (N) | | | | |
	Yemen[a]	Iraq	Other	Unknown	Total
Agreed	19	37	19	5	80
Did not agree	1	28	13	3	45
	20	65	32	8	125

[a]When Yemenites are compared with the rest, $\overline{X}^2 = 8.45$, $p < .01$.

Table 7. Degree of devotion to activity, by father's country of origin

| | Degree of devotion (%) | | | |
	Small	Medium	Great	Total
Yemen[a]	33.3	22.2	44.4	100
Iraq and Iran	48.0	34.1	17.1	100
North Africa	40.0	60.0	--	100
Turkey and Israel	--	75.0	25.0	100
Total	41.8	34.3	23.9	100

[a]When Yemenites are compared with the rest, good participation versus small and medium, $\overline{X}^2 = 4.48$, $p < .05$.

It is interesting to note that in the two previous experiments
we also found that Yemenites were more cooperative, although these
parents dealt with fostering general abilities and not with specific
skills. Apparently the Yemenite community traditionally attaches
more importance to learning than do other groups, and perhaps
patterns of parenting, including "teaching" roles, are rooted in
this community's tradition.

In any case, it is clear that the relationship we found between
parents' degree of cooperation and country of origin and the child's
sex emphasizes the influence of the cultural tradition on the parents'
attitude to the task suggested by the system. When attempting to
involve parents in fostering and teaching, one must take into consideration the existence of these influences on families.

Another background variable that was significantly related to
cooperation was the child's position in the sibling group. On the
child's position in the family, we have no data for those who did
not agree to participate. In practice, there is greater devotion
to first-born children than to children born later (Table 8).

Table 8. Degree of devotion to activity by child's position in
family[a]

Child's position in family	Distribution for degree of devotion (%)			
	Low	Medium	Good	Total
Eldest	25.0	25.0	50.0	100
Middle	37.0	40.7	22.3	100
Youngest	56.0	36.0	8.0	100
Total	41.8	34.3	23.9	100

[a]When eldest children are compared with others, good cooperation
versus low and medium, $\overline{X}^2 = 6.34$, $p < .05$.

With the first child it seems relatively easy to adopt non-
conventional parental roles, because the patterns of parenting
still retain a measure of flexibility. Also, the family is small
and the parents are less burdened and under less stress. But one
must be careful in assessing this finding because of the small
number of elder children (16) and because the number of children
in the family is related to the child's position in the sibling
group. Indeed, a certain relationship does exist between the number of children in the family and parents' cooperation, but this

relationship is not statistically significant.

Among families that agreed to participate in the experiment, there was a relatively high number of families with four children or fewer, while among those who refused, there were many families with a larger number of children. But, as mentioned before, the relationship is not significant.

Table 9. Agreeing to participate in the experiment by number of children in family

	2 to 4 children in family	5 children or more in family	Unknown	Total
Agreed	47	30	3	80
Did not agree	17	24	4	45
Total	64	54	7	125

A similar situation exists regarding devotion in practice (Table 10). Here, too, we see a tendency for greater devotion in smaller and medium-sized families and less devotion in the large families.

Table 10. Degree of devotion to activity by number of children in family

No. of children in family	Distribution for degree of devotion (%)			
	Low	Medium	Great	Total
2 to 4	38.6	34.1	27.3	100
5+	45.8	37.5	16.7	100
Total	41.8	34.3	23.9	100

Table 11 expresses the relation between devotion and number of children in another way. It seems that the difference by family size is mainly between those who show great devotion and all others.

Table 11.   Degree of devotion to activity by average number of chil-
            dren in family

Degree of participation	Low	Medium	Great
Average number of children in family	4.1	4.5	3.3

It is not surprising that large families find it more difficult
to come to meetings and to devote themselves to fostering one specific child, since they must overcome many obstacles. On the contrary, it is more surprising to find that in some large families
there was great devotion to the activity. Apparently family size is
not the main factor that influences parents' willingness to advance
their child and their readiness to preserve.

No difference was found between working mothers' devotion and
the devotion of mothers not working outside the house. Nor did
we find a relationship between father's occupational level (un-
skilled, semi-skilled, or skilled worker) and devotion to the activity. It must be remembered, though, that we are dealing with a
population that in this sense is homogeneous.

To conclude the discussion of factors connected with cooperation, it is important to emphasize that in all work with parents it
is vital to relate to the individual parents on two main levels:
first, the nature and quantity of stresses and difficulties with
which the family must deal (as expressed in our findings about the
child's position in the family and the number of children); and
second, the parents' attitude to the suggested activity itself,
its character, aims, and contents. This attitude is no doubt determined by several factors, among them cultural tradition (as expressed in our findings about sex of child and parents' country of
origin), patterns of parenting, personal interests, and self-confidenc
Even when a real willingness and readiness to perform the activity
exist, parents must overcome many difficulties, and it is important to
find out what inhibiting factors exist in the family in order to help
solve these problems, and not burden it still more.

Results Concerning the Learning Situation at Home

The information we have on the learning situation at home is
based mainly on parents' reports during the interview that took
place at the end of the experiment. The experimenter's ability to
assess the situation at home was limited, because she visited only
those homes where parents had not come to meetings. But her im-

pression, based on the group discussions, was that the picture presented at the interview was quite faithful. We examined a number of
subjects dealing with the learning situation at home.

Who is responsible for performing the activity? One of the subjects to which we attached importance (as a result of our experiences
in previous studies) related to the person responsible for performing the activity at home. From previous experiments we learned
that orderly and efficient action depends on the mother's cooperation,
even if she is not the only "teacher." In a considerable percentage
of families the siblings did most of the teaching, and this notwithstanding constant appeals from the experimenter not to let
siblings bear the main responsibility for the activity (Table 12).

It is interesting that only in a few houses was the activity
left mainly to the father. In most families, the mother was the
main "teacher," by herself or in cooperation with the father or
other siblings.

Table 12. Average attendance at meetings, by main teacher in the
home

Teacher	Number of subjects	Percent of subjects	Average attendance at meetings
Father	4	6.3	7.0
Mother	22	34.4	5.2
Father and mother	11	17.2	7.8
Siblings	24	37.5	a
Varying	3	4.7	4.4
Total	64	100.0	5.5

aInformation about 4 families is missing.

In Table 12 we also find confirmed the findings of previous
experiments, whereby it is important that the mother should be the
person mainly responsible for the activity. When siblings served
as "principal teacher," there was less participation in meetings
than when parents taught. Maximum devotion was attained when both
parents served as principal teachers.

It appears that the mother's active participation is necessary
not only for ensuring continuity in the activity, but also for
attaining scholastic achievements (Table 13).

Table 13.   Children's achievement in reading comprehension (answering content questions) by principal teacher at home

Principal teacher	Level of achievement, numerical distribution				Level of Achievement distribution in (%)			
	Low (0-5)	Medium (6-15)	High (16+)	Total	Low (0-5)	Medium (6-15)	High (16+)	Total
Father	2	2	--	4	50.0	50.0	--	100
Mother	9	6	7	22	41.0	27.3	31.8	100
Mother and father	1	4	6	11	9.1	36.4	54.5	100
Siblings	18	5	1	24	75.0	20.8	4.2	100
Varying	1	2	--	3	33.3	66.7	--	100
Total	31	19	14	64	48.4	29.7	21.9	100

The highest achievement is attained when both father and mother cooperate. The second best achievement is attained when the mother serves as principal teacher. When siblings are mainly responsible for the activity, achievement is very low (in a 2×3 table, parents compared with the rest, $\overline{X}^2$ = 11.9, p < .01). In all kinds of work with parents, it is thus important to first put the mother in a central position, and then try to gain some measure of cooperation from the father. It would seem that the father's participation is important mainly in terms of supporting the mother as an expression of common interest in the subject. The experimenter reported that there were several families in which both husband and wife came to the meetings and contributed greatly to the group discussion.

At the end of the year the parents were asked whether they thought the activity should continue in first grade. The number of positive answers to this question was higher among families where parents taught the child than where siblings were mainly responsible for the activity, but the difference was not significant (Table 14).

Enjoying the activity. The parents' enjoyment (or lack of it) of the activity is also very important. We asked the parents whether they had enjoyed the activity, and if they had, why. Tables 15 and 16 present the distribution of the answers.

Table 14.   Attitude to continuing the activity in first grade, by
            main teacher at home

| Main teacher | Attitude to continuation N | | Total |
	Positive	Negative or doubtful	
Parents	23	12	35
Siblings	14	11	25
Total	37	23	60

Table 15.   Distribution of answers to the question: Did you en-
            joy teaching your child?[a]

Reaction	Distribution (%)
1. Did not at all enjoy themselves	--
2.	4.8
3. Sometimes, with certain units	25.8
4.	9.7
5. Almost always enjoyed themselves	59.7
Total	100.0

[a]The experimenter marked the answer's position on a scale of
1 to 5, according to the tone of the parent's answer.

Table 16.   Distribution of reactions to question: Why did you en-
            joy teaching the child?

Reaction	Distribution (%)
Because the child enjoyed himself	8.2
Because you can see he is understanding	73.8
Teaching is interesting, fun for the parents	9.8
Other	8.2
Total	100.0

The parent's satisfaction and enjoyment are important in the highest degree for fostering activities. These parents are burdened by their own problems and difficulties, and if the fostering activity is not enjoyable and satisfying but serves as another source of frustration and stress, there is no chance that the activity will be continued or will help the child. On the contrary, a learning activity that is neither enjoyable nor satisfying serves as a focus for stress and fighting in the family. From the findings we see that a third of the parents did not enjoy the activity at all or did not enjoy it most of the time (Table 15).

Among parents who did enjoy themselves, only 10% enjoyed the activity of teaching in itself, whereas three-fourths of the parents derived enjoyment from the child's progress (Table 16). This finding suggests that one of the factors motivating parents is the recognition of the importance of the activity (the child's reading achievements) and the ability to see the child's progress as an important goal.

The fact that only 10% enjoyed the teaching activity itself confirms the argument concerning the conflict between parenting and teaching (we shall discuss this point further on). It may be that lack of intensive enjoyment is one of the main factors that led many parents to have reservations about continuing the activity in first grade, where the responsibility for the child's education and achievements clearly passes to the teacher. Therefore, if one wishes to have parents persevere in a fostering activity, ways and means must be found for parents to enjoy the activity itself, as an important factor in reinforcing the tie between parent and child and as a motivational factor for the fostering activity.

Difficulties in performing the activity. By means of a number of questions, we tried to examine the difficulties parents encountered because of the activity at home. The first question was: How much of a burden was the activity? (Table 17).

It seems that, notwithstanding the enjoyment that parents derive from the child's progress, performing the activity is not easy for them. Only a third of the parents did not report any difficulties, more than a third sometimes encountered difficulties, and about 27% found the activity very burdensome. These findings reinforce the claim we presented in the introduction, namely, that the special situation where parents serve as teachers for their children is complex and problematic.

Table 18 reflects the difficulties involved with the teaching role, which parents had taken upon themselves. About a fourth of the difficulties arise from the child's resistance to this new set of relations, where parent becomes teacher, the child becomes the parent's student. Another fourth of the problem is connected to

Table 17.   Distribution of reactions to the question: Was learn-
            ing at home much of a burden for you?

Reaction	Distribution (%)
Lack of time to come to meetings	10.6
Lack of time to teach	19.2
Problems with other siblings	6.4
Problems with younger siblings	21.3
Do not know how to teach	8.5
Child not interested	23.4
Other	10.6
Total	100.0

Table 18.   Distribution of reactions to question: What mainly made
            the teaching difficult?

Reaction	Distribution (%)
1. Very much	27.0
2.	3.2
3. A little, sometimes	33.3
4.	3.2
5. Not at all	33.3
Total	100.0

difficulties with other siblings, aroused by this new set of relations. There is also a small percentage of parents who see the
main difficulty in the teaching itself, i.e., in filling the teacher's
role. In any case, only 30% of the difficulties are connected to
objective factors such as lack of time, and 70% of the burden and
the difficulty are focused on the learning situation itself.

To better clarify the problems with the siblings, the parents
were asked a number of questions. As can be seen in Table 19, siblings usually wanted to participate.

In more than half of the families where siblings wanted to participate, the parents said they had in fact allowed them to be
present. In the other families, other employment was found for the
child (6 families), and in two cases activity was discontinued be-

Table 19. Reaction to question: Did the other siblings want to
           be present when teaching was taking place?

Reaction	Distribution (%)
Younger siblings	30.5
Older siblings	23.7
Only one child wanted	6.8
Were not interested	22.0
No siblings close in age	17.0
Total	100.0

cause of problems with siblings. From this we conclude that it is
important to consider all children in the family when performing a
fostering activity; care must be taken for the activity to include
all children. Parents must also be advised on how to deal with
problems that arise. Otherwise, the activity can cause more harm
than good.

About a fourth of the parents reported on problems arising
from the child's not being interested in the special learning
situation at home (Table 18). In Table 20 this difficulty is more
clearly expressed.

Table 20. Reaction to question: Did the child have to be forced
           to study or did he come willingly?

Reaction	Distribution (%)
1. There was need to force him	7.9
2.	6.4
3. Usually did not resist	39.7
4.	--
5. Was very interested	46.0
Total	100.0

With more than half of the children problems sometimes arose,
and in some cases the parents had to force the child, creating an
atmosphere of coercion around the task of learning and teaching.

Hence, it is necessary to find ways that will give satisfaction and
enjoyment to both parent and child and that will prevent the danger
of the learning activity's aggravating existing problems and creating new problems in the family.

Results Concerning Study Units

Parents welcomed the idea of teaching reading in kindergarten,
and according to the kindergarten teacher they were enthusiastic
when told they would be able to teach the children reading at home.
In the course of time it became apparent that in practice the parents
devoted most of their time to materials connected with reading, while
making little use of the other fostering units, and then only when
requested to do so. The parents seemed to fear that their children
would be tested and that the experimenter would see that the parents
had not done what she had asked them to do. But parents devoted
most of their time and attention to the different activities dealing with reading. Proudly they brought to the meetings the booklets
with stories the children had invented. The children glued on
words and letters, wrote down missing words, and drew. Gradually
they reached a point of giving the story a name, dividing it into
chapters, etc. The parents bought colorful cardboard papers so
that the children could bind the booklet and make it look like a
book. The children prepared these booklets as presents for relatives who were proud that the little ones in kindergarten were
reading, writing, and making books.

At the end of the experiment, the parents were asked in a personal interview to express their opinion (by means of an open
question) of the units they were given, both for developing cognitive skills and for teaching reading. We were surprised that
only very few made critical comments, either positive or negative.
Most parents gave vague answers: "It was very good," "Everything
was fine," "Thank you, it's good." Apparently, most parents sill
lacked or were unwilling to express critical judgment, or perhaps
they were afraid of offending the experimenter, who interviewed them
herself. But our feeling is that they really tended to accept the
material and the instructions unquestioningly, and also tended to
perform the activity quite rigidly from fear of deviating or from
lack of creativity in these matters. It would seem that much time
must be devoted to developing in parents the flexibility necessary
for successful fostering, to awaken in them the wish for creativity
and for diversity, and to develop in them the critical faculty.
In the meanwhile, either they apply the units exactly as was suggested to them, or they avoid using a given unit or material.

Since the parents cannot be expected to use all materials
creatively, it is best to give them a choice. It is important to
offer them a variety of units with different materials in each unit

so that they can choose from them those suitable for them and their
child.

Results Concerning the Child's Achievements

Reading achievements. At the end of the kindergarten school
year, all of the children were given an individual reading test.
Scores on this test reflect both the technical aspect of reading
(oral reading) and reading comprehension. Table 21 presents the
average achievements of the experimental group in this test, by
tested areas. In all subareas, the achievements of the experimental
group were higher than those of the control group, who learned
reading only in kindergarten.

Table 21. Reading achievement at end of kindergarten school year,
           by areas and groups

Tested areas	Experimental		Control	
	Mean	Standard deviation	Mean	Standard deviation
Reading words	7.7	6.64	3.4	5.43
Reading stories	30.3	29.17	10.0	15.28
Fluency	23.1	24.67	5.9	10.91
Ability to relate to content	12.4	14.47	1.8	3.36
Answers to comprehension questions	9.4	10.84	2.2	4.47

Since we are dealing with kindergarten children a considerable
percentage of them of course learned nothing (especially in the
control group), i.e., their score in the different areas was zero.
Children who did not want to read were not forced to do so; in contrast, some children received maximum grades. Since the distribution
is not normal, it is difficult to learn much from the means. In
the tables that follow, the score distribution of the experimental
group is compared with that of the control group (Tables 22-24).

In terms of reading and reading comprehension, parents did
indeed help their children progress considerably beyond the point
reached by children taught only by the kindergarten teacher (Tables
22, 23, 24). Of the control group children, 33% could do no technical reading at all, compared with only 12% of the experimental

Table 22. Distribution of reading scores, by groups

Group score[a]	Distribution (N)		Distribution (%)	
	Experimental	Control	Experimental	Control
0	8	25	11.8	36.8
1–15	15	25	22.1	36.8
16–30	27	14	39.7	20.6
31+	18	4	26.5	5.9
Total	68	68	100.0	100.0

[a] In a 2X2 table (0 to 15 scores compared with 16+), $\overline{x}^2 = 20.0$, $p < .01$.

Table 23. Distribution of reading comprehension scores (lack of ability to recount content of read text), by groups

Group score[a]	Distribution (N)		Distribution (%)	
	Experimental	Control	Experimental	Control
0	16	32	23.5	47.1
1–5	16	30	23.5	44.1
6–10	7	4	10.3	5.9
11+	29	2	42.7	2.9
Total	68	68	100.0	100.0

[a] In a 2X2 table (0 to 5 scores compared with 6+), $\overline{x}^2 = 29.0$, $p < .01$.

Table 24. Distribution of scores in reading comprehension b, answers to comprehension questions

Group score[a]	Distribution (N)		Distribution (%)	
	Experimental	Control	Experimental	Control
0	22	36	32.4	52.4
1–5	9	25	13.2	36.8
6–10	19	6	27.9	8.8
11+	18	1	26.5	1.5
Total	68	68	100.0	100.0

[a] In a 2X2 table (0 to 5 scores compared with 6+), $\overline{x}^2 = 28.3$, $p < .01$.

group children. Great differences were also found in reading comprehension, especially at the higher levels. Only a few of the
control group children reached the higher levels, while most of
the children who learned with their parents at home attained a
good comprehension of the text.

It is difficult to tell what caused the achievement of the
experimental group children to be so much higher. The question is
whether it was the actual teaching at home by parents and other
family members, or whether the children were influenced by motivational factors aroused by the parents' attention. Perhaps the
children were more open to learning reading in the kindergarten
because their parents showed an interest in their progress, visited
the kindergarten, and brought home materials. The findings concerning the relation between the parents' degree of devotion and
reading achievements, which will be presented later on, provide a
partial answer to this question.

Parents' devotion and reading achievements. We tried to discover what degree of relation exists between the number of times
parents came to meetings and children's achievement. The average
number of visits in each achievement level is presented in Table
25. Achievement levels were in two areas of reading comprehension:
the ability to recount the text, and answers to questions dealing
with the text.

Table 25. Average attendance at meetings in kindergarten, by
           achievements in reading comprehension

	Ability to recount text		Answers to comprehension questions		
Test grade	Number of subjects	Average attendance	Test grade	Number of subjects	Average attendance
0	16	3.8	0	22	4.1
1-5	16	4.6	1-5	9	4.2
6-10	7	5.4	6-10	19	5.9
11-15	13	6.3	11-15	3	8.7
16+	16	8.2	16+	15	7.9
Total	68	5.7		68	5.7

It seems clear that a relation exists between degree of parents'
participation in meetings and their children's level of achievement
in two types of reading comprehension tests. We might, therefore,

have claimed that parents who were more devoted caused their children
to have higher achievements. But we found that there is a relation
between degree of devotion and the children's I.Q. The correlation
between attendance at meetings and I.Q. score was 0.45. As we shall
see later on, this is an a priori relationship and is not a result
of the parents' participation. Therefore, it was important to see
whether a relation exists between achievement and degree of parents'
devotion when we control for I.Q. In Table 26 we present correlations and partial correlations between achievement and parents'
attendance, and children's I.Q.

Table 26. Correlations and partial correlations between parents'
          attendance at meetings, I.Q. scores, and children's
          achievement in two areas of reading comprehension

Variables	Score in recounting read text	Score in answering comprehension questions
I.Q. score	.45	.51
Attendance	.46	.46
I.Q. when attendance is controlled for	.30	.38
Participation when I.Q. is controlled for	.33	.31

Even if we control for the influence of a child's I.Q. score
on his or her achievement, a significant relationship is found between parents' attendance and achievement in reading comprehension
in the two areas tested. Thus we can attribute to the parents'
activity at home an influence on the child's achievement that is
independent of the child's intelligence. This is also clear from
the lowering of the correlation between I.Q. and achievement, when
controlling for parents' degree of devotion. We can say that
parents of intelligent children have a greater tendency to devote
themselves to the activity (no doubt because their efforts are reinforced by seeing the child's progress), but the devotion itself
has an independent influence over and above the child's intellectual level.

It is interesting that in the control group the correlation
between I.Q. and achievement in reading comprehension is lower than
in the experimental group: 0.36 for recounting the reading text
and 0.33 for answering comprehension questions. This phenomenon

is partly explained by the existence of a smaller variance in
achievement for the control group. But it is also possible that
the especially high correlations in the experimental group express both the direct influence of intelligence on achievement and
the indirect influence resulting from the greater devotion of
parents of intelligent children.

    In conclusion, we can state that fostering by parents (in
addition to fostering in kindergarten) clearly influences reading
achievement. From the relation that was found between degree of
parents' devotion and achievement, we can conclude that the learning activity at home, in itself, contributed to the child's achievement over and above the motivational factors aroused in the child
by the activity.

DISCUSSION

    In the Introduction we presented the theoretical basis for
cooperation between the educational system and parents in the
scholastic advancement of children. It was noted that the fulfillment of these tasks involves many problems, notwithstanding the
basic readiness of parents to take upon themselves teaching tasks
relating to their children (recognizing, as they do, the importance
of scholastic achievement). These difficulties were expressed in
our experimental research, in which parents participated in teaching their kindergarten children the elements of reading, parallel
to reading lessons given in the kindergarten.

    The experiment showed that many parents respond positively
to the request to teach their children, and that some parents also
show great devotion to the activity. It also appears from the
experiment that parents can indeed contribute to their children's
achievement in the units that they teach them.

    At the same time, teacher-like activities performed by the
parents seem to create considerable difficulties at home. In spite
of the initial readiness to undertake the activity, in the end a
considerable proportion of the parents do not devote themselves
to the activity with the child and rarely come to meetings to
receive materials and instructions. Upon the child's entrance
into first grade, some of the parents express resistance to continuing the activity, while the enthusiasm of other parents decreases. Moreover, a considerable proportion of parents reported
that the activity was an additional burden on them. Only about
half of the parents enjoyed the activity, and only about 10% of
these enjoyed in itself the act of being their child's teacher.
Most of the enjoyment was derived from feeling that the child was
making progress. The fact that some of the families reported an
atmosphere of pressure, and that in a few cases it was even neces-

sary to force the child to learn, is a worrisome negative finding.

The difficulties in applying educational activities at home apparently arise from two essentially different factors:

1.   Parents are burdened and stressed by the daily problems of the family and by their own personal problems. Parents who missed meetings explained that they could not stand the pressure because of great fatigue at the end of a workday and various household problems requiring both energy and time. Therefore, the parents find it difficult to fulfill the demands of the new task, which is an additional burden. (About 30 parents reported lack of time for performing the activity.)

2.   Parents seem to have great difficulty in fulfilling the new and, for them, deviant role of teacher, and children have difficulty in seeing the parent as teacher and in filling their own role of pupil at home. The difficulties reported by most parents (lack of interest on the child's part, difficulties with other siblings, helplessness in filling teacher role) provide evidence of this problem and of the emotional stress experienced by parents and children involved in educational activity at home. There is no doubt that the conditions of emotional distance, support, and objectivity necessary for teaching and learning do not exist here.

The non-positive aspects of the activity revealed in the findings raise the following question: Is the price the family pays for the teaching and learning activity at home worthwhile, taking into consideration both the child's achievement and the activity's effect upon the whole family?

A particularly bothersome question is: What feelings and thoughts have the parents who did not fulfill the performance demands?

In our opinion, cooperation between the educational system and the home must be expressed in a variety of ways, and not necessarily by involving the parents in teacher-like tasks. But in view of the academic achievement found in our experiment following the parents' activity, such a partnership must not be utterly rejected. Parents should be given a choice of areas (if any) in which they would like to work with their children. In each area, alternative ways and materials should be prepared to aid parents in helping their children to progress. Choosing from a variety of alternatives will make it possible for different families to choose an activity that has a chance of fulfilling the following necessary conditions: (1) the activity will be perceived by the parent as being important for the child and contributing to his or her development; (2) the activity will be enjoyable for both parent and child; (3) the parent will feel self-assured in filling the teacher's role in the chosen activity; and (4) the activity will suit the special conditions of the individual family. If these conditions are fulfilled, we can expect different parents to accomplish the task they have chosen without creating tension and stress at home; and parents will not experience conflict in filling the role they choose.

Even if parents can choose an activity that suits them best, it is important to provide instructions and reinforcements that will facilitate the creation of the right atmosphere and conditions for the activity. The parent-educator must relate to the parent as to the central figure in the process, and must be sensitive to the difficulties that the parent might encounter. Sometimes parents should be helped to stop the activity without feelings of guilt for having deprived the child. The parent-educator must also take into consideration the entire situation of the family, although the activity is focused around a given child.

Under these conditions, in families that choose to do so, educational fostering of children by their parents will be possible without paying too high a price.

FOOTNOTES

1. Smilansky, Sara & Shephathiah, Leah. Involving uneducated parents in fostering their children. *Research report 193*. Jerusalem: Szold Institute, 1976, pp. 59-61.
2. *Ibid.*, pp. 24-58.

REFERENCE

Smilansky, Sara & Shephatia, Lea. Involving uneducated parents in fostering their children. *Research report 193*. Jerusalem: Szold Institute, 1976.

MATERNAL INFLUENCES IN THE FORMATION OF SEX IDENTITY AND GENDER ROLE DESIGNATION AMONG DIFFERENTLY SEXED TWINS, TRIPLETS AND QUADRUPLETS

Esther R. Goshen-Gottstein

Bar-Ilan University
Israel

INTRODUCTION

Though Maccoby and Jacklin (1974) in their book on sex differences found surprisingly little differentiation in the ways in which parents socialize their male and female children, Birns (1976) and Block (1978) consider that early environmental shaping of sex-differentiated behavior in children does exist in several crucial areas.

In the varied strategies used by researchers to investigate if and how parents differentially socialize their sons and daughters, there is one strategy which appears to have been overlooked. Specifically, what might be called a "natural experimental condition" occurs when parents rear opposite-sexed multiple infants. In this situation the same parents are faced with two, three or four children of different sex but of the same age. As a consequence, both birth-order effects and parental variables such as age and child-rearing experience are held constant.

Using home-observations in the naturalistic environment the present study concentrated on mothers and multiple infants in order to assess maternal reactions to opposite-sexed twins' and same-sexed twins' aggressive, dependent and helping behaviors. Based on previous research, these behavior categories were seen as potentially important for differential sex role socialization. Moreover, evidence accumulated in recent years suggests that stereotypes, existing from the time of the infant's birth, play a role in shaping parental behavior. Such stereotypes can be initiated by assigning a sex label to the infant (Condry & Condry, 1976; Parke, 1978; Rubin, Provenzano & Luria, 1974). Labeling then becomes an organizing rubric around which the child constructs a sex-role defini-

253

tion (Kohlberg, 1966). Dressing the infant in sex-typed clothes
serves a similar function (Will, Self & Data, 1976). Based on
these studies, the mother's gender-linked talk and differentiation
of her children's appearances and activities on the basis of the
children's sex, were also investigated. Unless otherwise stated,
only mothers were observed interacting with their children since
fathers and grandmothers were seldom present.

SUBJECTS

Seven families consisting of two sets of twins, two sets of
triplets and three sets of quadruplets were studied--13 boys and
9 girls in all. Each set contained children of both sexes. The
twin and triplet families all lived in Jerusalem and were born
within the same year. The quadruplets were born in different parts
of Israel within the same time period.

PROCEDURE

The families were observed monthly in their homes by two psychologists. These monthly visits, each lasting for several hours,
began at the infants' fifth month of age and lasted until the end of
their second year. Thereafter, home visits took place every two
months until the children were 3 1/2 years old. Some children were
followed up to age 5 or 6 years.

The observers were non-participant; that is, they responded to
both mothers and children but did not initiate any interactions with
them.

Data from the transcripts of observed behavior descriptions
were later categorized into areas considered relevant to the study
of sex-determined differences in socialization.

Children's dependency, helping and aggressive behaviors were
all defined operationally and each behavior was evaluated per visit
on a three-point scale. Mothers' positive and negative reinforcement of dependency and aggression and her requests for children's
assistance also were evaluated per visit on a three-point scale.

The different names and descriptions used by a mother in relation to each child during each observation were also noted and
categorized, as were the children's clothes, hairstyles and play
activities.

RESULTS

Mothers' Differential Reinforcement of Dependency

In our families of multiple children no significant difference was observed between boys and girls on dependency behavior (boys $\overline{X}$ = 26.5, girls $\overline{X}$ = 23.2. Yet we found that boys had their dependency needs positively reinforced significantly more often by mothers than did girls ($\overline{X}$ = 18.5 for boys, $\overline{X}$ = 13.2 for girls; p = < 0.05).

In line with their greater dependency-reinforcement of boys, mothers also more frequently requested assistance from girls than from boys. Girls were asked to help an average of 5.7 times, while the boys were asked an average of 2.2 times (p = < 0.03). The daughters' assistance was sought not only in the caretaking of younger siblings but in any task that needed to be carried out around the home, such as tidying up or fetching. The girls were more helpful than were their brothers and helped $\overline{X}$ = 6.3 times each, compared with boys' $\overline{X}$ = 2.3 times each (p = < 0.02).

Child's Aggressive Behavior

There was no significant difference in aggressive behavior between boys and girls ($\overline{X}$ = 6.1 for boys compared with $\overline{X}$ = 4.9).

There was a trend for mothers to negatively reinforce their sons' aggressive behavior more frequently than that of their daughters ($\overline{X}$ = 5.4 compared with $\overline{X}$ = 3.4). However, this was not significant statistically. Mothers' tendency to positively reinforce their sons' aggressive behavior more frequently than they did that of their daughters ($\overline{X}$ = 1.2 compared with $\overline{X}$ = 0.6) was also not statistically significant.

Mothers' Gender-Linked Talk

Mothers in each of our families of triplets and quadruplets referred to the child who was the odd one out, as far as his or her sex was concerned, both by neuter names and by sexual labels. On the other hand, the children who were in the majority regarding their sex were almost exclusively referred to by neuter names only, unless they happened to be the mother's favorite at that time. Thus, while both the majority and minority sex children had an average of 15 neutral names each, the minority sex child had $\overline{X}$ = 7.2 gender-linked labels compared with the majority sex child who had only $\overline{X}$ = 0.5 such labels. On the randomization test for matched pairs the difference between the percentage of gender names in the minority and majority sex children was 37% ($\overline{X}$ = < 0.05). Consider the following examples:

> Ken, the only boy among the QU III quadruplets, was "the
> male" for his mother from the start. Stressing of his mas-
> culinity was already apparent in his fourth month when Mrs.
> QU III affectionately called him "sonny" and predicted that
> he would become a boxer. The following month she called him
> a football player. Father added that as a male, Ken ought
> to drink beer. During Ken's second year of life, mother
> tended to refer to him as "the man," (for instance, "The
> man is hungry"). At another time she predicted that Ken
> would become Samson the hero. She often addressed him as
> "Sir" and on his second birthday called him "Mr. B." On
> the other hand, the three girls among the quadruplets were
> addressed by mother with non-gender nouns or adjectives such
> as "dancer," "angel," "monkey," "doll," "beautiful," "naugh-
> ty," "sociable." A girl's gender was stressed only three
> times by mother during the entire observation period spent
> with this family. For example, mother once called Leah a
> "Beauty Queen."

The labeling of children on the basis of sex meant that mothers
perceived them as possessing certain qualities which they attributed to that particular sex. The qualities were often positive or
negative, based on mother's personal preferences and dislikes.
Usually they corresponded to the masculine and feminine stereotypes
prevalent in their culture. Thus:

> Mrs. TW I termed her boy twin, Ruben, age 7 months, "naughty,
> wild, starting to touch everything--a bandit." She added,
> "In my family the boys are more difficult than the girls."
> On the other hand, mother described the girl twin, Ruby,
> as, "Sweet, more delicate and easier. A good girl." She pre-
> dicted, "Ruby will be like her older sister, wanting to
> help me in everything. In our family the girls are better."
> The 2-year-old Ruben was referred to by his mother as, "King
> of the naughty ones and full of pepper." She did not even
> suspect Ruby of aggressive behavior, though it was she who
> repeatedly pulled her baby brother's hair. Yet during the
> same observation, mother twice wrongly suspected Ruben of
> hitting his baby brother. Mother obviously expected Ruben
> to be even more aggressive than he actually was.

What can be called "sex typing" did not take place merely on
the basis of positive or negative qualities exhibited by the child.
Yet it always revealed how a mother perceived her own or the
opposite sex. Thus:

> Mrs. QU II, mother of three boys and one girl quadruplet,
> saw the girl's behavior as gender-linked when her 22-month-

old daughter helped her fold the laundry. Mother told us that, "Helga likes to help. You can feel that she has to be a housewife." A few months later, Mrs. QU II related: "She is a girl, she likes to do things for me," though mother added: "They all like to fold clothes." No connotation of femininity or housewifeliness was apparent for this mother, however, when the boys carried out the same activities as their sister.

Mothers' Differentiation of Children's Appearances and Activities as a Function of the Child's Sex

When and how did mothers make their male and female twins, triplets and quadruplets look different from each other? The results show that mothers did not differentiate (in terms of clothing, hairstyles and the like) the appearance of their children until their third year of life.

a) *Hair-Styles:* The average age at which boys had their first hair cut was 29 months with a range of 27 to 36 months.

b) *Clothes:* Differentiation of children's clothes on the basis of sex also came relatively late. In only one family was there a pink/blue dichotomy for girls and boys, although this only began in the infants' fifth and ninth months. In all families, mothers dressed their twins/trips/quads in one another's clothes. The question of the ownership of clothes on the basis of sex did not usually arise until the fourth year of life.

Mothers generally let their daughters wear dresses from around their third year and even then only rarely. The earliest age a girl was observed wearing a dress was 26 months. Two other girls wore dresses at 34 and 41 months respectively. None of the remaining girls wore dresses at any of the home observations.

The skull-cap turned out to be a gender-distinguishing feature in children's clothes among all three traditionally oriented, religious families in our sample. Usually, religious families let their boys wear a skull-cap at least on the Sabbath from the end of their second year. Very religious families had an additional sex-distinguishing item of clothing--the *tsitsit,* a ritual, four-cornered, fringed garment, worn as part of his underwear by every religiously observant male. The TR I boys acquired their first *tsitsit* when 3 years old and Shula explained: "If a girl wears a *tsitsit,* she becomes a boy."

c) *Jewelry:* Mothers and children generally valued items of jewelry more than clothes for purposes of differentiating between

the sexes. Mrs. TW II, for example, emphasized, in relation to
her 1-year-old son, that a bracelet is not for boys. A year later
she would not let him wear a brooch. In all six remaining families,
it was only from the third year (range 28 to 43 months) that parents emphasized that jewelry is worn exclusively by girls.

Activities Including Play and the
Acquisition of Skills

Children were seldom actively discouraged from playing with
opposite sex-typed toys or encouraged to play with same sex-typed
toys by the parents in this study. Thus, Mrs. QU II was unique
among mothers when she presented 26-month-old Helga, her only girl
quad, with a doll and explained that, "A doll is for girls." At
the same time she gave Ari, one of the boy quads, a teddy bear.
All other mothers permitted both their sons and daughters to play
with dolls even when their children were 3 1/2 years old.

On rare occasions, a mother or grandmother did not permit one
of the children to engage in a certain activity because, in her
mind, that activity was linked with a particular gender, as demonstrated in the following example:

> The grandmother of the QU III quads brought wool and
> knitting-needles for the three girl quads when they were
> 40 months old. She withheld the wool and needles from Ken,
> explaining, "A man doesn't need to knit." Ken was deeply
> upset about this and repeatedly asked to be taught this
> skill until one of his sisters comforted him with, "When
> you'll be a girl, you can knit." On the other hand, Ken,
> at a later age, was regularly taken to football matches by
> father while the girls accompanied them only on occasion.

For very religious families, with a high degree of sex segregation, additional activities were differentiated on the basis of
gender.

> Among the TR I triplets only the boys had their hair cut for
> the first time in a special ceremony at the Wailing Wall.
> At this time the children were 3 years old. Only the boys
> were meant to light Hanukkah lights, although at age three
> Shula also insisted on lighting Hanukkah candles. Moreover,
> it was the boys who at 3 1/2 years were taken to Synagogue
> by father, while Shula stayed home with mother even on Purim
> (Feast of Esther) when children have special fun at the
> Synagogue Service. Mother explained to the observers that,
> "Father cannot look after three young children in Synagogue
> and boys have priority in this." When the triplets were

4 1/2 years old, mother stressed that only Shula had to help
her with the Passover spring cleaning. The boys had to help
their father to clean the books. At this time, Shula was no
longer unhappy not to be taken to Synagogue. She had become
reconciled to the fact that she would go there with her mother
only at the time of festivals. Additionally, she was no longer
interested in kindling Hanukkah lights. In fact, she proudly announced that she was a girl.

At age 2 1/2 years, the TR I boys were sent to a different
educational establishment than was their sister, and this
at a time when these triplets still wore their hair long
and were dressed in similar pants. The boys, at their all-
boy nursery-school, run in Yiddish by a male teacher, were
taught to read from the age of three. There was little play
and from the age of five boys learned until 4 p.m. Shula,
on the other hand, was sent to a nursery-school for girls,
run by women teachers in Hebrew, the language of the environment. Her school-day ended at 12 a.m. Not only was most of
the girls' time spent on play activities, but their vaca-
tions were also longer. Further, they were not taught to
read. Thus, the different sex roles were non-ambiguously
defined from the earliest years by the very religious society
in which the TR I family lived.

DISCUSSION

Observations of mothers' behavior in the actual child rearing
situation indicated that from the beginning they treat their
male and female infant twins/trips/quads differently, although
they appear unaware that they do so.

Mothers' Differential Reinforcement as a Function of the Child's Sex

a) Dependency: In this study, the boys' dependency was positively rewarded more frequently than that of the girls. Garai
and Scheinfeld (1968) suggest that since girls mature faster than
boys, it is likely that girls will be independent at earlier ages
than boys. If this premise is valid, it could be argued that
mothers encouraged the girls' earlier independence in order to
gain their assistance in caring for the other children. For a
mother who has to care for several young children at one time, a
relatively independent and helpful daughter would reduce the child-
care burden. Moreover, the daughters' independent and helpful behavior reinforces the stereotypical feminine image of helper. In
fact, this study provides clear evidence that mothers requested

help from their daughters significantly more than from their sons.

On the other hand, keeping the sons relatively dependent enabled mothers to have more physical contact with them. This proximity is especially enjoyed by mothers since the male child is
favored in the traditional Jewish and Oriental environments.

b) Aggressive Behavior: The boys' greater state of readiness
to display aggressive behavior was not confirmed by our weighted
score, although the tendency was as predicted. A larger sample of
subjects might have produced significant results. The tendency
for mothers to react both more negatively and more positively to
boys' aggression is in line with the findings of Maccoby and Jacklin
(1974).

Mothers' Gender-Linked Talk

Gender labeling was found to be the method most used by mothers
to distinguish clearly between their twins/trips/quads. In this
way they stressed the differences between their children. This
measure, probably used by mothers without their conscious awareness,
may also appear in relation to their single children. However, it
is the author's impression that mothers of multiple infants have
more recourse to this device, since the need to individualize the
children is greater in these instances (Goshen-Gottstein, 1980).

Mothers' Differentiation of Children's
Appearance and Activities

Mothers did not differentiate their children's appearance and
activities until the third year of the children's lives. Money
and Ehrhardt (1972) write that a newborn's sex is often publicly
declared by the color-coding of blue for boys and pink for girls,
long before the infant has enough hair for a boy's or a girl's hair-
cut. This did not apply to our sample since we are probably dealing with a cultural factor here.

This study demonstrated that mothers differentiated the appearances and activities of their sons and daughters relatively late
in the children's lives. As Stoller (1968) and Bandura and Walters
(1977) note, by age three children have already learned the concepts of male and female, have acquired the knowledge of stereotypes of masculinity and femininity prevalent in their culture and
have already developed sex-interests.

There is little evidence in this study that mothers discouraged
their children, especially their sons, from engaging in activities

they considered appropriate only for the opposite sex, contrary to the findings of Maccoby and Jacklin (1974). It would seem that mothers of twins/trips/quads expect their sons to engage in the same activities as their daughters, at least during their early childhood.

BIBLIOGRAPHY

Bandura, A. and Walters, R. *Social learning and personality development*. New York: Holt, Rinehart and Winston, 1977.

Birns, B. The emergence and socialization of sex differences in the earliest years, *Merrill Palmer Quarterly*, 1976, *22*, 229-254.

Block, J.H. Another look at sex differentiation in the socialization behaviors of mothers and fathers. In J.A. Sherman and F.L. Denmark (Eds.), *The psychology of women: Future directions in research*, New York: Psychological Dimensions, Inc., 1978.

Condry, J. & Condry S. Differences: A study of the eye of the beholder. *Child Development*, 1976, *47*, 812-819.

Garai, J.E. & Scheinfeld, A. Sex differences in mental and behavioral traits. *Genetic Psychology Monograph*, 1968, *77*, 169-299.

Goshen-Gottstein, E.R. The mothering of twins, triplets and quadruplets. *Psychiatry*, 1980, *43*, 189-204.

Kohlberg, L. A cognitive developmental analysis of children's sex role concepts and attitudes. In E.E. Maccoby (Ed.), *The development of sex differences*. Stanford, CA: Stanford University Press, 1966.

Maccoby, E.E. and Jacklin, C.N. *The psychology of sex differences*. Stanford, CA: Stanford University Press, 1974.

Money, J. & Ehrhardt, A.A. *Man and woman, boy and girl*. Baltimore and London: Johns Hopkins University Press, 1972.

Parke, R.D. Parent-infant interaction: progress, paradigms and problems. In G.P. Sackett (Ed.), *Observing behavior*, Vol. 1. Baltimore, MD: University Park Press, 1978.

Rubin, J.Z., Provenzano, F.J., & Luria, Z. The eye of the beholder: parents' view on sex of newborns. *American Journal of Orthopsychiatry*, 1974, *43*, 512-519.

Stoller, R.J. *Sex and gender*. New York: Science House, 1968.

Will, J.A., Self, P.A., & Data, N. Maternal behavior and perceived sex of infant. *American Journal of Orthopsychiatry*, 1976, *46*, 135-139.

PARENT-SCHOOL COOPERATION IN A CHANGING SOCIETY:

TEACHERS' LEARNING FROM DISADVANTAGED PARENTS*

Nechama Nir-Janiv

Ministry of Culture and Education
Bar-Ilan University

INTRODUCTION

I deeply believe that the self-trust and well-being of parents
are the most desirable goals of global society. The modern technological age has shattered the vulnerable human institutions of
the family. Parents, regardless of their backgrounds, countries
of origin or social class, have become disoriented, frustrated and
unhappy. Such parents raise unhappy, frustrated and disoriented
children. The K.E.D.M.A. project is geared to enable parents, especially disadvantaged parents, to feel more confident in themselves
as human beings and parents.

Parents have a very important influence on their children and
teachers who ignore this influence, the culture and beliefs of these
families and treat children and parents accordingly, are overlook-
ing very important factors. All parents care for their children,
and teachers have to learn how they care. Teachers who can develop
a more meaningful and relevant approach to children and who somehow restore parents' self-images are better teachers. I believe
that this kind of interaction between parents and teachers encourages children to develop into intelligent and integrated human beings.

_____

*This article will describe the findings of a project called
K.E.D.M.A., a Hebrew abbreviation for "Parents-Teachers Group
Discussions," which was conducted on behalf of the Ministry of
Education and sponsored by the Szold Institute of Research in
Jerusalem in 1972.

THEORETICAL BACKGROUND TO K.E.D.M.A.

There are three theoretical aspects to the K.E.D.M.A. project: the psychological, the educational, and the philosophical.

The Psychological Aspect: The failure of disadvantaged children at school is one of the greatest concerns of educators all over the world. Many systems, funds, curricula, theoretical thought, and experiments are dedicated to the clarification of the basic problems of children who fail at school in order to find efficient ways to prevent such failure and to lessen the resulting frustration of these children's parents. Most of the efforts mentioned are geared to the schools. Only in recent years has there been a movement in education towards involving parents in schools' programs. J. McVicker Hunt indicated in his book, *The Challenge of Incompetence and Poverty,* that parents are the cheapest and the best teachers for their children and that the greatest achievement of the seventies in terms of the different programs developed for disadvantaged children is that all the innovative programs in education have worked to involve and integrate parental involvement with these programs.

Until the last two or three years the direction in parent education was all one-sided in that teachers taught parents. Teachers taught parents psychology, education, child care, child nutrition, and so on. But in school, children continued to fail. The concepts, the information, the knowledge remained externalized. My hypothesis was that if teachers learned from parents they could better teach their students. My thinking was stimulated by one of the implications of Jean Piaget's theory, "The intellect organizes its own structure by virtue of experience with objects in space, causality and time, and the interrelationships of these environmental realities." The implication is that the child who comes to school at the age of 3, 4, or 5 already has an intellectual structure by virtue of his experience at home. His parents have already built into their child a cognitive pattern and a reservoir of associations, perhaps a way of learning, according to their own experiences and socio-cultural backgrounds. To study the cognitive patterns, social behaviors and aspirations of disadvantaged children in order to make children's schooling more effective and meaningful, teachers have to learn about the interaction of children and parents at home.

A study by Hess and Shipman (1968), reinforces the assumption above. The researchers tried to discover the cognitive pattern of children by observing how mothers from different social classes interacted in a teaching-learning situation. A focal point was the discrepancy between the behavior of families of different socio-economic classes and the requirements for academic performance set by schools. Study findings show that the social experiences of

children affect their cognitive behavior and eventually their academic performance. Patterns developed before formal schooling can
either impede or enhance the child's success in the academic setting. From the point of view of the researchers, the cognitive development of children can best be understood in terms of the mother-
child interaction.

Another concrete example that supports this point of view comes
from Israeli folklore specialists who found meaningful differences
between the story structure and the mode of telling stories in
Middle East cultures and those of Occident cultures. Parents from
the Middle East cultures are supposed to tell the moral of the story
to the children in order to make him "learn" from the story and
its moral. Teachers and parents from the Western cultures pre-
suppose that a child absorbs a moral. They do not want to "preach"
to the child verbally for they hope that the child will be able to
imply the moral autonomously. The folklorists think that the structure and the method of telling stories have an important influence
on a child's cognitive structure.

In summary then, teachers ignorant of parent-child interaction
at home can impede children's cognitive, emotional and social development and growth. Therefore, teachers must be aware of parents'
methods of teaching their children in order to create a more integrated environment, and to make schooling for young children meaningful and relevant.

The Educational Aspect: One of the major goals of the K.E.D.M.A.
project is to strengthen parents' self-concepts as worthwhile human
beings and parents. In a country where the dominant culture and
style of life clashes with the culture and style of life of new-
comers and immigrants, conflict occurs. The results of such a conflict are frustration, disorientation, disintegration, anger and
disappointment. Parents are frightened by their failure to confront the new reality and even more frightened by their children's
failure at school. They become more and more concerned with their
children's education because they are aware that success at school
means success in life. They ask for better education, for active
participation in the decision-making processes of the schools. In
order to make schools more effective parental involvement in the
schools is therefore essential. To sincerely involve parents from
disadvantaged communities there is a need for feelings of basic
trust and equality to develop between teachers and parents. In
order to promote their positive attitudes towards themselves and
their children, project K.E.D.M.A. tries to upgrade their pasts,
their cultures and their values. Such an approach can enhance
their roles as parents. On the other hand, teachers, in turn, discover a wide range of cultural values, a variety of habits and
interesting ways of child rearing. All this rich information and
understanding of families of different cultures can develop more

sensitive and flexible teachers and educators.

   The Philosophical Aspect: This pluralistic approach to culture honors the right to be different and equal. This is the basis
for creating the "I-Thou" dialogue between parents and teachers.
The child feels that the most "significant people" in his life,
mother, father, and teacher, together care for him and are cooperating to create an optimal environment and a meaningful cosmos where
he belongs, creates and acts. This kind of cooperation makes people
feel better, more secure, more oriented and more open to one another's
problems and concerns.

   In order to create a climate of empathy and openness, we tried
the method of group discussions. The teacher and the parents talked
and expressed their ideas and points of view about children's up-
bringing. The content of the group discussions dealt with parents'
past experiences, their biographies, their ways of celebrating
holidays, their opinions about the "good" child, how to teach the
child to be "good," and how their parents had taught them to be
"good." Another kind of question the parents discussed was the
"didactical" question: "How do you teach children to count, how
do you teach them colors, new words and stories, family relationships?" The teacher also asked the parents questions such as,
"What stories do you remember from your own childhood?"

   Parents were very active during the group discussions. In
the beginning they were, however, very reticent. They could not
believe that the teacher was asking them for advice. However, as
the year progressed they became more and more trusting and more and
more articulate.

EVALUATION OF THE EFFECTIVENESS OF K.E.D.M.A. PROJECT:
A RESEARCH STUDY

A. Methodology

   The sample for this study consisted of 269 parents from disadvantaged communities and 90 parents from middle class communities.
Only 19 parents dropped out of the study. There were 13 kindergarten teachers participating in the project: nine of them worked
with disadvantaged children and four with middle class children.
The teachers were selected on the basis of one criteria--they were
ready to spend their time working with parents. There were experienced teachers as well as young ones; very successful teachers
and average teachers. The children were 4- and 5-year-olds.

   Pilot Project: A pilot project was organized with 20 parents
from disadvantaged communities. I led a group discussion with them,

asking them how they teach their children. The parents were surprised
and amazed. "Why do you, the professional, ask us such a question?
We don't teach; teachers teach." A father was the first to become
aware that he teaches his child. "I teach my son arithmetic--I
teach him to count; we climb the stairs and we count: up - 1,2,3,4,5,
down - 5,4,3,2,1." A mother told us how she teaches her child to
count. "We are 10 members in our family; so--my daughter counts
everything: 10 beds, 10 shirts, 10 plates, etc." Another mother
told us how she teaches colors. "Red, white, green--my daughter,
she chooses always the red, she knows colors." The parents became
very excited and described our discussions as, "So beautiful, like
a wedding."

   Major Research Study: The actual research started with interviews of parents and teachers. The questionnaires dealt with the
following topics: parents' attitudes to their ethnic cultures;
parents' educational interactions with their children; and parents'
teaching strategies. Teachers were asked about their attitudes to
their profession, teachers' educational activities in the kindergarten, and their teaching strategies. The field work began in
January, 1971.

   Our budget was small and we could measure statistically only
one variable--the changes that occurred in teachers' attitudes to
parents, to their profession, and to their work.

   We chose two methods of evaluation--the pretest and the posttest method and a comparative method involving a control group.
The teachers were matched by age, teaching experience, level of
schooling, geographical area and the economic status of the children
they worked with. Teachers' answers were expressed in a written
form.

B.   The Findings

   Pretest & Postest: In comparing the answers of the pretest and
the postest, all 13 teachers expressed a deep appreciation of their
profession of kindergarten teaching. The common feeling reflected
in the postests was that after the group discussions with parents,
the teachers felt that their profession was even more meaningful,
that they became better people, more sensitive to the needs and
concerns of the parents, the teacher-aides and to other adults.
They were also more ready to listen to others.

   Teachers indicated that a new kind of relationship had been
born in which teachers trusted parents and parents trusted teachers.
Teachers discovered that parents from poor and disadvantaged communities are worthwhile human beings who can enrich teachers' personalities and add a new dimension to their educational interactions
with children.

Another interesting finding was that parents changed teachers' concepts of values. In the posttest they expressed a more relativistic-pluralistic approach to values. This is a very important shift for teachers who work in a multi-culture such as ours. One result of this change in values was that teachers began to integrate Middle East stories which they had learned from the parents during the group discussions into the school curriculum.

Teachers' attitudes toward their didactic activities were interesting. Five of the 13 teachers applied the method of group dynamics with the children. Two teachers asked the children the same questions they discussed with the parents, recorded the answers and then played back the answers to the parents.

Control Group: To validate the changes in teachers' attitudes we compared our experimental teachers with a control group. The difference between teachers' attitudes toward disadvantaged parents was statistically significant. The control group mistrusted parents as a source of information and indicated negative answers to the question, "Can parents change your personality?" They even rejected parents as active participants in school curricula.

Summary of Findings

To summarize the findings about the changes that occurred in the experimental group of teachers after the field work in K.E.D.M.A. we can point out the following:

1. Teachers' attitudes towards parents were enriched and enhanced by the group discussions and took a direction of mutual trust and respect. The "I-Thou" dialogue between parents and teachers strengthened parents' positive self-concepts and teachers' sense of meaning in their lives and in their professions.

2. Teachers' educational attitudes took a pluralistic-relativistic approach to values and norms.

3. Teachers' didactical methods and teaching strategies were enriched by new content which made their teaching more relevant.

AN UNEXPECTED FINDING: THE STORY OF MRS. DOUEK

I cannot finish this article on K.E.D.M.A. without mentioning a dramatic "finding"--we discovered a writer. Mrs. Madalene Douek, a newcomer from Tunis, was a poor, unknown housewife and mother of five children. The family was poor and unhappy and

Madelene was considered a peculiar woman. When the project began,
she became a very enthusiastic participant. People of her community
were suddenly very impressed by the ideas she expressed during the
group discussions. One day she could not come to the meeting and
sent a letter to the teacher. The teacher was amazed by the style
and power of her writing. We sent her to a publisher and now she
is writing a book about her childhood in the ghetto of Tunis. Her
life has changed completely: newspaper reporters write articles
about her and she speaks on the radio. She has become a celebrity
and a more worthwhile human being for herself, her children, and her
community.

BIBLIOGRAPHY

Auerbach, Aline, B. *Parents learn through discussion*. New York: John
     Wiley and Sons, Inc., 1967.
Carter, Barbara & Daper, Gloria. *School volunteers*. New York: New
     York Citation Press, 1967.
Feitelson, Dina. *The school and the parents*. Jerusalem. Ministry
     of Education and Culture, 1968.
Frankenstein, Carl. *The school without parents*. Jerusalem: Ministry
     of Education and Culture, 1968.
Goldman, Richard. *The cross cultural adaptation of a program to
     involve parents in their children's learning*. Haifa: Haifa
     University Press, 1972.
Hess, Robert D. & Bear, Roberta Meyer (Eds.). *Early education*.
     Chicago: Aldine Publishing Comp., 1968.
Hunt, J. McVicker. *The challenge of incompetence and poverty*. Urbana-
     Champaign: University of Illinois Press, 1969.
Newson, John & Newson, Elisabeth. *Four years old in the urban com-
     munity*. England: Penguin Books, 1968.
Pickarts, Evelyn & Fargo, Jean. *Parent education: Toward parental
     competence*. New York: Appleton Century Crofts, 1971.
Weikart, D. et al. *Longitudinal results of the Ypsilanti Perry
     Preschool Project*. Ypsilanti, MI: High Scope Educational
     Research Foundation, 1970.

ARITHMETIC DISABILITIES: THE RELATION BETWEEN

ARITHMETIC AND SOME PSYCHOLOGICAL ABILITIES--

A REANALYSIS*

J.J. Dumont and A.G. Ruyssenaars
University of Nijmegen
The Netherlands

J.H. Hamers
University of Utrecht
The Netherlands

INTRODUCTION

In the field of learning disabilities, by far the most attention is paid to reading and writing disabilities such as dyslexia
and dysorthographia, while considerably less attention is paid to
arithmetic disabilities. It is not very clear why this difference
in interest in these two kinds of learning problems should exist.
It may be that rather widespread opinion dictates that reading and
writing disabilities depend more on specific factors which are independent from intelligence, whereas arithmetic disabilities are
more dependent on the level of intelligence and are therefore less
prone to influence and improvement.

Since it has become clear, however, that arithmetic disabilities
can also occur with an otherwise normal intelligence level, attempts
to account for these disabilities through other psychological factors, or abilities such as memory or visuo-spatial aptitude, has
become common. In theory, two models of explanation are possible,
setting aside the general intelligence level as an hypothesis
accounting for arithmetic disabilities.

In the first place Schonell and Schonell (1962) have emphasized
the conditions in which the child has to learn arithmetic. Too
little practical experience, bad instruction, over-emphasis on
memorizing activities, negative motivation, emotional consequences
of physical stress and anxiety of failure do not provide favorable

*This research was made possible by a grant of the L.O.M. Founda-
tion at Mijmegen. The statistical analysis was carried out in collaboration with Dr. J.H. Oud of the University of Nijmegen.

conditions for success in arithmetic. Additionally, these factors
lessen ability to concentrate and promote hyperactivity.

In the second place the psychology of the structure of intelligence has led to identification of a number of factors that appear
to be related to the successful teaching of mathematics (Borghouts-
van Erp, 1978; Butcher, 1968; Eysenck, 1967; Smith, 1964; Vernon,
1971). In particular, the so-called visuo-spatial factor (indicated
by the symbol k or when combined with mechanical ability indicated
as k : m), together with the general intelligence factor g, appears
to be the most important predictor of arithmetic ability. Although
spatial ability seems to develop in the period between the eleventh
and fifteenth year of age (Fruchter, 1954; Vernon, 1971), it is
still questionable whether arithmetic at the elementary school
level is related to certain intellectual factors, and to visual
and spatial abilities. It was this question which prompted the
present study.

THE PROBLEM SET

If arithmetic is based on or related to specific conditions or
factors that can be identified in the structure of intelligence,
then the question is what are these factors. One method by which
these factors might be identified is factor analysis. An attempt
to do just that was made in 1977 by the authors of the present
paper. However, because interpretation of factors is not suited
to causal explanation, factor analysis failed to explain the nature
of the connections found among the variables. The authors decided
to repeat the study, but this time a reanalysis was undertaken and
the problem set was formulated in terms of functional dependency.

In the relevant literature a number of variables have been
suggested to explain arithmetic disabilities. In this study these
variables were operationalized and presented as independent variables
to explain the variance in a group of thirteen dependent variables,
which are supposed to be representative of the arithmetical performance of initial learners. All external variables relating to
environment, primary socialization, motivation, instruction, and
didactic style were left out of consideration as the intent was to
aim exclusively at variables which, as abilities or aptitudes within
the cognitive structure of the child, are supposed to influence the
initial arithmetical performance.

In addition to the choice of the ability-model as such and the
deletion of external variables there are other limitations to this
study. The sample of 120 children was a non-random sample and as
such cannot be regarded as representative of all children with arithmetic disabilities. Although conclusions will be limited for those

reasons, it is hoped that the understanding of arithmetic problems of young children will be furthered.

The problem can be formulated as follows: to what extent are performances on a number of arithmetic tests explained by variables which might influence those performances in a causal way?

INDEPENDENT VARIABLES

The selection of independent variables has been made on the basis of what has been put forward in the research literature as possible causes of failure in arithmetic.

Intelligence: This variable is important to understanding arithmetic problems as it facilitates the development of insight into the acquisition of strategies to solve intellectual problems (Dumont, 1976; Schonell & Schonell, 1962; Smith, 1964). In particular, the Wechsler Intelligence Scale for Children (WISC) subtests such as Block-Design and Insight are supposed to represent problem solving on a verbal and non-verbal level. In addition to these tests Vocabulary and Coding were included. Vocabulary was taken to demonstrate that it is indeed problem solving ability and not just verbal intelligence in general that is involved in arithmetic. In other words, poor vocabulary skill alone does not necessarily explain arithmetic disabilities. Coding was included because arithmetic can be conceptualized as the practical ability to transpose information of one code into output of another code. The flexibility required can possibly play an important role in automatizing arithmetical performances.

The Raven Progressive Matrices: These were used in order to assess to what extent general intelligence could be held responsible for arithmetic ability.

Specific Factors: In factor analytic studies it has been shown that visuo-spatial abilities are connected with mathematical performance in secondary education (Butcher, 1968; Smith, 1964; Vernon, 1971). It is possible that these same factors could account for arithmetic ability at the elementary school level. In this study the visual factor has been operationalized in the following variables: the Three-Dimensional Patterns from Leiter's International Performance Scale and the Paper Folding test from French's Kit of Referencece Tests. The spatial ability was represented by Card Rotation from French's Kit of Reference Tests and Space from a Dutch revision of Thurstone's Primary Mental Abilities Test.

Additional Variables: The following variables were included on the basis of several hypotheses put forward in other studies: .

• Memory: This was operationalized as memory for words and
memory for numbers. A study by van der Laan (1973) indicated that
memory can be regarded as a partial explanation of success or failure
in arithmetic.

• Fluency: This is an ability which enables the automatic
retrieval and output of verbal constructs and which can be conceived of as an indicator for automatization in learning arithmetic. This variable can be subdivided into a fluency-bound condition in which the child's production of words is governed by a
specific task and a fluency-free condition which requires the child
to mention as many words as he/she can within one minute (Bannatyne,
1973; Fruchter, 1948).

Classification and Seriation: These are two tests derived from
Piaget's theory of cognitive development which are conceptualized
as prerequisites and conditions for cardination and ordination
(Dumont, 1966). The classification task from Snijders-Oomen Non-
Verbal Intelligence Test (1967) and the dot estimation task from
Leiter's International Performance Scale were also included.

Dependent Variables

Arithmetical performance was assessed by:

1. *The "Schiedamse Reken Test" (S.R.T.):* This test provides
a sample of all arithmetic problems which figure in traditional arithmetic instruction. Included are computation, arithmetic reasoning and comprehensive arithmetic, and measuring
and computing with money.

2. *Addition (Arithmetic Operation 1) Exercises:* The numbers
1 through 20 were used as an operationalization of fast and
accurate performance of this first arithmetic operation.

3. *Subtraction (Arithmetic Operation 2) Exercises:* The numbers
1 through 20 were used as an analogous operationalization of
this second arithmetic operation.

Addition and subtraction were scored by assessing how many sums
could be done within one minute. For the S.R.T. there was no time
limit.

Sample

Children whose arithmetic ability was judged by their teachers
to be one or two years below that of their peers provided subjects
for this study. The degree of arithmetic retardation was also

assessed by means of the S.R.T. Because only children with arithmetic disabilities were to be included in the sample, a reading test
was administered to sort out those children who proved to have reading problems as well as arithmetic difficulties. This idea turned
out to be somewhat inappropriate as many children had both disabilities. In the end, however, 120 children (98 boys and 22 girls)
were selected from 12 schools for children with learning disabilities.
The age range of these children was between 9 and 11 years with a
mean of 123.8 months.

Analysis

     Frequency distributions, means and standard deviations were cal-
culated in order to compare the sample with normal primary school
children and multiple regression analysis was carried out with the
17 independent and 3 dependent variables. On the basis of the
standardized regression coefficients of the independent variables
a selection was made for a second analysis with 10 independent and
three dependent variables. Finally, some independent variables
were combined to trace what influence that would have on explaining
the variance. The sequence in which the independent variables were
introduced in the analysis was determined by the relative explanatory weight that was attributed to them on the basis of theoretical
considerations.

RESULTS

     Table 1 presents the means and standard deviations of all
variables concerned. These means and standard deviations show the
research sample to be a group of normal intelligence (Raven P.M.
for 10.6 years = 29; except for the WISC coding all WISC subtests
lay somewhere above the mean).

     The first regression analysis (see Table 2) was carried out
with the 17 independent and the three dependent variables. The
regression-coefficients are given in parentheses and the levels of
significance were set at the .05 and .01 levels. The independent
variables were introduced in the order which is shown below, because it was expected that in that way their relative weights
could be estimated in the most adequate manner. Inspection of
this table shows that some variables which were expected to play a
role in explaining the variables of the dependent variables did
not do so. From the values of the standardized regression coefficients it can be seen that several of the variables such as the
Raven P.M., Visualization, Classification and Seriation have no
connection with the dependent variables.

     On the basis of these results a second analysis was carried out

TABLE 1. Means and standard deviations for all variables

Dependent variables		
	M.	Sd.
1. S.R.T.	107.7	58.8
2. Addition	24.8	11.1
3. Subtraction	17.4	11.2
Independent variables		
	M.	Sd.
1. Age	123.8	9.2
2. Reading	35.2	23.1
3. Raven P.M.	24.9	8.4
4. WISC Vocabulary	41.6	8.4
5. WISC Insight	16.1	4.3
6. WISC Coding	29.3	7.8
7. Paper Folding	10.1	6.3
8. WISC Block Design	24.5	10.9
9. Three Dim. Patterns	6.6	2.7
10. Card Rotation	85.8	27.9
11. Thurstone Space	14.5	4.4
12. Word Memory	8.7	3.2
13. Number Memory	4.5	1.6
14. Fluency Free	25.6	7.9
15. Fluency Bound	16.6	4.3
16. Classification	6.2	2.4
17. Seriation	7.9	3.8

in which the number of independent variables was reduced to 10. The results of this analysis are presented in Table 3.

A final reduction of the number of independent variables was established by combining the separate visuo-spatial variables. The same procedure was used with the fluency-free and fluency-bound variables.

Although, from Table 4, a slight change in F-values is apparent, the overall picture of the analysis is maintained.

TABLE 2. Regression analysis

	SRT		Addition		Subtraction	
1. Age	52.8**	(.24*)	0.4	(.24*)	2.9	(.09)
2. Reading	21.5**	(.31*)	19.7**	(.47*)	0.0	(.39*)
3. Raven P.M.	8.4**	(-.06)	3.3	(-.08)	0.3	(-.01)
4. WISC Vocabulary	5.5*	(-.01)	0.5	(-.14)	0.7	(.00)
5. WISC Insight	11.6**	(.18*)	0.4	(.13)	0.3	(.17)
6. WISC Coding	5.3*	(.21*)	1.5	(.07)	11.2**	(.24*)
7. Paper Folding	7.3**	(.14)	0.0	(.12)	0.0	(.12)
8. WISC Block Design	9.4**	(.19*)	0.0	(.20*)	0.1	(.16)
9. Three Dim. Patterns	0.4	(.04)	0.6	(-.00)	0.1	(.00)
10. Card Rotation	7.1**	(-.20*)	4.5*	(-.02)	0.5	(.00)
11. Thurstone Space	0.4	(.07)	5.3*	(-.13)	0.0	(-.09)
12. Word Memory	0.6	(.08)	0.4	(.03)	0.1	(.12)
13. Number Memory	1.8	(-.11)	0.0	(-.12)	7.9**	(-.27*)
14. Fluency Free	0.5	(-.00)	9.1**	(.19*)	1.3	(.08)
15. Fluency Bound	3.5	(.13)	1.8	(.17)	0.5	(.11)
16. Classification	1.1	(.07)	2.1	(-.06)	1.0	(-.07)
17. Seriation	0.7	(.06)	0.3	(.00)	1.0	(-.04)
Variance accounted for	66.1%		55.2%		51.0%	

* $p = .05$

** $p = .01$

INTERPRETATION

Interpretation of the results is best based on Table 3, in which the 10 selected independent variables explain the variance of the three dependent variables. This selection by itself already leads to some conclusions. General Intelligence, as measured by a g-test like Raven P.M., did not sufficiently explain the different

TABLE 3.   Step-wise regression by separate variable

	SRT	Addition	Subtraction
1. Age	52.8** (.25*)	0.4 (.21*)	2.9 (.06)
2. Reading	21.5** (.30*)	19.7** (.44*)	0.0 (.38*)
3. WISC Insight	16.4** (.21*)	0.1 (.06)	0.7 (.16)
4. Paper Folding	14.2** (.15)	1.0 (.04)	0.0 (.07)
5. WISC Block Design	11.7** (.20*)	0.5 (.08)	0.0 (.09)
6. WISC Coding	6.5** (.15)	1.0 (.08)	11.1** (.24*)
7. Number Memory	0.3 (-.10)	0.6 (-.15)	6.0** (.27*)
8. Word Memory	1.6 (.09)	0.0 (.05)	1.2 (.12)
9. Fluency Free	1.1 (0.08)	12.5** (.17*)	0.2 (.08)
10. Fluency Bound	4.5* (.14)	0.7 (.13)	0.1 (.10)
	63.2%	51.7%	49.9%

```
*    p = .05
**   p = .01
```

TABLE 4.   Step-wise regression by grouped variable

	SRT	Addition	Subtraction
1. Age	52.8**	0.4	2.9
2. Reading	21.5**	19.7**	0.0
3. WISC Insight	16.4**	0.1	0.7
4. Paper Folding/5. Block Design	13.6**	0.7	0.0
6. WISC Coding	6.5**	1.0	11.1**
7. Number Memory/8. Word Memory	1.0	0.3	3.7*
9. Fluency Free/10. Fluency Bound	2.3	6.6**	0.2

```
*    p < .05
**   p < .01
```

performances of these children. This provides support for the hypothesis that arithmetic disabilities are independent of the general,
overall level of intelligence, and that these disabilities need to
be explained by more specific factors such as Block-design and Insight.
Arithmetic ability as measured by an achievement test like the S.R.T.
turns out to be primarily dependent on verbal and non-verbal problem
solving.

It should also be kept in mind that the child's age, despite
its small range, is a powerful factor in determining arithmetic
ability. The older child, simply by having spent longer in school,
will have progressed further and learned more.

The tasks of addition and subtraction are differentiated from
general achievement and from each other. The absence of a relationship of addition and subtraction with the WISC variables seems to
point out that in addition and subtraction specific tasks are involved. These tasks are conditioned by time-limits and can be described as automatization. Addition, in particular, can be explained
by the variables Reading and Fluency Free. To these two tasks
automatization is common. Performance of these tasks is based on
output production available in an automatic way. The more the child
masters automatization, the more he/she masters addition. Subtraction behaves in a markedly different way in all analyses. Obviously,
automatization is not as important in determining ability to sub-
tract as it is with addition. The connection of subtraction with
the subtests Coding and Memory for Numbers shows that subtraction
involves a different kind of information processing. The difference
in frequency not only shows a much longer reaction-time and/or less
accuracy of subtraction, but also a more reflexive activity. In
the process of subtraction numbers are memorized explicitly and
operated on explicitly. This activity contrasts very much with the
automatization of addition and could be termed explicitization or
semi-automatization.

CONCLUSIONS

On the basis of this study we can conclude that generally speaking, arithmetic disabilities are more dependent on verbal and non-
verbal problem solving than on general mental ability. Addition and
subtraction are distinguished from general arithmetic ability as
both of them are dependent on different abilities, described as
automatization and explicitization. Years of instruction proved to
be the best and most powerful explanation of arithmetic ability.
Specific prerequisites like classification and seriation no longer
played a role in accounting for the arithmetic ability of these
pupils.

Further research should aim at a task-analysis of the different arithmetic tasks. The two tasks addition and subtraction, although considered logically to constitute two parts of one operation, appear, in actuality to be two contrasting psychological tasks.

BIBLIOGRAPHY

Bannatyne, A.D. *Language, reading and learning disabilities*.
    Springfield, IL: Charles C Thomas, 1973.
Borghouts-van Erp, J.W.M. Rekenstoornissen. Een pleidooi voor visie.
    Tijdschrift voor Orthopedagogiek, 6, 1978.
Brus, B.T. & Voeten, M.J.M. *Een-minuut-test. Verantwoording en
    handleiding*. Nigmegen: Berkhout, 1973.
Butcher, H.J. *Human intelligence, its nature and assessment*. London:
    Methuen, 1968.
Coan, R.W. Facts, factors and artifacts: The quest for psychological
    meaning. *Psychological Review,* 1964, *71,* 123-140.
Cronbach, L.J. *Essentials of psychological testing*. London: Harper
    and Row, 1970.
Dodwell, P.C. Relationships between the understanding of the logic
    of classes and of cardinal number in children. *Canadian Journal
    of Psychology,* 1962, *14,* 191-205.
Dumont, J.J. *De ontwikkeling van de intelligentie*. Malmberg:
    Hertogenbosch, 1966.
Dumont, J.J. *Leerstoornissen I. Theorien en modellen*. Rotterdam:
    Lemniscaat, 1976.
Dumont, J.J. & Kok, J.F. *Curriculum Schoolrijpheid. Deel I*.
    Malmberg: Hertogenbosch, 1970.
Dumont, J.J., Hamers, J.H.M. & Ruyssenaars, A.J.J.M. Rekenstoornissen.
    De samenhang van technisch en begrijpend rekenen met enkele
    psychologische vaardigheden. *Pedagogische Studien,* 1977, *54,*
    386-397.
Eysenck, H.J. Intelligence assessment: A theoretical and experimental
    approach. *British Journal of Educational Psychology,* 1967,
    37, 81-89.
Ferguson, G.A. Human abilities. *Annual Review of Psychology,* 1965,
    16, 39-62.
French, J.W., Ekstrom, R.B. & Price, L.A. *Kit of reference tests for
    cognitive factors*. New Jersey: 1963.
Fruchter, B. The nature of verbal fluency. *Educational and
    Psychological Measurement,* 1948, *8,* 33-47.
Fruchter, B. Measurement of spatial abilities. *Educational and
    Psychological Measurement,* 1954, *14,* 387-395.
Getten van, L.M.H.J. Wat is intelligentie? De struktuurbenadering.
    Gedrag, Tijdschrift voor Psychologie, 19, 1971.
Hamel, B.R. *Children from 5 to 7*. Rotterdam: University Press, 1974.
Heesen, H., Strelitski, D. & Wissel van der, A. *Schiedamse rekentest.
    Handleiding*. Groningen: Wolters, 1970.
Humphreys, L.G. The organisation of human abilities. *American
    Psychologist,* 1962, *17,* 475-483.

Kaufmann, A.S. Piaget and Gesell: A psychometric analysis of tests
     built from their tasks. *Child Development*, 1971, *42*, 1341-1360.
Kema, G.N. *P.M.A. 2-4. Nederlandse bewerking.* Amsterdam: Swets en
     Zeitlinger, 1972.
Koster, K.B. *De ontwikkeling van het getalbegrip op de kleuterschool.*
     Groningen: Wolters-Noordhoff, 1975.
Laan, H. van der. *Leren lezen, schrijven en rekenen.* Groningen:
     Wolters-Noordhoff, 1973.
Michael, W.B. A suggested research approach to the identification
     of psychological processes associated with spatial-visualisa-
     tion factors. *Educational and Psychological Measurement*. 1954,
     14, 401-406.
Nunnally, J.C. *Psychometric theory*. New York: McGraw-Hill, 1967.
Piaget, J. Resag, K., Fricke, A., Hiele, P.M., van en Odenbach, K.
     Rekenonderwijs en getalbegrip. Baarn; Bosch en Keuning, 1973.
Schonell, F.J. & Schonell, F.E. *Diagnosis and remedial teaching in
     arithmetic*. London: Oliver and Boyd, 1962.
Smith, J.M. *Spatial ability. Its educational and social signifi-
     cance*. London: University of London Press, 1964.
Snijders, J.T. & Snijders-Oomen, N. *Nicht-verbale intelligenzunter-
     suchung.* Groningen: Wolters-Noordhoff, 1967.
Thurstone, T.G. Primary mental abilities of children. *Educational
     and Psychological Measurement*. 1941, *1*, 105-116.
Vernon, P.E. *The structure of human abilities*. London: Methuen,
     1971.
Wechsler, D. *Manual of the Wechsler Intelligence Scale for Children*.
     New York: 1949.
Wouters, P.A.M. & Boon van Ostade, A.H. Intelligentie: een algemene
     faktor of niet? *Gedrag, Tijdschrift voor Psychologie*, 1973, *1*,
     341-350.

WHY SOME CHILDREN DON'T CONSERVE:

IMPLICATIONS FOR EARLY CHILDHOOD EDUCATION

Doren L. Madey

NTS Research Corporation
Durham, North Carolina

Conservation occurs when a particular empirical factor (weight, volume, number) remains invariant in a child's mind throughout observed changes of state (Piaget & Inhelder, 1958). The present study began with a statement of fact: some children do not conserve. Studies supporting this fact abound (for example, Brainerd, 1973; Brainerd & Hopper, 1977; Bruner, 1966; Elkind, 1961; Higgins-Trenk & Looft, 1971; Lloyd, 1971; and Piaget, 1968). With this fact as a foundation, this study proceeded with the question: What is it about the task that prevents a child from conserving? The ability to conserve represents a sophisticated level of cognitive development in which many separate abilities are coordinated (Gelman, 1969, 1972); dissecting the task elucidates the skills a child needs to correctly solve a conservation problem.

The major aspects of the Piagetian conservation problem, regardless of its particular content, may be outlined symbolically. Each problem involves three consecutive time periods. Also involved are two stimuli, "A" and "B." A is the standard stimulus: it remains unchanged throughout the problem. B is the comparison stimulus: it undergoes a perceptual change at Time 2. Finally, and quite obviously, there must be a subject and an experimenter.

The subject is asked to make two separate, overt judgments regarding the quantitative equivalence (or difference) of the stimuli, once at Time 1 and again at Time 3. A third judgment is necessary for the successful completion of the problem, a judgment at Time 2, but this judgment occurs covertly.

At Time 1, A and B are equivalent in both the perceptual and quantitative senses. At Time 3, the two stimuli are equivalent only

283

in the quantitative sense. In the interim, Time 2, the experimenter
transforms the comparison stimulus, B to B^1, while the subject watches.
B^1 is quantitatively identical to B, but perceptually different from B.

Conservers and nonconservers are filtered out at Time 3. A conserver judges A quantitatively equivalent to B^1; a nonconserver judges
A quantitatively different from B^1.

The three-step conservation problem can be symbolized as follows:
Time 1:   A = B
     (The subject is questioned about the quantitative relation-
     ship between A and B. The subject judges A and B to be
     quantitatively equivalent. A and B are also perceptually
     equivalent.)
Time 2:   B → B^1
     (The experimenter transfers or transforms B to B^1. B and
     B^1 are quantitatively equivalent. B and B^1 are not per-
     ceptually equivalent. The subject must covertly judge this
     identity.)
Time 3:   A ? B^1
     (The subject is again questioned about the quantitative re-
     lationship between the two stimuli: a conserving subject
     judges A = B^1; a nonconserving subject judges A ≠ B^1.)

Any specific conservation problem fits this format. It is the
exact nature of the stimuli, the question, and the transformation that
differs from problem to problem. To solidify the symbolism just presented, Piaget's number conservation experiment has been dissected in
Figure 1.

In this study, the question, "Are there the same number of bars
in the two rows?" and the transformation (expansion) remain constant
while the stimuli are varied. The study is designed to test two hypotheses, one concerning type of stimulus or material and one concerning
number. The hypotheses are that, other things being equal, (1) the fre
quency of conservation responses varies significantly with the material
used, and (2) the frequency of conservation responses varies significantly with the number of objects used.

MATERIAL

Implicit in Piaget's work on quantity is the assumption that
comparisons with different materials tap the same conceptualizing
ability. Results from some studies support his assumption, but such
studies do not usually compare two nearly identical materials that differ only in the amount of meaning the child associates with each. Examples of two such materials are candy bars and wood bars. The candy
bars may have more meaning for the child: he can eat them.

Stimuli:

Two rows of objects identical in configuration, length,
shape, spacing, and actual number.

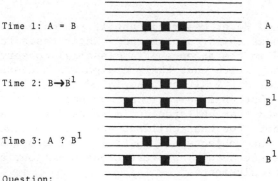

Question:

Are there the same number of objects in the two rows?

Transformation:

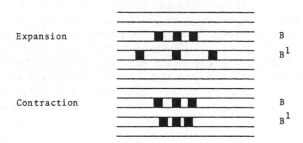

Figure 1.   A dissection of Piaget's number
conservation problem

Elkind's systematic replication (1961a) of one of Piaget's investigations supports Piaget's assumption. However, the three types
of materials Elkind used--sticks, liquids, and beads--differed in many
respects. And no evidence was offered that one of the materials had
more significance than another for the child. Gelman and Tucker
(1975) concluded that material heterogeneity did not affect accurate
number estimation. Here again the materials--different colored stars
and circles, toy soldiers, and toy mice--were of equal significance
to the child.

Of more interest are those studies that claim to disprove
Piaget's assumption. Mehler and Bever (1967) showed that very young

children are capable of discriminating the relative number of objects
in two rows. In their experiment, the authors used two materials--
plastic pellets and candy pellets--and concluded that a young child's
discriminative ability was better with the more relevant material, the
candy pellets (M & M's).

Mehler and Bever asserted that if you make the materials relevant you can make children conserve. Their basis for using the term
"conservation" in the absence of a classical conservation test was not
warranted. They state that their design was necessary to accommodate
the experimental difficulties associated with interviewing two-year-
old children. But their experiment was not a test for conservation:
it merely showed that children could recognize perceptual illusions.
The test did not show that children are able to conceptualize equality
or inequality when objects are spatially transformed. Conservation
implies invariance across an overt transformation, and Mehler and Bever
ignored this requirement.

Many experts have been critical of the Mehler and Bever study
(Beilin, 1968; Hunt, 1975; Piaget, 1968). Later attempts at replication have provided only limited substantiation (Calhoun, 1971; Willoughby & Trachy, 1972). Piaget (1968) even stated that Mehler and
Bever's research had nothing to do with conservation. Granted, this
team did not use the traditional conservation paradigm, but it is difficult to see how their results are completely unrelated to the conservation problem. Their controversial results provided the impetus
for one hypothesis of the present study, namely, that the frequency
of conservation responses varies significantly with the material used.
A relevant material (candy bars) and a nonrelevant material (wood
bars) are used in the present study.

NUMBER OF OBJECTS

Typical Piagetian conservation problems involve six, and often
ten, objects in each row (Lloyd, 1971; Piaget, 1952). Such large numbers, like irrelevant materials, may prevent young children from conserving. Several experiments have indicated that with small numbers
preschool children do treat quantity as invariant (Gelman, 1972;
Henry, 1976; Miller, 1976; Smither, Smiley, & Rees, 1974). But these
experiments did not prove number invariance using a conventional conservation task. For example, Gelman used a magic show paradigm,
thereby eliminating the overt transformation from the conservation
experiment. The children in her study were not confronted with the
contradictory perceptual information that children in a conventional
conservation experiment encounter. Gelman found that children can
tell that two objects are not the same as three objects. She demonstrated that young children do possess number invariance rules with
small numbers, but she did not demonstrate that these children possess
number invariance rules when they observe the transformation.

Interestingly, in a more recent investigation of the young child's conception of number, Gelman and Tucker (1975) do not relate their number invariance experiments to the conservation task. The second hypothesis in the present study was derived in an attempt to carry Gelman's study to its logical conclusion: to test young children for conservation (invariance across an overt transformation) with the small numbers she used to prove invariance. This second hypothesis states that the frequency of conserving responses varies significantly with the number of objects used. The hypothesis is tested by comparing each subjects responses to rows containing three, five, and seven objects.

METHOD

Subjects

Seventy preschool children, thirty-six males and thirty-four females, were tested. All subjects attended the Duke Memorial Weekday Preschool in Durham, North Carolina. Half of the subjects were randomly selected from three-year-old classes and the other half from four-year-old classes. The mean age of the entire sample was 51.78 months; standard deviation was 6.56.

Materials

Two types of stimuli were used: (1) miniature chocolate Hershey bars in their original dark brown wrappers and (2) miniature wood bars identical to the Hershey bars in dimension (4.4 mm X 2.4 mm X 0.6 mm), but lacking the relevant candy wrapper and chocolate smell. These wood bars were designed especially for the experiment; none of the subjects had ever seen such bars before. The two sets of fourteen bars were kept in individual boxes and were introduced to the children at separate times.

One low, nursery-school sized table was used for all the testing. The table's bright orange top contrasted well with the dark bars, and accented the spatial arrangement of these items. The table was divided in half by a piece of masking tape. During the testing, the experimenter and subject were seated opposite each other on matching nursery chairs at a level comfortable for the child.

Procedure

Each subject was individually tested with both the candy bars and the wood bars. With each stimulus type, the child was tested for conservation, using two rows of three objects, five objects, and seven objects. Thus each child was tested for conservation six times. For each test, the child was asked the same three questions.

The order in which the candy and the wood bars were presented was balanced for the subjects, as were the ascending (3-5-7) and descending (7-5-3) numerical arrangements. The row transformation in each conservation test was also balanced. The four resultant orders were as follows:

Order   I: Candy   3-5-7   Wood   3-5-7

Order II: Wood   3-5-7   Candy   3-5-7

Order III: Candy   7-5-3   Wood   7-5-3

Order IV: Wood   7-5-3   Candy   7-5-3

Eighteen subjects each were tested in Orders I and II; sixteen subjects each were tested in Orders III and IV. Each child was given the same introduction and instructions. The instructions which follow are based on Order I (Candy 3-5-7, Wood 3-5-7), but were easily altered for the other three orders.

Instructions:

Hi, my name is _____. Today we're going to play some games. See this table. It's divided into two parts by this piece of tape. This is your side (point to subject's side) and this is my side (point to experimenter's side). Now watch. I'm going to put some candy bars on your side and some on my side. (Three candy bars are placed evenly in two rows.)

Question 1: Now, (child's name), are there the same number of candy bars on your side as there are on my side? (Child answers. Experimenter moves one row of candy bars apart.)

Question 2: Now, are there the same number of candy bars on your side as there are on my side? (Child answers. Experimenter returns candy bars to original position, pauses, and then moves the other row apart.)

Question 3: Now, are there the same number of candy bars on your side as there are on my side? (Child answers. Experimenter returns candy bars to original position.)

(Experimenter adds two candy bars to each row and repeats the above procedure. Then the experimenter adds two more candy bars to each row, and repeats the procedure for a third time. The candy bars are put away, and the entire process is repeated using the wood bars.)

Each subject's test thus consisted of six identical sets of questions, one set for each of the six material-number combinations; each set was comprised of the above three questions. Each session lasted about fifteen minutes. The experimenter recorded the subject's responses during the session.

Scoring

The subject's answers to the six sets of questions were scored either pass or fail. A pass or conserving response was recorded only when the child answered an entire set of questions correctly. Any other result was recorded as a fail or nonconserving response. The child was labeled as a conserver, variable conserver, or nonconserver, depending on his or her answers. A conserver answered all six sets correctly; a nonconserver answered no sets correctly; a variable conserver answered between one and five sets correctly.

RESULTS

Two statistical analyses, as described by Siegel (1956), were used to test for significant differences in the number of conserving responses. The Wilcoxon Matched-Pairs Signed-Rank Test was used to compare differences between the two materials, candy and wood bars. The Cochran Q Test was used to compare differences among the numbers three, five, and seven.

Of the seventy children tested, twenty-five gave conserving responses all the time, twenty-five gave conserving responses part of the time, and the other twenty never gave conserving responses. The mean ages and standard deviation, in months, of the three groups were calculated: conservers, $\overline{X}$ = 51.7, SD = 6.16; variable conservers, $\overline{X}$ = 51.2, SD = 4.78; and nonconservers, $\overline{X}$ = 50.4, SD = 6.25. Of interest here are the variable conservers, twelve males and thirteen females. Some of these children were represented in each of the four orders. Inspection of the raw data revealed that approximately half of the variable conservers were in the 3-5-7 order and half in the 7-5-3 order.

As a test of the first hypothesis concerning materials, a Wilcoxon Matched-Pairs Signed-Rank Test was performed. Table 1 summarizes the results. Using this test, it was determined that children exhibit significantly more conserving responses when candy is used (p < .0001).

To test the second hypothesis concerning number of objects, the Cochran Q Test was used. Table 2 summarizes these results. It can be seen that the probabilities of conserving responses are significantly different with three, five, and seven objects (p < .001).

The responses of the variable conservers are summarized in bar-graph form in Figure 2. The ordinate of the histogram measures the proportion of conserving responses, and the abscissa represents all combinations of material and number. The histogram shows a decrease in conserving responses with the irrelevant material and larger numbers. It appears that the candy-3 condition is superior to the wood-3 condition. Likewise, the candy-5 condition may be superior

Table 1

Wilcoxon Matched-Pairs Signed-Rank Test
conserving and nonconserving responses (3-0)
with candy and wood

VARIABLE CONSERVER	NUMBER CONSERVING RESPONSES CANDY	NUMBER CONSERVING RESPONSES WOOD	d	RANK OF d	RANK WITH LESS FREQUENT SIGN
1	1	0	+1	7	
2	5	1	+2	16	
3	.3	1	+2	16	
4	3	2	+1	7	
5	1	0	+1	7	
6	2	2	0	-	
7	1	0	+1	7	
8	3	0	+3	20	
9	3	0	+3	20	
10	3	0	+3	20	
11	3	1	+2	16	
12	3	2	+1	7	
13	2	0	+2	16	
14	1	1	0	-	
15	3	1	+2	16	
16	1	0	+1	7	
17	1	0	+1	7	
18	3	2	+1	7	
19	2	3	-1	-7	7
20	2	2	0	-	
21	1	1	0	-	
22	1	0	+1	7	
23	1	0	+1	7	
24	3	2	+1	7	
25	3	2	+1	7	
					T = 7

Rank = 204
candy

Rank =   7
wood

$T_{(21)}$ = 7, p<.0001

to the wood-5 condition. Even more striking is the fact that the
variable conservers showed 100% responses with the candy-3 condition.

DISCUSSION

These results indicate that both material and number affect conservation ability. Young children are more successful at conserving
with candy bars as opposed to wood bars, and more successful with
smaller numbers than with larger numbers.

The material findings do not contradict Piaget's implied
assumption concerning different materials. The same conceptualizing
ability is tapped with both candy bars and wood bars. Using a more

Table 2

Cochran Q Test
conserving (1) and nonconserving responses (0) with
three, five, and seven objects

	3 objects	5 objects	7 objects	L_i	L_i^2
1	0	0	0	0	0
2	1	0	0	1	1
3	1	0	0	1	1
4	1	1	0	2	4
5	0	0	0	0	0
6	1	0	0	1	1
7	1	1	0	2	4
8	1	0	0	1	1
9	1	1	0	2	4
10	0	0	0	0	0
11	0	0	0	0	0
12	0	0	0	0	0
13	0	0	0	0	0
14	1	0	0	1	1
15	1	0	0	1	1
16	0	0	0	0	0
17	0	0	0	0	0
18	1	1	0	2	4
19	1	1	0	2	4
20	1	0	0	1	1
21	1	0	0	1	1
22	0	0	0	0	0
23	0	0	0	0	0
24	1	1	0	2	4
25	1	1	0	2	4

$G_1 = 15$ $\qquad$ $G_2 = 7$ $\qquad$ $G_3 = 0$ $\quad$ $L_i = 22$ $\quad$ $L_i^2 = 36$

$P < .001$, $Q(.001, 2) = 13.82$ $\qquad$ $Q_{(2)} = 22.53$, $P < .001$

relevant material just makes it easier for children to conserve.

The number findings extend Gelman's study (1974) to its logical conclusion and support the findings of Lawson, Baron, and Siegel
(1974). They indicate that young children are conservers more often
with smaller numbers than with larger numbers.

From the dissection of the number conservation problem, it is
evident that two interacting forces are operating: the child is
pulled one way by his logic and another way by his perceptions. Following a logical strategy, the child may think: "These two rows have
to be the same. All the experimenter did was move the objects apart."

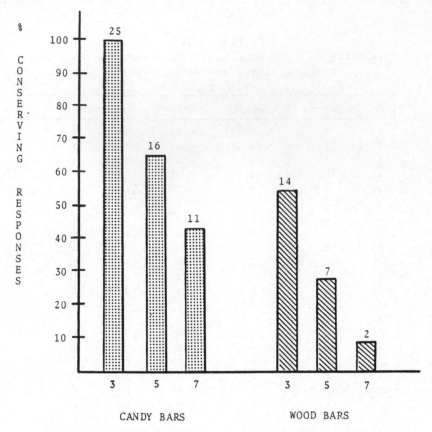

Figure 2. Number of conserving responses as the
joint effect of material and number

Using a perceptual strategy, the child might say: "But those two rows
look different." The child's answer to the conservation problem is
dependent upon the relative strength of these two interacting strategies. Conservation occurs when a child's logic wins over his perceptions. With a conserver, logic always wins; with a nonconserver, logic
never wins; and with a variable conserver, logic sometimes wins.

     In this study the variable conservers exhibited significantly
more conserving responses with the candy bars. It may be that with
this material the child was less likely to let the perceptual illusion dominate and more apt to actively use his logical strategy. With
the candy, a child might have responded: "Three candy bars taste like
three candy bars no matter how far apart they are." With the unfamiliar wood bars, the child may have had difficulty thinking in such con-

crete terms. With his logical strategy inactive, the child's immediate perceptions would dominate, and the child would give a nonconserving response. The fact that subjects exhibited fewer conserving responses with the wood bars probably indicates that this misleading perceptual strategy is more difficult to overcome.

The subjects in this study also responded as conservers significantly more often when the smaller numbers were used. The perceptual illusion with three objects was probably not as strong as it was with five objects, and both of these illusions were probably weaker than was the illusion with seven objects. Of course with any number of objects, the child did not necessarily use the relational information presented in the initial set and transformation to solve the final problem: he could have just counted the objects. This assumption is consistent with the results of the Gelman and Tucker absolute judgment experiment (1975). If a child counts, his logical strategy is not operating fully, and he is not conserving in the Piagetian sense. However, all of the subjects who behaved as variable conservers were not counting. Some of the subjects answered the questions too rapidly to have counted, even silently. Thus, for some subjects at least, the fact that more conserving responses were given with the smaller numbers probably indicates that such perceptual illusions are easier to overcome than those created with larger numbers. Children may perceive discretely with small numbers and yet take a global view of the problem when larger quantities are used.

Piaget (1952) was not interested in the perceptual illusion per se. He used the perceptual illusion inherent in the conservation task to show how children think. Mehler and Bever (1967) and Mehler, Bever, and Epstein (1968) just worked with the perceptual illusion; they showed that children were more successful at overcoming perceptual illusions with candy pellets in contrast to clay pellets. But their study did not say anything about conservation. This study has shown that children are more successful at conserving with candy bars as opposed to wood bars, and with smaller numbers in contrast to larger ones. From an educational or more practical perspective, the results suggest that using more relevant materials should facilitate a child's ability to learn. Making tasks more meaningful should nurture the development of a child's formal operational reasoning.

One defect of the present study deserves comment: the question format. By asking the question in only one form ("Are there the same number of candy bars on your side as there are on my side?"), there was room for an acquiescence response set. Rose (1973) has shown that young children tend to adopt an acquiescence response set. A subject could have attained conserver status just by repeatedly answering "yes"

to all questions. Likewise, a subject could be classified as a nonconserver just by saying "no" to all questions. The design could have
been balanced if half of the subjects had been asked the question in
an alternate form ("Is there a different number of candy bars on your
side and my side?"). However, since the analyses performed exclude
both the conservers and nonconservers, the acquiescence response set
cannot explain the higher performance with candy as compared with
wood bars. This response also will not account for the relative differences in the number of conserving responses with three, five, and
seven objects.

SUMMARY

In an effort to discover what it is about the number conservation task that prevents young children from conserving, the task was
dissected and two of its components were investigated: material and
number. Seventy preschool children were tested with two materials,
candy bars and wood bars, in rows containing three, five, and seven
objects. The results of the twenty-five variable conservers were
analyzed. Using the Wilcoxon Test, it was determined that children
exhibit significantly more conserving responses when candy is used
($p < .0001$). Using the Cochran Q Test, it was determined that the
probabilities of conserving responses are significantly different
with three, five, and seven objects ($p < .001$). These results indicate that large numbers and irrelevant materials may prevent young
children from conserving. These results were discussed in terms of
conservation as the case where a child's logic wins over his perceptions. The study's implications for early childhood education were
also discussed.

POSTSCRIPT

Since the time (June 1979) this paper was written for presentation at the International Congress on Early Childhood Education, additional research has been published which reinforces the major findings
of the present study. Of particular interest is the work by Acredolo
and Acredolo (1980, 1979) who hold that preoperational children are
torn between reliance upon their perception of the maintenance of
identity, which suggests conservation, and their perception of changes
in the other cues, which suggests nonconservation. What Acredolo and
Acredolo refer to as "perception of the maintenance of identity," was
called "logic" in the present study. Labels aside, the major educational implication of such studies is that making tasks more meaningful should nurture the development of a child's formal operational
reasoning.

BIBLIOGRAPHY

Acredolo, C., & Acredolo, L. P. The anticipation of conservation
    phenomenon: Conservation or pseudoconservation. *Child Develop-*
    ment, (in press).
Acredolo, C., & Acredolo, L. P. Identity, compensation, and con-
    servation. *Child Development,* 1979, *50,* 524-535.
Beilin, Harry. Cognitive capacities of young children: A replica-
    tion. *Science,* 1968, *62,* 920-921.
Brainerd, C. J. Feedback, rule knowledge, and conservation learning.
    Child Development, 1977, *48,* 404-411.
Brainerd, C. J., & Hooper, F. H. A methodological analysis of
    developmental studies of identity conservation and equivalence
    conservation. *Psychological Bulletin,* 1975, *82,* 725-737.
Bruner, J. S. On the conservation of liquids. In J. S. Bruner,
    R. R. Olver, P. M. Greenfield et al., *Studies in Cognitive*
    Growth. New York: Wiley, 1966.
Calhoun, L. G. Number conservation in very young children: The
    effect of age and mode of responding. *Child Development,* 1971,
    42, 561-572.
Elkind, David. The development of quantitative thinking: A systematic
    replication of Piaget's studies. *Journal of Genetic Psychology,*
    1961a, *98,* 31-46.
_____. Quantity conceptions in junior and senior high school
    students. *Child Development,* 1961b, *32,* 551-560.
Gelman, R. Conservation acquisition. *Journal of Experimental Child*
    Psychology, 1969, *7,* 67-87.
_____. Logical capacity of very young children: Number invari-
    ance rules. *Child Development,* 1972, *43,* 75-90.
Gelman, R., & Tucker, M. Further investigation of the young child's
    conception of number. *Child Development,* 1975, *46,* 167-175.
Henry, D. E. Interrelationships among attentional preferences,
    cardinal-ordinal ability and conservation. *Child Development,*
    1976, *47:* 750-758.
Higgins-Trenk, A., & Looft, W. Cognitive capacity of very young
    children: Yet another replication. *Journal of Psychology,*
    1971, *79,* 285-289.
Hunt, Trevor D. Early number 'conservation' and experimenter expec-
    tancy. *Child Development,* 1975, *46,* 984-987.
Lawson, J., Baron, J., & Siegel, L. The role of number and length
    cues in children's quantitative judgements. *Child Development,*
    1974, *45,* 731-736.
Lloyd, Barbara. Studies of conservation with Yoruba children:
    Differing ages and experience. *Child Development,* 1971, *42,*
    415-428.
Mehler, J., & Bever, G. Cognitive capacity of very young children.
    Science, 1967, *158,* 141-142.
Mehler, J., Bever, G., & Epstein, B. What children do in spite of
    what they know. *Science,* 1968, *162,* 921-924.

Miller, P. H., & West, R. F. Perceptual supports for one-to-one correspondence in the conservation of number. *Journal of Experimental Child Psychology*, June 1976, *21*: 417-424.

Piaget, Jean. *The child's conception of number*. New York: Humanities, 1952.

_____. Quantification, conservation, and nativism. *Science*, 1968, *162*, 976-979.

Piaget, J., & Inhelder, B. *The growth of logical thinking from childhood to adolescence*. New York: Basic Books, 1958.

Rose, S. Acquiescence and conservation. *Child Development*, 1973, *44*, 811-814.

Rothenberg, B. Conservation of number among 4 and 5 year old children: Some methodological considerations. *Child Development*, 1969, *40*, 383-406.

Siegel, S. *Nonparametric statistics*. New York: McGraw-Hill, 1956.

Smither, S. J., Smiley, S. S., & Rees, R. The use of perceptual cues for number judgment by young children. *Child Development*, 1974, *45*, 693-699.

Willoughby, R., & Trachy, S. Conservation of number in very young children: A failure to replicate Mehler and Bever. *Merrill-Palmer Quarterly*, 1972, *18*, 205-209.

FOOTNOTE

1. The author thanks Dr. Marcel Kinsbourne for his encouragement and advice during this research, and Mr. A. Jackson Stenner for his helpful comments during the writing of the manuscript. The author also thanks the children, teachers, and administrative staff of Duke Memorial Weekday Preschool in Durham, North Carolina

COMPREHENSION OF "BEFORE" AND "AFTER"

BY THE YOUNG CHILD

Barbara Perry-Sheldon
James Madison University

Gaile Cannella and Judith Reiff
University of Georgia

"When children enter a structured school environment they are, often for the first time, required to follow sequential directions rather explicitly" (Barrie-Blackley, 1973, p. 164). Clauses joined with time connectives are commonly used by teachers in explanations, directions, and requests to children. Some children have little difficulty following these temporal directions. Many young children are able to carry out the commands through selective ignoring of the time connectives either from practice--"washing hands after paint-ing"--or by observing the nonverbal actions of the adult or peers to see what is expected (Hatch, 1971). These contextual clues may be largely responsible for the child's comprehension of the directions even though he or she does not have a real understanding of some of the temporal words.

Teachers know that some children do have trouble understanding commands involving two or more parts connected with temporal con-junctions. Studies of words like "and," "first/last," "until," and "before/after" have indicated that particular time connectives used and their order of use affects comprehension. Commands connected with "and" are easily understood, indicating that memory is not the problem (Amidon & Carey, 1972), yet the same commands using "before/after" are misunderstood. In a similar manner, children are able to understand "first/last" commands more easily than "before/after" ones.

Two basic theories have emerged from research concerning "be-fore/after." Clark (1971) has proposed a semantic features model in which "before" and "after" are learned in a series of stages based on their semantic features or components. Under this model the child progresses from knowing neither "before" nor "after" and us-

297

ing an order-of-mention strategy, to knowing "before" and still using order-of-mention for "after." In the third stage the child knows "before," and "after" also means "before." In Clark's fourth stage the child knows both terms.

Another theory, advocated by Amidon and Carey, is based on a syntactic model. The syntactic model says that difficulty in understanding "before" and "after" is due to problems in processing subordinate clause structure. Studies under this theory have found "after" to be interpreted correctly more often than the term "before." This observation is the opposite of Clark's finding.

Coker (1978) has proposed that these studies overlook the confounding interaction of semantics and syntactic structure. Her study found no fixed order of acquisition. She did find that young children seem to understand the words first as prepositions and then as conjunctions. As subordinating conjunctions, order-of-mention and main-clause-first were two strategies employed by the child in interpreting the temporal terms.

CURRENT STUDY

The purpose of the present study was to investigate children's understanding of "before" and "after" in three situations: temporal directions, temporal questions, and pictorial events. The three interview methods used—"before/after" sentences, "before/after" pictures, and "before/after" production—were modeled on methods previously used in the study of temporal relationships.

The "before/after" sentence task consisted of twelve sentences representing four basic sentence types read to each child. The child was to act out the events presented in each sentence using a set of simple toys. The sentences were similar to those identified by Amidon and Carey (1972) and Ferreiro and Sinclair (1971) in their studies of temporal relationships. Examples of the sentences used are:

1. Before you string the beads, rub the cat.
2. After you give me a block, give me the pencil.
3. Pick up the pencil before you pick up the crayon.
4. Tell me your name after you give me a crayon.

The "before/after" picture task consisted of ten pairs of pictures illustrating a sequence of events that were randomly shown to each child. The child was asked to explain the events in terms of sequence. The pairs of pictures included such things as a whole apple and an apple core, a baby swinging and a baby falling from the swing, plus eight other pairs of events. Jarvella and Lubinsky (1975) had investigated the use of such pictures for testing understanding of temporal order by deaf children.

In the "before/after" picture task the child was asked to identify the order of two events acted out by the interviewer. Eight
pairs of events were illustrated using a set of toys. Following
each pair, the child was asked to identify when one of the events
occurred. For example, the interviewer would give the child a book
and then a pencil. The child was asked, "When did I give you a
pencil, before or after I gave you the book?" Ferreiro and Sinclair (1971) concluded that the use of "when" questions in similar
production tasks aided the child's understanding of the concept.

The subjects for the study were 62 children, ranging in age from
40 months to 80 months, enrolled in a half-day, private nursery/
kindergarten center. The children were white, middle-class mono-
linguals. There were 27 boys and 35 girls.

Each subject was interviewed individually by one of three investigators in a vacant room at the center. Each investigator
followed a set of written directions. The three "before/after"
tasks were part of a series of tasks completed by each child.

For each task, each subject received a score based on the
number of correct responses. A total "before/after" score represented the sum of the three tasks. A "before" score was computed
by counting the number of correct responses to "before" items on
the "before/after" sentence task and the "before/after" production
task. An "after" score was the sum of correct answers to the
"after" items on the same two tasks. All statistical analyses were
run using an SPSS (1975) computer program. An alpha level of 0.05
was selected.

A one-way analysis of variance on the total "before/after"
score showed significant differences by age, $F_{3,58} = 27.08$, $p =$
0.001. The 3- and 4-year-olds got less than 50% correct; the 5-
and 6-year-olds got more than 84% correct. Post hoc analysis using the Student Newman-Keuls procedure indicated homogeneous subsets for ages three and four and for the 5- and 6-year-olds. The
significant difference was between the subsets. Table 1 shows the
means and deviations by age.

Similar results were revealed by analysis of the "before"
score, $F_{3,58} = 35.39$, $p = 0.001$, and for the "after" score, $F_{3,58} =$
15.65, $p = 0.001$. Table 2 presents the means for "before" and
also for "after." The Newman-Keuls procedure indicated that 5- and
6-year-olds scored significantly higher than 3- and 4-year-olds on
both "before" and "after."

The "before" and the "after" scores were converted to percentages because there was an unequal number of items. A t-test

Table 1. Means and Standard Deviations by age for the before/
          after total

Age	n	M	SD
3	7	13.14*	3.18
4	15	14.67	7.11
5	25	25.96	4.35
6	15	26.26	3.96

*Maximum score was 30.

Table 2. Means and Standard Deviations for before and after by
          age

Age	Before*		After**	
	M	SD	M	SD
3	4.86	1.86	4.57	3.05
4	5.00	2.27	4.47	2.67
5	9.29	1.08	8.21	1.79
6	9.07	1.10	8.73	1.58

*There was a possible total of 11 "before" items.
**Maximum number of "after" items was 9.

using the converted scores revealed no significant differences between the concepts, $t_{61} = -1.11$, $p = 0.27$. The means were 0.54 for "before" and 0.59 for "after." The standard deviations were 1.25 and 1.52, respectively.

Pearson correlations, which revealed significant positive, moderate correlations between the tasks, ranged from 0.51 to 0.65 (Table 3).

Each task was analyzed using sex and combined ages, ages 3 with 4 and 5 with 6. Table 4 presents the analyses of variance. There were no significant differences by sex for any of the three tasks. There were significant differences by age, with the older group scoring significantly higher each time. Table 5 presents the means and deviations for each task.

Table 3. Correlational matrix of the before/after tasks

Task	1	2	3	4
Sentences (1)	1.00	0.51	0.56	0.83
Pictures (2)		1.00	0.65	0.85
Production (3)			1.00	0.86
Combined (4)				1.00

Table 4. Analysis of Variance for the three tasks

Source of variation	df	MS	F	p
Before/After Sentences				
Sex	1	1.56	0.25	0.999
Age	1	258.20	41.58	0.001
Sex × age	1	0.22	0.03	0.999
Within	58	6.21		
Total	61	10.51		
Before/After Pictures				
Sex	1	1.02	0.15	0.999
Age	1	187.00	27.72	0.001
Sex × age	1	0.56	0.08	0.999
Within	58	6.75		
Total	61	9.52		
Before/After Production				
Sex	1	1.23	0.28	0.999
Age	1	160.87	36.82	0.001
Sex × age	1	12.05	2.76	0.098
Within	58	4.37		
Total	61	7.00		

$\alpha = 0.05$

DISCUSSION

Our finding no difference between the mean responses to the
"before" items and to the "after" items indicates that comprehension
and interpretation of the two concepts are similar. This finding
fails to support the conflicting conclusions of Clark, who said
"before" precedes acquisition of "after," and Barrie-Blackley, who

Table 5.   Means and Standard Deviations for the three tasks by sex
           and age

	Boys	Girls	3 & 4	5 & 6
	Before/After Sentences			
M	9.04	8.80	5.95(50)*	10.31(86)*
SD	2.93	3.41	3.04	2.08
	Before/After Pictures			
M	7.19	7.51	4.85(49)**	8.57(86)**
SD	3.27	2.97	3.12	2.34
	Before/After Production			
M	5.70	5.49	3.25(41)***	6.69(84)***
SD	2.33	2.89	2.47	1.88

     *Percentage of maximum total of 12.
   **Percentage of maximum total of 10.
 ***Percentage of maximum total of 8.

found the opposite. The percentage of correct responses for all
ages, especially the 5- and 6-year-olds, seems to indicate that the
children in the study may have a better understanding of "before/
after" than would be expected from reviewing other research of temporal connectors.

     Some differences in understanding the combined concepts were
to be expected for the different ages. However, the sharp contrast
between the 4- and 5-year-olds raised some distinct questions. Why
was there such a large change in the number of correct responses?
Was the difference due to the developmental pattern of the young
children? If so, what was the nature of such differences? If the
differences were due to learning, then this implies that temporal
concepts may be taught. Amidon and Carey (1972) found that giving
children feedback about responses facilitated appropriate strategies
in attending to clauses involving temporal connectors.

     It must also be noted that a series of cognitive tasks and
some standardized cognitive measures given to the subjects in the
study correlated positively with the "before/after" scores. They
tended to correlate more highly with "after" than with "before."
These results need more study.

     The similar findings for each task and the correlations among
the tasks used in the study indicated that the three "before/after"
tasks are related. Each task seems suitable for investigating the

child's understanding of "before" and "after" in temporal directions, questions, and pictorial events.

IMPLICATIONS OF THE STUDY

Direct implications of our study and the research of others regarding temporal connectors indicate a need for teachers to be aware that children often fail to follow directions not out of willful disobedience or inattention, but from their lack of understanding of time connectives. Teachers must either modify their verbal interactions with children or enhance opportunities for children to learn the semantic/syntactical variances in our language.

Investigations of time connectives should be explored with more emphasis on assessing the cognitive levels of the children involved in the studies. Tentative analysis of data from this study indicated differences in correlations of "before/after" to number facility and spatial relations. (See Cannella, Perry & Reiff, 1979.)

A more general implication regards assessment of other aspects of a child's language development. Teachers should continuously observe and do informal surveys, using materials readily available to them. Assessment need not be limited to formal, standardized procedures. Results of the surveys should be applied in the classroom.

REFERENCES

Amidon, A., & Carey, P. Why five-year-olds cannot understand before and after. *Journal of Verbal Learning and Verbal Behavior*, 1972, *11*, 417-423.
Barrie-Blackley, S. Six-year-old children's understanding of sentences adjoined with time adverbs. *Journal of Psycholinguistic Research*, 1973, *2*, 153-165.
Cannella, G., Perry, B., & Reiff, J. Before and after acquisition through cognitive/intellectual understanding. Paper presented at the Georgia Educational Research Association's annual meeting, November, 1979.
Clark, E.V. On the acquisition of the meaning of before and after. *Journal of Verbal Learning and Verbal Behavior*, 1971, *10*, 266-275.
Coker, P.L. Syntactic and semantic factors in the acquisition of before and after. *Child Language*, 1978, *5*, 261-277.
Ferreiro, E., & Sinclair, H. Temporal relationships in language. *International Journal of Psychology*, 1971, *6*, 39-47.
Hatch, E. The young child's comprehension of time connectives. *Child Development*, 1971, *42*, 2111-2113.

Jarvella, R.J., & Lubinsky, J. Deaf and hearing children's use of
     language describing temporal order among events. *Journal of
     Speech and Hearing Research,* 1975, *18,* 58–73.
Nie, N., Hull, C., Jenkins, J., Steinbrenner, K., & Brent, D.
     Statistical package for the social sciences. New York: McGraw-
     Hill, 1975.

EFFECTS OF TRAINING ON THE DIVERGENT THINKING

ABILITY OF KINDERGARTEN CHILDREN

Mary Jo Cliatt and Jean M. Shaw

University of Mississippi

The increasing number and complexity of problems in the world today seem to indicate a need for fostering in children creative thinking abilities in the context of problem solving. Divergent thinking, the generation of many appropriate responses to a question or issue, is a valuable tool in problem solving. With adequate training, even young children can learn to think divergently.

The development of the creative and divergent thinking abilities of children should be an essential and basic part of education deserving the same attention as the traditional basic skill subjects (Feldhusen & Treffinger, 1977; Massialas & Zevin, 1967; Stein, 1974; Torrance, 1973, 1970). A variety of educational approaches have been used to increase problem solving and divergent thinking abilities of school-age children (Callahan & Renzulli, 1977; Christenson, Guilford, & Wilson, 1957; Davis, Raymond, Rawls, & Jordan, 1976; Goor & Rapoport, 1977; Huntsberger, 1976). Despite its importance, divergent thinking appears to be a neglected area in the development of younger children. The two studies which follow suggest ways teachers can encourage divergent thinking in children.

PURPOSES

The purposes of the first study were to assess the effects of a training procedure on the divergent thinking abilities of young children and to refine methods of training preservice teachers to encourage divergent thinking in young children.

METHOD

    Thirty-seven 5- and 6-year-old children, randomly assigned to
two kindergarten classrooms, served as subjects.[1] The researchers
designated one classroom as the experimental group (E) and the other
as the control group (C). They then administered the Torrance Test
of Creative Thinking, Form A, as a pretest to both groups E and C.
Pretest results established that groups E and C were initially
homogeneous with respect to variance. The pretest also established
the pretreatment levels of fluency, flexibility, originality, and
elaboration on verbal and figural subtests for individual children
and groups of children.

    Fifteen preservice teachers were assigned to the experimental
group (E). They were scheduled individually to work three hours a
week with children in one room of the University of Mississippi
kindergarten. These preservice teachers received intensive training in divergent thinking and questioning techniques.

    These preservice teachers administered an experimental treat-
ment to group E. Over a period of eight weeks, they asked the children in group E several divergent thinking questions each day.
They conducted these experiences daily in large and small group
sessions normally scheduled during the three-hour kindergarten program. Each preservice teacher conducted additional divergent thinking experiences on an individual basis by working with a selected
kindergarten child.

    Sixteen preservice teachers worked with the control group (C)
in a schedule similar to that of group E. Like the teachers of the
experimental group, these preservice teachers met weekly with their
supervisor. In the weekly sessions their supervisor instructed them
in methods of classroom management, ideas for self-concept building
in children, and other teaching techniques. The supervisor told
them they were to ask questions with the purpose of extending the
children's learning, but she did not suggest that they ask divergent
thinking questions.

    The researchers checked the questioning techniques of the pre-
service teachers of groups E and C in two ways: (1) Supervisors
audited and kept records of the teachers' interactions with the
children; and (2) preservice teachers turned in a written record
of the questions they asked the children. As a result of these
records, the researchers found that with group E over 250 instances
of divergent thinking had occurred while with group C, less than

---

[1]This portion of the study was done in collaboration with
Jeanne M. Sherwood, a doctoral student at the University of Mississippi.

twenty-five had taken place. To determine the children's growth
over the experimental period, the researchers administered Form B
of the Torrance Test of Creative Thinking as a posttest to groups
E and C.

RESULTS

    Analysis of posttest scores revealed that on all three verbal
subtests significant differences occurred between experimental and
control groups. When the investigators applied a t test to figural
subtest scores, they found no significant differences between groups
E and C. Table 1 gives a summary of t statistics.

DISCUSSION

    The results indicate that training at the kindergarten level
can increase the ability of children to think divergently. The
children primarily received a verbal treatment, and it was in the
verbal areas that the experimental group scores were significantly
higher than those of the control group. Although both groups made
higher mean scores on the figural posttests than on the pretests,
the differences between the two groups were not significant.

    Children whose teachers repeatedly exposed them to experi-
ences involving divergent thinking realized dramatic increases in

Table 1. Independent t-ratio results on subtest of the Torrance
          Test of Creative Thinking

Torrance Subtests	Group E $\overline{X}$	Group C $\overline{X}$	t-ratio
Verbal Subtests			
Fluency	40.16	23.00	4.95*
Flexibility	19.79	12.29	3.44*
Originality	42.89	25.81	3.10*
Figural Subtests			
Fluency	17.63	17.15	0.31
Flexibility	13.26	12.10	0.84
Originality	37.42	32.80	0.56
Elaboration	9.74	7.75	0.82

    *A t-ratio of 2.65 for 1 and 35 degrees of freedom is required
for significance at the .001 level.

divergent thinking abilities. If such increases in divergent thinking ability are deemed to be desirable traits in young children,
then teachers need to develop effective methods for fostering divergent thinking in the classroom.

FURTHER STUDY: TEACHER TRAINING

     Because of the positive results of the study on the divergent
thinking abilities of children, the researchers were motivated to
extend their study to refine methods for training preservice teachers
in using divergent thinking techniques with young children. In the
next study, the researchers measured preservice teachers' knowledge
and application of divergent thinking questioning techniques.

     The researchers used preservice teachers from two undergraduate
laboratory classes, EDEC 301, Experiences in Teaching in Early
Childhood Education, as their subjects. The preservice teachers
in these classes were individually scheduled to work three hours a
week teaching children in the University of Mississippi kindergartens.
They also met with their supervisors one hour and twenty minutes each
week for instruction and feedback on their work with children.

     Nineteen preservice teachers in one section of the class were
designated as an experimental group, E_T. They received intensive
training in divergent thinking and questioning techniques from their
supervisor. In weekly sessions, they were given information on the
various types of questions that teachers may ask young children and
the purposes that different types of questions serve. Their supervisor modeled asking open-ended, divergent thinking questions in the
training sessions. The preservice teachers worked in large and
small groups to learn to write and evaluate divergent thinking questions. The best divergent thinking questions were filed in a
"Think Tank" box. The preservice teachers also practiced asking
each other divergent thinking questions and received feedback from
their peers and supervisor on the quality of their questions. As
homework assignments, preservice teachers composed and judged more
questions. The preservice teachers planned divergent thinking questions related to activities they would carry out the following week
with the kindergarten children.

     Eighteen preservice teachers in another section were designated
as the control group, C_T. The control group also met in weekly
sessions with their supervisor. They received various instructions
on methods of working with young children. Although they were encouraged to plan and ask questions to extend children's learning,
their supervisor did not train them to ask divergent thinking questions.

In order to measure the preservice teachers' knowledge of questioning techniques and their abilities to create divergent thinking questions, the researchers devised parallel forms of a short written test. They administered Form A as a pretest. After nine weeks, they administered Form B as a posttest.

To ascertain the number of divergent thinking questions the preservice teachers actually asked, the supervisors required the students to hand in a written record of the questions they asked in the kindergarten each week. Supervisors helped to confirm the accuracy of the students' records by observing the preservice teachers as they worked with the children.

The researchers used analysis of covariance to compare the two measures for the experimental and control groups. Group means for test scores and the number of divergent thinking questions asked are shown in Table 2.

The researchers attributed the significant differences between the experimental and control groups to the training procedures. Since very few teachers ask divergent thinking questions automatically, training in such techniques is essential if teachers are to develop divergent questioning skills. Perhaps if other teacher-training programs employ this procedure, they may also notice impressive results.

Table 2.   Adjusted group means of preservice teachers on a measure of knowledge of questioning techniques and divergent thinking questions asked of children

Variable	Group E_T Adjusted $\overline{X}$	Group C_T Adjusted $\overline{X}$	Adjusted $\overline{X}_D$	F-Ratio
Test (Knowledge of Questioning)	10.67	7.24	3.43	15.02*
Questions asked of Children	19.53	4.94	14.59	51.42*

*An F-ratio of 7.44 for 1 and 34 degrees of freedom is required for significance at the 0.01 level.

BIBLIOGRAPHY

Callahan, C.M., & Renzulli, J.S. The effectiveness of a creativity
    training program in the language arts. *The Gifted Child Quart-*
    erly, 1977, *21*, 538-545.
Christensen, P.R., Guilford, J.P., & Wilson, R.C. Relations of
    creative responses to working time and instructions. *Journal*
    of Experimental Psychology, 1957, *53*, 82-88.
Davis, T., Raymond, A., Rawls, C.M., & Jordan, J. A comparison of
    achievement and creativity of elementary school students using
    project vs. textbook programs. *Journal of Research in Science*
    Teaching, 1976, *13*, 205-212.
Feldhusen, J.F., Hobson, S., & Treffinger, D.J. The effects of visual
    and verbal stimuli on divergent thinking. *The Gifted Child*
    Quarterly, 1975, *19*, 205-209.
Goor, A., & Rapoport, T. Enhancing creativity in an informal educa-
    tional framework, *Journal of Educational Psychology*, 1977, *69*,
    636-643.
Huntsberger, J. Developing divergent-productive thinking in element-
    ary school children using attribute games and problems. *Journal*
    of Research in Science Teaching, 1976, *13*, 185-191.
Massialas, B.C., & Zevin, J. *Creative encounters in the classroom*.
    New York: John Wiley and Sons, 1967.
Stein, M.I. *Stimulating creativity*. New York: Academic Press, 1974.
Torrance, E.P. *Encouraging creativity in the classroom*. Dubuque,
    IA: William C. Brown Co., 1970.
Torrance, E.P., & Torrance, J.P. *Is creativity teachable?* Blooming-
    ton, IN: Indiana University, 1973. (ERIC Document Reproduction
    Service No. ED 120 651).

STUDIES IN PRETENSE PLAY AND THE

CONSERVATION OF QUANTITY

Claire Golomb

University of Massachusetts

Boston

INTRODUCTION

In recent years psychologists and educators have shown a renewed interest in the nature of child play and have raised interesting questions about its possible significance for cognitive development. One of the early pioneering studies, published by the Israeli investigator Sara Smilansky (1968), stressed the importance of pretense or make-believe play in a social setting. Smilansky suggested that a number of important cognitive and social skills are being exercised when preschool children engage in sociodramatic play and that these skills are essential for success during the elementary school years. When children engage in role-play they must, of necessity, take the perspective of their own assumed role and that of the play partner, and coordinate their actions accordingly. Thus several students of role-play, stressing that role-taking implies perspective-taking skills, have attempted to establish the degree of correlation between role-play and perceptual, cognitive, and affective perspective-taking tasks (Feffer & Gourevich, 1960; Selman, 1971; Turnure, 1975). The results of these studies seem to lend some support to the notion that role-playing employs cognitive skills, but the data are not altogether consistent. Perhaps this ought not to be surprising to us, since the term "perspective-taking" probably refers to diverse rather than to unitary social and cognitive skills.

Own Studies: My own studies adopt a somewhat narrower focus and begin with an analysis of the specific cognitive operations that characterize pretense play. The child who engages in a game of make-believe assumes a role that deviates from his usual realistic one. For the duration of the game, the child, his partner, and the play objects are transformed, while simultaneously maintaining an imaginary duality of object and role. While adopting a role and enacting it, the child does not forget his "real" identity. If need be he can step momentarily out of his role, for example, to answer his mother's call or to have his shoelaces tied. The same is true of the identity he ascribes to the substitute objects. The child may treat a playdough blob as if it were a delicious birthday cake, but he carefully refrains from biting into it. He may pretend that a stick is his horse or that a shoebox is an imaginary airplane, but he does not attempt to defy the laws of gravity. He maintains the distinction between reality and fantasy throughout his games of pretense. Thus it appears that the playing child is capable of performing mental transformations, i.e., from the original real life identity to a pretense identity and back to the original and enduring identity.

These transformations are not matched by physical reality and are performed rather independently by the actor, who makes the transformations and cancels them as his play-theme indicates. Thus we are witnessing in the pretense situation of early childhood a form of reversible thought operation. Reversibility of thought, as Piaget defines it, is the ability of a mental operation to return to its point of departure, assuring the relative independence of cognition from perceptual domination (Piaget, 1950; 1960). Piaget considers reversibility essential for the development of conceptual thought and for the attainment of conservation. Conservation of quantity, for example, represents a form of thought that has freed itself from misleading perceptual cues. Piaget defines conservation as the cognition that certain properties (quantity, length, number) remain invariant in the face of certain transformations, and he views its acquisition as a necessary condition for all rational activity. Piaget maintains that the conservation problem requires a logical explanation in terms of identity, inversion, or compensation of relations. Thus, in order to solve the problem posed in the conservation task, the child must understand that the quantity, despite appearances to the contrary, remains unchanged, that it maintains its identity, that this can be demonstrated by cancelling the transformation and reestablishing equivalence, and that changes in one dimension are compensated for by changes in another dimension (e.g., height x width).

Piaget's analysis of the cognitive strategies employed in the solution of the conservation problem is also useful when we attempt to characterize pretense play. Quite analogously, in pretense play the child maintains his enduring identity despite the adoption of pretense identities. He cancels the pretense transformation at the end of his game, and he maintains complementary relations between his real and his assumed identities. The core property that characterizes both pretense play and conservation attainment is reversibility. In make-believe play the child employs an intuitive and unselfconscious form of reversibility: he performs reversible transformations that are not perceptually apparent and that are in fact mental transformations. In both conservation and pretense tasks, reality is dealt with via transformations.

Conceptual Analysis

Let me summarize the foregoing conceptual analysis and formulate the specific working hypothesis that guided the design of the following five empirical studies:

1. Symbolic, pretense, or make-believe play employs a primitive form of reversible thought operation.

2. This form of reversibility is akin to the reversibility that characterizes concrete operational thought.

3. Training in pretense play that draws the child's attention to the mental and reversible transformations that he spontaneously makes in his play (with particular emphasis on the dual identity that he assumes and also attributes to the play objects) will facilitate the application of these intuitive reversible thought operations to the solution of the conservation problem.

In our first study (Golomb & Cornelius, 1977), we selected a group of 15 nonconserving four-year-old middle-class children on the basis of conservation. We engaged these children over a three-day period in short pretense games of about 15 minutes each, followed by a verbal inquiry. This inquiry focused on the dual identity of the play object, namely, its pretense function and its function in real life. The child was questioned about the original identity, its transformation, and the ultimate return to the original identity of the play object. Conservation posttests that followed pretense play training indicated that 10 out of 15 children gave correct conserving judgments and explanations on at least some of the tasks. This score was not matched by the control group, which had played constructive games for a comparable amount of time.

In our second study, conducted with Jerry Adams, we wished to isolate the specific aspects of pretense play that facilitate the induction of conserving responses. We wanted to know whether it was pretense play per se or pretense play with verbal inquiry that was the effective mediator. We also examined the duration over time of the cognitive gains, and we included two delayed posttests. The results indicated that only pretense play with inquiry was an effective mediator of conserving responses and that the differences between the experimental and control groups reached statistical significance only on the third posttest ($p < .01$) 23 days after completion of

the play training. The scores for the pretense play group with inquiry gradually increased from posttest 1 to posttest 3.

     The third study, conducted jointly with Laura Friedman, com-
pared the effectiveness of pretense play training, direct conservation training, and a combination of pretense play and conservation
training. Only the combined condition yielded significantly better
results than the control groups ($p < .05$), although both pretense
play and conservation training produced some modest effects. Interestingly, the scores from posttest 1 to posttest 2 increased for
the pretense play training group, decreased for the conservation
training group, and remained stable for the combined group. Thus
we can say that the original effect of the first study was replicated but its magnitude considerably reduced.

     This attenuated effect made us aware of examiner variables.
It became clear to us that we had to maximize the child's attention
to the tasks and to assure his active participation in the development of a pretense theme. In the fourth study, conducted with Elaine
Gowing, we compared the effectiveness of the adult-initiated games
strategy, which we had used so far, with a new method that asked
the child to teach the adult a pretense game. The verbal inquiry
was also incorporated into this format. The results were reassuring: the adult-initiated games replicated the magnitude of the
original findings (67% conserved on the posttest). However, the
child-initiated game was significantly more effective than the
adult-initiated one (82% conserved on the posttest).

     The fifth and last study was conducted jointly with Shoshana
Bonen. For the first time we selected children from low income
families. The kindergarteners, aged five and six years, could be
described as socioeconomically deprived. Following the conservation
pretests, which established the nonconserving status of our 60 subjects, we gave our 40 experimental subjects a single session of
conservation training. We used a method found to be highly effec-
ive, namely, demonstrating a correct judgment and explanation and
then verbally correcting the child's own response. The following
day we posttested the children and discovered that only 10% (4
children) had benefitted from the training. Next, we assigned the
36 nonconservers to two additional training conditions: pretense
play or further conservation training over 3 days. Posttests indicated that both training conditions were effective inducers of
conserving responses, statistically significantly better than the
control ($p < .05$). Correct judgments and explanations were
also elicited on new, untrained tasks. The differences between
pretense play and additional conservation training were not statistically significant, a rather remarkable finding.

     How can the results from our five studies be interpreted?
The significance of our studies lies in the demonstration that

pretense play training can activate problem-solving strategies spontaneously engaged in when playing pretense games but usually not yet applied to the conservation task. Our symbolic play training studies have yielded a genuine conceptual reorganization in our preschool subjects, as manifested in the correct conserving judgments and explanations, in the duration of the effect, and in the generalization to new conservation tasks. Thus the subjects in our pretense play training condition were encouraged to draw upon familiar thought operations (pretense transformations) in a novel situation. Their successful application of this strategy supports the hypothesis that the underlying thought processes are to some degree analogous.

Finally, if imaginative activities provide an important link between preoperational and concrete operational thought, then symbolic play attains a new significance for the development of logical thought. From this perspective, symbolic or pretense play serves a distinct cognitive function: it exercises an early form of reversible thought operation and thus facilitates the construction of concrete operational structures. This represents a reassessment of the role of symbolic play for human development and suggests that pretense modes of reasoning should be exercised rather than merely overcome and outgrown. This interpretation carries important educational implications. For example, pretense games might be profitably employed with socioeconomically disadvantaged youngsters to teach them via a familiar and pleasurable activity some of the conceptual skills essential for academic success in the elementary school grades.

BIBLIOGRAPHY

Feffer, M.M., & Gourevich, V. Cognitive aspects of role-taking in children. *Journal of Personality*, 1960, 383-396.
Golomb, C., & Cornelius, C.B. Symbolic play and its cognitive significance. *Development Psychology*, 1977, *13*, 246-252.
Piaget, J. *The psychology of intelligence*. London: Routledge & Kegan Paul, 1950.
_____. *On the development of memory and identity*. Worcester, MA: Clark University Press, 1960.
Selman, R.L. Taking another's perspective: Role-taking development in early childhood. *Child Development*, 1971, *42*, 1721-1734.
Smilansky, S. *The effects of sociodramatic play on disadvantaged preschool children*. New York: Wiley, 1968.
Turnure, C. Cognitive development and role-taking ability in boys and girls from 7 to 12. *Developmental Psychology*, 1975, *11*, 202-209.

THE RELATIONSHIP BETWEEN THE DEVELOPMENT OF A
PEER SOCIAL SYSTEM AND ATTACHMENT

Ruth L. Wynn

Syracuse University

The opportunity for the very young child to establish social relationships with other children has not been considered an advantage or at least as beneficial as experiences with the mother. This attitude is evident in the current practice of home rearing within the nuclear family, which has heightened the importance of mother-child attachment while providing few opportunities for frequent peer contact. Group day care differs from home rearing in the nuclear family as a situation of daily separation from the mother and participation in a play group. Day care has not received unqualified acceptance for infants and toddlers because it has been thought that daily separation from the mother may be cause for some deviation in the "normal" mother-child attachment relationship (Bowlby, 1969, 1973; Ainsworth, 1963, 1973). This qualified acceptance has resulted in evaluations of the day care experience that have focused primarily on the effect of the child's attachment relationship with the mother without reference to other social relationships (Blehar, 1974; Brookhart & Hock, 1976; Caldwell, Wright, Honig & Tannenbaum, 1970; Doyle, 1975; Maccoby & Feldman, 1972; Ricciuti, 1974). It appears that, by focusing so narrowly on the mother-child relationship and separation experiences, we may be ignoring a positive aspect of the day care experience, namely, the importance of peer relations for infants and toddlers.

Of the psychologists, Bowlby and Ainsworth have attributed the greatest importance to the infant's formation of an attachment relationship with his or her mother. Their position is predicated on the assumption that social attachment is an evolved behavior system that has as its goal the maintenance of proximity to the mother as a means of reducing fear by providing maternal protection. Separation from the mother, an unfamiliar environment, and the

317

approach of a stranger all belong to a class of threatening conditions that activate the attachment system. However, several studies
reveal that other children are not viewed as members of the class
of threatening stimuli (Brooks & Lewis, 1976; Lewis & Brooks, 1974).
This absence of stranger anxiety gives credibility to Harlow's
theory (1965, 1971) of the emergence of a child-child affectional
system that allows the young child to tolerate the absence of the
mother. The major difference between Harlow and the Bowlby-Ainsworth position is that Harlow places considerable emphasis on innate
maturational changes that ensure an invariant shift in affectional
ties from the mother to age-mates, while Bowlby and Ainsworth claim
that there is no developmental discontinuity in attachment to the
mother.

The attachment relationship of the young child to his or her
mother appears to be more lasting and perhaps qualitatively different than the relationship Harlow observed in Rhesus monkeys. This
may reflect species differences or it may be an artifact of child
rearing within the nuclear family that emphasizes the mother-
child relationship and provides few opportunities for peer contact.
Lewis, Young, Brooks and Michaelson (1975) have proposed a third
model of social development in which the mother-child attachment
system and a peer system develop concurrently. Their model bridges
the differences between the Bowlby-Ainsworth approach and that
of Harlow by retaining the attachment system throughout the life
span, but granting a more important and independent role to the
child-child affectional system. In constructing this model, Lewis
et al. (1975) have challenged the current style of home rearing
within the nuclear family as being somewhat removed from that which
prevailed in former times. Both Harlow and Lewis et al. would view
early peer contacts as a natural occurrence in much the same way
that Bowlby and Ainsworth believe separation of the mother and young
child to be unnatural. Lewis et al. (1975) are stating a deprivation hypothesis of sorts, based on the assumption that the lack of
opportunity for peer group contact is a distortion of the natural
social pattern that existed in earlier forms of society. Studies
of the child-rearing patterns of such groups as the !Kung San
(Bushmen of the Kalahari) by Konner (1972, 1975) have revealed that
social interaction with other children occurs early in life and that
children are reared in multiaged peer groups from about eighteen
months onward. Group day care outside the home for infants and
toddlers may not be so culturally unique and artificial as might
first be supposed. In fact, it could be suggested that the rearing of children in a group that provides for social interaction with
other children early in life may have advantages for the individual
and the species.

Common everyday observation shows that children eventually
spend the major part of their time with other children away from
the mother. Cultural and situational factors have determined the

time for the emergence of this developmental shift by specifying
the age for separation from the mother and for encounters with other
children. It may be that the formation of social relationships with
age-mates signifies a developmental change in attachment behavior
whereby age-mates supplant the mother as a support for exploration
and play. In children this need not signal the termination of the
attachment relationship but rather that the two social systems coexist.

As yet there is little empirical information concerning the
developmental shift away from the mother to children as a function
of the child-rearing environment. A necessary condition for investigating the development of a child-child affectional system is a
situation that provides for frequent encounters with other children.
Group day care may be the only setting available in contemporary
society for the study of the development of a peer social system
in the very young child. A majority of studies (Brookhart & Hock,
1976; Caldwell, Wright, Honig and Tannenbaum, 1970; Doyle, 1975;
Maccoby & Feldman, 1972; Ricciuti, 1974) have found that there are
few differences in attachment behavior to consistently distinguish
children in group care from those reared at home. Konner (1972,
1975) also reports that attachment behavior and fear of strangers
develop in the !Kung San infants in a form very similar to that
found in Western home-reared infants. The present study was designed to test the hypothesis that a measurable shift in the
balance of attachment behavior and exploratory play with another
child would occur during the last half of the second year.

To explore this hypothesis I decided to examine whether another
child could supplant the mother as a support for exploration and
play as a function of prior social exposure to children and if the
presence of the other child would elicit social play that could
disrupt the proximity-maintaining behavior of the attachment system.
Toddlers were chosen for study because infant attachment patterns
appear to decline around the second birthday (Cox & Campbell, 1968;
Kotelchuck, Zalazo, Kagan & Spelke, 1975; Rheingold & Eckerman, 1970).
Paralleling the attenuation of infant attachment behavior, there
appears to be an increase in social interaction with peers (Anderson,
1972; Eckerman, Whatley, & Kutz, 1975). In order to investigate
this developmental shift in the balance of attachment behavior and
exploratory play with children, it was essential to adopt an approach in which both attachment behavior and social play with another
child could be studied at the same time. A procedure that gives
the child a choice between the mother and a child playmate with
access to both would permit this. A modification of the strange
situation developed by Ainsworth and Wittig (1969) that incorporates
such a forced-choice situation and replaces the adult female stranger with a child stranger not only made this approach possible, but
allowed for assessment of attachment behavior by established
method and criteria.

METHOD

Subjects

The subjects were 20 middle-class day-care children, half
between the ages of 18 and 24 months and half between 24 and 30
months, and 20 home-reared children also equally divided into the
two age groups. Equal numbers of boys and girls were selected
for each of the age levels within rearing groups. All of the
day-care children were attending a day-care center for at least
40 hours a week immediately preceding participation in the study.
The mean length of time in attendance was 10 months, with a range
of 4 to 24 months. The 20 home-reared children were principally
cared for in their own homes by their mothers. The two rearing
groups differed significantly on the mean number of hours of group
experience out of the home in the absence of the mother ($\overline{X}$ = 158
hours for the home-reared children in contrast to $\overline{X}$ = 2,128 hours
for the day-care children).

In order to demonstrate the equivalence of the day-care and
home-reared samples for other than the rearing situation, measures
of family composition and home experience were obtained via a questionnaire completed by the mother. Items about the family composition included mother's age, father's age, mother's years of education, father's years of education, and number of siblings. Items
about the home experience (Schwarz & Wynn, 1971) were those assumed
to be closest to the situation encountered in a day-care center,
which involves contact with several peer-age children and adults
other than family members in the absence of the mother. The items
were size of the child's home play group, how often the child played
at a friend's house, number of times the family went out leaving
the child with a sitter, and the number of different sitters used
by the family. Both family composition and home experience were
investigated for the rearing situation by multivariate analysis of
variance (MANOVA) (Clyde, 1969). Neither family composition nor
home experience discriminated between the day-care and the home-reared
groups. Family composition and home experience variables were also
computed for sex of the child. Neither family composition nor home
experience discriminated differences between boys and girls.

Procedures

Subjects were observed in a laboratory playroom while the
mother sat in an adjacent room completing the questionnaire. She
was seated within the visual field of her child looking through the
playroom doorway, and contact was not prevented. In order to create
the forced-choice situation, age-appropriate but immovable toys were
located at the end of the play room farthest from the doorway to the
mother's room. The play session followed the scenario of the

Ainsworth strange situation.

Six 5-year-old female children served as the child strangers. They were instructed to remain in the playroom in the vicinity of the toys and to attempt to engage the child in play. The child strangers were trained during pilot sessions, but there were observed differences in their play with a younger unfamiliar child. Because of this, a different playmate was chosen for each child within each of the eight groups.

The behavior of the three participants was videotaped through a one-way vision mirror in the playroom. A microphone recorded speech and vocalization. The videotaped records were coded to extract quantifiable measures of exploratory play and attachment behavior. Exploration was measured by greatest maximum distance from the mother, time away from the mother, time out of the visual field of the mother, exploratory toy play, and social exploratory play. Attachment behavior was measured by visual contact seeking, crying, search behavior, proximity-seeking behavior, and proximity-avoiding behavior. Distance, frequency-intervals, and intensity measures were utilized. Intercoder reliability averaged 0.94 across measures with a range of 0.99 to 0.75. The effects of age, sex, and rearing condition were tested by computing repeated measure multivariate analyses of variance or covariance (MANOVAs) for each of the ten dependent measures.

RESULTS

The anticipated significant effects for episodes are consistent with the results reported by other investigators (Blehar, 1974; Feldman & Ingham, 1975; Maccoby & Feldman, 1972) who have employed the strange situation with children who are about two years of age.

No significant differences were found between day-care and home-reared children for any of the five measures of attachment behavior.

Age of the children affected exploratory and attachment behaviors. The older children ventured a greater maximum distance from the mother, $F(3,30) = 3.089$, $p < .042$, and exhibited less crying associated with separation, $F(7,26) = 2.505$, $p < .041$. The differences are in the direction expected, although finding significance for only one measure out of five for each of the two categories of behavior is less than substantial.

There were three significant differences between rearing groups on measures of exploratory behavior. The day-care children ventured a greater maximum distance from the mother, $F(3,30) = 5.589$, $p < .004$; spent more time away from the mother, $F(3,30) = 4.085$, $p < .015$; and more time out of the mother's visual field, $F(3,30) =$

3.562, p < .026. Exploratory toy play was marginally significant, $F(7,26)$ = 2.329, p < .055. The day-care group, however, did not participate in social play with the unfamiliar child more than did the home-reared group.

Significant interactions based on rearing by sex of the child were found for the four measures based on the child's proximity to the mother: greatest maximum distance from the mother, $F(3,30)$ = 4.562, p < .010; time away from the mother, $F(3,30)$ = 3.438, p < .029; time out of the visual field of the mother, $F(3,30)$ = 4.112, p <.015; and visual contact seeking, $F(3,30)$ = 3.605, p < .025. These several rearing-by-sex effects appear to be related to the introduction of the unfamiliar playmate. The day-care girls were the most hesitant during the familiarization period, episode 3, withdrawing from the playmate to the area in the playroom where the mother was visible. This wariness was very shortlasting. No further decreases occurred, and in fact day-care girls spent more time in social play and exploration than did the other three groups during the final, most stressful episodes of the strange situation. The other three groups behaved in just the opposite fashion: attracted by the playmate's presence initially, followed by a sharp decline in exploration. Actually, each of the four rearing-by-sex groups differed in their strange situation behavior inasmuch as the quadratic trend was significant for those measures.

Search behavior revealed significant differences for sex of the child, $F(3,30)$ = 3.061, p < .043. Girls did the most active searching after the mother's first departure, and this did not change when the girls were left alone. The boys, however, became most active in searching for the mother when they were alone. The scores for boys and girls were quite similar in episode 7 with the arrival of the playmate.

DISCUSSION

The hypothesis advanced in this study was based on the premise that an unfamiliar child is viewed as a highly attractive social object by toddlers, rather than as a threatening stimulus. This is consistent with the hypothesis of an emerging peer affectional system. The findings of this study indicate that there was a tendency for the children to engage in friendly social interaction with the unfamiliar playmate with little hesitancy. During the first three-minute encounter with the unfamiliar playmate, 75% of the children spent at least some time in social play. In addition, 75% of the children increased the amount of time spent in the playroom away from the mother, and 63% of the children spent more time in the playroom where they could not see the mother after the playmate arrived than they did before her arrival. Visual contact seeking decreased for the 50% of the children in the presence of

the unfamiliar playmate. These findings suggest that the proximity-
maintaining behaviors of the attachment system can be disrupted by
the presence of another child, at least at the ages examined in
this study.

The differences between rearing groups also found in the present
study suggest that early experience with other children in group care
facilitates the development of peer relations that are supportive
of exploration and play in the mother's absence. The differences
between rearing groups in exploration do not conform to the results
reported by other investigators (Blehar, 1974; Brookhart & Hock,
1976; Maccoby & Feldman, 1972). These conflicting results may be
related to the behaviors directed toward the stranger. Other investigators (Blehar, 1974; Brookhart & Hock, 1976; Maccoby & Feldman,
1972) found that day-care children were more avoidant of the adult
stranger than were home-reared children. One conclusion that may
be drawn is that the adult stranger may have inhibited exploration.
In the present study, however, the presence of a child stranger appeared to have the opposite effect. It is reasonable to assume
that, compared with day-care children, home-reared children spend
more time with adults or alone than with other children. The rearing
situations appear to provide different socialization experiences
that are reflected in a child's ability to feel comfortable in the
presence of an unfamiliar child or an unfamiliar adult.

The several rearing-by-sex effects were not expected and warrant
consideration. They suggest that there are more basic differences
between day-care and home-reared boys and girls than the differences
in wariness, which was not a good predictor of social interaction
with another child. Kagan, Kearsley, and Zalazo (1975) have suggested that wariness is indicative of the child's inability to
resolve questions about whether the actions of the unfamiliar child
will be friendly or not. On the basis of results from their longitudinal study of day-care and home-reared children, the authors
concluded that the exhibition of wariness in the presence of an unfamiliar child was a function of both cognitive maturity and experience. The cognitive precocity of females reported by Kegan, *et al.*,
(1975), suggests that the day-care girls in the present study were
likely to form questions about the other child. Their experience
in daily interactions with other young children may have given them
cause to hesitate before responding to another child. They may
have been considering the fact that not all children make good play-
mates and were waiting for some signal of friendliness. Once this
occurred, the day-care girls found the company of the other child
highly attractive and were the most socially interactive group.

The home-reared girls behaved in an opposite fashion, perhaps
because of their prior experience. It seems reasonable to assume
that their previous experience with other children consisted of play-
mates selected by the mother on the basis of the children's ability

to play in a friendly fashion.   These encounters probably occurred
in the presence of one or the other child's mother. If this were
the case, the home-reared girls in the present study might have
been able to resolve quickly in the affirmative the question raised
concerning the unfamiliar child.   This resolution would account for
the most marked increases in social play and exploration for the
home-reared girls with the appearance of the other child, but overall they spent the least amount of time in exploration and play
away from the mother.

The boys did not display any wariness toward the unfamiliar
child, but the play behaviors were different for day-care and home-
reared boys in the presence of the playmate.   The home-reared boys,
while remaining in the playroom and away from the mother, were involved in solitary play with toys.   This behavior suggests more a
lack of social skill than the inhibition of exploration associated
with wariness.   The day-care boys appeared to have a repertoire
of social skills and engaged in play with the unfamiliar child.

Kagan et al. (1975) suggest that because boys are more interactive than girls in the day-care situation, the daily contact with
peers has a more substantial influence on reducing uncertainty for
boys than for the less active girls.   The home setting does not produce this difference.   It may be that less vigorous play is permitted
in the home than is likely to occur in a day-care center.   When
gross motor equipment such as a slide is unavailable, boys engage
in more rough-and-tumble play than girls (Blurton-Jones, 1972).   This
type of equipment is less common in the home than in day-care centers.
Boys may therefore receive more negative reinforcement for their
social interactions in the home than do the less active girls.   This
may result in home-reared boys having fewer social skills for interacting with the playmate than day-care boys or home-reared girls.

One conclusion that may be drawn is that the day-care experience tends to reduce differences in boys and girls.   For example,
girls tend to engage in as much rough-and-tumble play near a slide
as do boys (Blurton-Jones, 1972).   In more global terms, the day-
care experience may be considered one that facilitates the development of independence from the mother.   Home-rearing, on the other
hand, may encourage sex stereotyping, which would tend to produce
more dependency in girls than in boys.   These findings are also
supported by Cornelius and Denny (1975), who found no differences
between day-care boys and girls, although home-reared girls sought
proximity to the mother more than did home-reared boys.

The day-care experience is a complex social event.   Other
studies are needed to gain a more thorough understanding of its
effect on the young child.   The present study has indicated that
the social responsiveness of the young child toward another child
may be enhanced by daily contacts with other children, and that

the development of these social skills may facilitate the growth
of independence in both boys and girls. Contrary to the Bowlby-
Ainsworth position, which assumes that daily separation from the
mother is detrimental to the mother-child attachment relationship,
this study also suggests that the day-care experience is not associated with any deviation in the "normal" mother-child attachment relationship.

BIBLIOGRAPHY

Ainsworth, M.D.S. The development of infant-mother interaction
    among the Ganda. In B. M. Foss (Ed.), *Determinants of infant
    behavior II*. London: Methuen; New York: Wiley, 1963, 67-112.
_____. The development of infant-mother attachment. In B. M.
    Caldwell and H. N. Ricciuti (Eds.), *Review of child develop-
    ment research, Vol. 3*. University of Chicago Press, 1973.
Ainsworth, M.D.S., & Wittig, B.A. Attachment and exploratory be-
    havior of one-year-olds in a strange situation. In B.M. Foss
    (Ed.), *Determinants of infant behavior IV*. London: Methuen,
    1969, 111-136.
Anderson, J.W. Attachment behavior out of doors. In N. Blurton-
    Jones (Ed.), *Ethological studies of child behavior*. Cambridge:
    Cambridge University Press, 1972, 199-215.
Blehar, M.P. Anxious attachment and defensive reactions associated
    with day care. *Child Development*, 1974, *45*, 683-692.
Blurton-Jones, N. Categories of child-child interaction. In N.
    Blurton-Jones (Ed.), *Ethological studies of child behavior*.
    Cambridge: Cambridge University Press, 1972, 97-127.
Bowlby, J. *Attachment and loss: Vol. 1 Attachment*. London: Hogarth;
    New York: Basic Books, 1969,
_____. *Attachment and loss: Vol. 2 Separation*. London: Hogarth;
    New York: Basic Books, 1973.
Brookhart, J., & Hock, E. The effects of experimental context and
    experimental background on infants' behavior toward their
    mothers and a stranger. *Child Development*, 1976, *41*, 333-340.
Brooks, J., & Lewis, M. Infants' responses to strangers: Midget,
    adult and child. *Child Development*, 1976, *47*, 323-332.
Caldwell, B.M., Wright, C.M., Honig, A.S., & Tannenbaum, J. Infant
    care and attachment. *American Journal of Orthopsychiatry*,
    1970, *40*, 397-412.
Clyde, D.J. *Multivariate analysis of variance on large computers*.
    Clyde Computing Service, 1969.
Cornelius, S.W., & Denny, N.W. Dependency in day-care and home-
    care children. *Developmental Psychology*, 1975, *2*, 575-582.
Cox, F.N., & Campbell, D. Young children in a new situation with
    and without their mothers. *Child Development*, 1968, *39*, 123-
    131.
Doyle, A. Development in day care. *Developmental Psychology*, 1975,
    2, 655-656.

Eckerman, C., Whatley, J., & Kutz, S. Growth of social play with peers during the second year of life. *Developmental Psychology,* 1975, *11,* 42–49.

Feldman, S.S., & Ingham, M.E. Attachment behavior: A validation study in two groups. *Child Development,* 1975, *46,* 319–330.

Harlow, H.F. *Learning to love.* San Francisco: Albion, 1971.

Harlow, H.F., & Harlow, M.K. The affectional systems. In A. M. Schrier, H. F. Harlow, and F. Stollnitz (Eds.), *Behavior of non-human primates.* New York: Academic Press, 1965, 287–334.

Kagan, J., Kearsley, R.B., & Zalazo, P.R. The emergence of initial apprehension to unfamiliar peers. In M. Lewis and L.A. Rosenblum (Eds.), *Friendship and peer relations.* New York: Wiley, 1975, 187–206.

Konner, M. Relations among infants and juveniles in a comparative perspective. In M. Lewis and L.A. Rosenblum (Eds.), *Friendship and peer relations.* New York: Wiley, 1975, 99–129.

_____. Aspects of the developmental ethology of a foraging people. In N. Blurton-Jones (Ed.), *Ethological studies of child behavior.* Cambridge: Cambridge University Press, 1972, 285–304.

Kotelchuck, M., Zalazo, P.R., Kagan, J., & Spelke, E. Infant reaction to parental separations when left with familiar and unfamiliar adults. *Journal of Genetic Psychology,* 1975, *126,* 252–262.

Lewis, M., & Brooks, J. Self, other, and fear: Infants' reactions to people. In M. Lewis and L. A. Rosenblum (Eds.), *The origins of fear.* New York: Wiley, 1974, 195–227.

Lewis, M., Young, G., Brooks, J., & Michalson, L. The beginnings of friendship. In M. Lewis and L.A. Rosenblum (Eds.), *Friendship and peer relations.* New York: Wiley, 1975, 27–66.

Maccoby, E.E., & Feldman, S.S. Mother-attachment and stranger reactions in the third year of life. *Monographs of the Society for Research in Child Development,* 1972, *37.*

Rheingold, H.L., & Eckerman, C.O. The infant separates himself from his mother. *Science,* 1970, *168,* 78–83.

Ricciuti, H.N. Fear and the development of social attachments in the first year of life. In M. Lewis and L.A. Rosenblum (Eds.), *The origins of fear.* New York: Wiley, 1974, 73–106.

Schwarz, J.C., & Wynn, R. The effects of mothers' presence and previsits on children's emotional reactions to starting nursery school. *Child Development,* 1971, *42,* 871–881.

AN EXPLORATORY STUDY OF PROBLEM SOLVING

IN THE NATURAL HABITAT

Myrtle Scott

Indiana University

A major task of researchers interested in human development during the early years as well as across the life span is the continued search for the major influencers of development and the apportionment of the variance attributable to each. An even more important task, however, is the attempt to discover the interconnected and dynamic laws which govern the course of this development. [Recent work on a transactional model of development by Sameroff & Chandler (1975) and a dialectic model by Riegel (1976) appear helpful in this regard.] Nowhere are these laws more urgently needed than in the area of problem solving. Davis (1973) recently summarized research on problem solving and identified a variety of models and techniques (including Gestalt, cognitive, stimulus-response and computer models, brainstorming, simulations, synectics and bionics) which have been used to investigate the phenomenon.

HISTORY OF THE EXPLORATION OF THE PROBLEM

Early psychometric models such as those of Binet (1905), Guilford (1966), Spearman (1927), and Thurstone (1938) began the specification of the components of human intellectual or cognitive functioning. Piaget (1970) provided a dynamic cognitive developmental model which has been very fruitful for American researchers. At the same time he also tied cognitive functioning to its underlying biological organization as did Hebb (1959).

Kretch (1972) and his colleagues made the important link between intelligence and the environment and showed that variations in experience produce not only changes in learning but also changes in basic brain structure and chemical functioning. Hunt (1961) pointed to the interactional nature of the relationship between the child and his or her environment and identified some psychological dimensions of the environment which were thought to be important in enrichment (Hunt, 1964). Bronfenbrenner (1979) has recently provided an expanded model of the environment which includes variables at the microsystem, mesosystem, exosystem and macrosystem levels.

A Promising New Development

Roger Barker (1968) and his colleagues identified systematic, lawful units in the environment which coerce certain behaviors from children and prohibit others. These units, called behavior settings, have some physical and some social characteristics. These coercive forces in the natural habitat have now been studied for individual children (Barker, 1963; Barker & Wright, 1955/1971; Gump, 1964; Wright, 1967), for preschoolers and their teachers (Kounin, 1970; Kounin & Gump, 1974; Scott, 1977) and for entire communities (Barker & Schoggen, 1973; Barker & Wright, 1955/1971). This group of researchers has also developed methods which permit the examination of a child's naturally occurring, ongoing behavior in his or her own natural habitat without interruption or interference by an investigator or experimenter. This approach was used in the present study.

SUBJECTS

Subjects were seven boys and girls with no apparent physical or mental abnormalities who were from a small Kansas town. The age range of the children was from 2 to 10 years.

METHOD

The data for the present study were full day specimen records of individual children's behavior collected at the Midwest Psychological Field Station in Kansas. Rotating teams of observers followed each child from the time he or she awoke in the morning until the child was asleep again that night. The procedures for making specimen records have been described fully elsewhere (Schoggen, 1964; Wright, 1967). A total of 93 hours and 30 minutes of observational data was collected.

All records were analyzed into Problem Solving Events (PSEs). A PSE is defined as (1) a naturally occurring unit (2) within the normal everyday perspective of the subject (3) which has a recognizable beginning and end point, (4) which proceeds in the same psychological direction throughout its course, and (5) which shows clear evidence of some situation requiring a solution, some barrier to be overcome or some tension to be reduced. Each PSE was then judged according to an 11-category system.

RESULTS

Four analyses were conducted in this preliminary study in order to examine (1) the types of problems encountered by the children; (2) the solution strategies which children selected to solve their problems; (3) the contexts of the problems which children encountered in their natural habitats; and (4) the initiation and termination of the PSE.

Analysis 1: The highest percentage of problems which all children encountered was social problems. Cognitive problems, in contrast, showed a very low rate. Environmental problems appeared to show an age trend, with their occurrence dropping somewhat as the child grew older.

Analysis 2: All children employed multiple strategies more than half the time in attempting to solve their problems. There appeared to be some sex differences in this regard with girls using a single strategy 29% of the time on the average and boys using a single strategy 47% of the time on the average. The most frequent problem solving strategy used by children was a physical one. Talking or negotiating ranked second and thinking about the problem third.

Analysis 3: The majority of children's PSEs occurred in the presence of others. Younger children, however, encountered more PSEs when alone than did older children.

Analysis 4: Children, in general, initiated their own PSEs 45% of the time on the average. Again, some sex differences appeared in this regard with girls initiating 57% of their PSEs while boys initiated only 28%.

SUMMARY

In summary, this exploration study suggests several things: (1) an ecological methodology appears fruitful for studying children's problem solving in the natural habitat; (2) specific problems can be reliably identified in naturally occurring child behavior; (3) these problems and the child's handling of them show some general developmental trends (for example, as children get older the nature of the problems which they encounter changes); and (4) individual differences are also apparent in child problem solving (for example, boys and girls tend to respond somewhat differently to problems). Further research needs to be carried out in order to determine the generalizability of these findings.

REFERENCES

Barker, R.G. *Stream of behavior*. New York: Appleton-Century-Crofts, 1963.

Barker, R.G. *Ecological psychology*. Stanford, CA: Stanford Universit Press, 1968.

Barker, R.G. & Wright, H.F. *Midwest and its children*. Hamden, CT: Archon Books, 1955/1971.

Barker, R.G. & Schoggen, P. *Qualities of community life*. San Francisco Jossey-Bass, 1973.

Binet, A. & Simon, T. Méthodes nouvelles pour le diagnostic du niveau intellectual des anormaux. *L'Année Psychologique*, 1905, *2*, 191-244.

Bronfenbrenner, U. *The ecology of human development*. Cambridge: Harvard University Press, 1979.

Davis, G. *Psychology of problem solving*. New York: Basic Books, 1973.

Guilford, J.P. Intelligence: 1965 model. *American Psychologist*, 1966, *21*, 20-26.

Gump, P.V. Environmental guidance of the classroom behavioral system. In B.J. Biddle & W.J. Ellena (Eds.), *Contemporary research on teacher effectiveness*. New York: Holt, Rinehart & Winston, 1964.

Hebb, D.O. A neuropsychological theory. In S. Koch (Ed.), *Psychology: A study of science*. Vol. 1. New York: McGraw-Hill, 1959.

Hunt, J.McV. *Intelligence and experience*. New York: The Ronald Press Book Co., 1961.

Hunt, J.McV. The psychological basis for using pre-school enrichment as an antidote for cultural deprivation. *Merrill Palmer Quarterly*, 1964, *3*, 209-247.

Kounin, J.S. *Discipline and group management in classrooms*. New York: Holt, Rinehart & Winston, 1970.

Kounin, J.S. & Gump, P.V. Signal systems of lesson settings and the ta involvement of children. *Journal of Educational Psychology*, 1974, *66*, 159-164.

Kretch, D. Psychoneurobiochemeducation. In H.W. Bernard & W.C. Huckins (Eds.), *Exploring human development*. Boston: Allyn and Bacon, 1972.

Piaget, J. Piaget's theory. In P. Mussen (Ed.), *Carmichael's manual of child psychology*. New York: Wiley, 1970.

Riegel, K.F. The dialectics of human development. *American Psychologist*, 1976, *31*, 689-700.

Sameroff, A.J. & Chandler, M.J. Reproductive risk and the continuum of caretaking casualty. In F.D. Horowitz & E.M. Hetherington (Eds.), *Review of Child Development Research*. Vol. 4. Chicago: University of Chicago Press, 1975.

Schoggen, P. Mechanical aids for making specimen records of behavior. *Child Development*, 1964, *35*, 985-988.

Scott, M. Some parameters of teacher effectiveness as assessed by an ecological approach. *Journal of Educational Psychology*, 1977, *69*, 217-226.

Spearman, C. *The abilities of man*. New York: Macmillan, 1927.
Thurstone, L.L. *Primary mental abilities*. Chicago: The University of
     Chicago Press, 1938.
Wright, H.F. *Recording and analyzing child behavior*. New York: Harper
     and Row, 1967.

AN INTERNATIONAL AND COMPARATIVE STUDY OF CHILDREN'S
PLAY SPACE REQUIREMENTS IN RESIDENTIAL ENVIRONMENTS

Steen Esbensen

University of Quebec
Hull, Canada

INTRODUCTION

Early childhood educators have consistently concerned themselves with the development of research and practice in an effort
to affect and improve the environment for young children. The term
environment, however, means different things to different people
and professional disciplines use the term environment according
to their training. Early childhood educators have defined the optimum learning and developing environment for young children as one
which encompasses the home, the school and the community. Further
analysis reveals that the interactive role of people such as teachers, paraprofessionals and parents has been of primary importance
in the debate over what constitutes an optimum environment.

The construction of an optimum environment in either the home,
school or community is dependent upon the particular qualities found
throughout five dimensions: people, time, curriculum, materials,
and space. Professional activities of both researchers and practitioners in the field of early childhood education have concentrated more on the significance of the first four factors.

PEOPLE

A variety of adult competencies and behaviors have demonstrated
the effect that different modes of interaction may have on the motivation or play behaviors of children. An adult may be tuned in
and genuinely involved with children or may be more distant and
didactic in approach by philosophical choice. The particular behavioral
mode will influence the child's motivation and play behavior, not to mention the child's development of human relations.

333

TIME

Children develop a sense of time through their experiences;
time to clean up, time to eat, time to go out, time to nap, time
to go home. In addition to specific references to time, research
reports indicate that early childhood programs which offer children
the opportunity to stay with a project and to finish it at their
own pace are more likely to develop motivation and longer on task
behaviors than are programs which limit the children's activities
to 10- to 22-minute time intervals.

CURRICULUM

The learning theories developed through recent educational
innovations have caused many teachers to question which curriculum program they should follow. On the other hand the variety of
program prototypes has helped school districts provide teachers with
specific curriculum programs. The different curriculum programs
in early childhood education have been grouped and classified according to these categories: (a) verbal didactic model, (b) verbal
cognitive model, (c) sensory cognitive model, and (d) child development model.

MATERIALS

A range of didactic and open ended play materials have been
developed for young children during the twentieth century. The
quality, durability and flexibility of such materials either facilitate or inhibit play potential. Equally important and often overlooked in early childhood education programs is the actual presentation of materials, their orderliness in the play environment
and their presentation throughout the play environment.

SPACE

The factor of space has been dealt with by researchers in an
attempt to understand the child's development of a concept of space.
In daily application practitioners in early childhood education
have given only limited attention to the impact of the built environmental factors. This is true both in relation to the spatial
planning of a learning environment and in the use of space in the
community. This paper will report the findings of a study of public policies dealing with play spaces for children. This study
was prepared for the United Nations Committee on non-governmental
organizations in Geneva, Switzerland, for the International Year of
the Child.

The International Playground Association coordinated the U.N.
committee and commissioned "An International and Comparative Study
of Legislation and Guidelines for Children's Play Spaces in the
Residential Environment" to be directed by the author. Through the
auspices of the Canada Mortgage and Housing Corporation and the
Université de Québec à Hull the study was completed and will be discussed in the subsequent pages.

PROBLEM

The availability of spaces for children to play within close
distance to their homes has been of very little concern for past
generations of children. During the twentieth century, however,
urbanization has increasingly encroached upon the spaces for
leisure and play activities, thus dramatically affecting the opportunities available for children to play. Some countries have
developed public policies at various levels of government in order
to deal with this problem. However, how such policies come about
and at what levels of government such strategies exist is not known.

This study reveals that some countries have developed public
policy strategies for partially assuring the availability of play
spaces for children in the future. The public policy mechanisms
used to deal with this issue vary from legislation and guideline recommendations, to global "motherhood" statements of the rights of the
child. This report has thus selected two major distinctions of
public policy. Public policies which are created through legislation and which imply enforcement are known as standards while
statements such as recommendations are defined as guidelines.

SCOPE OF THE STUDY

Within this frame of reference "planning for children's play
is considerably more than just putting playgrounds into completed
housing developments. Planning for play is in itself town and
country planning" (Bengtsson, 1974). The distinction between playgrounds and play space opportunities is often not clear in the
minds of decision makers, developers and citizens as a whole. A
playground with a slide, swings, and climbing equipment is a western
phenomenon which implies the need to furnish elaborate and often
costly equipment for children to be motivated to play. In fact
such "spaces" might partially respond to the child's interest and
provide children with positive physical and social experiences.
Playgrounds are thus included in this study of play space requirements in the residential environment.

This report deals not only with play grounds or facilities,
but rather with the greater problem of play space availability

within a close distance to the home. Such spaces are not available
when landscaping features such as gardens and vegetation are clearly designated as aesthetic camouflage. Nor is the parking garage
or parking lot in the front yard typically an appropriate play space.
The issue of providing appropriate quality to the design and development of a residential development which will facilitate play opportunities for children of different ages is contingent upon the extent to which public policies for children have been developed.

LIMITATIONS OF THE STUDY

This study is thus clearly related to the more complex issue
of land use and development. The distribution of land through
practicing economy in land use (keeping costs down) and access to
affordable and quality housing has increasingly forced developed
and developing nations to establish measurable criteria for the
distribution of open spaces, amenity areas (spaces used by residents
for leisure and recreation activities), and parking facilities.

Public parks or open spaces in the community have been given
significant attention from urban planners and educators. Such
spaces are not exclusively used by the residents of a building
or group of buildings and thus are not included in this study. The
objective of this study is to focus primarily on the open space
recreational or amenity areas made available to child residents of
typical residential developments as indicated through public policies such as standards or guidelines in different countries. As
indicated earlier, in many instances these areas have commonly been
defined as children's playgrounds. In this study the term play
space is used to articulate and describe areas where children of
different age groups can have ready access to play. In the clarification of "ready access" it is important to note that such access
is related to proximity to the residential environment. These
play spaces are intended principally for use by inhabitants of a
particular residential development and are not designed for general
public use.

METHODOLOGY

This study was conducted through the distribution of a tightly
constructed questionnaire mailed to 100 professionals in 38
countries representing the four corners of the globe as can be
seen in the following lists.

List of Countries Contacted: Australia, Austria, Bangladesh,
Belgium, Brazil, Canada, Denmark, Egypt, England, Finland, France,
Greece, Holland, Hong Kong, India, Ireland, Israel, Italy, Japan,
Malaysia, Malta, New Zealand, Nigeria, Norway, Pakistan, Peru,

Phillipines, Portugal, South Africa, Spain, Sweden, Switzerland, Thailand, United States, USSR, West Germany, Yugoslavia, Zambia.

No Response From: India, Ireland, Italy, Japan, Malaysia, Malta, Nigeria, Pakistan, Peru, Philippines, South Africa, United States, Zambia.

CONSTRAINTS

     Developing quantifiable standards or guidelines does impose certain constraints. Most prevalent are the problems which arise in calculating spaces in different units of measure. It has often been said that comparing space requirements for children's play spaces in different countries is like comparing apples to oranges. This is clearly an indication of the difficulty of acquiring ac- curate information and of finding out how the spaces are calculated. In fact, the data which was provided by respondents to this survey was relatively free of confusion despite the variety of measures used. In all cases the respondents clarified the measures used in their country so as to enable the researcher to establish a common measure and thus develop a comparative analysis of standards and guidelines in the different countries.

     The means used in calculating the play space requirement con- sisted of a range indicated on the questionnaire. Play space re- quirements are determined in different countries by the means listed below:

a)   the number of m^2 per bedroom
b)   the number of m^2 per bedroom excluding master bedroom
c)   the number of m^2 per unit
d)   the number of m^2 per child
e)   the number of m^2 per child space
f)   the number of m^2 per person
g)   the number of persons per hectare

(Note: m = meter or circa 1 yard 3 inches.)

     The major analysis problem was thus to determine equivalencies for each unit of measure and to convert the space requirement into a common unit of measure. Once the common measure was resolved, it was important to assess the degree of control a municipality or country exercised to ensure the availability of children's play spaces in the residential environment. Such was the challenge of developing a meaningful inventory and comparative study of children's play space requirements.

CONVERSION MODEL

Canadian and Danish play space requirements have been compared successfully in a previous document (Esbensen, 1979) through the application of a conversion model which uses the 3-bedroom home as the "common" family residence. Residences may vary from apartment high rises, walk-up apartment blocks, row houses, stacked houses, to single, semi-attached or single family homes. With a hypothetical family of four living in a typical 3-bedroom family unit, a conversion from the above range of space requirements is possible. The resulting conversion makes it possible to compare the per unit play space requirements or recommendations in different countries.

RESPONSES

The survey consisted of 100 questionnaires mailed to representatives in 38 countries. Thirty-two responses were received from 25 different countries. The final report is thus inclusive of the residential play space criteria from 25 countries. The quality of the responses from the 25 countries varied considerably; some respondents filled out every question in great detail, while others responded very briefly. The information necessary to establish a comparative inventory of play space requirements was provided, however. The following summaries reflect the responses provided to the questions.

STANDARDS

Ten of the countries indicated that they have standards for children's play spaces in the residential environment. Of these ten countries, nine have national standards, while only Brazil reports standards at the municipal level in the cities of Rio de Janeiro and São Paulo. The following countries have national standards: Canada, Denmark, England, Finland, Norway, Spain, West Germany, USSR, and Sweden. The criteria are very quantitative, and indeed enforceable in the USSR, Denmark, Sweden, Finland and Spain. In the other nations the standard is primarily advisory, in the sense that the municipalities can choose to apply the national standards or to ignore them. Thus in Canada, England, Norway and West Germany there are strong indications that great variations exist in the provisions made for play. The differences are often attributed to the local level of interest or lack of interest in developing children's play environments close to the children's homes. Thus, play space implementation varies considerably in these countries if one considers the lack of standards at the municipal level and lack of implementation of national standards at the regional or the municipal level.

GUIDELINES

Returned questionnaires from the 10 countries responding positively to the existence of standards revealed that all have developed guidelines. These guidelines serve as recommendations to
assist municipal authorities, architects, and planners in creating
appropriate spaces for children's play. While only 10 countries
have both standards and guidelines it is interesting to note that
18 of the 25 countries do have guidelines which recommend that play
spaces be made available, that these spaces be located within certain proximities of the dwelling and that such spaces be of a relatively specific size to accommodate the play of children. Of these
18 countries, 15 have established guidelines at the national level;
however, Brazil, Hong Kong and Portugal operate only with municipal
or town planning act guidelines.

NATIONAL STANDARDS USING CONVERSION MODEL

National standards for children's play spaces in the residential
environment are established in the following nine countries listed
according to the stringency of their quantitative requirements.

Denmark	35 m^2/unit for 40 units or more
Sweden	27 m^2/unit
Norway	5-20 m^2/ unit depending on size of the development
Spain	18 m^2/unit
Finland	10 m^2/unit
England	9 m^2/unit
Canada	5 m^2/unit for 20 units or more
West Germany	3-5 m^2/unit
USSR	not known

LOCAL STANDARDS USING CONVERSION MODEL

Standards at the local/municipal level for children's play
spaces exist in the following nine countries. (England does not have
the municipal requirements, but Brazil has joined the list with the
municipal policies in two cities.)

Denmark	35 m^2/unit for 40 units or more
Sweden	27 m^2/unit
Norway	5-20 m^2/unit depending upon the size of the project
Spain	18 m^2/unit
Finland	10 m^2/unit
England	9 m^2/unit
Canada	5 m^2/unit

West Germany $3-5$ m^2/unit
Brazil $4-5$ m^2/unit for resident's amenity
                                space
USSR   not known

It is noteworthy that even the countries that responded that no
requirements existed stated an interest and concern that perhaps
requirements would be needed in the future to prevent past errors
in which haphazard planning resulted in undesirable living environments.

In Denmark, Finland, Spain and Sweden the law applies automatically to municipalities. This format often creates greater consistency in the allocation of land for play spaces. In Canada,
England, Norway, and West Germany the municipalities are able to
determine the appropriateness of the play space standards for the
family housing developments. In Canada, the Canada Mortgage and
Housing Corporation requirements are applied to comprehensively
planned developments covered under the National Housing Act insured
lending program; however, local authorities often negotiate their
way around the existing standards. Consequently, there is great
variance among municipalities in the provision of play space facilities across Canada. In Norway, 220 of the 450 municipalities
have adopted modified versions of the national standards and have
put the criteria into the municipal loan planning policies as a
"should." Thus local variances and enforcement practices are still
possible. Such practice is not common in Canada where only half
a dozen municipalities have reportedly developed play space policies
within the town planning policies for family housing developments.

In England the standards are also national but apply only to
council housing developments. Again, local planning authorities
may choose to adopt these standards for purposes of development
control. Information as to the extent of municipal adoption is
not available at the present time.

A small unpublished survey reported by the English respondent
showed that approximately 15% of the public housing developments
provide play spaces to and often above the standard and another 15%
are constructed to a lower standard. In cases of unsubsidized
housing five percent of the housing schemes surveyed had below standard
play spaces. There is, however, no published information as to
the extent of municipal adoption of the national standards.

Finland established play space requirements in 1974 which
made the national level standards and guidelines for play spaces
applicable at the municipal level. While the criteria is established for the whole country it is not known whether they are appropriately implemented. In Spain, the national legislation also
applies at the municipal level. The standards are strictly en-

forced.   There appears to be an inclination towards providing a
range of play space opportunities for children in residential environments in Spain.   Spaces are developed to provide for physical,
social, and intellectual activities and concern about meeting the
emotional needs of the children is increasingly expressed.

Sweden has also established national standards and guidelines.
The requirements apply to all family housing developments based on
27 m^2/unit.   Sweden, however, has attempted to limit its focus
on playground equipment in recent years and increasingly is concerned with preserving nature and the play ability of the natural
components in the residential environment.

Questionnaire responses from Hong Kong, New Zealand and Thailand
indicate the existence of guidelines but close examination of
responses and a review of the accompanying documents reveals that
the guidelines in these places are not specific to children's play
spaces in the residential environment.   In fact the criteria mentioned in the guidelines of these countries deals with the total
amenity space, that is the open spaces for all user groups including
children.   The responses from these countries are not directly related to the scope of this study, but provide interesting and valuable information nonetheless.   It is interesting to note that in
Hong Kong and Thailand the open space requirements for amenity areas
are assigned so as to provide urban residents with spaces for re-
laxed family outings, e.g. a walk in the park.   The availability
of spaces for incidental play of children close to home happens on
the front door step which, depending upon location, is more or less
safe.   The scarcity of land, the cost and the population density of
Hong Kong and Thailand make the space problem difficult to resolve.
Both countries have established social recreational and cultural
centers which are part of an attempt to provide organized places
such as facilities and organizations to provide children with places
to "play."

In Brazil it is reported that people live mostly in buildings
such as high rise apartments.   The municipal edification (building) codes of the municipalities of Rio de Janeiro and São Paulo
have reportedly developed standards and guidelines for children's
play spaces.   The requirements for Rio apply to buildings of more
than 7 units, and consist of 1 m^2 per room.   In reality this requirement is the space from which all recreation areas are derived.
The actual space allocation for children's play spaces is very
limited within this code.   Consequently, efforts to organize activities for children in Brazil have followed patterns similar to
those provided in Hong Kong, that is, activities of a social, cultural and "play" nature.

The elimination of the above respondents from the list of
countries with either standards or guidelines thus leaves 14 of

the 25 countries studied with criteria for children's play
spaces.

CONCLUSION

This paper has summarized, compared and analyzed the public
policies as represented through standards and guidelines of 25
countries from around the world. It is evident that all the countries involved in this study are cognizant of the problem faced by
children living in the residential environments around the world.
The extent to which the problem is recognized and dealt with is
greater in some of the more densely populated western European
countries.

Cultural and social values may affect the extent to which a
country chooses to deal with the provision of children's play
spaces in the residential environment. The problem of allocating
the space from scarce resources is a common concern. In the majority of the countries contacted in this study the requirements
for amenity spaces for the residents of a community are often sufficient to provide more space for the children. In these instances
it is the recommendation that the national, regional and municipal
policies become more consistent with the play needs of children.
Several of the countries have demonstrated their ability to establish such policies, guidelines and standards for children's play
spaces. This study reveals that the countries which have developed
the most stringent quantitative requirements have adopted the
strategy of having both standards and guidelines. The countries
where such requirements are established are most consistent in their
ability to apply the requirements across the country.

The findings clearly indicate that it is those countries which
have articulated a strong "pro-child" position which have developed
public policies supporting that position. Interestingly, it is
also those countries which have the most stringent requirements for
the allocation of play spaces for children. In view of the findings, it is very plausible that the absence of stringent quantitative requirements for the allocation of children's play spaces will
cause startling inadequacies in family housing projects of the
future.

Although the findings are alarming, this author is optimistic
that those countries with an interest in protecting the rights of
children will learn from those which have developed strong public
policies to support the child's right to play. This optimism is
balanced however, by the reality that the free enterprise system in
which residential areas are simply developed for profit without
regard for children is stronger than the children's advocacy movement.

The information provided in this report is designed to help public policy decision makers in governments throughout the world develop the necessary policies to ensure that the children of today and those to come will have ample opportunities for play within their living environments.

Early childhood educators have a vital role in helping families with young children become knowledgeable about the environmental influences on the development of young children. Their role as teachers of the young child provides opportune moments to discuss and to share their concerns for quality living environments for children.

This research has documented the gaps in public policies for children's play spaces in residential environments. Researchers, practitioners, parents and administrators concerned with the well being of future generations of children now have the basic information with which to act. It is hoped that the information provided in this report will enable others to develop the necessary measures to assure that the children of today and those to come will have ample opportunities for play within their living environments. For a more detailed report of the findings please write to the Children's Environments Advisory Service, Canada Mortgage and Housing Corporation, Montreal Rd., Ottawa, Ontario, Canada.

BIBLIOGRAPHY

Bengtsson, A. *The child's right to play*. International Playground
    Association, Sheffield: 1974.
Esbensen, S.B. A place to play, a place to grow. *Habitat*, 1979, *22*,
    15-19.
Esbensen, S.B. *An international inventory and comparative study of
    legislation and guidelines for children's play spaces in the
    residential environment*. Ottawa: Canada Mortgage and Housing
    Corporation, 1979.

THE FROEBELIAN KINDERGARTEN AS AN

INTERNATIONAL MOVEMENT

Dorothy W. Hewes

San Diego State University

In the dawn of June 21, 1852, there died in a remote Prussian
mountain village a man so supremely self-confident that he predicted
his ideas on education and human relationships would not be adopted
for two centuries. Called "The Old Fool" by his neighbors and "The
Seer" by a devoted following of educators and philosophers, he died
serenely despite the knowledge that his life's work had just been
outlawed by a hostile government. Few outside the field of early
childhood education have heard the name of Friedrich Froebel, yet
most lives in the literate world have been touched by his intellectual legacy. Perhaps the time has already come for Froebel to be
understood. His theories are in the contemporary mood of Piaget
and the child-centered educators. Stripped of the sentimental veneers
that were applied during the Victorian age, these theories emphasized
development of cognitive skills and of a positive self-image that would
sustain a student over a lifetime of learning.

The principles upon which Froebel based his educational theories
reflected a number of streams of thought. A product of the romantic
post-Napoleonic era, affected by the philosophers of pre-Darwin
Europe, he studied with Pestalozzi and was also influenced by his
minister father's Lutheranism. Primarily, however, he was a trained
scientist, guided by his detailed observations of children and his
understanding of human nature. The heart of his system was his faith
in the active nature of learning, the concept of learning through
play. He insisted on the natural unfolding of each child's capa-
bilities within a community of mutual love and democracy where each
individual was helped to gain self-realization from positive interaction with others.

Within twenty years after his death in 1852, Froebel's kinder-

345

gartens had been established throughout Europe. After Queen Victoria
was persuaded by Charles Dickens to send her children to one in London,
royalty all over Europe followed her example. Children of the industrialized slums were taken into philanthropic kindergartens to
keep them out of the gutters and rich children had an identical curriculum to keep them from being spoiled. There were only ten or
twelve kindergartens in the United States in 1870, but by 1880 there
were over four hundred in thirty states. Missionaries took the
Froebelian method to the Sandwich Isles, Japan, Africa--and what
was then Palestine.

The strength of the Froebelian movement in Israel, however, was
not the result of American missionaries' work with the Arabs. Instead, it is a particularly good example of the synergism between
two dynamic ideas. According to Bentwich (1965), the first Hebrew
kindergarten was opened in the agricultural settlement of Rishon-le-
Zion in 1898. Its teacher was a local girl who had trained at the
Evelina Girls' School in Jerusalem. The link between the first kindergarten and Froebel may lie in the French origins of that early
settlement and of Hebrew as a written language under the patronage
of Baron Rothschild. Froebel's own rich benefactor, the Baroness
Marenholtz-Bulow, travelled through Europe to spread his ideas. When
she went to Paris in 1858, Barnard (1890) says she summoned to her
parlor-lectures the most distinguished representatives of all religious denominations to stress the "universal humanity" of the
kindergarten. Under further impetus of the Committee of Education of
the Congress of Philosophers that met from 1867 to 1872, the kindergartens spread throughout France. At the Evelina Girls' School, as
at the normal school in Jerusalem, there were French-trained teachers
who were Froebelians.

What is the connection between the kindergarten and the revival
of Hebrew? As is so common, young children served an adult purpose.
Although there had been various Hebrew classes in Jerusalem and the
outlying areas, its adoption as an everyday language began with those
early settlements like Rishon-le-Zion. Kindergartens were opened
in conjunction with the elementary schools, as they were in France,
and the children learned to play and sing in both French and Hebrew.
Bentwich comments that ever since, the kindergarten has been an organic element of the Jewish educational system and has helped
"children of immigrants to transfer easily and naturally to the--for
them now--language of the country" (Bentwich, 1965, p. 11).

Spodek recently described the kindergarten of Froebel and its
theory of learning through self-activity. He spoke of the "common
belief system" and unity of those kindergarteners who a century back
formed an international network. We still have many commonalities.
I once recognized the movement play in a Yugoslavian kindergarten
as the familiar "Cobbler, cobbler, mend my shoe" and then two years

later was delighted to visit a classroom in Bangkok where the children were chanting it in Thai. It would be a fascinating project to see how many similarities we have, but I believe the most important is our preservation of Froebel's faith in children's need to learn through activity, and to call that activity "play."

Because of recent emphasis on infant programs, it seems particularly important to point out that one reason for the decline of the Froebelian kindergarten by the turn of the century was its enthusiastic misapplication of materials designed for babies. The kindergarten was planned as part of the continuum which begins with birth and extends into adulthood. Froebel placed great emphasis upon infancy because self-realization began with an awareness of the environment, with the need to "make the inner outer and the outer inner" which we now are familiar with under Piaget's terms of assimilation and accommodation. He also wrote about the three-fold nature of development, similar to our affective, cognitive, and physical domains, emphasizing that activity is the first phenomena of awakening child-life and must be fostered. "For this instinct corresponds to man's triune activity of doing, feeling, and thinking. It corresponds to the essential nature of humanity, which is to have power and understanding, to become ever more and more self-conscious and self-determining" (Jarvis, p. 24).

As Froebel originally presented his system, the play materials and activities that he called gifts and occupations were not rigidly sequenced and used in routine dictated lessons as they were later on. He began with the mother-play book, *Mutter und Koselieder,* with its etchings and verses to teach parents games like "pat-a-cake" or "all-gone." Its intricate detailed pictures were intended for older children to study, but toddlers would recognize such concepts as an empty bowl being licked by the family dog. He wrote that infants need to have bright objects to look at, and he suggested mirrors to flash "light birds" onto the walls, or caged live birds.

Froebel's motto was "Come, let us live with our children." Older family members were to begin using Froebel gifts as soon as the infant could focus its eyes well. The First Gift was a set of bright yarn balls in primary colors, to be dangled on a string while the adult talked or sang about them. The Second Gift, a wooden ball and block, acquainted the older baby with qualities of hardness and contrast. The Third Gift, a 2-inch cube cut into 8 blocks, satisfied the need of a toddler to take apart and put together. Montessori later was to follow Froebel's admonition that these were to be made of natural wood, since the child could only learn one thing at a time and color would distract. Note that these were all home toys. By two and a half, kindergarten should start. And by age three, Froebel said, children should be provided with clay and drawing materials so that they could begin to symbolize their ideas, as well

as with bigger blocks and accessories so that they could reproduce
the world around them.

What actually happened in the kindergartens of the 1890s?
Teachers produced by normal schools began to use those first three
gifts with older children for whom there was no developmental significance. They memorized and routinized the Mother Play Book, and
they expected children to follow dictated lessons. Manufacturers
of school supplies produced kindergarten materials and included
directions for their rote use. Both public and private school systems increased the numbers of children from Froebel's limit of fifteen to as many as forty or fifty per teacher, and the age span of
two to seven was reduced to the fourth and fifth year only.

There were significant political, social, and economic changes
in the world during this time, also. Froebel envisioned the kindergarten as a nurturant place for children. In the 1880s, it was as
if the world had become receptive of the seeds of concern for young
children that had been scattered broadcast upon it. It was a period
following widespread revolutions, when newly democratic governments
were aware of the rights of women and the children, when economic
prosperity made utopian ideals seem affordable and when innovation
occurred in education and many other areas. It was also a time of
much moving about of political exiles.

By the mid-1890s, a worldwide economic depression meant that
philanthropies and government funds dwindled to almost nothing for
young children. The leaders of the kindergarten movement began to
squabble over details. This period was followed, early in this
century, by what might be called the age of scientism. The intuitive
methods of the Froebelian kindergarten were replaced by questionnaires and habit-training and measurements. The child study movement
became the new gospel. With that new atmosphere of professionalism,
it was the social worker instead of the kindergarten teacher who was
depended upon for the family support system. By the end of World War
I, Froebel's name was rarely mentioned. And yet, underneath, there
was still a valiant effort on the part of many individuals to maintain respect for learning through play. It emerged in the Montessori Method, in the nursery schools of the 1930s, and in what we
call the British Infant School or alternative education.

What can be learned from history? The most important lessons
may be these:

1. If we believe in education through self-activity, we must
continue to plan programs responsive to the needs of the children
enrolled, with age-appropriate environments and materials. We must
never again depend upon the magic of manufactured equipment and prescribed rote teaching.

2.   Teachers should have specific educational and experiential backgrounds so that they understand and respect and relate to young children.   Textbooks and passing scores on examinations are not enough.

3.   Group size is critical to learning through play.   Recent research has verified the original kindergarten ratio of one teacher, two assistants, and about fifteen children.

4.   Just as we cannot ignore infancy as an important developmental period, neither can we emphasize any one age level.   With Froebel, we can see that there is a continuum in which each period should be valued for itself.

5.   Because of time constraints, it is impossible to discuss the implications of differences of opinion about the education of young children today.   However, the greatest lesson we can learn from the past hundred years is that we must stick together.   We have more agreements than disagreements.   Because of the kindergarten network established a hundred years ago, we have a solid core of beliefs.

It is doubtful that we will ever have another receptive period like that of the 1880s, but the kindergarten pioneers would be proud of what we are accomplishing.   The education of young children has a great future, as well as a historic past.

BIBLIOGRAPHY

Bentwich, J.S. *Education in Israel*. Philadelphia: American Jewish
    Publications Society, 1965.
Hailmann, W.N. *Four lectures on early child culture*. Milwaukee, WI:
    Doerflinger, 1880.
Heinemann, A. H. *Froebel letters*. Boston: Lothrop, Lee & Shepard,
    1893.
Jarvis, J. *Friedrich Froebel's pedagogics of the kindergarten*. New
    York: D. Appleton, 1904.
Michaelis, E. & Moore, H.K. *Froebel's letters on the kindergarten*.
    London: Swan Sonnenschein, 1889.
Spodek, B. Early childhood education: A synoptic view. Paper pre-
    sented at International Congress on Early Childhood Education,
    January 1980.
The crèche and child culture in France. In H. Bernard (Ed.), *Papers
    on Froebel's kindergarten*. Hartford, CN: 1890.

EARLY CHILDHOOD EDUCATION IN THE KIBBUTZ

Gideon Lewin

Study Centre for Children's Activity
Oranim, Israel

In this paper I am going to report some ideas about early childhood in the Kibbutz. This is not going to be a report about a research project. A Kibbutz is not a project. A Kibbutz is not an
experiment. It is a way of life; it is another society within the
western society chosen voluntarily by its members and builders. The
other day a colleague from Europe asked about some criticisms he
had heard from Israeli friends about the Kibbutz. He wanted to
know if this criticism was based on true facts. My answer was that
many non-Kibbutz people want to see the Kibbutz as a paradise. A
paradise, by definition, is a place where people from outside want
to come in and those living inside want to get out. The Kibbutz
is no paradise. It is a social, economic, cultural and political
reality. My second remark relates to this reality. I am going to
speak about children of reality, not children of a dream. A dream,
being a very private, intimate affair, teaches us more about the
dreamer than about the persons appearing in the dream.

History rarely provides the opportunity to create an educational
system from the very beginning of the community. This fortunate
event happened to the Kibbutz movement, the collective agro-indus-
trial settlements that began their pioneering work 70 years ago.
Kibbutzes started as groups of youngsters for whom the first families-
and the first children — were events of extraordinary significance,
who gave their communities a deep sense of togetherness, of belonging,
of shared responsibilities. It was the beginning of an ongoing
search and confrontation where the facts of life, very hard facts
indeed, had to be met, confronted and changed according to social
ideals and hopes. The system of collective education as it exists
today in 240 settlements with a total population of about 120,000
people, takes care of about 12 thousand children of early childhood

or preschool age.

   One of the basic pedagogic and psychological principles of
collective education is the community's responsiblity for the education of the children from birth to adolescence. I do not know of
any other modern society where family and community share their
joint effort of educating the young in such close, direct and mutual
patterns. Therefore, we can state that the children grow up in a
life cycle with two emotional centers: the family and the children's
group with its educators. These two centers are not opposite poles,
antagonistic or competitive. Love and professional care join easily
together because the real life of the grownups is based on common
social ideas and ideals. Therefore, the child's identity evolves
with a sense of belonging to a family which belongs to the community
as a circle inside a circle. This identity gives "the ego the capacity to sustain sameness and continuity in the face of a changing
fate" as Eric Erickson said. The children live in small groups
of three to five children of baby age, eight to twelve children
of toddler age, and fifteen to twenty children of kindergarten age.
If education's role is to introduce children into the basics of
human culture, then the educational system has to provide three
basic elements "food, clothes and shelter." These three essentials
are given to children first, whatever the economic conditions of the
adult community. After these basic elements have been introduced
the essential elements of culture are introduced: knowledge of tradition and tradition of knowledge, skills of work and work of skills,
structures of activities and activities of structures which are at
the core of any development.

   We do, therefore, consider our children's houses not as institutions where children are taken care of by alien professionals. Our
children's houses are the children's home, the region of life and
development where the children live and play, eat and sleep, work
and create — a whole life cycle, just like that of their parents. I
believe that a serious problem of modern society lies in its being
a consumer society where even education is big business. You sell
knowledge, use pre-prepared instant lectures; even pop-psychology
tries to intervene in education. In order to adorn this dull system,
the worship of creativity came into existence. The educational
system of the Kibbutz was and is open to these influences of the
surrounding society. However, we try to give our children a sense
of the necessity of being productive before being creative, being
active before being a user, being involved before being a critic,
joining forces before being competitive, and being responsible before
being selfish.

   Hope, will, purpose, competence--these are the four virtues
Erickson tells us should grow out of early childhood years. He says
that without them other values and goodnesses lack vitality. In
order to achieve these virtues we try to trust the vitality and

wisdom of children's activities, the closeness of the adults' ideas
with the educational practices, the identity of the collective way
of life with the basic human needs.

If we consider the quantity, if not always the quality, of the
many research studies about Kibbutz education published in the United
States, Japan, Germany, England and other countries by psychologists,
anthropologists, educators and others we must come to the conclusion
that there seems to be in modern society a desperate need to look for
alternative ways of early childhood education. This need seeks answers to the many frustrations society faces in regard to family life,
mass life in the mega-cities, the need to integrate a growing number of
uprooted people who wander over the globe looking for peace and a
place to start a new life and the realization that more and more
children are deprived of their basic rights, so generously granted
them by UNESCO. Although I believe, after 40 years' experience
as a Kibbutz member, that the Kibbutz creates indeed an alternative
way of life, and a better one, it cannot be said that our educational
practices can be copied and transferred easily into other societies.
But with all modesty we may say that the collective educational
system has contributed some different viewpoints, practices and
reflections to modern psychology and education. I may mention the
following topics: No harm is inflicted upon babies when people other
than the mother alone takes care of them. Bowlby's theory has been
proven once more to be unfounded. The educator in the baby-house
is not only a professional who knows the baby's physiological, psychological and hygienic needs. She assists the mother. She often
knows health problems before the pediatrician detects them. She
is not a mother substitute as some researchers have defined her role.
She is a professional assistant, a caregiver both to child and mother.
She is there in case of need, and in the background if not needed,
but always available to help.

It is impossible to speak about collective education in early
childhood without mentioning the caregiver or metapelet, as we
call her. She is not the traditional "nanny" nor is she a mother
substitute; she is not a professional nurse. She is not the
shepherd who took care of Laiius' and Jokasta's deserted son. She
is all this and much more: she is a member of the Kibbutz and she
creates the atmosphere of the child's house. She is a main factor
in the process of socialization. She is constantly engaged in the
reciprocal process of interaction with the children in relation to
their needs, activities and competences within the ever widening
circle of their physical and social surroundings. She is not a
hired worker but a member of the same collective settlement as the
child's parents and family. Most metapelets have professional training; 60% of them were themselves born and raised in the Kibbutz.
This is our "educational infantry" and their secret strength is their
love for their children, their home and community, combined with
their social commitment. Care, commitment and competence create

a structure with a special flavor, a reliable source from which
children get trust and confidence which prepares them for a world
in which they will need all their strength just to exist.

Bringing up children in small groups with an understanding
educator not only furthers socio-emotional development but spurs
intellectual abilities as well. The emotional tie of a child
to his family is not a question of geography. It is a question of
the specific role each member of the family fulfills in the child's
life space and how he or she does this. Peter Neubauer comments
in *Children in Collectives* that the quality of the emotional
relationships between parents and child cannot be measured by the
geographic distance between parental quarters and children's homes.
He also comments that the Kibbutz never set out to offer substitu-
tional care but to develop a collective care program (thus eliminating the traditional dichotomy of family care or community care).
Neubauer suggests that the mother's participation and the care-giver's
involvement successfully provide a new form of communal care. The
concept of strangers is completely different. Strangers are easily
accepted as child-loving members of the community. The sense of
belonging and, therefore, of security is strongly influenced by the
group of children.

The role of the family, the children's group, and the processes
of identity formation and ego strength are some of the fields in
which generally accepted views of psychological development in the
western world had to be changed. The implication seems to be clear:
Early childhood's educational practices and theories are an outcome
of the adult ways of life. Collective education is named collective
not because children live in groups but because their parents live
a collective way of life. Every society uses its children to define
itself. The Kibbutz society, at least, declares this openly and
proudly.

How can one judge the results of our educational practices?
We have in the Kibbutz now a third and fourth generation. A true
educator is never satisfied with the outcome of his system, even if
he is satisfied with each child. A child is not a statistic — as
the president of the United States once said. The educational system
is a question of ethics, a way of life, a declaration of confidence
and forever a belief in a better human society. The results of
different educational systems and approaches are difficult to compare. You cannot measure them but you can see, feel and observe
them. It is clear that the differences are related to values,
virtues and judgements. There are differences in the way one
lives one's life and spends one's childhood. If we, as educators,
provide our children with a happy childhood, with deep roots in
their community and a belief in their own competence as well as
a sense of responsibility for their fellow human beings, then we
may say that we indeed preach what we believe, do what we preach,

and act as we do with conscience and without fear so that we may serve as guides and mentors for new generations to come.

BIBLIOGRAPHY

Neubauer, Peter (Ed.) *Children in collectives: Child rearing aims and practices in the kibbutz.* Springfield, IL: Charles C Thomas, 1965.

THE STRUCTURE OF CHILDREN'S ACTIVITIES: A REPORT ON THE

WORK OF THE STUDY CENTRE FOR CHILDREN'S ACTIVITIES

Gideon Lewin

Study Centre for Children's Activity
Oranim, Israel

The interest in children's activities is constantly growing.
Understanding the structure and meaning of these activities is the
king's road to better educational approaches. When a child is engaged in any activity--painting, singing, building, make-believe,
experimenting, exploring or whatever--there is an easily recognizable surface quality to his doings. His activities have a certain
style which may reflect the child's physical or social surroundings.
They are executed according to the child's skill and competence and
are dependent to a greater or lesser degree on the equipment, tools,
materials or utensils a child may use. This surface quality of children's activities varies according to his or her social, ethnic, economic and personal living conditions. But beyond this surface quality
of activities there seems to exist a hidden, deep set of constraining
rules of activities. It may even be possible to speak of a set of
rules, a "Grammar of Activity." These constraints seem to be universal and independent of the ethnic, social or economic backgrounds
of the children but based on innate human systems such as the nervous,
muscular and others. Our Study Centre for Children's Activities
has for a few years observed, recorded and analyzed various activities of kindergarten children who came from different strata of the
Israeli population: Jewish and Arab, city and rural, well-to-do
and deprived, Kibbutz children and new immigrants.

During the last five years we have worked with more than 1500
children, observed and recorded their activities, and are now working on our data. We hope to present more detailed results in the
near future. Meanwhile, we can report the following reflections.
When we observe children's activities we see three stages: The
first is doing things with and to objects, tools or equipment.
This is a stage of finding out what the object, tool or material

is, how it behaves, if it has a will of its own. In the second stage
the child tries to explore what he or she can do with the tools and
the different materials. This is a decisive stage for the acquisition
of skill and handling tools and is a significant step toward the
humanization of the child. It might be the beginning of human culture. The child learns how to master and handle materials instead
of being overwhelmed by them. Now the first significant combinations
appear: Combinations of some pieces of equipment, combinations of
tools and materials and objects, combinations of acts, combinations
of words, sentences and deeds. In the more difficult third stage,
skillful, effective and purposeful handling of tools, objects and
ideas evolve in order to achieve a given goal or in order to carry
out some experiments. It is of great importance for educators to
see, define and understand these different stages in various activities in order to relate to, intervene with and encourage children in
their activities.

We have concentrated our observations thus far on certain activities such as block-building, the home-area, spontaneous musical
activities and activities at the sand table and water table. In all
these activities, and possibly in others as well, we can detect a
hierarchical complexity unfolding which is the same in sequence and
order in all the different activities and populations we observed.
This hierarchy of complexity appears as a kind of syntax of activity.
It is possible to define the structures of activities as a sequence
of combinations--a syntax--which develops possibly because of innate
human abilities, which become cultivated by competence and experience
and might be facilitated by the child's environment. It might be
possible to see the development of human culture as the development
of ever more complex combinations in technology, language, the arts
and crafts and social organization. This same schema of development
is observable in the child's development of competent behavior. The
hierarchical complexity appears in the form of organization of materials, objects and concepts the child uses. When we consider these
surface organizations it becomes clear that they behave according
to some organizing principles. One of these seems to be the need for
an equilibrium of forces, materials and compositions. The child will
be satisfied with his activity only when the product of this activity
has a balance in form, content or action. The quest for balance,
which seems to be a biological one, is one of these organizing principles.

Just as the miracle of human language is that an almost unlimited
number of words, sentences and concepts can be created from 20-25 different letters so it may be that by using a limited number of senso-
motoric skills and components a practically unlimited number of pro-
ducts can be created. Human activity is the generative instrument
that enables the child not only to react to stimuli but to choose between them and to react or use only those which appear to fit his or
her competence. The choosing of stimuli for reaction is the creative

aspect of our activities. When we observe children's activities we can see the performed manifestation of rules which are idiosyncratic to a given activity. It is possible that along with these manifest rules universal underlying rules exist such as the hierarchical complexity, the need for balance and symmetry, the need to express concepts and ideas through manual or mental activities and the need to incorporate the personal symbolic meaning of one's deeds into an ever-widening social-symbolic meaning.

This report is only a beginning. To observe the idiosyncrasies of a certain activity is a first step in pointing out stages of development. It is, however, a necessary step if we want to establish a theory of human activity that is governed by universal rules. The practical educational implication of such a structural theory could be of great value for the improvement of work with children. It might have immense impact on teacher training which usually lags behind in responsiveness to children's needs. In early childhood education we could then concentrate mainly on encouraging the child's own initiative and curiosity and skills and experiences rather than on content-bound, information-consuming curricula. We are encouraged by the work at our Centre which points clearly to the benefits of this direction.

A DEMONSTRATION PROGRAM FOR

CAMPUS INFANT CARE

Helen Warren Ross

San Diego State University

In the United States, the need for programs for infant care
outside the home as well as interventions within the infant's home
is increasing rapidly. There are numerous reasons why the field of
infant care is burgeoning. With the advent of Hunt's book *Intelligence and Experience* (1961) the laissez-faire attitude toward the
education of the young child began to change rapidly. Programs
such as Head Start and Home Start have become as much a part of our
educational system as public kindergartens. The results of research
on these innovation programs suggest that intervention earlier than
when children are 3 or 4 years of age may be important for children's
later outcomes in terms of cognitive and social emotional development. Therefore, many intervention programs for infants have been
developed.

Additionally, many mothers are now working as more families
feel the need for a second income. Many women are returning to
jobs or job training soon after their children are born, placing
their children in infant care facilities instead of remaining home
as a full-time mother during the first few years of their baby's
life. Women are no longer willing to wait until Johnny goes to
first grade or completes high school to embark on a career. Further,
with the phenomenal increase in single parent families, the child's
primary caregiver may be pressed into the labor force. More and
more women either desire or are forced to return to a career or
school while their children are but babes.

In order to meet the increasing demand for trained infant caregivers, the School of Family Studies and Consumer Sciences at San
Diego State University launched a program to provide students with
experience in the organization of infant care facilities and to

teach them program planning strategies. One portion of the infant
care program is sponsored by the students to provide care for the
children of students. This care program is staffed by one part-time
coordinator and two assistants. Additional help is provided by
parents and students who are enrolled in a course on Infant Development offered in the School of Family Studies and Consumer Sciences.

A second part of the program, on which this paper will focus,
provides advanced students with the opportunity to work in an infant
laboratory two days a week for a total of nine hours. The primary
purpose of this lab is not to provide mothers with surrogate care
but to provide students with the experience of working with infants
and giving students the responsibility, under guidance, for care of
infants in groups. Students also are responsible for parent meetings
and home visits since the relationship between parents and caregivers
is crucial to the infant's well-being. This program allows students from various disciplines to observe infant development first-
hand. Students from psychology, sociology, nursing, speech pathology,
physical education and special education use the facility. Other
colleges and high schools are also invited to come visit and observe. In order to enhance the learning experience for the observers
as well as for the student caregiver, questions are encouraged from
observers and demonstrations of motor and language skills and problem solving by the infants are given.

Training strategies for caregivers in an infant program must
be far different from the typical nursery curricula. Infants as
young as two weeks are now being cared for outside the home. During
the period considered infant care, the average infant undergoes a
metamorphosis from a supine/prone, somewhat passive organizer of
his surroundings to a top-heavy, partially-upright active explorer
of his environment. What does all this mean for the caregiver of
one or many infants? The first consideration in providing care for
infants is that of health and safety. During the first few months
the infant will need food, protection from the elements, and safe
storage. He must be in a position not to fall, be dropped, or run
over. Later, when he is able to maneuver in space safe care means
containment or a safe environment in which to explore. The infant
at this age is primarily a learning machine and given an environment
that responds in a contingent fashion to his input he develops his
own curriculum. In order to provide a contingent relationship between infant and environment during the first few months of life,
the caregiver's role is like that of Sherlock Holmes. He/she must
respond to and consider every clue which may solve the mystery of
the infant's communication. As the caregiver responds to specific
signals but not to others the infant develops a more precise means
of communication and the caregiver's behavior becomes attuned to
the infant's signals. At first when a baby is developing his reflex-
ively organized action patterns he must be provided with ample opportunity to practice, since practice makes perfect with infants as

well as with adults. This means having fingers to suck, voices to
hear, patterns to see, rattles to hold. As his reflexes become
better integrated he will often startle himself. He may shake a
rattle too vigorously or scratch his face while searching for a
thumb. During this beginning stage when the infant is immobile and
cannot control his position in space, he should be allowed the opportunity to look at the world in a vertical position; since he
cannot go after all those interesting sights he should have them
within his visual distance and arms' reach. The immobile infant
enjoys the intriguing battery of toys placed within arms' reach.
Later, while still at the mercy of gravity and unable to move in
space he gains more control over his limbs and becomes adept at
getting his thumb to his mouth, shaking a rattle rhythmically or
talking to a mobile. The baby watches his fingers with fascination
and chews his toes with glee. He learns that his body is a creative
plaything. At this time the baby becomes comfortable with objects
in relation to each other and in relation to himself.

In the latter half of the first year the infant will propel
herself in space, be adept with eye-hand coordination and demonstrate a knowledge of the world around her.

As the baby becomes more mobile one can observe that he moves
an object to obtain a desired goal or will use one object to reach
another. He no longer literally follows the ball to pick it up when
its motion ceases but can take the more direct route. Now the
nascent formulations of sign and symbol appear. The baby is not yet
ready to "picture" or keep in mind the absent object but he can locate it if it is partially hidden.

Now and then the infant's reach may exceed her grasp; however,
her knowledge is sufficiently limited that the environment must
offer challenge and provide safety. As she begins to explore in an
upright position, she defies gravity; she may take many spills. As
she does so she learns more about how she fits into the environment.
She will also manipulate toys in a manner that may appear to be
destructive. She is really learning how far she can throw, how
heavy an object is, how it feels, and tastes, whether she can take
it apart . . . all important aspects of learning. This behavior
would concern a teacher of the nursery age child but the 1- or
2-year-old is learning about the property of different materials
as well as about what she can do with her body, fingers, and eyes.

There may be many cranky periods during this time. Teething
is rarely pleasant and for many infants, the limitation of their
motor skills may be frustrating. The infant may see a solution but
her immature motor system may render her incapable of solving the
problem. Once the infant begins to crawl, she needs safe space
which may sometimes make it necessary to confine her in a play pen.

She will actively explore and needs space to try out her new navigational skills. This means crawling through, in, out, under, and playing with toys that can be manipulated and mouthed.

During this period the infant defines boundaries between self and nonself. This is a crucial step in development. It is not until this externalization of the environment occurs, even in its most inchoate form, that the child can begin to develop a relationship with others. Her relationship with the environment changes from the reactive to active and caregiving must respond to this rapid and important metamorphosis.

BABIES AT COLLEGE

Thus far, over a period of five years there have been 100 infants enrolled and 27 students (plus one professor of Special Education on sabbatical leave in the Family Studies and Consumer Sciences Infant Laboratory) have participated in the program. We ask that parents remain with their infants until they feel that the baby is comfortable in the new environment. We have had some mothers who remain with the baby--not to care for the infant but because they enjoy the atmosphere and the opportunity to be with other adults and infants.

These "college" babies come from the community (69%), students (12%), professors (13%) and university staff (6%). The ethnic mix includes Mexican Americans, Blacks, and Anglos. Our sex ratio is 61 percent male to 39 percent female. The families include educators, professionals and welfare recipients. Three of our infants were diagnosed as developmentally delayed and one was born prematurely. This varied mix has supplied us with valuable information. As we reviewed the population of babies that we had cared for over the years we became interested in what sort of baby goes to college. We noted that we had a large number of breast-fed babies and that most of the breast-fed infants were female. Fifty-nine percent of the total group were breast-fed for three months or longer. This is a large number but it is even more striking that 81 percent of our female infants were breast-fed this length of time while only 32 percent of our male infants were thus fed ($\overline{X}^2 = 12.00$, $p < .05$). This difference led us to look at other differences between the sexes. The number of subjects is small, 100 in all, but we thought we might find some interesting sex differences. Both birth order and sex of the child appear to be related to age of placement. More males are placed at a younger age than females and more second or later borns were placed at less than three months. More male first-borns are placed than female. Thus in our experience a first-born female is less likely to be placed than a male. The very young infant is likely to be male and later born. None of these differences is reliable but the differences do pose interesting questions.

CAREGIVING AND CAREGIVERS

   In terms of caregiving for babies it was found that the most
important determinant of care, or curriculum if you will, was the
infant. As we envisioned the program, the philosophy was to provide
a warm and supportive system which would further cognitive as well
as emotional development. We hoped to serve as an extension of home
care and were determined not to interfere with parenting styles
unless the emotional or physical well-being of the baby appeared
to be in jeopardy.

   In order to maintain optimal health standards and provide the
infant with optimal emotional and cognitive support several policies
were established. These guidelines had to be flexible despite the
fact that we believed that our way was the "right way." One policy
was that infants were not to be left in cribs with a bottle. There
are sound reasons for this from a health standpoint. Furthermore,
we also knew the psychological benefits of cuddling and talking to
the infant while feeding, and we wanted to impress on the mother
that bottle propping was a very definite "no no." Our baptism by
fire was bound to come and so it did in the form of a robust one-
month-old Mexican infant whose mother spoke no English. This baby
screamed when held and would not take his bottle. By means of
rather inept Spanish we learned that he had always had his bottle
propped. Our Spanish was too limited to convince his mother that
she should hold her infant when she fed him but we did discover
an alternative feeding position for the baby. We found if we were
to place him in an "en face" position with his head on the caregiver's
knees and his feet against his or her stomach he could still have
eye contact, could be talked to, was secure, and was not enraged by
being restricted in the usual feeding position.

   This infant also taught us our second important lesson. We
provide mobiles for the very young infant and, depending on the
child, around four months of age we place by the baby bright objects
which can be batted, fingered and eventually tugged. One young boy
always came with mittens and his mother urged "no sacarles" (do not
take them off). We were distressed as the mittens interfered with
hand to mouth activity as well as full use of the mobiles. At one
point the mitten simply came off and we noted that the baby's nails
were uncut. My interpretation, which I knowingly shared with the
students, was that his young mother was afraid to cut his nails and
I would give her a demonstration. Indeed she was afraid! As I
later learned, in the culture from which this baby came, it is believed that if one cuts a baby's nails before he is six months he
will go blind. Well, the handsome lad is not blind and his mother
and I still speak. Despite the outcome I wish I had not so im-
periously imposed my standard as a result of ignorance, thereby
creating undue anxiety in a new mother.

Other conflicts with home and out-of-home care involve such simple issues as caring for the crying infant. We have learned that in some instances the baby must cry and we must be brave. We have also discovered that the care of babies reduces social barriers and enhances companionship between people who might not ordinarily have the opportunity to meet. Finally, we've learned that babies do play with each other, form attachments to each other, and to caregivers; we've learned to look, to listen and to touch the baby and his family for we have much to learn and they have much to teach. We are also relearning that the primary models for the individual from birth to death are the original family. Therefore, if early learning is important and families transmit this knowledge and if the infant "teaches" the parent how to parent then we must be involved with the family, not just the infant. This principle will remain constant despite the fact that the thrust of a program may be intervention or to provide care for the infant while the mother works. We simply cannot serve an infant, mother, father, or sibling in isolation.

This period of infancy precedes the development of a complex biological organism with a nervous system capable of altering his environment in ways which stagger the imagination. How is it that this infant with no language but a cry when first born and controlled largely by environmental stimuli develops in a mere 18 months all the basic skills necessary for later complex problem solving? In this short span he becomes aware of the basic principles of such sophisticated disciplines as physics and mathematics, as well as basic human relations. This first experience, whether occurring at home or out of home, is crucial to the integration of all later experience. Therefore, it is incumbent upon those of us who are concerned with the education of young children to assure the best for the youngest.

INFANT DEVELOPMENT

Infant	Physical Environment	Personal Social
0-1 month refinement of reflexes, short periods of quiet-alert-awake, many periods of sleeping, fussing	objects of a size which can be held by small infant, sucked easily; visual stimuli, not too complex within 8-12 inches; some babies at this early age suffer from too much stimulation and will be fussy	caregiver responding to distress signals, rocking and holding soothes most infants; some will be soothed by voice and attentive to talking; baby will often cease feeding momentarily to engage caregiver in eye

Infant	Physical Environment	Personal Social
		contact or in response to voice.

1-4 months

Infant	Physical Environment	Personal Social
repetitive, practice behavior, i.e. hand watching, playing with toes, vocalizing, beginnings eye-hand coordination, very social, usually prefers people to objects	more complex visual stimuli, mobiles, patterned sheets, objects within reach for batting and pulling; look for toys that respond to babies' actions	caregiver may carry on conversation with baby; be sure not to interrupt, simple games . . . peek-a-boo; a blow on the tummy is likely to produce peals of laughter, a very social time

4-8 months

Infant	Physical Environment	Personal Social
many major motor accomplishments, crawling, sitting, refinement of eye, hand coordination, evidence of many cognitive skills; looking for objects out of sight	safe space, many cubbies to crawl into, toys that can be held when crawling, lots of containers to put toys in and take them out, interesting manipulable toys, protective safe environment	infant is working on the beginning of separating from his primary caregiver, no longer intrigued with people, will commence games of give and take, often impatient with too much cuddling . . . has left the lap to explore the world

8-12 months

Infant	Physical Environment	Personal Social
becomes more mobile, more objective; the exploratory play during this period may look aimless or destructive but it is very important; may still be working on motor skills, i.e., crawling, pulling to stand, cruising jargon apparent and perhaps a few labels		many infants during this period become occupied with the world of things; they demonstrate strong preferences for specific persons and may show definite signs of separation anxiety, aware of new and different places and people, will "converse" with adults or self and enjoys simple games

SUGGESTED BOOKS FOR INFANT CAREGIVERS

American Academy of Pediatrics. *Standards for day care centers for infants and children under three years of age*. Evanston, IL: The American Academy of Pediatrics, 1971. Basic health and safety standards for group care are listed.

Gordon, I. J. *Baby learning through baby play*. New York: St. Martin's Press, 1970. This book is basically addressed to parents but is most useful for caregivers. It suggests simple games that are enjoyable for adult and infant.

Herbert-Jackson, E., O'Brien, M., Porterfield, J., & Risley, T. *The infant care center*. Baltimore, MD: University Park Press, 1977. This is a complete guide to organizing and managing infant day care. It is somewhat sterile in its approach but could be useful as a training tool for organization and planning.

Hirshen, S., & Ouye, J. *The infant care center*. Washington, D.C.: Day Care and Child Development Council of America, 1973. A brief innovative outline of an architect's view of the optimal environment for infants in group care. Spaces are divided by age groups according to developmental patterns.

Honig, A., & Lally, J. *Assessing the behavior of caregivers*. (Available American Psychological Association, JSAS, 1200 Seventeenth Street, N.W., Washington, D.C. 20036), 1973. A checklist for monitoring the behavior of adult teachers with infants. Items are clustered into language facilitation, Piagetian tasks, social-emotional caregiving and physical development. Also a useful tool for caregivers.

Hunt, J. McV. *Intelligence and experience*. New York: The Ronald Press Book Co., 1961.

Segal, M. *From birth to one year*. Rolling Hills Estates, CA: B.L. Winick & Associates, 1974. A fine collection of photos and suggested activities month by month with specific suggestions for toys which can be made at home. The reader should be aware that these activities might be appropriate for some babies but might provide too much stimulation for others. Also, the author makes poor suggestions vis-a-vis snacks such as lollipops and candies.

Segal, M., & Adcock, D. *From one to two years*. Rolling Hills Estates, CA: B.L. Winick & Associates, 1976. This book is divided into parts which cover specific age groups. The photographs are excellent and advice sound which does not imply "superior" knowledge or expertise. Again note the caveat about the use of lollipops and cookies. Otherwise easy to read and charming with excellent selections.

Willis, A., & Ricciuti, A. *A good beginning for babies: guidelines for group care*. Washington, D.C.: National Association for the Education of Young Children, 1973. A superior book which covers all facets of infant care. A fine section on toys; perhaps the section on safety and health could be expanded. Emphasis is on the individuality of infants and the importance of working with the family to care for the infant.

BIBLIOGRAPHY

Hunt, J. McV. *Intelligence and experience*. New York: The Ronald
    Press Book Co., 1961.

DIALOGICAL APPROACH APPLIED TO NON-FORMAL EDUCATION

IN POOR AREAS OF UNDERDEVELOPED COUNTRIES

Salomón Magendzo

Interdisciplinary Program of Educational Research (PIIE)
Santiago, Chile

Modes and forms of education that have been applied in under-developed countries to preschool education have largely been patterned on models essentially foreign to these nations. Most of these models were created using concepts common to North American or European educational designs which in the long run are irrelevant to the needs of underdeveloped countries.

Typical formal school systems enforce their own distinctive standards simply ignoring those who, for whatever reasons, do not meet or cannot meet the criteria. Therefore, many times, non-formal education has provided a means of reaching those large masses of people who do not "match" the pattern of formal schooling. Non-formal education appears to be a possible solution for underdeveloped countries.

The link between education in the home and in the community is essential in preschool education. It is no longer the case that most children spend their early years in the exclusive care of their families. Responsibility for the care of young children, and for the provision of their development is being "shared" with the organizers of preschool education. Responsibility for many aspects of children's socialization is being removed from the family and put in the hands of professionals. However, there is concern that placing functions normally associated with the family in the hands of professionals undermines parents' self confidence and further alienates parents from their role as the first and most important educators of their children.

Preschool education affects only 10% of the children in Latin America. In recent years numerous research projects have been

371

conducted to evaluate the effectiveness of formal preschool education in promoting the cognitive and linguistic development of children. With few exceptions these studies have indicated the limited
potential of preschool curricula in affecting children's development. At best, short-term improvements have been observed. The
relative failure of these compensatory programs has been interpreted as pointing out the pervasive influence of the home and family
on a child's development. Different values are often taught at
school and, therefore, the school is often thought to deny the
values, attitudes and experiences of the home.

It is imperative and essential that the importance of the role
of parents as educators be restored, but a humanistic approach
rather than a "banking education" is needed.

Parents' education, specifically for those parents in deprived
areas, has become mostly a "banking education." Freire has defined
banking education as an act of depositing knowledge in the mind of
those who are ignorant. In "banking education" knowledge is a
gift bestowed on those who are considered to know nothing. An
"expert" provides a curriculum to be used by parents in order to
compensate their children for what they are lacking for their complete development.

The opposite of "banking education" is a humanistic approach
towards education which helps people, through dialogue and experience, become aware of their own potential and needs and see themselves
as creators of their destiny. Man is not a spectator but an active
person. Through dialogue he perceives his responsibility and commitment. Dialogue becomes an encounter between men, a sharing of
ideas, a creative process of reflection and action. By the process
of thinking about their realities people become aware of their
problems and may become interested in searching for specific solutions.

THE DIALOGICAL APPROACH

The dialogical approach is based on a specific assumption:
Parents, through dialogical relations and the sharing of healthy
experiences, should create a curriculum and facilities for their
children which are based on their own needs and reflect life itself.
The dialogical approach allows people to become aware that any experience the child has with reality forms part of its learning
process and that there should be no control or need for an artificial setting such as institutional preschool education. The
curriculum created by the parents is a natural one and emerges
from the parents' and children's daily experiences.

The dialogical approach could be divided into three main
aspects:

1. The motivational process
2. The stimulation process
3. The action process.

THE MOTIVATIONAL PROCESS

The motivational process includes all the steps which are being developed in order to get parents interested in:

a) assuming the responsibility for their children's education
b) searching for solutions to situations which hinder their own and their children's development.

The motivational process starts with a special invitation to interest the parents (and others) in becoming acquainted with a specific program and continues with strategies to help them so that the program fulfills their own needs. The motivation should sensitize everyone to the program and develop people's skills so that they can organize themselves to achieve their own objectives.

THE STIMULATION PROCESS

The stimulation process contains those procedures which will materialize the objectives. Parents make a commitment to meet every week in order to

a) share ideas about specific topics related to the parents' reality and the children's necessities
b) develop a curriculum for their children and
c) search for solutions for the problems which hinder their own and their children's development.

The stimuli represent a series of experiences which encourage parents to become aware of their own ideas, potential and knowledge about raising children. It is through this experience that parents get to conceptualize their ideas and assimilate new ones.

These stimuli include the cognitive, affective and social domains. The cognitive area tends to expose the parents to specific experiences which are related principally to the intellectual aspects of the child. Language, world knowledge, motor development, perceptual development, classification, series, numbers, time, space, relations, play activities, etc. are included in the cognitive area.

The affective domain includes stimuli which will influence the sharing of emotional experiences important for the child. It includes aspects such as punishment, reinforcement, love and expression of emotions.

The social area tends to reinforce the parent attitudes and behaviors which will promote the development of their children
socially: group collaboration, creativity, independence, etc.

.The stimulation process always permits the parents to become
aware of their own experience and the way they are relating to
their children. Here are two examples:

Cognitive Area: The World Around Us

Stimulus: An unknown object.
Objective: The parents will become aware of the way they ap-
                proach an object unknown to them. This will permit
                them to observe the way children get to know the
                world and their own reactions to their children.

To reach the objective many activities are developed with the
parents and the children. Parents share their experiences.

Affective Area: Love

Stimulus: Slides with pictures of parents sharing love.
Objective: The parents will become aware of the importance of
                love.

To reach the objective the parents ought to decodify the slides,
and share the experiences of their own lives where love has had an
impact (gifts, being together with parents, caresses, etc.).

These stimuli are presented weekly by a facilitator who is a
member of the community elected by the group of parents. He is
trained specifically in a non-directive approach. His job is to
introduce the stimuli which will permit the parents to get in touch
with their experiences and share ideas.

THE ACTION PROCESS

The action process is related to specific and realistic commitments in which the parents become involved in order to:

a) actualize what they achieve in the groups.
b) resolve problems which hinder their own community develop-
    ment and that of their children.
c) be responsible for their children's education .

In order to achieve these goals parents who are developing the curriculum of their children commit themselves to forming groups composed of preschool children. These groups meet for 2 or 3 hours each day in a home in the community, in a parent's house or in a club. These meetings are conducted by a monitor who is a parent or an adolescent from the community who helps develop his curriculum by working with the parents in the weekly revisions. He shares the development of the group with the parents who are also committed to help him once a week with the children. The curriculum then is not only child centered but also community and family centered. The child is considered not only in his psychological context but also in his social and cultural context.

The weekly sessions permit the parents to develop their children's curriculum and also to organize themselves to solve community problems.

A CONTRIBUTION TO THE EVALUATION AND DESIGN OF NON-FORMAL

PRESCHOOL PROGRAMS IN MARGINAL COMMUNITIES

Salomón Magendzo & Carmen Luz Latorre

Interdisciplinary Program of Educational Research (PIIE)
Santiago, Chile

INTRODUCTION

During the 1960s the developing countries focused their efforts on the achievement of sustained economic growth as a means of bridging the gap between developing and developed countries and improving their populations' standards of living. By the end of the decade, however, it became evident that despite the great increase observed in the national product and even in the per capita income, the gap between developed and underdeveloped countries still existed and had even increased. Additionally, large sectors of the population of the latter remained in a condition of severe deprivation. Consequently, a "unified approach to development" was proposed by the United Nations.[1] This approach put economic and social development on an equal footing. The concern which had been centered on "growth" shifted into a concern for "development." In recent years, this concept has been translated into a concern for deprived sectors, the study of their characteristics and the strategies meant to support marginal communities. In practice, the trend of support measures for communities has been basically to compensate the most deprived groups for the problems resulting from the "style of development" in Latin American economies. This trend indicates a positive step in focusing compensatory policies on a specific approach to marginal sectors rather than on "global social indicators."

A clear counterpart to this evolution of Latin American sentiment is seen in different viewpoints on childhood observed throughout the years.[2] In the 1960s, childhood was considered a human resource requiring investment in order to obtain efficient productive agents for the process of growth while later there was more concern with the child itself, particularly in the early years.

377

This concern was based on the findings of a variety of research studies which show how crucial the first years are for the future development of the individual.

Assistance programs for preschool children originated mainly after the crisis of the 1930s. Their goal was to provide health and nutritional assistance to the children of working mothers. Then, after the 1950s, program emphasis shifted to education in Latin American countries. Centers arose which were devoted to providing basic training or school entry to children between 4 and 6 years of age. The number of children served by these pre-primary school centers is low; they operate with highly trained personnel which results in high costs and low feasibility for developing centers to serve greater numbers of children. Finally, during the 1970s, multiple programs with a more integral vision (in regard to child's dimensions) were created. These programs were designed to be effective and less expensive alternatives to those provided by pre-primary school centers and are possible mainly because human resources available within the family and within the community are employed for stimulating preschool children.

Thus, at present, there are multiple systems offering services for preschoolers ranging from formal assistance programs to integral, non-formal programs, in Latin America. The number of children in all these systems, however, is extremely limited, reaching a maximum of 10% of the population.[3] Moreover, no basic information on the value of these kinds of preschool experiences is available as a result of research and program evaluations.

Although some evaluations of preschool programs have been carried out they have generally been made by the program creators themselves and mainly give account of the efforts made and precarious measurements of the effects observed. Usually such evaluations are subjective opinions rather than measurements, and there are few measurement techniques which attempt to deal with cognitive aspects of the child's development. Little effort has been made to keep a record of the program effects on the family and the community.

Costs of implementing the programs are occasionally registered in the reports of these non-formal systems. Normally, when attempts are made in this respect, the costs supplied are historical (a reflection of the costs in a particular period of time, which, given the inflation in our countries, is far from an accurate indication of what the breakoff of the program has meant from a financial point of view). In addition, when information is supplied on operating costs, it relates to direct expenses of the program (direct payment to the personnel, and materials) and does not take into account the contributions made by the families and by the community in terms of money and goods. Obviously, these factors have to be considered since those resources have an alternative use and, therefore, mean a cost to society.

Chile has followed the Latin American pattern as to type and scope of preschool services. In 1977 the formal systems of preschool assistance covered 9.6% of the population between 0 and 6 years old and only 13.2% of the severely deprived children population. Yearly costs per child ranged between US$ 127 and US$ 361[4] making it almost impossible to cover 100% of the population needing this attention. As an answer to this difficulty, non-formal programs have arisen which are devoted fundamentally to marginal sectors. Among these the most important are:

Early Stimulation Program: Program of diagnosis and stimulation of psychomotor development in children aged 0 to 2. This program is provided by the Health Department and is intended to cover the whole country.

Square for Preschool Children: This program makes use of a town square and some community adolescents and is intended for children aged 2 to 6. It operates in a marginal barrio in the city of Santiago.

Parent-Son Program: This program involves parent groups in urban and rural communities in an active-participatory approach and was specially designed for children aged 4 to 6.

Although these programs differ in the strategies employed, in the agents involved, in the degree of community commitment required, in the age of the target population, etc., the three are all intended to solve a specific problem: to offer a better expectation for the development of preschool children in marginal sectors.

Consequently, by the end of 1978, the authors set forth the urgent need for carrying out a preliminary cost-effectiveness analysis of the three programs. Financial support from UNICEF was subsequently obtained.

This evaluation facilitated the understanding and analysis of the internal dynamics of the programs, their basic elements, the achievements within the population involved and the cost implied by program implementation.

As a result of this experience, together with the review of other non-formal preschool programs in Latin America, the investigators found two fundamental aspects related to:

a) The evaluation of non-formal preschool programs in marginal communities, and
b) The basic elements for effective preschool attention in marginal sectors.

EVALUATION OF NON-FORMAL PRESCHOOL PROGRAMS IN
MARGINAL COMMUNITIES

The experience gained in the evaluation of non-formal preschool programs in marginal areas led the evaluators to become
aware of the importance of understanding the role that the community plays, a role which must be assumed by the evaluators when
they are analyzing a program that affects and involves them.

The first step in the fulfillment of such an evaluation is to
become aware of the importance of the legitimization of the evaluators so that the community itself is willing to analyze the program
involving its own members. The evaluators' goal is then to be
accepted as mere stimulators for community reflection leading to
the evaluation process.

The evaluators must understand that it is the community itself
which can determine if a program is being effective, if it satisfies
its needs, interests and aspirations, if the effort that is being
made is the best alternative, and which elements are favoring or
hindering its effectiveness.

In this sense, non-formal preschool programs, because of their
usual integral character and due to their involvement in the culture,
require an evaluative model with the characteristics of participatory research (Hall, 1975), that is: (i) that the evaluation offer
a direct benefit to society; (ii) that the community involve itself
in the evaluative process; and (iii) that the community feel that
the evaluation is part of its educational experience.

It is necessary then that the evaluators let the community
know that the central role of the evaluation must be played by
community members themselves. The role of an evaluator must be
understood by the community to be that of co-evaluator.

In order to achieve these goals the evaluators must be able
to specify strategies of approach to the community that allow them
to shift from an acquaintance with the programs to a real involvement.

When the suggested strategies are used, the evaluative process
of preschool programs acquires a systematic dimension in which the
evaluator is interested in analyzing the effort made by the program
to achieve the stipulated goals, the effect that this effort has
over the direct and indirect beneficiaries, and the elements that
can explain the development or hindrance of the program.

Thus, the evaluation of non-formal preschool programs requires fixing evaluative categories as a frame for diverse questions arising throughout the evaluation.

From this perspective, the evaluators play a double role. On the one hand, they are external agents, which allows them to analyze each experience within a global evaluation frame formed by theoretical background and knowledge of other preschool programs in similar environments. On the other hand, they are internal agents since they have to be able to become part of the evaluation group formed by the community.

As a result of the experience carried out by the authors the following model of evaluation was designed:

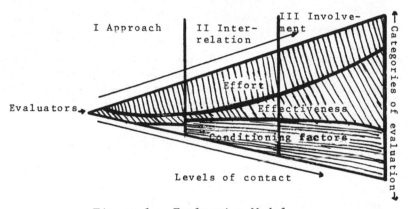

Figure 1.   Evaluation Model

As observed in the model, the authors had two parameters in mind: Evaluation Categories and Levels of Contact.

1.   Evaluation Categories

Effort, effectiveness, processes. The evaluation categories are the parameters which act as a frame for the questions that arise as the evaluators come into contact with the program.

a) *Effort:* Effort is related to the input or energy invested in both quantitative and qualitative aspects in order to achieve the goals stipulated in the program. In this sense, the description of costs, the type of personnel, the populations to be covered and the strategies are part of the effort made to achieve program goals.

b) Effectiveness: Effectiveness addresses the achievements attained by the program through the effort made. The effectiveness is not understood as the program's scope with respect to the needs of the population, but rather as the fulfillment of the specific goals of the program and of other goals which appear to be important in the light of the evaluators' conceptualization throughout the process.

c) Conditioning Factors: The conditioning factors address the analysis of the elements that might be favoring or hindering the effectiveness. The conditioning factors, finally, indicate to the evaluators the interactions of factors having an influence on the effectiveness of the program.

These three categories are present at all levels of contact.

2. Levels of Contact

The levels of contact address the way in which the evaluators get acquainted with the programs. Each level indicates the different degree of depth that the evaluators reach in each program in order to have a better understanding of the evaluation categories: effort, effectiveness and process.

The levels of contact are:

a) Approach: As observed in the diagram, the first level of contact is the approach the evaluators use as they make use of and analyze the documents about a program. However, the initial learning becomes enhanced as the evaluators move to other levels of contact.

b) Interrelation: Interrelation is established in workshops held among the evaluators, the creators and the people responsible for the program. These meetings allow the evaluators to have access to richer documentation usually employed internally by the experts responsible for the program.

c) Involvement: Involvement takes place when the evaluator has acquired through the preceding levels a vision of the effort, effectiveness, and conditioning factors of the program to be evaluated. This provides the framework with which to approach the community in which the program has been developed and creates the basic conditions for co-evaluation. The reason that the term involvement is used is that the evaluator incorporates with the community for the purpose of evaluating the program along with the creators and beneficiaries of the program.

This growing insight into the learning and understanding of a program enables the evaluators to stop being mere external agents and to become co-evaluators.

Cost Analysis

The cost analysis of educational programs belongs to the evaluative category: Effort. Discussion about this subject was thought necessary given the limited methodology specifications and the frequent lack of such data in preschool programs.

Some considerations regarding the determination of preschool program costs are required.

a) The scarce information available for determining costs along with the urgent need for such data obliges one to make multiple assumptions about the information that is missing (for instance, assumptions about the specific skills of the participants, the characteristics of the buildings, etc.). In spite of this, the costs so determined are quite useful as long as the assumptions are clearly stated so that those who make use of them are aware of their limitations. On the other hand, pointing out the missing data serves a useful purpose in demonstrating to the people in charge of the programs the need to record information on costs at the same time as they keep a record on the program's achievements.

b) In addition to estimating the real costs for the institution in charge of the program (private cost), the real cost that the actualization of the program represents to society must be included as even more important. The reason for this is that authorities and researchers of Latin America who are concerned with the subject will then have more solid backgrounds to judge the feasibility of program implementation in another context.

Given the scarce resources and the multiple needs existing in Latin America, such resources have many alternative uses. It is obvious that a State must determine priorities among alternative projects--based on the social rentability of each one of them and taking into account the benefits that the application of resources to a massive program focusing on preschool offers to society in contrast with the benefits offered by the same resources applied to alternative projects.

The valuation of the social costs of non-formal programs implies taking into account all the contributions made by the community which represent no expenses at all for the institution in charge of the program. Contributions include direct contributions in goods and time devoted to the program by community members (for example, those who earn a lower income than that of the market or those who receive no income at all).

In determining the social costs the following specifications can be made:

• Although the programs have been subject to adaptations at different times and the elements to be taken into account to estimate the social cost in each stage may be pointed out, the estimation itself is made exclusively for the benefit of the current development of the program. This is based on the fact that it is assumed that the continuous review and adaptation of the program addresses an optimum combination of factors to fulfill the objectives proposed.

• The use of human resources can be valued according to the market price offered to a person having similar skills and experience, considering that in this pricing process the following assumption is implicit: there exists a competitive and undistorted market so that wages and salaries tend to reflect the marginal productivity of labor. A good example of distortion is the existence of taxes on the use of labor and on the sale of services by the worker (employer's and employee's contribution to the State). This general assumption implies a sub-estimation of marginal labor productivity.

• In determining the income, the skills and age of an individual must be considered (the latter as a reflection of experience). In doing so it is possible to use the income of an individual whose skills and experience are equivalent to those of the individual whose income is to be estimated. The existence of a quasi-monopoly by the State for certain professions allows use of figures corresponding to the State income scale.

• For valuation of material lasting one year or less market prices without taxes shall be considered.

• For the valuation of land, buildings and equipment lasting more than one year it is necessary to consider the corresponding depreciation plus the interest that the resources invested there would have produced if they had been given an alternative use (social cost of capital).

• Given that current market prices are generally used for the different qualifications, it is necessary to modify them according to the unemployment rate for that level of qualification.

c) One of the purposes of analyzing preschool programs is to gather information to compare alternatives.

Given that non-formal preschool programs have extremely diverse specific objectives as well as a basic common objective, it
is convenient to insist that the cost analysis of the programs
cannot be carried out in isolation, without taking into account
either all the other specific objectives or the effectiveness of
the program in fulfilling its basic and specific objectives.

Basic Elements for a More Efficient Community Preschool Action

The evaluation of the three non-formal preschool education
programs described above and the examination of seven programs in
Latin America (in Colombia, Venezuela and Mexico) through documents, workshops and field work resulted in the identification of
basic elements needed for more effective community preschool action. This evaluation method allows the evaluators to obtain not
only quantitative but also qualitative data representing dynamic
factors that can predict educational action.

It is necessary to point out that the following elements result from field observation and from the judgment of the evaluators
as to the role that the community can and must play in a community
educational action.

These elements can be summarized as follows:

Community selection

Motivation process

Implementation of the program   Evaluation

The following is an operative definition of each of these items
and of the elements which best predict an effective community action.

1. Community Selection

Community selection is the mechanism through which the creators
of a preschool program detect--by means of pre-established indicators--
the communities that apparently require the implementation of the
proposed program. Selection of these communities is validated
through contact with key community agents in order to get feedback
as to the need for the program.

Elements: The selection of the communities must result from
a real understanding of community members' needs. Given that there
is an urgent need for the implementation of preschool programs as
a result of the existence of large sections of the population in a
situation of deprivation and also because of the low level of
service offered by the formal education systems, community selection should be very strict, involving in the first place those communities in most urgent need.

The selection shall involve the global community rather than
isolated groups which may have been created for other purposes.
It is necessary to create an ad-hoc and specific community organization for carrying out a preschool program.

2. Motivation Process

The motivation process is an action which tends to create a
favorable predisposition towards the program by the members of the
selected communities and to commit them to attend and take part in
the activities required for the implementation of the program.

Elements: In the motivation process it is most relevant that
the community acknowledges the program and those people who are
responsible for its implementation. This acknowledgment implies
that the creators of the program must be able to become active
members and be accepted by the community.

It is most important to effectively motivate the acknowledged
and key people in the community in order to stimulate its members
to enter the program.

The creation of active groups as models provides motivation
for other community members to become interested in entering the
program and/or creating new groups. The degree of correspondence
between the needs of the community and the program offered affects
motivation to participate. The variety of programs offered to a
community at any particular moment influences the motivation that
the community may have to take part in a specific program.

3. Implementation of the Program

a) The Community Takes Over the Administrative and Educational Management of the Program: The curricular and financial aspects of the organization of a preschool program must arise from
the community members themselves. The contribution of a financial
source is important but the management of the resources should be
delegated to the community members themselves.

• Investigation shows that only a sustained action with the preschool child over a period of time has a true education-al effect. Therefore, actions which do not truly involve the parents result in temporary, non-permanent progress.

• Criticism and self-criticism as formative elements observed in non-formal preschool-education programs are elements that should be used.

• Reflection by community members on their own preschool pro-grams creates a wider word-consciousness and stimulates the generation of a preschool curriculum arising from their own needs. The curriculum shall not be imposed by an expert but shall be developed and recreated by the parents themselves through dialogue with each other.

• Materials such as slides, paper-drawn images, picture books, and diagrams, stimulate people to reflect, arousing conscious-ness and leading to action.

• Employing coordinators selected by the community groups themselves favors the reflection-action process or self-educa-tion arising from the group.

• The continuous training of such coordinators according to an active-participant and self-training concept is a basic element for their personal evolution and for the role they play within the groups.

• The community selects the monitors employed to work with the children.

• In order to bridge the gap between these monitors and the people in the groups, monitor training should be carried out along with the development of the group. The monitors can then acquire knowledge through exchanging ideas with the parent group which will include parents, brothers and monitors.

• The employment of recreative and interrelation elements is an essential factor for group unification and continuity.

• The consolidation of particular community groups, rather than isolated centers belonging to different communities, pro-vides cohesion and facilitates the search for common interests and solutions to problems.

  b) The Community is Enhanced by the Program: The creation of different groups and children's participation in the different acti-vities created by these groups increases the contact between the children and the community, which in turn results in greater community involvement.

> • Stimulating the involvement of other people who are in contact with preschool children (shopkeepers, gardeners, butchers, masons, etc.) so that they become aware of their likely role in the educational action--through strategies created by the groups themselves--enhances community commitment.

> • A place where children can meet periodically favors the unification of parents and children.

> • The creation of preschool children's groups in which parents can actualize what they have discussed within their own groups is a factor that helps to enforce and to put into practice what has been learned, and to bring it to reality in their homes.

> • The community houses shall be taken advantage of as educational and cost-saving elements.

> • Making use of adolescents and brothers as monitors serves an important educational role. A strategy is needed to allow these helpers to receive some income in return for what they do, but they should not feel they are "employees." The search for strategies to involve adolescents, who for some reason have withdrawn from the community interests, seems essential. Usually, programs tend to employ those human resources who for some reason have become motivated or are old enough to take part in a community action.

4. Evaluation

Participatory evaluation is a model that fits preschool programs in marginal sectors. By means of certain specific techniques the community members become the evaluators of their own programs.

FOOTNOTES

1. United Nations. Report on a unified approach to development analysis and planning. Commission on Social Development, 39th Session, October, 1972.
2. For further examination of the vision on childhood and of the concept of development through time, see Latorre, C.L., Filp, Johanna, & Vera, Rodrigo. *Políticas en beneficio de la niñez desvalida en edades tempranas.* 1980.

3. UNESCO. *Evaluacion y situacion actual de la educación en America Latina.* Santillana, S.A.; Madrid: UNESCO, 1977.
4. Filp, Johanna, & Latorre, Carmen Luz. *Antecedentes generales sobre la educación prescolar en Chile.* CIDE, 1978.
5. The evaluation categories employed in this model are an adaptation of those defined by Edward Suchman in *Evaluative research-- principles and practice in public services and social action programs.* New York: Russell Sage Foundation, 1967.

BIBLIOGRAPHY

Filp, Johanna, & Latorre, Carmen Luz. *Antecedentes generales sobre la educatión prescolar en Chile.* CIDE, 1978.
Latorre, C.L., Filp, Johanna, & Vera, Rodrigo. *Políticas en bene- ficio de la niñez desvalida en edades tempranas.* 1980.
Suchman, Edward. *Evaluative research-principles and practice in public services and social action programs.* New York: Russell Sage Foundation, 1967.
United Nations. Report on a unified approach to development analysis and planning. Commission on Social Development. 39th Session, October 1972.
UNESCO. Evaluación y situación actual de la educación en América Latina. Santillana, S.A.; Madrid: UNESCO, 1977.

CHANGES IN AFFECTIVE PERCEPTIONS WITH CHANGES
IN ACADEMIC ACHIEVEMENT: A Preliminary
Study of Three Twelve-Year-Old Boys*

M. Gootman
University of Georgia

D. R. Steg
Drexel University

THE SCILS PROGRAM

At Drexel University in 1967, the Self-Controlled Interactive
Learning System (SCILS) Program was started to implement a unique
approach developed for teaching basic reading and other academic
skills. The SCILS Program revolves around a learner, a monitor,
courseware, and equipment. The monitor supervises the SCILS experience, observes the learner while he or she is working with the equipment, and plans the appropriate sequence of learning activities based
on the learner's specific requirements.

The talking page is an audio-visual, multi-media desk-top learning system. The learner uses a lever to coordinate what he sees in
the lesson book with what he hears from a record. The learner uses
a pencil to write words and sentences in the lesson book. Oralographic, linguistic, and experience courseware accompany the talking page.

The voice mirror is a modified tape recorder which is used in
conjunction with the talking page. It allows the learner to record
and listen to his voice without having to rewind the tape.

The increasingly positive annual results of the SCILS Program
in teaching reading to young children led to a decision to explore

*This study has been partially funded by the Bernard van Leer
Foundation. Support is gratefully acknowledged.

the potential of SCILS for helping older non-readers. The SCILS
Program appears to be particularly well-suited to meet the needs of
students who consistently fail to read throughout their elementary
years, regardless of the remedial actions taken by the school. Unlike many other methods designed to help non-readers, this method
allows the child to remain in control of the environment throughout the learning experience. In addition, the learner is exposed
to material which is designed to meet his or her interest and ability
levels rather than material which is either too juvenile or too
difficult. Conventional reading programs often carry a stigma and
children tend to view them as an extension of the same materials and
approaches with which they are not succeeding in the classroom, or
they tend to view them as punishment for failure. The novelty of
the SCILS experience, its privacy, and its total separation and distinction from the classroom and previous learning encounters hold
promise for placing it in a totally different perspective from conventional reading programs.

THE REMEDIATION STUDY

This section presents the results of a pilot study designed to
determine the feasibility of implementing the SCILS Program with
older non-readers using the talking page, voice-mirror, and parent
volunteers as monitors.

Three children from a Philadelphia public elementary school
located one block from Drexel University were selected to participate in this pilot study. The principal of this school had wit-
nessed the successes of former SCILS students in his school and was
consequently anxious to use the SCILS Program to help the school's
older non-readers. The principal and the guidance counselor selected three boys who were in the sixth grade, but who could barely
read. All three were from low socioeconomic status families and were
black. These three students were selected for the study on the basis
of four criteria: they were extremely poor students; they had average intellectual abilities; other remedial efforts had failed with
them; and, yet, they appeared to be anxious to learn to read. While
their parents granted permission for the study, in at least two of
the three cases, parental apathy towards the child's learning was
evident.

Three parents of other children in this school volunteered to
be the monitors for the project. After 20 hours (in about two weeks)
of intensive training by a SCILS Instructional Specialist, these three
volunteers were able to assume complete responsibility for monitoring
the three students on the SCILS equipment.

Objective measures of reading achievement, auditory perception,
socialization, control of aggression, and attitude to learning were

obtained both before and after participation in the program. At the
conclusion of the project, subjective information about the students'
progress and attitudes was extracted from interviews with the students, the volunteers, and their classroom teacher. Previous SCILS
research (Steg, 1969, 1972, 1978; Steg, D'Annunzio, & Fox, 1974,
1978; Steg, D'Annunzio, Fox, & Gootman, 1978) has indicated that a
minimum of 30 hours instructional time appears to be the critical
turning point for successful reading achievement by SCILS students.
The research also indicates that the achievement gains increase
incrementally with time, well after the student is no longer working
with SCILS equipment.

Dramatic gains in achievement were not expected during the pilot
study since students spent only three months in the program. However, it was hoped that at least the negative trend could be reversed.

The Wide Range Reading Test (WRR) was used as the measure of
reading achievement. The results in Table 1 indicate that all three
students made at least modest gains in reading achievement as measured by the WRR. Although these gains might not appear to be unusual for the average sixth grader, they are exceptionally large for
children who have been making insignificant progress or who have
been regressing throughout their school years (note their pre-test
scores).

Since the SCILS Program provides both auditory and visual approaches to reading, the auditory component of the Illinois Test
of Psycholinguistic Abilities was administered to these three students. Although all three sub-tests of the auditory component were
administered, it is important to note that the SCILS equipment
and programs are specifically designed to enhance the kinds of auditory skills tested by the auditory closure and sound-blending tests
but that they do not deal with auditory sequential memory. Indeed,
the three students made large gains in sound-blending and auditory
closure, which are verbal auditory skills and they made no gains or

Table 1. Pre- and post-WRR scores for SCILS pilot study students

Child	Pre-test	Post-test	SCILS time
S	3.8	4.1*	57 hours
D	2.1	2.9	43 hours
A	3.3	3.5	19 hours

*Since 4.0 is considered to be the point at which independent
reading begins, this child made a major and vital advance in reading while enrolled in the SCILS Program.

regressed slightly in auditory sequential memory, which is a numerical auditory skill (see Table 2).

The results of the WRR and the ITPA-Auditory suggest that the SCILS Program was beginning to reverse the trend of negative achievement for these students. They already appeared to be making gains in achievement in spite of the fact that one student had not yet reached the critical turning point of 30 hours of instructional time and in spite of the fact that insufficient time had elapsed to witness the SCILS gains that occur incrementally over time.

Certain tasks in the Tasks of Emotional Development Test (T.E.D.) by Cohen and Weil (1975) were selected to examine the effects of emotional and attitudinal perception of the SCILS program on these three students. For each task, a photograph was presented to the child who was asked to tell the test administrator what is going on in the picture, what the people might be doing, feeling, and thinking and how the story ends. The three photographs selected from the T.E.D. Test were presented to the pilot students both before and after their participation in the SCILS Program.

The socialization photograph gauges the child's ability to reach out and communicate with peers and to benefit from and participate in group activities. This task was used to examine whether the knowledge and competence gained from SCILS helped these children to interact with their peers in a healthier manner. Another photograph that was used examines the acceptance and control of aggressive feelings toward peers. Aggression was examined since it has been observed

Table 2. Pre- and post-ITPA-Auditory scores for SCILS pilot study students

Child	Test	Pre-test	Post-test	SCILS Time
S	SB*	7-7 (18)**	8-7 (21)	57 hours
	AC***	5-6 (16)	6-5 (19)	
	ASM****	3-2 (9)	2-7 (6)	
D	SB	7-7 (18)	8-7 (25)*****	43 hours
	AC	7-3 (21)	9-4 (24)	
	ASM	4-2 (14)	4-2 (14)	
A	SB	8-2 (20)	>8-7 (25)	19 hours
	AC	6-1 (18)	8-5 (23)	
	ASM	4-2 (14)	4-0 (13)	

```
  *Sound Blending              ****Auditory Sequential Memory
 **Raw score in parentheses   *****Maximum obtainable score
***Auditory Closure
```

in individual cases that the SCILS equipment is often a tool for
channeling aggression in positive directions, as well as a means for
overcoming passivity in learning. Most important is the photograph
which is designed to determine whether the child has established a
positive attitude toward academic learning. This task was selected
to determine whether participation in the SCILS Program changed
these three students' attitudes toward academic learning.

The first photo administered was the socialization task. This
picture shows ". . . four children in a group, apparently interacting with each other; a fifth is at some distance from the group
facing it and in a position to walk toward the children" (Cohen &
Weil, 1965, p. 13).

Child S. initially told a story about how the fifth child wanted to be part of the group, but they wouldn't let him in because,
"He is not qualified . . . he just looks at them. He knows he wants
to do it, but they might laugh at him." Although S. has the child
socialize in the story, the socialization occurs only after much
hesitation and deliberation. However, S.'s post-test story reveals
a boy who is curious about the other children's activities, asks if
he can join them and then joins them immediately. Perhaps S's
responses to this photo before and after his participation in the
project reflect a change in how he relates to his peers. While his
lack of abilities may have previously subjected him to much ridicule
(as reflected by peers' laughing at him) and he may have felt isolated
from his peers (as reflected by the boy not qualifying), S. interpreted
the picture in a healthier manner after he began to achieve a modest
amount of success in SCILS.

D. did not allow the boy to socialize in either the pre- or
post-tests. However, initially he stated that the others would not
let the boy join because they were angry at him. The second time,
he said that the children did not play with the boy because he was
new. Perhaps this suggests a slight improvement in socialization--
at least in the second instance, D. did not perceive the situation
as being hostile.

In A.'s pre-test story, the boy goes home and does not socialize while in the post-test story he ends up playing with the others.

Lack of achievement is often a stigma which impedes proper
socialization. The underachiever is frequently subjected to ridicule and exclusion. The results of the six pre- and post-social-
ization tests suggest that all three boys' ability to socialize
improved after exposure to the SCILS Program. Perhaps, as they
began to encounter success in learning, their self-confidence in
interpersonal relations was strengthened.

The photograph used to examine the acceptance and control of

aggressive feelings towards peers shows two children facing each
other. One of the children looks ready to fight. The other child
is standing with his arms by his sides.

The subjects' responses on both were healthy and there were
no perceivable differences between these responses. Consequently,
it was not possible to evaluate the effects of SCILS on aggression,
and it remains an open question as to whether or not SCILS can
positively affect initial negative responses in this subtest.

The photograph to determine the establishment of positive attitudes toward academic learning shows a child sitting on a chair
at a desk, holding a pencil, and looking at an open book on the
desk.

In the pre-test, S. stated that the child "doesn't feel so
good. He wants to do it but deep inside he doesn't like it but he
does it anyway so he can go to another school or do his homework."
However, in the post-test S. says, "He wants to do it. It's interesting. He's happy he's doing it." The change in S's attitude is
quite dramatic. From ambivalence and dislike about homework, he has
switched to enjoyment in only three months.

In the responses given by D. and A., the most striking feature
was that while in the pre-tests each perceived that the objective
of studying was to be able to pass a test, in the post-tests they
each perceived more distant objectives. D. said, "He passed his
test cause he's studying. When he got older he'd get a job," while
A. remarked, "He's doing his work, nobody's bothering him. He's
trying to go to college." The pre-tests reflected a concern for
immediate gratification such as good grades and passed tests while
the post-tests reflect postponed gratification and the realization
of the ultimate purpose of studying for tests. Perhaps their successes in the SCILS program made D. and A. begin to conceive of themselves as actually being capable of eventually achieving academic
success and its rewards.

The achievement and attitude changes suggested by the objective
tests discussed above are also suggested by the self-reports of
the students and interviews with the volunteers and the classroom
teacher. When asked what he tells his friends about Drexel, D. said,
"I tell them I came here to learn." All three boys discussed their
attendance at Drexel very enthusiastically. D. states, "I've
had a lot of improvement. It helps in class--reading class and
social studies sometimes when we read and stuff." A., in discussing
how SCILS has helped him in school, comments, "It helps you in sound-
ing out words, you read better."

The volunteer monitors were eager to discuss the progress of
their students. They noted that all have improved noticeably in

spite of the fact that in some instances their family's private
problems interfered with the learning. When asked whether the
children enjoyed the program, one of the volunteers exclaimed,
"Yes, that's why there's improvement. Their peers aren't here to
ridicule them if they make a mistake and my relationship [with a
child] is different from [the usual] teacher-child relationship."

While the children's 6th grade teacher does not yet see any
academic improvement, she has noted the enthusiasm of the children:
"I know they enjoy it. One child has a low frustration level, but
whatever you're doing there is evidently not frustrating him. If
anything even looks difficult before he tries it, he doesn't want
to try--but he's trying in your program."

Although great caution must be taken in drawing conclusions
when working with only three children for the short period of three
months, certain trends have clearly emerged from the experience.
The children have been conscientiously attending the sessions and
appear to be extremely excited at the prospect of finally successfully learning how to read, and already they have made modest gains
in achievement. They have also made positive advances in their
attitudes toward academic learning. The parent volunteers who came
from within the local community were fully capable of being trained
by a competent instructor, took their responsibilities seriously
and successfully implemented the SCILS Program. Furthermore, the
classroom teacher of these three children has observed changes in
these students' learning behaviors and attitudes.

These preliminary findings suggest that the SCILS Program holds
great promise for helping older non-readers to learn basic reading
skills. An expanded project is now warranted and should be undertaken to confirm and strengthen the results suggested by this pilot
study.

BIBLIOGRAPHY

Cohen, H., & Weil, G. *Tasks of emotional development*. Brookline,
    MA: T.E.D. Associates, 1975.
Steg, D.R., Mattleman, M., & Hammil, D. Effects of individual pro-
    grammed instruction on initial reading skills and language
    behavior in early childhood. International Reading Association,
    6 Tyre Avenue, Newark, Delaware, April 1969.
Steg, D.R., & D'Annunzio, A. Helping problem learners during the
    early childhood years. Early Childhood Education II Session
    (C-14), 1972 American Educational Research Association, Palmer
    House, Chicago, April 6, 1972.
Steg, D.R. Cybernetics revisited (1978). Frontiers of Strategic
    Management, International Conference. TIMS/ORSA (The Interna-
    tional Management Science and Operations Research Society of

America), Americana Hotel, New York, NY: May 1, 1978.

Steg, D.R. Some theoretical and experimental considerations of responsive environments, learning and social development. In J. Rose (Ed.), *Progress of Cybernetics,* Vol. 3, London: Gordon & Breach Science Publishers, 1979.

Steg, D.R., D'Annunzio, A., & Fox, C. Deviation amplifying processes and individual human growth and behavior. In J. Rose (Ed.), *Advances in cybernetics and systems: 1646-1655.* New York: Gordon & Breach, 1974 (ERIC Document ED 077587).

Steg, D.R., D'Annunzio, A., & Fox, C. *Deviation amplification, two case studies of cognitive development: A seven year report (1969-1976).* VIIIth International Congress on Cybernetics, Namur, Belgium, International Association of Cybernetics, September 6, 1976. Publication 1978.

Steg, D.R., D'Annunzio, A., Fox, C., & Gootman, M. Two case studies in cognitive development. A nine-year report (1969-1978). Council for Exceptional Children, 56th Annual International Convention, Kansas City, May 4, 1978 (ERIC Document 153 431).

A UNIQUE BLENDING OF TECHNOLOGY AND EDUCATION USING

THE SELF-CONTROLLED INTERACTIVE LEARNING SYSTEMS

(SCILS) IN AN ON-GOING EARLY CHILDHOOD PROGRAM

Lois Baker

Drexel University

INTRODUCTION

To function adequately in society today, one of the most important skills one is expected to attain is literacy. In the past,
the criteria for literacy for all but the select few were merely the
abilities to read and write one's name or read from a religious text.
However, society has changed and the expectations of today are much
greater. Now, individuals are expected not only to "learn to read"
but also to "read to learn."[1]

More and more rapidly, new information is circulating in contemporary society. As a consequence, previously accepted devices
for teaching reading are no longer adequate and new techniques and
tools must be devised to enable individuals to comprehend, evaluate
and utilize this wealth of data.

The purpose of this paper is to demonstrate how a well organized, traditional program, run by the Drexel Early Childhood Center
at Drexel University in Philadelphia faced the problem and how its
practices began to change as the research results made sharper the
differences between desired practices and actual practices. The
many successes as well as difficulties encountered at the inception
of this program, our findings (both predicted and unpredicted) during the ongoing work, study, and research of the program, and the
practical interface of the program will be discussed.

THE DREXEL EARLY CHILDHOOD CENTER: ITS
PHILOSOPHY AND CHARACTER

The opening of the Drexel Early Childhood Center in September
1928 coincided with the beginnings of child study institutes across
the United States. If one were to visit our Center, situated in an
attractive nineteenth century Philadelphia home on the edge of the
campus and near the community which it serves, one would find forty
3-, 4-, and 5-year-old, culturally, socioeconomically, and racially
integrated children in two classrooms or on a playground equipped
with the traditional items of blocks, puzzles, child-sized furniture,
climbing apparatus, and so on. In addition, however, one would find
such things as two talking typewriters, three talking pages, three
voice mirrors and a large assortment of linguistic, phonetic, experience based, and mathematical courseware which individual children
use in a sound-proofed booth. These items constitute the Self-
Controlled Interactive Learning System (SCILS) which contribute to
the uniqueness of our program.

For more than 50 years the Center has had a philosophy based
on an understanding of child development and has endeavored to preserve the practices of the past while introducing innovations necessary to keep pace with the needs of the future. In both these en-
deavors children have been viewed as:

  . being active and curious
  . requiring a secure environment which they can explore and
    control
  . requiring a responsiveness which reflects an understanding
    of their individuality
  . requiring significant adults (whether parents, teachers,
    or others) in their lives who are able to work together for
    their well-being.[2]

One might be curious as to why innovations were necessary in a traditional program which had long been successful. The answer is that
Center program staff came to the conclusion that it was important
to ascertain if what they said was happening really was happening.
As a result, in 1967, Dr. Doreen Steg, in cooperation with the
Director (the author) of the Drexel Early Childhood Center, began
research into the relationship of academic achievement in reading,
comprehension and arithmetic to the use of educational technology.

RESEARCH STUDY

Difficulties Encountered

In the beginning, the study met with much opposition and

skepticism--even negativism. Concerns and apprehensions were frequently expressed about the physical setting. Some adult conceptions of the apparent "closed," "sterile," and "isolated" environment of the child's booth seemed far more disturbing to the adults
than to the children. It took a long time to convince some of the
classroom teachers that their own attitudes and classroom practices
were most important (even critical) to the attitudes and feelings
expressed by the children. It cannot be stressed enough that in
order to have a successful program it is imperative to have staff--
and parents--willing to be supportive and to keep an open mind.
Too often, adults were impatient to see immediate results and to
question the wisdom of the approaches used in the program.[3] For
example, in regard to the former, an over-zealous parent might
chastise the child for not going to the typewriter when invited,
or for not knowing certain information he or she felt the child
should have known. Consequently, to avoid undue pressures on the
child, parents were not permitted to observe their own children in
the booths.

Another issue that arose was how much time children should
spend in the booths. Some teachers preferred children to participate in their regular classroom activities rather than permitting
the children to spend twenty minutes of their time in SCILS. On
the other hand, some enthusiastic SCILS monitors or supervisors
permitted children to overstay their time which resulted in physically drained, although emotionally exhilarated children. These
concerns indicated that neither children nor adults were always the
best judges of the point of diminishing return. The research of
Dr. Steg and her associates was of particular value in addressing
these types of issues.

Research Results

As research began to sharpen the differences between the desired
practices and the actual practices of the program our approach began
to change. Now. after over ten years of work, observations, studies,
and replications, Dr. Steg and her associates have not only established viable guidelines for our program but have discovered that
children need to spend at least 30 hours with the SCILS program in
order to receive maximum benefit. We now make sure that every child
leaving our Center has spent this amount of time in this part of our
program.

Consistent results have been obtained in our recent cross-
sectional and annual studies of kindergarten children. Some of these
results are as follows:

Results using criterion-referenced measures developed at Drexel

in order to determine whether program objectives are being achieved,
show that by the end of kindergarten, children participating in
SCILS are able to:

. match and name colors
. match and identify their names
. match and verbally identify letter names and sounds
. recognize some names and demonstrate facility with a beginning sight vocabulary

(2) At the beginning and end of each academic year the SCILS
children and two groups of control children (similar in background
to the SCILS children but enrolled in two nearby early childhood
programs) are tested with standardized tests. The SCILS children
consistently make greater grains on both the Frostig Test of Visual
Perception and the Illinois Test of Psycholinguistic Abilities.
These gains are statistically significant.

By the end of kindergarten, SCILS children have a higher mean
score on the Wide Range Reading Test than do both control groups.
The SCILS groups show an average increase of 5.1 months in reading
ability while control groups I and II show average increases of 2.4
months and 1.9 months respectively.

SUPPORT FROM THE COMMUNITY FOR THE PROGRAM

Our work with parents has fostered enthusiasm, support and communication. Although our program is only for 3-, 4- and 5-year-old
children, parents are asking that the program be extended into the
lower elementary grades.

Response from the general community and cooperating educational sources has also been positive. Teachers and principals who have,
or have had, some of the program's former children attending their
elementary schools have expressed enthusiasm for the program. In
some instances, these educators have used the SCILS program for
remedial reading purposes for their older students and have noted
favorable results.

SUPPORT FROM THE CHILDREN FOR THE PROGRAM

The enjoyment the children receive from the program is evidenced
in the following quotations from two of our "graduates."

Ten-Year-Old Girl: It was nice, we learned a lot . . .
I learned how to spell, put my vowels together, sentences
. . . Every day I had a turn . . . so when I went to

another school they were just teaching me more stuff about what I learned here.

Eleven-Year-Old Boy: I found out how to write and type the words, and I would study them, and then I would go on to some different words and I would study them. It helps you learn more words, how to spell them correctly . . . cat, dog, boat, and all that . . . It's fun to do.[3]

INNOVATIONS

The information, preparation, and related coursework required for the SCILS program and the special training required for the SCILS program for both classroom teachers and monitors in child development have enabled us to combine the two programs into a total, continuous and compatible whole. As a result, the teachers in the two programs now plan cooperatively and there is free interchange of ideas between them. Additionally, the classroom teachers are now helping the children with their notebooks (the book each child keeps and into which he or she writes a letter or word each day). Previously this activity was carried on by the SCILS teacher.

A relatively recent change has been made in the manner in which the children are asked to become involved in the program; now, instead of the SCILS teachers merely inviting or asking a child to have a turn with the talking typewriter, they arrange an "appointment" with the child. Interestingly, this has resulted in the children placing great importance on their attendance and has increased their enthusiasm and involvement in this program. Children who might frequently have refused the teachers' invitations are happy to comply with the "appointment."

There have been some children, however, who have not been enticed by the appointment. In these situations, special techniques are necessary to help children change their attitudes towards using SCILS. One young boy, for example, preferred to play with his trucks in the classroom to participating in the SCILS program. An observant SCILS teacher sensitive to this preference worked with the child to develop a program about trucks for the typewriter. This little boy now goes eagerly to the typewriter.

CONCLUSION

Through the wise use of the tools and systems of educational technology and the input of loving, caring and understanding adults, children can be provided with a greater capacity to understand and manage their active learning in today's world.

FOOTNOTES

1. Steg, D.R. *Self controlled interactive learning systems*. De-
    partment of Human Behavior and Development, Nesbitt College,
    Drexel University, Philadelphia, PA: 1978, p. 3.
2. *Ibid* p. 2.
3. Teachers were fearful at first of using the SCILS technology and
    concerned at using this technology with such young children (3,
    4, and 5 years of age). These fears accounted for the efforts
    required to convince the teachers of the importance of their
    input into the SCILS program.
4. *Ibid* p. 17.

BIBLIOGRAPHY

Steg, D.R. *Self controlled interactive learning systems*. Department
    of Human Behavior and Development, Nesbitt College, Drexel
    University, Philadelphia, PA: 1978.

THE SELF CONTROLLED INTERACTION LEARNING SYSTEMS (SCILS):

A COMMUNICATION MODEL OF LEARNING*

D. R. Steg
Drexel University

M. Mattleman
Temple University

C. Fox
MATSCO, General Electric

PART I: THE SCILS PROGRAM

INTRODUCTION

The Self Controlled Interactive Learning Systems (SCILS) program involves the use of a "talking typewriter," a "talking page,"
and a "voice-mirror" to teach reading, typing, writing, and
mathematics to children at the Drexel Early Childhood Center, Drexel
University, Philadelphia. Its premise is that learning involves
both the acquisition of skills (training) and the going beyond past
experience to the formation of new concepts (education). The proper
use of instructional technology is to enable the learner to acquire
skills which can be utilized in new concept formation. The teacher's
role shifts from concentration on training to involvement in education. However, if instructional technology is to be effective it should
incorporate control by the student, responsiveness to the student,
and instantaneous feedback to the learner which allows for self-
correction. (For a more detailed explanation of the theoretical
principles underlying the SCILS program see Part II of this paper.)

Specifically, learning in the SCILS program involves the following:

*This study has been partially funded by the Bernard van Leer Founda-
tion grant to D. R. Steg (No. 648). Support is gratefully acknowledged.

405

. Multi-sensory engagement of the learner;
. Learner control of the environment;
. Responsiveness to the actions of the learner;
. Instantaneous feedback allowing the learner to evaluate his
  actions in relation to his goals.

These features enable substantial learner progress. Further,
these learning principles are not age-specific or culture-specific;
rather, they are principles which can be universally applied to any
learner. One of the main goals of the program is to enable the
child, or adult, to become an independent learner. Because SCILS
involves an interactive environment which the child can control with
a minimum of effort, it is especially suited to this purpose.

The designs of the hardware, courseware and software components
of SCILS embody the above learning principles and the use of this
automated and non-automated equipment provides the child with the
opportunity for exploration and investigation using discovery techniques.

COMPONENTS OF THE SCILS PROGRAM

A) Hardware

The Talking Typewriter:[1] The "Talking Typewriter" is a computer
based typewriter which involves the child totally in a learning experience. Secluded within a small sound proof booth, the child is free
to do as he wishes, away from the approval or disapproval of adults
and peers, in a practically indestructible environment. The child's
visual interest is secured by the color-coded keys of the typewriter,
by the images projected on the viewing screen, and by the letters and
other symbols which appear on the paper when he types.

Auditory stimulation comes from the voice recordings played by
the equipment in programs of exploratory typing and in replay of the
child's own voice when included in the format of a program. The
child receives tactile input from the typing action itself. A
sense of accomplishment is quickly established as every typing
motion can trigger a simultaneous auditory, visual, and/or
kinesthetic response.

The Talking Page and Voice Mirror:[2] Lessons introduced on the
Talking Typewriter are reviewed and expanded on the Talking Page.
In a sound-proof environment, similar to that of the talking typewriter, the child's interest is again held by the tactile stimuli of
handling the record, paper and pencil, by the visual input of the
lesson book, by his own writing, and by the auditory input of the
recorded voice. Used in conjunction with the Talking Page, the Voice
Mirror, a basic tape recorder with simplified controls for recording

and instant playback, allows the learner to hear his own
voice.

B.   Courseware

The Drexel program has developed its own courseware, based on
the needs of each child. The focus of the courseware designed over
the last ten years has been to emphasize:

. Control of the learning process by the children;
. The desires, interests and experiences of the children;
. Regularities of the English language wherever possible;
. Auditory or visual modalities;
. The children's own experience stories;
. Interesting literary materials;
. Concepts in arithmetic and mathematics.

C.   Oralographic Courseware

The Oralographic courseware was developed specifically for use
with the Talking Typewriter and the Talking Page by Richard and Edith
Kobler for Prentice-Hall. One of the essential features is the enhancement of self-transformation and self-correcting actions on the
part of the learner.

The SCILS equipment, used in conjunction with the Oralographic
courseware will pronounce, analyze, and synthesize words, syllables,
letter sounds, and sentences with absolute reliable clarity and with
a repeatability which is totally in control of the learner. The learner determines and executes on the instrument the repetition of acousti-
cal statements. The learner is at liberty to skip forward or backward
and cannot only utter but also record his own speech as frequently as
he wants to and compare it with the model.

The Oralographic method involves learner totally from the very
start: he looks at the text material; he listens to explanations
and instructions; he speaks either together with the recorded voice
of the instrument or records his own voice; he listens again to his
own voice and the equipment's voice in a comparison attempt; and he
writes much of what he hears, sees, and says. It is of great importance that Oralography involves not only the passive receptor-senses
of looking and listening, but also, to an equal extent, the active
responses of speaking and writing (tactile response). Writing is not
only necessary because of its intrinsic value as a skill but also because in the Oralographic modes of Dictation, Speech Analysis, and
Scrambling, writing is a necessary response-tool on the part of the
learner.

SCILS PROGRAM OBJECTIVES

The specific program objectives of the SCILS training are demonstrable skills in: (1) recognizing alphabet letters, numbers and other symbols on the keyboard; (2) typing alphabet letters from dictation; (3) reading words orally; (4) composing stories; (5) recognizing and understanding concepts in arithmetic and mathematics.

In addition to the educational services available to the children and to the community, each year Drexel has conducted applied research in early childhood learning behavior, using the SCILS system. Emphasis has been on various aspects of "pre-school" child development and learning, using standardized tests and criterion referenced instruments to measure effectiveness.

PROJECT ACTIVITIES

Each child can go to the SCILS training area three times a week. He may use either the Talking Typewriter and/or the Talking Page and Voice Mirror. The monitor assists each child who comes to the equipment and chooses the phase and lesson appropriate to that child. The length of time (between 15 to 30 minutes) the child spends with the equipment and other anecdotal material is recorded. The area is cleared of all materials, except those to be used during the session. If there are observers in the room, the observers are asked to move out of the view of the child. Before going into the SCILS Typewriter booth, the fingernails of the child are painted by the child to correspond with the colors on the keyboard. The monitor says the name of each color or has the child say the name of each color as the nails are being painted. This helps the child learn his colors and to match the letters and colors on the typewriter keys. The child is not told why the nails are painted.

As the child begins the session, the monitor adjusts the equipment button so that time and stroke count are recorded. He then depresses the push-period "start" and puts the SCILS in the phase and language track appropriate to the child.

Each week the progress of the children is reviewed in a staff meeting and documented in summary statements. From the information obtained, the supervisors of the program compose a weekly suggestion sheet for each child which is posted in the SCILS room. The monitor then initiates the suggestions on this sheet when selecting activities for the child.

Play with the Talking Typewriter

Play with the Talking Typewriter involves five phases.

Phase I: This phase is used by the staff to prepare courseware. Children are not involved in this phase.

Phase II: Labeled the exploratory phase, this phase is used during a child's initial sessions. This phase can be either interspersed with other phases during a session or be used again at the request of the child. Past experience has shown that the ways of approaching SCILS during this phase are as varied as the subjects who use the equipment.

During phase II the typewriter is set so that any key can be depressed. When a key is depressed, the sound, or name, of the character is given and the character is typed. Exploration allows the child to familiarize himself with the keyboard and the booth environment, to realize that he is in control of the enviroment, and to begin to generalize about the results of his actions. Also, in this phase, the child is able to begin to organize his actions according to his own particular style. As an example, some children may begin by focusing their attention on the characters appearing on the paper, while others may begin by listening to the auditory cues, and repeating characters on specific keys with their related sounds.

To initiate phase II for the child, the monitor turns the dial on the control panel to phase II. He also adjusts the key voice to the appropriate track--for example, letters, sounds, colors, and the like. The child then begins to type without any directions from the monitor.

Phase III: This phase is known as the semi-automated stage and is used in order to enable the child to match characters of his own choosing. The monitor gives the child either cards on which there can be colors, letters or numerals, or instructions on the intercom, so that the child can type material of his own choosing. The monitor observes the child through the one-way mirror next to the control panel, the lid of which is up, thus locking the keyboard. When the child selects a card, the monitor waits until the child's finger is above the matching character. The monitor then depresses the button on the control which unlocks the keyboard, allowing the child to depress the desired key.

Phase IV: This is the more advanced courseware presentation phase. The child is presented with programs which have been designed by the staff or which have been composed by the child. Programs may be introduced at the beginning of a session or during a session. In either case, the monitor tells the child, "I am going to put a story on for you." If the child refuses a story, the monitor honors his refusal. However, if the child's refusal is based on the selection of a particular program, the monitor can ask the child if he would like to hear another story, or use the oralographic courseware.

The monitor allows the child to proceed with the program without interruption unless it becomes evident that the selection program is too difficult or too long. In these cases, the monitor terminates the program.

Phase V: The final phase involves experience stories. In most cases, experience stories are developed from classroom activities. However, there are times when a child is excited about an event and begins to tell the monitor about it. When this occurs, the monitor can use the session to have the child record his experience on a program card which is replayed to allow the child to hear his own voice. He can also allow the child to illustrate the experience on slides. After the session, the monitor selects key words and/or phrases used by the child and encodes them for typing. During his next session, the child can be presented with a program which includes his voice recording, slides and the typing instructions.

At the termination of the typewriter session, the monitor enters the booth and removes the child's paper from the typewriter. The child and monitor leave the booth and sit at a table in the corner of the room where they review what the child has typed. The child sits close to the blackboard. A timer on the table is set so that the session does not run over 5 minutes. The monitor then uses several methods to have the child examine his or her paper, such as, "Can you find me a T on your paper?" or "Match the letters on the board to the ones on your paper." The monitor uses auditory, visual, tactile and kinesthetic approaches whenever possible, for example, tracing felt letters with the fingers.

If the child is in the exploratory phase, the post-session is spent recognizing shapes, colors, letters and numbers. If the child is in phase III, the VAKT (visual, audio, kinesthetic, tactile) approach can be used. In this approach, the child is given a paper with the word printed on it that he has just typed during that day's session. The monitor says the word twice and asks the child to trace the word with his or her "two magic fingers" (the index and middle fingers). When the child feels he is ready, he turns the paper over and writes the word. This approach can also be used in teaching letters, numbers, and so on. In addition to the above, the monitor is free to use his or her own imagination and creativity when it comes to the post-session, by connecting it in some way to what the child has typed.

The session is terminated at the 5-minute mark or before if the child so requests. The two copies of the paper from the Talking Typewriter are separated. One is given to the child and the other is filed in the records.

In recording the session in a child's book, the monitor includes the following:

1. Date, monitor's name, time session started and ended, amount
    of time spent in SCILS booth, amount of time spent at post-
    session, number of typing strokes;
2. The colors the child named or matched;
3. Description of session--child's behavior and reactions;
4. Phase or program used;
5. Post-session description.

Record books are filed by the child's first name and typewriter
papers are filed by last name.

Work with the Talking Page and Voice Mirror

This system brings the printed page to life. It is an audiovisual, multi-media desk-top or booth learning system designed to
totally involve the learner.

The Talking Page plays records, but it does more than talk--it
also responds. To use the Talking Page, the student places a Talking
Page book on the flat surface of the instrument, slips a Talking Page
record into the slot at the rear, and then presses the "Close" button.
To hear messages, he moves the pointer handle to any of the 33 positions along the left edge of the Talking Page, and lifts the handle
up. This automatically tunes in a message to which the student can
listen again and again if he wishes, or he may skip passages at his
discretion.

The Talking Page book is opened to the lesson that the child is
working on. The child is encouraged to complete one lesson, in order
that he may start on a new one the next session. If he does not complete it, he starts from the beginning of the lesson at the next
session, not from where he left off.

Each page of a Talking Page is marked by one or more tiny printed
boxes at the left edge of the page. If the student moves the pointer
to any box on the page, he will hear a message about something he sees
on that part of the page, or he may use the page as an index to locate a message he wants to hear on the recording. The monitor records
the lesson the child has completed and the date and the time of the
lesson.

RESEARCH ON THE SCILS PROGRAM

The SCILS program has generated a number of research questions,
some of which have already been explored. A summary of these questions and some of the answers to date, as well as a more detailed
look at one longitudinal study are presented below.

A.   Summary of Research Questions

1.   When a child between 3 and 6 years old participates in SCILS:

a.   What progress does he make in reading skills during his early childhood years? (Cross-sectional studies)

b.   What progress does he make in reading skills and comprehension during his elementary years? (Longitudinal studies)

c.   What long term effects does participation in SCILS have on a child's emotional development and a child's creativity? (Pilot studies)

2.   Can SCILS help children who are emotionally disturbed, developmentally delayed, or learning disabled? (Case studies)

3.   What is the cost-benefit ratio to the individual and to society when SCILS is used to teach reading? (Economic cost-benefit analysis).

B.   Summary of Results

1.   a.   During kindergarten SCILS children make significantly greater progress in reading skills than control kindergarten children.

b.   Lower and middle socioeconomic status (SES) children who spend a minimum of 10 hours in SCILS achieve at or above grade level in reading (Wide Range Reading Test) during their elementary years (grades 1 through 6).

c.   Lower and middle SES children who spend a minimum of 30 hours in SCILS at the Drexel Early Childhood Center achieve at or above grade level in reading, comprehension and arithmetic during their elementary years (grades 1 through 6).

d.   Preliminary studies suggest that SCILS can have a positive effect on a child's self-concept and creativity.

2.   Case studies delineate in detail how emotionally disturbed, developmentally delayed and learning disabled children can progress through using SCILS.

3.   The cost-benefit analysis shows a beneficial return on investment in SCILS for the individual and for society.

C. Longitudinal Study

The purpose of this study was to consider some theoretical aspects of the concept of "self-controlled environments" and its relation to learning as well as to some recent experimental findings. This problem has reached crucial proportions as is clearly indicated by the current controversies of the validity, substantiation and/or justification of reinforcement theories of learning versus control theories of learning. The distinction to be made between communication or cybernetic control and reinforcement control delineates clearly the difference between "sensory feedback" and the feedback concept of "knowledge of results" or "reinforcements," and has far reaching meaning for the application of control theory to human activity. An experimental environment of a "self-controlled" nature has been researched since 1967 at Drexel University's "Early Childhood Center," under the direction of the Department of Human Behavior and Development. Findings suggest that early stimulation (ages 2.5 to 6 years) seems to be effective in specific language and reading skills including alphabet recognition, decoding, reading comprehension, language facility, and typing ability. Unexpected results in areas other than academic skills have become evident, particularly in the areas of emotional and social development. Children who were unable to use a similar non-automated program, owing to rather severe behavioral difficulties, were successfully involved in the automated program.

Twenty-three Get-Set (Philadelphia Head Start Program) children who were enrolled in Drexel's Early Childhood Center for an average of 2.54 years were the subjects of this study. Fourteen of the subjects were followed through the sixth grade and one through the seventh.

Treatment consisted of daily sessions, ranging in length from 15 to 25 minutes. The primary component of this treatment was work on the Talking Typewriter and Talking Page. Work was arranged primarily to accentuate auditory perceptual strengths of subjects and secondarily to remediate weaknesses. The objectives of the programming were the demonstration of skills in (a) recognizing alphabet letters, (b) typing letters from dictation, (c) reading words orally, and (d) composing stories. Monitors also worked with children on individual experience stories which were then programmed for the equipment.

Commencing with Kindergarten, the following tests were given to the children annually: the Peabody Picture Vocabulary Test (PPVT); the Wide Range Arithmetic Test (WRA); the Informal Word Recognition Test (IWR); and an Informal Reading Inventory (IRI). The California Achievement Tests (CAT) scores for all subtests were made available annually through the cooperation of the Philadelphia Board of Education.

Using descriptive analysis as well as correlation and regression analysis, the following results were obtained:

- Achievement of children in the areas of word recognition and arithmetic correlated significantly with time on equipment (SCILS Time).

- All children with a minimum of 10 hours of instructional time in SCILS, regardless of pre-tested IQ level, achieved at or above grade level in reading.

- All children with a minimum of 30 hours of instructional time, regardless of pre-tested IQ level, achieved at or above grade level in reading, comprehension and arithmetic.

- Long term gains appear to be sustained 6 years after the children have left the Center.

- These long term gains are incremental, that is, they increase year by year.

- Achievement of low socioeconomic status (SES) children in the areas of reading and arithmetic correlated significantly with attendance at the Early Childhood Center. A pre-test mean IQ score of 71.8 (with two children untestable) was obtained at initial testing and a post-test mean IQ score of 94.6 (with the two previously untestable children now included) was obtained from the same sample at the end of the treatment.

- No significant correlation between initial IQ and achievement was obtained.

By present indications use of the SCILS program in the early childhood years points to better performance by children in reading and arithmetic than would otherwise be the case. The program also leads to increasing levels of understanding and comprehension, and its effects do not disappear but increase as the child grows older. By grade 2, SCILS time begins to relate to Wide Range Reading (WRR) and by grades 3, 4, 5, and 6, it relates much more with WRR and even more with Informal Word Recognition (IWR).

Educational Significance of the Program

The literature contains many studies which appear to indicate a continual decline, after the fourth grade, in academic skills (Chall, 1967; Deutsch, 1963).

Since early exposure to structured learning experience has been shown to correlate with later achievement, it would seem es-

sential, especially during the formative years of 3 to 6, to provide children with the opportunity to learn. For most children, this
evidently is not a problem, since learning takes place with little
apparent difficulty. But for a substantial minority, this learning
does not take place as normative data indicates. Further, for these
children, this lack of learning is associated with a decrease in self-
esteem and an increase in impulsive, sometimes destructive behavior
towards themselves and others.

   Whether or not these levels of achievement will be further maintained and accrued to, remains to be seen through further longitudinal
study of these children and of others leaving the Center. However,
given the levels of significance for correlations between (1) time .
spent on the typewriter and achievement, and (2) the time enrolled in
the early childhood program and achievement, it is not probable that
this performance pattern will break down in the future to any great
extent.

PART II: THEORETICAL BACKGROUND TO SCILS PROGRAM

   In 1948 Wiener published his "Cybernetics: Control and Communication in the Animal and Machine." In the intervening years, this
second industrial revolution, as cybernetics is known, has developed
toward general theories of Communication and Control within complex
systems. Its scientific content has been markedly elaborated. For
example:

   . Work on complex networks of communication has suggested the
     notion of organization as the prime focus of cybernetics
     (Warren S. McCulloch, Heinz von Foerster);
   . Studies of circular flows of information, mutual causality
     and the dynamics they imply have associated with theories of
     control that are entirely neutral and predictive in orienta-
     tion (Norbert Wiener, Magoroh Maruyama);
   . Research on decision-making and on information transmission
     together with advances in recursive theories of computation
     have lead cybernetics to describe living organisms as adap-
     tively changing information processors (John von Neumann),
     or adaptingly changing the environment to suit the individual
     (D.R. Steg);
   . Philosophical analyses have identified cybernetics as the
     science of models, including those of self-reference (W.
     Rose Ashby, Anthony Wilden);
   . Generalizations from ecology which see man in interaction
     with his environment of physical, social and informational
     contingencies have relativised the notion of mind (Gregory
     Bateson) and that of man as a self-governing being (Karl W.
     Deutsch).

Each of the above key concepts--organization, control, adaptivity, modeling, self-reference and self-governing being--can be coalesced within an empirical substantiated general theory,[3] which is applicable to all complex social systems. This framework has been developed since 1962 (Steg, 1974, 1973, 1966, 1964, 1962; Steg, D'Annunzio & Fox, 1976; Steg, 1974; Steg & Schulman, 1973).

BEHAVIOR: ADAPTIVE VERSUS ADAPTING

Adaptive

Automatic activity of man, animal or machine is an adaptive control system, by its very nature. It is safe to assume that as with the laws of physics, the laws governing control systems apply equally to animal, man or machine. In the language of the system engineer, this is a closed-loop control system. The control system pattern consists of (1) an input signal that triggers some action, (2) a feedback signal as the result of this action to compare with the input signal, (3) a closing of the loop and a summation of the two signals and (4) effective action to counteract this summating signal. A persistent residuary signal can be made to affect memory which results in "learning." In a control system, work is triggered as a result of an actual error input.[4] The error is essential to the activity of any control system. These mechanical patterns apply to automatic machinery, animal behavior, and man's everyday automatic activity.

Adapting

An important deviation from the automatic pattern occurs when the automaticity of a system is eliminated. Non-automatic activity will not necessarily be subjected to the adaptive nature of the control system and trigger its own energy to cancel the disturbance. Non-automatic activity makes possible other activities which change the environment instead of being changed by the environment. A seal automatically grows a thicker coat of fur as the temperature drops, but man can control the temperature in a room, using knowledge of physics and chemistry.

With the automaticity eliminated the response to a disturbance is chosen after the disturbance has been analyzed as to its source, the energy involved in the disturbance, and the possible response and resulting consequences, including analysis and assessment of energy sources and energy balances. In other words, understanding is replacing automatic response.

To recapitulate, an adaptive control system is subject to the effect of the environment on its sensing elements and has no

freedom to control the effect of the environment on its sensing
elements. It can only adapt the system by using its own energy to
satisfy the requirement from the environment conveyed through the
sensors.

Opposed to this automaticity is the human ability of adapting
an environment by means that extend human reach in a specific
fashion, including in the process the use of tools, machines, psychological, socio-political, economic, educational and other instruments. Specifically, the human mechanism directs the signal-triggered
action with a view to the adaptation of the environment to eliminate
the differential between the feedback signal resulting from the modified environment and the original input signal. The mechanism involved in the latter system or disturbance is subject to the "filter"
of intelligence, thus creating an "art image" of the environment to
an "art" or "dream image."

As defined by Dewey, art is "to select what is significant and
to reject by the very same impulse what is irrelevant and thereby
compressing and intensifying the significant" (Dewey, 1934). We
should add to the statement that both the "significant" and the
"irrelevant" are dynamic concepts that continuously change position.
Because machines have only automatic, adaptive responses, and thus
have built-in the qualitative aspects, or "significant aspects,"
"creativity" is impossible.

Education (formal and/or informal) is the phenomenon which
initiates a control activity, triggered by the element of relation,
association or construction that appears, for example, when an artist
produces an image unlike the one achieved by a camera. It also
appears in all scientific discovery, as a change from the accepted
previous concept. In other words, education centers on the "art"
created image and its involvement in control system activity.

Adapting behavior depends on education and not training alone.
Training involves learning some specified pattern of behavior, be it
prestidigitation or tightrope walking, while education is new concept
formation. The result of education is creativity, while the result
of training is performance involving skill.

While one can decide which behavior one wishes to enhance, it is
well to realize that the trend is fairly clear in the area of consumer
behavior, or in the field of learning (such as the acquisition of skills
for example). While conceivably these behaviors are unique, it is
certainly not likely. They have been generalized to social (Buckley,
1968), and political (Deutsch, 1974), as well as ethical (Steg, 1978),
psychological (Steg, 1973; Steg & D'Annunzio, 1978), and economic
(Steg, 1973, 1966, 1964, 1963; Steg & Schulman, 1978) behavior.

If adapting behavior is aimed for, then the following are critical: (1) ways of handling variety[5] and (2) access to information, or, selectivity of information (Ashby, p. 252).

Beyond deviation-counteracting feedback or negative feedback, there is also the possibility of a deviation-amplifying component, or positive feedback (Steg et al., 1976; Steg et al., 1978).

We have, thus, a model of thinking which contains quality as an essential element and operates pragmatically as a closed self-organizing loop. It accounts in a new way for teleological processes like problem-solving, "planning," foresight, and "mechanistic" behavior. It allows for an infinite variety of awareness-cognition-response feedback systems.

FEEDBACK-CONTROL

The principle of feedback-control was recognized by training psychologists more than 25 years ago. However, its introduction as a formal behavioral concept dates back to 1948, when Wiener published his book "Cybernetics." His term Cybernetics called attention to the study of human control mechanism and the principle of feedback control.

Feedback control visualizes an elementary system of control by which the sensing elements of an organism can obtain information and feed it back internally for guidance of its operative motor nerve centers. Such feedback was a commonplace of the physiologist long before the engineer found common ground with him in "cybernetics." This principle of steermanship by feedback has undoubtedly played a very important evolutionary role in animal life possibly even before life appeared.

Behavioral scientists have indicated a rather widespread acceptance of the principle of feedback. However, feedback and knowledge of results are being used synonymously, and knowledge of results is thought to function as reward as well as information. In the "Psychological Abstracts," feedback is indexed as "See also knowledge of results, Reinforcement." One can thus see why many theorists took the term feedback to mean reinforcement.

In the latter analogy the feedback signal is interpreted as having reinforcing properties. The smaller the magnitude of the error, the greater the reinforcement value of the signal. It is understood then that the response that minimizes error is presumably strengthened or learned.

It has been observed experimentally that providing knowledge of results, rather than reducing or withholding knowledge, does lead

to more effective learning. It is also true that immediate knowledge
is more effective than delayed knowledge. However, this does not
automatically enhance efficiency of performance and learning. Yet,
it is generally assumed that learning can be enhanced if it is followed
by reinforcement.

In other words, dynamic sensory feedback provides an intrinsic
means of regulating motion in relation to the environment while
knowledge of results given after a response is a static after-effect
which may give information about accuracy, but does not give dynamic
regulating stimuli. Dynamic feedback indication of "error" would
thus be expected to be more effective in performance and learning
than static knowledge of results.

Furthermore, the efficacy of reinforcement assumes an active need
or drive state while feedback theory assumes that the organism is built
as an action system and thus energizes itself. Hence, body needs are
satisfied by behavior that is structured primarily according to perceptual organizational mechanisms and require programs that communicate. (Bruner, 1963, 1970; Bruner & Kalnins, in press; Dewey &
Bentley, 1949).

Systematic transformation of sensory feedback patterns are affected by the use of tools, be they symbols, socio-psychological,
economic, or other instruments. Opposed to this, reinforcement theory
describes learning as due to the effects of reinforcement that bear
no systematic relation to the different kinds of behavior learned.

We can now judge why reinforcement of a child turning his head
to the right to be reinforced by a sucrose solution sucked from a
bottle takes hundreds of tries, with a 30% rate of failure, whereas
Bruner's baby with the $20,000 pacifier needs only a few tries (taking
about five seconds) before he learns to focus upon a picture of his
mother when he is not even hungry. The bottle experiment is a stimulus-
response model, while the pacifier experiment is a true cybernetic
feedback model (Bruner, 1963, 1970; Bruner & Kalnins, in press;
Steg, 1973).

TRANSFORMATION OF CONTROL

A theory of behavior organizations should enable us to conceptualize an orderly progression from relatively simple overt response patterns seen in very young children to the complicated skills,
symbolic responses, and other abstract thinking that an individual
can exhibit. These human processes can be analyzed in terms of
systematic transformations of sensory-feedback patterns. Implicitly
this denies the general validity of association and reinforcement
models as total explanatory models.

What appears to be different types of thinking may actually be considered as differences in patterns of feedback control. There are no distinctive categories in learning except in a general descriptive sense (Smith & Smith, 1966).

  (1) Verbal learning and instrumental learning differ because the systematic transformations of closed-loop regulation of behavior are different in these two areas.
  (2) Instrumental learning and unaided psychomotor learning differ since the use of tools and machines involves spatial, temporal and kinetic transformations of feedback. This in turn changes the pattern of control.
  (3) Psychomotor learning incorporates the feedback mechanisms of manipulative movements.
  (4) Orientation learning involves integration of the larger transport and postural movements of the body into a more general pattern of control.

Classical conditioning differs from orientation learning because the subjects are restrained and deprived of much of the varied sensory feedback used in normal adaptive responses. Feedback theory can account for a variety of behavior (from relatively simply overt responses to complex overt and symbolic skills). Thus, cybernetic research in learning may well provide a framework for understanding and studying a variety of learning patterns (Smith & Smith, 1966).

COMMUNICATION AND SOCIAL DEVELOPMENT

In communication there are at least two different systems that can be involved. There can be communication with a person or communication without a person, or rather, communication by means of an intermediary, an object. It need hardly be emphasized that communication through objects is different from communication with a person.

Until recently, education and training have been dependent on relations between people. Usually a child learns by being in communication with another person, whether child, or adult.

In the case of communication through objects, there is a direct relationship between the individual and the object. Such a system is different from the one in which there is direct contact between people. As a result, the field of teaching systems is just that much enlarged, although interrelations between people and objects are all subject to the person to person relations.

All teaching is about (1) science (object-to-object relation), (2) applied science (person-to-object relation), and (3) humanities (person-to-person relation). The person-to-person relation is common to all teaching, be it between pupil and teacher or parent and child.

However, in technology teaching-learning (pupil and object) there is
now a different system involved.

In case one immediately worries about the competition this may
present to the other system, consider that an airplane does not interfere with walking. Furthermore, we suggest that SCILS (Self-Controlled
Interactive Learning System) should be used at an early age when
systems of communication are being developed.

The people-object relation is as essential as the people-to-
people relation. However, people-people relations work best when
people share similar experiences. People-people contact is basically
inhibited by different educational backgrounds, and by the fact that
people have not had similar past experiences. However, if both
teachers and students had people-object relationships, and shared
some experiences, then education, which is a people-people relation,
would become easier to achieve.

SOCIAL AND SELF-CONTROLLED ENVIRONMENT

The social environment is a matter of give and take, but relations between people and objects are not. It is argued that a child
who has not yet established a people-people relation (an autistic child
for instance) runs the risk of establishing only a people-object relation and may remain satisfied with that. But it may well be that it
is the other way around, in which a person may be involved in a people-
object system--the non-give-and-take system. A person involved in a
system relation with objects has learned that there is a certain af-
finity possible with the outside world which is the relation between
people and objects. The next possible step may then be when one of the
objects in the outside world is in fact a person. It is thus possible
that a relation which does not have a give and take may soon change
into one that does. Experimental evidence at Drexel University's Early
Childhood Center, in working with mentally and physically handicapped
children, who have been mainstreamed seems to support this (Steg &
D'Annunzio, 1978; Steg, et al., 1978).

EMPIRICAL SUBSTANTIATION IN EDUCATION

The premises of the SCILS program are that learning involves
both the acquisition of skills (training) and the formation of new
concepts (education) and that the proper use of instructional technology
is to enable the child to acquire skills which can be utilized in new
concept formation. The teacher's role then shifts from concentration
on training to involvement in education. However, if instructional
technology is to be effective it should incorporate responsiveness to
the student, control by the student, and instantaneous feedback to the
student which allows for self-correction.

SCILS, a technologically based communication or cybernetic learning environment drawn from this theory, demonstrates continued incremental long-term gains in reading from early intervention (ages 3-6). One can reach independent reading level (upper 3rd grade) with a minimal investment of time of 60 to 180 hours.

CONCLUSION

We have found a pattern of "Adapting" behavior where the environment is changed to suit the requirements of the child, as opposed to the child changing to suit the requirements of the environment. This is a true communication or cybernetic activity. Exhibited adapting behavior is evidenced in a communication or cybernetic situation wherein the individual takes choices, relates to information selectively, and refuses to be "brainwashed" or influenced in choosing what he desires. We are not indoctrinating, propagandizing, conditioning or even suggesting.

In summary the term C^3 (Communication, Command and Control) or more academically "Cybernetics" is well known and comfortable in the simple world of high technology, military strategy and weapons systems. Having achieved some insight into behavior in the much more complex world of social system we may be ready to attempt some modest contributions in the social/behavioral sciences, particularly in education.

FOOTNOTES

1. Developed by Richard Kobler from a concept developed by O.K. Moore and Ruth Moore.
2. Hardware and Oralographic Courseware from the Prentice-Hall Developmental Learning Systems.
3. The modest empiricism in human transaction herein exemplified is developed from a general theory of adapting behavior (Steg, 1973; Steg & D'Annunzio, 1978; Steg, et al., 1978).
4. The term "error input" is an engineering term commonly accepted to mean a disturbance.
5. In large social systems, the difficulty is the variety in the disturbances that is regulated against, particularly since there is a limit to the amount of regulation and control that can be achieved. This is contrary to what is usually thought of as size being the critical feature. (Ashby, P., p. 244)

BIBLIOGRAPHY

Ashby, W.R. *An introduction to cybernetics*. London: Methuen & Company, Ltd., 1964.

Bergstrom, T.C. & Goodman, R.P. Private demands for public goods. *American Economic Review,* 1973, *3, 280-296.*

Bruner, J.S. Up from helplessness. In J.P. DeCecco (Ed.), *Readings in educational psychology.* Del Mar, CA: CMR Books, 1970.

Bruner, J.S. *Studies in cognitive growth: Infancy.* (Volume III, Heinz Werner Lecture Series). Worcester, MA: Clark University Press with Barre Publishers, 1963.

Bruner, J.S. & Kalnins, I.V. The coordination of visual observation and instrumental behavior in early infancy. *Perception,* in press.

Buckley, W. (Ed.) *Modern systems research for the behavioral scientist.* Chicago: Aldine Publishing Company, 1968.

Chall, Jeanne. Learning to read: The great debate. New York: McGraw Hill Company, 1967.

Deutsch, K.W. *Politics and government: How people decide their fate.* Boston: Houghton Mifflin Company, 1968.

Deutsch, Martin. The disadvantaged child and the learning process. A. Harry Passour (Ed.), *Education in depressed areas.* New York: Teachers College, Columbia University, 1963.

Dewey, J. *Art as experience.* New York: Minton Balch, 1934.

Dewey, J. & Bentley, A.F. *Knowing and the known.* Boston: The Beacon Press, 1949.

Scriven, M. Teaching ourselves by learning machines. *Journal of Philosophy,* 1970, *67, 898-908.*

Smith, K.U. & Smith, M.F. *Cybernetic principles of learning and educational design.* New York: Holt, Rinehart and Winston, Inc., 1966.

Steg, D.R. Some system concepts in the human system and a review of some recent experiments in infant behavior. Proceeding, VIIIth International Congress of Cybernetics, Place Andre Ryckmans, Namur, Belgium, 1973.

_____. Programmed teaching and learning. In F.T. Villemain (Ed.), *Proceedings of philosophy of education society.* Edwardsville, IL: Southern Illinois University, 1973.

_____. System rules and ethics. In F.T. Villemain (Ed.), *Proceedings of philosophy of education society.* Edwardsville, IL: Southern Illinois University, 1963.

Steg, D.R., D'Annunzio, A., Fox, C. & Gootman, M. Two case-studies in cognitive development. A nine year report. Council for Exceptional Children, 56th International Convention, May 4, 1978.

Steg, D.R., D'Annunzio, A. & Fox, C. Deviation-amplifying processes and individual human growth and behavior. In J. Rose (Ed.), *Advances in cybernetics and systems. Vol. III.* New York: Gordon Breach, 1976.

Steg, D.R. & D'Annunzio, A. Kindergarten children and SCILS: A comparative assessment of progress, 1976-1977. Paper presented at Eastern Educational Research Association, Williamsburg, VA, March 11, 1978.

Steg, D.R., Fox, C., Mattleman, M., Kean, M., Schulman, R. & D'Annunzio, A. Early intervention through technology found: Continued incremental long term gains in reading through SCILS (Self Controlled Interactive Learning Systems). Paper presented at AERA Toronto, Canada, March 30, 1978.

Steg, D.R., Mattleman, M. & Hammil, D. *Effects of individual programmed instruction on initial reading skills and language behavior in early childhood*. Newark, DE: International Reading Association, 1969.

Steg, D.R. & Schulman, R. Human transaction and adapting behavior. In K. Krippendorf (Ed.), *Communication and control in society*. New York: Gordon Breach, 1978.

Steg, D.R. & Schulman, R. An interdisciplinary theory of adapting behavior. Office of Naval Research Technical Report, NR 151-1356X, September, 1974.

Steg, D.R. & Schulman, R. A general theory of adapting behavior. *VIIIth International Congress on Cybernetics*. Namur: Association Internationale de Cybernetique, 1973.

Weikart, W. *Bulletin of the High/Scope Foundation*, Fall, 1977, *4*, 4-5.

SUGGESTIONS FOR IMPROVING KINDERGARTEN EDUCATION

IN THE ARABIC SECTOR

Anahet Avakian

Ministry of Education and Culture
Israel

In the past few years, parents have begun to recognize the values and concepts that a child acquires in the kindergarten. I have become aware of this development through my visits to kindergartens and through talks with teachers, headmasters, and others on the subject.

Nevertheless, there is still much to be done in the field of parent education. In order to tackle these tasks, let me present a brief survey of the problems:

1. As you all know, children up to three years old get their educational values and acquire concepts mainly from their homes. Most of these families are uneducated, and have no idea of helping their children by using teaching (educational) instruments. They may even think that this is a waste of money. They have no idea of the importance of these educational instruments.

2. Besides the influence of the home there is the influence of the street. To my disappointment, the street often has a negative effect which must be tackled in the kindergarten.

3. Children are asked to enter the kindergarten at the age of five. Most of them have not attended any educational institute before this time. The teaching in the kindergartens is mainly collective teaching with individual treatment for specific children.

In order to overcome these problems the following suggestions are made:

a) Open classes for children before the age of five--i.e., pre-kindergarten. It should be mentioned here that some pre-kindergartens

have been opened in the last few years in certain places in the Arabic
sector but attendance is not compulsory and depends on the parents'
initiative.

b) Prepare good kindergarten teachers and train them to use different teaching materials such as television, games, children's stories
and so on. Provide assistance to teachers so they will be trained adequately because they play a serious part in the educational process.
In-service training courses need to be widely available for kindergarten
teachers and their assistants.

c) Plan a program for underdeveloped children who come from big,
poor families.

d) Train parents to educate their children adequately through
right conversation, plays, tasks and correct parental contact with
them. Here I suggest introducing an educational teaching forum in
order to guide parents in the treatment of their children.

e) Adapt the children's library books that are used in Hebrew
kindergartens and others that are used in the Arab countries. In order
to choose suitable books (stories), I suggest that a committee of
teachers, inspectors, and children's book writers be established. Some
of the kindergarten teachers in the Arab sector do not know Hebrew well;
they have been teaching since the time of the mandate.

f) Provide medical treatment for kindergarten children, either
by a doctor or a specialized nurse.

g) Because the headmaster of a school is responsible for the
kindergartens in his school I suggest that headmasters have to have
suitable educational ideas about teaching and learning in the kindergartens in order to help their work as helpers and facilitators of the
kindergarten teachers.

h) At present, inspection in the kindergartens for Druzes and
Bedouins is in the hands of inspectors who do not know Arabic which
is the language of both teacher and children. A kindergarten inspector should know the language medium used in the kindergarten.

i) It would be valuable to prepare a television program for Arab
children that takes into account their environment, social and educational requirements. Also, it is advisable to prepare television programs to guide the parents in treating their children.

j) Local councils in the Arab villages are responsible for kindergarten buildings; most of them need guidance and help in order to
build suitable kindergartens.

k)   A number of kindergarten teachers are needed to replace those who leave their kindergartens for special holidays or on other occasions.

COGNITIVE PERFORMANCE OF KINDERGARTEN CHILDREN

WHEN TESTED BY PARENTS AND STRANGERS

Pnina S. Klein

Bar-Ilan University
Israel

Tests of readiness have proliferated over the last two decades as professionals have developed an awareness of what basic abilities are necessary for academic success in the early school years (i.e., Bloom, 1963; Bryant, 1964; Butler, Gotts, Quisenberry & Thompson, 1971; Hammill & Bartel, 1975; Kirk, 1971; Wallace & Larsen, 1978). Most testing situations involve an interaction between the tester and the testee. Test administration procedures have been standardized in order to minimize the possible effects of different testers. However, variations in performance of young children in response to one tester as compared to another are to be expected, especially when the "other tester" is the child's own parent. Since the practice of parent testing is relatively new, the question of differences in children's performance in response to their parents as compared to strangers has not yet been explored.

It has become more apparent in recent years that for optimal chances of academic success active parent participation is a necessity. The status of direct parental involvement in pre-school education programs has changed dramatically since the 1960s (Evans, 1975). Tijossen (1978) summarizes the conference on Intervention Strategies for High Risk Infants by stating that parents as full partners in every stage of the educational process of their children are the main factor contributing to the success of an intervention program. Shearer and Shearer (1978) summarize their model for early childhood intervention, The Portage Program, with a similar conclusion, i.e., that one of the major elements contributing to the successful outcome of the program is the enhancement of the belief that parents are the child's first teachers and, potentially, his best teachers. Baker and Heifetz (1978), working on the Read Project, as well as Denhoff and Hyman (1978), working on several parent pro-

grams for developmental management, stress the central role of
direct parental involvement in its various forms. Although the need
for direct parental involvement in early education programs has been
well recognized, parental involvement in testing situations has remained unexplored. If one considers the purpose of testing to be a
prediction of academic success in school, then theoretically, testing
by strangers may have more predictive validity than parent testing,
since the child will be required to interact with strangers in the
early days of schooling. If one considers the objective of testing
to be the evaluation of the child's best performance or profile of
abilities for the purpose of matching the child to a suitable educational program, then children's performance should be evaluated under
what may be the most favorable conditions for them; for these purposes
parent testing could be considered a natural choice. Differences in
performance of children under both testing conditions may suggest some
possible avenues for planning optimal learning environments and
educational programs.

The objective of the current study was to examine the effects
of the tester, i.e., parent versus stranger, on the performance of
preschool children on a battery of cognitive tests. Specifically,
the basic questions considered were: (1) Does a child's performance
on a series of cognitive tests vary with variations in tester? and
(2) Is the effect of parent-versus stranger-testing related to the
child's age, sex and socioeconomic status?

METHOD

Subjects

Subjects were 589 kindergarten children from 20 kindergarten
classes in various towns around Tel-Aviv. Their ages ranged between
4.6 and 6.2 years with a mean age of 5.5 years. The participating
kindergartens included children of Low SES (LSES) and of Middle SES
(MSES) as determined by area of residence, parental education and
ethnic origin. Teachers of the participating children volunteered
to participate in the study.

Procedure

All 20 participating kindergartens were randomly divided into
two groups; one group was designated for parental administration of
the tests, the other for stranger administration. No significant
differences were found between the two groups in age, sex-ratio and
level of SES.

In four participating kindergarten classes, N = 80, testing
was carried out twice, i.e., by both parents and strangers. Two of

these classes were of LSES; the others were of MSES.

Stranger administration: Eight female testers, previously
unknown to the children, administered the tests. Each child was
tested individually in the kindergarten in one testing session.

Parental administration: Parents were informed by letter from
the kindergarten teacher that they were invited to participate in
a project in which they would be taught how to test their own child's
learning abilities. Parental participation approached 100%. Parents
were invited to school in groups of four to six. An introductory
session lasting approximately 30 minutes preceded the testing. During this session, parents were presented with a test booklet and
the instructions were read and explained to them. The main objective
of the introductory session was to clarify to the parents the differences between their usual role as parents and teachers and their
new role as testers (e.g., "refraining from helping" through both
verbal and nonverbal communication). The objective of the test as
an indicator of a profile of learning abilities was suggested to the
parents. Following the introductory session each parent-child pair
was seated separately from other pairs and testing began. Parent-
child interactions were observed by either the school psychologist,
guidance counselor or teachers, who also responded to parents' questions if assistance was requested. Following the testing, the parents were instructed on how to score the test and how to construct
the profile of their child's abilities.

For those subjects who were tested by both strangers and parents, parental administration was observed and recorded by trained
observers; one observer was assigned to two parent-child pairs. An
average of two to three weeks elapsed between one type of testing
and the other. The order of testing, that is, stranger versus parent, was counterbalanced.

Although not directly related to the research objective discussed here, test results were discussed with the parents in two
sessions: one, clarifying the relationship between the test activities and school performance; the other, more specifically geared
towards choices of games and activities which could help a child
develop each of the abilities measured by the test.

Materials

Children's cognitive profiles were assessed by the APART
(Adelphi Parent-Administered Readiness Test, Klein, 1979). This
measure was especially constructed for administration by nonpro-
fessionals and requires little preadministration preparation. The
APART includes ten tests, four of which are directly related to
actual performance on tool subjects taught in school, i.e., Letter

form recognition, Comprehension, Writing ability and Number concept.
These tests were included since the closer the measures are to the
abilities one attempts to predict, the closer prediction gets to
identification and thus the less risk there is in prediction. Four
other tests, i.e., Visual perception, Visual memory, Concept formation and Auditory sequential memory were included, based on theory
and research suggesting their predictive validity for school achievement. In addition, APART includes a measure of ideational fluency
as an indicator of divergent thinking expressed through words and
drawings, and a test measuring understanding of facial expressions
of emotions which taps nonverbal learning related to social sensitivity.

The tests are described below in the order in which they are
administered.:

Concept Formation: The child is required to examine four pictures of objects and decide on a common characteristic shared
by three of the pictures, excluding the fourth one.

Letter Form Recognition: The child is shown one letter of the
alphabet and asked to choose among four choices and underline
a form just like the model presented.

Writing Ability: The child is asked to copy geometric and letter
forms of models printed on the test page into predesignated
spaces.

Number Concept: The child is asked to respond to questions involving decisions of "more," "less," "as many as" and relations
between digits and number of objects they represent.

Comprehension and Memory: Two brief, four-sentence stories
are read to the child followed by four comprehension questions
for each story.

Visual Memory: An achromatic detailed line drawing of children
playing is presented to the child. He is asked to study the
picture so he can tell later, when the picture is removed, all
the things he has seen.

Visual Perception: In order to distinguish between verbal fluency and memory, the same picture as in Visual Memory is presented again. This time, the child is asked to look at the
picture and say what he sees.

Immediate Sequential Memory: Series of digits, gradually increasing in length, are read to the child, one series at a
time, and the child is asked to repeat them immediately following presentation. The rate of digit presentation is two per

second, as in the Illinois Test of Psycholinguistic Abilities.

Recognition of Facial Expressions of Emotion: The child is asked to associate between a verbal description of situations arousing emotions read to him, and the schematic facial expression most commonly expressing the emotions appropriate for the specific situation described.

Creativity/Performance: The child is asked to draw as many things as he can that look like circles or have circles in them.

Creativity/Verbal: The child is asked to tell (not draw) as many things as he can that look like squares or have squares in them.

It should be noted that APART (excluding the tests of Creativity and Recognition of Facial Expressions) correlated with the Metropolitan Readiness Test (N = 383), r = .61, p < .001.

FINDINGS

For each of the APART measures an analysis of variance for tester (parent vs. stranger) by age (4.6 to 5.0, 5.0 to 5.6, and 5.6 to 6.0) and sex was carried out. A significant main effect for tester was found for the following tests: Concept Formation, Letter Form Discrimination, Writing Ability, Visual Memory and Comprehension and Memory (Table 1). On almost all the tests children scored higher when tested by their parents, as compared to strangers.

Are there any differences between younger and older subjects in response to parents as compared to stranger testing? A main effect for age was found for the following tests: Letter Form Discrimination, Writing Ability, Number Concept, and Visual Memory, indicating that on these tests older subjects perform better than the younger ones, regardless of tester (Table 1). A two-way interaction Tester by Age was found for Writing Ability (F = 4.06, df = 2, 504, p < .05). The younger subjects, i.e., 4.6-to 5.0-year-olds scored higher when tested by strangers as compared to parents, whereas a reversed trend was observed for the older subjects, i.e., the 5.6- to 6.0-year-olds (Fig. 1).

Are there differences between boys' and girls' performance in response to parents' as compared to strangers' testing? Although no significant differences were found between the scores of boys and girls on all tests (Table 1), a significant interaction, Tester by Sex, was found for Creativity/Verbal (F = 5.11, df = 1, 580, p < .05). Girls tested by parents scored highest of all groups; for boys there was no difference in score, when tested by parents

Table 1.   Values of F from ANOVA for tester by age and sex (N = 589)

	Tester	Age	Sex
Concept formation	30.85*	0.66	0.03
Letter form discrimination	18.84*	4.51*	1.37
Writing ability	11.86*	3.82*	2.43
Number concept	2.02	9.19*	0.12
Comprehension and memory	16.06*	2.28	0.14
Immediate sequential memory	0.41	0.28	1.43
Recognition of facial expression of emotions	2.72	1.67	0.05
Creativity/performance	0.57	0.56	0.06
Creativity/verbal	2.05	0.20	3.24
Visual memory	5.35*	4.11*	0.03
Visual perception	3.23	2.56	0.16

*p < .05

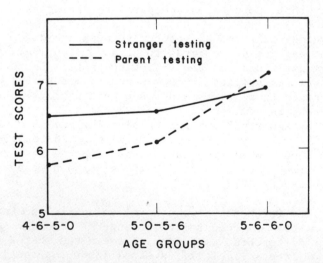

Figure 1.   Mean scores of 4.6 to 5.0, 5.0 to 5.6, and 5.6 to 6.0-year-old children on the Writing Ability Test.

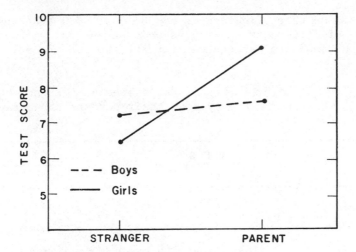

Figure 2.   Mean scores of boys and girls on the Creativity/Verbal
Test when tested by strangers and parents.

as compared to strangers (Fig. 2).   While no differences were found
between boys and girls with regard to the number of responses on
Creativity/Performance, a main effect for sex was found for this test
when scored for the level of elaboration in the drawings.   The level
of elaboration was evaluated by an independent judge and ranked on
a four-point scale.   The girls were found to score higher than the
boys with regard to the level of creative elaboration on the Creativ-
ity/Performance Test ($F = 7.67$, $df = 1$, 580, $p < .01$).

For subjects tested by both parents and strangers, t tests for
dependent samples were carried out to make a comparison between the
test score of each child when tested by his parent as compared to
his score when tested by a stranger.   A separate analysis was carried
out for each SES group.

Are there any differences between MSES and LSES subjects in
response to parent vs. stranger testing?   For the MSES group differences between parent vs. stranger evaluation were found only in
Comprehension and Memory ($t = 2.2$, $df = 39$, $p < .05$), and in Creativ-
ity/Verbal ($t = 2.53$, $df = 39$, $p < .05$), whereas for the LSES group
differences between parent vs. stranger testing were found for the
following tests: Concept Formation ($t = 7.78$, $df = 39$, $p < .01$);
Letter Form Discrimination ($t = 4.72$, $df = 39$, $p < .01$); Writing
Ability ($t = 7.78$, $df = 39$, $p < .05$); Number Concept ($t = 2.38$, $df =
39$, $p < .01$); Visual Memory ($t = 2.53$, $df = 39$, $p < .05$); Compre-
hension and Memory ($t = 2.29$, $df = 39$, $p < .01$); Immediate Sequential Memory ($t = 4.30$, $df = 39$, $p < .01$).

Based on these findings it may be concluded that the basic question of differences in scores on a parent vs. stranger testing should be considered separately for the two SES groups.

Table 2. Mean and S.D. for all HBT scores of LSES and MSES children who were tested by both their parents and strangers (N = 80)

Test	LSES		MSES	
	Parent	Stranger	Parent	Stranger
Concept formation	7.35 (1.06)	5.59 (1.59)[*]	7.36 (1.31)	7.25 (1.27)
Letter form discrimination	8.08 (2.38)	6.22 (1.85)[*]	8.82 (1.44)	8.71 (1.96)
Writing ability	6.45 (1.71)	5.59 (1.84)[*]	7.39 (0.92)	7.14 (1.24)
Number concept	6.36 (1.62)	5.47 (1.84)[*]	7.33 (1.47	6.78 (1.63)
Comprehension and memory	6.94 (1.12)	6.14 (1.42)[*]	7.14 (1.01)	6.64 (1.37)[*]
Immediate sequential memory	5.69 (1.57)	4.66 (1.03)[*]	6.25 (1.46)	6.40 (1.45)
Recognition of facial expression of emotions	4.50 (1.56)	4.58 (1.46)	5.30 (1.26)	5.12 (1.42)
Creativity/performance	6.24 (3.83)	7.17 (3.42)	7.78 (4.26)	6.04 (4.60)
Creativity/verbal	5.63 (2.86)	5.21 (3.24)	9.00 (4.48)	6.12 (4.45)[*]
Visual memory	9.47 (3.32)	8.08 (2.45)[*]	10.39 (3.62)	10.86 (3.79)
Visual perception	12.28 (4.36)	12.28 (3.02)	14.74 (4.74)	13.41 (4.59)

[*] $p < .05$

The findings support the assumption that test situational variables, such as the person who tests the child, have significant effects on test results, especially for LSES children.

As can be seen in Table 2, parent vs. stranger testing has a different effect for LSES, as compared to MSES, children. There are seven tests for which significant differences between parent and stranger testing were found for the LSES group, as compared with only two such tests for the MSES. Thus, it can generally be stated that parental testing in the LSES group has a greater effect on children's scores than it does in the MSES group. The seven tests affected in the LSES group included all three tests of memory (Comprehension and Memory, Immediate Sequential Memory, and Visual

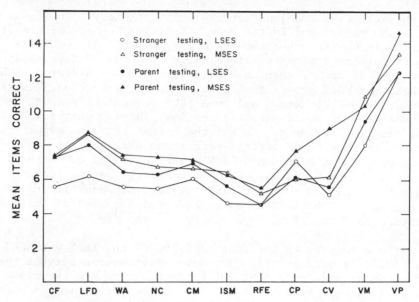

Figure 3.   Means of all test scores of Low and Middle SES children
            when tested by strangers and parents.
            Note: CF – Concept Formation; LFR – Letter Form Recog-
            nition; WA – Writing Ability; NC – Number Concept; CM –
            Comprehension and Memory; ISM – Immediate Sequential
            Memory; RFE – Recognition of Facial Expressions of Emo-
            tions; CP – Creativity/Performance; CV – Creativity/
            Verbal; VM – Visual Memory; VP – Visual Perception.

Memory), two tests of concept formation (Concept Formation and
Number Concept), as well as a test of visual-motor coordination
(Writing Ability) and a test of visual attention, form discrimination and understanding of location in space. Among the tests that
were not affected by parental administration in the LSES group were
the test of Visual Perception requiring visual perception, verbal
labeling and verbal fluency, as well as both measures of creativity,
tapping divergent thinking and ideational fluency. Although not
significantly so, LSES children actually scored higher on Creativ-
ity/Performance when tested by strangers as compared with parents
(Fig. 3). The wide spectrum of functions affected by parental
evaluation in the LSES group may suggest that parent testing could
have affected a basic ability or abilities that, in turn, affected
the specific tasks tested.

On what basic abilities could parental testing have had an
effect? As can be seen in Figure 3, the greatest differences in
test scores between the LSES and MSES children, when tested by
strangers, were in Letter Form Discrimination, Visual Memory,

Concept Formation and Immediate Sequential Memory. The tests of
Concept Formation and Letter Form Discrimination are of a multiple
choice nature; the other two are memory tests. All of these tests
require careful immediate attention and control of impulsivity in
response. As can be seen in Figure 3, the major differences between
the LSES and MSES groups in Letter Form Discrimination, Visual
Memory, Concept Formation and Immediate Sequential Memory, have almost disappeared under parental testing, leaving only slight insignificant differences. On all the latter tests no significant
differences were found between parent and stranger testing in the
MSES group, and the LSES and MSES groups differed on these tests
under the stranger testing, but not under the parent testing. Thus,
it may be concluded that the parental testing selectively improved
the scores of LSES children on tasks requiring careful immediate
attention and control of impulsivity in response.

If one focuses on the test profiles of the LSES and MSES groups
when tested by parents (Fig. 3), major differences between these
groups can be seen on the Visual Perception and the two creativity
tests. It should be noted that these differences emerged under the
parent testing condition only. The creativity tests, as well as
the Visual Perception test, require verbal fluency and ideational
fluency. Whereas parents in the LSES group affected their children's scores mainly on tasks requiring careful examination of the
test stimuli and immediate retention, parents of the MSES were
found to encourage their children's performance on tasks requiring
a free flow of ideas and words. Furthermore, although not statistically significant, LSES children scored lower on Creativity/Per-
formance when tested by their parents as compared to testing by a
stranger (Table 2). The tendency of the LSES parents to encourage
their child's careful performance on the test may lead to improved
performance on tasks requiring careful attention at the expense of
those calling for more free divergent thinking or verbal fluency.

No overall differences in mean testing time were found between
the groups (Parent vs. Stranger, and LSES vs. MSES). However, it
should be noted that the MSES parents allowed their children more
time on the creativity tests as compared to the LSES parents.
Based on observations of Parent-Child pairs in the testing situation,
it is suggested that the differences in parental effects on test
scores could be related to differences in the style of mother-child
interactions of LSES and MSES groups. The participating observers
concluded independently that most MSES mothers coached their children mainly on tasks allowing for more responses, using mainly positive reinforcement, whereas LSES mothers most commonly used remarks
such as "you are not paying attention," and "slow down."

In summary, preschool children were found to perform better
under the condition of parental testing as compared to stranger
testing. This was especially significant for the LSES children.

Girls, as compared to boys, performed for parents better than for strangers on a task requiring verbal and ideational fluency, i.e., Creativity/Verbal. The 4.6- to 5.0-year-old subjects performed on a visual-motor coordination test of copying, i.e., writing ability, better for strangers than for parents, whereas the older subjects actually showed a reversed trend, i.e., they performed better for parents.

Based on the findings, it may be concluded that differences exist between LSES and MSES groups with regard to the effects of immediate mother-child interactions on cognitive performance. The LSES parental testing led to higher scores on tasks requiring careful examination of stimuli and choice-making, while the MSES parental testing affected mainly creative flow of ideas and words.

As for the question of school-readiness testing, it may be concluded that test-situational variables, such as tester, do have a significant effect on test results, especially for LSES children, a point which puts in question the validity of stranger testing of the "potential" of these children. Further research is needed to explore the immediate effects of different messages in interpersonal relations on the cognitive performance of young children, especially in their interactions with their first and most important teachers-- their parents.

REFERENCES

Baker, B.L., & Heifetz, L.J. The Read project: Teaching manuals for parents of retarded children. In T. D. Tijossen (Ed.), *Intervention strategies for high risk infants and young children*. Baltimore, MD: University Park Press, 1978.

Bloom, B. (Ed.). *Taxonomy of educational objectives*. New York: D. McKay, 1963.

Butler, A., Gotts, E.E., Quisenberry, N.L., & Thompson, R.P. *Literature search and development of an evaluation system in early childhood education*. Bloomington, IN: Indiana University, 1971 (ERIC Document 059 780).

Denhoff, E., & Hyman, I. Parent programs for developmental management. In T. D. Tijossen (Ed.), *Intervention strategies for high risk infants and young children*. Baltimore, MD: University Park Press, 1978.

Evans, E. *Contemporary influence in early childhood education*. New York: Holt, Rinehart and Winston, Inc., 1975.

Hammill, D.D., & Bartel, N.R. *Teaching children with learning and behavior problems*. Boston: Allyn & Bacon, Inc., 1975.

Keogh, B.K., & Becker, L.D. Early identification procedures. *Exceptional Children*, 1973, *40*, 9-11.

Kirk, S. From labels to actions. In D. Hammill and N. Bartel (Eds.), *Educational perspectives in learning disabilities*. New York:

        Wiley, 1971.
Klein, P.S. *Adelphi parent administered readiness test (APART).*
        Johnstown, Pennsylvania: Mafex Associates, 1981.
Shearer, D.E., & Shearer, M.S. The Portage project: A model for
        early childhood intervention. In T. D. Tijossen (Ed.), *Inter-
        vention strategies for high risk infants and young children.*
        Baltimore, MD: University Park Press, 1978.
Tijossen, T.D. *Intervention strategies for high risk infants and
        young children.* Baltimore, MD: University Park Press, 1978.
Wallace, G., & Larsen, S.C. *Educational assessment of learning
        problems: testing for teaching.* Boston: Allyn and Bacon, Inc.,
        1978.

BEYOND EARLY IDENTIFICATION OF CHILDREN'S

ABILITIES AND DISABILITIES

Iain Davidson

Ontario Institute for Studies in Education
Canada

INTRODUCTION

The term "early identification" is typically used to refer to
the identification of children at an early stage in their schooling,
usually because these children present problems for the school system. This early discernment of problems is intended primarily to
reduce, by early remediation, the number of children who might
later require "special educational help." This traditional view
of early identification has a connotation of the "different," the
"special" and the clinical (psychological or medical) rather than
of general education.

My discussion of early identification, both as notion and
practice, is based on the general understanding that I have developed of societal provision, including education, for young
children, and especially of the type of teaching appropriate for
them. Within this framework reference will also be made to the findings of a survey conducted by the author and Dr. Harry Silverman
at the Department of Special Education, the Ontario Institute for
Studies in Education (OISE), Toronto.

THE SITUATION IN ONTARIO

From the mid-1960s onwards, many school boards in Ontario
began work in the early identification of children entering
schools. The Ministry of Education supported a number of research
studies and gave strong encouragement to the development of identification procedures, although typically from a special education

441

viewpoint. In a short study from 1978 to 1979, Dr. Silverman and
I attempted to survey the practice, degree of development, and to
some extent, the attitudes of school boards towards the work of
early identification. An initial questionnaire survey of virtually
all elementary school boards in Ontario provided a general overview.
A second, representative sample was chosen consisting of 21 boards;
to these were added six boards with extensive experience in early
identification work. A new, more detailed, questionnaire was sent
to these 27 boards and personnel from them were interviewed in
order to establish school board practice in more detail. The attitude of the province was ascertained through these questionnaires
and interviews and through a conference organized by OISE and the
Ministry in June 1979, which dealt with all aspects of early identification.

Practices, attitudes and theory in relation to early identification in Ontario show both similarities and dissimilarities to
those in other countries, but these will not be dealt with here.
Comparison between Ontario and other areas, however, has proved
very useful in developing the basic position I now hold, some aspects of which are now presented.

SOME BASIC PERSPECTIVES

The following ideas have been selected as salient; they are
representative rather than comprehensive and I hope that the brevity
with which they are presented does not distort them. They are not
claimed as original nor dramatic, and although relationships between them are occasionally obvious, they of course require much more
detailed exposition in order to establish those relationships. It
is my hope, however, that the presentation of these points will encourage readers to analyze more closely the basic assumptions of
early identification work.

1. In studying early identification, I have become strongly
aware of two facts: (1) that educational practice derives from
values, ideologies, attitudes and beliefs about children, education,
life and society; and (2) that the values and attitudes which dic-
tate practice need to be made explicit before and while practice
is carried out. Thus, before one develops early identification
procedures (or when one examines such work in practice) it is necessary to be clear about one's assumptions and to list them explicitly.
For instance, in the Ontario survey, school boards often found it
difficult to list the goals or the focus of their programs. Additionally, boards often shared goals but not procedures with other
boards and vice versa. Perhaps the greatest danger is that early
identification procedures may contain implicit goals and directions which are not noticed by those conducting such work, but
which are nevertheless directive of that work. This situation leads

to confusion.

   2. The early identification process occurs, and indeed exists,
because of something else, some other function, which pre-exists
and indeed defines it, namely teaching; yet too often the literature
yields the impression that early identification work focuses on
children as entities independent of the educational process. It
is necessary for a teacher to know what she or he is aiming to teach
and what conceptualization of the child she or he holds, before choosing an identification procedure to deal specifically with areas of
curriculum.

   Procedures are commonly established more on the basis of existing techniques (such as tests), or on traditional and familiar
areas of a psychological sort (such as intelligence and perception)
than on the basis of what is educationally important. The reader
is often left with the suspicion that what is being measured is
what is measurable rather than what is worth measuring. It would
seem that educators tend to think within a narrow range of psychological constructs, and to act according to the conventions that
derive from psychology rather than to choose from a variety of
modes of thinking.

   In the Ontario survey, interviews with the 27 selected boards
revealed that board members tended to talk in terms of traditional
categories (language, perception, fine and gross motor skills and
the like) used in the educational assessment of young children.
This tendency was probably caused, in part, by such traditional
constructs being presented to them in the first, written questionnaire. However, even in the free-flowing interview discussions,
it was apparent that these traditional constructs were seen as being of primary importance. The personnel involved typically went
on to discuss how such information about a child was then translated into information which could be used by classroom teachers.
This second stage process was more ad hoc and less formalized than
the ascertainment of a child's level of functioning on, for example, language and perception, although it was considered by
board personnel to be of great importance. It is clear that the
conceptualization of children as learners was a derivative and consequence of a conceptualization of children as perceivers, language
users, fine motor performers and so on. While a case can be made
for this conceptualization as a legitimate psychological perspective; it is too static, not sufficiently dynamic, and depends on
constructs that are too narrow for educational use.

   3. Related to the above point but important enough to be
discussed on its own is an idea which, though again not original,
has become for me the most important single emphasis in my position
on early identification work. In fact, the exposition of this
idea necessarily involves this paper taking a radically different

direction and almost abolishing the term "early identification" or
at least reducing it to a subordinate status. In brief, I propose
that the most useful service that can be performed for young children and their teachers is to carry out an early review of each
batch of school entrants, with the aim of covering all areas of
functioning in school, and providing information of a sort that
will give teachers a "flying start" in programming, teaching and
further enquiring about all their children. In order to give
teachers this start the information provided by such a review must
be educationally relevant, immediately usable (that is, requiring
little translation from the language of other disciplines), and
stated in functional terms. Information must be teaching-oriented
and descriptive of a child's current status. Such information
enables a teacher to pinpoint a child's developmental status in a
given area and thus to know at which stage to begin teaching the
child. Prediction is not an aim of this process; indeed, it is
probably inimical to the emphasis on current functioning for immediate teaching.

Such a developmental review procedure will yield a developmental profile for each child; many of these profiles will, of
course, demonstrate current performance which is either above or
below age expectations, and/or wide differences within a profile
between areas of functioning. Without recourse to any finite
labelling, teachers can readily keep an eye on children with such
profiles, emphasizing in the programming and/or teaching of such
children components they consider may encourage more rapid or complete development. Routine monitoring by the teachers will provide evidence of the degree of success (or otherwise) of such teaching.

The developmental review of children's abilities contains
within it the notion of early identification of children's difficulties while avoiding directive labelling, psychological or
physical segregation, and categorization as "different." Further,
the same framework easily encourages investigating further those
children who cause concern or puzzlement as a result of a general
assessment. Following this, more specialized and detailed investigation can and should be conducted and the results fed back to the
teacher for programming, teaching, monitoring and further assessment. Developmental review can thus be a two-stage process for
any child requiring such investigation. However, it would be a
mistake to think of developmental review as essentially an initial
assessment for all and an initial and second assessment for some.
Instead, developmental review should be conceived of as a process
of ongoing assessment throughout a child's early school experience,
perhaps through his or her first (typically kindergarten) year, with
the teacher continuously checking the developmental progress of
the child. The initial stage of the process should be the most intensive, as at this time the child is unfamiliar to the teacher.

This stage should also involve a concentration of personnel and procedures (interviews, tests, observations and so on), but the information generated from this initial stage must be seen and used as initial, and not predictive or definitive information.

4. A fact that many school board personnel seem reluctant to realize is that the process of early identification--and I would now add developmental review--requires continuous decision-making. Further, the points or stages at which decisions are required are often not understood. First, it needs to be recognized that developmental review or early identification are in fact processes and dimensions of educational provision. In the Ontario survey it often seemed that early identification was perceived as an adjunct or "extra" to the educational system. Secondly, there needs to be acknowledgement or establishment of a body which will conduct the process and have overall responsibility for it. Often this does not happen. Apart from the creation of groups or committees for specific activities such as selection of tests there is little recognition that such a body is required.

Three major groupings of decisions are identitiable; all require to be seen within the same framework (of developmental review or early identification) and to be handled by the same group of personnel. The first grouping is at the level of board policy. The second is concerned with decisions of a procedural sort: who does the initial assessment work, at what times in the school year is it carried out, how are parents to be used or involved, and how is information to be recorded.

Finally, decisions related to choosing specific assessment techniques and materials are necessary. The process of evaluation of monitoring is also of ongoing importance throughout any system of developmental review or early identification. Again, decisions have to be made about how this is to be done, and supervision and application of its results are critical. Relative to this, materials need to be analyzed and critically examined for relevance and psychometric characteristics such as validity.

Typically, boards in the Ontario survey did not have a well-established supervisory body and the level of systematic evaluation was minimal, both in terms of procedures in general and of materials in particular. In fact, it could be argued that these attitudes reflect early identification or developmental review practice in most countries.

Not only did the composition of an organizational group vary in the Ontario survey but it also varies in the literature. Too often, the deficit emphasis of early identification is reflected in the predominant special education orientation of a committee. My preference is for a group composed mainly of early childhood and curriculum department personnel, supplemented by special education and psychology department representatives. Personnel from the latter two areas tend to have more experience in techniques of assessment and use of materials as well as being the appropriate groups to deal with second stage assessment of children showing unusual developmental patterns. However, because the focus of developmental review and early identification is on provision of information and guidance for teachers, the composition of the organizational body should reflect this. Consequently, it is the specialists in early childhood education and curriculum who are typically the best equipped to provide a teaching focus, and to relate or direct procedures to the teachers concerned.

5. A fifth principle of early developmental review and early identification work is that the key role of classroom teachers should be explicitly recognized by intensive in-service preparation and ongoing training in the principles and practice of all aspects of such work. It is ironic to note that while teachers are given the key role in the teaching of children involved in developmental review or early identification procedures and in intervention programs, as one moves back through the stages of this work and away from the classroom, teachers' contributions become less important. In the Ontario survey, which again reflects practice typical in the literature, while teachers did much of the assessment work, they were often under the supervision or aegis of special education or psychological service personnel. Teachers were also less involved in the selection of either assessment instruments or packaged programs for teaching, and at the board decision-making level no more than half of the boards involved the teachers in a committee overviewing the early identification procedures.

Major shifts in perspective are also required regarding the role of both teachers and their employers. Teachers traditionally see themselves as less professional than psychologists, consultants, special educators and the like; they do not generally consider themselves competent to decide what should be assessed in children and how to do it. They see themselves as the recipients of information and guidance but not as having a share in the development of the basic information which guides programming and teaching. Boards tend to see teachers in the same way. Further, specialist work such as special education and psychological assessment continues to wear a cloak of mystery, of "specialness" that it does not deserve. Territoriality, the poverty of pre-service training, and traditional societal attitudes are all involved. Although these themes will not be developed here, they would need to be addressed on an in-service basis, but the training must go far beyond simple and casual use of professional development days or an occasional workshop. There must be systematic training, in stages if needed, with the required levels of competence both established and demonstrated. Outside help may well be required by the boards. Certainly, this process would cost boards money,

time, effort, and a great deal of discussion before decisions could
be made, but the quality of developmental review work depends on
the quality of the teachers involved, and that in turn rests on
solid training. In the Ontario survey teachers were very much emphasized but in-service training was typically informal and casual.
Incidental training through use of consultants, for instance, is
one component but much more is needed. Strong leadership is required
from the boards, superintendents and directors, ministries and departments of education.

6. Developmental review gives schools and school systems an
excellent opportunity to blend the different types of attention
given to children from three sources--school, families and preschool agencies. It would seem that schools are now in a position
to give leadership of a most valuable sort from the moment children
first enter them. After all, children are captives of the school
system for many years and the latter can do much at this point to
determine both the quality of a child's attitude to school, and the
relationship of the school and the family. Therefore, I should
like to see a greatly extended set of arrangements for introducing
new parents to the school system, especially immigrant parents and
those in disadvantaged settings. Interviews, relating to the
school's mode of functioning and to the child's way of behaving, can
be held before children enter the school. Parents can be asked to
observe, using very general checklists, and to discuss their observations at a later date. Assessment results can be conveyed,
and the school's program outlined to parents. Suggestions of how
to support the school's program by activities at home can also be
made. Parent workshops can be arranged to cover all aspects of
the developmental review process within a general framework of
introducing the parents to the school's work. All of this may seem
to involve much more work, but in actuality I think it represents
a rearrangement and improvement of existing workloads rather than
the introduction of radically new types of work.

In terms of developmental review one untapped resource of growing importance in Ontario, of great importance in Israel, and of
varying importance in other countries is day nurseries, nursery
schools and equivalent agencies. The organization, systematic
attention and developmental focus of preschools are really pre-
cursors of the school system and as such it is wasteful not to take
note of what children have done during their time in the preschool.
Interviews could be arranged with personnel of these agencies,
mutual visits, and at least the transfer of documents could be made
well before the child enters the school system.

7. A last point is that developmental review is a process
rather than a set of techniques, not merely something that can be
filtered or injected into an educational system or attached to it
but a dimension of it. Every board or system has to develop the

procedures that suit it ideologically and practically; its developmental review system will be necessarily unique. There is no one
way to conduct developmental review or even early identification,
although many boards in the Ontario survey and many systems in the
literature seem to think within this sort of framework. Furthermore, early development criteria which are established in one's own
system on the basis of those of other systems must be explicit,
continuously reviewed and developed, and not harden into fixed
regulations.

CONCLUSION

The conceptual approach of this paper reflects both educational
first principles and work occurring, albeit in patches, in Ontario,
Israel, the United States, the United Kingdom and Continental
Europe. While recommendations on how to carry out the ideas suggested here can only be made in a local setting in the light of local
conditions the time is ripe for bold demands and strong conceptualizations. The early evaluation of children in school has much to
commend it in principle, but current practice requires it to be re-
conceptualized rather than tinkered with or consolidated in its
details.

THE BAR-ILAN PICTURE TEST: A SEMI-PROJECTIVE TECHNIQUE FOR DIAGNOSING PROBLEMS RELATED TO THE EDUCATIONAL ENVIRONMENT IN ELEMENTARY SCHOOL

Rivka Itskowitz and Helen Strauss

Bar-Ilan University
Israel

The Bar-Ilan Picture Test for Young Children (Itskowitz & Strauss, 1977) is a semi-projective device which depicts realistic and meaningful situations dealing with issues generally encountered in the educational setting of young children. It enables one to pinpoint children's perceptions of their place in society, in their formal educational setting, and in their homes, as well as their perceptions of what constitutes their weaker points and their potentials for coping with life. The test is suitable for children in kindergarten and elementary school, that is, 4- to 10-year-olds, but has been used successfully with children up to 16 years of age.

The test is not intended to probe the deeper layers of personality such as the "Freudian" variables. These are dealt with by existing tests such as Children's Apperception Test (Bellak, 1975), and the Blacky Test (Blum, 1950). On the contrary, the demand characteristics of the pictures are such that they elicit information from the child which is specific to the problem at hand--information which would be more difficult to obtain from the fully projective techniques. Furthermore, this semi-projective technique makes it possible to impart the raw information gleaned from the test to the educational practitioner. Ultimately, it is hoped that the test will be used as a diagnostic tool by a wider range of people engaged in direct work with the child, such as counselors, social workers, and senior teachers who are supervised by psychologists.

Description of the Test

The test consists of nine basic pictures, six of which have
separate versions for boys and girls; thus, there are 15 pictures
in all. Each picture represents a situation from school or from
home. The order of presentation emphasizes the importance of school
as the pictures depicting school situations precede those depicting
home situations. The sequence is as follows: 1. on the way to
school; 2. in the classroom; 3. in the schoolyard; 4. at home with
mother; 5. at home with father; 6. two children in their room, one
playing and one studying; 7. siblings; 8. parents by themselves;
9. group of children with invalid child.

Rationale

Various aspects of the impact of school were chosen to represent different degrees of physical and psychological distance from
school and from others who may influence the attitudes of the child
such as the teacher, the parents, siblings, and the peer-group.
The various physical distances were scaled as follows: in the classroom; in the playground; on the way to school; and at home. The
relative importance of significant others is useful in providing insights into education at home and its relationship towards the
school.

The pictures are characterized by their simplicity. The figures
were drawn primarily in outline form, and only the most important
details were included. During planning of the test, attention was
paid to the various subpopulations for whom it was intended--that is,
different age groups, subcultures, and levels of perceptual functioning. Accordingly, an endeavor was made to construct the pictures so
that various subgroups of children would identify with and respond
to them.

The presentation of each picture is accompanied by standard
questions which are designed to ascertain the child's thoughts,
feelings, and behavior in relation to the specific situation.
Questions may be varied by the experienced tester according to the
special problems of the child. (For a more detailed description of
the test, its reliability and validity, see the test's manual.)

Various Uses of the Test

Originally, the test was intended for diagnosis of individual
children. However, it has also proved valuable as a means of screening an entire class as was demonstrated when the test was administered to several classes from the second through sixth grade. The

children were asked to write their answers on an answer sheet and it
was found that their involvement in the task was such that even slow
pupils who generally have difficulties in writing succeeded in expressing themselves. Essentially, however, information was obtained
about the pupils' perceptions of themselves as learners and their
attitudes towards teachers, peers, and home in order to detect mal-
adjusted children.

Another use of the test is to study the sensitivity of the teachers towards their pupils. In relation to this premise two classes
were tested and the answers of the pupils were analyzed according
to a number of categories such as feelings towards school, the teacher, parents, being called to the blackboard, and the like. The
teachers of the two classes were asked to write what they thought
would be the answers of the pupils according to the same categories.
One of the teachers was very experienced and sensitive while the
other teacher was new in the profession. The results indicated that
both teachers' perceptions of the atmosphere of the home corresponded
highly with the answers of the pupils. Only 12% of the answers of
the experienced teacher and 27% of those of the inexperienced teacher did not fit with the children's answers in this area. However,
when the teachers had to estimate the feelings of the children towards
situations in the school setting the degree of agreement was much
smaller. In relation to anxiety felt by the children on their way
to school (picture 1) the percentage of the first teacher's correct
answers was 64 while for the second teacher the percentage of correct
answers was 35. With the fear in the classroom situation (picture 2)
the correct estimates decreased even more: the first teacher perceived correctly the fear of her pupils towards herself in 53% of
the cases while the second teacher's responses were correct only in
23% of the cases. The estimation of the children's fear of being
called to the blackboard was nearly the same as that of the picture
2 situation: 47% in the case of the first teacher and 30% in the
case of the second one. Feelings towards class in general were correctly guessed in 60% and 48% respectively of the cases.

On the whole, both teachers judged the children as being less
frightened than the children expressed themselves to be. Although
the experienced teacher was more sensitive to the children than was
the unexperienced teacher even she found it difficult to perceive
the feelings of her pupils towards school. On the other hand both
teachers perceived quite correctly the feelings of their pupils
towards home. The same results were found in a kindergarten in which
the same test procedure was carried out (see the test manual). It
seems that when the teacher herself is part of the situation it is
more difficult for her to perceive it correctly, possibly because
her professional image may be threatened.

The test may also be used as a means of studying the attitudes
of teachers towards their pupils and the school situation. Twenty-

five teachers were shown pictures 2 (the classroom) and 3 (the schoolyard) and were then asked the following questions: 1. What can one
do in class? 2. Do the children like to go to school? 3. What does
the teacher say to the child? 4. How does the child feel about it?
5. What do his/her classmates think about it? 6. If the child does
not know how to handle a problem, what will he/she do? 7. What will
the teacher do when the child does not know how to cope with a problem? 8. If the child would be able to change the learning situation
what would he/she change? 9. What may the child decide in class?
10. What do the children in the schoolyard do? 11. What are they
talking about? 12. What does the child (standing a little apart)
say? 13. Why is he/she standing there? 14. What can he/she do if
rejected? 15. What else can he/she do? (Questions 14 and 15 are asked
only if the teacher perceives that the child has been rejected.)

Answers to the first question indicated a variety of responses.
Thirty-four percent of the answers related to general behaviors such
as walking about, talking to friends, and so on. Nearly half of
these types of answers contained behaviors such as quarrelling and
disturbing class mates. Twenty-nine percent of the reactions described learning behaviors such as writing, reading, and listening,
and 14% of the reactions related to play. Creativity, mostly in the
form of drawing, was mentioned in 10% of the answers, while another
10% dealt with the contents of learning such as subject matter. The
last 3% referred to making friends.

In terms of questions relating to interaction between the teacher and the child, 67% of the teachers saw such interaction as disciplinary in nature: the child had done something wrong and was
thus being reprimanded by the teacher. The rest of the teachers
often saw this interaction as a negative learning situation, that
is, the child was not able to cope with his task and the teacher
related negatively to the child. Likewise, the teachers perceived
the actions of the child's peers to the child as being mostly negative. Seventy-one percent described the other children as ridicul-
ing, envying, or pitying the child, while only 14% perceived the
reactions of the peers as positive. Fifteen percent saw the children
as being unaware of the interaction between child and teacher, although some of them ventured the explanation that the children were
accustomed to seeing their classmates approaching the teacher and
talking to her during the lesson.

Responses to the question of how a child copes with a situation
he or she is not familiar with revealed that 41% of the teachers stated
that the child would usually turn to the teacher. Thirty-two percent responded that the child would turn to a classmate, and the remaining 21% of the reactions assumed that the child would give up or
get angry. Only 4% of the answers referred to the child as trying
to cope with the situation alone.

Thirty-two percent of the teachers' reactions to the question of how the teacher could help a child cope with a problem stated that the teacher would explain to the child how to go about solving the problem. Eighteen percent of the reactions stressed directing the child towards the solution, 18% suggested scolding him or her for not having listened, and 14% advised telling the child exactly what to do.

As to decision making, most teachers agreed that the child could not decide anything by himself. Only 17% mentioned that the child could make some decisions without help from the teacher.

In relation to picture 2 (How do the children feel in the class-room?) most teachers considered that pupils were bored in the class-room (44%) or they refrained from answering this question (20%). The remaining 34% of the teachers saw the children as being more in-volved in the learning situation. However, when dealing with the child's wishes as to how changes in school life should be effected, most teachers were aware that the present situation leaves much to be desired. Thus, 63% of the answers dealt with aspects of "open education" such as working on subjects which interest the children and which they can handle, working in groups, and introducing more play into the class setting. The remaining 37% of the answers were in the direction of the child's acceptance of the existing situation as the most suitable one or of the child's desire to improve his or her own behavior.

The reactions of the teachers to the picture of the children in the playground (picture 3) were as follows: 54% of the teachers saw the child standing apart as being rejected, 37.5% saw him as neutral, while only 8.5% perceived the child as being accepted by the other children. As to the questions about how the child might cope with the situation of not being accepted by the group 26% of the answers were in the direction of the child trying again to be accepted, 37% stated that the child was trying to form a group of children around him or her or was playing alone, while 37% mentioned negative behaviors such as disturbing others, passivity, turning to an adult for help in order to gain adult support in having the other children accept him or her rather than trying to gain acceptance by himself or herself, or even trying to bribe the other children to accept him or her.

These findings indicate that the activity of the children in class as perceived by the teachers is characterized by learning be-haviors such as reading, writing, and listening versus general be-haviors such as walking about, talking to others, and misbehavior. Little reference was made to the contents of learning, such as spe-cific subjects or tasks.

Interaction between pupil and teacher was mainly seen as relating to disciplinary problems while a few answers related to learning, some of them in a negative way. Furthermore, lack of independence was mostly attributed to the children both in regard to their ability to cope with problems and to their taking part in decision making processes. Therefore, it does not come as a surprise that the teachers perceived the pupils as being dissatisfied with the existing situation and as being exposed to negative reactions both in class and in the peer group.

Actually, the teachers themselves became aware of the negative tinge of their answers and it became possible to discuss the implications of their attitudes with them. As a result of the discussion, teachers began to work to change their attitudes in a more positive direction.

Changing the attitudes of teachers is thus another use to which the Bar-Ilan Test may be put. Individual or group discussion on topics of concern to teachers aids them in becoming aware of their self-perceptions and of their pupils in the school setting. Lately, the test has been introduced as a tool in sensitivity training for teachers. A study by Alon, Itskowitz, and Strauss (1980) revealed that a group of teachers who underwent sensitivity training by means of the Bar-Ilan Test improved significantly more than another group of teachers who underwent a less structured sensitivity training within the same length of time.

The test has also been used in several studies of children's attitudes towards school and home and in studies of preschoolers' expectations of school. Scales for grading the answers to the test for purposes of research have been constructed and are provided in the test manual. Recently Niv (1980) introduced a multiple-choice version of part of the test in order to study the perceptions of deaf eleven-year-old boys.

In conclusion, the Bar-Ilan Test may be used for individual diagnosis of the problems of children, class screening, probing attitudes of teachers and changing their attitudes, and also for research.

BIBLIOGRAPHY

Alon, M., Itskowitz, R., & Strauss, H. *Increasing sensitivity in teachers towards pupils' reactions by means of structured sensitivity training*. Paper presented at the 4th International Colloquium in School Psychology. Jerusalem: July 1980.

Bellak, L. *The T.A.T., C.A.T. and S.A.T. in clinical use*. New York: Grune & Stratton, 1975.

Blum, G.S. *The Blacky pictures: A technique for the exploration of personality dynamics.* New York: The Psychological Corporation, 1950.

Itskowitz, R. & Strauss, H. *The Bar-Ilan Picture Test for Young Children.* Jerusalem: Ministry of Education, 1977. (Enlarged manual in press.)

Niv, D. *The attitudes of the deaf child to his handicap and to the kind of educational setting in which he learns.* Unpublished study (Hebrew), Bar-Ilan University, 1980.

TEACHER EVALUATION IN EARLY CHILDHOOD EDUCATION:

APPLICATION OF A MODEL

Jerry B. Ayers

Tennessee Technological University

The problem of evaluating graduates of teacher education programs has been a concern of institutions of higher education for a number of years. The need for institutions of higher education to evaluate their teacher education programs was emphasized in the standards adopted in 1970 and 1977 by the National Council for the Accreditation of Teacher Education (Standards, 1970 & 1977). Standard 6.1 states "The institution . . . engages in systematic efforts to evaluate the quality of its graduates upon completion of their program of study and after they enter the teaching profession. This evaluation includes evidence of their performance in relation to program objectives." (p. 11) Standard 6.2 emphasized the use of evaluation results in program improvement and states "The institution regularly evaluates its teacher education programs and uses the results of its evaluation in the modification and improvement of those programs." (p. 11)

In order to meet the above standards and gather sufficient information for curriculum development and improvement, Tennessee Technological University in 1970 initiated a program of systematic followup studies of the graduates of the teacher education program. Due emphasis was given to the graduates of the programs for the preparation of teachers entering the area of early childhood education. These early studies led to the development and implementation, in 1973, of the Tennessee Technological University Teacher Evaluation Model. Among the major objectives of the evaluation program of the University were the following:

1. To evaluate the objectives of the teacher education program of the University through a systematic study of the graduates.

2. To provide information for faculty and administration concerned with teacher education programs at the University in
making decisions pertinent to curriculum evaluation and development.

3. To aid in the process of making long-range plans for improving the total program of the University with particular emphasis
on teacher education.

TENNESSEE TECHNOLOGICAL UNIVERSITY TEACHER EVALUATION MODEL

The Tennessee Technological University longitudinal model was
based in part on the work of Sandefur (1970). The major purposes
of the study resulting from implementation of the model were to evaluate graduates of the teacher education program and to apply the results to the process of making long-range plans for improving the
total program of the University with particular emphasis on teacher
education (Ayers, 1975, 1976a,b, 1977, 1978).

The basic evaluation model provides input from four sources
including (1) graduates of the teacher education program, (2) their
supervisors (principals), (3) their students, and (4) independent
observers. Following is a brief description of the instruments and
methods used for collecting data from the four basic sources.

Graduates: Career base-line data including such variables as
demographic information, ratings of the level of achievement of objectives of the teacher education program of the University, and self-
ratings of teaching ability are collected from a sample of graduates
by use of questionnaires. Grade averages, courses completed, and
standardized test scores from such instruments as the National
Teacher Examinations are obtained from University permanent records
and a measure of the graduate's personality is obtained by administration of the California F-Scale Forms 45 and 40 (Adorno et al., 1964).

Supervisors: Principals' evaluations are obtained using the
Teacher Evaluation by Supervisor Instrument (Sandefur, 1970). This
instrument allows for the rating of the graduates in four areas:
(1) subject matter competence, (2) relations with students, (3)
appropriateness of assignments and academic expectations, and (4)
overall classroom effectiveness. A second instrument, also completed
by the principals, is designed to obtain a rating of the graduates'
level of achievement of the objectives of the teacher education program.

Pupils: There is considerable evidence that pupil evaluations
of the teacher are a valid source of information. The Student Evaluation of Teaching (SET-I) developed by Veldman and Peck (Veldman, 1970)
is utilized to obtain five dimensions of teacher behavior in grades

4-12. These dimensions include: (1) Friendly and Cheerful, (2) Knowledgeable and Poised, (3) Lively and Interesting, (4) Firm Control, and (5) Democratic Procedure. A second version of the instrument (SET-II) has been developed by Haak, Kleiber and Peck (1972) for use in grades K-3. This instrument is used to assess five dimensions of teacher behavior as follows: (1) Rapport, (2) Interactional Competence, (3) Interaction Style, (4) Unreasonable Negativity, and (5) Fosterance of Self-Esteem.

Independent Observers: Three direct classroom observation systems are employed in the model including: (1) a ten-category system of interaction analysis (Amidon & Flanders, 1971), (2) the Classroom Observation Record (COR) developed by Ryans (1960), and (3) the Tuckman Teacher Feedback Form (Tuckman, 1976).

The ten-category interaction analysis system is used by trained research assistants to assess in a quantifiable manner the behavior of teachers and students engaged in the teaching-learning process. The COR measures four dimensions of student behavior and 18 dimensions of teacher behavior. Each dimension of pupil and teacher behavior was carefully described and defined in a glossary accompanying the recording form. A polarized seven-point interval is used by the research assistants to rate each pupil and teacher behavior dimension. The Tuckman Teacher Feedback Form measures four dimensions of teacher characteristics including (1) Creativity, (2) Dynamism, (3) Organized Demeanor, and (4) Warmth and Acceptance.

Data Collection

Collection of data with the above instrumentation is being accomplished in two ways. First, extensive use has been made of the mail for collecting initial data from graduates of the teacher education programs and for making contact with graduates after they have entered the teaching profession. Initially, all graduates are contacted in the fall of the year after graduation for the collection of initial demographic information. In turn, those graduates who are teaching within a 100-mile radius of the University are asked to participate in the longitudinal study. For the past seven years, about 55-60 graduates (each year) who have completed either the Bachelor of Science (B.S.) or Master of Arts (M.A.) degrees have volunteered to participate in the project.

These graduates are visited by specially trained graduate assistants for purposes of collecting additional data. The assistants spend approximately a half day in each participant's classroom completing the observation instruments, interviewing the graduates and principals, and collecting data for computer processing.

Application of the Model to Graduates in Early Childhood Education

During the course of the operation of the model, various subgroups of graduates participated in the project, including 115
individuals who were teaching in grades K-3. This group consisted
of 85 individuals who had completed the B.S. and 30 who had completed
the M.A. Following is a summary of the results of the application
of the model to the total group. Data presented were collected during the first year after the individuals had completed their respective degrees.

Seventy-seven B.S. graduates had completed the National Teacher
Examinations. The mean score on the Weighted Commons Examination for
this group was 1163 (SD = 134) which placed them at about the 48th
percentile when compared with national samples. The 13 M.A. graduates
had achieved a slightly higher mean score on the Weighted Commons
Examination ($\overline{X}$ = 1186, SD = 151). Mean teaching area examination
scores for both groups were approximately 604 (SD = 72), which placed
them at the 52nd percentile when compared to national norms. Scores
on the American College Test completed by the graduates prior to ad-
mission to the University indicated that both groups were near the
national average for entering freshmen with a mean score of 19 (SD =
5.0).

During the first year of participation in the project, all graduates completed the California F-Scale. The mean score for the 75
B.S. graduates completing the test was 105 (SD = 21) while the 21
M.A. subjects achieved a mean score of 94 (SD = 22). There was no
significant difference between the groups. It appeared that older
subjects with more teaching experience and formal education were more
open-minded in their beliefs.

Both B.S. and M.A. graduates were rated highly by their principals. Table 1 shows the mean ratings given by the principals. It
will be noted that in all cases, M.A. graduates were rated higher than
B.S. graduates.

The Student Evaluation of Teaching instrument, SET-II, was administered in the classroom to all subjects. Mean scores on the five
dimensions of the instrument are shown in Table 2. Again, it will be
noted that M.A. graduates scored higher than B.S. graduates. Based
on comparisons of the data with national norms developed by the
Research and Development Center at the University of Texas, the graduates in the study appeared to be scoring somewhat low in the area
of interactional competence.

A ten category interaction analysis system was utilized to record observed classroom behavior. This system was basically described

TABLE 1.   Mean principal ratings of four dimensions of teaching.

Dimensions	B.S. (N=47)		M.A. (N=16)	
	X	SD	X	SD
Subject Matter Competence	4.1	0.8	4.6	0.6
Relations with Students	4.2	0.9	4.5	0.7
Appropriateness of Assignments	4.2	0.8	4.5	0.5
Overall Effectiveness	4.0	1.0	4.5	0.6

TABLE 2.   Comparison of mean scores from the student evaluation of teaching.

Factor	B.S. (N=58)		M.A. (N=19)	
	X	SD	X	SD
Rapport	5.5	1.3	5.6	1.0
Interactional Competence	4.6	0.8	4.9	0.8
Stimulating, Interaction Style	10.1	2.2	10.7	1.7
Unreasonable Negativity	8.1	1.6	8.2	0.8
Fosterance of Self-Esteem	6.7	1.1	7.3	1.0

by Amidon and Flanders (1971) and consisted of four categories of indirect teacher talk, three categories of direct teacher talk, two categories of student talk and one non-verbal category. Following are the ten categories: (1) Accepts Feelings, (2) Praises or Encourages, (3) Accepts or Uses Ideas of Students, (4) Asks Questions, (5) Lecturing, (6) Giving Directions, (7) Criticizing or Justifying Authority, (8) Student Talk-Response, (9) Student Talk-Initiation, and (10) Silence or Confusion. The observers recorded a numerical value corresponding to a particular category every three seconds or every time the categories changed.   Thus, an objective record was obtained of the variable interaction within the classroom.   Three to six twenty-minute observations per subject were recorded during each half-day visit. Ratios (see Table 3) were computed to reflect the climate of the classroom.

TABLE 3.   Comparison of mean ratios from interaction analysis.

Ratio	B.S. (N=47)		M.A. (N=16)	
	X	SD	X	SD
i/d	0.50	0.29	0.52	0.25
I/D	0.52	0.24	0.55	0.20
ST/TT	0.49	0.20	0.52	0.21
Lec/TT	0.35	0.23	0.32	0.14
Sil/TT	0.35	0.17	0.31	0.16

i/d   Indirect to Direct Ratio =
       Sum of categories 1, 2, 3, divided by sum of categories
       6, 7

I/D   Indirect to Direct Ratio =
       Sum of categories 1,2,3,4 divided by sum of categories
       5,6,7

ST/TT   Student Talk to Teacher Talk =
        Sum of categories 8,9 divided by sum of categories 1-7

Lec/Tot   Lecture to Total Teaching =
          Category 5 divided by sum of categories 1-7

Sil/Tot   Silence to Total Teaching =
          Category 10 divided by sum of categories 1-7

The ratios presented in Table 3 are comparable with those from other studies. Again, M.A. graduates appeared to be teaching at a more refined level than B.S. graduates. The indirect to direct teaching ratios were below those reported for graduates teaching in the upper elementary and high school grades.

The Classroom Observation Record consists of 18 dimensions of teacher behavior and four dimensions of student behavior. This instrument was completed at the end of each observation session. Based on previous work of the author (Ayers, 1977) the results of the use of the instrument have been factor analyzed. It appeared that three factors were present and have been termed I, Cognitive Style; II, Affective Style; and III, Student Behavior. Table 4 shows the factor scores for the two groups of graduates. Again, it will be noted that the M.A. graduates achieved higher scores.

The Tuckman Teacher Feedback Form is completed at the end of each observation session. The results of the use of this instrument are shown in Table 5. Again, it will be noted that M.A. graduates were consistently rated higher in their performance in the classroom.

TABLE 4. Comparison of mean scores from three factors of the COR.

Factor	B.S. (N=84)		M.A. (N=23)	
	$\overline{X}$	SD	$\overline{X}$	SD
I	40.0	8.0	43.6	3.5
II	61.5	5.1	66.7	7.2
III	21.7	5.1	23.9	2.8

TABLE 5. Comparison of mean scores from the Tuckman Teacher Feedback Form.

Factor	B.S. (N=31)		M.A. (N=13)	
	$\overline{X}$	SD	$\overline{X}$	SD
Creativity	29.2	6.7	31.2	5.8
Dynamism	29.3	6.4	31.8	4.9
Organized Demeanor	34.3	5.1	36.0	4.0
Warmth and Acceptance	35.7	6.4	37.6	5.1

Correlations of the variables for the B.S. graduates are shown in Table 6. In general, intercorrelations between the variables of an instrument were high and positive, as would be expected. Significant correlations of interest include negative correlations and scores from the Tuckman Teacher Feedback Form. Several positive significant correlations were noted between other variables, but no explanation can be offered for the results.

USE OF EVALUATION RESULTS

Program development at Tennessee Technological University is an ongoing process within the teacher education programs. Program development, operation and evaluation can best be described as a cyclic process that is continuous. The use of evaluation results is the key element in examining the total process for curriculum development and improvement.

Evaluation reports of the application of the model have been

TABLE 6. Correlations of the variables for the B.S. graduates.

Scores	1	2	3	4	5	6	7	8	9	10	11	12	13	14	15	16	17	18	19	20	21	22	23	24
1. NTE Commons	1000	476	-046	-049	-019	007	-355	139	158	116	129	143	012	012	012	187	107	173	221	177	097	350	128	286
2. Gr. Pt. Av.		1000	228	234	-224	245	-176	075	053	064	058	045	004	004	004	-020	-037	-066	019	-054	392	302	337	352
3. Prin. I			1000	587	499	623	-271	012	056	032	-010	-012	083	083	083	-145	107	-112	-092	-102	240	-062	125	·113
4. Prin. II				1000	354	722	-083	-042	-011	005	-037	-019	147	147	147	108	071	-017	-225	063	202	-094	-034	-118
5. Prin. III					1000	500	-288	-043	-023	-018	-029	-026	031	031	031	241	021	106	-066	127	185	-146	007	-089
6. Prin. IV						1000	-209	006	021	026	012	001	044	044	044	255	-003	072	070	151	019	-230	-208	-220
7. F-Scale							1000	097	097	127	117	131	-064	-064	-064	060	116	015	-109	033	-287	-491	-224	-320
8. i/d								1000	910	906	904	922	125	142	023	-052	-042	-219	065	-059	113	309	195	119
9. I/D									1000	927	919	942	151	166	048	-026	-042	-035	026	001	067	246	128	110
10. ST/TT										1000	966	981	045	034	-062	-036	-028	-015	007	-021	045	187	101	041
11. Sil/TT											1000	986	-015	003	-104	-008	-034	011	067	-011	053	192	082	046
12. Lec/TT												1000	040	043	-087	-021	-017	-006	069	-010	037	184	086	036
13. COR-I													1000	980	985	-375	-250	-430	-442	-489	726	515	754	762
14. COR-II														1000	975	-375	-250	-430	-442	-489	744	610	744	806
15. COR-III															1000	-373	-249	-430	-441	-486	560	370	505	733
16. SET-1																1000	252	787	146	664	000	-136	-200	-117
17. SET-2																	1000	290	094	393	047	141	056	097
18. SET-3																		1000	288	756	-080	-177	-212	-093
19. SET-4																			1000	192	-021	304	199	026
20. SET-5																				1000	021	037	-079	-002
21. TUCK-I																					1000	618	802	850
22. TUCK-II																						1000	614	671
23. TUCK-III																							1000	776
24. TUCK-IV																								1000

*Decimal points omitted. Underlined values significant at or beyond .05 level.

disseminated to all faculty in teacher education, University administrators and other interested individuals. Meetings have been held
for the purpose of discussing the results of the studies, and a special curriculum study committee has been formed from the faculty
within the teacher education programs of the University. This group
has been charged with the responsibility of examining the results
of the studies in depth and on a continuing basis. Following is a
listing of some of the more important changes and curricula improvements at the bachelor's level in early childhood education that are
directly attributable to the implementation of the evaluation model.

1. Addition of more practicum and laboratory experiences into
the teacher education program. Included under this broad area
are more contacts in working with children in the schools at an
earlier level.

2. Courses in the history, philosophy, and social foundations
of education were modified.

3. Overlap and duplication among courses has been eliminated.

4. Additional courses were created to meet special needs of
various groups, i.e., science methods and reading courses.

5. Reconceptualization of the teacher's role is taking place
on a continuing basis.

6. Modifications in the requirements for a major in elementary
education have taken place and the total program has been made
more field oriented.

7. A course has been developed in the area of special education
that is now required for all students prior to graduation.

8. Methods instructors have become more active in the public
schools through actually assuming the role of the classroom
teacher.

9. Efforts have been made to provide greater assistance to graduates in locating employment and in providing assistance after
entry into the profession.

10. Additional human relations training has been introduced
into the curriculum.

CONCLUSIONS AND SUMMARY

The purpose of this paper was to present a summary description
of an evaluation model that appears to be an effective tool to gather

data for the improvement of teachers in early childhood education. No attempt was made to draw elaborate conclusions from the study since there are many other factors that must be considered. It is obvious, however, that individuals who have achieved the M.A. degree (or who are more experienced teachers) appeared to be better teachers in the classroom.

Evaluation is an integral part of the teacher education programs of Tennessee Technological University. A systematic plan has been developed and implemented for collecting information, performing necessary analyses, and dissemination of results. In turn, the evaluation efforts have been used in the cyclic process for program modification, improvement and development. Systematic evaluation is essential to the total process for the training of teachers and should be an integral part of every such process. However, change is a slow process and means need to be developed to expedite the process.

The model outlined in this paper can be used by schools and other agencies for the improvement of teachers. The main element to be kept in mind in the implementation of such a process is consistency of the plan of action and appropriate use of the evaluation.

BIBLIOGRAPHY

Adorno, T.W. et al. *The authoritarian personality*. New York: John Wiley & Sons Inc., 1964.
Amidon, E.J., & Flanders, N.A. *The role of the teacher in the classroom*. Minneapolis: Association for Productive Teaching, 1971.
Ayers, J.B. *Report 75-4. Tennessee Technological University teacher evaluation model*. Cookeville, TN: Tennessee Technological University, 1975. (ERIC Document Reproduction Service No. ED 123 210)
Ayers, J.B. *Report 76-1. Tennessee Technological University teacher evaluation model*. Cookeville, TN: Tennessee Technological University 1976a. (ERIC Document Reproduction Service No. ED 126 085)
Ayers, J.B. Implementation of a longitudinal model for teacher evaluation, *Education*, 1976b, *96*, 3, 218-221.
Ayers, J.B. *Report 77-2. Tennessee Technological University teacher evaluation model*. Cookeville, TN: Tennessee Technological University, 1977. (ERIC Document Reproduction Service No. ED 148 778)
Ayers, J.B. *Report 78-2. Tennessee Technological University teacher evaluation model*. Cookeville, TN: Tennessee Technological University, 1978.
Haak, R.A., Kleiber, D.A., & Peck, R.F. *Student evaluation of teacher instrument, II*. Austin, TX: The Research and Development Center for Teacher Education, University of Texas, 1972.

Ryans, D.G. *Characteristics of teachers*. Washington: American Council on Education, 1960.

Sandefur, J.T. *An illustrated model for the evaluation of teacher education graduates*. Washington: American Association of Colleges for Teacher Education, 1970.

Standards for accreditation of teacher education. Washington: National Council for Accreditation of Teacher Education, 1970.

Standards for accreditation of teacher education. Washington: National Council for Accreditation of Teacher Education, 1977.

Tuckman, Bruce W. The Tuckman Teacher Feedback From (TTFF), *Journal of Educational Measurement*, 1976, *13*, 3, 233-237.

Veldman, D.J. *Comprehensive personal assessment system for teacher education programs*. Austin, TX: The Research and Development Center for Teacher Education, University of Texas, 1971.

LASTING EFFECTS AFTER PRESCHOOL*

Richard B. Darlington

Cornell University

BACKGROUND OF CONSORTIUM

The Consortium for Longitudinal Studies was formed in 1975.
In that year a group of early childhood investigators who had in-
dependently conducted experimental infant and preschool programs
for low-income children in the 1960s began a series of meetings
chaired by Irving Lazar of Cornell University. Originally named
the Consortium for Developmental Continuity, the group included:
E. Kuno Beller, Temple University; Martin and Cynthia Deutsch,
New York University; Ira Gordon, deceased September, 1978; Susan
Gray, George Peabody College; Merle Karnes, University of Illinois;
Phyllis Levenstein, Verbal Interaction Project; Louise Miller,
University of Louisville; Francis Palmer, Merrill-Palmer Institute;
David Weikart, High/Score Foundation; Myron Woolman, Institute for
Educational Research; and Edward Zigler, Yale University.

Several concerns led to the formation of the Consortium.
Since the release of the Westinghouse Report on Project Head Start
in 1969, most people assumed that the effects of preschool lasted
little past the end of the program. The Consortium members felt
that their subjects (aged 8 to 18 at that time) were old enough to
provide a test of the long-term effects of preschool.

The meetings resulted in a decision to pool the data that each
investigator had collected individually and to collaborate on a
common follow-up data collection and analysis effort. Each investi-

---

*This paper was prepared by Jacqueline Royce, Ann Snipper,
Harry Murray, Irving Lazar, and myself. Longer reports are available.

469

gator agreed to send his or her original raw data and common follow-up data to Cornell to form a Consortium data bank. Parallel or pooled analyses with raw data were to be undertaken at Cornell, but each member retained full rights to release raw data to others and to publish his or her own findings. I joined the Consortium in 1977 to direct Consortium data collection and analyses with Irving Lazar. Robert Jester of the University of Florida, now a principal investigator for the Gordon project, became a Consortium member after Ira Gordon's death. The Consortium for Longitudinal Studies originated and continues to exist principally through a strong commitment to a collaborative effort.

DESCRIPTION OF CONSORTIUM EARLY
CHILD DEVELOPMENT STUDIES

The early education programs in the Consortium studies were located in urban and rural sites in the Northeast, Southeast, and Midwest (see Table 1). The programs were active from 1962 to 1972; only Levenstein's Verbal Interaction Project, Weikart's Perry Preschool Program, and Karnes's GOAL programs are in operation at the present time. Depending on the theoretical interest of the investigator, curricula included programs based on the Bank Street child development model, Montessori methods, Piagetian theory, the Bereiter-Engelmann method, and others.

The Consortium studies can be categorized as center-based, home-based, or combination home visit/center programs. Center-based studies typically provided nursery school programs for 3- or 4-year-olds with varying degrees of structure in the program curriculum. Instruction generally took place in small groups, but in some cases was on a one-to-one basis.

Home-based studies directed their educational efforts primarily toward the parent, usually the mother, as the major instrument of change and influence in the child's life. Activities, toys, and games were brought to the family home by a parent educator or home visitor, who taught the mother to use the materials and to promote her child's development through parent-child interaction. These programs served infants and toddlers.

The third group of studies combined these approaches, providing a center-based nursery school program along with periodic home visits that involved both parent and child. In some programs the emphasis during the home visit was closely related to the center programs; in others, the content was more general.

The 1976 follow-up sample was composed of 2,008 children from 11 projects. The median project had 64.9% of the children enrolled

TABLE 1. Characteristics of early education programs and ages of subjects for each data set

Principal investigator	Early education program	Location	Type of delivery system	Subject birth year	Age at entry to program	Length of program	Years of program
Beller	The Philadelphia Project	Philadelphia, Pennsylvania	Center	1959	4 years	1 year	1963-64
Deutsch	Institute for Developmental Studies	New York, New York	Center	1958-61	4 years	5 years	1963-71
Gordon	The Parent Education Program	Gainesville, Florida	Home	1966-67	3 mo. to 2 years	3 years	1966-70
Gray	The Early Training Project (ETP)	Murfreesboro, Tennessee	Center/home	1958	3.8 or 4.8 years	14 mo. or 26 mo.	1962-65
Gray	The Family-Oriented Home Visitor Program	Nashville, Tennessee	Home	1971	birth to 1 year	1 or 2 years	1970-73
Karnes	Curriculum Comparison Study	Champaign-Urbana, Illinois	Center	1961-63	4 years	1 year	1965-66 (2 waves)
Levenstein	The Mother-Child Home Program	Glen Cove, Manhasset & Freeport, Long Island, New York	Home	1964-68	2 years & 3 years	1 to 1 1/2 years	1967-72
Miller	Experimental Variation of Head Start Curricula	Louisville, Kentucky	Center & center/home	1964	4 years	1 year	1968-69

TABLE 1. (cont.)

Principal investigator	Early education program	Location	Type of delivery system	Subject birth year	Age at entry to program	Length of program	Years of program
Palmer	Harlem Training Project	New York, New York	Center	1964	2 or 3 years	1 or 2 years	1966–68
Weikart	Perry Preschool Project	Ypsilanti, Michigan	Center/home	1958–62	3 years (1st wave) 4 years	2 years (1st wave) 1 year	1962–67 (5 waves)
Weikart	Curriculum Demonstration Project	Ypsilanti, Michigan	Center/home	1964–65	3 years	2 years	1966–70
Weikart	Carnegie Infant Program	Ypsilanti, Michigan	Home	1968	3 mo. to 2 years	16 mo.	1967–70
Woolman	Micro-Social Learning System	Vineland, New Jersey	Center	1966–68	4 to 5 years	1 to 4 years	1969–73
Zigler	New Haven Follow-Through Study	New Haven, Connecticut	Center	1962–64	5 years	4 years	1967–71

in the program, 94.8% of whom were black, and 50% female.   The
medians on the follow-up sample for background variables measured
at the time of entry into the projects were: mother's education of
10.4 years; socioeconomic status (Hollingshead ISP) of 64.0; 3.2
siblings; and pretest Standford-Binet IQ score of 92.1.   The 1976
follow-up sample was very similar to the original sample despite
the attrition and changes in groups and projects included in the
follow-up.

MEASURES

     A wide variety of status and process variables were collected
by individual investigators over four waves or time periods of data
collection.   Before the formation of the Consortium (1962 to 1975),
investigators collected diverse, preprogram, child and family
measures (wave 1) and then numerous and varied postprogram outcome
measures over several years (wave 2).   In the Consortium follow-ups
of 1976 and 1979 (waves 3 and 4), a core of common measures was
collected.   The measures included in the Consortium data bank are
described below.

     All investigators, with the exception of Beller, collected
preprogram background data such as education and occupation of
mother and father, number of siblings, and father presence in the
home, as well as sex and ethnicity of child, mother's age at child-
birth, and other variables.   Beller collected background demographic
data retrospectively as part of the 1976 Consortium Parent Interview.

     The second wave of testing, also conducted independently by
the investigators, consisted primarily of standardized IQ and achievement tests and project-developed tests.   The majority of projects
collected Stanford-Binet and the Peabody Picture Vocabulary Test
(PPVT) IQ scores at the various wave 2 follow-up testing periods.

     In 1976 five types of follow-up data were collected in a
common format: an individually administered intelligence test
(Wechsler), school record information, scores on school-administered
standardized achievement tests, and interviews with the participant
and his or her parent (usually the mother).

     To guard against artifactual results due to differences between
the programs, subjects were never pooled into a single large sample.
Instead, all hypothesis tests compared treatment children to control
children from the same project site, and the results were pooled
using the pooled-z technique (Mosteller & Bush, 1954).   For each
project the exact p value of the result was calculated and converted
to a z score with the sign corresponding to the direction of the
effect.   The z scores were then summed: $z = \Sigma z_i / \sqrt{k}$, where z_i is
the z score from project i and k is the number of projects.   The

significance of the pooled z score was then determined. Since contrary results in different projects cancel one another out, this tests the "average" effect of preschool. When results were tested by chi-square, uncorrected chi-squares were calculated (Camilli & Hopkins, 1978).

This method tests the null hypothesis that on the average across our various programs, preschool has no effect on later school performance. (A less conservative null hypothesis would be: preschool has no effect on children's later school performance. This hypothesis could be rejected on the basis of the successful outcome of a single program.)

To ensure that no single program accounted for a significant pooled result, results were tested for what we called "robustness" by deleting the program with the strongest result from the analysis and recalculating the pooled-z score. Projects with designs most appropriate to test the effectiveness of preschool were analyzed separately from the quasi-experimental projects. The p values reported here are two-tailed.

Attrition due to mobility, death, or other events is a serious threat to the validity of a longitudinal study. The projects used in the pooled-z analyses reported here had a median recovery rate of 75%. Virtually all attrition was due to inability to find subjects; less than 3% of the recovered subjects refused to participate.

Analyses were performed to assess whether the total samples found on follow-up differed from the total original samples, whether the found treatment group subjects differed from the found control group subjects, and whether the pattern of attrition differed for treatment and control groups. These analyses yielded results consistent with the hypothesis that attrition was essentially random, introducing no known biases into our results.

RESULTS

Our findings replicated results on IQ reported by many previous investigators--large effects when children are tested soon after the program, tapering down to smaller but statistically significant effects three or four years after preschool, and vanishing thereafter. This finding has a positive aspect: if one year of enrichment has effects three or four years later, then twelve years of enriched schooling might have lifelong effects. IQ scores, however, are merely indirect predictors of school success; our most important analyses concerned the effect of preschool on direct measures of school success.

In the 1976 follow-up, investigators examined school records to determine whether their subjects were progressing with their age

mates or had run into difficulty and were assigned to special education classes or retained in grade at any time in their school
careers. For the median project, for example, subjects were in
7th grade when school data were collected. Special education placements included classrooms for children diagnosed as mentally retarded (educable or trainable), learning disabled, or emotionally
disturbed. Speech and hearing problems were not classified with
special education placements. We combined the two indicators to
form a composite variable: students who met school requirements
versus children who failed to meet school requirements and were
placed in special education classes or retained. Because schools
have different policies, practices, and resources for students who
fail, each Consortium program group was compared with its own control
group within a school district. Results were tested for robustness
by deleting the data set with the strongest finding.

Preschool graduates had significantly fewer school failure
experiences than did the control groups (Table 2). Across the seven
projects with appropriate data, the median rate of failure to meet
school requirements was 45% in the control group but only 24% in
the program group. The results were statistically significant for
the group of seven data sets ($p < .001$) and robust after deleting
the strongest project. The results were even stronger for data
sets with experimental research designs.

When the two indicators of school competence were analyzed
separately, preschool apparently had a stronger effect on rate
of special education assignment than on grade retention. The median
rate of assignment to special education classes was 29% for the
control group but only 14% in the program group among the six data
sets with appropriate data (Table 3). The combined results were
statistically significant ($p < .001$) and robust. For grade retention (not shown) across the eight data sets with appropriate data,
program children were significantly less likely to experience grade
retention than controls ($p = .018$), but this result was not robust.
The median rate of grade retention was 25% in the program group compared with 31% in the controls.

Although program and control groups generally did not differ
significantly on background variables measured before preschool,
we used standard multiple regression to control for observed differences in school competence analyses. Covariates controlled in
this way were: level of maternal education (in grades completed),
father presence versus absence, number of siblings, sex, ethnicity
(black versus white), and preprogram IQ score. On the average,
when controlled for background and initial cognitive ability factors,
16% more of the preschool graduates than controls were on grade in
regular classes rather than assigned to special education classes
or retained in grade. Results were significant (pooled $p < .001$)
and robust.

TABLE 2. Percent of students failing to meet school requirements (placed in special education classes and/or retained in grade), program vs. control[a]

Project (n)	Program, %	Control, %	Chi-square	p (2-tail)	Pooled z	Pooled p (2-tail)
Closely approximating experimental design						
Gordon (82)	39.1	61.5	2.25	.134		
Gray (55)	52.8	68.4	1.25	.263		
Palmer (221)	24.1	44.7	7.66	.006		
Weikart (123)	17.2	38.5	6.78	.009		
Median (481)	31.6	53.1			4.00	< .001
Quasi-experimental						
Beller (69)	45.9	50.0	.11	.737		
Levenstein (127)	22.1	43.5	4.47	.035		
Miller (125)	20.6	11.1	.89	.356		
Median all projects (802)	24.1	44.7			3.59	< .001

[a]Data were collected when most of the children were in the following grades: Gordon, 5th grade; Gray, 12th grade; Palmer, 7th grade; Weikart, 4th grade; Beller, 12th grade; Levenstein, 3rd grade; and Miller, 7th grade. Certain control groups were excluded so that the program-control comparison would be as close to experimental as possible.

TABLE 3. Percent of subjects placed in special education classes, program vs. control[a]

Project (n)	Program, %	Control, %	Chi-square	p (2-tail)	Pooled z	Pooled p (2-tail)
Closely approximating experimental design						
Gordon (82)	23.2	53.8	5.10	.0244		
Gray (53)	2.8	29.4	8.16	.0044		
Weikart (123)	13.8	27.7	3.55	.0602		
Median	13.8	29.4			4.04	< .001
Quasi-experimental						
Beller (66)	5.7	3.2	.23	.6315		
Levenstein (125)	13.7	39.1	8.07	.0046		
Miller (109)	20.4	12.5	.55	.4656		
Median all projects (558)	13.8	28.5			3.52	.001

[a]Data were collected when most of the children were in the following grades: Gordon, 5th grade; Gray, 12th grade; Weikart, 4th grade; Beller, 12th grade; Levenstein, 3rd grade; and Miller, 7th grade. Certain control groups were excluded so that the program-control comparison would be as close to experimental as possible.

An analysis of the special education data by program variation confirms this result. All but one of the projects with special education data included more than one variation of the preschool program. Altogether there were seven different program variations that could be compared with well-matched control groups on frequency of placement in regular classes instead of special education classes. In all seven programs the proportion of the program children placed in regular classes exceeded the proportion of control-group children so placed. The probability that this would occur by chance is 0.020. The seven programs were ranked on effectiveness, as measured by the difference between proportions of program and control children placed in regular classrooms. In the median program on this ranking, 29.4% of the control-group children were placed in special education classes compared with only 5.3% of the experimental-group children.

The second question we addressed was whether certain kinds of children benefited from preschool (the differential effects of the school competence outcome measures). This question derives from a widely held assumption that, for example, children with higher initial IQ scores or those from relatively higher SES backgrounds benefit more than other children from preschool programs. We used regression analysis to test for evidence of differential effectiveness. We found that the positive effects of preschool on school competence were not affected by the child's preprogram IQ score, gender, mother's educational level, family structure, family size, or ethnic group.

The effect of preschool on IQ scores over time was also analyzed. Overall results indicated that preschool had a significant effect on intelligence test scores for up to three or four years after the end of the preschool program. Similarly, the difference was significant for experimental projects only at immediate post-test, one year after and two years after. Thus, results indicate that preschool increased children's IQ scores for at least two years after the program, with some evidence of an increase for three or four years afterwards. Analysis of the WISC-R data collected in 1976 indicated that the effect of preschool on IQ scores is not permanent. Results were not pooled across projects because the tests were administered at different ages and at different number of years after the programs. Only the projects with the youngest samples had IQ score differences in 1976 (see Consortium, 1978).

We also examined the possibility of differential effects of preschool on IQ scores, i.e., the possibility that preschool affected different types of children in different ways. Results did not indicate any differential effects.

Analysis of achievement test data collected by the schools involved far greater methodological problems than any of our other analyses because of more missing data, children taking different tests or different versions or levels of a test, etc. The achievement test analyses are still going on. Initial pooled results indicate a significant difference favoring the program groups in mathematics subtests, but not in reading, at the fourth grade, the grade for which most projects had data.

Our work is described in more detail in a work in the Child Development Monograph series, which should appear later this year. In addition, a government report of about 250 pages is now available for $6; a 58-page summary is also available.

We believe that our work has been important in two recent developments in the United States. The annual budget for Head Start preschool programs was increased by about $160 million after years of neglect. And the United States Department of Defense has recently decided that preschool programs should be provided for children of military personnel at all military bases.

These school performance results indicate that the prevailing pessimism about the long-term effects of early education programs was premature. Preschool helped low-income children meet the requirements of their schools. Children who participated in Consortium preschool programs were significantly more likely than controls to be on grade in regular classrooms rather than assigned to special education classrooms or retained in grade during their school careers. These outcome measures of school success or failure are direct indications of social competence (Zigler & Trickett, 1978). The child has met society's initial expectations, thereby increasing his or her future options.

SUMMARY

The Consortium for Longitudinal Studies has provided evidence that early childhood programs can have an impact on the academic careers of low-income children. This effect can be measured both in terms of performance on standardized tests and in terms of actually meeting the requirements of normal progression as defined by the schools. The four waves of data collection continue to provide an opportunity to evaluate the effect of preschool on various outcomes as children in the sample reach young adulthood.

FOOTNOTE

1. A full description of Consortium programs can be found in Consortium, 1977; Consortium, 1978; Lazar, Royce, Murray,

Snipper & Darlington, in press; and individual project reports
listed in the reference list.

BIBLIOGRAPHY

Beller, E.K. Research on organized programs of early education.
    In R. Travers (Ed.), *Handbook of Research on Teaching*.
    Chicago: Rand McNally & Co., 1973.
Camilli, G., & Hopkins, K. Applicability of chi-square to 2 X 2
    contingency tables with small expected cell frequencies.
    Psychological Bulletin, 1978, *85*(1), 163-167.
The Consortium on Developmental Continuity. *The persistence of
    preschool effects*. Final report, Grant No. 18-76-07843 from
    the Administration for Children, Youth, and Families, Office
    of Human Development Services, U.S. Department of Health,
    Education, and Welfare, October, 1977.
Consortium for Longitudinal Studies. *Lasting effects after preschool*.
    Final report, Grant No. 90C-1311 from the Administration for
    Children, Youth, and Families, Office of Human Development
    Services, U.S. Department of Health, Education, and Welfare,
    October, 1978.
Deutsch, M., Taleporos, E., & Victor, J. A brief synopsis of an
    initial enrichment program in early childhood. In S. Ryan
    (Ed.), *A report on longitudinal evaluations* (Vol. 1). Washing-
    ton, D.C.: Office of Child Development, DHEW Publication No.
    (OHD) 74-24, 1974, pp. 49-60.
Gordon, I.J., Guinagh, B., & Jester, R.E. The Florida parent educa-
    tion infant and toddler programs. In M.C. Day and R.K. Parker
    (Eds.), *The preschool in action: Exploring early childhood
    programs* (2nd ed.). Boston: Allyn and Bacon, Inc., 1977.
Karnes, M.B., Zehrback, R.R., & Teska, J.A. Conceptualization of
    the GOAL (game-oriented activities for learning) curriculum.
    In M.C. Day and R.K. Parker (Eds.), *The preschool in action:
    Exploring early childhood programs* (2nd ed.). Boston: Allyn
    & Bacon, 1977.
Klaus, R.A., & Gray, S.W. The early training project for disad-
    vantaged children: A report after five years. *Monographs of
    the Society for Research in Child Development*, 1968, *33*, (4,
    Serial No. 120).
Lazar, I., Royce, J., Murray, H., Snipper, A., & Darlington, R.
    Lasting effects after preschool. *Monographs of the Society for
    Research in Child Development*, in press.
Levenstein, P. The mother-child home program. In M.C. Day and
    R.C. Parker (Eds.), *The preschool in action: Exploring early
    childhood programs* (2nd ed.). Boston: Allyn & Bacon, 1977.
Miller, L., & Dyer, J.L. Four preschool programs: Their dimensions
    and effects. *Monographs of the Society for Research in Child
    Development*, 1975, *40* (5-6, Serial No. 162).

Mosteller, F., & Bush, R.R. Selected quantitative techniques.   In
    G. Lindzey (Ed.), *Handbook of social psychology* (Vol. 1).
    Reading, MA: Addison-Wesley, 1954.
Palmer, F.H., & Siegel, R.J. Minimal intervention at ages two and
    three and subsequent intellective changes. In M.C. Day and
    R.K. Parker (Eds.), *The preschool in action: Exploring early
    childhood programs* (2nd ed.).   Boston: Allyn & Bacon, 1977.
Seitz, V., Apfel, N., & Efron, C. Long-term effects of early inter-
    vention: The New Haven project. In B. Brown (Ed.), *Found:
    Long-term gains from early intervention.* Boulder, CO: Westview
    Press, 1978. (Zigler project).
Weikart, D.P., Bond, J.T., & McNeil, J.T. The Ypsilanti Perry pre-
    school project: Preschool years and longitudinal results.
    Monographs of the High/Scope Educational Research Foundation,
    (No. 3), 1978.
Weikart, D., Deloria, D., Lawser, S., & Weigerink, R. Longitudinal
    results of the Ypsilanti Perry preschool project. *Monographs
    of the High/Scope Educational Research Foundation,* (No. 1),
    1970.
    1974, pp. 125-133.
Weikart, D., Deloria, D., Lawser, S., & Weigerink, R. Longtiduinal
    results of the Ypsilanti Perry preschool project. *Monographs
    of the High/Scope Educational Research Foundation,* (No. 1)
    1970.
Woolman, M. *Learning for cognition: The micro-social learning system.*
    Report to the New Jersey State Department of Education, 1971.
Zigler, E., & Trickett, P.K. IQ, social competence, and evaluation
    of early childhood education programs. *American Psychologist,*
    1978, *33,* 789-798.

SELECTED ATTITUDES OF TEACHERS AND STUDENT

PERCEPTIONS OF INSTRUCTION AT THE PRIMARY LEVEL

Jacques S. Benninga and Thomas R. Guskey
University of Kentucky

Kathy R. Thornburg
University of Missouri

In 1970, Flanders stressed that "teaching behavior is the most potent, single, controllable factor that can alter learning opportunities in the classroom" (Flanders, 1970, p. 13). Since that time a growing number of educational studies have shown that teaching behavior is indeed an important variable in classroom research. However, these studies have also shown that the distinction between teaching behaviors and the attitudes and perceptions of teachers is not a clear one. For example, many of the labels associated with behavioral characteristics such as honest, aggressive, authoritarian, destructive, democratic, are the same labels used to describe teachers' attitudes and personalities. There appears to be no general agreement as to whether changes in behavior lead to attitudinal changes or if changes in attitudes lead to behavioral change. It is generally agreed, however, that attitudinal or behavioral change is most often evident among those individuals who sense some reason for change. If the attitudes and behaviors of teachers stem from the role they have defined for themselves as teachers (Brophy & Good, 1974, p. 130), it seems plausible that clarification or redefinition of that role might lead to particular attitudinal or behavioral changes.

The one common element which runs through summaries of research on teacher effectiveness seems to be its inconsistency. The Rand Corporation report (Averch, Carroll, Donaldson, Kiesling & Pincus, 1972) for instance, summarized this research by concluding that ". . . research has found nothing that consistently and unambiguously makes a difference in students' outcomes." At the same time, certain trends do seem to be apparent. Ryans (1964), found that teachers receiving high observer assessments on his three major patterns of teacher classroom behavior (i.e., warm vs. aloof; responsive vs. evading; stimulating vs. dull) could be clearly distinguish-

ed from those teachers receiving low observer assessments. The high
group was (a) more favorable in its opinions of students, (b) more
prone to democratic classroom procedures, and (c) represented by a
mean inventory response suggesting superior emotional adjustment (p.
88). Weber (1971), focusing on the characteristics of four inner-
city schools in which reading achievement was above the national
norm, found that among other characteristics, teachers in all four
schools had "high expectations" for all of their students. Similarly, a study by Brookover and Lezotte (1979) emphasized the importance of teacher attitudes in relation to school achievement. This
research was conducted in schools identified by the Michigan Department of Education as showing either academic improvement or academic
decline. Based upon questionnaires and interviews with the respective faculties, the following discrepancies were found:

a.   There is a clear contrast in the evaluations that teachers
and principals make of the students in the improving and declining schools. The staffs of the improving schools tend to
believe that *all* of their students can master the basic objectives; and furthermore, the teachers perceive that the principal shares this belief. They tend to report higher and increasing levels of student ability, while the declining school
teachers project the belief that students' ability levels are
low, and therefore, they cannot master even these objectives.

b.   The staff members of the improving schools hold decidedly
higher and apparently increasing levels of expectations
with regard to the educational accomplishments of their students. In contrast, staff members of the declining schools
are much less likely to believe that their students will
complete high school or college.

c.   In contrast to the declining schools, the teachers and
principals of the improving schools are much more likely to
assume responsibility for teaching the basic reading and math
skills and are much more committed to doing so. The staffs
of the declining schools feel there is not much that teachers
can do to influence the achievement of their students. They
tend to displace the responsibility for skill learning on
the parents or the students themselves.

d.   Since the teachers in the declining schools believe that
there is little they can do to influence basic skill learning,
it follows they spend less time in direct reading instruction than do teachers in the improving schools. With the
greater emphasis on reading and math objectives in the improving schools, the staffs in these schools devote a much
greater amount of time toward achieving reading and math
objectives.

e. Generally, teachers in the improving schools are less satisfied than the staffs in the declining schools. The higher
levels of reported staff satisfaction and morale in the declining schools seem to reflect a pattern of complacency and satisfaction with the current levels of educational attainment. On
the other hand, the improving school staff members appear more
likely to experience some tension and dissatisfaction with the
existing condition (pp. 66–68).

While it is apparent that home and family background, racial-
ethnic group membership, certain motivational factors (Mayeske et al.,
1973) and teacher behavior (Dunkin & Biddle, 1974) are predictive
of academic school success, the attitudes that teachers exhibit in
their interactions with their students should not be overlooked.
According to Brophy and Good (1974),

. . . attitudes can affect teacher-student interaction in much
the same way that teacher expectations can. That is, once a
teacher forms a particular attitude toward an individual student, the teacher is likely to begin to treat this student in
individualized ways. Attitudes, like expectations, will be communicated. A student whom the teacher particularly likes will
probably know it, and so will his classmates. The same goes
for a student whom the teacher dislikes. This knowledge is
likely to affect the responses of the students to the teacher,
probably causing them to behave in ways that will reinforce the
teacher's attitudes. Thus, students the teachers like will
probably begin to behave in ways that will make the teacher
like them even more, while rejected students will probably begin to respond in ways that will increase the teacher's degree
of rejection (p. 130).

With this argument in mind, the logical next question is whether
young children can indeed accurately perceive and evaluate the attitudinal differences in teachers. Little evidence exists relative to
this question. While it has been shown that students in the middle
grades and in high school can discriminate between their teachers
(Symonds, 1955; Amatora, 1952; Tuckman & Oliver, 1968), young children appear to be less able to do so (McDonald, 1972, as reported in
Brophy & Good, 1974; Pittman, 1952; Davis & Slobodian, 1967).

In a recent effort, however, after reviewing a large body of
research related to student evaluations of instruction, Haak, Kleiber
and Peck (1972) conclude that a case can be argued ". . . at least
tentatively (for) the reasonableness of assessing teacher behavior
by obtaining young students' perceptions of it . . ." (p. 13). These
authors found a 'remarkable degree of agreement' in the literature
suggesting that,

>The warm and friendly teacher who is rated as superior by the students is a mature adult whose focus is outwardly directed toward the children and, furthermore, a person who views the children in a very positive and generous kind of light. The poor teacher appears to be thoroughly ego-centric, concerned with herself, interpreting the students' actions as personally directed toward her own discomfort, and disposed to impugn the motives of others (p. 29).

As a result of their review Haak, Kleiber and Peck felt that sufficient evidence did exist to warrant the development of a group instrument to measure student ratings of teachers at the lower primary level.

The present research is a further attempt to delineate the interaction between certain teacher attitudes and student perceptions of teaching. Our aim was to generate a profile of teacher attitudes and perceptions similar to Ryans' (1964). This profile was based on teacher responses to five questionnaires and certain demographic information (grade level taught and years of teaching experience). In addition, students evaluated their teachers along four dimensions: rapport with students, interactional competence, unreasonable negativity and fosterance of self-esteem.

It was hypothesized that student evaluations would be more positive for those teachers who felt a greater responsibility for and commitment to student outcomes.

METHOD

Subjects

A total of 42 classroom units, including all of the first, second, and third grades in a school district adjacent to a large metropolitan area were selected for the study. The majority of parents of the children attending the sampled schools were either connected with one of several colleges and universities in the area or worked at other skilled or professional jobs. They would be considered solidly middle class. Teachers sampled from this district (all of the first, second, and third grade teachers) had experience in the classroom ranging from one to over thirty years with a mean of 8.3 years. Forty of the teachers were female and all were white.

All of the children in attendance on the testing dates were sampled. Included from the three elementary schools in the district were 378 first graders, 405 second graders and 365 third graders, for a total of 1148 primary-level children. There were 606 boys and 541 girls. Testing was completed by the end of October, approx-

imately two and one-half months after the beginning of the school
year.

Design

    The study emphasized the relationship of several teacher atti-
tudes to the students' perceptions of the teaching milieu. To
assess these relationships, measures of teachers' attitudes, teachers' perceptions of their own teaching and children's evaluations of
the instruction were used. The latter measure was designated the
dependent variable. Independent variables (measures of teacher attitudes and perceptions of teaching) included measures of authori-
tarianism, control, teaching self-concept, perception of causation
and affect toward teaching. Nineteen of the 42 teachers did not
complete the biographical information requested; thus, while information was collected on all teachers and their classrooms, complete
information regarding the relationship of teacher attitudes to student perceptions was available for only 23 teachers and their classrooms.

Instrumentation

    Independent Variables: All of the independent variables were
measured by self-report questionnaires which were individually distributed to each teacher. The authors collected the completed questionnaires several days after dissemination.

    The first teacher attitude measure was obtained using the F-
Scale, Forms 45 and 40, developed by Adorno, Frenkel-Brunswick,
Levinson and Sandford (1950). The F-Scale is designed to measure
individual prejudices and anti-democratic tendencies. This scale
was originally developed in an effort to identify the attitudes which
would describe an acceptance of authoritarian beliefs. Scale items
relate to tendencies toward belief in such attitudes as conventional-
ism, authoritarian submission, superstition, power, destructiveness
and projectivity. A higher score on the F-Scale indicates a greater
authoritarian tendency.

    The second teachers' attitude measure was the Attitude Toward
the Freedom of Children Scale (Shaw & Wright, 1967). This scale
contains 33 statements concerning children's rights and liberties.
Scores on the scale are determined from the median scale values of
items with which the subject agrees. A higher score on this scale
indicates a greater need to control children's behavior, whereas a
lower score indicates a more laissez-faire, child-centered attitude
in dealing with children.

    Three perceptual measures on teachers were obtained through the
use of instruments developed in the research of Guskey (1979). The

first of these instruments was designed to measure how confident
teachers are of themselves, or their teaching self-concept. This
questionnaire consisted of 30 Likert-type, rating scale items. Most
of these items were adapted from behaviorally based items for assessing self-concept developed by Brookover (1973) and Dolan (1979).
Each item asked the teacher to rate herself in relation to particular behaviors or characteristics. Five options were available for
the rating: superior, good, average, below average, or poor. An
example of an item would be: "Most students learn well what I set
out to teach." Each teacher would then assign herself a rating on
this item from superior to poor.

A second perceptual questionnaire was designed to measure
teachers' affect toward teaching. This section also consisted of 30
Likert-type rating scale items. These items were derived from two
sources. Several items were adapted from those developed by Dolan
(1979) for assessing affect toward school. The majority of the items,
however, were adapted from items contained in the Self Observational
Scales (SOS) for students, an instrument developed by Katzenmeyer
and Stenner (1974) of the National Testing Service. The items adapted for the questionnaire were from the SOS scales which assessed
school affiliation and teacher affiliation. Each of the items in
the affect toward teaching questionnaire asked the teacher to indicate her feelings in regard to particular statements. Again there
were five options available for the rating: strongly agree, agree,
not sure, disagree, or strongly disagree. Statements were both
positive and negative. An example of a positive item would be:
"I enjoy learning about new classroom techniques." A negative item
would be: "I often get bored in discussions about education."

The final perceptual questionnaire was designed to measure the
perceptions of causation of teachers. This questionnaire consisted
of 30 forced-choice type items in which teachers were asked to assign
weights to both of the two options. These weights were to be assigned
according to the feelings or preferences of the teacher. The weights
assigned to both options were to total "100" in all cases; in other
words, a simple percentage divided between the two options. Items
contained in this section were derived from items on the Achievement
Responsibility Scale for students, developed by Crandall, Katkovsky
and Crandall (1965). These items were again both positive and negative, assessing perceptions of the causes of academic success and
perceptions of the causes of academic failure. An example of a positive item from this section of the questionnaire would be: "If a
child does well in your class, would it probably be (a) because he
had the natural ability to do well, or (b) because of the encouragement you offered?" For this item, the greater the weight a teacher
assigns to option (b), the greater the measure of internality of
responsibility (locus of control) for academic achievement, and the
greater the measure of alterability of cause for the teacher.

Dependent Variable: The children's perceptions of teachers were obtained by using the Student Evaluation of Teaching II (SET II), a group measure developed by Haak, Kleiber and Peck (1972). This instrument contained a series of 23 statements, on cards, individually packaged for each child. Each child was then asked to determine if the statements were "about your teacher" or "not about your teacher" by sorting the cards into one of two separate folders. The scoring divided the statements into three major factors: stimulating interaction style, classroom climate (unreasonable negativity), and fosterance of self-esteem.

RESULTS

Our first step in analyzing the data was to calculate the scale score means and standard deviations for each of the teacher and student variables. These are shown in Table 1. Since the teacher was the appropriate analytical unit in this first part of our analysis, scores on the three dependent variables represent the average teacher ratings by students on these variables.

Table 2 shows the intercorrelations between measures of the teacher variables. Several of these correlations were statistically significant. In addition, the direction of the interrelationships between several of these variables indicates a number of interesting tendencies.

Teachers' perceptions of causation, affect toward teaching, freedom of children measures, and F-Scale measures were all in a direction consistent with expected trends. That is, the more

Table 1. Means and standard deviations of teacher and student variables.

Variable	N	Mean	Standard Deviation
Perceptions of causation	42	49.62	3.20
Affect toward teaching	42	52.13	5.10
Teaching self-concept	42	95.88	4.77
Freedom of children	42	6.03	.70
F-Scale	37	3.52	.78
Interaction style	23	10.21	.54
Negativity	23	8.73	.50
Fostering self-esteem	23	7.09	.37

Table 2.   Correlations between selected teacher variables (corrected
           for attenuation) (N = 42)

	Perceptions of causation	Affect toward teaching	Teaching self-concept	Freedom of children	F-Scale
Perceptions of causation (r = .857)	1.000				
Affect toward teaching (r = .757)	.202	1.000			
Teaching self-concept (r = .943)	-.333*	.017	1.000		
Freedom of children (r = .97)	.217	-.323*	.210	1.000	
F-Scale	-.113	-.237	.287	.190	1.000

*p < .05

responsibility teachers assume for the learning of their students,
the more they like teaching, the more freedom they feel children
should have, and the more democratic their values tend to be. However,
all of these measures are inversely related to self-concept measures.
In other words, the more confident teachers appear to feel less
responsibility, like teaching less, feel more restrictive in regard
to children's freedom, and tend to be more authoritarian.

     The next step in the analysis was to look at mean scores in
measures of the student variables across various groupings of teachers.   The sample of 23 teachers for whom student data could be analyzed was subdivided, first with respect to teaching grade level, and
second, with respect to number of years of teaching experience.   This
data indicated that the grade level at which a teacher teaches (within this narrow range) had little effect upon students' ratings of
the teacher.   Grade 1 teachers do, however, tend to receive consistently more positive ratings than do Grade 3 teachers.   In regard
to years of teaching experience, again there was little difference
between the groups.   There was, however, a tendency for less experienced teachers to receive more positive ratings from their students
than did teachers with many years of experience.

     Finally, we looked at the means of scores given teachers by
students of different sexes.   Male students consistently rated their

teachers more positively than did female students, but again this difference was not statistically significant.

DISCUSSION

Several generalizations may be drawn from these results. First,
as teachers feel more responsibility for student learning (perception
of causation) their affect-towards-teaching score increases but their
teaching self-concept score decreases significantly. These teachers
view their interactions with children as being more permissive and
democratic. When, on the other hand, teachers feel they are not
responsible for the learning of their students, an opposite effect
appears to take place. That is, teachers who view themselves as not
responsible for student learning (i.e., who feel that learning is
more determined by factors external to the teacher), apparently tend
to assign importance to other aspects of the school program. When the
teacher cannot assume major responsibility for student progress, the
tendency to control behavior seems to become more dominant. A teacher
with these characteristics is therefore likely to construct an environment allowing for less freedom. By necessity she becomes more authoritarian.

These results can be interpreted as both a corroboration and
extension of Brookover and Lezotte's study (1977). Those teachers
who feel that learning is determined by factors external to themselves would tend (with little provocation) to hold lower expectations for and consequently spend less time in direct instruction
with their students. These teachers would not like teaching but
would, at the same time, feel confident about their teaching abilities. The less confident teacher is the one who feels responsibility
for student outcomes, yet is never quite confident that she is doing
all she can for each student. Consequently, she would have a lower
teaching self-concept. We can speculate that this teacher is the
one who constantly searches for new ideas and strategies which may
prove to be more successful with individual students.

Future research should examine these trends. It may be that if
teachers are given a consistent philosophical and theoretical perspective from which to view children, and subsequent teaching strategies relating directly to this core framework, their perceptions of
causation may change towards the acceptance of more internal responsibility for student learning. We could then expect that teachers would
like teaching more and be more involved in meeting individual needs.
Such diverse approaches as DISTAR, Mastery Learning and Montessori
are attempts in this direction.

Secondly, first, second and third grade students all rated their
teachers positively. First graders did tend to rate their teachers
more highly than did third graders. A developmental interpretation
may help clarify this tendency. Young, preoperational children tend

to be egocentric.   Interpreted from a social perspective, young
children, because of their egocentricity, tend to have unilateral
respect for authority figures (see, for example, Piaget's "Moral
Judgment of the Child," 1965).   Thus, the youngest children would
interpret almost any action of the authority as the correct action,
and, therefore, teacher ratings would be high.   As children develop,
this social orientation changes from one of unilateral respect to
one of cooperation.   Cooperation implies the gratification of needs
on both sides.   Thus, as children mature, one could expect them to
become more discriminating in the evaluation of their teachers.
Given the wide discrepancy in personality types found in this study
and the uniformity of student evaluations, the foregoing explanation seems justifiable, especially in light of recent research
(Etaugh & Harlow, 1975; Lee & Wolinsky, 1973; Brophy & Good, 1974)
that teachers tend to be more disapproving of male students.   In
the present study, by contrast, male students tended to rate their
teachers slightly higher than did females.

The results of this study, while preliminary, suggest that
certain teacher characteristics may be predictive of classroom
climate.   The data suggest that the more confident teacher is the
teacher who feels less responsibility for student learning and that
students at the primary level do not discriminate well between
personality types on a group-administered test.

BIBLIOGRAPHY

Adorno, T., Frenkel-Brunswik, W., Levinson, D., & Sanford, R. *The
     authoritarian personality*. New York: Norton & Co., Inc., 1950.
Amatora, Sr. M. Can elementary school children discriminate certain
     traits in their teachers? *Child Development*, 1952, *23*, 75-80.
Averch, H.A., Carroll, S.J., Donaldson, T.S., Kiesling, H.J., &
     Pincus, J. *How effective is schooling? A critical review and
     synthesis of research findings*. Santa Monica, CA: The Rand
     Corporation, 1972.
Bloom, B.S. *Human characteristics and school learning*. New York:
     McGraw-Hill, 1976.
Brookover, W.B. *Identification and analysis of elementary school
     social environment characteristics associated with differential
     school performance, socio-economic status and racial composi-
     tion of the schools controlled*.   USOE Co-op Research Project.
     East Lansing, MI: Michigan State University, 1973.
Brookover, W.B., & Lezotte, L.W. *Changes in school characteristics
     coincident with changes in student achievement*. East Lansing, MI:
     Michigan State University, Institute for Research on Teaching,
     1979.
Brophy, J.E., & Good, T.L. *Teacher-student relationships: Causes
     and consequences*. New York: Holt, Rinehart & Winston, Inc.,
     1974.

Crandall, V.C., Katkovsky, W., & Crandall, V.J. Children's beliefs in their own control of reinforcements in intellectual-academic achievement situations. *Child Development*, 1965, *36*, 91-106.

Davis, O.L., & Slobodian, J.J. Teacher behavior toward boys and girls during first grade reading instruction. *American Education Research Journal*, 1967, *4*, 261-270.

Dolan, L.J. *The affective consequences of home concern, instructional quality and achievement: A quasi-longitudinal study.* Unpublished doctoral dissertation, University of Chicago, 1979.

Duby, P.B. *Attributions and school learning.* Unpublished doctoral dissertation, University of Chicago, 1979.

Dunkin, M.J. & Biddle, B.J. *The study of teaching.* New York: Holt, Rinehart & Winston, Inc., 1974.

Ekstrom, R. Teacher aptitudes, knowledge, attitudes, and cognitive style as predictors of teacher behavior. *Journal of Teacher Education*, 1976, *17*, 329-331.

Etaugh, Claire, & Harlow, Heidi. Behaviors of male and female teachers as related to behaviors and attitudes of elementary school children. *Journal of Genetic Psychology*, 1975, *127*, 163-170.

Flanders, N. Teacher influence, pupil attitudes, and achievement. *Cooperative research monograph, No. 12.* Washington, D.C.: U.S. Government Printing Office, U.S. Department of H.E.W., 1965.

Flanders, N. *Analyzing teacher behavior.* Reading, MA: Addison-Wesley Publishing Company, 1970.

Getzels, J.W., & Jackson, P.W. The teacher's personality and characteristics. In N.L. Gage (Ed.), *Handbook of research on teaching.* Chicago: Rand McNally, 1963.

Gum, M.F. *The adient and abient types of teachers as conceptualized by students.* Unpublished doctoral dissertation, University of Chicago, 1961.

Guskey, T.R. *Inservice education, classroom results and teacher change.* Unpublished doctoral dissertation, University of Chicago, 1979.

Haak, R.A., Kleiber, D.A., & Peck, F. *Student evaluation of teacher instrument II.* Austin, TX: Research and Development Center for Teacher Education, University of Texas, 1972.

Katzenmeyer, W.G. & Stenner, A.J. *Self observational scales (SOS).* Durham, N.C.: National Testing Service, 1974.

Lee, Patrick, & Wolinsky, Annie. Male teachers of young children: A preliminary empirical study. *Young Children*, 1973, *27*, 342-352.

Martin, C. The emotional, social and psychological make-up of the teacher and its relationship to teaching. *Childhood Education*, 1967, *44*, 235-238.

Murry, H., & Staebler, B. Teachers' locus of control and student achievement gains. *Journal of School Psychology*, 1974, *12*, 305-309.

Palardy, J.M. What teachers believe-what children achieve. *The Elementary School Journal*, 1976, *69*, 370-374.

Pittman, J.A. A study of the suitability of an attitude-gauging instrument for assaying the attitude-toward-schooling of a group of sixth grade Negro pupils. *Journal of Negro Education*, 1952, *2*, 136-147.

Rosenshine, B., & Furst, N. Research in teacher performance criteria. In B.O. Smith (Ed.), *Research in teacher education: A symposium*. Englewood Cliffs, NJ: Prentice-Hall, 1971.

Ryans, D.G. The prediction of teacher effectiveness. In *Encyclopedia of Educational Research*. New York: MacMillan, 1960.

Ryans, D.G. Research on teacher behavior in the context of the teacher characteristics study. In J. Biddle and W. Ellena (Eds.), *Contemporary research on teacher effectiveness*. New York: Holt, Rinehart, & Winston, 1964.

Shaw, M., & Wright, J. *Scales for the measurement of attitudes*. New York: McGraw-Hill, 1967.

Symonds, P.M. Characteristics of the effective teacher based on pupil evaluations. *Journal of Experimental Education*, 1955, *23*, 289-310.

Tuckman, B.W., & Oliver, W.F. Effectiveness of feedback to teachers as a function of source. *Journal of Educational Psychology*, 1968, *59*, 297-301.

Turner, R., & Denny, D. Teacher characteristics, teacher behavior and changes in pupil creativity. *The Elementary School Journal*, 1969, *69*, 265-270.

Weber, G. *Inner-city children can be taught to read: Four successful schools*. Washington, D.C.: Council for Basic Education, 1971.

APPENDICES

Teacher Measure 1
The F-Scale

Name _____

Directions:

The following statements refer to opinions regarding social groups and issues, about which some people agree and others disagree. Please mark each statement in the left-hand margin according to your agreement or disagreement as follows:

        +1: slight support, agreement
        +2: moderate support, agreement
        +3: strong support, agreement
        -1: slight oposition, disagreement
        -2: moderate opposition, disagreement
        -3: strong opposition, disagreement

_____ 1. Obedience and respect for authority are the most important virtues children should learn.

_____ 2. A person who has bad manners, habits, and breeding can hardly expect to get along with decent people.

_____ 3. If people would talk less and work more, everybody would be better off.

_____ 4. The business man and the manufacturer are much more important to society than the artist and the professor.

_____ 5. Science has its place, but there are many important things that can never be understood by the human mind.

_____ 6. Every person should have complete faith in some supernatural power whose decisions he obeys without question.

_____ 7. Young people sometimes get rebellious ideas, but as they grow up they ought to get over them and settle down.

_____ 8. What this country needs most, more than laws and political programs is a few courageous, tireless, devoted leaders in whom the people can put their faith.

_____ 9. Nobody ever learned anything really important except through suffering.

_____ 10. No sane, normal, decent person could ever think of hurting a close friend or relative.

_____ 11. What the youth need most is strict discipline, rugged determination and the will to work and fight for family and country.

_____ 12. An insult to our honor should always be punished.

_____ 13. Sex crimes, such as rape and attacks on children, deserve more than mere imprisonment; such criminals ought to be publicly whipped, or worse.

_____ 14. There is hardly anything lower than a person who does not feel a great love, gratitude, and respect for his parents.

_____ 15. Most of our social problems would be solved if we could somehow get rid of the immoral, crooked, and feeble-minded people.

_____ 16. Homosexuals are hardly better than criminals and ought to be severely punished.

_____ 17. When a person has a problem or worry, it is best for him not to think about it, but to keep busy with more cheerful things.

_____ 18. Nowadays more and more people are prying into matters that should remain personal and private.

_____ 19. Some people are born with an urge to jump from high places.

_____ 20. People can be divided into two distinct classes: the weak and the strong.

_____ 21. Some day it will probably be shown that astrology can explain a lot of things.

_____ 22. Wars and social trouble may someday be ended by an earthquake or flood that will destroy the whole world.

_____ 23. No weakness or difficulty can hold us back if we have enough will power.

_____ 24. Most people don't realize how much our lives are controlled by plots hatched in secret places.

_____ 25. Human nature being what it is, there will always be war and conflict.

_____ 26. Familiarity breeds contempt.

_____ 27. Nowadays when so many different kinds of people move around and mix together so much, a person has to protect himself especially carefully against catching an infection from them.

_____ 28. The wild sex life of the old Greeks and Romans was tame compared to some of the goings-on in this country, even in places where people might least expect it.

_____ 29. The true American way of life is disappearing so fast that force may be necessary to preserve it.

_____ 30. The trouble with letting everybody have a say in running the government is that so many people are just naturally stupid or full of wild ideas.

Teacher Measure 2
Attitude toward the Freedom of Children Scale

Name _____

Directions:

Following you will find thirty-three statements expressing different attitudes toward the question of children's rights and liberties.

    Put a plus (+) if you *agree* with the statement.
    Put a zero (0) if you *disagree* with the statement.

If you cannot decide about a statement, you may mark it with a question mark. This is not an examination. People differ in their opinions about what is right and wrong on this issue.

_____ 1. A young child must be disciplined until he has learned not to touch those objects in his environment which he cannot handle without damaging.

_____ 2. When a child's wants and those of an adult are in conflict, the child should receive the more consideration.

_____ 3. Parents should feel called upon to give reasons to the young child for the restrictions imposed, only when he is capable of understanding.

_____ 4. A pre-school child should never be allowed to have his own way.

_____ 5. A child who is entangled in a disciplinary problem should be allowed to explain his point of view.

_____ 6. A child should be restricted only when he is infringing upon the rights of others.

_____ 7. Adults should give no suggestions which will influence the form of a child's play constructs.

_____ 8. Play activities should never be supervised.

_____ 9. Implicit obedience is always desirable.

_____ 10. Leniency in restricting the liberties of a child is better than too much severity.

_____ 11. A child's whims and impulsive desires should never be humored.

_____ 12. Children should be given reasons for the restrictions placed on them.

_____ 13. It is necessary to teach a child that he cannot always have his own way.

_____ 14. A pre-school child should, from the time he shows any inclination to do so, be allowed to choose the dress or suit he is to wear.

_____ 15. Children are being allowed too much freedom.

_____ 16. The wishes of the child should usually be respected.

_____ 17. I would have the child ask permission before engaging in activities that are new or strange.

_____ 18. A pre-school child should be allowed freedom of action except in matters pertaining to his health and physical safety.

_____ 19. A child should be forced to obey if he does not do immediately as he is told.

_____ 20. I would place no restriction on the child's activity except in time of grave danger to himself or others.

_____ 21. A child should be given anything he wants to eat.

_____ 22. The child should be allowed free choice in the matter of associates.

_____ 23. Matters of conduct should be decided by the parent and the child together.

_____ 24. A child should be required to say "please" whenever he makes a request.

_____ 25. When a child's wants and those of an adult are in conflict, the adult should be given the more consideration.

_____ 26. Restrictions should not be imposed when they will discourage the child's spontaneous efforts.

_____ 27. A child should be taught to obey an adult unquestioningly.

_____ 28. The parent should choose the group with which the child is to associate, but the child should be allowed free choice with respect to his companions within the group.

_____ 29. A child should obey his parents because they are his parents.

_____ 30. The parent should comply with every demand of the child.

_____ 31. A child should be required to obey immediately in matters pertaining to health and physical routine.

_____ 32. Children's activities, when they seem to an adult to be destructive or wasteful, should be restricted.

_____ 33. A child's playthings are not his to do with as he
        pleases.

Teacher Measure 3
Teaching Self-Concept

Name _____

Directions:

The following statements describe characteristics which are sometimes
used to evaluate teachers. As honestly as you can, please rate
yourself in relation to these characteristics, using the ratings:

        A. Superior   D. Below average
        B. Good   E. Poor
        C. Average

_____ 1. Students find the ideas I am trying to communicate impor-
          tant.
_____ 2. Most of my students participate in discussions.
_____ 3. Few students are unhappy in my class.
_____ 4. Most students work hard on their classwork.
_____ 5. Students do not resent assignments I make.
_____ 6. Most of my students feel school is important.
_____ 7. Most students feel what I teach is worthwhile.
_____ 8. I recognize not only results but also students' efforts.
_____ 9. Most of my students actively participate in the class.
_____ 10. I give my students cues to aid them in their learning.
_____ 11. I often get positive feedback from my students.
_____ 12. Many students look forward to my class.
_____ 13. Students seem to learn a lot through my teaching methods.
_____ 14. Most students try very hard in my class.
_____ 15. I am able to help students understand difficult concepts.
_____ 16. Students often tell me I'm a good teacher.
_____ 17. I often review my teaching methods.
_____ 18. I am successful with most of my students.
_____ 19. Most students remember the ideas I stress.
_____ 20. I use my classroom time effectively.
_____ 21. Students find my class interesting.
_____ 22. Most students learn well what I set out to teach.
_____ 23. I am able to control my class well.
_____ 24. Most students feel comfortable in my class.
_____ 25. I let my students know what I think is important.
_____ 26. Very few of my students fail.
_____ 27. Most students keep up with assignments I make.
_____ 28. Discipline is not a problem in my class.
_____ 29. Most students are successful in my class.

_____ 30. I let students know regularly how well their learning
          progress is going.

Teacher Measure 4
Affect towards Teaching

Name _____

Directions:

Place the letter of the response which comes closest to your feelings
in regard to each of statements on the blank in front of each number.
The responses are:

    A. Strongly agree
    B. Agree
    C. Not sure either way
    D. Disagree
    E. Strongly disagree

_____ 1. I am encouraged with my success as a teacher.
_____ 2. I am often bored in discussions about education.
_____ 3. I look forward to school starting in September.
_____ 4. I often can't wait for the school day to end.
_____ 5. I probably won't make a lasting impression upon my students.
_____ 6. I often doubt the importance of my work as a teacher.
_____ 7. I look forward to coming to school in the morning.
_____ 8. I think most students will remember my class.
_____ 9. I often doubt my effectiveness as a teacher.
_____ 10. I enjoy learning about new classroom techniques.
_____ 11. I generally enjoy my time away from school more than my
           time in school.
_____ 12. The greatest rewards of teaching come from students.
_____ 13. I'm an important influence in the lives of my students.
_____ 14. I usually feel good when I am at school.
_____ 15. I often worry about my performance as a teacher.
_____ 16. Students generally have little respect for teachers.
_____ 17. Teaching is what I feel I'm best at.
_____ 18. The everyday hassles of school upset me.
_____ 19. I am now a better teacher than I was a year ago.
_____ 20. Teaching is a profession, not just a job.
_____ 21. It's hard for me to get to school on time.
_____ 22. I enjoy helping students with learning difficulties.
_____ 23. Most of my students have many difficulties in school.
_____ 24. Motivating students seems harder each year.
_____ 25. Teaching is a job with very few rewards.
_____ 26. I like getting to school early.
_____ 27. I'm usually anxious to leave school at the end of the day.

_____ 28. I like teaching much better than I used to.
_____ 29. I usually like my students.
_____ 30. There are a lot of negative aspects to teaching.

Teacher Measure 5
Perception of Causation
Teacher Questionnaire

Name _____   School _____

Date _____   Grade Level _____

                                     No. of Years Teaching _____

This questionnaire is being used to get a general idea of teachers'
perspectives. The results will be kept confidential, so please answer
as honestly as you can. Read each question carefully and mark your
choices accordingly.

Directions:

For each of the following questions, please give a weight or percent
to each of the two choices according to your preferences. For example:

        Do most students complete home assignments because of

        _____ a. personal motivation, or
        _____ b. parents checking on their school work?

You may feel that students complete their work much more because of
personal motivation than because of parent insistence. In that case,
you might answer

        97% a.
         3% b.

Or you may feel quite the opposite. The percentage will vary according to how strongly you feel about each alternative. You may see
choice (b) almost totally responsible for students completing assignments and might give it 99% . Choice (a) would then get   1% . The
two must always add to 100% .

1. If a child is doing well in your class, is it probably
        _____ a. because he has the natural ability to do well, or
        _____ b. because of the encouragement you've offered him?
2. When your class is having trouble understanding something you
      have taught, is it usually

_____ a. because you didn't explain it very clearly, or
_____ b. because your students are just slow in understanding dif-
           ficult concepts?
3. When most of your students do well on a task, is it more likely
   to be
_____ a. because the task was a very easy one, or
_____ b. because you let them know what you expected?
4. When a child in your class can't remember something you said
   just moments before, is it usually
_____ a. because you didn't stress the point strongly enough, or
_____ b. because some students just don't pay attention?
5. Suppose your principal says you are doing a fine job. Is that
   likely to happen
_____ a. because you've been successful with most of your students,
           or
_____ b. because principals say that sort of thing to motivate
           teachers?
6. Suppose you are particularly successful with one class. Would
   that probably happen
_____ a. because you helped them overcome their learning difficul-
           ties, or
_____ b. because these students usually did well in school?
7. If your students learn an idea quickly, is it
_____ a. because you were successful in encouraging their learning
           efforts, or
_____ b. because your students are basically intelligent?
8. If your principal suggests you change some of your class procedures, is it more likely
_____ a. because of his personal ideas about teaching methodology, or
_____ b. because your students haven't been doing well?
9. When a large percent of the students in your class are doing
   poorly, does it usually happen
_____ a. because they have done poorly before and are used to it, or
_____ b. because you haven't had the time to give them all the help
           they need?
10. When your students seem to learn something easily, is it usually
_____ a. because they were already interested in it, or
_____ b. because you have helped them organize the concepts?
11. When students in your class forget something that you explained
    before, is it usually
_____ a. because most students forget new concepts quickly, or
_____ b. because you didn't get them actively involved in learning
           it?
12. When you find it hard to get a lesson across to a class, is it
_____ a. because you haven't insisted on their learning earlier
           lessons, or
_____ b. because they are just slow in understanding and learning?
13. Suppose you present a new idea to your students and most of them
    remember it. Is it likely to be

_____ a. because you reviewed and re-explained the difficult parts, or
_____ b. because they were interested in it even before you explained it?

14. When your students do poorly on a task, is it
_____ a. because they didn't really expect to do well, or
_____ b. because you didn't insist they prepare adequately?

15. When parents commend you on the work you do, is it usually
_____ **a. because you have made a special effort with their child, or**
_____ **b. because their child is generally a good student?**

16. If a child does not do well in your class, would it probably be
_____ a. because he did not work very hard, or
_____ b. because you didn't provide the proper motivation for him?

17. Suppose you don't have as much success as usual with a particular class. Would this probably happen
_____ a. because you didn't plan as carefully as usual, or
_____ b. because these students just had less ability than others?

18. If one of your students says, "Ya know, you're a pretty good teacher," is it probably
_____ a. because you make school interesting for him, or
_____ b. because students generally think you are warm and kind?

19. Suppose you find that many students are anxious to be in your class. Is this likely
_____ a. because most students feel you have a nice personality, or
_____ b. because you encourage most of your students to learn well?

20. Suppose you are showing a student how to work out a particular problem and he is having trouble with it. Would that happen,
_____ a. because you may not have been explaining it at his level, or
_____ b. because he is not used to being helped by adults?

21. When you find it easy to get a lesson across to a class, is it
_____ a. because you got most students to participate in the lesson, or
_____ b. because the lesson was a simple one?

22. When a student in your class remembers something you talked about weeks before, is it usually
_____ a. because some students have that potential to remember things well, or
_____ b. because you made the point interesting for him?

23. If you are working with a child who can't understand a concept and he suddenly gets it, is it likely to be
_____ a. because you gave him regular feedback on each learning step, or
_____ b. because he usually works on something until he gets it?

24. When you are having a hard time getting your students interested in a lesson, is it usually
_____ a. because you didn't have time to plan the presentation well, or
_____ b. because your students are hard to motivate in general?

25. If one of your students says, "You're a crummy teacher!" is it probably
_____ a. because many of your students have learning problems, or
_____ b. because you haven't been able to get him to work on his particular difficulties?
26. When your students seem interested in your lesson right from the beginning, is it
_____ a. because the topic is one which usually interests students, or
_____ b. because you were able to get most of the students involved?
27. If you were to find that most of the students in your class were doing very well, would it probably be
_____ a. because their parents were supporting the school's efforts, or
_____ b. because you had motivated them to work hard?
28. When your students seem to have difficulty learning something, is it usually
_____ a. because they were not willing to work at it, or
_____ b. because you weren't able to make it interesting to them?
29. If a parent is critical of you as a teacher, is it likely to be
_____ a. because you have difficulty getting the child to do required work, or
_____ b. because the child is not developmentally ready to do well in your grade?
30. On those days when you are depressed about teaching, is it
_____ a. because learning is a difficult activity for many of your students, or
_____ b. because you aren't able to motivate students to work as hard as they should?

A FIELD-BASED APPROACH TO THE VALIDATION OF

BEHAVIORAL COMPETENCIES FOR YOUNG CHILDREN

Jack V. Powell

University of Georgia

INTRODUCTION

Contemporary theory and practice suggest numerous alternatives
for providing educational programs for preschool and early kindergarten years (Powell, 1977). These programs such as the child-
development-oriented nursery schools, Montessori Preschools, academically oriented preschools, the British infant schools, and structured
vs. nonstructured programs have all emerged as a result of research
and theoretical issues on child development, motivation, and the
psychological nature of learning.

Amid the controversy in determining appropriate programs for
educating young children, the practitioner must turn to the psychology of child behavior for guidance in making curricular decisions.
Good and Brophy (1973) stated that teachers should acquire and be able
to implement a variety of teaching approaches because of the uniqueness
of individual needs and the variety of learning techniques that are
required to stimulate their learning behavior. In a similar context,
Hyman (1974) recommended specific criteria which teachers should consider in making their teaching methods relevant to student needs.
These are:

> the context of the teaching situation (time and place); the
> number, ability, interests, and previous experience of the
> students; the nature of the subject matter; the teacher's
> own abilities and inclinations; and what he wishes to empha-
> size in his teaching--skills, knowledge or values.

According to Mosher and Purpel (1972), and Howsam (1976), instructional strategies and innovative techniques in public education

505

often reflect conventional pedagogy while leaning on the developer's
personal educational experiences. If education means a continuous
growth process, then we cannot afford to permit tradition to over-
shadow current research in an era of educational accountability; therefore, a classroom teacher needs to keep abreast of current trends in an
effort to perform the best possible tasks in classroom teaching and
learning.

PURPOSE

The long-range goals of this project are to (1) solicit responses
from in-service and pre-service teachers relative to behaviors believed
to be appropriate and essential for young children, (2) develop a theoretical base for utilization through undergraduate field-based classes,
and (3) provide a practical textbook for the in-service or pre-service
classroom teacher educator.

It is recognized that the psychology of child growth and development in conjunction with the educational benefits of individualized
instruction should give direction to the education of young children.
Their instructional program should be developmentally flexible considering both learner characteristics and the nature of the resources
upon which the activities are based. With these factors in mind, a
broadly based textbook will be proposed that will be sequentially
structured, and comprehensive enough to provide optimum curricular
integration.

METHODS AND PROCEDURES

In Spring 1974, a list of 42 behaviors developed by the author
was initially presented to the 50 faculty members of the Athens,
Georgia Child Development Centers. They were mainly concerned with
what types of cognitive activities children should encounter in preschool with implications for developmental activities through early
primary grades.

After a four-day workshop, each participant was given a questionnaire on which to rate each behavior. They were asked to respond to

each item on the list as being (1) Most Appropriate, (2) Appropriate,
(3) Essential, but not relative to preschool-early primary curriculum,
or (4) Inappropriate. Each behavior was then analyzed in terms of responses given. Thirty-six of the items were rated as "Most Appropriate" or "Appropriate" during the first validation process.

From Summer 1974 until the end of Winter quarter 1979, a total
of 615 subjects had responded to the list, thus resulting in a final
taxonomy of 27 behaviors. These respondents were preschool, kindergarten, and elementary teachers participating in 14 staff development
workshops, as well as undergraduate and graduate students enrolled
in the early childhood program at the University of Georgia.

Each behavioral statement on the list is being field tested for
relevancy of developmental sequence and instructional activities. A
terminal product will be a resource for preschool and early childhood
curriculum development and implementation.

Behavioral Classification. The 27 items which will form the nucleus
for the text have been related to the theory of Bloom, Gagné, and
Briggs. This organization will not only establish a framework for
instructional planning but will also offer developmental guidance in
the planning process.

SUMMARY

Over a 4-year period, 615 beginning and experienced classroom
teachers in early childhood and elementary education participated in
the validation process of a taxonomy of behaviors for preschool and
primary curriculum development.

This field-based research culminated in a final list of 27 behaviors believed to be appropriate for the education of young children. The final product will be a textbook for practitioners in early
childhood education and a reference for anyone involved in or contemplating curriculum development for this age level.

TABLE I   Classification of Behavioral Statements

BEHAVIOR	AUTHOR'S INTERPRETATION	TAXONOMIC ANALYSIS (BLOOM)	TYPE OF LEARNING (GAGNE)	SUGGESTED MEDIUM (BRIGGS)
The child will:				
1. Know left and right.	When he can raise right or left hand on command; move to right or left on command; & recognize the right and left sides of a sheet of paper	1.11 Knowledge of terminology	Stimulus-Response Learning	Practice with spatial directions and left-right concepts; given commands
2. Follow directions.	When given step by step on a selected task	3.00 Application	Chaining	Requires oral or printed verbal units presented in sequence
3. Print his name.	Perform (independently) on papers, etc., by using upper and lower case letters	3.00 Application	Chaining	May require practice in addition to printing name on classwork
4. Print numerals 1-10.	While teacher is writing the example on the chalkboard; write on paper (by memory) on command	1.20 Knowledge of ways and means of dealing with specifics	Chaining	Written units on reproducing numbers in sequences
5. Use scissors properly.	Hold correctly and cut to some degree of accuracy	3.00 Application	Chaining	Practice in cutting out pictures, geometric shapes, etc.
6. Tie his shoes.	Not assisted until the need arises	3.00 Application	Chaining	Practice with actual objects
7. Repeat the letters of the alphabet from A-Z.	Perform orally in sequence; recognize individual letters out of sequence; print alphabet correctly	1.22 Knowledge of Trends & Sequences	Verbal Association	Practice with oral units in and out of sequence
8. Count to fifteen.	When asked to do so rotely	1.20 Knowledge of ways and means of dealing with specifics	Verbal Association	Practice with oral units in sequence
9. Recite short poems or songs after hearing them a selected number of times.	Repeat fingerplays & songs in group situation; encourage individuals to volunteer	1.22 Knowledge of Trends and Sequences	Verbal Association	Practice with oral units
10. Recognize his own name.	When called out among several others; when he sees it in print	1.11 Knowledge of terminology	Multiple Discrimination	Oral or written exercises requiring name recognition among others; situational and contextual tasks

BEHAVIOR	AUTHOR'S INTERPRETATION	TAXONOMIC ANALYSIS (BLOOM)	TYPE OF LEARNING (GAGNE)	SUGGESTED MEDIUM (BRIGGS)
11. Match various colors.	Can say the names of colors and match oral word with concrete color named; point to color when named; locate specified color somewhere in classroom	4.20 Analysis of Relationships	Multiple Discrimination	Exercises using color charts or colored geometric shapes
12. Discriminate between likenesses & differences in shapes, designs, and pictures.	Verbally differentiate; match like things on paper	4.20 Analysis of Relationships	Multiple Discrimination	Actual objects or pictures; oral, written and manipulative exercises
13. Match sets of objects to corresponding numerals as *** are ___ stars.	Perform a one-to-one correspondence up to 10	3.00 Application	Multiple Discrimination	Exercises in pairing objects with words or pictures
14. Point out letters in newspapers or books and name them.	Incidental exercises for reinforcement and/or motivation	3.00 Application	Multiple Discrimination	Drill in context of identified paragraphs or isolated verbal material
15. Associate color words from paper to a color chart.	Initially learned by incidental association	2.10 Translation	Multiple Discrimination	Exercises in associating words with their appropriate color
16. Read labels on signs, cans, etc.	Labels put on selected objects (chairs, desks, windows, tables, items in "play" store) by teacher; child independently reads them	3.00 Application	Multiple Discrimination	Present actual objects or pictures in real or simulated setting
17. Classify according to selected grouping, e.g.: building, people, fruit, flowers, animals, dishes, furniture, toys, and clothing.	Establish categories from given variables	3.00 Application	Concept Learning	Requires exercises dealing with identifiable concrete experiences--objects and pictures

(continued)

TABLE I (Continued)

	BEHAVIOR	AUTHOR'S INTERPRETATION	TAXONOMIC ANALYSIS (BLOOM)	TYPE OF LEARNING (GAGNE)	SUGGESTED MEDIUM (BRIGGS)
18.	Discriminate between selected variables such as large and small, more or less, high and low, in and out, fast and slow, hot and cold, heavy and light, most and fewest.	Point to objects to show understanding of large--small, hot--cold, show understanding of fast--slow, heavy--light through movements; manipulate objects or quantities to show more--less, most--fewest	3.00 Application	Concept Learning	Requires situational and concrete experiences
19.	Select appropriate placement of objects according to teacher verbal questions/statements, e.g.: the ball is under the ___ (table), the book is on the ___ (desk), etc.	Respond according to given statements or questions	3.00 Application	Concept Learning	Requires situational exercises that are verbal in nature
20.	Demonstrate a knowledge of basic geometric shapes by drawing a circle, a square, a triangle, a cross, and a straight line.	Select (from given figures) the appropriate shape(s) and draw it when asked	2.20 Interpretation	Concept Learning	Exercises emphasizing reproduction as indicated by oral or printed stimuli
21.	Demonstrate the ability to use top to bottom and left to right page procedure in reading & writing.	Identify the top and bottom, left and right of a page by pointing; write name in upper left-hand corner of paper	2.20 Interpretation	Concept Learning	Situational experience reinforced through observational procedures
22.	Discriminate between lower case & upper case letters.	Select the correct lower case letter among a group of lower and upper case letters when presented. Follow same procedure with upper case letters	2.20 Interpretation	Concept Learning	Oral exercises on identifying size and shape of letters

BEHAVIOR	AUTHOR'S INTERPRETATION	TAXONOMIC ANALYSIS (BLOOM)	TYPE OF LEARING (GAGNE)	SUGGESTED MEDIUM (BRIGGS)
23. Utilize instructional games in learing situations.	Play such games as Color and Shape Bingo, Alphabet Bingo, and Lotto in small group settings	3.00 Application	Principle Learning	Actual objects or pictures
24. Demonstrate evidence of listening skills while others are talking.	Orally answer questions about things covered in small group discussions	3.00 Application	Principle Learning	Situational experience reinforced through observational procedures
25. Reconstruct familiar stories without omitting significant details.	Satisfactorily dramatize the story to include all important events	5.10 Production of a unique communication	Problem Solving	Oral or verbal speech patterns
26. Interpret short stories as told or read.	Draw pictures to interpret story after listening to it	4.10 Analysis of Elements	Problem Solving	Requires art work and/or drawing exercises
27. Relate pictures to story content.	Put in correct order a sequence story puzzle such as "The Three Bears"	4.10 Analysis of Elements	Problem Solving	Requires a variety of oral or written exercises, both structured and isolated

REFERENCES

Good, Thomas L., & Brophy, Jere E. *Looking in classrooms*. New York:
    Harper and Row, 1973.
Howsam, R.B., Corrigan, D.C., Denmark, G.W., & Nash, R.J. *Educating
    a profession*. Washington, D.C.: American Association of Col-
    leges for Teacher Education, 1976.
Hyman, Ronald T. *Ways of teaching*. Philadelphia: Lippincott Com-
    pany, 1974.
Mosher, R.L., & Purpel, D.E. *Supervision: The reluctant profession*.
    Boston: Houghton-Mifflin, 1972.
Powell, Jack V. Behavioral classification of competencies for early
    childhood education. *Reading Improvement, 1977, 14,* pp. 258-264.

CURRENT ISSUES IN THE EVALUATION OF

EARLY CHILDHOOD PROGRAMS

Herbert Zimiles

Bank Street College of Education

In this paper, I wish to comment on some recent trends in the evaluation of early childhood programs. My interest in evaluation is based on two considerations. First, and obviously, there has to be accountability in educational programs. We have a responsibility to develop a technology for gauging the effectiveness of educational programs. We may criticize existing modes of educational evaluation because they fail to achieve adequate levels of validity, but our criticism needs to be aimed at improving, not eliminating efforts to evaluate.

My second reason for pursuing the problem of evaluation is that current methods of evaluation are biased against nontraditional modes of education. Since I am primarily interested in the development and propagation of child-centered education, I am disturbed by the fact that alternative approaches to education are made to appear less effective than they are because of the way in which programs are evaluated. Traditional evaluation methods use achievement tests which are devised to assess the mastery of traditionally conceived curricula. They focus on factual material which is most likely mastered by means of rote learning. The fragmentary way in which subject matter is dealt with in most tests tends to mirror both the form and content of traditional forms of education. In effect, traditional forms of evaluation penalize those educational programs that do not conform to the traditional mode. We need to develop less biased, alternative methods of evaluation.

The evaluation of early childhood programs, a newer enterprise, has been both more and less adversely affected by the biasing character of evaluation. On the one hand, because it has not been possible to use group tests to assess very young children, the extent

513

to which segmented, factual content fitted to a multiple-choice
format could be used for evaluation purposes has been reduced.
On the other hand, it has been assumed that the gains made by very
young children in preschool are as accessible to measurement by
means of nomothetic assessment procedures as are the gains made by
older children in elementary school--a dubious assumption.

Major evaluation studies of Project Head Start, as well as
programs for much younger children, are beginning to surface. Most
notable among the newer studies is the National Day Care Study recently completed by Abt Associates (1979). Well funded and thor-
oughly conducted, this effort to guide child development policy by
means of a comprehensive evaluation study illustrates both the advances and the continuing flaws of evaluation work. I will refer
to it from time to time in this paper.

Evaluations of programs for young children have been criticized
on grounds that are by now familiar. First, such studies place too
much emphasis on cognitive functioning, in part because cognitive
phenomena are more easily measurable. Second, the manner in which
cognitive phenomena are assessed tends to severely restrict their
definition. The test format is hospitable to a map of the cognitive
domain that consists of discrete bits of disconnected knowledge.
Thus, specific cognitive skills and elements of information are
what is measured by most multi-itemed tests of intellectual functioning in young children. Accordingly, there is little opportunity to
assess what I have elsewhere called cognitive dispositions, attributes that support effective cognitive functioning but which are
more organically tied to the developing self--such traits as resourcefulness, inquisitiveness, perseverance, problem-solving effectiveness, and the like.

Efforts to assess affective elements of children's development
that might be influenced by their educational experience--such
characteristics as self-esteem, self-knowledge, impulse control,
expressiveness of feeling, relatedness to other children and adults,
dependency, and even more integrative traits such as ego strength--
seem doomed to failure because of technical and theoretical limitations that have bedeviled personality assessment for decades. The
tests which were developed in the early years of Head Start to measure affective traits betrayed the serious problems that surround
this difficult technical task.

Recent studies illustrate the ways in which evaluation methods
are changing and the ways in which they remain stymied by longstanding methodological problems. Major evaluations of preschool
programs continue to rely on tests whose validity and adequacy
were questioned years ago. For example, the National Day Care
Study used the Preschool Inventory and the Peabody Picture Vocabu-

lary Test. To be sure, pretest-posttest comparisons were combined
with observation studies to yield a thoughtful assessment of the
quality of day care, but it nevertheless remains true that tests
whose limitations and deficiencies were well known many years ago
are still being used as a basic means of assessing the impact of
early education programs. Despite the heightened activity and commitment to developing new methods of assessing the psychological development of young children, few valuable new measures are available for use in evaluation studies.

Many of the new evaluation studies rely more heavily on observation data to record characteristics of both the educational
setting and teachers' assessments of child functioning. Part of
this shift to observation procedures is dictated by the fact that
many evaluation studies focus on programs for toddlers and infants.
Such children obviously cannot take group tests; assessment must of
necessity be based on observations of children's responses to more
or less controlled stimulus situations. The use of observation procedures opens the way to a broader range of assessment, but questions
remain whether behavior observations are capable of achieving the
level of refinement and accuracy required by evaluation studies.

The expansion of programs for very young children introduces
a new perspective to program evaluation. Since many of these programs are introduced not because they are regarded as desirable,
but because the circumstances of some young children's families
make them necessary, the focus of evaluation studies is on gauging
their potential harmfulness. Instead of expecting programs to
demonstrate that they are fostering growth and development in excess of what might otherwise be expected, as is the case in conventional evaluation studies, the only evidence sought pertains to
whether participating children are not harmed. In effect, failure
to reject the null hypothesis is regarded as a sound basis for af-
firming the value of these programs.

Some of the new trends in evaluation research seem to be contradictory. There is, on the one hand, a concerted effort to upgrade the quality of such work by searching for more valid assessment of child variables and devising statistical procedures that
allow for more precise control of extraneous variables in an evaluation design. On the other hand, at the government's behest and
in order to muster political support for federally funded programs,
there is an increasing tendency to involve parents and community
members in both planning and executing the evaluation. It is not
uncommon for community groups to help determine the criterion variables of an evaluation. Thus, political considerations, along with
the need to trim personnel costs associated with individual testing
and/or observation, have led to a pattern of designing evaluation
studies so that they can be staffed and conducted by community-based
para-professional workers.

These trends function at cross-purposes. The search for more
refined and powerful methods of measurement is more likely to be
successful if we use the most experienced and knowledgeable observers available and allow for the most intensive and probing assessment and observation. It would seem important to first establish
the most valid evaluation procedure attainable irrespective of cost
and level of expertise entailed. It is essential to demonstrate
what a valid evaluation of an early childhood program looks like
before turning to ways of achieving such measurement inexpensively
and within a politically supportive framework. The field needs to
be shown a sound evaluation even if it is costly and can only be
conducted by highly skilled and experienced specialists. The task
of adapting the method for use by para-professionals and to a more
restricted budget comes later. It is self-defeating to undertake
this exceptionally difficult work with a set of undermining constraints.

There are other trends that do not necessarily represent progress. The advances made in computerized statistical analysis tend
to yield findings that are so elaborately adjusted (mathematically)
that they bear no discernable relationship to the original raw
scores. As a result, information regarding the progress made by
program participants must be taken on faith. The practitioner often
has no primary understanding of the findings. When the results of
an evaluation study are fed back to the practitioner for the purpose
of guiding program changes, the more the practitioner can feel related to the evaluation and have some basic grasp of what was measured and how much change was recorded, the more meaningful will be
the findings and the more likely they are to influence the quality
of teaching. Further, the more the practitioner understands the
meaning of the scores, the more he or she is in a position to comment
on the validity of the findings and attest to their reasonableness.
The elaborate methods of analysis ushered in by the computer make
it virtually impossible for the practitioner to fathom the results
except in terms of their bare outlines.

There are also grounds for distrusting the elaborate findings
generated by the computers. Data analyses are so easily attainable
and can be conducted in such an infinity of ways that it behooves
the eager-to-please data analyst to present a huge spread of findings, one which is so large that it is likely to include one or two
morsels that the client will find especially palatable. The extent
to which chance is operating to create interesting findings, and
the degree to which an error or inappropriate application of method
contributes to the results are more difficult than ever to ascertain.
In this regard, the report of the National Day Care Study contains
the following statement: "Potential statistical pitfalls have been
examined and shown not to threaten reported conclusions." (p. 83)
It is not very reassuring to have to be reassured along these lines.
With one hand the evaluators are drawing the practitioners closer

to them and asking them to participate in the design of the evaluation
and, with the other, they are moving them away from a basic understanding of the meaning of the findings.

But the most serious problem that afflicts educational evaluation
continues to be our inability to measure with validity the basic
psychological processes affected by educational programs. We lack
the technical capacity to measure with sufficient precision for purposes of assessing the impact of educational programs. In many cases
our measurement is too crude and, in other cases, it is simply not
attainable. Much of our observation and assessment is based on mere
glimpses of the phenomena we are attempting to study. No one would
dare review a play based on seeing one or two scenes or on viewing
it from a point so remote that the action could neither be seen nor
heard clearly. Yet we delude ourselves into believing that just such
glimpses provide the kind of detailed and precise information that
is required to evaluate the influence of a program. We tend to lose
sight of the degree of precision and refinement of measurement that
is needed to assess the relatively small increments produced by
programs. We have grown so accustomed to the crudity of psychological measurement that we have come to accept it for more than it is.
Variables that are especially difficult to measure are dismissed as
too complicated, or, worse, as nonexistent, even though they may
have great theoretical significance. Instead, dimensions which are
far less salient, but nonetheless measurable, become the focus of
evaluation.

Let us consider a far-fetched example. Let us pretend that
someone has come forth with the radical proposition that we tend
to exaggerate the importance of feeding children, that it would make
little difference if children were given but one meal every three
days instead of three meals every single day. Most of us would
reject such a suggestion out of hand, pointing to theoretical knowledge regarding the effects of nutrition as well as abundant personal experience, anecdotal evidence, and case study material. But the
proponent of this proposition would probably prevail by noting that
this specific hypothesis has never been subjected to experimental
test and that, therefore, there is no basis for dismissing the idea.
So we reluctantly proceed with the study. Let us add to this hypothetical situation the fact that we are limited in our measurement
of the dependent variable, body weight, to a balance with a set of
20-pound weights. Given such restrictions in measurement, it is
likely that we will fail to uncover discernible effects of starvation after a three-day test period. Thus, the absurd hypothesis
would be sustained.

I cite this unlikely example for two reasons: First, it illustrates the degree to which we distrust our theoretical understanding
of phenomena. We feel obligated to subject every trivial hypothesis
to experimental test irrespective of the degree to which it flies

in the face of our accumulated theoretical and empirical knowledge. Instead of building on what we already know so that we can advance knowledge and technology, we seem to be caught in dealing with endless challenges to what is already known by theoretically naive champions of experimental empiricism. Secondly, and more importantly, this improbable example points to the fact that we may arrive at the wrong conclusion despite an elegant experimental design because of crudity of measurement. In fact, a balance with a set of 20-pound weights achieves a more relevant and refined measurement of the dimension of weight than we are usually able to obtain in psychological measurement.

In choosing so extreme an example, I am not implying that the effects of early education are likely to be as disastrous as starvation. But I do think that efforts to evaluate group day care for very young children and infants by demonstrating that such programs do not have an adverse effect on development are ill-advised. The processes of human bonding, for example, are too delicate and complex to assess by the relatively simple procedures required by large-scale evaluation studies. When measurements are crude, we are likely not to find a difference between the treatment effects. It would be a grave error to interpret the findings of no differences in attachment as demonstrating the lack of adverse influence of infant day care. The effects of separation experiences are so extraordinarily difficult to disentangle and understand, even under conditions of prolonged psychotherapy, that it is illusory to think that they can be captured by routine observation procedures.

What are we to believe about such findings? Can we believe that it is all right for babies to be reared by strangers in institutions rather than by parents at home? (And which babies and in which centers?) Can we really draw such powerful inferences from the failure to reject the null hypothesis in a study using crude measurements? One of the dangers of such findings is that they are likely to lull us into believing that it makes little difference how very young children are treated. Psychological research is filled with studies which show no difference--largely because of faulty measurement and/or theoretical analysis. Were we to take all such studies seriously, we would conclude that hardly anything makes a difference. Given such a framework, the more elusive and covert emotional experiences that are believed to have a decisive effect on development are likely to be altogether excluded from consideration.

For example, after reviewing the research data, some specialists have recently questioned whether the psychological consequences of incest are as serious as had been alleged. It is extremely difficult for psychologists to demonstrate the effects of serious forms of deprivation and trauma in a research design, although clinicians can provide ample case histories of their adverse effects. All of

us know individuals who appear to have survived extremely adverse
conditions of living--whether it was physical abuse, illness, aban-
donment, or other forms of deprivation. The fact that there does
not seem to be a one-to-one relation between certain traumas and
particular consequences should not necessarily lead us to revise
our assessment of the overall negative impact of such influences.
The consequences of such experiences are often more complicated than
our simple measures of impact allow us to see. And yet, we seem,
in the case of early institutional care for young children, to be on
the verge of using the meager evidence of no difference to revise
our conception of the psychological influence of early development.
I am not suggesting that we should never doubt our assumptions or
that there is no room for more precise experimental evaluation of
our accumulated theoretical knowledge, but I do maintain that we
must carefully consider the crudity of measurement in interpreting
the significance of evaluation and research data before we reject
what has been learned from years of clinical experience.

There is little doubt that institutional care for many children
is needed and that such services should be improved and expanded.
For many children, even poor institutional care is better than what
they would otherwise receive. And some institutional care is excellent and far superior to what their clients would otherwise receive. When families with special child-care needs are used as
their own control group, so to speak, then group care is likely to
be shown to be advantageous. But it is a different matter to extend
such emergency care to the entire population, to make it universal,
and to assume that its overall impact will be unremarkable. Yet,
given the increasing tendency for married women to work, the ideology of the women's movement, and what appears to be a declining
readiness to assume responsibility and capacity to endure hardship
and discomfort, it is likely that institutional care of young children
will become the predominant mode as reports of no adverse effects
are circulated. If we adopt a sanguine attitude toward group care
for young children on the basis of faulty evaluation data, if we
fail to reject the null hypothesis when in fact it should be rejected, the effects of this error may not be noticed for decades. Nor
will it be possible to trace the formative influence after so long
and complicated an intervening period. In the meantime, we will have
embarked on a new style of child rearing whose effects are likely
to be irreversible.

Perhaps the only experiment that has already been carried out
along these lines has been among the kibbutzim in Israel. However,
the data are not all in from this experiment and, more important,
the caretakers of children reared collectively in the kibbutzim are
members of the children's community and, in a manner of speaking,
are members of each child's extended family. The caretakers are
assigned by the community to serve as parent surrogates and child
advocates and have chosen to live in a communal society. Such

affective bonds between child-care workers and their children are
seldom duplicated in most child-care centers.

Taking into account the aforementioned obstacles to evaluation,
and bearing in mind that educational evaluation needs to be definitive if it is to be useful (and, perhaps more problematic, is likely to be interpreted as being definitive even if it is not), the
search for more comprehensive and valid evaluation by means of
measurement of relevant child variables, is, in the short run, illusory. It is not realistic to expect to devise valid and precise
methods of measuring what needs to be measured in order to arrive
at a thorough and relevant assessment of the impact of educational
programs on participating children. As long as we persist in expecting educational evaluation to focus on gathering evidence of
program impact, we are destined to have evaluations based on what
can be measured rather than what should be measured.

Reluctant to proceed on so unsatisfactory a basis, I have suggested that we should base our evaluations on an assessment of the
educational setting, on a description and analysis of the educational environment that defines the essential features of the program experienced by participating children (Zimiles, 1977). It is
more feasible to describe the nature of a program that impinges on
the child and to infer its potential impact than to attempt to
measure the impact directly. Such a framework, although it seems
radical and regressive, is in fact the one we usually adopt when we
are called upon to make important educational evaluations. If we
are considering enrolling our own children in a particular school,
we are more likely to be influenced by what we learn by directly
observing the educational setting or by what others think who have
already observed the setting in depth than by an analysis of
differences between pretest and posttest scores. We know that test
scores do not deal with the most relevant issues and that they are
influenced by characteristics of the children that have little to
do with the properties of the program. We turn, instead, for a
definitive assessment, to an examination of the actual educational
conditions to which our children will be subjected and then proceed
to make inferences about their potential impact. I have proposed
that such an approach become systematized and codified so that it
can serve as the basic methodological framework for evaluating
educational programs until the time comes when we finally succeed
in devising valid methods of assessing those variables that are most
relevant for describing the impact of educational programs on children.

The National Day Care Study has at least partially adopted
such a framework. In searching for the manipulable and, therefore,
policy-related antecedents of high quality day care, they defined
quality as a composite of observation data describing how the children were treated by teachers, how the children behaved, and outcome

measures based on standardized tests. In effect, the study developed a strategy midway between traditional exclusive reliance on
outcome measures and the stance advocated here. It is a hopeful
sign that evaluators are beginning to confront honestly the falli-
bility of their measures and to consider alternative methodological
frameworks.

BIBLIOGRAPHY

Abt Associates. *Children at the center: Summary findings and their
    implications* (Vol. I). Final report of the National Day Care
    Study. Prepared for the Day Care Division, Administration for
    Children, Youth, and Families, Office of Human Development
    Services, U.S. Department of Health, Education, and Welfare
    (Contract No. 105-74-1100), March 1979.
Zimiles, H. A radical and regressive solution to the problem of
    evaluation. In L. G. Katz (Ed.), *Current topics in early child-
    hood education* (Vol. I). Norwood, NJ: Ablex Publishing Corp.,
    1977.

LIST OF CONTRIBUTORS

Anahet Avakian
Ministry of Education and Culture
Haifa, Israel

Jerry B. Ayers
College of Education
Tennessee Technological University
Box 5116/Cookeville, TN 38501

Lois Baker
Department of Human Behavior and Development
Drexel University
Philadelphia, PA 19104

Evelyn A. Benas
Merritt Community College
Hayward, CA 94540

Jacques S. Benninga
Dept. of Curriculum and Instruction
College of Education
University of Kentucky
Lexington, KY 40506

Gaile Cannella
University of Georgia
Athens, Georgia 30602

Mary Jo Cliatt
School of Education, University of Mississippi
University, MS 38677

Rivka Dagan
Ministry of Education and Culture
Beer Sheva, Israel

Richard B. Darlington
Department of Human Service Studies
N135 MVR Hall
Cornell University
Ithaca, NY 14853

Iain F.W.K. Davidson
Ontario Institute for Studies in Education
252 Bloor Street, W.
Toronto, Ontario, Canada

J.J. Dumont
Institute for Orthopedagogics
University of Nijmegen
Erasmuslaan 40-16
6525 GG Nijmegen, The Netherlands

Steen B. Esbensen
University of Quebec (HULL)
283, boul. Tache, CP. 1250
Hull, Quebec, J8X3X, Canada

C. Fox
MATSCO
General Electric
Valley Forge, PA 19481

Roberta J. Goldberg
Moore Hall, UCLA
405 Hilgard Avenue
Los Angeles, CA 90024

Claire Golomb
Department of Psychology
University of Massachusetts at Boston
Harbor Campus
Boston, MA 02125

Marilyn C. Gootman
College of Education
University of Georgia
Athens, GA 30602

Esther R. Goshen-Gottstein
Clinical Psychologist
17 Jabotinsky Road
Jerusalem, Israel

Thomas Guskey
Department of Curriculum and Instruction
College of Education
University of Kentucky
Lexington, KY 40506

J.H. Hamers
University of Utrecht
Utrecht, The Netherlands

Zevulum Hammer
Ministry of Education and Culture
Jerusalem, Israel

George W. Harrison
Natal Training College
P.O. Box 566
Pietermaritzburg, South Africa

Dorothy W. Hewes
School of Family Studies
San Diego State University
San Diego, CA 92182

J. McVicker Hunt
Professor Emeritus, Department of Psychology
University of Illinois at Urbana-Champaign
Urbana, IL 61801

Rachel Inselberg
Department of Education and Professional Development
Western Michigan University
Kalamazoo, MI 49008

Rivka Itskowitz
Department of Psychology
Bar-Ilan University
Ramat Gan, Israel

Lilian G. Katz
Department of Elementary and Early Childhood Education
University of Illinois at Urbana-Champaign
Urbana, Il 61801

Pnina S. Klein
School of Education
Bar-Ilan University
Ramat Gan, Israel

Carmen Luz Latorre
Interdisciplinary Program of Educational Research
PIIE - Luis Videla Herrera 2360
Santiago 9, Chile

Gideon Lewin
Hamisrad L'Limood P'i'Looyot Hayeled
Seminar Oranim
Kiryat Tivon, Israel

Mary S. Lewis
Child Development Specialist
HEW Region IX
Administration for Children, Youth, and Families
50 United Nations Plaza
San Francisco, CA 94102

Avima Lombard
School of Education, The Hebrew University
Jerusalem, Israel

Doren L. Madey
Senior Research Analyst
NTS Research Corp.
2634 Chapel Hill Blvd.
Durham, NC 27707

Salomón Magendzo
Interdisciplinary Program of Educational Research
PIIE
Luis Videla Herrera 2360
Santiago 9, Chile

M. Mattleman
Department of Elementary Education
Temple University
Philadelphia, PA 19122

Nechama Nir-Janiv
Ministry of Education and Culture
Bar-Ilan University
Ramat Gan, Israel

Jolene Oswald
Kalamazoo Public Schools
Kalamazoo, MI 49008

Marion Perlmutter
Institute of Child Development
51 East River Road
University of Minnesota
Minneapolis, MN 55455

Barbara Perry-Sheldon
James Madison University
Harrisonburg, VA 22807

Jack V. Powell
College of Education
University of Georgia
427 Aderhold Hall
Athens, GA 30601

Yaacov Rand
Research Institute
6 Karmon Street Beit Hakerem
Jerusalem, Israel

Judith C. Reiff
University of Georgia
Athens, GA 30602

Mildred Robeck
Department of Education
University of Oregon
Eugene, OR 97403

Helen Warren Ross
Family Studies and Consumer Sciences Department
San Diego State University
San Diego, CA 92115

A.J. Ruyssenaars
Institute for Orthopedagogics
University of Nijmegen
Erasmuslaan 40-16
6525 GG Nijmegen
The Netherlands

D. Royce Sadler
Department of Education
University of Queensland
St. Lucia, Brisbane, Australia 4067

Myrtle Scott
Smith Research Center, Rm. 141
Indiana University
Bloomington, IN 47401

Leah Shepathiah
Department of Psychology
Tel Aviv University
Tel Aviv, Israel

Jean Shaw
School of Education
University of Mississippi
University, MS 38677

Michael Siegal
Department of Psychology
University of Queensland
St. Lucia, Brisbane, Australia 4067

Anne Silcock
Department of Education
University of Queensland
St. Lucia, Brisbane, Australia 4067

Sarah Smilansky
Department of Psychology
Tel Aviv University
Tel Aviv, Israel

Bernard Spodek
Department of Elementary and Early Childhood Education
College of Education
University of Illinois at Urbana-Champaign
Urbana, IL 61801

Dina Stachel
School of Education
Tel Aviv University
Ramat Aviv, Tel Aviv
Israel

Doreen Ray Steg
Department of Human Behavior and Development
Drexel University
Philadelphia, PA 19104

Helen Strauss
Department of Psychology
Bar-Ilan University
Ramat Gan, Israel

Kathy Thornburg
University of Missouri
St. Louis, MO 63121

Sarah S. Van Camp
College of Human Resources
University of Delaware
Newark, DE 19711

Ruth L. Wynn
Department of Child and Family Studies
College for Human Development
Syracuse University
Syracuse, NY 13210

Herbert Zimiles
Bank Street College of Education
610 West 112th Street
New York, NY 10025

ISRAELI ORGANIZING COMMITTEE AND ADVISORY BOARDS

Organizing Committee

Nir-Janiv, Nechama — Chairman of the Congress; Ministry of Education
                  and Culture; Bar-Ilan University
Feitelson, Dina — Haifa University
Jasik, Lynne — The Hebrew University; O.M.E.P.
Stern-Katan, Sara — Member of the Knesset (Israeli Parliament)
Lewin, Gideon — Study Centre for Children's Activities, Oranim
Lewin, Isaac — Bar-Ilan University
Lombard, Avima — The Hebrew University
Mashat-Pnini, Mazal — Ministry of Education and Culture
Rokach, Ephraim — Ministry of Education and Culture
Smilansky, Sarah — Tel Aviv University
Winter, Zahava — Ministry of Education and Culture

Advisory Board

Ginsburg, Lilli — Teachers' Association
Gur, Rita — WIZO
Harman, Zena — Israel National Committee for U.N.I.C.E.F.
Horowitz, Rivka — Israel Association for Internation Cooperation
Lobalski, Masha — Na'amat
Portugaly, Drora — Ministry of Education and Culture
Ram, Gila — Teachers' Association
Rand, Yaacov — Bar-Ilan University
Shach, Tamara — The Ministry of Labor
Shraga, Mordechai — Municipality of Jerusalem
Weiss, Hedva — Teachers' Association
Zinder, Hemdah — Israel National Commission for U.N.E.S.C.O.

International Advisory Board

Hunt, J. McVicker — Honorary Chairman of the Congress: University
                        of Illinois at Urbana-Champaign, U.S.A.
Amarel, A. — Educational Testing Service, U.S.A.
Andersson, Bengt-Erik — Department of Education Research, Sweden
Bowles, Samuel V. — University of Massachusetts at Amherst, U.S.A.
Boyd, Richard — Cornell University, U.S.A.
Calfee, Robert — Stanford University, U.S.A.
Cazden, Courtney — Harvard University, U.S.A.
Condry, John — Cornell University, U.S.A.
Cross, William E. — Cornell University, U.S.A.
Duncan, Dorothy — Goldsmiths College, U.K.
Dworkin, Nancy — Temple University, U.S.A.
Ethchegoyhen de Lorenzo, Elosia Garcia — Organization de los Estados
                                          Americanos, Uruguay
Fox, Cheryl — Center for Self-Controlled Learning, U.S.A.
Fromberg, Doris — Hofstra University, U.S.A.
Ginsberg, Herb — University of Maryland, U.S.A.
Gordon, Ira (Deceased) — University of North Carolina, U.S.A.
Green, Maxine — Columbia University, U.S.A.
Horowitz, Frances Degen — University of Kansas, U.S.A.
Ishigaki, Emiko — Seiwa Women's College, Japan

INDEX